JOSS WHEDON

THE COMPLETE COMPANION
THE TV SERIES, THE MOVIES, THE COMIC BOOKS AND MORE

JOSS WHEDON: THE COMPLETE COMPANION (REVISED AND UPDATED EDITION)
ISBN: 9781783293599

Published by
Titan Books
A division of Titan Publishing Group Ltd.
144 Southwark St.
London
SE1 0UP

First edition: April 2015
10 9 8 7 6 5 4 3 2 1

Did you enjoy this book? We love to hear from our readers. Please e-mail us at:
readerfeedback@titanemail.com or write to Reader Feedback at the above address.

To receive advance information, news, competitions, and exclusive offers online, please sign
up for the Titan newsletter on our website: **www.titanbooks.com**

A CIP catalogue record for this title is available from the British Library.

Printed and bound in the USA.

JOSS WHEDON

THE COMPLETE COMPANION
THE TV SERIES, THE MOVIES, THE COMIC BOOKS AND MORE

TITAN BOOKS

CONTENTS

ANGEL

FIREFLY and SERENITY

COMICS

DR. HORRIBLE'S SING-ALONG BLOG

DOLLHOUSE

MARVEL'S AGENTS OF S.H.I.E.L.D.

FILMS

APPENDICES

New Content in This Edition

For this revised and updated edition of *The Complete Companion*, we've added the following new articles in our attempt to keep up with the ever creative and prolific Joss Whedon:

0.01
Introduction
Why another examination of Joss Whedon?
Robert Moore

I promise that that question really did make sense at one point. I first posed the question on March 3, 2011, on the first day of the six-week online event on Popmatters.com that served as the basis for the first edition of this book. Both in March 2011 and the spring of 2012, before the release of *The Avengers*, which became the third largest selling film in history and propelled Joss Whedon from cult figure to A List, that question made sense. But here is the most important thing to keep in mind: Joss Whedon's importance as an artist has nothing to do with the staggering box office success of *The Avengers*. The questions raised in the second edition of this book deserve answering for the very same reasons that they deserved answering when Joss was an icon for the few rather than the many.

Even when we were doing the online event in the spring of 2011, Joss Whedon laid claim to fame as the most intensely studied TV creator in popular culture, with dozens of books and thousands of essays covering and re-covering every aspect of his television series, movies, and comics. What is it that has generated such unprecedented interest? Why do so many people care so deeply about his television series, comics, movies, and Internet musicals?[1]

Whedon's influence on pop culture has been so deep and wide-ranging it is hard to realize that we are less than twenty years removed from the debut of *Buffy the Vampire Slayer* on the fledgling WB network. The WB is long gone at this point—as is UPN, where *Buffy* relocated after a dispute between Twentieth Century Fox and the WB over money—but *Buffy* continues to obsess and delight fans to a degree matched by only a handful of shows.

---

1 To grasp how wide-ranging and intense the interest has been in only two of his creations, *Buffy the Vampire Slayer* and *Angel*, see Don Macnaughton's *The Buffyverse Catalog: A Complete Guide to* Buffy the Vampire Slayer *and* Angel *in Print, Film, Television, Comics, Games and Other Media, 1992–2010.* What is striking about many of the publications recorded there is how many are either serious critical pieces or academic essays. While the *Star Trek* franchise can surpass *Buffy* and *Angel* in terms of merchandise, neither it nor any other television series has inspired anything approaching the same degree of serious critical and scholarly attention.

Lest one try to marginalize the show by assigning it "cult TV" status, one should also keep in mind that *Buffy* remains the most intensely studied television series by television critics and scholars in the history of television, which does not preclude its being a cult show, though it would be a most unusual one. Unlike many other series targeted by TV scholars, such as the shows making up the *Star Trek* franchise, studies of *Buffy* are almost entirely textual analyses of the show's content instead of studies of the show's fandom. People remain primarily concerned with what *Buffy*, *Angel*, *Firefly*, and *Dollhouse* have to *say* about culture almost to the complete exclusion of questions about who watches these shows or why.

Writing was almost literally in Joseph Hill Whedon's blood (he later morphed his first name into "Joss"). While his mother was an active feminist, his father Tom was a television writer, working on series like *Benson*, *The Golden Girls*, and *Electric Company*. Joss's grandfather was also a television writer, enabling his grandson to assert that he was the world's first third-generation television writer. Grandfather John wrote for such famous 1950s and 1960s shows as *The Donna Reed Show*, *The Dick Van Dyke Show*, and *The Andy Griffith Show*. Joss's brothers Jed and Zack have followed in the family tradition, while Jed's wife Maurissa Tancharoen (the self-described "Asian Whedon") is also a TV writer.

Although Joss Whedon had a more than a minor impact on popular culture prior to *Buffy*—through his writing on *Roseanne*, screenplays for *Titan A.E.*, *Toy Story* (doing an important late rewrite of the script that helped the film net an Oscar nomination for best screenplay), *Alien Resurrection*, and (perhaps most famously) the film version of *Buffy the Vampire Slayer*, and for his work as a script doctor on films like *Speed*, *Twister*, and *Waterworld*—his real impact came on television. The success of *Buffy* on TV created the demand for the spinoff *Angel* and the opportunity for the space Western *Firefly*, which although quickly cancelled by Fox TV after it failed to be the hit replacement for *The X-Files* that they hoped it to be, went on to become one of the most beloved series ever. Due to remarkably strong DVD sales, *Firefly* was continued in the feature film *Serenity*, which while not a box office success (though it has gone on to be a consistent seller on DVD and Blu-ray, so that the film has turned a substantial profit for Universal Studios, which had purchased the film rights from Twentieth Century Fox), has grown in critical regard and today persistently makes lists of the best science-fiction movies ever made.

After the cancellation of *Angel* by the WB and the box office failure of *Serenity*, Whedon turned to comics. While still working on *Buffy* he had produced the critically acclaimed comic *Fray*, a story of a vampire slayer in the future, while his later work with famed artist John Cassaday on *Astonishing X-Men* resulted in one of the more celebrated superhero stories of recent years. Typically, Whedon elevated a female heroine, creating *the* Kitty Pryde story. He later took over from creator Brian K. Vaughan on *Runaways*, a comic that itself had been deeply influenced by *Buffy*.

Joss then embarked on his most ambitious comic-book project, working with the Dark Horse label to continue Buffy's story by producing Season 8 in comic book form. Although there have been many comic-book continuances of movies and television series, having new and canonical versions of series with full involvement of the creator was practically unheard of at the time (since then others have followed Whedon's example). Whedon has continued other series in comics as well, having done prequels to *Serenity*, while *Angel* has ended on IDW and become *Angel and Faith* with Dark Horse, while *Buffy* has moved into Season 10.

Whedon returned to television in the flawed but often brilliant *Dollhouse*, a series that was lightly watched—not least because Fox put it in its notorious "Friday Night Death Slot"—but which did evolve into a fascinating series that showed enormous potential. Like *Firefly*, it may in the long run prove to have been a series that was a bit too far ahead of its time.

Immediately after the announcement by Fox of the greenlighting of *Dollhouse*, Hollywood was hit by a Screen Writers Guild strike. During the strike, Whedon conceived of writing a direct-to-Internet musical, which he proceeded to write with his brothers Zack and Jed and sister-in-law Maurissa Tancharoen. The musical, taking the form of an Internet video blog, was *Dr. Horrible's Sing-Along Blog*, and starred Neil Patrick Harris as Dr. Horrible, a would-be member of the Evil League of Evil, though in fact a bit of a moral anarchist trying to cause the downfall of the capitalist system through acts of terrorism (fighting the status quo, which, he says, is "not quo"). The story also focused on the doctor vying with his arch nemesis Captain Hammer (Nathan Fillion) for the affections of Penny (Felicia Day), and contained a string of catchy original songs that were appealingly performed by the participants. *Dr. Horrible* was shown online for free on three consecutive days in July 2008. Later it was sold via iTunes and on DVD/Blu-ray (with a truly funny musical cast commentary) in an attempt to make back production costs and put a little money in the pockets of the people who made it.

Dr. Horrible is in many ways Whedon's most unique achievement, and could in the long run prove to be one of his most important. Many regarded as the first great thing produced directly for the Internet, and the way the participants self-funded the project could provide a template for other producers of scripted content who want to work outside the studio system. The entertainment industry didn't quite know how to categorize the musical. The American Film Institute dubbed it one of "Eight Moments of Significance" of 2008, while it won an Emmy despite never having appeared on TV (though when Neil Patrick Harris hosted the Emmys, he and his fellow *Dr. Horrible* cast members did a short reprisal of their roles onstage). But what *Dr. Horrible* showed was that it was possible to produce exceptionally fine direct-to-Internet content without the help of the studio system, something that *Dr. Horrible* female lead Felicia Day has demonstrated as well, producing a number of Internet series, most famously *The Guild*, an online series about a MMORPG gaming guild, which she not only starred in but also wrote and produced.

I would like to argue that what Whedon did with *Dr. Horrible*, bypassing the traditional movie distribution network, has to some degree found fulfillment on Netflix. Whether doing original series such as *Orange is the New Black* or *House of Cards*, or reviving series cancelled by other networks such as *Arrested Development*, Netflix is rewriting the rules for television. In fact, there was a Whedonesque feel to the blockbuster announcement that Marvel would be doing series focused on four different superheroes (though in the case of Jessica Jones, the question is why she is no longer a superhero)— Daredevil, Luke Cage, the Immortal Iron Fist, and Jessica Jones—before uniting the four of them in the miniseries *The Defenders*. It is no surprise that Whedon alumni Drew Goddard and Steven DeKnight have both been involved with *Daredevil* at different stages of its development.

In the future, the Internet could well be where Whedon does much of his work, or perhaps also as low-to-no-budget film maker. Since *The Avengers*, Whedon has completed two independent films, both released directly to the public. *Much Ado About Nothing*, his delightful retelling of Shakespeare's comedy, was released directly on DVD and Blu-Ray, while *In Your Eyes*, another low-budget film that is part romantic comedy and part fantasy (and unfortunately the weakest work he has been engaged in to date) was released for direct download after it failed to find a distributor.

Three major events have conspired to change Joss Whedon's status from cult favorite to A-Lister. The first was the release of *The Cabin in the Woods* a month before the release of *The Avengers*. Although not the hit the latter was, it was nonetheless well received and garnered excellent reviews. The second was the release of *The Avengers*, which was even more of a megahit than was anticipated. It was, if anything, a much, much better movie than even his most avid fans hoped for. On every level the film was a triumph, even making the Hulk, a dud in two previous feature films, a completely delightful character.

The next step in Joss Whedon's ascendance to superstar writer/director/ producer/creature was Marvel's asking him to create the studio's first live-action TV series in decades, after several name changes eventually known as *Marvel's Agents of S.H.I.E.L.D.* My own belief is that Joss Whedon's involvement on the series has been somewhat minimal. Everything seems to indicate that most of the work on the show is undertaken by Jeffrey Bell from a production standpoint and Jed Whedon and Maurissa Tancharoen from a writing one. Most of Joss's attention in Season 1 was directed towards *The Avengers 2: The Age of Ultron*; it will be interesting to see if his involvement on the show increases as production on *The Avengers* wraps up.

The essays and interviews in this collection cover in detail all of the TV series, comics, and movies that have been mentioned here. Some of the essays examine themes in particular shows, while others trace ideas that cut across all of Whedon's work. Some essays explore specific characters in detail, while others ask what his work has meant for the depiction of gender or heroism or sexuality. Other writers examine specific episodes in especial detail, while others look at his struggles with studios or how his work has inspired fans to assert their power in new and innovative ways. Meanwhile "Joss Whedon 101" essays serve as introductions to all of Whedon's best-known productions and even many of his minor ones, from *Buffy the Vampire Slayer* all the way down to his one-shot comic *Sugarshock*. We also feature in-depth interviews with prominent figures from the Whedonverse.

WHY DO WHEDON'S CREATIONS RESONATE SO STRONGLY WITH HIS FANS?

His various projects do inspire a passion that is rare in the industry, something that conforms with Whedon's explicit intentions; he has said that he would rather have 100 viewers who *had* to watch one of his shows than 1,000 who *liked* to watch. What are some of the qualities that have made viewing his shows or reading his comics so compulsory? Why do so many of us *have* to watch (and re-watch) his shows and films?

Answering the last question adequately would require its own book, and even in a short essay a dozen or so possible answers are possible. The essays comprising this book provide several answers to this question, but let me touch on three things that suggest some of the reasons his work is so entrancing for so many.

1. JOSS WHEDON LIKES WHAT WE LIKE

In an August 2010 interview with io9.com, writer China Miéville explained why he dislikes J.J. Abrams's science-fiction films:

I've never met [J.J. Abrams]. I am not a member of his fan club or anti-fan club. I disliked *Cloverfield* a very great deal. I disliked *Star Trek* intensely. I thought it was terrible. And I think part of my problem is that I feel like the relationship between J.J. Abrams' projects and geek culture is one of relatively unloving repackaging—sort of cynical. I taste contempt in the air. Now I'm not a child—I know that all big sci-fi projects are suffused with the contempt of big money for its own target audience. But there's something about [J.J.'s projects] that makes me particularly uncomfortable. As compared to somebody like Joss Whedon, who—even when there are misfires—I feel likes me and loves me and is on some cultural level my brother and comrade. And I don't feel that way about J.J. Abrams.

Without passing judgment on J.J. Abrams [for my part I suspect that he cares for science fiction and fantasy more than Miéville imagines; after all he has continually returned to action, science fiction, and fantasy genres, and even *Felicity*—a show grounded in everyday reality if any is—featured an alternative reality segment near the end of its final season], there is no question that Joss Whedon is not merely a TV creator and writer; he is a fan. He has frequently expressed his love for other TV series, such as *Veronica Mars* and *Battlestar Galactica*, appearing in a guest cameo in the former and allegedly being invited to direct an episode of the latter, though work on the *Dollhouse* pilot prevented his involvement. He writes comic books as an insider, and his shows are littered with references to other TV series, movies, books, and comic books.

Many TV series name check movies, TV series, and comics, but all too frequently with the unloving care that Miéville detects. Not Whedon. His shows are filled with geeks and nerds, and even when their obsessions are treated humorously, it is done so with a degree of affection. Take the Season 6 episode of *Buffy* ("Smashed" 6.9) in which Spike goes to Warren and his fellow geek villains to have him verify whether or not the chip the Initiative implanted in his skull was still working. Warren initially refuses, and Spike, unable to hurt Warren or his friends because of the chip, sees their Boba Fett figurine and realizes how he can force them to cooperate:

Spike: Examine my chip, or else Mister [looks at label] Fett here is the first to die.

Jonathan: [panicking] Hey, all right, let's not, let's not do anything crazy here.

Andrew: That's a limited edition, 1979 mint condition Boba Fett.

Warren: All right, dude. Chill. You can still make it right. You know you don't wanna do this.

Spike: What I want is answers, nimrod.

Warren: Right. But you don't wanna hurt the Fett, 'cause man, you're *not* coming back from that. You know, you don't just do that and walk away.

To the degree that he is able—given network and studio interference—Whedon tells the stories he does because he belongs to his target audience. Miéville's criticism of Abrams is grounded in the fact that he believes Abrams is an outsider and that his movies and shows are imbued with condescension and cynicism. Whether this is true of Abrams, it is true that too many science fiction series and movies feel like they were made by people who look down on those they hope will buy tickets to see their films or tune in on their TVs.

This is one reason why the announcement of Marvel Studios' decision to have Whedon direct *The Avengers* was greeted with such enthusiasm: he not only likes comics but writes them. One senses a deep affection for these characters on the part of Whedon.

Buffy, Angel, Firefly, Dollhouse, Fray, Amazing X-Men, and *Dr. Horrible* were all made by a science fiction and fantasy insider for people who love science fiction and fantasy stories. And while he has directed memorable episodes of other shows—he has directed especially fine episodes of *The Office* and *Glee*—the kinds of genre shows he has excelled in represent a kind of home base for him.

2. JOSS WHEDON THINKS WE ARE SMART

Most TV writers assume that their viewers are idiots, completely gullible, or at least not terribly intelligent. A significant number of series are invariably targeted at the lowest common denominator and only rarely demand that the viewer pay close attention to what is going on. Whedon, on the other hand, credits his viewers with a high degree of intelligence and assumes that they are capable of absorbing a considerable degree of detail. He assumes a high level of literacy on the part of his audience, and frequently makes reference to classic films and books in addition to pop culture. For instance, in the *Buffy* episode "Goodbye Iowa" (4.14) the Cyborg Adam encounters a young boy in a scene that is supposed to remind viewers of a comparable scene in James Whale's original *Frankenstein* (1931), in which the Monster meets a little girl as he first goes out in the world. You can still enjoy the scene if you don't get the reference, but it is all the more satisfying if you do.

Or take the Season 6 episode "Older and Far Away" (6.14), in which all the guests at Buffy's birthday party are trapped after Dawn made an unfortunate wish to the vengeance demon Halfrek. Dawn complains that everyone she knows keeps leaving and wishes that they wouldn't. As a result of her wish none of the party guests are able to leave the Summers' residence. Foreign film buffs will recognize the plot as deriving from the Luis Buñuel film *The Exterminating Angel* (1962). In both film and episode there is no discernable physical barrier keeping the guests from leaving, but something mysterious and ineffable, the only difference being that in *Buffy* we discover the magical cause, while in the Buñuel film we never learn why they are unable to leave. Again, knowing the film is no hindrance to enjoying the *Buffy* episode (even Kenneth Topping in his usually incredibly informative *The Complete Slayer* fails to note the connection to *The Exterminating Angel*), but it adds to the fun.

Sometimes the writing requires at least a little knowledge to make sense of a scene, and if you don't possess the knowledge, Whedon doesn't have his writers go out of their way to explain the reference. When Oz is captured by the Initiative ("New Moon Rising" 4.19), Buffy and the Scoobies break into the Initiative's underground bunker and rescue him, taking its leader hostage. When they run into a group of soldiers, Buffy quickly holds a crossbow to the head of the commanding officer and orders the soldiers to keep away:

Buffy: Stay back, or I'll pull a William Burroughs on your leader here.

Xander: You'll bore him to death with free prose?

Buffy: Was I the only one awake in English that day?

If the viewer is unaware that William S. Burroughs often employed free association in his writing (so Xander was in fact paying a little bit of attention in class) one might not get Xander's reference, but if one is also unaware that Burroughs accidentally shot and killed his wife while playing a game of "William Tell" while drunk, one would not get Buffy's.

Watching Whedon's shows carefully repays all the effort one expends, with the payoff coming in both big and small ways. Near the end of Season 6 of *Buffy*, after her girlfriend Tara has been killed by a stray bullet, Willow is literally hell-bent on revenge. Catching up with the gunman, Warren, in the woods, he frantically begs for his life before Willow says "Bored now" and through magic flays him alive. Viewers familiar with the series instantly recognize the phrase from Season 3 when we meet a vampire version of Willow from an alternate world. That Willow, thoroughly evil, often tells others "Bored now" ("Doppelgängland" 3.16). The implication is that our Willow—goodhearted, sweet, reliable Willow—whom viewers have loved for six full seasons of *Buffy*, has become as corrupt as her evil doppelganger. Marti Noxon, the writer of the episode, does not underscore or emphasize the reference, and not getting it doesn't detract much from enjoying the episode, but for those who recognize the reference, it provides an additional layer of explanation for just how dark Willow has gone. It also tells us what has happened to *our* Willow. Just as the other Willow turned evil upon losing her soul after becoming a vampire, so ours has become evil after losing Tara, which is for her tantamount to losing her soul.

The same kind of intelligent care has gone into the narrative structuring of the show. Stories are planned not merely over several episodes but even into future seasons. Although Buffy's sister Dawn does not appear until Season 5, it is something foreshadowed in a Season 4 dream sequence in which Buffy and the rogue slayer Faith are making a bed together. Recognizing that Buffy needs to leave, Faith remarks, "Little sis coming, I know. So much to do before she gets here" ("This Year's Girl" 4.15). No explanation is given as to what Faith means; the hint is just left hanging in the air. But fans re-watching the episode after Dawn's mysterious appearance at the beginning of Season 5 find the reference delightful, just as they can Tara's words to Buffy in another dream sequence in the Season 4 finale "Restless" (4.22): "Be back before dawn."

All this points to the depth of Whedon's shows, the sheer quantity not merely of text but subtext. That Whedon is aware of the layering is obvious. Giles even remarks to Buffy in one episode that subtext had become text; that is perpetually true of the show.

In a Season 2 episode, Giles, Buffy's middle-aged Watcher, becomes interested in asking his fellow teacher Jenny Calendar out on a date. When Xander, Willow, and Buffy—who have been discussing a classmate they believe has been collecting body parts to reanimate his dead brother—see Giles nervously waiting for Jenny in order to ask her out, Xander suddenly says:

Xander: And speaking of love.

Willow: [Confused] We were talking of the reanimation of dead tissue

Xander: Do I deconstruct your segues?

Xander, of course, is cleverly suggesting that Giles's—whom they all regard as impossibly old—romantic interest in Jenny is the reanimating of a different kind of dead tissue.

It is the deep embrace of subtext that has resulted in the exhaustive examination of productions like *Buffy*, *Angel*, *Firefly*, *Serenity*, *Dr. Horrible*, and *Dollhouse* by television critics and scholars. *Buffy* has inspired countless narratives about its narratives. Seven years after the final episode of *Buffy* there is no end in sight of books and essays and academic conferences covering every conceivable aspect of the show. Even critically acclaimed series like *The Sopranos* and *The Wire* receive only a small percentage of the critical attention that *Buffy* does. The reason lies in the rich subtext that undergirds the show. We can say so much about *Buffy* and Whedon's other work because it says so much to begin with.

3. JOSS WHEDON TRULY LIKES AND RESPECTS WOMEN

Buffy Summers was not the first female hero on television, but her appearance was a pivotal moment in the history of women there. Prior to Buffy, one could count the number of heroic females in television on the fingers of both hands with several digits left over. But after Buffy, there has been an unceasing string of female heroes who follow the pattern established on *Buffy*. (See my essay elsewhere in this volume on "How *Buffy* Changed Television" for greater detail on the role *Buffy* played in establishing a major presence of female heroes on TV.)

Because so many other essays in this book will delve into Whedon's regard for women there is no need to explore it more fully here. His shows reflect again and again his respect for and appreciation of women, and he consistently places heroic women in his projects. Anyone who has heard his remarkable acceptance speech upon being presented an award by Equality Now understands much of what goes into his portrayal of strong female characters. And this is clearly one of reasons his shows have been so passionately embraced.

Why is this important? Why particularly is it crucial that there be these vital, strong, heroic women?

To answer this question I must turn to the personal. As a single father raising a young girl, I quickly learned to appreciate how desperately my daughter wanted to see heroic girls and women in movies and on TV. Watching *Peter Pan*, she unexpectedly viewed Wendy as the hero of the story. Many classic films were rejected when we visited the video store, Elizabeth asking instead for movies "with girl heroes." This was immediately pre-*Buffy*, but after *The Wizard of Oz*, *The Journey of Natty Gann*, and *Nausicaä of the Valley of the Wind* pickings were slim.

All this changed with *Buffy*. Instead of the occasional movie or television series with strong females, there now are a host. It is possible that shows, such as *Roswell*, *Farscape*, *Dark Angel*, *Alias*, *Veronica Mars*, *Battlestar Galactica*, *Terminator: The Sarah Connor Chronicles*, and *Fringe* would have appeared anyway, but the fact is that it was only after *Buffy* that such shows hit the networks in any quantity.

I learned firsthand through my daughter just how important it is for young girls—or even older girls—to have examples of women who demonstrate that it is good to be strong. It is just as important for men to grasp and understand that men are not really strong unless women are also strong. Men are not strengthened by the diminishing of women and vice versa.

My daughter wanted "girl heroes" that she could identify with and whose exploits she could enjoy. Unfortunately, she had few. Today, post-*Buffy*, there are many. Anyone who has helped change the cultural landscape to that degree deserves considerably more than a mere book.

CHAPTER 1

BUFFY THE VAMPIRE SLAYER

1.01
Joss Whedon 101:
Buffy the Vampire Slayer
Robert Moore

The story of the transformation of *Buffy the Vampire Slayer* from a low-budget feature film into a critically acclaimed television series is an improbable one. Joss Whedon was not, in fact, the instigator. That credit goes to producer Gail Berman, who in the mid-1990s was looking for new projects to develop for television. In 1992 the film version of *Buffy* had been released, based on Whedon's original screenplay. Exasperated with changes being made to his script during filming, he eventually left the set and avoided the studio during the later stages of filming. Whedon had gone on to enjoy a flourishing and highly remunerative career as writer and script doctor and had, in fact, put *Buffy* behind him by the time Berman approached him about the possibility of turning the film into a television series. Berman had presciently anticipated that the movie would provide the basis for an excellent series and sold Whedon on the idea (Whedon 25). Although she would later be mercilessly castigated as the villain who pulled the plug on *Firefly* when she was head of programming at Fox TV, the fact is that without Berman's initiative, neither *Buffy* nor *Firefly* would ever have been produced.

Berman and Whedon took the idea of *Buffy* to all of the major networks but were rejected by each one. The fledgling WB network, however, was in search of original programming and ordered a pilot. Although they did not place it on their schedule for the fall of 1996, they did order it to series as a mid-season replacement in the winter of 1997. While a number of major TV critics were immediately taken with *Buffy*'s clever dialogue and meshing of comedy and drama alongside fighting vampires and demons (Matt Roush of *TV Guide* was perhaps the show's first high profile fan), the ratings through its first season were never strong and renewal was uncertain. The WB finally decided to give the show another chance and during its second season, with greatly improved writing and a larger budget that made possible higher production values, the show became a hit.

The TV series picks up three months after the end of the movie, with Buffy Summers relocating from Los Angeles to a new school in Sunnydale, California. The move by Buffy and her mother was forced by her expulsion from her former high school after she burned down the gym, which was filled with vampires, an event contained in the film's screenplay but which was eliminated due to budgetary limitations. The TV series is, therefore, strictly speaking not a sequel to the movie, but to the screenplay that Joss wrote that the movie was based on. Those wishing to see something like what he had in mind in writing the screenplay should see "Buffy: The Origin" in the *Buffy the Vampire Slayer Omnibus*, a comic that was "Adapted from Joss Whedon's original screenplay" by Dan Brereton and Christopher Golden (35-102).

In the film high school cheerleader Buffy Summers learns that she was the Chosen One; the formulation is sharpened in the TV series: "Into every generation a Slayer is born: one girl in all the world, a chosen one. She alone will wield the strength and skill to fight the vampires, demons, and the forces of darkness; to stop the spread of their evil and the swell of their numbers. She is The Slayer."

As Joss Whedon has pointed out, as silly as the title of the show is, it hints at several major aspects of the series. "Buffy" is intrinsically comical and leads the viewer to expect humor; "Vampire" indicates that the viewer can anticipate the scary and supernatural; while "Slayer" promises action, with the expectation that the action will involve girl with the silly name.

One of the central themes in the show is Buffy's reluctance to embrace her calling, from denying it in the show's pilot, to begrudgingly acknowledging its inevitability in the next few seasons, until fully embracing it in Season 5. Being The Slayer, the Chosen One, was thrust upon her, without her having a say in it. Although the show is frequently comic in tone, Buffy's story is at its core a tragic one. Why? Because one only becomes The Slayer when someone else has died, which points to the future and one's own inevitable death, which is likely to be violent. As Buffy tells Giles in Season 5, "Look I realize that every Slayer comes with an expiration date on the package, but I want mine to be a long time from now. Like a cheeto" ("Fool for Love" 5.7). But the brute fact is that for Buffy many of the dreams she had when fifteen are no longer possibilities; instead her life situation is truly Hobbesian, a perpetual war against vampires and demons in which her life could well prove to be "solitary, poor, nasty, brutish, and short."

Though, in fact, not solitary. One of the major differences between the film and the series is that in the movie Buffy, though with some help from her love interest Pike, fights more or less on her own; in the series she instantly acquires a group of friends who form a team to aid her in her struggle against the demons and vampires. Willow and Xander, along with her watcher Giles, form the core of the Scooby Gang—whose ranks swell and ebb as the series progresses—who aid Buffy both as friends and sidekicks, in addition to engaging in the ceaseless research that backgrounds all their activity. The more frequent paradigm of the hero—such as Clint Eastwood's Man with No Name—is of a loner, someone who neither desires nor can afford friends or companions. Although Buffy is the most powerful of the Scoobies (though she is rivaled in later seasons by Willow's emergence as a witch) and the only one who has no choice about fighting the powers of darkness, what sets her apart as a hero is the support she receives from friends and family. As the vampire Spike (later himself to be a member of the Scoobies) remarks after his first encounter with Buffy, "A Slayer with family and friends, that sure as hell wasn't in the brochure" ("School Hard" 2.3).

The narrative format of *Buffy* was established in Season 1. A Big Bad (in the first season, an extremely ancient vampire known as The Master) is introduced, against whom Buffy engages in a season-long confrontation. Each season features several standalone episodes, but even in these some portion of the longer narrative is developed. The season-long arcs are focused mainly on the struggle against that year's Big Bad. The arcs of the various characters are not, however, necessarily limited to a single season, but extend over two or more seasons. While neither Buffy's, Willow's, nor Xander's personal stories are articulated in single-season chunks, those of The Master, The Mayor, and Glory are.

Joss Whedon is a risk taker, and that fact accounts for some of the most thrilling as well as some of the most disappointing moments in *Buffy*. The upside of taking risks is that when they pay off, the results can be extraordinary. Seasons 2, 3, and 5 show what can happen when the risks pay off, these being some of the most compelling seasons of any show in the history of TV. The downside of risk taking is that gambles don't always pay off. Season 4, with its rather unconvincing and somewhat off-putting arc dealing with The Initiative, never really becomes particularly compelling, while the cyborg Adam is one of *Buffy*'s least interesting Big Bads. Season 4 is one of the show's weakest, despite an abundance of outstanding standalone episodes. But despite this plethora of great episodes ("Wild at Heart" 4.6, "Something Blue" 4.9, "Hush" 4.10, "A New Man" 4.12, "This Year's Girl"/"Who Are You?" 4.15-16, "Superstar" 4.17, and "Restless" 4.22, to name only a few), they could not compensate for the weak central narrative.

Buffy was the WB's flagship series through Season 5. Then, after bitter contract negotiations between Twentieth Century Fox, the studio that produced the series, and the WB broke down, the show moved over to UPN.

The final two seasons are generally not felt to be *Buffy*'s finest. Both seasons were dark and featured too many weak episodes, while the Big Bads were not up to the level of previous baddies. The show nonetheless managed some spectacular episodes, such as the unforgettable musical episode "Once More, With Feeling" (6.7), "Conversations With Dead People" (7.7) and "Chosen" (7.22), the series finale. The show continued to take risks and refused to repeat itself; if the risks did not quite pay off, neither can it be said that Whedon and new show runner Marti Noxon were ever willing to stand pat.

The story of *Buffy*'s success remains one of the most improbable in the history of TV. After all, most attempts at converting films to TV involve successful films, not failures. Not merely a successful television series, the show not only created a cultural icon in the character of Buffy Summers, but established new precedents in what it was possible to do with television. Few seeing the film in 1992 would have imagined that the little blonde vampire-slaying cheerleader would become an indelible feature of our cultural landscape.

Works Cited

Brereton, Dan, and Christopher Golden. "Buffy: The Origin." Adapted from Joss Whedon's original screenplay. *Buffy the Vampire Slayer Omnibus*. Vol. 1. Milwaukee, OR: Dark Horse, 2007. Print.

Buffy the Vampire Slayer: *The Chosen Collection*. Cr. Joss Whedon. Perf. Sarah Michelle Gellar, Alyson Hannigan, Nicholas Brendon, Michelle Trachtenberg, and Anthony Stewart Head. Twentieth Century Fox Home Entertainment, 2006. DVD.

"Chosen." 7.22. Writ. and dir. Joss Whedon. *Buffy*.

"Conversations with Dead People." 7.7. Writ. Jane Espenson and Drew Goddard. Dir. Nick Marck. *Buffy*.

"Fool for Love." 5.7. Writ. Doug Petrie. Dir. David Solomon. *Buffy*.

"Hush." 4.10. Writ. and dir. Joss Whedon. *Buffy*.

"A New Man." 4.12. Writ. Jane Espenson. Dir. Michael Gershman. *Buffy*.

"Once More With Feeling." 6.7. Writ., dir., and music by Joss Whedon. *Buffy*.

"Restless." 4.22. Writ. and dir. Joss Whedon. *Buffy*.

"School Hard." 2.3. Writ. David Greenwalt and Joss Whedon. Dir. John T. Kretchmer. *Buffy*.

"Something Blue." 4.9. Writ. Tracey Forbes. Dir. Nick Marck. *Buffy*.

"Superstar." 4.17. Writ. Jane Espenson. Dir. David Grossman. *Buffy*.

"This Year's Girl" (part 1 of 2). 4.15. Writ. Douglas Petrie. Dir. David Grossman. *Buffy*.

Whedon, Joss. Interview by Tasha Robinson. *The A.V. Club.com*. 5 Sep. 2001. Onion. Web. *Joss Whedon: Conversations*. Ed. David Lavery and Cynthia Burkhead. Jackson: UP of Mississippi, 2011. 23-33. Print. Television Conversations Series.

"Wild at Heart." 4.6. Writ. Marti Noxon. Dir. David Grossman. *Buffy*.

"Who Are You?" (part 2 of 2). 4.16. Writ. and dir. Joss Whedon. *Buffy*.

1.02
"Raise Your Hand If You're Invulnerable!": An Interview with Harry Groener

Tanya R. Cochran

First published in "Spotlight: Joss Whedon," PopMatters.com, 11 March 2011.
On Monday, January 24, 2011, I had the privilege of spending some phone-time with Harry Groener. A versatile and seasoned actor, Groener may best be known to readers as the third-season *Buffy the Vampire Slayer* antagonist Mayor Richard Wilkins, a frontrunner for *Buffy* fans' favorite villain. Yet Groener has been acting for decades, commanding both screen and stage. In the following interview, Groener answers questions about what it means to be honored by his peers and remain rooted in the theatre, what it was like to work with Joss Whedon and *Buffy* actors Sarah Michelle Gellar and Eliza Dushku, what constitutes a healthy actor–fan relationship, and what he's excited about concerning his latest project.

PopMatters (PM): First and foremost, congratulations on the 2010 Ovation Award for *Equivocation*. After quite a few prestigious nominations—including nominations for several American Theatre Wing Tony Awards®—over your career, what does this particular award mean to you? How does it feel to be recognized in this way?

Harry Groener (HG): It's recognition by the community of my work, and it means a lot because of the play itself. I love the play, and I adore Bill Cain who wrote it. The experience was a very meaningful one for me, so it meant a lot that [my role in *Equivocation*] was the one that was pulled out and was recognized. It's always good when your peers in the community recognize you for your work. It makes you feel good! And it is good to be nominated. People make fun of saying that, but it is, in fact, true. Somebody has to win because that's the contest, right? Those are the rules. But in truth—and this is the way I felt about the other nominations—the fact that you are singled out as one of the few for that season does mean a lot to me. Winning is the icing, the recognition of it, the acknowledgment of it. It means a lot.

PM: I know that you and your wife Dawn Didawick are among the founding members of the Antaeus Company in North Hollywood, California, and that the theatre's mission includes helping actor-members stay grounded and rejuvenated, mentoring each other, and reaching out to the community. As a teacher myself, I'm interested in the teaching roles you have taken on in the company (or on the sets of your various projects) and what you enjoy most about teaching others—actors or community members—your craft.

HG: Well, this is funny because I've been asked if I wanted to teach. At the moment, what I enjoy doing are the question and answer sessions with the younger actors, as opposed to master classes. Going in and working on scene work... I still have a reluctance to do any of that, only because I feel that I'm still working it out myself so I don't know that I'm... I don't want to say "qualified" because I think there is a certain qualification that I have to give out information. But as far as being in a classroom situation, I'm a little uncomfortable with that at the moment. I might not be later on. But I'm *not* uncomfortable in the question and answer format. I know that benefited us greatly when I was [a student] at the University of Washington and we had actors come in. We would pump them for information and get as much as we could about what it was like "out there." And I liked that. It opens up all kinds of subjects. And if that leads to some demonstration, that's one thing... but it's that type of work that I enjoy. As far as [The Antaeus Company's] concerned, I've done some of that. We're very involved and we have a wonderful outreach program and we go out to schools. Our company does mainly classical plays, so we try to bring those plays to a younger audience and try to help build [the art] because we're losing that audience to computers and other media. We have to try to find a way to bring them into the theatre, and I enjoy that. In fact, many people in the company enjoy that. We have a lot of good teachers in the company, many who teach Shakespeare classes and all kinds of other things.

PM: Yes, I looked at the list of members, and you have an impressive group of people working together there.

HG: Yes, yes. It really is. It's an amazing company: over a hundred actors. Not all working at the same time. Most of the actors work in television and film and other places. There are usually between 40 and 60 who are available at one time to do a project, and even that gets mixed up because one of the tenets of our company is that we double cast all of our plays. That was something set up by Dakin Matthews who, along with Lillian Garrett-Groag, started the company as a way to function in Los Angeles where you come to do television and film not theatre. And [Matthews] said, "How do we do this?" Well, if you double cast, you're free to go and do and make the money you need to survive, to live. And the integrity of the play is not compromised because you have an equally wonderful actor in the role who takes over for the time that you're gone. At one point it was even thought maybe we could go as deep as triple casting, but that would have been insane! Yet that was thought of, to cover our bases.

From the beginning, we knew that we would be different, very different than an understudy situation. There are actors, including myself, who realize you're doing it for nothing. Yes, you're doing it for love, but it's time consuming. Part of the deal is that you actually get to perform. Nobody wants to work in an understudy situation; no one would take that responsibility on because it's too much time. And so who would take on an understudy position? Well, the actors who need the experience and need the work and might not be as proficient in their work yet, and so the quality of the production is diminished—or can be or possibly is diminished—to some extent, and that's not something our company wants to deal with. There's a lot of talk about the double-casting situation because it's difficult primarily on the directors, unless they really come into it knowing it's going to be difficult and they accept it, but it's really hard for them. It's harder for them, I think, and for the stage manager in terms of scheduling, than it is for the actors. There are some actors in the company who don't like it, who don't want to do it. They would prefer to have a single cast, but that isn't always possible. *I* think it's impossible. For the company to survive, I think you have to double cast. In fact, I couldn't work with the company unless it double cast.

PM: In a 2002 interview with Nancy Rosati of *Talkin' Broadway*, you say, "The goal is really the same whether it's television, film, or theater, and that's to tell a good story." You feature prominently in the third-season narrative arc of *Buffy the Vampire Slayer*. Would you define that season's story as "good," and if so, what specifically made it good?

HG: Yes, I *would* say that it was good, and I think the fans confirm that it was good. I think it was probably the way the mayor was set up and then the way he was written. Joss was very specific, very clear about what he wanted with this particular guy. [Mayor Richard Wilkins] was innocuous. [Whedon] didn't want someone with a very thin moustache saying, "You must pay the rent, you must pay the rent," and if ever I crossed over into that sphere, he would say, "No, no, no. Don't worry about that. Throw it away, throw it away, throw it away." He was very clear about selling that story. And what I thought was wonderful, and what I got from a lot of the fans, was that the mayor was much more scary because he didn't have any horns or scales or fangs or whatever. He was like your guy next door. He was like your uncle. And he was dangerous and deadly. Don't we see that all the time in the news? We see very plain-looking people and they're evil and they kill children. Awful people. I think it's the way that [Whedon] told this particular story. You locked into that arc. And you really got it. The mayor seemed unstoppable, the way they were setting him up. Of course, you all knew in the back of your head that Buffy was going to win—she had to win—but the way they were setting it up, [viewers] kept wondering, *When is it going to happen? He's getting stronger and stronger, and he's gonna win, he's gonna!* It's the way Joss wrote it that made it a really good story. They gave me great, great things to do. Very funny things. The humor was very important along with the danger of it.

PM: You have performed in a wide variety of roles, venues, and genres. Yet I suppose there is something unique about each one. What made working on *Buffy* distinctive?

HG: Well, distinctive from other television, from other episodics. It was distinctive certainly because of Joss and his mind and where they took the character. It was distinctive in that it was the longest run of a character that I've ever had other than a series in an episodic like that, in that kind of role. And it was the cast. The cast was so wonderful and conscientious and funny and committed. Sarah [Michelle Gellar] was just divine. You know, she's been acting ever since she was as high as your knee. And such a pro, I mean a real pro. Always came prepared. Never threw any scenes. Sometimes you hear, I guess you hear in the tabloids, about people doing that. I have yet to witness any of it. I've certainly seen in my lifetime maybe one or two self-indulgent actors throwing a hissy fit, but I rarely, rarely see it in this business—whether stage, television, or film. Everyone behaves really well, behaves as ladies and gentlemen; they do their work. It's only a very tiny, tiny percentage of people who behave in a certain way who get published in the tabloids, and those people would behave like that whether they were in show business or not. What distinguishes the show for me is all of that and the character that I was able to play, what they allowed me to do. Also, the strange relationship with Faith that [the mayor] had. She is the daughter he never had, and he's the father who loved her unconditionally, absolutely unconditionally. She had never experienced that before. She'd never had that love before, so it made it stronger and stronger, their bond together. And I thought that was strangely wonderful and sick all at the same time [laughs].

PM: Many viewers recognize the on-screen synergy between your Mayor Wilkins and Eliza Dushku's Faith. Can you talk a little bit about how that chemistry came about during rehearsals and/or during filming?

HG: Well, she's such a lovely girl. We got along right from the beginning. She's very sweet and smart and very professional and really had a handle on the part. It was actually quite simple. There was nothing really to do other than show up and sort of understand. We both enjoyed that relationship and that story line. It was full. There was a lot going on, whether it was written on the page or not. And that's, again, in the writing. When you can look at a scene and you really get what's going on, there's more to play than the written word. And that is a testament to Joss. To the degree that here's Faith, and she's this tough, leather-wearing vampire killer [laughs]. At the same time, there's this wonderful scene when the mayor puts her up in an apartment, and he gives her all that kind of stuff. He buys her this beautiful, little summer frock. He says she'd look so pretty in this and gives it to her. And she actually tries it on and wears it for him as the daughter. For Faith to actually do that and not say, "What the hell's going on!" The fact that she did that means she *did* understand their relationship, and there wasn't something kinky and weird going on. There wasn't. There wasn't *anything* kinky and weird. It was pure, as pure as those two people could be in how they felt about each other, in what she was to him and what he was to her. That was very clear and pure and good—[laughs] on a certain level, right?! But I thought that was very, very sweet for Joss to come up with that [scene with the dress]. It made the story richer. [Dushku] was delightful to work with, and she's a lovely woman. She made my character very, very easy to play.

PM: As a professional actor working with Joss Whedon as a professional writer/director, what can you say you learned from Whedon while on the set of *Buffy*?

HG: I wish I could say I learned a lot. I don't know what I learned from [Whedon] specifically. What I learned about the business through him was interesting. He's so brilliant in his work—in his writing, his mind, and his imagination. You think that everything in television is fairly controlled, and it is. Pretty much. Things don't go so crazy. Yet for the last two episodes [of the third season], we didn't have a script. We were given synopses at the end of the evening about what they were going to film the next day. But no words, no script, no anything. They just said, "Come on in, and when we have it, we'll give it to you."

PM: Sounds a little scary to me! [Both laugh.]

HG: Yes, I've always had a script. There's never been just a synopsis. You go to work, you get ready to work. What Joss was doing was actually writing it as we were traveling, getting there. And we'd wait. Finally, they'd say, "We have the first scene." You'd get the scene; then you'd go and rehearse it. They'd light it. And while they were lighting it or rehearsing it, Joss was over there in the corner on the set, literally over in the corner, writing the next scene. You think, *Well, that I've never seen before.* You're amazed that that can happen, especially now when you have a room full of people deciding on one little thing. That's fascinating. You learn more about the business and how the mechanism works. [Whedon] did behave like a director sometimes. He'd say, "Don't do the obvious. Go the other way, go the other way." That's something a director can always show you. No matter how old you are or how much experience you have, you can always fall into that trap [of doing the obvious]. It's always good to be reminded [not to do that].

PM: You have quite a few devoted fans, some whom have followed your entire career, some who are particularly interested in your work with Whedon. From an actor's point of view (i.e. being the object of many people's fandom), how would characterize a healthy actor/fan relationship?

HG: Probably one that's limited to "Please sign my photo" and "Thank you very much." I don't think that it's healthy to get too involved with any fan, although there is one friend [Melanie Alford] whom I met a long time ago who started out as a fan—and is still a fan—of *Buffy*, and she, in fact, put together the unofficial Harry Groener website [www.harrygroener.com]. You have to be careful, because I didn't know about Melanie right in the beginning. But she seemed very nice and she would write. You have to be careful because you can get strange people who want to communicate, and you have to discourage that type of communication. But with Melanie, it was different. She also said, "I have an idea for some stories. Can I send you what I have written? It would really save my life." I said to go ahead and send it, and it turned out that she's actually a lovely and wonderful writer, she really is. Very, very good writer. But she's had a very tough life. We've met a number of times—in New York, in Indiana at plays I was in. I've met her and her mother both. She's actually quite nice and has had some terrible tragedies in her life. She had a terrible accident that crippled her in a terrible way. A car accident. A drunk driver hit her as she was coming home late from work one night. She was in the hospital and was very bad, and I called her in the hospital and I think that really helped out. She's turned out *not* to be crazy! [Laughs.] She's very, very nice. We correspond a little bit here and there and wish each other well for holidays and things like that. And *I* don't know what's going on. Sometimes I look at the fan site as well and say, "Oh, it was that year that I did that." I don't keep up. I don't remember when I did certain things.

PM: Yes, fans are very good at keeping track of those details.

HG: Yes, they can be really good at keeping track of that. But generally, as a rule, I feel you should not get involved other than a "I'm happy to take a picture with you" or when you go to conventions and sign something. Although, most people at the conventions are sweet and dear and terrific, and I enjoy talking to them because I'm a sci-fi nut myself. So I enjoy talking about that world, and it's really fun. I understand the mindset, so I really do like it. But you have to be careful, especially with those who write to you and ask you to help out with this or that, who latch on. You have to discourage that. You have to be judicious, careful. That, I think, is a healthy relationship.

PM: Are you aware that your work with Whedon is studied and praised by scholars? In other words, do you ever read academic scholarship on your work with *Buffy*?

HG: No, I don't. I had no idea that Whedon's work is studied. That's quite complimentary! No, I had no idea, and I don't read any of that, as I don't read reviews. I don't read any of that stuff. I do read the articles occasionally to help me know, yes, that person did get it right. That's always good to know because I've been in situations where people have not taken the time and trouble to care and gotten things completely wrong. That's always discouraging. There was one interview I had with a man who was very sweet and had been doing this for a long time and didn't have anything to record with. He wrote everything down and got everything right! [Laughs.] Every single thing absolutely right! He was a vet, had a good memory. The detail was freakin' impressive!

PM: What are you currently working on? And what are you most excited about regarding the project?

HG: Currently, I'm working on playing King George in *The Madness of King George III*. It's Alan Bennett's play, and there's a movie by the same name. Nigel Hawthorne played the lead. It'll be with Chicago Shakespeare Theatre, and I've never worked there so that's pretty exciting. It's a lovely theatre… I'm excited about being in Chicago. I love Chicago. I've played there a number of times. When we're close to the opening, my wife will come out and be there for the rest of the run. I'm looking forward to this play, and I'm really enjoying the research of it because when you're playing an actual historical person, it's going back to school and learning about a whole other culture, time, and society. And what I love about that is that you learn there really isn't much that's different other than the costumes and some of the rules. And certainly now, technology.

In the last hundred years or so, technology has changed more than it ever has in the entire history of human beings and is growing exponentially. That's a major, major difference. But the bottom line, at its core, there is so much of how people lived hundreds and thousands of years ago that is *exactly* the same. Relationships are the same—same problems between men and women, power struggles, politics. People enjoy the same things. Kids did the same things; they enjoyed the same toys. In many ways, [our predecessors] were smarter, more educated. Their education was much more well-rounded. They spoke more languages. At least, those who were educated; you certainly can't say that about everybody—women, for example. Women weren't always allowed to educate themselves. And that exists now in certain places in the world where women aren't allowed to educate themselves or vote or anything like that… I just love the research part of [playing a role]. I've read five books so far about King George III, and I'm waiting on one more book to get to me about him and this whole time period. I'm rereading and getting details to put into the script. I've been learning all the lines. I have the lines; I'm off book and ready to go. I couldn't wait for the time when I could sit down, get in there, and write down all these little pieces of information and all these little things that are going to hopefully help make the character richer and deeper. You get into it more when you have the research, and I really, really like that.

PM: Thank you so much. It has been such a pleasure.

HG: Thank you. I really enjoyed talking to you.

Notes

I have taken the title of this piece from Groener's Mayor Richard Wilkins in the *Buffy* episode "Choices" (3.19).

I wish to thank Harry Groener for generously sharing his time and responses, Jason Kendziera of the Susan Smith Company for helpfully arranging the interview, and Melanie Alford for carefully maintaining the valuable *Somewhat Official Harry Groener Site*.

1.03
"Note to Self, Religion Freaky": When Buffy Met Biblical Studies

Ronald Helfrich

While the wide arc of the globe is turning
We feel it moving through the dark
—B-52s, "Revolution Earth"

No doubt some of you are scratching your head at the subtitle of my paper and saying to yourself, "When *Buffy* Met Biblical Studies, when did *Buffy* meet Biblical Studies?" Some of you might be thinking to yourselves, "I recall a few instances where the TV show *Buffy the Vampire Slayer* wove religious issues into the program. There was the religious tyrant Genevieve Holt who ran that brutish children's home in "Where the Wild Things Are" (4.18). There were Willow's occasional references to her Jewishness ("Bad Eggs" 2.12, "Passion" 2.17, "Amends" 3.10, "The Body" 5.16, "Hell's Bells" 6.16, "Help" 7.4). There was the time when Riley was on his way to church ("Who Are You?" 4.16). There were the several references to Wicca ("Hush" 4.10). And there was that line that Buffy famously uttered in response to something Giles said to the Buffster as he and she were on their way into a crypt to see what Spike's minions were looking for and which, of course, serves as the title of my paper: "Note to self, religion freaky" ("What's My Line, Part 1" 2.9). But *Buffy* meeting Biblical Studies? Come on!"

Let's see if I can explain why I chose this title. As with any "intellectual" or "academic" fan boy or fan girl paper this paper will, if you scratch hard enough below the surface, tell you something about me and about the social, cultural, and ideological contexts I came of age in. When I first matriculated at college I was a Biblical Studies major. I even had romantic visions of a once upon some time in the near future when I would be teaching Biblical Studies at a major college or university somewhere in the English-speaking world.

Though my academic fairy tale has not come true—it took me a long time to recognize that I didn't want to spend a significant proportion of my academic life studying languages, that my interests in religion were broader and more cultural and theoretical than Biblical Studies allowed, and that trying to find a job in academia with a very specialized degree in a smallish field would be difficult. So I ended up in cultural anthropology and later history. Talk about job opportunities! I did, nevertheless, learn a lot during my intellectual journey through the labyrinth of Biblical Studies. One of the things I learned was that the Torah/Pentateuch/Five Books of Moses (Genesis, Exodus, Leviticus, Numbers, and Deuteronomy) could not have been written by the man tradition claimed had written them, Moses.

It is Baruch Spinoza, a Jew living in seventeenth-century Holland, who is arguably the father of modern "scientific" Torah Studies. In his *Theological-Political Treatise* Spinoza brought Renaissance methods to bear on the Pentateuch, questioning whether Moses actually wrote the five books of the Torah. Spinoza instead attributed their authorship to a historian writing hundreds of years after the event.

Spinoza's assertion about the authorship of the Torah would really take hold in intellectual culture and eventually the academy beginning in the late eighteenth-century and continuing through the nineteenth. Under the impact of the Renaissance, the Scientific Revolution, and the Enlightenment (a holy trinity I view as three-in-one) a number of scholars, many of them German (something American evangelist Billy Sunday would make hay of when he argued during the first World War that the Allies were God's instrument to punish heretical Germany for its higher biblical criticism), came to the same conclusion Spinoza had years earlier. Arguing that the Torah could not have been written until urbanism, the monarchy, and a priestly caste had arisen in Ancient Israel, they argued that the five books of the Torah could not have been written by Moses. Instead they maintained that the Torah was the product of several sources, the J or Y source, the document which used the term *Yahweh* for god, the E source, the document which used the term *Elohim* for god, the P source, the priestly document which contained regulatory and ritual sources relating to the priesthood in Ancient Israel, and the D source, the book II Kings 22 says King Josiah "discovered" in the temple in Jerusalem in 622 BCE. The Deuteronomist would also, claim "scientific" biblical critics, play an important role in the editing of the books of Joshua, Judges, Samuel, and Kings. Scholars date J to the 10th century BCE, an era of increasing urbanism, professionalization (the development of a priestly caste), and bureaucratization (the development of priest/scribes) in Ancient Israel, E to the eighth century BCE, D to the seventh century BCE, and P to the sixth.

I am sure many of you at this point are still scratching your heads and still wondering, at least to yourselves, what all of this has to do with *Buffy* Studies? Let me see if I can explain.

Buffy the Vampire Slayer, as I am sure we all know, came on the air as a mid-season replacement on the WB network in March of 1997. Almost immediately the show generated not only an intense and devoted fan base but also an impressive amount of scholarly and critical intellectual analysis. In fact, no other TV show anywhere in the known universe has generated the academic discourse *Buffy* has at this point. This academic analysis, it turns out, has read *Buffy*, to borrow the title of a Clint Eastwood film, about every which way it can. Academics have used *Buffy* as a platform from which to praise the show for its postmodernist, feminist, social ethical, girl power, "undemonising," liberal, radical, and conservative themes and damn it for its liberal, conservative, Manichean, paternalist, racist, sexist, and classist ones.

A few examples of the latter:

For Neal King ("Brownskirts: Fascism, Christianity, and the Eternal Demon," ed. James B. South, *Buffy the Vampire Slayer and Philosophy* 197-211) *Buffy* is not so much about the girl next door as the proto if not outright vigilante fascist down the street who leads the forces of "good" against a host of "evil" others. For King, *Buffy*, with its dualistic distinction between good humans and evil vampires, demons, monsters, and witches is nothing more than another ugly ethnocentric Manichean fairy tale about us the "good" and them the "bad." In King's mental world the Scoobies, Buffy's companions in the war against evil, are the jackbooted and brownskirted or brownshirted defenders of a vicious human nationalism that won't stop goose slaying their way through Sunnydale until every "evil" vamp, demon, monster, and witch in their way is dead (note the "politically correct" liberalism here).

To Michael Levine and Steven Jay Schneider ("Feeling for *Buffy*: The Girl Next Door" in South 294-308) *Buffy* is just another unconscious Freudian reality tale starring the proverbial girly girl next door. Schneider's and Levine's Buffy, like every other woman in the universe apparently, is yet another virgin/whore object of the ever-present voyeuristic male gaze, males who want either to marry her—fortunately or unfortunately this "m" word breeds limpness in males—or seek no more than the zipless happy with her, making her, in the process, into just another one of the many wenches who serve to satisfy their insatiable lusts. She, in turn, is the stuff Freudian dreams are made of. She is Buffy the frigid and Buffy the slutty (categories ironically parodied by Buffy in the first episode of the show, "Welcome to the Hellmouth" 1.1).

For a number of other commentators the prejudicial ugliness of *Buffy the Vampire Slayer* lies in its racism, sexism, middle classism, and ageism. For Elyce Rae Helford ("My Emotions Give Me Power: The Containment of Girls Anger in *Buffy*," ed. Rhonda Wilcox and David Lavery, *Fighting the Forces* 85-97) the show reveals different types of racist, sexist, and bourgeois stereotypes in its depiction of anger in its three Slayers—Buffy, Kendra, and Faith—undermining in the process any potentially positive moment (note the radiant utopian ideology here) of social change in the process (the text in the service of the status quo?). According to Helford, Buffy—the white, middle-class Slayer—controls, redirects, and uses humor to diffuse her anger while upholding, in the process, a middle-class ladylike identity. Kendra, a black Jamaican Slayer, on the other hand, rarely expresses her anger and never uses humor while working-class Slayer Faith is rarely humorous, is almost always rebellious, expresses her anger openly, and is often sexually explicit while hiding, all the while, feelings of self-loathing. The characteristics of each Slayer, claims Helford, and the differences between them mark Buffy off as insider to Kendra's and Faith's black and working-class outsiders (note the concentration or race and class here both central symbols of much contemporary criticism).

Others move beyond the supposed class bias of Buffy's anger when condemning the show. For Helford (Introduction, ed. Helford, *Fantasy Girl* 1-9) *Buffy*'s portrayals of women are regressive. *Buffy*, she claims, markets cleavage to the masses in the form of simulated girl power. For Lorna Jowett (*Sex and the Slayer* 37) the death of Anya (Emma Caulfield) in the final episode of the series ("Chosen" 7.22), a female character Jowett characterizes as "minor," "disposable," and "powerless," is a product of misogyny in the *Buffy* text. For AmiJo Comeford ("Cordelia Chase: Sunnydale Cheerleader and L.A. 'Rogue Demon Huntress': The Feminine Myth Deconstructed," paper given at the Slayage Conference 3, Henderson State University, Arkadelphia, AR, 5-8 June 2008; and "Cordelia Chase as Failed Feminist Gesture," ed. Durand, *Buffy Meets the Academy* 150-60.) the victimization of Cordelia Chase, in *Buffy* and its spinoff *Angel*, is evidence of sexism in Whedonverse texts.

For Alissa Wilts ("Evil, Skanky, and Kinda Gay: Lesbian Images and Issues," ed. Edwards, Rambo, and South, *Buffy Goes Dark* 41-56) the death of Tara in "Seeing Red" (6.19) and Willow's response to it—Tara and Willow were lovers—is yet another instance of the dead lesbian and the evil lesbian clichés in the media as well as a homophobia that occasionally rears its ugly head in the Buffyverse. For Kent Ono and Vivian Chinn (Ono, "To Be a Vampire on *Buffy the Vampire Slayer*," ed. Helford, *Fantasy Girls* 163-86 and Chin; "Buffy? She's Like Me, She's Not Like Me—She's Rad" in ed. Early and Kennedy, *Athena's Daughters* 92-104). *Buffy*'s vampires are really metaphors for the people of color who are the genocidal fodder for the Scoobies white middle-class vigilantism. For Lynne Edwards ("Slaying in Black and White: Kendra as Tragic Mulatta in *Buffy*," Wilcox and Lavery, *Fighting the Forces* 85-97) the portrayal of the Jamaican Vampire Slayer Kendra draws on the tragic mulatta myth in which a fair-skinned black women, usually of mixed racial heritage, tries to pass for white with tragic consequences and thus reveals the existence of racism in the Buffyverse.

For J.P. Williams ("Choosing Your Own Mother: Mother-Daughter Conflicts in *Buffy*," ed. Wilcox and Lavery, *Fighting the Forces* 61-72) *Buffy*'s portrayal of knowing teenagers, unknowing parents (Joyce Summers and Sheila Rosenberg, Buffy's and Willow's mothers respectively) and the killing of Jenny Calendar, the assertive techno-pagan computer science teacher who loves Buffy's Watcher Rupert Giles and mentors Scooby Willow, is evidence that the program harbors ageist prejudices against mothers and surrogate mother figures.

It is here in the text centered criticisms of *Buffy* that, I think, *Buffy* meets Biblical Studies (of both the scientific and literalist varieties). Though the "documentary hypothesis" has been around since the late nineteenth-century the only evidence for it is textual. The different names for god in the biblical text (Yahweh, *Elohim*) are believed to show that there was a Yahwist document and an Elohist document (and presumably it means that to modern humans the ancient Hebrews were unable to play with synonyms).

The two creation stories in the Book of Genesis, for instance, are attributed to the P or Priestly source (Genesis 1.1, "When *Elohim* began to create heaven and earth" is this a "sacred" tale which justifies the position of the priests in the Hebrew state?) and the Yahwist (Genesis 2.4b, "When *Yahweh Elohim* made earth and heaven..."). *Buffy*'s interpreters King, Levine and Schneider, Helford, Jowett, Comeford, Wilts, Ono and Chin, and Edwards assume that historic Western prejudices consciously or unconsciously leave their mark on the *Buffy* text but they offer no extra-textual evidence for any of this. King elides the fact that there are historical debates over precisely what fascism is and he simply can't accept that for whatever reason real evil exits, at least narratively, in the Buffyverse. Levine and Schneider offer no extra-textual evidence for the Freudianism they claim to find in *Buffy*. Ono and Chin offer no extra-textual evidence for their contention that *Buffy* is racist and that *Buffy*'s vampires are representations of ethnic and racial "others." Helford does not engage the numerous interviews in which *Buffy*'s creator Joss Whedon (Commentary: "Welcome to the Hellmouth," *Buffy the Vampire Slayer: The Complete First Season on DVD*) claims that he meant *Buffy* to be "feminist." Nor does she, if we want to focus exclusively on the textual level, bring third-wave feminist positions to bear on her second-wave feminist contentions that *Buffy* is sexist.

Comeford offers no evidence statistical or otherwise that Cordelia Chase is anymore victimized and hence damaged than say Angel or Spike or any other major character in the *Buffy* or *Angel* text, male or female. Edwards ignores the fact that Kendra is never described as a mulatta in either the shooting script or the final script ("What's My Line Shooting Script," *Buffy the Vampire Slayer: Complete Second Season DVD* and "What's My Line," *Buffy the Vampire Slayer: Complete Second Season DVD*) of "What's My Line" (2.9 and 2.10). Finally, Jowett's attribution of Anya's death to misogyny ignores Whedon's statement in his commentary (Commentary: "Chosen," *Buffy the Vampire Slayer: Complete Seventh Season on DVD*) on the episode "Chosen" (7.22) that he killed Anya for narrative reasons—someone had to die—and that he chose Anya because Emma Caulfield had decided that five years of playing Anya was enough.

Biblical Torah Studies and *Buffy* Studies are also similar in their attempts to put their respective texts into broader contexts. The redaction of the Torah is said to be a product of urbanism, the rise of a monarchy, and the rise of a professional priestly caste. The *Buffy* text is thought to reveal, like a crystal ball (I owe this metaphor to my colleague Jonathan Nash), anything we might want to know about in this instance, American and presumably Western ethnocentric, political, gender, class, age prejudices, and class prejudices.

OK, some of you now might be saying to yourselves, yes I can see your point. There is, on some level at least, a similarity between Biblical Torah Studies and Crystal Ball *Buffy* Studies. Both of them center their analysis on the text. But so what? What's the big deal about this?

Now that I may have some of you with me I want to deconstruct a bit of the argument I have just been making and see if I can explain to you in the process what the big deal is about the connection between Biblical Torah Studies and *Buffy* Studies.

Yes there are similarities between Biblical Studies and *Buffy* Studies, but there are also differences between them. Biblical Studies, unlike contemporary crystal ball textual criticism—which film critic David Bordwell (in his

Making Meaning) calls symptomatic criticism—is grounded in classical critical approaches that go back to Plato and Aristotle which emphasize the close analysis of the text (lower criticism) and the analysis of the textual sources of that text (higher criticism)—Bordwell calls this form of criticism explicative criticism. This form of exegetical criticism is very different from the crystal ball textualism that dominates so much literary, cinema, and television criticism today. In symptomatic criticism the sources of the text are not simply other texts but primarily the social and cultural contexts or discourses into which that text "fits."

Crystal ball textualists tend to skip the close analysis of the text as text altogether in favor of a social and cultural contextualization of the text (the text as ethnocentric, racial, sexist, classist, ageist). This crystal ball approach to contexts is of an entirely different order and quality than those of Biblical Torah scholars in that urbanism and professionalization are extra-textual historical processes while the crystal ball textualist approach which sees ethnocentrism, racism, sexism, classism, and ageism as discourses that are both outside of and inherent to "texts" of all types (a kind of Holy Spirit of the textual world?).

The difficult trick, at least from a historical perspective, is how crystal ball textualism gets from text to context without an engagement with primary source materials. Crystal ball textualists rarely engage in primary source material analysis beyond the text as I noted. None of the essays on *Buffy* I have been examining in this paper, for instance, explore production material from Twentieth-Century Fox or Mutant Enemy. None of them draw on interviews with any of *Buffy*'s creative personnel including *Buffy* creator Joss Whedon. Why? Since the 1960s the academic disciplines of Cultural and English Studies have experienced a theoretical sea change. Once enamored of auteurist textual criticism, today Cultural Studies and English Studies are dominated by scholars and critics who are less interested in authors, authorial intentions, and "texts" per se than in how "texts" of all kinds reflect *underlying* social, cultural, and psychological contexts. These changes have forced those in Cultural and English Studies to reconfigure the theoretical mental terrain in which they reside, creating, in the process, a veritable theoretical smorgasbord feast of mix and match social theory from semiotic to structuralist, feminist to psychoanalytic, racist to classist, Marxist to cognitive, and phenomenological to hermeneutic theory.

As a result of this theoretical smorgasbord and the theoretical bricolage that has resulted from the synthesis of many of these theoretical perspectives questions of nationalism, race, gender, class, and age have become central to the contemporary crystal ball textual enterprise while primary source research isn't even an afterthought for most crystal ball textualists because it isn't regarded as essential. They assume that the author is dead and that it is society and culture that does its ethnocentric, racist, sexist, classist, and ageist work through the text via the medium of the "author."

HOW VALID ARE THE INTERPRETATIONS OF BUFFY'S CRYSTAL BALL TEXTUALISTS?

In the final part of this paper I want to briefly explore another question: How valid are the interpretations of *Buffy*'s crystal ball textualists? Is *Buffy* really ethnocentric, racist, sexist, classist, and ageist as *Buffy*'s crystal ball textualist critics claim? It is important to note that not every commentator, not even every academic commentator, has read *Buffy* in these ways. Frances Early ("Staking Her Claim: *Buffy the Vampire Slayer* as Transgressive Woman Warrior," *Journal of Popular Culture* 35.3 (2001): 11-28) characterizes Buffy as a transcendent female warrior. Patricia Pender ("'Kicking Ass is Comfort Food': Buffy as Third Wave Feminist Icon" in ed. Gillis, Howie, and Munford, *Third Wave Feminism* 164-74) raises questions about whether one can apply the canons of second-wave feminism to third-wave feminism television shows. Joss Whedon (Commentary: "Welcome to the Hellmouth" (1.1), *Buffy the Vampire Slayer: Complete Season One on DVD* and Commentary: "Chosen" (7.22), *Buffy the Vampire Slayer: Complete Seventh Season on DVD*) says that he intended *Buffy* to be feminist and has directly contradicted Lorna Jowett's contention that Anya was killed off in the final episode because she was a woman (Commentary: "Chosen" (7.22), and quoted in *TV Guide Insider* 23 May 2003). I could also find counterexamples to the contention that *Buffy* is ethnocentric, racist, classist, and ageist but I have limited space.

So how do we square this contradictory circle? Should we throw up our hands and assert that *Buffy* is a contradictory text? Is *Buffy* both ethnocentric and nonethnocentric, racist and nonracist, sexist and nonsexist, ageist and nonageist all at the same time? Or does crystal ball textualism, because it generally doesn't engage in research in primary source material, open itself up to the criticism that it can say and has said virtually anything it wants as long as it recapitulates its preexisting assumptions that ethnocentrism, racism, sexism, classism, and ageism are omnipresent in US and Western society and culture and hence its texts (the joys of tautology?)? Does the fact that few symptomatic critics do primary source research mean that there are absolutely no evidentiary checks and balances in crystal ball textualism because there is no checking or balancing of textual claims against primary source materials? While we can verify, extra-textually, whether there was an increase in urbanization, the monarchy, and professionalization in Ancient Israel can we do the same thing for the claims of crystal ball textual critics given that extra textual and textual "evidence" is collapsed in symptomatic criticism?

Academics really need to take a look in the mirror once in a while and reflect on the history of academia and the social and cultural forces that have played a role in structuring knowledges within the Ivy Tower. One of the questions we could pose while looking in this mirror is this: Do Biblical Torah Studies and *Buffy* Studies reflect social and cultural ideologies that reflect the evolution of notions of expertise and professionalism since the Enlightenment?

Students of the Torah, on some level, assume that the Pentateuch is a human document. Crystal ball textualists make certain assumptions as well. One can see these in their discussion of character in the Buffyverse. The *Buffy* papers I have been analyzing all tend to counterpoint their own preferred socially and cultural constructed and (generally unexpressed) nonfascist, nonracist, nonsexist, nonclassist, and nonageist ideal depictions of vampires, demons, monsters, black women, working class women, mothers, and surrogate mothers against their fascist, racist, sexist, middle class, and ageist opposites establishing, in the process, binary pairs of opposites one of which is coded as good, the other of which is coded as evil. In this Manichean mental world the only possible nonracist and nonsexist depiction of a black female Slayer, for instance, is one in which she is apparently never teased, never criticized, always central to the show, always disobedient of patriarchal authority, and alive for the entire run of the show, while the only nonageist depiction of Jenny Calendar would be one in which she never betrays the Scoobies, always fights the patriarchal forces, trains Willow in how to be a witch, and never dies at the hands of Angelus. Such a Slayer and such a Jenny Calendar would invariably be rather shallow and one-dimensional characters which border on, if not become, caricatures and stereotypes. Is this ideological exemplar criticism? Is this normative criticism grounded in notions of ideological correctness? Do you really want to see such stereotyped and caricatured characters in a TV show?

As I noted the questions I have been asking raise questions about the nature of symptomatic criticism. Is it a kind of ideologically correct enterprise? If it is a kind of ideologically correct textual enterprise does this raise questions about the dispassionate and descriptive nature of such criticism? What if our crystal ball textual Slayers aren't in possession of the Du Lac cross of right textual analysis? When crystal ball textualists read a text are they revealing their own biases and prejudices and giving us insight, in the process, into their own social and cultural contexts? Does this raise questions about the readings themselves? Are the readings of crystal ball textualists, in other words, a species of reader response or audience analysis? Are they reflective of the academic obsessions of the day—ethnocentrism, racism, sexism, classism, and ageism?

So what can be done to move *Buffy* Studies beyond this virtually exclusive focus on the text, which, by the way, I am not saying is not an entirely bad thing if the focus is exegetical and we move beyond the text toward more empirical terrain that is verifiable by checking and balancing interpretations against primary source material (exegesis-hermeneutics-homiletics). We need to understand that television is people (the men and women who made *Buffy* happen including creators, writers, producers, craftspeople, actors, executives), a business (the industrial society and culture in which *Buffy* developed and which includes personnel connected to the networks and the studios), technology (technological factors that impacted *Buffy*), forms (the genres and languages *Buffy* deploys), representations (What does *Buffy* tell us about the US society and culture and the wider world), and something viewers react to (Who watches *Buffy*? Where? Under what conditions? How have viewers, real viewers not just academic readers, responded to *Buffy*).

We need to understand television's modes of production, means of production, relations of production, hierarchies of power, star system, production system, technologies, stylistic, representational, and narrative practices, and histories. We need to understand the relationship of the television industry to other corporate entities both nationally and globally and the role television plays in structuring and replicating ideologies. We need to understand what TV's writers thought they were writing, what TV's directors thought they were directing, what TV's producers thought they were producing, what TV's craftspeople thought they were crafting, what TV's actors thought they were acting, and what a TV's readers thought they were reading (compare Michael Temple and Michael Witt's Introduction to their edited collection, *The French Cinema Book* 1-5).

These are not the only things we need to recognize about television. We need to recognize that there are the budgetary constraints within which TV operates. According to writer Drew Goddard and director David Solomon (Commentary: "The Killer in Me," *Buffy the Vampire Slayer: Complete Seventh Season on DVD*) the episode "The Killer in Me" (7.13) had a budget which didn't allow for the appearance of more than a few Potentials because of this lack of money. David Fury and James Contner (Commentary: "Grave," *Buffy the Vampire Slayer: The Complete Sixth Season on DVD*)

BUFFY THE VAMPIRE SLAYER 1.03

claim that most of the budget for Season 6 was, in fact, spent on "Once More with Feeling" (6.7). We need to recognize that there are constraints related to availability of actors in the Hollywood community and the salaries actors draw.

According to writers David Fury and Drew Goddard (Commentary: *Buffy the Vampire Slayer: Complete Seventh Season on DVD*) Mutant Enemy, Joss Whedon's production company, had trouble finding competent British actors to play British parts in the Buffyverse. We need to recognize that there are constraints associated with the roles network executives play in the casting a television series. Rumors have long circulated that WB executives balked at having the womanly Riff Reagan who played the role of Willow in the pilot play the role of Willow in the series.

We need to understand the role contingency sometimes plays in television production. According to Kristine Sutherland (Kristine Sutherland; Interview; Season Four Overview, *Buffy the Vampire Slayer: Complete Fourth Season*) the fact that she was living in Italy for most of Season 4 meant that her character Joyce only appeared limitedly that season. This allowed the writers to move Buffy into a dorm at the University of California in Sunnydale and to explore Buffy's feelings of displacement.

The decision by Seth Green (Oz) to move on to the "greener pastures" of the movie world forced the writers to make changes to Season 4 and allowed the writers to take Willow's sexuality in new directions.

The decision by Anthony Stewart Head (Giles) to spend more time in England with his daughters during Season 6 and less time on the show allowed the writers to focus even more strongly on the growing up and responsibility themes of that season and the show.

Bianca Lawson's decision not to take the part of Cordelia allowed her to play the part of Kendra and Charisma Carpenter to take the role of Cordelia Chase (*Sex and the Slayer* 200, note 8.).

Drew Goddard's decision to write a scene between Eliza Dushku (Faith) and James Marsters (Spike) in "Dirty Girls" (7.18) was an attempt to showcase the two together in order to see if they had the necessary chemistry so that Mutant Enemy might propose a series built around them to network executives (Commentary: "Dirty Girls," *Buffy the Vampire Slayer: Complete Seventh Season on DVD*).

The decision by Joss Whedon to finally write a musical episode of *Buffy* ("Once More with Feeling" 6.7) was predicated on the skills of Joss's actors and James Marsters' persistence in asking Joss to write a musical (Commentary: "Once More, With Feeling," *Buffy the Vampire Slayer: Complete Fifth Season on DVD*).

I have already noted that Whedon's decision to kill Anya in the final episode of the series, "Chosen" (7.22), was occasioned by Emma Caufield's decision not to renew her contract because of her wish to move onto other acting roles and challenges (Joss Whedon; Commentary: "Chosen" (7.22), *Buffy the Vampire Slayer: Complete Seventh Season on DVD* and Whedon quoted in *TV Guide Insider* 23 May 2003).

And we need to realize that TV writers don't always express their own viewpoints in their work. Whedon has discussed how he has his characters take stands that he doesn't necessarily agree with for the sake of narrative structure (Whedon; Commentary: "Conviction" (5.1), *Angel: Complete Fifth Season on DVD;* and Rob Thomas, editorial comments in ed. Thomas, *Neptune Noir: Unauthorized Investigations into Veronica Mars* 1-7, 34, 46, 94, and 170). We need more studies, in other words, like those of Julie D'Acci on *Cagney and Lacey* (Julie D'Acci; *Defining Women: Television and the Case of Cagney and Lacey,* 1994) and Matthew Pateman on Jane Espenson's scripts on *Buffy, Angel,* and *Firefly* (Matthew Pateman; "'Shallow Like Us': a Bit of a Chat About a TV," keynote address at the Slayage Conference 3, Henderson State College, Arkadelphia, AR, 5-8 June 2008).

I know I have posed a lot of questions already in this brief paper but I want to close this paper with four more: Isn't it about time that we proclaim the death of the death of the auteur? Isn't it about time that we give a renewed emphasis to exegesis? Isn't it about time that we renew our emphasis on primary source research? And isn't it about time that, if we are going to make claims about how texts are read that we actually ask people beyond the ivy walls who read *Buffy* how they "read" the *Buffy* text (survey and ethnographic work perhaps?)? All four are indeed a big deal.

1.04
You're Strong. I'm Stronger:
Vampires, Masculinity & Language in *Buffy*
Malgorzata Drewniok

Although Joss Whedon's *Buffy the Vampire Slayer* aired from 1997 till 2003 (running for seven seasons), it is still a hugely popular series. Much has been written about the show, e.g., Wilcox and Lavery's *Fighting the Forces* (2002) and Wilcox's *Why Buffy Matters* (2005). Language is one of the show's most distinctive features. It has been extensively explored in certain aspects by scholars from many disciplines, including Overbey and Preston-Matto (2002), Adams (2003), Kirchner (2006), and others in the special issue of *Slayage: The Journal of the Whedon Studies Association* devoted to *Buffy* language (*Slayage* 5.4, 2006), as well as Mandala (2007). There is still much to be said about *Buffy*'s language, however, especially when it comes to its chief villains: vampires.

The long running nature of the series means that the writers were able to develop an extremely wide variety of vampire types. There are background vampires and there are more prominent ones; there are conventional vampires, embracing a figure we know from the 19th century Gothic novel, as well as more contemporary ones. There are even "good" vampires, who have a soul and do not kill. It is clear then that to construct a vampire in *Buffy the Vampire Slayer* one needs more than just a black Bela Lugosi cape. The vampires in the show are constructed through acting, clothes, and props, but also through language.

I will explore here the relationship between masculinity and the language the vampires in *Buffy the Vampire Slayer* use: macho vampires vs. the Slayer. The show aimed to abolish the stereotyped vampire and to propose a new incarnation of this creature, but to do that, it had to depict such a vampire first. The vampires at the beginning of the series embrace the "macho" monster style, achieved partly through the way they speak. Lorna Jowett discussed gender in *Buffy in Sex and the Slayer* (2005) and Jennifer K. Stuller looked at Buffy as a superheroine in *Ink-Stained Amazons* (2010). I would like to look at how vampire macho attitude is reflected in language.

THE CONVENTIONAL VAMPIRE

When the series begins with the two-part pilot, "Welcome to the Hellmouth" (1.1) and "The Harvest" (1.2), Buffy has to face a group of stereotypical vampires called the Order of Aurelius. Its leader, the Master, is trapped underground in a ruined church (sunk by an earthquake) and confined by a magical force field. He is dependent on his second in command, Luke, and other minions, to get food, i.e. human victims. In the very first episode two vampires, Thomas and Darla, are sent to bring some "offering" to the Master but are prevented by a new girl in town, Buffy. In order to rescue her new friend Willow, Buffy fights Darla and Thomas, whom she stakes. Then Luke, a more powerful vampire, appears and is surprised that such a petite girl is fighting his brethren. He dismisses Darla, saying, "I'll see if I can handle the little girl." He attacks Buffy and realizes she is not what she appears to be. But Luke is not intimidated. He tells her, "You're strong" and a moment later sends her flying across the room, commenting: "I'm stronger." The fight between Luke and Buffy continues for the last few minutes of the episode and the vampire finally gets impatient. He complains, "You're wasting my time." And when Buffy does not give up and hits him again and again, he smirks, "You think you can stop me? Stop us? You have no idea what you're dealing with" ("Welcome to the Hellmouth" 1.1).

Although in the next episode we learn that Luke realizes who Buffy is, his words express his disdain and lack of respect for this strong female fighting him. He describes her as a "little girl," and although he acknowledges her strength, he still seems to think she is out of her league, that she is not worth his effort. But Buffy does not back off and in time Luke needs to increase his sense of authority: his self-correction ("Stop me? Stop us?") shows he feels the need of backing himself up with others, building his identity—and strength—as a part of a group, not an individual. His last utterance is an open threat: "You have no idea what you're dealing with."

It is important to point out here that Luke's chauvinist attitude comes from his leader. The Master, an ancient vampire with vast magical power, but confined physically underground, is dismissive of Buffy even when he learns she is the Slayer, the chosen one who stands alone to fight vampires. They first meet in "Nightmares" (1.10) when everyone's nightmares come to life. In this dream reality the Master is able to temporarily leave his confines because he is the embodiment of Buffy's nightmares. He greets her with, "So! This is the Slayer! You're prettier than the last one." By this short utterance the Master emphasizes his age and experience—although there is only one Slayer in every generation, he implies he has met at least one more, and possibly more than that. He points to Buffy's prettiness to depreciate her strength. His words also sound like a threat: the Master appears to be a very strong vampire; therefore it is quite possible that his encounter with the other Slayer ended with her death. In this instance the Master succeeds, terrifying Buffy to the extent in which she cannot say a word, and buries her alive ("Nightmares").

Luckily, this was just an alternative reality; Buffy survives and she faces the Master again in the Season 1 finale, "Prophecy Girl" (1.12). This time they both know this encounter is final—one of them is going to die. According to a prophecy Buffy is supposed to fight the Master and die. Despite initial doubts she is now determined to face him, to save the world. She goes down to his lair and he greets her with "Welcome." She is frightened but tries to keep a brave face and uses one of her weapons: a witty remark. But the Master sees right through her and "the feeble banter portion of the fight," denying her power. When she tries to shoot him with a crossbow, he catches the bolt and dismisses her attack: "You're not going to kill me with that thing." Not only is he stronger and faster than she; he also constantly depreciates her verbally, not even allowing her weapon a proper name, just a "thing." Buffy is more and more petrified but the Master taunts her, "I'm waiting for you. I want this moment to last" ("Prophecy Girl"). Out of context those words sound like those of a lover seducing his lady. But here the Master's words are menacing: he revels in Buffy's fear and her seemingly imminent death. He is using a seductive line and giving it a new meaning: of a threat.

Finally Buffy succumbs to her opponent; the Master drinks from her and leaves her drowned. He is so sure of himself he does not bother to check whether he really has killed the Slayer. He leaves his lair, freed by the power of feeding from the Slayer. Found by Angel and resuscitated by Xander, the Slayer again faces the vampire leader, but now the power shifts. She takes him by surprise: he exclaims, shocked, "You're dead!" Buffy uses witty remarks to distract him, but he still believes she cannot possibly defeat him. Even when he fails to hypnotize her, he says, "Did you really think you could best me here when you couldn't below?" And when she laughs because she has already spotted her chance to defeat him, he asks, "You laugh when my hell is on earth?" But a moment later Buffy throws him over the skylight into the room below and onto an upturned wooden table and thus impales and kills him ("Prophecy Girl").

As a conventional vampire, representing a stereotype we know thanks to Bram Stoker, the Master uses old-fashioned language and is a chauvinist when it comes to the Slayer. His attitude is also reflected in those of his minions, like Luke mentioned earlier. The Master knows she has the power to fight vampires; however, his self-confidence never falters and he cannot even imagine being defeated by this Slayer, especially this petite, delicate girl.

MODERN VAMPIRES

The Master dies at the end of Season 1 and the second season sees a different kind of vampire, new in town. In the third episode, "School Hard," a vampire couple arrives in Sunnydale and immediately causes a stir. One of them is Spike—a punk vampire in a black leather coat and with bleached hair. He does not acknowledge any authority and makes it known when he introduces himself and his companion to the Order of Aurelius: "You've got Slayer problems. That's a bad piece of luck. Do you know what I find works real good with Slayers? Killing them." The Slayer is always a young female and Spike seems very dismissive of such a girl, even though she is always powerful. He is boastful: "I did a couple of Slayers in my time. I don't like to brag. Who am I kidding? I love to brag! There was this one Slayer during the Boxer Rebellion and…" ("School Hard" 2.3). At this point in the narrative we do not know whether he is speaking the truth or just boasting. However, later the series, in Season 5, his back-story is revealed, and it is shown that Spike really did kill two Slayers, one in China during the Boxer Rebellion, and the other in New York in 1977 ("Fool for Love" 5.7).

I believe Spike is the most dynamic of all the characters in the series, not only among the vampires. He starts as a cruel and clever vampire (his nickname comes from his favorite torture tool) and the Slayer's enemy, but as the series progresses he switches sides, joins the Scoobies (Buffy and her friends), and becomes Buffy's friend and lover and eventually her champion. That is why it is so interesting to observe the way he projects his "macho" persona when he first appears in town, when he boasts about killing Slayers. He does that to make himself more important, to prove he is manlier than the rest of the vampires who struggle in the fight against the Slayer. He makes a deal with the others: he will kill the Slayer and in return they will leave him and his companion, Drusilla, in peace.

SPIKE AND THE SLAYER

When Spike first meets the Slayer, he sets her up to fight a vampire weakling in a dark alley, and when she stakes him without much effort, Spike comes out of the shadows with a smirk on his face, saying, "Nice work, love." Later on in the series he will often use pet names, but addressing the Slayer as "love" is definitely depreciating here. The next time they meet he is not subtle—he wreaks havoc in her school and searches the building for her, bellowing, "Slaaayer! Here, kitty, kittyyyy. I find one of your friends first, I'm gonna suck them dry. And then use their bones to bash your head in" ("School Hard" 2.3). He diminishes her power by calling her "kitty" as if she were literally a pet.

Spike starts off macho, dismissing any power a "girl" can have. But at the end of the series, in Season 7 it is Spike who comforts the Slayer when she is temporarily expelled from her home. He says: "I love what you are, what you do, how you try. I've seen your kindness and your strength. I've seen the best and the worst of you. And I understand with perfect clarity exactly what you are. You're a hell of a woman. You're the one, Buffy" ("Touched" 7.20).

There is also another modern vampire around: Angel, Buffy's romantic interest and helper, a reluctant vampire, a vampire with a soul. He appears in the very first episode of the series and follows Buffy. She feels it and leads him into a dark alley where she attacks him. He smiles as she pins him down to the ground, "Ah, heh. Is there a problem, ma'am?" With this exaggerated politeness he pretends he does not know who she is. But when she finally lets him get up, he admits, "Truth is, I thought you'd be taller, or bigger muscles and all that. You're pretty spry though" ("Welcome to the Hellmouth" 1.1). At this point there can be three interpretations of his words: first, because she knocked him down, he assumed she must be bigger; second, he has met other Slayers—but that implies that he knows about vampires and Slayers as well as that he is old; and third, he heard about her from other vampires in Sunnydale. Whichever the interpretation, Angel employs a patronizing tone, like Luke acknowledging Buffy's physical strength, but not entirely believing in her Slayer powers. Since the story is just beginning, she does not know yet he is a vampire; therefore she is not bothered by his words.

In the next few seasons Buffy and Angel have a stormy relationship. Buffy is attracted to him, but she cannot initially imagine being with a vampire, a creature she is destined to kill. However, they eventually give in to their feelings and become a couple. When Spike arrives in Sunnydale, it is revealed he is acquainted with Angel. The latter pretends to be the still evil Angelus whom Spike remembers (before Angelus was cursed with a soul and became Angel). Spike asks him about Buffy, and he replies, "She's cute. Not too bright though. Gave the puppy dog 'I'm all tortured' act. Keeps her off my back when I feed." To hide his transformation Angel reverts to a lie, playing on stereotypes that blondes are gullible and stupid.

Later on in the series it is shown how Spike was turned into a vampire and joined Angelus' pack. In one of the flashbacks in "Fool for Love" the pack is hiding in a coal mine in Yorkshire. Angelus is the supposed leader of the pack; Spike does not want to submit to him. Angelus scolds Spike for his behavior: "You've got me and my women hiding in the luxury of a mine shaft, all because William the Bloody [Spike] likes the attention." This is a power struggle between the two. On the one side we have Angelus, who speaks possessively of *his* women (Darla and Drusilla) and claims killing requires a "certain amount of finesse," that it is "pure artistry." On the other side we have rebellious Spike who calls Angelus "a poofter" and expresses his disagreement with "bollocks" and "sod off" ("Fool for Love"). The vampires cultivate their macho image not only when facing the Slayer but also among themselves (although still in the presence of females: Darla and Drusilla).

A VAMPIRE UP-TO-DATE

There is another macho vampire worth mentioning here. Although the conventional vampire embodied by the Master was defeated at the end of Season 1, the series comes back to this idea at the beginning of Season 5 in "Buffy vs. Dracula." In the Buffyverse Count Dracula is still alive and comes to Sunnydale to meet the famous Slayer. He is presented as an elegant, civilized man rather than a dangerous vampire. He observes Buffy from the shadows when she stakes a vampire and comments, "Very impressive hunt." By choosing to use "hunt" rather than "kill" he gives Buffy an elevated status, that of a hunter. It is curious because "vampire slayer" and "vampire hunter" have become interchangeable in recent popular culture, for instance in Laurell K. Hamilton's *Anita Blake: Vampire Hunter* series (1993-) and Jeaniene Frost's *Night Huntress* series (2007-). But Buffy in fact is not a hunter. She patrols and usually kills vampires to prevent them from hurting humans; she does not hunt them for pleasure. Dracula in the series shows his admiration by adding, "such power." Instead of attacking the Slayer, he is admiring her from a distance. When she asks who he is, he says, "I apologize. I assumed you knew. I'm Dracula." She does not believe but he insists, "You know who I am. As I would know without question that you are Buffy Summers." He recognizes her power. And then he gives the reason of his visit: "I came to meet the renowned... killer" ("Buffy vs. Dracula" 5.1). Again, he chooses not to use the term "Slayer" and as he elevated her with "hunter" a moment earlier, now he depreciates her role by calling her a "killer." It is notable he takes time to choose the right word: he pauses before saying "killer," thus accentuating the word. It seems he implies Buffy is not a noble Slayer, defender of innocents, but rather a killer who preys on his kind.

Their meeting is brief and when they meet again, he gives her more words of admiration, "You're magnificent... You are different. Kindred." And here lies his true meaning: Dracula admires Buffy because in his eyes she is like him, a civilized killer, a kindred spirit, a powerful creature. Buffy is of course appalled. But he continues, "I have searched the world over for you. I have yearned for you. For a creature whose darkness rivals my own" ("Buffy vs. Dracula"). This is in fact an insult. Dracula claims Buffy is dark like him, evil and not human. It is also curious that Dracula's words foreshadow what happens to Buffy at the end of this (fifth) season: she will sacrifice her life to save the world and then will be magically resurrected in the following season, but she will be different, changed.

It is also remarkable that Dracula's words echo those of the Master. In the Season 1 finale, the Master uses a specific register: that of a seducer/rapist. Dracula does the same in Season 5. The Master tells Buffy, "I'm waiting for you. I want this moment to last." Buffy replies, "I don't," but he dismisses it with "I understand" and still drinks from her ("Prophecy Girl" 1.12). When Dracula visits Buffy in Sunnydale, he tells her, "You're magnificent" and, "I have searched the world over for you. I have yearned for you." When he leans towards her neck, she feebly says, "No," but he dismisses it with "Do not fight," and drinks from her ("Buffy vs. Dracula"). Later when they meet again:

Dracula: Are you afraid I will bite you? Slayer, that's why you came.

Buffy: Last night... it's not gonna happen again.

Dracula: Stop me. Stake me."

Buffy: Any minute now.

Dracula: "Do you know why you cannot resist? Because you do not want to."

In addition, Dracula himself makes a reference to the Master, commenting: "You have been tasted" and Buffy replies, "He was... unworthy" ("Buffy vs. Dracula"). It is a very subtle but humorous way of mocking the monstrous Master, although the audience still knows Dracula is as stereotypical.

Buffy the Vampire Slayer touches upon many issues and is linguistically rich. The show's aim—as stated by its creator, Joss Whedon—was to show high school as a horror experience. But the series also succeeded in proposing a new kind of vampire. First the conventional vampire was portrayed as one to be quickly disposed of. Vampires with a "macho" attitude towards the Slayer either met death (Luke and the Master) or changed their ways (Angel and Spike), or, in the case of Dracula, simply left the scene after being staked and re-staked. One of the Slayer's weapons is language and through language the "macho" vampires tried to depreciate her. But eventually it was always Buffy who could stand over each of them and say: "You're strong. I'm stronger."

Works Cited

Adams, Michael. "Beyond Slayer Slang: Pragmatics, Discourse, and Style in *Buffy the Vampire Slayer.*" *Slayage: The Online International Journal of Buffy Studies* 5.4 (2006). Web.

---. *Slayer Slang: A* Buffy the Vampire Slayer *Lexicon*. New York: Oxford U P, 2003. Print.

Buffy the Vampire Slayer: *The Complete DVD Collection*. Region 2. Twentieth Century Fox, 2004. DVD.

"Buffy vs. Dracula." 5.1. Writ. Marti Noxon. Dir. David Solomon. *Buffy.*

"Fool for Love." 5.7. Writ. Doug Petrie. Dir. Nick Marck. *Buffy.*

Frost, Jeaniene. *Halfway to the Grave*. New York: Avon, 2007. Print. The Night Huntress Series #1.

Hamilton, Laurell K. *Guilty Pleasures*. New York: Ace, 1993. Print. Anita Blake: Vampire Hunter Series #1.

"The Harvest (Part 2 of 2)." 1.2. Writ. Joss Whedon. Dir. John T, Kretchmer. *Buffy.*

Jowett, Lorna. *Sex and the Slayer: A Gender Studies Primer for the* Buffy *Fan*. Middletown, CT: Wesleyan U P, 2005. Print.

Kirchner, Jesse Saba. "And in Some Language That's English? Slayer Slang and Artificial Computer Generation." *Slayage: The Online International Journal of Buffy Studies* 5.4 (2006). Web.

Mandala, Susan. "Solidarity and the Scoobies: An Analysis of the -y Suffix in the Television Series *Buffy the Vampire Slayer.*" *Language and Literature* 16.1 (2007): 53-73. Print.

"Nightmares." 1.10. Writ. Joss Whedon and David Greenwalt. Dir. Bruce Seth Green. *Buffy.*

Overbey, Karen, and Lahney Preston-Matto. (2002). "Staking in Tongues: Speech Act as Weapon in *Buffy.*" Wilcox and Lavery, 73-84.

"Prophecy Girl." 1.12. Writ. and dir. Joss Whedon. *Buffy.*

"School Hard." 2.3. Writ. David Greenwalt and Joss Whedon. Dir. John T. Kretchmer. *Buffy.*

Stuller, Jennifer K. *Ink-Stained Amazons and Cinematic Warriors: Superwomen in Modern Mythology*. London: Tauris, 2010. Print.

"Welcome to the Hellmouth (Part 1 of 2)." 1.1. Writ. and dir. Joss Whedon. *Buffy.*

Wilcox, Rhonda V. *Why Buffy Matters: The Art of Buffy the Vampire Slayer*. London: Tauris, 2005. Print.

--- and David Lavery, ed. *Fighting the Forces: What's at Stake in Buffy the Vampire Slayer*. Lanham, MD: Rowman, 2002. Print.

1.05
Failure of the Everyman:
The Lost Character That Was Xander Harris
Kyle Garret

From the moment he rides his skateboard on to the screen in "Welcome to the Hellmouth," Alexander LaVelle Harris stakes his claim as the outsider looking in on each aspect of the *Buffy the Vampire Slayer* universe. Xander is placed as the Everyman in the midst of both the natural and supernatural worlds. He is the awkward, geeky boy in high school, the shiftless townie in college, and the lone member of the Scooby Gang without powers or abilities above and beyond the normal human being (at least until the arrival of Dawn). More so than any of the other characters, Xander's story arcs are tethered to the real world. Yet the resolutions to those stories are supernatural in nature, and in turn undermine their real world significance. This becomes problematic in the later seasons of the show, when the rest of the cast continues to delve deeper and deeper into supernatural realms and Xander's Everyman role becomes harder to maintain.

During the first two seasons of *Buffy*, Xander's standing on the show is less distinct, as the entire cast is still being fleshed out. While Willow may be a borderline genius, her intelligence is not regularly a benefit to the group's missions. She, Xander, and Cordelia are all civilians pulled into a super-powered world familiar only to Buffy and Giles, both of whom have specific skill sets that make them essential. When Xander's desire to be a part of the popular high school crowd comes to a head in Season 1's "The Pack" (1.6), its supernatural resolution doesn't seem at odds with the character. At this point, he represents nothing more than an awkward teenage boy who tries too hard and says the wrong thing too often. His run-in with hyena spirits is no better or worse than Willow's relationship with a medieval demon in "I, Robot... You, Jane" (1.8). Even as late as episode 2.16, "Bewitched, Bothered, and Bewildered," Xander has still yet to be thematically ostracized from the rest of the gang, so his magic-gone-awry attempt at winning back Cordelia doesn't come off as particularly strange.

It's not until Season 3 when Xander's future status on the show is clearly laid out with the appropriately titled "The Zeppo" (3.13). While the rest of the gang, which now features an additional Slayer in Faith and the ever more powerful witch Willow, engage in an epic battle, Xander is sent away for his own protection. The fact that Xander is not bound by the rules of the Buffyverse is underscored when he interrupts a stereotypical Buffy/Angel moment that parodies their usual melodrama. At this point, the show itself is still maintaining a fine balance of real world problems told through a supernatural lens. It is a balance that keeps Xander's role on the show from becoming forced.

The climax of Xander's overarching story comes in episode 5.3, "The Replacement." This is the moment of Xander's self-actualization, the pinnacle of his role as the Everyman. Every aspect of this episode is set up to establish that Xander's world is at odds with the supernatural world his friends live in. While he might spend time with them in that world, when Xander is the center of his universe, all is normal, all is mundane. His girlfriend might be an ex-demon, but her mortality is underscored by her injured arm; it's her current, human form that matters. Xander moves into an apartment of his own, escaping from the basement that has been the center of so many Buffy-related adventures. His new home isn't a gathering place for the Scooby Gang; it's a home for him and his all too human girlfriend. This is his refuge, his way of establishing his own identity, one that is not beholden to Buffy or her influence. By the end of "The Replacement," Xander owns his role as the Everyman.

The difficulty, then, lies in writing a character that has ostensibly reached the end of his journey, but continues to appear in episodic stories for nearly three more seasons. Even more problematic is the fact that the show, now saddled with continuity spanning four plus seasons, became ever more and more dependent upon plot, moving further and further away from metaphor as its central conceit. This meant that Xander's newfound solidarity would not last. Soon, the supernatural elements of the show were crashing down on Xander's real world problems in increasingly less subtle ways.

The epitome of this new era in the life of the character came in Season 6, with "Hell's Bells" (6.16).

From the very beginning of the show, there have been ominous, often heartbreaking hints about Xander's upbringing. The issue was seldom addressed directly, but the offhand comments sprinkled throughout each season indicated that Xander came from a dysfunctional family, one filled with, at the very least, verbally abusive drunks. The story of Xander's family was intentionally kept away from the week-in and week-out adventures in an effort to keep it untouched by the fantasy elements of the show. The fact that Xander never talked about his family in any detail gave the entire story a certain realism that the majority of the show lacked. In many ways, it was the most tragic story line on the show.

In Season 6, however, all of that was thrown out the window. We finally meet Xander's family in "Hell's Bells," and instead of getting the smart, nuanced story we had been teased for so long, we get buffoonery. Gone is any attempt to keep such a well-orchestrated story by itself, away from the ever more ridiculous, supernatural elements of the show. Anya's side of the wedding aisle is filled with outlandish demons, whose cover as "circus folk" would be mildly groan-worthy in an ordinary episode of *Buffy*, but is a failure given the weight of the story up until now. At this point in the show's run, all things must now include some kind of spectacle to be engaging, so Xander and Anya's wedding is crushed beneath the weight of demons, magic, and even time travel. The episode leaves Xander emotionally broken, but it seems that it's less because of what has happened and more because of how.

The desperate attempt to do something with Xander by turning his wedding into a fight scene only served to delay the inevitable. There was still more than a full season of episodes of *Buffy* left, and it was clear that Xander had truly become a lost character, one who had peaked too early. The attempt at forcing him into Buffy's world by surrounding him with demons and amplifying Anya's heritage had been a disaster, so in Season 7 he was taken in another direction, one more in keeping with the Everyman character he'd been before. Unfortunately, the specifics of this new direction seemed to come out of the blue, and support for it was then fabricated after the fact as a way of again thrusting Xander squarely into the supernatural world.

The end of episode 7.12, "Potential," is a near perfect moment for Xander, when he finally puts into words what has been so apparent for nearly seven years. It's a moment that is at odds with "Hell's Bells," but in keeping with the climax seen in "The Replacement." Dawn has just discovered that she is not, as she believed, a potential Slayer. She's disappointed by this fact, thinking that not being one of the chosen ones, not being supernatural in some way, makes her inferior to those who are. After nearly seven years of living in the shadows of his friends, Xander finally verbalizes his position while comforting Dawn. He tells her how those with powers will never understand how it is to be without them, that he stands aside and sees everything though he feels helpless to affect events. It underscores how significant it is that Xander is the Everyman, that he is not fully in the supernatural world, and thrives outside the Buffy spotlight. Taken on its own, Xander's near soliloquy is a wonderful summation of the character.

But that summation is soon picked apart a few episodes later in "Dirty Girls" (7.18). Once again, we see an organic aspect of Xander's Everyman role pulled kicking and screaming into Buffy's world, and once again it comes across as a forced way of including Xander in the action. A nice, but ultimately innocuous line at the end of Xander's moment in "Potential" suddenly becomes something more, or at least an indelicate implication of something more. The moment is so heavy-handed that Xander is literally maimed by it, losing an eye for the sake of the story. Caleb, an emissary of the First Evil, actually says "You're the one who sees everything, aren't you?" just before he gouges Xander's eye out. Finally, the show has done it; Xander is no longer the Everyman, and can never be that character again, as he now has a constant reminder of how his life has been taken over by the supernatural.

In the end, the role that Xander had played so well is cast aside, and he becomes a normal human being trying to stay afloat in a sea of the abnormal. He doesn't have the necessary skills to stay above water, so he becomes lost, his greatest feature having been stripped of him by the increasing demands of an episodic genre story.

Works Cited

"Bewitched, Bothered, and Bewildered." 2.16. Writ. Marti Noxon. Dir. James A. Contner. *Buffy*.

Buffy the Vampire Slayer: The Chosen Collection. DVD Boxed Set. Created by Joss Whedon. Twentieth Century Fox Home Entertainment, 2006. DVD.

"Dirty Girls." 7.18. Writ. Drew Goddard. Dir. Michael Gershman. *Buffy*.

"Hell's Bells." 6.16. Writ. Rebecca Rand Kirshner. Dir. David Solomon. *Buffy*.

"I Robot... You Jane." 1.8. Writ. David Greenwalt. Dir. Scott Brazil. *Buffy*.

"The Pack." 1.6. Writ. Matt Kiene and Joe Reinkemeyer. Dir. Bruce Seth Green. *Buffy*.

"Potential." 7.12. Writ. Rebecca Rand Kirshner. Dir. James A. Contner. *Buffy*.

"The Replacement." 5.3. Writ. Jane Espenson. Writ. James A. Contner. *Buffy*.

"The Zeppo." 3.13. Writ. Dan Vebber. Dir. James Whitmore, Jr. *Buffy*.

1.06
Buffy the Vampire Slayer in the Fantasy Canon
Nathan Pensky

Buffy the Vampire Slayer was famously "a teen drama…with vampires," equally involved with representing realistic teens as with showing these teens fighting monsters and demons. Creator and showrunner Joss Whedon once said that his original conception of the landmark show came from an impulse to give substance to the buxom blonde so easily disposed of by monsters in horror movies.

To view *Buffy*, then, as a revisionist entry in the fantastical horror genre would seem apt. But it's interesting to notice that it's not the fantastical elements Whedon inherited from horror movies that are most revised, but the realistic ones. *Buffy* is original for focusing on realistic characters—their language, their psychological motivations, their humanity—as much as on their involvement in a fantasy world. *Buffy* is traditionalist in the horror genre, but innovative in attending to realism as readily as fantasy. And the show's success as fantasy illustrates the importance of a strong sense of reality in effective fantasy stories.

To even begin to talk about a fantastical world, one has to seriously consider its relation to reality. There is reality as it actually exists; there is a facsimile of this reality as we experience it, projected into a medium that bends to the whims of imagination; and finally there is a fantasy world that makes certain alterations upon this facsimile. The latter two both take place in "fiction," or the not-real. But the enjoyment of fantasy worlds always requires a groundwork of necessary plausibility. For us to go into a wonderland, we must first understand what a "land" is; for us to enjoyably follow the exploits of a superman, we must first know what a "man" is, and how the superman differs from him. One imagines passing through a series of doors into larger and larger rooms, the structural integrity of each subsequent room depending entirely on that of the former. Fantasy stories require of their audience two concepts of "the real," one of which is "actually real" and commonly experienced in reality and another that is an abstraction of the real, which constantly references this common experience but which also has a certain imaginative malleability.

Also, one notices right away that the subtler the malleability of abstracted realities, the greater their artistic effect. While great fantasy stories make un-real claims upon literary projections of real experiences, the demands of their un-reality end up being really not very great. For instance, consider the dragon. Here is a creature quintessential to many fantasy worlds but the novelty of which rests entirely upon the combination of very normal creatures. Broken into parts, the dragon is a cat, a snake, and a bat. The dragon's most fantastical attribute, breathing fire, is also an amalgam of two very normal things. We know of fire; we know of breathing. To suppose that something could breathe fire is not an exercise in recreation but rearrangement. Given these observations, does the dragon seem more or less real than, say, Blair from *Gossip Girl*, whose novelty occurs within the projected realities that fantasy uses as its substructure? Blair supposes a "new woman" (and very effectively, too) whereas a dragon only supposes our old conceptions of fire, breathing, cats, bats, etc. and combines them.

Whereas "realistic" stories rewrite history, fantasy is much more indebted to history as it has already been written.

The giant is a man whose bigness gives humanity a beastliness, makes him "other." But his menace is his sameness, not his otherness. The vampire is the human form given aspects of certain parasites, worms, insects, and bats. But we are more frightened of vampires when they take the form of a man than when they appear as mists. Very little actual fantasy is required for a fantasy story, and subtle forms of fantasy are much more effective than those that go over the top. One could tell a story about a "normal day"—a character working in an office, fighting traffic, paying too much for lunch—and then have him bump into only *one* unicorn, after meeting a thousand objects and people of everyday quality, and *presto change-o*, the story barrels headlong into fantasy. This is only a short stretch of the imagination, in some ways much smaller than to suppose an ordinarily fictional "something that could have happened but did not."

This is significant to *Buffy*, because while the show would seem an "innovation" or a "revision," it is really more a throwback, a return to form. By focusing on what is real in its telling of fantasy stories, it illustrates the indebtedness of all fantasy stories to reality, and positions itself within a long tradition of like fantasy stories. With *Buffy* we get a television show about teens much more real than those in *Gossip Girl* but who also happen to be destined to fight the demonic forces of evil. Rather than the fantasy of one aspect of this show undermining the real, fantasy and reality are completely dependent upon the other and thus they reinforce each other in a way that is not necessarily required in shows like *Gossip Girl* and *90210*, the fantasy of which is much less overt but also much greater. As effective fantasy finds itself indebted to effectively real characters, so effective fantasy stories often contain characters strikingly true to life.

REALISM, FANTASY, AND MAGIC REALISM

Like fantasy, realistic fiction or "realism" is a literature constructed from a reaction to reality itself, and this often not an altogether realistic reaction. Realism is not so much a reflection of "the real" as an emphasis of certain aspects of it.

The construction of the realistic aesthetic is, in a way, much less indebted to reality itself than that of fantasy. Realism does not necessarily build from the experience of the reader but asks him or her, in a sense, to throw that experience out the window and, instead, to take into account someone else's experience. Since reality itself is not a plane from which realism launches its own imaginative vision but rather one from which it reactively rebuilds, realism has no particular loyalty to reality. The difference is somewhat like that between a picture of a dragon and a cubist painting of a woman. The former is real in medium, unreal in that which is being depicted; the latter is unreal in medium, real in that which is being depicted. The cubist painting of the woman assumes an experience of "woman-ness," but one that is not necessarily shown in the art itself. The point of the cubist painting lies in a perceived difference as compared to an actual sameness, whereas the picture of the dragon highlights the reverse, a perceived sameness as compared to an actual difference. One can only guess at to what a cubist painting of an imaginary creature would be; someone might try, but it wouldn't work unless we first knew what the creature looked like. So we could understand a cubist painting of a dragon, but only because we've already seen much more "realistic" drawings up to that point.

Realism makes use of the difference between that which "did or did not happen" much more liberally than that which "could or could not happen." The effectiveness of the latter difference is built upon the former and, in a sense, enforces its veracity; in not addressing the latter difference, realism often does not take the trouble to enforce such veracity, or at least often requires it in a less representative way. This is not to say that realists do not need to know what reality is, or that the good writers among them do not need to assume that their readers do. But where fantasists build upon existing realities, realists tear down existing realities only to rebuild them. Again, where realism rewrites, fantasy rearranges.

Another key difference between realism and fantasy is that realism focuses on novelties of human interaction, while fantasy focuses on ordinary human interaction in new worlds. Fantasy wants the container of the story to be new, the setting and circumstance, while realism wants the contained or what goes into the container to be new, the characters. Realism wants new men fighting against the old world, while fantasy wants ordinary men who find themselves in new worlds. And this is why fantasy stories are thought to be less personal than realistic ones.

Fantasy stories often feature very "ordinary" protagonists in un-real circumstance, while realism features the exact opposite—un-ordinary protagonists in ordinary circumstance. But as "ordinariness" in literature is often a measure of how close we are allowed to look, and all characters stop being ordinary if one is allowed to live inside their thoughts, fantasy with its rendition of the misplaced everyman as seen from the outside often comes off as less personal, while realism with its psychological emphasis of interior perspective becomes more so.

By recognizing the narrowness of "what is personal" in the above description, we can see the important innovation of magic realism, which somewhat reconciles the personal and the fantastical by allowing fantastical elements to represent the personal. Magic realism recognizes that a character's personality can be addressed as profoundly through his or her actions within a new world, as by addressing the psychological motivations of those actions. It addresses the question of whether or not fantasy stories are personal by addressing fantasy's relation to "the real," that reality is always personal.

Magic realism writers—like Gabriel García Márquez, Jorge Luis Borges, Italo Calvino, and Salman Rushdie—altogether bypass the argument of the impersonality of fantasy stories. They maintain the literary embellishment of realism, that of a closer-than-life perspective and emphasis of detail, while doing away with its core characteristic, a re-writing of actual experience. With the magic realists, we get the mannerisms and stylizations of realism with an allowance for different worlds or literary containers. Magic realists rearrange real like fantasists but look closely at those real things like realists. Here, we get un-ordinary protagonists, because we are allowed to live within their perspective and can looks closely at all their peccadilloes, in the un-ordinary circumstance of magic. And often the new worlds and characters of magic realism are made to interact with are projections of internal, personal struggles. Here, we enjoy close perspective, as in realism, but we also formally rely upon the real, as in fantasy.

Buffy the Vampire Slayer belongs in the tradition of magic realism. Buffy is an ordinary girl, yet her interiority is writ large in adventure. Her powers do not threaten her ordinariness; they are, in fact, significant projections of her quite plain interiority. Supernatural powers do not make the characters of *Buffy* less recognizable. Their powers are an exercise in perspective, an exercise in showing graphically what a novel by Henry James would explore psychologically through inner monologue. Our "closeness" to Buffy Summers, by way of her interiority being significantly projected into a shown medium, formally comprises her status as a vulnerable, human hero.

This is illustrated well in one of the most poignant moments of the series. It is a turning point for the character of Faith, the "other Slayer," and in differentiating Faith's slip from reality against Buffy's steadfastness. The moment occurs in "Bad Girls" (3.14) when Faith accidentally kills a human, thinking that he is a vampire. Buffy, who "dusts" vampires on a daily basis, is visibly shaken by the death of an actual human being. Faith is not so outwardly shaken, and she continues down the arc that had been already established this season, further into evil and inhumanity. Her projected psychology falls into the blank monochromatic mood swings of all evil characters while Buffy's maintains its hue and nuance.

DIVING FURTHER INTO FANTASY

Fantasy stories vary in whole and in part by the distances they remove themselves from the real. They are divided here in three categories by A, B, and C, though the difference among the types is very fluid and perhaps better represented along a continuum than in groups.

Type A Fantasy is a story in which the difference between the imagined fantastical world and that of the reader is very large; the world as we know is not in plain view. Common objects may persist between the two worlds, as in the "sword and sorcery" sub-genre; swords exist in our own real world, though maybe they have never been put to quite such good use on our own plane. People look generally the same, though with heightened features. Heroes are impossibly strong, helper dwarves are impossibly ugly, villains either specter-like or dark-side versions of the hero, with equal strength but thwarted morality and thus distorted outward physicality. Commonalities between this kind of fantasy and the real—and thus in the dynamic by which this kind of fantasy is spring-loaded, as it were—are established by way of abstraction and of emphasis. These stories see heightened (and usually simplified) versions of real situations played out in epic battles between good and evil. Characters imbued with this kind of fantasy can throw farther, ride longer, hit harder. They do some of the things that we do, only much better, which ultimately gives them a difference of quality rather than degree.

Examples of Type A Fantasy are the *Lord of the Rings* and *Star Wars* sagas, where the action occurs "in a land far, far away" or so "long ago" that reality itself seems to have a markedly different nature than ours. Characters can ride horses for days on end, or jump up huge walls with perfect balance. They use "the Force," which can perhaps be the most pure expression of Type A Fantasy. Where we can move things by way of abstracting them, or by harnessing them with technology, they can move objects physically with their minds, which is a kind of mental exercise so great as to become "other."

Type B Fantasy exists when definite portals exist between the worlds. Fantasy and reality merge significantly. Or more aptly, fantasy and reality have to deal with each other. Fairy tales are of this Type B—as the rich man's house in "Cinderella," or the woods in "Hansel and Gretel," or the abject poverty described at the beginning of "Jack and the Bean Stalk."

These places and things were more or less real in history, though they seem remote from modern sensibilities and have been so infiltrated by magic entities since their historical moment that it is sometimes hard to think of them as ever being real. The *Harry Potter* books are perhaps a more obvious example of Type B Fantasy, as well as the *Narnia* books.

Certain totemistic magical items can also be said to be in the tradition of Type B Fantasy. We have rings in our world; magic rings are not necessarily made magic as a result of their being greater or "more ring-y," as Type A's difference of emphasis would dictate. Conan's sword used in the Type A sense, for example, becomes "more a sword" in his hands; its function is heightened. But the faculty of Arthur's sword, Excalibur, to choose the King of Logres is totemistic, and not necessarily as a function of its being a sword. Excalibur in other ways is Type A but not in this one. A cup or a crown could have just as easily chosen Arthur to be king.

Type C Fantasy is story-telling in which the real exists as a literary device by which to view the fantastic. With Type C, the reader/audience is totally immersed in fantasy, but usually through the eyes of a very normal type of person. The modern obstinacy of the protagonists of *Alice in Wonderland* and *The Phantom Tollbooth*, as well as the simple goodness of Dorothy in *The Wizard of Oz* and, to a certain degree, the Hobbits in *Lord of the Rings*, are all examples of Type C Fantasy tradition; in either case, "normalcy" hinders an understanding of each respective magical world but also enables our own enjoyment of those worlds. Alice, Milo, and Dorothy maintain their real-ness in their magical worlds to give the viewer a portal by which to view said worlds. They are the eye of the fantastical hurricane, and the eyes of the reader/audience.

Magical objects of the Type C variety include those chosen for their homeliness, like the owls or the Ford Anglia in the *Harry Potter* series, or like the ways Chewbacca resembles a faithful dog in *Star Wars*. These objects are not only totemistic but also homely; their associations are to ideas small rather than great; they are characterized not by their being a symbolic portal between the ordinary and the other-world but as being totally at home in our own world. Their "otherness" in fantasy worlds, then, is all the stranger for being recognizable. We identify with them and are not overawed by them, except in their being magic, and feel the difference of their being magical *because* we identify with them. Type C magic in itself perhaps most aptly encapsulates the dynamic of fantasy being indebted to reality.

The best examples of Type A are the most simple in their abstraction, the most complex in the narrative layering of said abstraction, as in the *Lord of the*

Rings. Type B, however, improves with complexity; here we find sneak-thief heroes and sympathetic villains. For example, while most characters in *Lord of the Rings* are Type A, Frodo and Gollum are Type B, which is why they have a kind of kinship, and why they both must leave the world in the end. They are pushed out by Middle-earth's being mostly of the Type A variety. Many fantastical stories have elements of all three, though in such examples each type is still distinctive and yields themes representative of said distinctions.

Buffy shows all three types at different times. Willow's nerdiness coupled with her extreme power as a witch can be said to have Type C significance, while her intelligence has Type A. One should view her intelligence and her nerdiness separately, as they are not necessarily two sides of the same coin, which is demonstrated through the character of Xander, who is definitely nerdy but not particularly intelligent. Buffy's strength is, of course, Type A, while the spells and rituals performed on the show are part of the Type B tradition.

The character of Giles is interesting for very clearly showing all three types at various times during the run of the series. At first he shows definite symptoms of Type C, exuding fatherly homeliness and approachability in his status as Buffy's Watcher, yet obvious magical tendencies. As the Watchers' Council begins to expand its influence over Buffy's world, Giles begins to take on Type B totemistic qualities. Through the course of the series, Giles's resourcefulness—and indeed that of all the characters—approaches Type A levels. All the *Buffy* characters at one point take on different types, though maybe no other character exists so comfortably in all three as Giles.

BUFFY THE VAMPIRE SLAYER AS MAGIC REALISM

Buffy the Vampire Slayer is a significant example of magic realism. The formal intermingling of reality and fantasy are interestingly (and as it turns out, inversely) paralleled in storylines and characterizations. Buffy is very ordinary—indeed she often flees *from* fantasy *into* the real—a character who confronts her mortal and immortal enemies with all parts of her personality intact and on display.

Buffy is conflicted, scared, remorseful, reluctant; her appropriation of fantastical elements is as awkward as that of the show's realism to fantasy is fluent. And this is a crucial quality of the show: a formal fluency between the real and the unreal reflected in characters whose narrative transitions between reality and unreality are anything but fluid. We watch Buffy fight demons, and yet our emotions in watching her do so are feelings we would recognize anywhere.

Another extremely interesting aspect of the story is its sheer number of fantastical characters. Fantasy becomes almost commonplace on the show, such that there is very little "othering" of magical creatures. Many stories with large and various fantastical casts have a Type C "normal" character who remains couched in reality and gives the audience a sense of "a man on the ground." Think Luke in the "Mos Eisley scene" of *Star Wars*, Alice in her Wonderland, or even Harry Potter, who in the magical world of Hogwarts and Diagon Alley never seems to stop being amazed by it all. Not so in *Buffy*; vampires and magic becomes prosaic very quickly on the series, and surprises are those of plot and character rather than of a heightened fantasy. The character closest to performing this Type C function is Xander, but he is too situated in his role as the lovable fool to serve as a Type C everyman.

As stated before, the peccadilloes of interiority that would comprise a story's placement within the tradition of realism are in Buffy drawn as fantastical. Whatever is personal or unusual about the real selves of human beings is on the show drawn as fantasy. The core conflict of the series is Buffy's own personal struggle with her magical self, and thus, her reluctance to be thrown headlong into her own personality and "become herself." She is a character that over the course of the series transforms from the thoughtless, easily-killed blonde of horror movies into the heroine of her own epic story.

No other story arc typifies this transformation more clearly than Buffy's romance with Angel. She feels deeply for him on a real-world level, yet her feelings run contrary to what is safe on a fantastical one. Complications arise between them only after they are unmasked as, respectively, Slayer and vampire. Buffy and Angel's love is perhaps the most fantastical element in the series, in that it runs against every rule set up in their magical cultures, and yet it is the most recognizable: the star-crossed lovers. Yet even before being revealed as a vampire, Angel is always dangerous to Buffy. That his danger is reflected and confirmed across the line between reality and fantasy speaks volumes to the show's ability to exist within both worlds.

A sense of drama being played out on two levels occurs everywhere on the series, often mirroring typical teen television clichés with equally trite horror-fantastical clichés, their amalgam comprising something unique and meaningful. One example of this is the evil Mayor character from Season 3. He is relentlessly cheerful, a politician. Yet his cheer hides a menace perhaps unplumbed by any other character in the show's run—except for Nathan Fillion's maniacal preacher Caleb.

But the best example of television drama clichés being mirrored by fantasy cliché, with the combination informing and enriching each and together creating something special, is the inclusion of the Dawn character at the beginning of Season 5, perhaps the show's most profound moment of fantasy.

Television is known for throwing new characters into the mix willy-nilly, long-lost cousins who suddenly move into town and become part of "the gang," neighbors who had always lived right next door but whom the audience had never seen. In this case, the Dawn character uses the audience's ignorance against itself. She is presented at the beginning of Season 5 as "Buffy's sister," treated as if she had always been there. Even faithful viewers doubted themselves, not remembering any mention of a long-lost sister but having no reason to disbelieve the Summers' knowledge of their own family. Maybe the audience had forgotten some scene where Michelle Trachtenberg had been shooed away to private school, and had only recently returned.

This would be par for the course for TV. There was no indication that any funny business was afoot until we had already run through the surprise of seeing her and had accepted her as just another TV cliché, as we had been taught by so many other series. But as always, *Buffy* shows us what we've seen on television, then shows us something more. The explanation of the appearance of Dawn fuses formal television technique and magical content in a wholly new way. Our sense of reality is involved significantly in the moment, as with all great fantasy.

1.07
Pedagogy of the Possessed:
Teaching and Learning in *Buffy*
Michael Curtis Nelson

For the last ten years audiences have watched young wizards learn to negotiate the supernatural in a rigid, hierarchical academy for the magically gifted. Joss Whedon's series *Buffy the Vampire Slayer*—set first in a California public high school, later in a university—offers a very different view of instruction in the dark arts, one that not only comports with Americans' suspicion of formal education and preference for pragmatic, on-the-job instruction but also reflects its creator's pessimistic view of the perfectibility of culture. Joss Whedon has structured *Buffy* as an amalgam of an American television staple, the high-school comedy-drama, and the traditional horror story, whose frequent reliance on a research component makes it a good complement to the school setting. Elevating a character type usually relegated to supporting cast status, the juvenile delinquent, Whedon makes his heroine an average pupil at odds with school administration, adept only at an alternative, secret curriculum that the series valorizes over traditional classroom instruction.

Aside from fleeting moments of insight in the classroom, Buffy's substantive education takes place under the tutelage of Watcher and mentor Rupert Giles (Anthony Stewart Head). Working undercover as the school librarian, Giles instructs Buffy (Sarah Michelle Gellar) in the dark lore she must master in order to dispatch the creatures she's been called to slay. Buffy's course of study plays like a dream curriculum founded in principles of active learning. Providing access to primary documents (thanks to Giles, Sunnydale High has an impressive collection of occult texts) and taking his charge into the field for hands-on instruction, Giles turns Buffy's education into a literal internship from—and in—hell.

Yet *Buffy* is hardly an endorsement of experiential education, a favorite American pedagogical approach with an emphasis on individual growth and societal change, whose roots go back to psychologist and educational reformer John Dewey. Neither is it a call to revolution, like Brazilian Paulo Freire's influential and still controversial treatise on the transformative potential of schooling, *Pedagogy of the Oppressed*. Instead *Buffy* mocks earnest, issues-of-the-day writing common in shows from *Room 222* to *Beverly Hills, 90210* to *Joan of Arcadia* by grafting teen narratives about drug abuse, domestic violence, or sexual orientation onto horror plots, a practice that simultaneously reinvigorates such themes while disavowing the belief in progressive educational goals that usually accompany them.

Just as Sunnydale's Hellmouth attracts an impressive array of supernatural creatures—mummies, shape shifters, and soul-sucking demons, in addition to vampires—so the local high school employs a lengthy parade of pedagogues, whose rapid turnover is insured by the predations of the former group. At Sunnydale High, teachers, principals, and advisors have the shelf lives of Spinal Tap drummers, and their evanescent tenures enable writers to represent (and parody) a wide range of teaching styles and instructional approaches.

Principal Flutie, in charge of Sunnydale High when the series begins, subscribes to the permissive, self-esteem approach to educating teens, welcoming Buffy and giving her a clean slate, despite her spotty record at her old school in L.A. After he proves too indecisive to lead a school built on the portal to hell (in conference with Buffy he tears up her record, then, after glimpsing what it contains, anxiously tapes it back together as they talk in "Welcome to the Hellmouth [Part 1 of 2]" (1.1), the hapless Flutie is later torn apart by students possessed by hyena spirits ("The Pack" 1.6). Principal Snyder (Armin Shimerman), Flutie's law-and-order successor, more interested in integrating "antisocial types" like Buffy into the school, declares that "Sunnydale has touched and felt for the last time" ("The Puppet Show" 1.9).

Good teaching manages to manifest itself despite Snyder's harsh tactics. Season 1's "Teacher's Pet" features a science teacher who sees past Buffy's reputation, but insists on discipline. Mr. Gregory tells her that she "has a first-class mind," and encourages her to apply herself. She does, and for once, carries out the pre-slaying homework—usually tackled by Giles and Willow (Alyson Hannigan)—that saves the day. Before he can establish a lasting connection with Buffy, however, Mr. Gregory loses his head to a she-mantis impersonating a Sunnydale teacher and seducing, then feeding on, male virgins ("Teacher's Pet" 1.4). Computer instructor Ms. Jenny Calendar (Robia LaMorte), self-described "techno-pagan," wins over the Scooby Gang (Buffy, Willow, and Xander [Nicholas Brendon]) with her frankness and open classroom in Season 2. Angel (David Boreanaz) kills her later the same season when he temporarily loses his soul ("Passion" 2.17). Guidance counselor Mr. Platt also reaches Buffy, in Season 3, albeit briefly. "The hope I bring you is, demons can be fought; people can change," he confides, shortly before his death at the hands of a student dabbling in a Jekyll-Hyde potion ("Beauty and the Beasts" 3.4).

The pattern continues at UC Sunnydale. Professor Maggie Walsh (Lindsay Crouse), like Mr. Gregory, challenges Buffy to excel, and she responds, at one point writing a paper that makes brainy Willow jealous. But the professor who refuses to "coddle" her students secretly heads the sadistic "Initiative," which captures vampires and demons and subjects them to behavioral modification. Oh, and she also creates a prototype human-demon-robot hybrid named Adam (Season 4).

In the time-honored tradition of the high school comedy-drama, teaching moments serve to introduce episode themes in *Buffy*. Season 1's "Out of Mind, Out of Sight" introduces the topic of marginalization and persecution, when English teacher Ms. Miller reads Shylock's soliloquy from Shakespeare's *Merchant of Venice*. Just to underscore the point, during the following discussion, Cordelia (Charisma Carpenter) gives her self-absorbed condemnation of self-victimization, even as she exhibits that very tendency. In "Bad Eggs" (2.12) a health class exercise in mock parenting establishes the theme of responsibility. The teaching moment that introduces an episode's subject carries over into college. Professor Walsh lectures on Freudian theory—defining the id, ego, superego, and Pleasure Principle—in "Beer Bad" (4.5), highlighting the issues of impulse control and ethical behavior, in an episode that follows Buffy's reaction to rejection after a sexual encounter with a classmate.

In each instance, there is a supernatural or paranormal dimension to the theme. A marginalized student becomes invisible and carries out her revenge on those who ignored her. Egg parasites turn students and faculty into pod people. Doctored brew transforms Buffy and a clutch of pretentious undergrad boys into cave teens. Thus *Buffy* puts a clever, ironic, often ghoulish twist on themes, which serves both to lampoon over-serious, ripped-from-the-headlines topical television but also, oddly enough, to give these tired subjects a resonance they lack in TV instructional settings that don't involve snake-men and fungus demons. It's the inside joke that *Buffy* sustained for seven seasons: rendering teen dilemmas as life-or-death struggles with the forces of darkness, with the fate of the world hanging in the balance, better captures the experience of being young than any attempt at verisimilitude can.

At the same time, portraits of teachers—good and bad—and alternative pedagogies, serve to set off in sharp relief the series' ideal teacher: Giles, whose relationship with Buffy is the heart of *Buffy*. Part John Keating from *Dead Poets Society*, part Henry Higgins, Giles pushes his mentoring beyond the pragmatic to provide life lessons to guide Buffy's path to independence as a Slayer and young woman, always reminding her that ultimately, she's on her own.

Teacher and student evolve together in a relationship with plenty of rough patches. Season 1 shows the pair growing into their roles, learning to accommodate each other's idiosyncrasies. "You're like a textbook with arms," Buffy tells her Watcher early on ("Welcome to the Hellmouth [Part 1 of 2]"). "We're doomed," Giles mutters to himself, aghast at the Scooby Gang's nonchalance. "We feel our way as we go along," Giles admits to Buffy in a typically frank confession ("Never Kill a Boy on the First Date" 1.5). In Season 2, Buffy opens up more to her Watcher, who in turn reveals more of his past. Giles's instruction takes on more depth, and he provides the reflection requisite for all successful experiential education (acknowledging, for example, the "issues" plaguing Buffy after her death at the hands of the Master at the end of Season 1), and as a result their relationship becomes as much therapeutic as instructional.

When Kendra—the Slayer summoned when the Master killed Buffy—arrives in Sunnydale, the contrast between the two Slayers, as well as the differences between Giles and Kendra's Watcher, further illuminate Giles's pedagogy.

"With Buffy, however, some flexibility's required," Giles tells Kendra, by way of explaining his departures from Watcher orthodoxy ("What's My Line [Part 2 of 2]" 2.10). Buffy discovers that, despite his bookishness, Giles has not been teaching her by the book. The Slayer Handbook (yes, it exists!) that Kendra has memorized has played no part in Buffy's education, because, Giles explains, it "would be of no use in your case." Kendra is shocked to discover that Buffy has been allowed to attend school and date boys, since her own experience has been more like a Chinese gymnast's: given to her Watcher by her parents when she was so young that she no longer remembers them, Kendra has spent her entire life training ("What's My Line [Part 2 of 2]"). Her preparation has more in common with the apprenticeship model of indoctrination that passes for education in the demon world of *Buffy* than with Giles's tutelage.

Season 3 reveals that Kendra's Watcher was no aberration. Defrocked Watcher Gwendolyn Post and Watcher Wesley Wyndam-Pryce, an official Council emissary sent from England to investigate newly-Watcherless Slayer Faith (Eliza Dushku) and evaluate Giles, both react as Kendra did: they see Giles as inappropriately permissive. Wesley says he's behind the times. Gwendolyn goes so far as to tell Giles he's become Americanized. When the council relieves Giles of his Watcher duties, they justify their actions by accusing him of acting as a father to Buffy. It's a charge Buffy's mother echoes, when she confronts Giles after Buffy's disappearance following the events of the Season 2 finale. Giles, she claims, established a relationship with her daughter "behind my back"; "I feel you've taken her away from me," she concludes ("Anne" 3.1).

Giles finds himself in the same position vis-à-vis the Council that Buffy endures with respect to the high school administration. Both are rebels, and, except for the Scooby Gang, *isolatos*—that is to say, typical Whedon heroes. Perhaps because it's so hard to think of Giles as an outsider, Whedon gives us Season 3's "Band Candy" (3.6), in which Sunnydale adults become teenagers again. Giles's adolescent self is pure juvenile delinquent, complete with violent tendencies and a working-class accent. It's a reminder that he, like Buffy, remains an outsider.

For the balance of the series Giles moves back and forth from official Watcher status to consultant capacity, while Buffy gradually assumes her own teaching duties, with sister Dawn (Michelle Trachtenberg), students at the new Sunnydale High (as a part-time advisor), and fledgling Slayers as the series finale approaches.

Buffy first gets a taste of the role of teacher with Kendra. In a heated discussion with the new Slayer, Buffy insists that emotions are "total assets," while Kendra considers them a weakness. Both girls admit that Kendra has better technique than Buffy, but Buffy claims the newcomer lacks "imagination." "Power alone isn't enough," Buffy explains; a Slayer needs to "improvise, go with the flow." Improvisation, incidentally, characterizes Giles's instructional relationship with Buffy, and is the element the Council finds most distasteful, most "American." Buffy goes on to prove her point by staging a teaching moment. She goads Kendra, then asks, "You feel it, right? How the anger gives you fire? A Slayer needs that" ("Becoming [Part 1 of 2]," 2.21).

Buffy's on-the-job training of Dawn follows the same contours. "Who has the power?" she asks her little sister as they watch a new vampire climb from his grave in "Lessons" (7.1), the final season opener. Letting Dawn fight the newbie until he's about to bite her drives home the lesson: the baddies always have the power. "It's real. It's the only lesson, Dawn. It's always real," Buffy sums up. It's the first lesson Buffy gives four Potentials when they arrive in Sunnydale after the destruction of the Watchers' Council. When Giles wants to consult with Buffy in secret, she disagrees. "No time to coddle them, Giles," she says, echoing Professor Walsh. "Welcome to the war room, guys." At this point, Buffy has become Giles's pedagogic equal, and he cedes responsibility for the new Slayers to her ("Bring on the Night" 7.10). Other characters also acknowledge Buffy's new status. Principal Wood and Dawn's classmates all assume that Buffy is Dawn's mother, not her sister. It's played for laughs, but in a way her newly embraced adult responsibilities show that Buffy reaches the end of her character's development before *Buffy* concludes, which might explain the lack of drama in many of the final season's episodes. If the series is really about Giles and Buffy, there's nothing more to tell.

Joss Whedon's oft-quoted comment about the setting of *Firefly*—"nothing will change in the future: technology will advance, but we will still have the same political, moral, and ethical problems as today"—holds true for the vision of history that informs *Buffy*. The series posits an endless cycle of good battling evil in the place of real social progress, and while this perspective stands in stark contrast to the educational reform worldview, Giles nevertheless shares with John Dewey faith in the educability of the individual, and the belief that "to prepare [the child] for the future life means to give him command of himself; it means so to train him that he will have the full and ready use of all his capacities" (Dewey). "I didn't make Buffy who she is," Giles tells Joyce Summers after she blames him for her daughter's disappearance. Indeed, but he certainly has succeeded in giving her command of herself.

Works Cited

"Anne." 3.1. Writ. and dir. Joss Whedon. *Buffy*.

"Bad Eggs." 2.12. Writ. Marti Noxon. Dir. David Greenwalt. *Buffy*.

"Band Candy." 3.6. Writ. Jane Espenson. Dir. Michael Lang. *Buffy*.

"Beauty and the Beasts." 3.4. Writ. Marti Noxon. Dir. James Whitmore, Jr. *Buffy*.

"Becoming (Part 1 of 2)." 2.21. Writ. and dir. Joss Whedon. *Buffy*.

"Beer Bad." 4.5. Writ. Tracey Forbes. Dir. David Solomon. *Buffy*.

Buffy the Vampire Slayer: *The Chosen Collection* DVD Boxed Set. Twentieth Century Fox Home Entertainment, 2006. DVD.

Dewey, John. "My Pedagogic Creed." *School Journal* 54 (Jan. 1897): 77-80. *dewey.pragmatism. org*. Web. 4 Jan. 2012.

Freire, Paulo. *Pedagogy of the Oppressed*. 1968. Trans. Myra Bergman. 30th anniversary ed. London and New York: Continuum International, 2000. Print.

"Lessons." 7.1. Writ. Joss Whedon. Dir. David Solomon. *Buffy*.

"Never Kill a Boy on the First Date." 1.5. Writ. Rob Des Hotel and Dean Batali. Dir. David Semel. *Buffy*.

"Out of Mind, Out of Sight." 1.11. Writ. Joss Whedon, Askley Gable, and Thomas A. Swyden. Dir. Reza Badiyi. *Buffy*.

"The Pack." 1.6. Writ. Matt Kiene and Joe Reinkemeyer. Dir. Bruce Seth Green. *Buffy*.

"Passion." 2.17. Writ. Ty King. Dir. Michael E. Gershman. *Buffy*.

"The Puppet Show." 1.9. Writ. Rob Des Hotel and Dean Batali. Dir. Ellen S. Pressman. *Buffy*.

"Teacher's Pet." 1.4. Writ. David Greenwalt. Dir. Bruce Seth Green. *Buffy*.

"Welcome to the Hellmouth (Part 1 of 2)." 1.1. Writ. Joss Whedon. Dir. Charles Martin Smith. *Buffy*.

"What's My Line (Part 2 of 2)." 2.10. Writ. Marti Noxon. Dir. David Semel. *Buffy*.

Whedon, Joss. "Introduction: Relighting The *Firefly*." Bonus features. Serenity. Universal, 2005. DVD.

1.08
The Big Bad Universe:
Good and Evil According to Joss Whedon
Nandini Ramachandran

Joss Whedon's great gift is his ability to extrapolate into the clear blue sky from mundane speculative fiction stereotypes: fairy tales, space travel, mind control. It was this uncanny momentum that lifted *Dollhouse*'s torpid first season into the sublime second season; that allowed *Firefly* to dive into *Serenity*. The most consistent application of this talent was in the crafting of his "Big Bads." Whedon might not have invented the seasonal arc on television, but he certainly made great strides towards perfecting it; and he did it largely by dancing through shadows.

Buffy the Vampire Slayer, Joss Whedon's most influential cultural product, chronicles the rebellion of a champion. Buffy is the Chosen One, strong enough to bear the weight of the world, until she finds a way to scatter and delegate her burden. The superhuman strength is an imposed fate, it is her destiny to be the Slayer. Her true skill lies in an ability to forge friendships and build pragmatic alliances; with a little help from her friends, the Scoobies, she helps protect human civilization against the forces of chaos and anarchy. Yet, it is only by breaking ancient laws that she ultimately liberates herself, and the evidence is clear: sometimes you have to break the rules to preserve them. Whether this is an improvement remains to be seen. The *Season Eight* comics delve into the consequences of creating an army of Slayers, but this essay is restricted to Whedon's work on television.

In fandom a lot has been made of Joss Whedon's adaptation of Joseph Campbell's work. A quick scan of *Hero with a Thousand Faces* reveals his debt, and certainly the narrative structure of *Buffy* draws heavily upon the monomyth of the hero. I think, however, that the emphasis on Campbell elides more important themes within Whedon's television, and evades his central *cultural* point: that evil is an empirical question, not an epistemological one.

Evil is as *does*, not *how* it is conceived. Evil is a behavior, not an ineffable Kantian category. Like all behavior, it is mutable and socially constructed. The hero and the devil in the Whedonverse are interdependent, and morality is born in the space between the within and the without. One generation's savior is another generation's terrorist; ethical positions exist only in the eye of the beholder. The Initiative's experimentation upon demons in *Buffy* is as repellent as the Alliance's experiments on River in *Firefly*; the humans who trap demons to fight as gladiators in *Angel* ("The Ring" 1.16) are as surely villainous as the demons who trap humans for slave labor in *Buffy* ("Anne" 3.1).

What makes the world run is neither good nor evil, but rather the balance between them, the paradox that neither has any meaning without the other. This paradox is at the crux of all Whedon's television shows, whether inspired by the tech-heavy future or fantastic pasts. Like all speculative fiction, they are a comment about the here-and-now, not about the far future or a mystical alternate reality. It is true they deploy different modes and tropes; *Buffy* is epic and *Angel* tragic; *Firefly* is satirical and *Dollhouse* dystopic. But this is typical of Whedon's holistic conception of human experience, as his prophet, Joseph Campbell, explains:

"The happy ending of the fairytale, the myth, and the divine comedy is to be read, not as a contradiction, but as a transcendence of the individual tragedy of man. The objective world remains what it was, but, because of a shift in emphasis within the subject, it is beheld as though transformed. Where formerly life and death contended, now enduring being is made manifest—as indifferent to the accidents of time as water boiling in a pot is to the destiny of a bubble, or as the cosmos is to the appearance and disappearance of a galaxy of stars. Tragedy is the shattering of forms and of our attachment to them; comedy the wild and careless, inexhaustible joy of life invincible... [T]ogether [they] constitute the totality of the revelation that is life, and which the individual must know and love if he is to be purged... of the contagion of sin... and death... It is the business of mythology proper, and of the fairy tale, to reveal the specific dangers and techniques of the dark interior way from tragedy to comedy" (28-29).

Whedon makes his point in several layers, woven into the plot, the people, the philosophy of the Whedonverse, his "metaplay," or "theatre whose leading metaphors state that life is a dream and the world a stage." His people are not classical heroes—everyone's emphatically self-conscious—but they are reluctant, if not ignorant, heroes. He takes the personal-identity crisis furthest with Echo in *Dollhouse*, but the dilemma of alternate personalities exists early in *Buffy*. For every Buffy there must be a Faith, for every Giles an Ethan Rayne. "Doppelgangland" (*Buffy* 3.16), for a Willow fan, is the best thing about Season 3. Later in *Buffy*, Whedon focuses more sharply on the *human* self—that pesky soul—as a source of ethical conflict.

This is a theme that marks its appearance with that existential Frankenstein, Adam, in Season 4 and finds an apotheosis in Dark Willow and the nerdy Trio in Season 6. In Season 5, which featured Whedon's first god, the Grandiloquent Glorificus, the biggest betrayal of all was by her human alter-ego, Ben. Gods, even malignant, capricious gods, are no match for what humanity is willing to do to itself. With questions of the self squared away, *Buffy* moves on yet again in Season 7, debating choice (Demon Anya) and free will (Spike).

With Spike, admittedly, the conflict muddies, for re-souled Spike is not recognizably different from de-souled Spike. Angel(us) does us the favor of being schizophrenic—Angel is as "good" as Angelus is "evil"—especially in the early seasons of *Buffy*. No such switch exists for Spike. As demons go, Spike has always been capable of reckless love and relentless pragmatism. He concedes as much in the episode "Lover's Walk" (*Buffy* 3.8): "I might be love's bitch, but at least I'm man enough to admit it." He allies with Buffy to keep "Happy Meals with legs" kicking along in Season 2. Spike's noblest moment isn't Season 7's gibbering lunatic, nor is it his stint as champion in *Angel*. It occurs long before the acquisition of his soul, when he protects Dawn from Glory in Season 5 of *Buffy*.

The question boils down to this: does having a soul mitigate attempted rape, even assuming that lack of free will does mitigate murder? It is true the Buffy–Spike sexual relationship is exploitative on *both* sides, which is perhaps more justified in a demon like Spike than in a hero like Buffy. She abuses his affection for her almost as badly as he attempts to abuse her. The bathroom-rape is a touchy subject for Spike fans—does recognizing that both parties enjoyed hurting each other make the question of consent irrelevant? What makes the scene most jarring is that it is inconsistent with Spike as a person, rather than as a vampire. It is his pride, not his soul, that one presumes will prevent such abhorrent behavior. Plenty of human men, after all, are capable of rape, souls or not. All this agency placed on the fragile soul in the Buffyverse makes one wonder: what makes humans so magnificent that it comes as part of our packaging, while demons must undergo terrific trials to attain it? There are as many valorous, compassionate demons as there are shiftless, sadistic humans, so why attach metaphysics to destructive impulses?

In *Angel*, human evil becomes the dominant motif, and the ranks of helpful demons greatly multiply. Doyle dies trying to prevent demon-on-demon genocide, and the worst evil in town is a bunch of corporate lawyers. In the industrial city, good and evil have never been considered distinct. The city and its sewers learned to coexist long ago; the apocalypse chugs comfortably along in the slums whilst the party proceeds apace uptown. *Angel*'s central theme is that there is no true innocence in this world, that life is a series of competing betrayals. The entire cast of *Angel* is corruptible, and corrupted, over the five seasons. It is Angel, not Angelus, who tells Darla that sex with her was "perfect despair," Angel who treats her so shabbily upon learning about her impossible pregnancy. It is Angel who sires Sam Lawson on the submarine, though he could probably have convinced Spike to do it. It is Angel who agrees to take over the L.A. offices of Wolfram & Hart in order to protect his son (ineffectually, as it turns out).

Angel is all about atonement, redemption, remorse; it highlights the scar tissue of learning to live with oneself rather than with a cruel world. It is *Angel*, more than *Buffy*, that is the spiritual predecessor to all the soulful vamps and Cylons that litter this decade's popular culture. What *Angel* sought to do with tragedy and angst, *Being Human*'s Mitchell seeks to do with humor and perspective. With Mitchell, being a vampire is an extension of being human, rather than a perversion, something that Whedon's tormented Angel could never get himself to believe. Despite the fact that Mitchell's bloodlust must be intolerably worse than Angel's— *Being Human*'s vamps can't satisfy their thirst with bottled blood—his overcoming of it isn't portrayed to be a victory for human nobility, merely for human decency. This profound shift in the paradigm of the vampire, from someone intrinsically evil to someone battling addiction, would have been impossible without the dialogue about the nature of evil that *Angel* began in speculative television.

WHEDON'S SKILLFUL SHADOWING GOES PAST PERSONALITY...

"It's as if the world today were a cinder of yesterday's fire." —Borges.

Whedon's skillful shadowing goes past personality; even the institutions of good and evil in the Buffyverse are built to reflect one another: the Watchers' Council here, Wolfram & Hart there. As Lucifer Morningstar once told Dream of the Endless in Neil Gaiman's *Sandman*, "Hell is heaven's shadow, its dark reflection inverted upon the lake of reality." The clearest instance of this balance is the Ra'tet', a collection of five entities responsible for the sun's journey across the sky. Two are evil, two good, and one is human.

Consider, for a more dominant metaphor, the two "families" we track through the Buffyverse: the Scoobies and the Order of Aurelius. If the Scoobies are all facets of what we consider "the greater good"—as the adjoining spell in "Primeval" (*Buffy* 4.21) indicates—the vampires are all embodiments of aspects within the greater darkness. The Aurelians symbolize the sum total of the "dangerous classes"—Darla (vice), Angelus (predation), Drusilla (madness), Spike (aggression)—the very impulse from which the fantastic was born.

Scholars of the genre draw its protohistory back to the nineteenth century, arguing that the fantastic was founded upon schisms that the Industrial and French revolutions introduced into genteel European society. "The sleep [or dream] of reason produces monsters" to quote from a famous Goya painting. It was a genre beloved by the romantics, with their wild and varied crazes, and imbued with their inconstancy, flippancy, and eternal doubt. The Buffyverse, in its distinctive postmodern way—Buffy is very much a 20th-century Slayer—draws hugely on this conflict between reason and romance that so animated earlier centuries. It is no coincidence that the chief vampires in both *Buffy* and *Angel* were all sired prior to 1900; each represents a different ethos in the evolution of modern thought.

Whedon's penchant for the long narrative makes *Dollhouse* and *Firefly* peculiar pleasures. Everything feels condensed, accelerated, unresolved; barely is the Big Picture revealed when the plot halts. The early episodes of *Dollhouse* notwithstanding, Whedon's foray into science fiction matches the best of the Buffyverse. *Firefly* is a satire on colonialism, a lesson about the price of hubris. The plot details the exploits of a band of pirates—let us call them the malcontents—that crew the spaceship *Serenity*. The backdrop is a throwback to nineteenth-century imperialism with its bandits, cowboys, and outlaws. *Firefly* is a story from back when the metropolis and the colonies were presumed to be mutually exclusive, each quarantined in its little bubble of privilege or squalor.

The movie *Serenity* is a twist on the Slayer origin myth revealed in Season 7 of *Buffy*. The shadow-men invested the first Slayer with the heart of a demon through magic; the Alliance manufactures superheroes with technology. In both cases, the girl herself is considered little more than a weapon, and the forces that foster her also propel evil. Demons are the living embodiment of the perils of magic, Reavers of the perils of technology.

Slayers presage monsters, and *Serenity* explores, appropriately, the origin of demons and heroes alike. Whedon is making the same point with the Reavers of *Firefly/Serenity* as he did with the power-that-was, Jasmine, in *Angel*: to pacify humanity is to enslave humanity. Unmitigated "good," in Whedon's worlds, is as dangerous to humanity as unmitigated "evil." Peace can be as brutal as war for those caught on the side that lost; for most, the war is never over. Angel Investigations and the malcontents fight, as champions of the underrepresented, for their own survival as much as anyone else's. Neither the Alliance's Pax nor Jasmine's World Peace has any place for rebels, and survival is a constant battle at blurred boundaries of humankind.

The Jasmine arc in Season 4 of *Angel* was much maligned, buried as it was behind many episodes of Oedipal frenzy. Deficient fathers and prodigal sons are a persistent feature of *Angel*; and disappointing parents are a feature of the Whedonverse generally. Joyce Summers is the best parent in the universe, yet she manages to entirely overlook two years of slayage. Amy's mother snatches away her youth, River Tam's parents allow the government to experiment on their daughter. Whedon inverts this tendency to devastating effect in *Angel*. "The father will kill the son" reads the false prophecy, while it is the sons of *Angel* that are forever plotting to kill their parents. Another *Angel* staple is the Implausible Impregnation of Cordelia with an assortment of grisly demon-spawn. In Season 4, one such pregnancy comes to term after an apocalyptic com-shuk with Angel's son (I warned you). Cordy finally dies, swallowed whole by her fertility, and Jasmine is born.

Jasmine is an aspect of the powers-that-be, the purest force for "good" in the Buffyverse. Like the First Evil, the powers prefer to work through intermediaries; oracles and seers opposing lawyers and preachers. Embodied, as with Jasmine, they are every bit as dangerous and megalomaniacal as the First. The First has the legions of hell intent on destroying humanity;

Jasmine has legions of "saved" humans crusading against demonkind. The opposition is predictably symmetrical: while the First Evil is unleashing itself in Sunnydale, Jasmine and her minion Beast are wreaking havoc in L.A. and driving demons to the Hellmouth. With *Angel*'s Jasmine, as with *Serenity*'s Miranda, the price of salvation is savagery; the relinquishing of nuance and judgment. They are both, in effect, anti-utopias.

"Therefore God becomes as we are, that we may be as he is." —Blake

Dollhouse carries this skepticism forward into a full-fledged *dystopia*, which is where utopia meets tragedy. The people of *Dollhouse* begin as slaves and shells, ensnared by and enamored of the Big Bad. Some of them—Adele, Topher—are acquiescent harbingers of catastrophe, wholly immoral if somewhat benevolent. Perversely, they are thus the only people capable of averting the apocalypse, which is perhaps why they fail so remarkably. Where powers-that-were and ancient evils fail, the modern corporation succeeds. Rossum's Attic is the only part of the Whedonverse in which previous centuries fall away, for a dystopia, more than any other literary form, is born of the crucible of the present.

In "A Utopia of Fine Dust," analyzing the futurists Fourier and Saint-Simon, Italo Calvino once argued that the trial by fire for utopias lies is the narrowing of their distance from reality. The more the imaginary world breaches into to our own, the more potent are the values it seeks to convey. "Utopia," he writes,

"is a city that cannot be founded by us, it can only found itself in us, build itself brick by brick in our ability to imagine it, to think it out to the ultimate degree. It is a city that claims to inhabit us, not to be inhabited, thus making us possible inhabitants of a third city… a city born of the mutual impact of new conditionings, both inner and outer". In the 21st century, utopias have mostly given way to dystopias, and the values to warnings, but the form itself remains unchanged. It elaborates worlds that, like utopias "must be sought in the folds, in the shadowy places, in the countless involuntary effects that the most calculated system creates without being aware that perhaps its truth lies right there" (Calvino 245-255).

Dystopias reveal worlds where the best of intentions are married to the most cynical of outcomes. They are stories about the cost of custom-tailored humanity. In *Brave New World*, a new humanity was fabricated with hedonism and eugenics, in *1984* with repression and rage; in *Dollhouse* it is done with technology and desire. In each, the price is free will and individuality, and in each the protagonists are subtly different from fellow drones and thus capable of transcending their conditioning. Slowly, out of the cohesion of Society, the individual is born and betrayed—John Savage, Winston Smith, and Echo/Caroline—returning, in the end, right where they began. Savage goes back to the wild, Winston to his bleak acceptance, Echo to the Dollhouse. Unlike the others, Echo has a family to fall back upon, and thus survives to set the world right; how far and how well, we will never know.

In the last decade, dystopias have proliferated as a format in popular culture, spawning endless movies, television shows, books, and videogames. Even that most cheery of movie formats—animation—explored dystopia in *Wall-E*, while television shows like *V* and books like *The Hunger Games* have made it a familiar feature of 2012's cultural landscape. It says a lot, I imagine, about the human condition that all we see everywhere are tragic futures, the pathetic mangling of the illusions of progress and human perfectibility. Yet, if one is to draw a line between *Brave New World* and our present deluge of dystopias, it must be done mindful of the circumstances they mediate. If Huxley wondered, "Can humans become robots?" back in 1932, today we wonder, "Can robots become human?" Our conclusions, nonetheless, need not differ from Huxley's, who condemned mankind to either lunacy or insanity. Joss Whedon, less pessimistic, relies on his unconventional families—such as Adele's Rebels in *Dollhouse*—to recover the world from its apocalypse. Are we likely to be as lucky?

Works Cited

Angel *Collector's Set: Seasons 1-5*. Box set. Twentieth Century Fox Home Entertainment, 2007. DVD.

"Anne." 3.1. Writ. and dir. Joss Whedon. *Buffy*.

Being Human. Created by Toby Whitehouse. Perf. Russell Tovey, Lenora Crichlow, and Aidan Turner. BBC and BBC America, 2008-2011. Television.

Buffy the Vampire Slayer: *The Complete Series*. Twentieth Century Fox Home Entertainment, 2005. DVD.

Calvino, Italo. "On Fourier: III. Envoi: A Utopia of Fine Dust." *The Literature Machine*. Trans. Patrick Creagh. London: Pan/Secker and Warburg, 1987. 244-55. Print.

Campbell, Joseph. *The Hero with a Thousand Faces*. 1949. New York: MJF Books, 1996. Print.

"Doppelgangland." 3.16. Writ. and dir. Joss Whedon. *Buffy*.

Dollhouse: *The Complete Season 2*. Twentieth Century Fox Home Entertainment, 2010. DVD.

Dollhouse: *Season One*. Twentieth Century Fox Home Entertainment, 2009. DVD.

Firefly: *The Complete Series*. Twentieth Century Fox Home Entertainment, 2002. DVD.

Goya y Lucientes, Francisco. *The Sleep of Reason Produces Monsters*. 1799. Plate 43 of The

Caprices (Los Caprichos). Etching. The Metropolitan Museum of Art, New York. *Met Museum*. Web. 8 Jan. 2012.

"Lovers Walk." 3.8. Writ. Dan Vebber. Dir. David Semel. *Buffy*.

"Primeval." 4.21. Writ. and dir. David Fury. *Buffy*.

"The Ring." 1.16. Writ. Howard Gordon. Dir. Nick Marck. *Angel*.

The Sandman. 75 issues. Story by Neil Gaiman. Pencils by Sam Keith, Mike Dringenberg, and others. New York: DC / Vertigo, 1989-1996. Print.

Serenity. Writ. and dir. Joss Whedon. Universal, 2005. DVD.

1.09
Women Who Hate Women:
Female Competition in *Buffy the Vampire Slayer*
Faye Murray and Holly Golding

Buffy the Vampire Slayer is one of those decidedly rare television series where not only is the ratio of male to female characters almost equal but women are portrayed as being able to have meaningful and significant relationships with other women. Furthermore, such relationships and interactions often take center stage on the show, serving to advance plots, develop characterization, and anchor the series in reality, while appreciably contributing towards its emotional heart. As such, it is no surprise that *Buffy* consistently passes the Bechdel Test with flying colors; that is, virtually every episode has at least one scene in which two named female characters talk to each other about something other than men (*Bechdel Test Movie List*). Nor is it remarkable that *Buffy* is widely lauded as a landmark feminist show given its reliance on interesting, multi-dimensional female characters who are in constant communication with one another, and whose female-female relationships are integral to the series' narrative.

Buffy is often acclaimed as a feminist TV series on another count too: the frequency with which the show subverts and reverses traditional gender roles. Such reversals are commonplace on *Buffy* with women possessing an equal—and sometimes greater—degree of both mental and physical strength than men, and inhabiting positions of power traditionally held by men in society. Creator Joss Whedon explicitly explains this gender role reversal in *Buffy* in his "Welcome to the Hellmouth" DVD Commentary: "The first thing I ever thought of when I thought of *Buffy: The Movie* was the little… blonde girl who goes into a dark alley and gets killed, in every horror movie. The idea of *Buffy* was to subvert that idea, that image, and create someone who was a hero where she had always been a victim. That element of surprise... [and] genre-busting is very much at the heart of both the movie and the series."

The shift in the male-female power dynamic on the show is also reflected by the male characters, who tend to assume conventionally feminine traits such as physical weakness, irrationality, tenderness, and passivity.

However, perhaps regarding *Buffy* as presenting us with such a straightforward feminist paradigm is too simplistic an interpretation of what the female-female relationships on the show actually promote, especially when on closer inspection it becomes apparent that there is a notable lack of enduring female friendships on the show. Rather, relationships between women on the show are repeatedly characterized by rivalry and competition, even when both parties work together to defeat common enemies. These relationships generally possess a bitchy undertone, with barbs about clothing, appearance, and physical attractiveness being commonplace. A similar pattern can be seen in the relationships between the female protagonists and their female antagonists, whether these are monster of the week, villains such as Sunday in "The Freshman" (4.1), or recurring characters such as Glory in Season 5.

This essay will dissect and analyze the different types of female-female relationships presented on the show—with a focus on female competition through a discussion of the female characters' sexuality and their relationships with men—in order to come to a conclusion about whether the portrayal of female relationships complicates the idea of *Buffy the Vampire Slayer* as a feminist work, or whether it can be considered one aspect of Whedon's attempting to subvert traditional gender roles.

ENDURING FEMALE RELATIONSHIPS/FRIENDSHIPS ON *BUFFY*

The best example of an enduring female friendship on *Buffy* is the relationship between Buffy and Willow, which is set up in the first episode of the series, "Welcome to the Hellmouth." Although their friendship is certainly stronger in the earlier seasons, it still functions as one of the fundamental and enduring stable relationships of the show. Moreover, Willow best exemplifies the role of "sidekick" in relation to the "hero," Buffy, even when compared to Xander and Giles, the two other core members of the Scooby Gang. It is Willow who provides Buffy with support, not only through her witchcraft and ever-growing knowledge of the supernatural but also emotionally, often acting as a sounding board for Buffy's expressions of her emotions and inner turmoil.

As Sharon Ross points out in "Female Friendship and Heroism in *Xena* and *Buffy*," Buffy and Willow rely on each other in order to navigate through life's challenges and make difficult decisions; they do this through discussion, through the "expression of their emotional knowledge," and through the validation of the other's feelings and thoughts (248). In this way they are better able to deal with the adversity and suffering they encounter during the progression of the series: their emotional openness and ability to communicate makes them, as women, better equipped to confront the problems women face in our patriarchal society. Through the Buffy-Willow friendship Whedon is showing that not only do women need to communicate and form positive, supportive relationships with other women in order to advance in society and break down the existing patriarchal framework but also that this can actually be achieved through interdependence, through the sharing of power between women in preference to "relying on a patriarchal model that organizes power and leadership linearly and hierarchically" (Ross 241). Willow transcends her status as sidekick through her friendship with Buffy, helping Buffy to realize that the conventional "lone hero" model is archaic and that "the toughest hero is a flexible one who relies on others" (Ross 233).

The Buffy-Willow relationship is also progressive in that their friendship is never centered on their romantic relationships, although said relationships do frequently enter into their discourse. Additionally, when their friendship is at risk of being marginalized by their romantic relationships, this is shown to be a negative development. In the Season 1 episode "I Robot... You Jane" (1.8), for instance, Willow neglects her blossoming friendship with Buffy in order to spend time with her boyfriend Malcolm, who is later revealed to be the villain of the episode. Willow's behavior throughout the episode is critiqued as she isolates herself from the rest of her friends and begins to spend all of her time communicating with Malcolm. Buffy in particular does not accept this marginalization of their friendship and, after growing increasingly concerned, takes action; by the end of the episode all friendships are re-established. The weakening of the Buffy-Willow friendship is also an integral part of the main arc of Season 4 as they gradually drift apart, due in part to their preoccupation with new romantic relationships. This is again shown to be a negative development, and is something which Spike recognizes, and takes full advantage of in "The Yoko Factor" (4.20). Only when Buffy and Willow reconcile and the Scooby Gang joins together, both literally and figuratively, are they able to defeat the season's Big Bad, Adam.

But why then are there so few examples of enduring female-female relationships on *Buffy*; why is the Buffy-Willow relationship such an anomaly?

At least part of the answer to this question becomes apparent when examining the characters' sexuality. During the early seasons of the show Willow is the archetypal high school geek: she is bookish, lacks confidence, and by her own admission is dressed by her mother. Contrast this with Buffy, who is assertive, fashionable, athletic, and aware that she is a sexually attractive female. Both are aware, at least subconsciously, that this distinction exists and as a result Buffy does not perceive Willow as a sexual threat. Willow recognizes that she is deemed by society in general as being less sexually desirable than Buffy, and does not challenge this perception despite being involved in a love triangle of sorts with Xander and Buffy during the early episodes of the series. This love triangle ends when Buffy begins dating Angel, and Willow begins dating Oz; again, at this point Willow poses no threat sexually to Buffy as both are in stable relationships with devoted partners.

In Season 4 Buffy and Willow both find themselves unattached again. Willow is now much more assertive and sexually confident, to the point that she might potentially be perceived as a sexual threat by Buffy, and thus a strain is placed on their friendship. It is at this point, however, that Willow discovers her lesbian identity, and enters into a relationship with Tara, meaning that once again she is no longer a feasible sexual competitor to Buffy.

Interestingly, Tara is the only character on *Buffy* able to have numerous amiable and positive relationships with other women. For instance, during the Season 5 episode "The Body" and throughout Season 6 she provides emotional support for Buffy, and although Buffy and Tara are never as close as Buffy and Willow, there is never any animosity between them, only mutual trust and respect. The Tara-Dawn relationship is also notably close with Tara often filling the role of older sister to Dawn; this closeness means that Tara still looks after Dawn and remains in frequent contact with her, even after she breaks up with Willow and moves out of the Summers' house. Tara is even able to maintain a steady friendship with Anya. Yet again, this ability to maintain friendships with the other women on the show can be attributed to her sexuality; as a lesbian she poses no sexual threat to the heterosexual female characters and therefore presents no competition when it comes to dating and attracting male attention.

FEMALE-FEMALE ANTAGONISM BETWEEN ALLIES ON *BUFFY*

With the exception of the Buffy-Willow relationship, much of the interaction among female allies throughout the series is characterized as antagonistic. This is especially apparent in Cordelia. From Season 2 until her departure at the end of Season 3, Cordelia consistently aids the Scooby Gang in defeating supernatural foes, but in spite of this she never forms any significant ties with any of them, excepting her romantic relationship with Xander. Her relationships with Willow and Buffy range from grudging acceptance to coldness, indifference, and disdain. Catty gibes about appearance and status often accompany exchanges between Buffy and Cordelia, and sometimes these taunts have sexual connotations, as in the Season 3 episode "Homecoming" (3.5):

Cordelia: (to Buffy) You crazy freak!

Buffy: Vapid whore!

The nature of Cordelia's relationship with Willow, although possessing a similar dynamic to the Buffy-Cordelia relationship, is subtly different. Throughout the first season all of the insults come from Cordelia, and are directed at Willow primarily because she is an easy target. As Cordelia gradually becomes integrated into the group, she stops directing insults towards Willow, although there is still the odd insensitive remark directed at both Buffy and Willow, as in the Season 2 episode "Passion" (2.17):

Buffy: You know, Cordelia, we've already done your car. Call it a night if you want.

Cordelia: Right. Thanks. And you know I'd do the same for you if you had a social life.

As Cordelia's relationship with Xander is discovered, however, most of the antagonism is now on Willow's side as she makes snide comments about Cordelia behind her back. Eventually, the antagonism on both sides subsides only to return after Xander and Willow's illicit relationship is exposed.

It might be easy to dismiss this bitchy behavior as being solely due to Cordelia and her conduct throughout Season 1 were it not for the existence of similar figures such as Anya later in the series, the various love triangles influencing these relationships, and the fact that Willow and Buffy do occasionally instigate and retaliate. It is important to note that both Willow and Buffy, at one time or another, have been in romantic competition with Cordelia. In the episodes "Some Assembly Required" (2.2), "Reptile Boy" (2.5), and "Halloween" (2.6) it is apparent that Cordelia has a romantic interest in Angel, something which she openly acknowledges to Buffy. In "Halloween," Cordelia says: "You know what I think? I just think you're trying to scare me off 'cause you're afraid of the competition. Look, Buffy, you may be hot stuff when it comes to demonology or whatever, but when it comes to dating, I'm the Slayer."

At this point in the series Buffy and Angel's relationship has not been established, although Buffy's interest in pursuing a relationship with Angel is clear. This triangle serves to reinforce Angel's heteromasculinity (in that both women covet him) and Buffy's heterosexual desirability (in that Angel chooses Buffy over Cordelia), while also functioning as an example of the conventional "two women fighting over a man" scenario. Although a staple in pop culture, such a scenario acts to maintain and perpetuate the myths of women as being "more interested in men than in preserving female friendships and thus promoting heteronormativity" (Buckman 55), and while Cordelia fits this paradigm perfectly, as Buckman observes, the show regularly critiques her behavior as "superficial and emotionally immature" (55).

After Cordelia's departure from the show, Anya steps neatly into Cordelia's position within this paradigm, although, as with Cordelia, Anya's behavior is often critiqued as shallow and emotionally immature while also being played for laughs. Anya is never especially close to any of her female allies either; instead she tends to form much closer bonds with male characters such as Xander, Giles, Spike, and later Andrew. This dichotomy is probably best exemplified by the Anya-Willow relationship—or lack thereof—something which is dealt with directly in the Season 5 episode "Triangle" (5.11):

Willow: Xander's my best friend!

Anya: Oh, and you don't want anyone else to have him. I know what broke up him and Cordelia, you know. It was you! And your lips!

Willow: No it was not! Well, yes it was so, but... That was a long time ago. Do you think I'd do that again?

Anya: Why not?

Willow: Well, hello, gay now.

Anya: But you're always doing everything you can to, to point out how much I'm an outsider. You've known him since you were squalling infants together. You'll always know him better than I do. You could sweep in and, and poison his mind against me.

Willow: You're insane! I am not gonna take him away and I am not gonna hurt him.

Anya: Well, I'm not either!

As this scene illustrates, Anya perceives Willow as a sexual threat due to Willow's history with Xander, and in particular his dalliance with Willow while he was still dating Cordelia. The fact that Anya still harbors these feelings of unease and animosity towards Willow, despite Willow's sexuality, suggests that her anxiety is at least in part due to Willow's status as Xander's best friend. Willow's perception of Anya is no kinder; throughout the show we see that Willow feels Anya is not good enough for Xander, and is concerned that Anya may even end up harming Xander in some way. Essentially Willow perceives herself as Xander's protector—a role generally occupied by a male—leaving Xander to fill the traditional female role of requiring protection: another instance of Whedon's gender role reversal. By the conclusion of the episode both characters learn that they must work together, and respect each other's significance in Xander's life in order to deal with the current threat. Despite this realization, Anya does not become closer to either Buffy or Willow, and in the Season 7 episode "Selfless" (7.5), neither Buffy nor Anya hesitates at the prospect of killing the other:

Xander: You don't understand. This isn't an intervention. Buffy's coming to kill you.

Anya: She's coming to try.

Xander: Did everybody have their crazy flakes today? You guys are friends. How could you talk like this?

Anya: I have a job to do. And so does Buffy. Xander, you've always seen what you wanted to. But you knew, sooner or later, it would come to this.

FEMALE-FEMALE ANTAGONISM BETWEEN ENEMIES ON *BUFFY*

The Buffy-Faith relationship is interesting to analyze in that it could also have come under the category of antagonism between allies, given their interactions during early Season 3 and late Season 7. In fact, the rivalry between Buffy and Faith is apparent before Faith actually does anything to warrant it, and can be seen from Faith's first appearance in "Faith, Hope, and Trick" (3.3). Buffy takes an immediate dislike to Faith as soon as she appears on the scene, and Buffy's behavior throughout the next few episodes (in particular, "Revelations," 3.7) effectively destroys their relationship before it even begins. In "Faith, Hope, and Trick." Buffy is seen to be jealous of Willow and Xander's fascination with Faith, Giles's appreciation of her "zest," and Joyce's admiration of her attitude ("I like this girl, Buffy"). Buffy is self-aware enough to recognize her jealousy and petty behavior, but this doesn't change her attitude towards Faith:

Buffy: She's very personable. She gets along with my friends, my Watcher, my mom. Look, now she's getting along with my fries. [From the next room they see Faith remove food from Buffy's plate]

Joyce: Now, Buffy...

Buffy: Plus, at school today, she was making eyes at my not-boyfriend. This is creepy.

Joyce: Does anybody else think Faith is creepy?

Buffy: No, but I'm the one getting single-white-femaled here.

Joyce: It's probably good you were an only child.

Buffy: Mom, I'm just getting my life back. I'm not looking to go halfsies on it.

Even in Season 7, when a newly reformed Faith returns to Sunnydale to help Buffy train the new Potentials, Buffy falls back into familiar habits. In "Dirty Girls" (7.18), Buffy interrupts a conversation between Faith and Spike:

Faith: Wow. Everybody's just full of surprises. Hey, B.

Buffy: (tersely) Well, it's nice to see you two getting along so well.

The suspicion and unhappiness with which Buffy greets any personal interaction between Faith and Spike is similar to her responses in Season 3 to Faith's relationship with Angel. Indeed, it is worth noting that Buffy and Faith do not fully become enemies in Season 3 until Faith makes a move on Angel, in the aptly titled "Enemies" (3.17). Additionally, it is during this episode that Faith's jealously of Buffy, previously only implied, becomes explicit:

Faith: You know, I come to Sunnydale. I'm the Slayer. I do my job kicking ass better than anyone. What do I hear about everywhere I go? Buffy. So I slay, I behave, I do the good little girl routine. And who's everybody thank? Buffy.

Buffy: It's not my fault.

Faith: Everybody always asks, why can't you be more like Buffy? But did anyone ever ask if you could be more like me?

Angel: I know I didn't.

Faith: You get the Watcher. You get the mom. You get the little Scooby Gang. What do I get? Jack squat. This is supposed to be my town!

Buffy: Faith, listen to me!

Faith: Why? So you can impart some special Buffy wisdom, that it? Do you think you're better than me? Do you? Say it, you think you're better than me.

Buffy: I am. Always have been.

Faith: Um, maybe you didn't notice. Angel's with me.

Buffy: And how did you get him, Faith? Magic? Cast some sort of spell? Cause in the real world, Angel would never touch you and we both know it.

It is particularly striking that Faith draws on her apparent relationship with Angel to hurt Buffy and, more than this, seems to believe that this relationship secures her status as being better than Buffy, not just as a slayer, but as a woman. Once again, the male romantic interest has been utilized, both by the show and by Faith as a character, to make a female competitor jealous, and in this way develop the rivalry between the female characters. Later in Season 4 Faith once again targets Buffy through her then boyfriend Riley, going so far as to actually sleep with Riley while inhabiting Buffy's body ("Who Are You?" 4.17).

Another noteworthy female antagonist to Buffy is Glory, the Big Bad of Season 5. Much has been written about Glory as an evil counterpart to Buffy, and for good reason; they share numerous traits commonly associated with the blond bimbo stereotype. Both can be flighty and use Valley Girl colloquialisms, both possess an interest in fashion, and both are attractive, petite blonds. However, as is customary in Whedon's works, these tropes are subverted; Glory is a god, and physically the strongest villain Buffy ever faces. While many of Buffy's battles include the trading of hostile remarks and quips, her exchanges with Glory in particular are characterized by stereotypical bitchiness and insults focusing on physical appearance. Even Dawn is perceptive enough to identify the bitchiness which underlies all of the Buffy-Glory interactions:

Dawn: I just think you're freaking out 'cause you have to fight someone prettier than you. That is the case, right?

Buffy: Glory is evil. And powerful. And in no way prettier than me." ("Blood Ties" 5.13)

Similarly, not even the more minor, episodic villains are exempt from this kind of stereotypical bitchiness, as seen in the Season 1 episode "Angel" (1.7):

Darla: Do you know what the saddest thing in the world is?

Buffy: Bad hair on top of that outfit?

Darla: To love someone who used to love you.

Buffy: Well, you been around since Columbus, you are bound to pile up a few exes. You're older than him, right? Just between us girls, you are looking a little worn around the eyes.

From the Season 4 episode "The Freshman" (4.1):

Buffy: I thought people were supposed to get smarter in college?

Sunday: Yeah, I think you had a lot of misconceptions about college. Like that anyone would be caught dead wearing that.

Again, the interaction between female antagonists on the show frequently goes beyond simple fight talk, with spiteful comments about appearance being the norm. Additionally, although all the above examples center on Buffy, other major female characters do engage in this kind of behavior too. Willow refers to Faith as a "superbitch" ("This Year's Girl" 4.15), calls Riley's wife a "bitch" to appease Buffy after having spent an episode bonding with her ("As You Were" 6.15), and has the following to say about Veruca in "Beer Bad" (4.5): "Buff, have you heard of this Veruca chick? Dresses like Faith, voice like an albatross."

IN SUMMARY

Within the series, Whedon certainly attempts to address female competition, and the bitchiness that can arise from it, by presenting it in a negative light through characters such as Cordelia. There are even entire episodes of *Buffy* dedicated to showing the detrimental effects that competitive female relationships can have, not only on the women themselves, but also on the incidental individuals surrounding them. For instance, in the episodes "Bewitched, Bothered and Bewildered" (2.16) and "Him" (7.6), large numbers of women are shown fighting over a man as the result of magic; chaos ensues, the bitchiness escalates ("slut-bag hussy," "Anna Nicole Smith thinks you look tacky"), and things quickly become violent. The Buffy-Dawn relationship is a particular focus of the episode "Him" (7.6) with the long-running sisterly tension between the two of them coming to the fore: "You've always been the special one. Hot little Buffy with her boyfriends. The Slayer. And now someone likes me, and you just can't stand that I'm getting the attention. What am I—gonna compete with you? You're older and hotter and have sex that's rough and kill people. I don't have any of that stuff."

Only when Buffy expresses to Dawn that their relationship is more important than any romantic interest is the spell broken. Thus the damaging aspects of female competition are examined, and the importance of female relationships highlighted. Furthermore, Whedon reinforces the need for positive female–female relationships, most significantly through the Buffy and Willow friendship, which provides us with an example of two women consistently supporting each other and working together to overcome problems that range from the fantastic to the everyday.

However, although competition and antagonism in certain situations are critiqued, in others they go unmentioned. Buffy and Willow are both capable of bitchiness and competitiveness, and this is often left uncontested, especially when the object of their criticism is either evil, or portrayed as a sexual threat. There appears to be a pervading idea that some women are deserving of this harsh treatment; while it is made clear that competition between, for example, Buffy and Dawn is destructive, it is acceptable when it relates to characters such as Faith and Veruca. This is indicative of an implicit association between sexuality, or sexual promiscuity, and punishment; the female antagonists on the show are routinely presented as licentious or sexually deviant, thus any bitchy remarks directed towards them are deemed acceptable.

Of course, it could be argued that the female protagonists on the show exchange their fair share of cutting remarks with male antagonists ("You're one creepy little dweeb, Warren" ["I Was Made to Love You" 5.15]) thus putting them on a level playing field with their female counterparts. However, upon closer examination it becomes apparent that such comments tend to differ in nature; Buffy's taunts to male villains revolve around their impending defeat, inadequacies as villains and relative lack of strength ("The prom's a go and you're pathetic", and "Luckily for me, you're an incompetent maladjust" ["The Prom" 3.20]) rather than personal observations about their attractiveness. At no point does Buffy mock Spike for his clothing choices, or tell Angelus that he looks a little "worn around the eyes."

Additionally, *Buffy* presents us with a world where female friendship can only exist where women aren't competing for men. While Whedon critiques the idea of competition for men in episodes such as "Bewitched, Bothered and Bewildered" and "Him", many more examples go unexamined. But can Whedon really be held to account for this? After all, *Buffy* is still a TV show and as such its writers still need to create a compelling drama by relying on TV conventions and tropes such as the love triangle, which inevitably causes competition and hostility among the characters involved. Moreover it could be reasoned that on *Buffy* Whedon is actually being rather progressive, in that the vast majority of the love triangles presented on *Buffy* involve two females and one male. In this way traditional gender roles are again being subverted; we are presented with dominant female characters aggressively fighting for the right to more passive, submissive men.

Ultimately, Whedon performs a difficult balancing act. On the one hand he is endeavoring to illustrate the positive relationships necessary between women and provide examples of such friendships; on the other he is bound by the dramatic needs of the show, and as a result must rely on certain storytelling conventions such as the love triangle. Although the presentation of female relationships on the show is perhaps not as progressive as one might hope, Whedon's attempts to represent and encourage female solidarity are surely admirable. Certainly *Buffy* offers far more successful attempts to portray positive female relationships than can be found in most contemporary popular culture (or indeed some of Whedon's other projects; *Angel* in particular offers very few examples of female-female interaction, let alone positive relationships). Perhaps, then, *Buffy* should be viewed not as an unproblematic feminist manifesto, but rather as a move in the right direction with respect to the representation of female relationships on TV, and therefore as a show which many current series would do well to refer to when developing their own female relationships.

Works Cited

"As You Were." 6.15. Writ., dir. Douglas Petrie. *Buffy*.
Bechdel Test Movie List. N.p. [2011.] Web. 23 Oct. 2011. bechdeltest.com.

"Beer Bad." 4.5. Writ. Tracey Forbes. Dir. David Solomon. Buffy.

"Bewitched, Bothered and Bewildered." 2.16. Writ. Marti Noxon. Dir. James A. Contner. Buffy.

Buckman, Alyson R. "Triangulated Desire in Angel and Buffy." Sexual Rhetoric in the Works of Joss Whedon: New Essays. Ed. Eric B. Waggoner. Jefferson, NC: McFarland, 2010. 48-92. Print.

Buffy the Vampire Slayer: The Chosen Collection. Boxed Set. Created by Joss Whedon, Perf. Sarah Michelle Gellar, Nicholas Brendon, Alyson Hannigan. 20th Century Fox Home Entertainment, 2006. DVD.

"Dirty Girls." 7.18. Writ. Drew Goddard. Dir. Michael Gershman. Buffy.

"Enemies." 3.27. Writ. Douglas Petrie. Dir. David Grossman. Buffy.

"Faith, Hope, and Trick." 3.3. Writ. Jane Espenson. Dir. James A. Contner. Buffy.

"The Freshman." 4.1. Writ., dir. Joss Whedon. Buffy.

"Halloween." 2.6. Writ. Carl Ellsworth. Dir. Bruce Seth Green. Buffy.

"Him." 7.6. Writ. Drew Z. Greenberg. Dir. Michael Gershman. Buffy.

"Homecoming." 3.5. Writ., dir. David Greenwalt. Buffy.

"I Robot... You Jane." 1.8. Writ. Askley Gable and Thomas A. Swyden. Dir. Stephen Posey. Buffy.

"I Was Made to Love You." 5.15. Writ. Jane Espenson. Dir. James A. Contner. Buffy.

"Passion." 2.17. Writ. Ty King. Dir. Michael E. Gershman. Buffy.

"The Prom." 3.20. Writ. Marti Noxon. Dir. David Solomon. Buffy.

"Reptile Boy." 2.5. Writ., dir. David Greenwalt. Buffy.

"Revelations." 3.7. Writ. Douglas Petrie. Dir. James A. Contner. Buffy.

Ross, Sharon. "Female Friendship and Heroism in Xena and Buffy." Action Chicks: New Images of Tough Women in Popular Culture. Ed. Sherrie A. Inness. New York: Palgrave Macmillan, 2004. 231-56. Print.

"Some Assembly Required." 2.2. Writ. Ty King. Dir. Bruce Seth Green. Buffy.

"This Year's Girl." 4.15. Writ. Douglas Petrie. Dir. David Grossman. Buffy.

"Welcome to the Hellmouth." 1.1. Writ. Joss Whedon. Dir. Charles Martin Smith. Buffy.

Whedon, Joss. Commentary. "Welcome to the Hellmouth" Buffy.

"Who Are You?" 4.16. Writ. dir. Joss Whedon. Buffy.

"The Yoko Factor." 4.20. Writ. Douglas Petrie. Dir. David Grossman. Buffy.

1.10
Coming Out of the Broom Closet:
Willow's Sexuality and Empowerment in *Buffy*
Jessica Ford

Joss Whedon's *Buffy the Vampire Slayer* locates lesbians and lesbianism in a place of power over others and within the magical. The character of Willow is empowered by her sexuality, as her journey of sexual discovery is paralleled by her increasing agency within the Scooby Gang.

Buffy is founded on the overarching metaphor that high school is hell; the horrors of life are made literal and take on various forms and guises throughout the series (see, for instance, Little 282; Chandler; Wilcox). An extension of this use of metaphor can be seen in the character development of Willow. Her sexual evolution is a metaphor for her sexual awakening and empowerment. Other representations of homosexual teenagers on television focus on disempowerment and social rejection, for example Jack from *Dawson's Creek*, Kurt from *Glee*, and Anna from *One Tree Hill*. In contrast, Willow's exploration of her sexuality coincides with her evolution from nerdy sidekick to powerful witch. Willow is simultaneously empowered by her evolving magical abilities and her sexuality. Through an examination of the facets that make up the character of Willow, in particular the Willow/Tara relationship, it is evident that Willow's increasing sexual agency and magical abilities are constructed in order to empower her as a queer character.

While it is not ideal to define anyone, even fictional characters, by their relationships with others, the trajectory of Willow's story is shaped by her burgeoning sexuality and the impact of her lovers on her development. Willow's transformation from nerdy, impotent girl to the most powerful member of the Scooby Gang reflects a different way of telling queer stories. The formative years of Willow's development are spent yearning for the oblivious Xander, until she is pulled into the world of Oz, who is himself a supernatural being. After enduring the loss of Oz to the darkness of his inner werewolf, Willow develops an unexpected and sensual relationship with Tara, whose influence on Willow is undeniable and shapes her magical and sexual developments. Yet it is the loss of Tara that drives Willow to her darkest place and her powerful yet evil unleashing of magic at the end of Season 6. Finally it is Kennedy who restores Willow's confidence sexually and magically and enables her to change the Buffyverse forever.

When the show first introduces her, Willow is a sweet but geeky girl who adores her best friend Xander, but her feelings are not reciprocated. She is a weak individual in a show dominated by characters with supernatural powers. Xander is Willow's equal in terms of agency, because they both lack the ability to alter events around them. Throughout Season 1 and into Season 2 Willow's computer hacking skills develop and her role within the Scooby Gang becomes more important, as she surpasses her seemingly juvenile feelings for Xander.

Willow's sexual development really starts in Season 2 when she begins a relationship with Oz: guitarist and werewolf. Oz is powerful and cool, attributes that Willow does not see in herself. Yet Oz is drawn to Willow, such as in the episode "Inca Mummy Girl" (2.4) in which Oz notices Willow dressed as an Eskimo, over other more scantily clad ladies. In the episode "Halloween" (2.6) Oz sees Willow walking past his van and asks, "Who is that girl?" with intense fascination. During their relationship Willow discovers magic and Oz becomes a werewolf after being bitten by an infant relative. As Willow learns about and accepts Oz's darker, wolfish impulses she begins to explore her own relationship to magic. The end of Season 2 sees the culmination of the confidence Oz has given Willow and her willingness to delve into the magical. In "Becoming, Part 2" (2.22) Willow attempts a spell far beyond her proficiency and experience with magic. What she doesn't realize at the time is that she was successful in restoring Angel's soul; however, this advance is minimal compared to abilities she acquires during her relationship with Tara.

In Season 3 the audience realizes that there may be more deviance to Willow than what her baggy sweaters portray when Vampire-Willow pays Sunnydale a visit in the episode "Doppelgangland" (3.16). Vamp-Willow is empowered by her supernatural abilities; she is overtly sexualized to the point that Willow notes about her alter ego: "I think I'm kinda gay" ("Doppelgangland" 3.16). Edwina Bartlem looks at the character of Willow in her article "Coming Out on a Hellmouth" and notes that "Vampire Willow is not simply Willow's externalized other, rather she appears to be a reflection of a different aspect of Willow's character...implying that Willow has the potential to be queer, seductive, powerful and evil" (Bartlem). This kind of foreshadowing is a common trope of the show, but it also reflects the strong relationship between sexual agency and supernatural power.

As high school graduation approaches, Willow considers her place within the Scooby Gang and asserts her desire to become a "bad-ass wicca" ("Choices" 3.19). Yet her wishes do not come into fruition until she encounters Tara and is forced to outgrow and move beyond her high school boyfriend in Season 4. When Oz decides to leave, she is forced to reevaluate who she is and what she wants ("Wild at Heart" 4.6). She has been left powerless and it is this need for utility that drives her towards Tara. There is a decisive shift in the episode "New Moon Rising" (4.19) when Willow is forced to make a choice between Oz and Tara. Willow is forced to externalize what she and the audience has known for much of Season 4: her relationship with Tara is sexual, magical, and powerful. Ultimately Willow's relationship with Oz is about his power and his inability to control his inner darkness, which is not constructive for Willow's growth. In contrast Tara is a powerful and positive force in Willow's life that enhances her sexual and magical life.

The progress of Willow's relationship with Tara and the exploration of her magical abilities are key influences on Willow's character arc. It is through her relationship with Tara that she finds confidence in herself as a sexual being and is encouraged to pursue magic. Her feelings of impotence are voiced in the first episode of the series "Welcome to the Hellmouth" (1.1) when Willow tells Buffy how she loses the power of speech when around boys she likes. Willow does not value her own sexual agency, because she doesn't think she has any, until she meets Tara.

Within the Willow/Tara relationship, choice and agency work simultaneously. In the "coming out" episode "New Moon Rising" Willow is forced to choose between Oz and Tara, past and future, wolfy-impotency and magical power. As Rebecca Beirne points out, "Willow... believes that Tara gives her her sexuality" (Beirne). This is correct from the perspective of Willow; however, for the audience it appears to be power in the realm of magic that empowers her sexual agency. As a show *Buffy*, is highly aware of this:

Tara: Even when I'm at my worst, you always make me feel special. How you do that?

Willow: Magic. ("Family" 5.06)

Willow and Tara's relationship is constructed within the realms of witchcraft and magic, and thus the associations with empowerment are innate. While Farah Mendlesohn is more concerned with the Buffy/Willow relationship, she makes some interesting points about the rise of Willow's agency throughout the series, noting that her witchcraft becomes an invaluable tool to the Slayer (Mendlesohn 47). By coding the characters' progressions in terms of relative power gains, the choices made are seemingly self-evident; however, Willow and Tara's relationship is more complex than a simple power grab.

A QUEER CHARACTER, INDEED

Through the development of Willow and Tara's relationship both characters become more powerful. Power is an essential part of the show's premise, as many of the characters are defined in terms of their relative power. To the Scooby Gang, Willow and Tara are most useful as witches, but they're also imperative to each other's growth:

Willow: You've been spell gal night and day lately.

Tara: Well, I just wanna keep up with you, and I'm... well, I just like to be useful. You know, to the gang? I just... never... feel useful.

Willow: You are. You're essential. ("Family" 5.6)

Willow is correct, because without Tara, Willow would be unable to make the magical advances that she does; it is through the trust and understanding she gains from their relationship that Willow is able to further her magical prowess. The Willow/Tara relationship is understood from the outset in terms of magic, as in their first connection in "Hush" (4.10) when they lose the power of speech and join together to protect themselves magically from The Gentlemen. The line between their physical and magical interaction becomes increasingly blurred as the series continues. It is clear from the relationship's conception that "magical experimentation is a close metaphor for sexual experimentation" (Winslade). Willow's sexual development is essential to her magical one, as all of the progress she makes throughout the series contributes to her empowerment.

The Willow and Tara relationship is between two women, but also between two witches. As the primary representation of witchcraft and queer women within the show, Willow and Tara are portrayed as "wicca good... love the earth and woman power," as Xander sings in "Once More, With Feeling" (6.7). Dominique Wilson discusses how the portrayal of witches in *Buffy* is fluid and varying according to context; thus it is reflective of contemporary Western values and represents good and evil as not black and white (Wilson 146). Willow and Tara are portrayed using various symbols taken from the occult and witchcraft and appropriating them for the Buffyverse. Within the show "witchcraft is set up as the domain of women and is frequently linked to the powers of beauty and love" (Krzywinska 186). Willow becomes the primary embodiment of witchcraft throughout the show, thus "witchcraft gets partially freed from many of the traditional trappings of transgression" (Krzywinska 187).

As Willow is an established character within the series, the audience is more likely to trust and identify with her. In a way witchcraft is normalized in the context of *Buffy* through Willow; this is also the case for lesbianism, as same-sex relationships are as central to the show as heterosexual ones. Willow and Tara's relationship represents the only lasting loving relationship on the show, one that was cut short by means beyond their control. All other relationships in the Buffyverse ended either by choice or due to irreconcilable differences. Willow and Tara reflect a relationship based on love and stability, which is evidenced when they take on parental roles for Dawn at the beginning of Season 6 after Buffy and Joyce have died. Placing a homosexual couple at the top of the domestic hierarchy further normalizes their place as within the show.

Sexuality and intimacy between Willow and Tara is expressed through magic. It is commonly acknowledged that predominantly in *Buffy* "lesbian sex... is presented using the conventions of fantasy" (Bartlem). An example is the deflowering of a rose in "Who Are You?" (4.16). Levitation, like the rose, is a common trope used throughout the show to represent Willow and Tara's intimate scenes, such as in "Once More, With Feeling" when Tara is levitated off the bed in a moment of sexual pleasure; or in the conclusion of "Family," when the two embrace and float above the floor while dancing at the Bronze. Bartlem states that this representation may be problematic, as the "depiction of lesbian sex as a form of magic, situates it as being beyond the material world, outside the physical body and beyond reality."

While this holds weight in terms of a larger political agenda, when this representation is contextualized as part of the larger construction of the show, the representation is consistent. It is difficult to compare the sexual relations between Willow and Tara to the relations between other characters. Buffy has sexual relations with Angel, Spike, and Riley; power for these characters manifests itself in physical strength. Thus sparring and combat became a sexual metaphor, representing a form of foreplay. The representation of Willow and Tara's sex life as spells and witchcraft is reflective of the characters' shy personalities as well as a construction through which to explore the nature of a same-sex relationship between witches.

Throughout her evolution as a lesbian character Willow retains her femininity, which is essential to her representation as a witch and a lesbian. Tanya R. Cochran notes that the characters are not "lipstick lesbians," but they still retain their feminine locks and flowing, floral dresses (Cochran 53). Their style seems to be taken more from Wicca culture than from lesbian stereotypes; their flowing skirts are reminiscent of boho-chic and play into ideas of wicca woman power. Whedon appears to want to avoid any stereotyping of the characters as "butch" and "femme" and they are represented as equals. Cochran argues that in the eyes of the audience this is "fortifying its normality and ambiguity" (Cochran 53). Thus further emphasizing that for Willow her sense of self and identity comes from being a witch, as well as being queer. In a conversation with Buffy, Willow reveals her fears about how interconnected her sexual desirability and magic are:

Buffy: Will, there's nothing wrong with you. You don't need magic to be special.

Willow: Don't I? I mean, Buffy, who was I? Just... some girl. Tara didn't even know that girl. ("Wrecked" 6.10)

Willow connects her sexual desirability with witchcraft and Tara's gaze. Willow's self-worth throughout the show is heavily connected with her usefulness; she stays in Sunnydale, as she says in "Graduation Day (Part 1)" (3.21) in Season 3, "to help people." Her conception of herself is intrinsically linked with her relationship with Tara, as she expresses: "the only thing I had going for me... were the moments, just moments, when Tara would look at me and I was wonderful" ("Villains" 6.20). Beirne contends that Willow attributes her desire to sleep with women with her love for Tara, which is evident in the awkwardness of her courting Kennedy in Season 7 (Beirne). Willow's understanding of herself as a lesbian is shaped by her sexual agency and thus her conception of empowerment.

In Season 6 when Tara is killed by a stray bullet we see the full potential of Willow's power. Her self-control is bound only by her love for Tara, and when that is destroyed she sees no reason for restraint and becomes unrestrainedly evil. A comprehensive understanding of Willow's character at this point is difficult to negotiate. Beirne asserts that we are presented with an "unmistakably queer character, whose desires are wholly unnatural, and whose will must be obeyed" (Beirne). Yet can these characteristics be attributed to the fact that she is a lesbian, a witch or just because she is Willow? The Willow/Tara relationship began with the creation of magic and in a disturbing way it makes sense that it may end with the destruction of magic, along with everything else. Made literal, love is creation; loss is destruction.

The loss of Tara is just as essential to the character arc of Willow as is her relationship with Tara. By gaining all power at the end of Season 6 Willow creates a new niche for herself within the group and gains further agency by the end of Season 7; however, it is a slow process for Willow to regain both her sexual and magical confidence and control. It is no coincidence that as Willow's relationship with Kennedy develops, so does her magical control. The idea of power becomes an important issue in the fight against The First and Willow's willingness to use it becomes imperative:

Kennedy: Willow, she's not even the most powerful one in this room. With you here, she's not close.

Buffy: You're new here, and you're wrong. Because I use the power that I have. ("Get It Done" 7.15)

After Tara's death Willow eventually comes back into the fold, and she reverts to the impotency of the early seasons, relying on her computer hacking skills. Yet at the end of Season 7, Willow's power becomes the lynchpin in a plan to save the world. Willow has to be willing to use the magic she once used to try and destroy the world, only this time to save it. In a way this is Tara's final gift to Willow, and she becomes a "goddess" ("Chosen" 7.22). Not without, however, the confidence in her sexuality and womanhood that has been gained from her blossoming relationship with Kennedy. Willow's role within the group evolved over the years to ensure that Willow's "spells are part of the armoury of the Scooby Gang" (Krzywinska

188). In "Chosen," Willow's transformation finally culminates in her ability to empower others, by making every Potential a Slayer.

In seven seasons Willow has gone from impotent, geeky friend of the Slayer to an essential power player within the Buffyverse. Her development in sexuality throughout the series has shaped the audience's understanding of power, lesbianism, and witchcraft in *Buffy the Vampire Slayer*. Willow is a queer character in many senses of the term, which takes on various burdens of representation. Whether she is a positive role model or an accurate representation of queer society is debatable, but we do know that she is empowered.

Works Cited

Bartlem, Edwina. "Coming Out on a Hell Mouth," *Refractory: A Journal of Entertainment Media* 2 (2003). 5 June 2009. Web.

"Becoming (Part 2)." 2.22. Writ. and dir. Joss Whedon. *Buffy*.

Beirne, Rebecca. "Queering the Slayer-text: Reading Possibilities in Buffy the Vampire Slayer," *Refractory: A Journal of Entertainment Media* 5 (2004). 5 June 2009. Web.

Buffy the Vampire Slayer: *The Complete DVD Collection*. Region 2. Twentieth Century Fox, 2004. DVD.

Chandler, Holly. "Slaying the Patriarchy: Transfusions of the Vampire Metaphor in *Buffy the Vampire Slayer*," *Slayage: The Online International Journal of Buffy Studies* 1.3 (2003). Web.

"Choices." 3.19. Writ. David Fury. Dir. James A. Contner. *Buffy*.

"Chosen." 7.22. Writ. and dir. Joss Whedon. *Buffy*.

Cochran, Tanya R. "Complicating the Open Closet: The Visual Rhetoric of *Buffy the Vampire Slayer*'s Sapphic Lovers," *Televising Queer Women*. Ed. Rebecca Beirne. New York: Palgrave, 2008. 49-64. Print.

"Doppelgangland." 3.16. Writ. and dir. Joss Whedon. *Buffy*.

"Family." 5.6. Writ. and dir. Joss Whedon. *Buffy*.

"Get It Done." 7.15. Writ. Douglas Petrie. Dir. David Solomon. *Buffy*.

"Graduation Day (Part 1)." Writ. and dir. Joss Whedon. *Buffy*.

"Halloween." 2.6. Writ. Carl Ellsworth. Dir. Bruce Seth Green. *Buffy*.

"Hush." 4.10. Writ. and dir. Joss Whedon. *Buffy*.

"Inca Mummy Girl." 2.4. Writ. Matt Kiene and Joe Reinkemeyer. Dir. Ellen S. Pressman. *Buffy*.

Krzywinska, Tanya. "Hubble-Bubble, Herbs and Grimoires: Magic, Manichaeanism, and Witchcraft in Buffy." Wilcox and Lavery 178-94.

Little, Tracy. "High School Is Hell: Metaphor Made Literal in *Buffy the Vampire Slayer*." Buffy the Vampire Slayer *and Philosophy*. Ed. James B. South. Chicago: Open Court, 2003. 282-93. Print.

Mendlesohn, Farah. "Surpassing the Love of Vampires: Or, Why (and How) a Queer Reading of the Buffy/Willow relationship Is Denied." Wilcox and Lavery 45-60.

"New Moon Rising." 4.19. Writ. Marti Noxon. Dir. James A. Contner. *Buffy*.

"Once More, With Feeling." 6.7. Writ., dir., and music Joss Whedon. *Buffy.*

"Villains." 6.20. Writ. Marti Noxon. Dir. David Solomon. *Buffy.*

"Welcome to the Hellmouth." 1.1. Writ. Joss Whedon. Dir. Charles Martin Smith. *Buffy.*

"Who Are You? (Part 2 of 2)" 4.16. Writ. and dir. Joss Whedon. *Buffy.*

Wilcox, Rhonda V. "There Will Never Be a "Very Special" *Buffy*: Buffy and the Monsters of Teen Life." *Slayage: The Online International Journal of Buffy Studies.* 1.2 (1999). Web.

--- and David Lavery, ed. *Fighting the Forces: What's at Stake in* Buffy the Vampire Slayer. New York: Rowman, 2002. Print.

"Wild at Heart." 4.6. Writ. Marti Noxon. Dir. David Grossman. *Buffy.*

Wilson, Dominique. "Willow and Witch Craft? The Portrayal of Witchcraft in Joss Whedon's *Buffy the Vampire Slayer." The Buddha of Suburbia: Proceedings of the Eighth Australian and International Religion, Literature and the Arts Conference 2004.* Ed. Carole M. Cusack, Frances DiLauro, and Christopher Hartney. Sydney: RLA Press, 2005. 146-58.

Winslade, J. Lawton. "Teen Witches, Wiccan, and "Wanna-Blessed-Be's": Pop-Culture Magic in *Buffy the Vampire Slayer." Slayage:The Online International Journal of Buffy Studies* 1.1 (2001). Web.

"Wrecked." 6.10. Writ. Marti Noxon. Dir. David Solomon. *Buffy.*

1.11
The Darkness of "Passion": Visuals and Voiceovers, Sound and Shadow
Rhonda V. Wilcox

In the little booklet accompanying the *Chosen* DVD set, Joss Whedon names his twelve top-ten *Buffy* episodes not "shot" by himself—among them, "Passion." He also notes that his list is meant in part "to brag about episodes I worked on less visibly." "Passion" was written by Ty King and directed by Michael E. Gershman. Of course, Whedon (the former Hollywood script doctor) often rewrote or added passages for *Buffy*, collaborating with the credited writers. Most of us nowadays understand that a television show has many parents. Whatever its precise parentage, "Passion" is a wonderful creature—or perhaps I should say creation, but it does seem almost alive to me. Its director, Michael Gershman, was the longtime Director of Photography for the series, and he shot the episode beautifully (it was the first he directed, but not the last). It is one of the visually darkest episodes of *Buffy*, and Gershman uses the interplay of light and dark to develop the emotions and ideas of the story. The writing is also particularly beautiful; and perhaps one of its most noteworthy elements is the memorable voiceover, enhanced by an extraordinarily effective use of music and sound. Those visuals and that voiceover work together to make "Passion" one of the great episodes of television.

"Passion" is the 17th episode of the second season of *Buffy*, many people's favorite season. The show comes as one of an intense sequence of episodes. In the two-part 13th/14th, "Surprise"/"Innocence," the vampire Angel loses his soul (which gypsies had returned to him only to torment him) when he enjoys a moment of pure happiness as he and Buffy make love for the first time. So: Episode 14, Angel turns evil; episode 15, Oz turns werewolf (though Willow still kisses him); in episode 16, Cordelia comes out, publicly claiming Xander as her boyfriend. In other words, we have shows about (among other things) Buffy and Angel; Willow and Oz; Xander and Cordelia. We might say that the next episode, "Passion," is about the adults—Buffy's Watcher, the librarian Rupert Giles, and computer teacher Jenny Calendar—and it is indeed the episode in which Buffy in effect gives Jenny her forgiveness for Jenny's part in supporting the gypsy curse and her blessing on a reconciliation between Jenny and Giles ("I don't want him to be lonely. I don't want anyone to be"). It is the fourth episode in a row about the central characters' romantic relationships.

But it is also the episode in which Jenny dies. Thus it is the first instance of a Whedon trademark, the death of a character in whom the audience is invested, the death of a character who is *alive* for the audience. Something similar occurs in the pilot, with the death of Xander's best friend Jesse, but the effect is not as strong there, because in Jenny's case, the long-term narrative form of television has been operating to create something like a relationship: we have known Jenny (played by Robia LaMorte) almost as long as the rest of the characters, now in their second season. In an interview on "Passion" recorded for the *Chosen* DVD, Whedon calls Jenny Calendar's death a "very specifically placed pivotal moment in the show. We needed to kill somebody, because we needed to tell the audience that not everything is safe." I must confess that I couldn't help thinking, "Who better to kill than someone whose last name is LaMorte?"—but that is simple serendipity, enjoyable though the wordplay might be. In any case, it seems clear that in "Passion" we see one climax of a set of stories about relationships driving towards a moment of mortality—or, to put it another way, "Passion" is about sex and death, among many other things. (In *Buffy*, there are always other things.) Almost every scene is ripe with meaning, and few more so than the opening of "Passion."

OPENING RHYTHMS: VISUAL AND VOICE

The first shot of "Passion" gives us an unusual camera angle: we are looking down on the heads of dancers in the Bronze as they move to slowly swinging music in the dim light. We hear a female voice coolly singing about slipping the net and cutting free. Buffy and Xander dance while conversing, though we cannot hear their words; Cordelia and Willow chat at a table in the background; and even farther back, unseen by the others, is Angel, gazing at Buffy from the dark. Only we see him. The other characters' unawareness of his gaze makes them seem vulnerable; makes him seem powerful. Back in 1975, film scholar Laura Mulvey wrote a now-famous Freudian analysis of the male gaze ("Visual Pleasure and Narrative Cinema"). Whatever one's view about the Freudian specifics of her argument, is there anyone who hasn't felt, at one time or another, the unnerving sensation that someone is watching? The power goes to the watcher (and I'm not talking about Quentin Travers). From Gershman's opening shot looking down on the dancers throughout the rest of the scene (or, indeed, the rest of the episode), it is clear that the one gazing is exerting a kind of power.

But Angel's (or Angelus's) visual stalking is not the only element in the scene that indicates such power. As the female voice sings, we begin to hear a male voice speak: David Boreanaz voicing Angel. His words take over, though he begins almost in a whisper: "Passion. It lies in all of us—sleeping, waiting—and though unwanted, unbidden, it will stir—open its jaws and howl." The words begin in quiet but end with animal rage, though the voice is quiet still. Just as the other characters are unaware of his gaze, so too they are unaware of his voice. Again, only we share that knowledge; his voice surrounds the scene. If not an omniscient "voice of God," a voiceover is usually given to the protagonist, recalling events or commenting as they proceed; normally, the voiceover gives the viewer a place to locate, often a character to identify with or at least pull for. How chilling is it, then, that the most dangerous antagonist gives the voiceover here? J. P. Telotte, author of *Voices in the Dark*, confirms that this is a rarity (I emailed him to ask). Voiceovers are characteristic of film noir, and there are many film noir elements of this episode, some of which I'll touch on later. But giving the villain the voiceover is *not* characteristic, because giving a character the voiceover normally means giving the character power. So: unaware of his voice, unaware of his gaze, the others dance on.

Additional uses of sound and sight in the opening amplify the emotion. The diegetic music, the opening song in the Bronze, gives way to Christophe Beck's non-diegetic score as the Scoobies move into the night. As they emerge, smiling, from the club, again we cannot hear their voices, but the rhythm of their walking works with the music of the female singer ("Think I'd learn by now," she tells us). The music shifts to the strings of the score as we see Angel with a victim in the night, dropping her drained body to the ground (foreshadowing another body to be dropped later in the episode). Percussion reminiscent of a slow heartbeat (slow with the nearness of death?) weaves through the sound of the strings. We seem to look over Angel's shoulder in a shot in which a close-up of the dark back of his head and his black coat take up nearly a third of the screen, while the small figures of Buffy, Willow, Xander, and Cordelia walk away into a narrow space between buildings. Again the visual makes this dangerous figure predominant, looming over the others. Having seen him murder while the others are unknowing, we share his view and hear his voice; we are immersed in the darkness with him.

This is not the most ominous part of the opening, however. The music, percussive notes cascading down like distant thunder, rolls into the next scene, carrying the feeling of danger with it. We are looking into Buffy's room through her window as she moves around in the light, preparing for bed. She senses something is out there and looks through the blinds, through the glass of her window, the glass of our screen. Then our viewpoint shifts; we are inside. In one of the darkest episodes ever, we have here one of the darkest scenes: After Buffy turns her lamp off, there is only a glint of light on the coverlet, on her face. We might not even see, on first viewing, Angel's head outside, behind the blinds, as he gazes in and then slips aside, out of sight; I confess that I did not. But when the moment comes, when one *does* see him—it is shocking. And then, in the next shot, with more light on her sleeping face (has some time passed?), we see a *shadow* move towards it. The shadow is Angel. His hand gently touches her face, and she lies unaware of the danger. In the most literal sense, the stalker in the room is dreadful. The musical score is beautiful but ominous; and the images tell us just how dark the moment is. In the last shot of the scene, there is darkness dominating in the center of the screen, with window light to the left and right. As he sits on her girlhood bed, Angel's head is in the center of the darkness, and his shadow falls towards her, though her face still catches the light: two faces together in the dark. Now Angel is silent as he gazes. With the camera, we pull back from, we retreat from, this beautiful scene so full of the fearful power of potential violence, still aware of the love that came before. All of this comes before the credits.

WINDOWS

As attentive *Buffy* watchers will recall, Buffy's bedroom window is a significant place for the long-term story. Framed against that window was Buffy and Angel's first kiss—a shot repeatedly shown throughout the years of the series; it was also the place of the visual revelation that Angel is a vampire. Her blinds provide a noir backdrop for that scene. She often uses the window as a door, a way to secretly get out of her house to patrol, and just as often uses it to allow Angel in to visit her—at first to warn her of danger, and later for more pleasant purposes. We see them kissing through the window, as well as by it. It is nothing new to suggest that, especially in vampire stories, the image of a threshold (whether door or window) can be connected with the idea of sexuality. In fact, it is a rather comforting part of vampire myth to think that the vampire can only enter where invited— making for a kind of safe sexual fantasy. But once invited, the vampire can always return (one can't re-virgin oneself). In this very episode, we find a reminder of the sexual suggestion when Buffy searches for a spell to disinvite the vampire: Xander tells her and Cordelia that the situation should be a warning against "inviting strange men into your bedrooms." The open window seems a reasonable symbol for female sexuality.

I would never argue, however, that *Buffy* is a one-to-one allegory; symbols can have more than one meaning (and indeed, if they live in more than one mind, they must, to one degree or another; none of us see things exactly alike). In this episode, there is a cluster of window images, all of them important. What I would like to suggest is that they color one another— they echo in one another (to use both sight and sound to try to express the idea). I will limit myself to discussing only three in any depth. The first we have already covered: Buffy's bedroom window, which was a central place for the expression of their love but has become, in the opening of "Passion," the entry for a predator; as David Kociemba says in a brilliant essay on the episode, "Angelus systematically rewrites the settings" (par. 19). The second is the window that frames Jenny Calendar's death. The third is the window through which we see Buffy and Willow's reaction to Jenny's death.

Threshold imagery can evoke either sex or death (or both; the French call the moment of sexual climax "la petite mort," after all). The threshold is a place of crossing over, in one way or another; you aren't where you were before, physically or emotionally. For Jenny, the window is a place of death. She has been working late, alone in her computer classroom, trying to create a transliteration of the lost gypsy ritual of restoration, to return Angel's soul once more. In the dimness of late afternoon, Giles visits her, and when she reports her conversation with Buffy and tells him she may have news, he invites her to come to his home later: it seems their relationship will be restored along with Angel's soul. In the next scene in Jenny's classroom, she is still working, and it is much darker; the only light comes from noir-slatted windows and the computer screen. Just after her program successfully creates the transliteration, she saves it on disk. (She backs up her work! Angel would have been eternally damned if I'd been the one at that computer.) And then she sees Angel sitting in the darkness, watching, waiting. He taunts her, toys with her, destroys both the computer and the printout of the spell. She has earlier obtained an orb of Thessala to hold his soul when she draws it from the ether; as Jenny held it in the magic shop, the director focused in close-up on Robia LaMorte's face, lit by the intermittently glowing orb, her own eyes glowing as she spoke of returning Angel's soul. Now, in the darkened classroom, the orb glows again as Angel holds it, and his face is divided almost completely in half between dark and light.

Stacey Abbott has written of how just such visuals—half dark, half light—indicate Angel's two-sided nature (30). In this scene in "Passion," Angel smashes the orb—smashes the light—and throws Jenny through the locked door: premonitory violence. As she runs through the colonnaded outer hallways of the school, light and dark seem to strobe over her. Film scholar Jeanine Basinger (Joss Whedon's college professor), addressing the biennial *Slayage* conference on the Whedonverse, spoke of the art of the rhythm of editing (in fact, she was referring to the work of another famous student of hers). There is another kind of rhythm here, of music and movement. The opening scene I have already described shows a slower rhythm as the characters dance and stroll in oblivious happiness; here, Jenny's desperate motion matches the speed of the intense musical score, just as the strobing shadows do. We have sped to a climax.

Her race ends up a stairway, at the landing, by the window. Angel, who seemed behind, has reached it before her. The two figures are framed by the half-circle of the large window. This shot, like the shot of Buffy and Angel's first kiss, is a memorable one, often re-shown; many viewers probably have it clearly in mind. In the structure of the window, seven arrowing lines of wood point towards the center, where Jenny and Angel stand. She is to the left, he is to the right; as he breaks her neck, his arm reaches straight up the center, moving with the musical score. She drops gracefully into the darkness as his body moves into the center of the space, clearly marked by the window's lines. The visuals and the music have the emotional force of beautifully performed ballet, horrific though the scene is. The lighting and the framing are provided by the incomplete circle of the window (no symbolic ring of immortality here). And we are with them inside the dark place; only outside, through the window, is there light.

The window of Jenny's death, then, is the second such image. It is also, of course, the window through which we clearly see Angel's killing—which, with all the anonymous and minor characters he has killed before, we have perhaps not truly seen. As Whedon says in the "Passion" interview, they "wanted to show that—No, Angel isn't just pretending to be evil, he's not just a little bit evil... he's her enemy."

The next major window image shows us Angel watching again, savoring the reaction to this murder. Both the voiceover and the secret gaze return. The voiceover starts just after the discovery of Jenny's dead body and bleeds over into the scene in which Buffy and Willow get the phone call from Giles telling them what has happened, as Angel greedily watches from outside. Passion, his voiceover tells us, is in "the joy of love, the clarity of hatred, the ecstasy of grief." The ecstasy of grief indeed: as Angel watches from the dark, the view through the Summers' window is softened by sheer, translucent curtains, but we can still see the faces. Once again we cannot hear their words (except for Willow's "No!")—but we can hear the tones of their voices; we can hear and see their pain. With the framing of the window, we are made conscious of the fact of observation; somehow their grief seems both more distant and more real. This window shows us the human vulnerability to loss. And outside, Angel gloats.

SHADOWS AND FIRE

In "Passion," Angel is the figure most connected with the dark. But there are others who are shadowed as well. We have already touched on the shadow moving towards Buffy. When Jenny sits in her computer classroom, bars of shadow fall on the board behind her, noir-fashion. The same imagery, bars of shadow on dimly lit walls, appeared in the magic shop she visited—and even more darkly when the vampire Drusilla entered the shop later to kill the owner. Angel's incestuously connected fellow vampire Spike, Drusilla's lover, who formerly seemed the greatest threat to Buffy but now is confined to a wheelchair, is represented with the large shadow of a chain on the wall beside him as Angel taunts him with his confinement. Giles, having discovered Jenny's dead body placed in his own bed by Angel, stands literally up against the wall by the threshold of his home as he talks to the police; as he does so, his shadow rises large on the wall behind him, while the police lights revolve outside the open door. Like Buffy, Giles has been touched by Angel's darkness. The angel of death has penetrated Jenny's body and Giles's home.

The scene of Giles's discovery is, like most of the episode, set in darkness; but small candles have been placed on every step of the stairs that Giles, carrying a bottle of wine, mounts to find Jenny. He assumes that they have been put there by Jenny as part of a romantic invitation, but it is Angel that has placed them there, just as he has placed the love duet of *La Bohème* on the record player. At the highest note, Giles drops the wine in perfect rhythm: the glass crashes, the liquid spills.

Those small candle flames suggest passion. There are two other noteworthy instances of fire in the episode. More than one viewer has complained about the fact that, when Angel destroys Jenny's computer, it bursts into flame. Visual symbolism takes precedence over verisimilitude here: the sight of Angel warming his hands at this hellish little flame gives us a premonition of the scene's emotional direction; it is a sign of his savagery. And later in the story, Giles creates a much larger blaze as he tries to take vengeance on Angel. (As Whedon says in the *Chosen* booklet, "Death, *La Bohème*, and Tony Head with a flaming baseball bat. Come ON, people" [2].) Giles not only strikes Angel but sets the whole Factory (Angel, Drusilla, and Spike's home) afire. But as Buffy has warned Xander, Willow, and Cordelia, the problem with this scenario is that it could get Giles killed; in fact, it seems that may have been one of his goals. ("Are you trying to get yourself killed?" she asks him after she runs to the rescue.) Following a futile battle with Angel, Buffy turns away to save Giles; and the action closes with a scene that combines the imagery of windows and fiery passion: Buffy drags Giles out of the flames and hugs him, both of them huddled on the ground outside, framed by a window full of fire behind them. "You can't leave me—I can't do this alone," she tells him. She has lost Angel and he has lost Jenny. But Giles and Buffy must step outside their passions and go on.

VOICES, -OVER AND –OFF

Angel's voiceover has, from the start of the episode, suggested power, just as his unseen gaze has. As Kaja Silverman observes in *The Acoustic Mirror*, voiceovers in Hollywood cinema had long been almost "exclusively male" (48). In more recent televisual terms, we have heard more female voiceovers (in *Roswell*; in *Veronica Mars*; in *Gossip Girl*—both of the latter two by Kristen Bell; and one could go on). But here the male is the voice-from-above. Furthermore, and much more unusually, the voice is the voice of the enemy (as I've noted earlier). The effect is to make the forces marshaled against Buffy seem particularly threatening.

However, the situation is much more complicated than that. Throughout the episode, Angel is stalking Buffy, her friends, and her mother. When Buffy tries to give her mother a censored version of what has happened with Angel, Joyce summarizes, "He's changed; he's not the same guy you fell for." But Willow later reminds Buffy that, different though he is, "You're still the only thing he thinks about." Many fans of the series distinguish between Angel with a soul and Angel without a soul by using the names Angel and Angelus, respectively. Some may have wondered why I have not used the same distinction. Sometimes I do, but in this discussion I have chosen not to, because one of the things I think "Passion" makes us uncomfortably aware of is that the two are much closer than we might like to imagine. Any of the beautiful sentences in the voiceover could have been spoken by either. The words are dangerous because they're true. "Without passion, we'd be truly dead"—and who better to tell us than the undead lover?

But the episode does not just leave us with the danger of the beautiful darkness. (And may I say: one reason this episode is so impressive in its operatic expressiveness is that all the major actors were particularly beautiful at this season of their lives.) There is yet another aesthetic twist in the power of the voiceover. *Buffy* is known for the power of its language (i.e., Whedon and the other writers are known for the power of their language), but in this episode Buffy has ceded that power to Angel. Until the end; and then she takes back her voice and the voiceover. As Kaja Silverman reminds us, we sometimes hear not a voiceover but a voice-off—"so designated because its ostensible source is not visible at the moment of emission" (48). It is much more likely to be female than is a voiceover, she notes, and is much less powerful in effect. Repeatedly in this episode we see Buffy speaking without being able to hear her. I would argue that at the end of "Passion," Buffy's voice moves from the status of normal character's voice to voice-off to voiceover, and thus to regained power.

In the scene following Buffy's rescue of Giles, Buffy stands with him at Jenny Calendar's gravesite in the cool daylight. The two of them mourn her, and Buffy says, "I'm sorry I couldn't kill him for you—for her—when I had the chance." Then we move from the visual of the gravestone to the sight of Willow substituting in Ms. Calendar's room. Just as happened at some points with Angel's voiceover, we hear words of characters in the scene—mixed back and forth with the voice from outside the scene—in this case, Buffy's, spoken by Sarah Michelle Gellar. As her voice bleeds over from the graveyard to the classroom, she says, "I wasn't ready. But I think I finally am"; then we hear Willow's quiet words to the class about following Ms. Calendar's lessons; and then Buffy's voice again. It may be from "off," but it also seems "above," as she asserts the course to come: "I can't hold onto the past anymore. Angel is gone. Nothing's ever gonna bring him back."

Taking the voiceover position, Buffy is taking back her strength in the fight. And the contrast in the voices is revealing, too: Angel's words are abstract and elegant; Buffy's are conversational, simple. Writers such as Karen Eileen Overbey and Lahney Preston-Matto (among many others) have pointed out that Buffy's language is one of her weapons, a lively, witty force (75-76). But her language here is tired and quiet, with little in the way of figurative speech or grand generalizations. Angel is telling us the meaning of life; Buffy is simply facing her own facts. But hers is the final voice of the episode; Buffy has the last word.

The episode, however, does not end with words; it ends with an image. Buffy's voice, remember, has spread out from her own place (in the cemetery with Giles) over the outside world (in the school with Willow and the other students). But as she speaks the final words, we see the computer disk with the restoration spell for Angel slide unnoticed off the desk to land between it and a computer stand. In this episode full of darkness, the last shot is of a slice of light between two walls of darkness: the disk, in close-up, cuts across the light between the shadows, as the sound of its falling echoes portentously. The visual ironically undercuts Buffy's declaration that nothing will bring Angel back—or at least it does in potential; when we first see it, we do not know whether or not the restoration spell will ever be used again—or, indeed, should be. As Whedon says in the interview, "We wanted to make it as hard for our characters and for the audience as possible. We wanted to make them as unhappy as possible, and we wanted to make them know that redeeming or getting Angel back would be either impossible or so difficult and fraught with consequences that they themselves would be unsure whether they wanted to." The visual, then, undercuts Buffy's voiceover; hers is definitely not the voice-of-God type, but more the damaged noir hero voice: not all-knowing, but all the more human in its imperfection of knowledge and language—and all the more heroic, too.

Jenny Calendar's secret knowledge, falling like her body, is waiting to be revived—though she never will be. We, the audience, have been guided by Angel's voice; we have gazed from his viewpoint. On Jenny's blackboard, the night of her death, the word "mirror" is writ large. How much of ourselves do we see here? In our unoperatic existences, is there still some danger from that flame? Do we peer through that window? By the end of "Passion," the hero's voice prevails. But still, by the end of "Passion," we have seen a little more of the darkness.

Works Cited

Abbott, Stacey. *Angel*. Detroit: Wayne State UP, 2009. Print. TV Milestones Series.

Basinger, Jeanine. "Joss Whedon, Film Major: A+ All the Way." The Third Biennial *Slayage* Conference on the Whedonverses. Henderson State University. Arkadelphia, AK. 5-8 June 2008. Keynote lecture.

Buffy the Vampire Slayer: The Chosen Collection DVD Boxed Set. Twentieth Century Fox Home Entertainment, 2006. DVD.

Kociemba, David. "'Over-Identify Much?': Passion, 'Passion,' and the Author-Audience Feedback Loop in *Buffy the Vampire Slayer*." *Slayage: The Online International Journal of Buffy Studies* 5.3 (2006). 39 pars. Web. 20 Oct. 2011.

Mulvey, Laura. "Visual Pleasure and Narrative Cinema." *Screen* 16.3 (1975): 6-18. Print.

Overbey, Karen Eileen, and Lahney Preston-Matto. "Staking in Tongues: Speech Act as Weapon in *Buffy*." *Fighting the Forces: What's at Stake in* Buffy the Vampire Slayer. Ed. Rhonda V. Wilcox and David Lavery. Lanham, MD: Rowman & Littlefield, 2002. 73-84. Print.

"Passion." 2.17. Writ. Ty King, dir. Michael E. Gershman. *Buffy*. Disk 5.

Silverman, Kaja. *The Acoustic Mirror: The Female Voice in Psychoanalysis and Cinema*. Bloomington: Indiana UP, 1988. Print.

Telotte, J. P. Email to the author. 11 Feb. 2011.

---. *Voices in the Dark: The Narrative Patterns of* Film Noir. Urbana-Champaign: U of Illinois P, 1989. Print.

Whedon, Joss. "Interview with Joss Whedon: Passion." Special Features. *Buffy*. Disk 5.

---. "Joss Whedon's Selection of His Favorite Buffy Episodes." *Buffy: The Chosen Collection* DVD Boxed Set Episode Guide. [1-4.] Print.

1.12
Returning to the Basement:
Excavating the Unconscious in *Buffy's* "Restless"

Laura Berger and Keri Ferencz

"I believe the subtext here is rapidly becoming text."
—Rupert Giles, "Ted," *Buffy The Vampire Slayer* (2.11)

Dreams have been identified as "an important narrative element of *Buffy the Vampire Slayer*" (Keller 165), both in the frequency of their occurrences— about thirty dreams in the first four seasons of the show (Keller 165)—and in terms of their significance, as they provide viewers the opportunity to penetrate the exteriority of each character and explore the realms of his or her unconscious. The episode which best illustrates the importance of dreams within the *Buffy* universe is "Restless" (4.22), written and directed by Joss Whedon; each of the four dreams in this episode can be seen as an explication and dramatization of the irreconcilable tension between who one is and who one *should* be. The pages that follow will explore this tension with reference to psychoanalytic theory including the Lacanian understanding of the self, namely the division between the self and its ego-ideal or "ideal-I," and Judith Butler's gender theory that speaks to the external pressures on the self to conform to societal gender norms. Ultimately, the narrative decision to allow viewers entry to the interior dream lives of characters allows these tensions visibility, resulting in a deeper understanding of the characters as conflicted subjects becoming available to viewers.

Before beginning an analysis of "Restless," it is useful to briefly explore the relevant aspects of both psychoanalytic and gender theory that will inform our interpretation. Psychoanalytic theory, originally developed by Sigmund Freud, seeks to understand the nature of persons by exploring the unconscious mind, because human consciousness is riddled with gaps (Freud, *The Unconscious* 50). Thus, the unconscious is the key to understanding fully the subject—to repair the gaps in consciousness. The primary way of uncovering the unconscious in psychoanalytic practice is through the interpretation of dreams because they allow a privileged glimpse of the unconscious at work (Eagleton 157). Dreams can be seen as "picture-puzzles" (Freud, *Interpretation of Dreams* 924) or "symbolic texts" (Eagleton 157) because the difference between latent meanings and manifest details is so extreme in dream-form. Dreams, then, must be translated or deciphered in order to be understood. This process of probing allows for the discovery of the dream's latent meanings—the unconscious fears and desires of the subject. Since the psychoanalytic approach to literary criticism is also concerned with discovering the latent meanings hidden in manifest details, applying psychoanalytic dream interpretation techniques to "Restless" is an ideal approach, for it will enable a more complete exploration of the episode's underlying meanings.

In addition to Freud's writings on the unconscious and the interpretation of dreams, we shall make reference to the theory of the mirror stage posited by psychoanalyst Jacques Lacan, whose primary concern is the constitution of the human subject as a being or an "I." Lacan conceives of the mirror stage as a process occurring during infancy that leaves lifelong tension within the subject. Sean Homer notes that "the sense of a unified self is acquired at the price of this self being an other" (Homer 25). It is important to make explicit that the duality of self that develops in the mirror stage does not simply disappear as the infant matures; the sense of Otherness within the infant's ego remains, and the tension inherent in the duality only increases with greater awareness on the part of the subject as he or she ages. Lacan notes that the ego is unable to live up to the expectations imposed on it by the ideal-I, as evidenced by the dreams of Willow, Xander, Giles, and Buffy in "Restless."

It is not merely internal tensions related to the self that are illuminated in dreams but also tensions related to social norms, including traditional notions of gender. Prominent queer theorist Judith Butler suggests that gender is a result of social conditions, not an innate identity. As such, Butler asks that we consider gender as an act that is both "intentional" and "performative" (*Subversive Bodily Acts* 380): an invention with no origin, a circumstance and not a state. We are *assigned* a gender on the basis of sex, and it is our duty to "perform" that gender with an audience in mind, real or imagined. *Buffy the Vampire Slayer* is celebrated for characters who defy confining configurations of "maleness" and "femaleness," but doing so is a struggle. "Restless" brings that struggle into the light, subtly showing the way that each character grapples with notions of gender and his or her own perceived failings in the performance of assigned gender roles.

WILLOW'S DREAM

The first dream of the episode is Willow's, and though it explores both the tension between the self and its ideal-I and the impositions on the self by societal expectations of gender, the dream's focus is the performative aspects of selfhood in relation to preconceived notions of who one *should* be. Willow's narrative arc across the first four seasons of *Buffy the Vampire Slayer* is a dramatic one; she transitions from an introverted, bookish loner in the first season to a more socially integrated teenager in Seasons 2 and 3, and truly blossoms in the fourth season, discovering at college an adult romantic love. Willow believes that with Tara, she has become the woman she was meant to be. Broadly speaking, then, Willow's dream is a nightmare, for she devolves from what she considers her ideal self back to the stunted outsider she was in high school.

The first moments of Willow's dream echo Peter Greenaway's film *The Pillow Book* (1996) as well as Jeanette Winterson's *Written on the Body* quite explicitly. In the latter work, the unnamed, ungendered narrator finds in her lover Louise one who is able to translate and understand a bodily "secret code" (Winterson 89); in other words, Louise is able to understand her lover on the deepest levels. In the opening moments of her dream, Willow is painting poetry—literally writing—on the back of her lover Tara, which suggests a similarly deep connection between the characters. Emphasizing this, Willow tells Tara, "I never worry here. I'm safe here." Though this feeling of safety is not to last, this initial scene is essential, for it positions Willow as comfortable in her own skin, in her most whole form, and thus representative of having achieved her ideal-I. Tara breaks the idyllic spell of the dream's opening moments when she tells Willow, "They will find out, you know. About you." It is important to note that although her sexual identification as a lesbian is central to Willow's sense of self, social opinion surrounding her sexual orientation is not something that plays a role in the anxiety she feels in the dream; rather, as was intimated above, Tara (as a corporeal representation of sexuality) represents Willow's safe place where she is free from the anxiety of identity performance.

Willow's dream begins its transition to nightmare when she finds herself enrolled in a drama class. Though she has a history of academic excellence, drama class represents an uncomfortable situation for her. When Willow arrives at what is meant to be the initial class and finds that not only is she late, but she is to take part in a performance being given expressly for everyone whom she has ever known, her anxiety increases dramatically. In this way, her repressed anxiety about "performance of identity on a day-to-day basis" (Pateman 132) is transfigured into a floundering and lack of preparedness for the performance being given in class. Giles appears as the director, but does nothing to calm the anxieties Willow is feeling by telling the assembled cast that the audience longs to "strip you and eat you alive," suggesting that those with whom Willow has surrounded herself are constantly trying to destroy her fragile, newly-developed sense of self. Giles further notes that "acting isn't about behaving, it's about hiding," emphasizing that the masks one wears in life do not accurately define who we are, but rather conceal our real identities from prying eyes.

As Willow arrives to class, Buffy approaches her and expresses jealousy over the fact that Willow is already in costume and character. This points directly to the performative nature of self as well as the inferiority that Willow has begun to feel. All the people around her are dressed in what could never be mistaken for anything but costumes: Harmony is a milkmaid, Buffy a 1920s flapper, and Riley a cowboy. Buffy's suggestion that Willow, in her everyday clothes, is somehow costumed highlights the fact that she knows Willow to be playing a role in everyday life. Though she tries to comfort Willow by telling her, "No one's going to know the truth… you know, about you," Willow has begun to understand that her newly developed sense of self is merely a mask, and one that others can see it as such.

Attempting to find respite from her anxiety, Willow escapes into the velvety folds of the proscenium's red curtains, which, series creator Joss Whedon notes in his DVD commentary on "Restless," evoke images of female genitalia. As this is an effort to return to safety and comfort, it is unsurprising that it is at this point that Tara resurfaces in the dream, offering Willow a momentary sense of stability, as well as a deeper understanding of that which her dream is seeking to communicate. Tara tells Willow that she is being followed, and within the narrative of the dream, what seems to be hunting Willow is the shadow of her former self. Tara retreats deeper into the safety of the cerulean curtains, exiting Willow's dream for good, but not before issuing the warning that "everyone's starting to wonder about... the real you. If they find out, they'll punish you," suggesting once again that if Willow's true self is revealed, she will be alone, having lost all that she has spent her adolescence fighting to gain: self-confidence, friendship, and love. Immediately following Tara's disappearance, the curtains transform into a site of violence, with Willow being attacked from all sides by a faceless, menacing entity.

The transition into the final act of Willow's dream marks the true descent into nightmare territory, for it is here that Willow fully devolves into her high school self. Pulled from the no-longer-safe space of her sexuality by Buffy, who wonders aloud what Willow has done to prompt a demon to hunt her, Willow is returned to a classroom at Sunnydale High School. After being told that "everyone already knows," Willow's "costume"—which she finally acknowledges as being representative of a security blanket when she insists that she "needs" it—is violently removed so that she stands before the class looking exactly as she did in the years before her transition out of geekdom. It is in this, the final scene of Willow's dream, that the Lacanian notion of "organic insufficiency" (Lacan 6) is clearest—Willow's repressed knowledge that she is still the awkward, insular, immature being she always was rather than the personification of her ideal-I comes to the surface. Revisiting her teenage years and the self-doubt and insecurity that came with them suggests to Willow that she is still somehow "less-than" both her friends and her internalized image of herself. The dream ends with Willow being directly attacked by the demon who has been haunting her; a demon that, as has been previously noted, represents her former self. Ultimately then, Willow is attacking herself for being foolish enough to believe that she could overcome her true self in order to become her ideal-I.

XANDER'S DREAM

Moving chronologically through "Restless," the next dream belongs to Xander. His dream, like Willow's before him, is concerned with tensions between self and ideal-I, but unlike Willow's, it also addresses the tensions between self and societally-imposed notions of gender. Xander's lack of physical strength, intelligence, and supernatural gifts creates within the character a feeling of inferiority to those around him. Additionally, the fact that "'real men' in *Buffy*... are often monsters" (Jowett 95) nearly guarantees Xander's inability to become an ideal of masculinity. The focal point of his dream is his struggle against repressed feelings of inferiority as both a man and, more broadly, a human being.

In a way that is again similar to Willow's dream, Xander's begins in an idyllic fashion and transitions into a nightmare. Those readers familiar with the early seasons of *Buffy the Vampire Slayer* will recall Xander's unrequited love for the title character. Though references to this love have all but disappeared by Season 4, Xander's dream shows that these feelings have not vanished, but have merely been repressed and displaced onto Buffy's mother, Joyce, who attempts to seduce Xander in the early part of his dream. With Xander calling himself both a "conquistador" and a "comfortador," this opening scene firmly positions him as the man he longs to be, or what Lacan would call his ideal-I. Accepting Joyce's proposal for a "rest," Xander excuses himself for a moment to freshen up, marking the beginning of his dream's shift into nightmare territory.

We have noted above that Xander's dream concerns itself with the ways in which he perceives himself as inadequate, and immediately upon leaving Joyce's bedroom, the sexual element of this inadequacy becomes clear. Alone in the bathroom, Xander begins to urinate only to discover that he has been transported to a laboratory, with white coat-clad doctors and members of the Initiative watching his member intently. His discomfort clearly stems from the pressures of having an audience, suggesting that he has concerns regarding the size and functioning of his manhood, the phallus being representative of masculinity in a broader sense.

Fleeing the bathroom/laboratory, Xander searches for another place in which to relieve himself, and finds himself in the basement apartment within his parent's home, a place which is a site of great internal conflict for him as it is a physical reminder of all the ways he is not living up to the expectations placed on him. Dark, dank, and depressing, Xander inadvertently returns to his home multiple times throughout his dream, stressing how he sees his post-high school life as stunted. Just how strongly he feels his inferiority becomes clear later in the dream, when he answers "the basement, mostly," when asked where he is from. Applying Xander's basement dwelling to Freud's notion of the tri-partite soul, which is commonly represented as a house, we can suggest that he is mired in the "cauldron full of seething excitations"

(*Dissection* 91) that comprises his id. In psychoanalysis, the id is the site of all human desires, desires that are in constant conflict, negating any possibility for action. As such, Xander's basement apartment can be seen to represent not only his stunted life but also his inability to escape this stasis. Though he is unable to escape the basement, an unknown entity is constantly trying to enter into his home, and although we never see this entity, it is reasonable to posit that he is being stalked by some reminder of his ideal-I.

Much of what follows in Xander's dream are attempts to escape his prison-like dwelling and that which is coming after him, only to inadvertently return. The changing environments he escapes into are, however, worth a brief discussion, for they serve to illuminate the areas in which he sees himself as inferior. His initial escape brings him into contact with Buffy, Giles, and Spike, all three of whom represent elements of his feelings of inferiority. This scene is important in the larger narrative of Xander's dream, for it is here that he begins to feel alienated from those who have traditionally accepted him, failings and all. Buffy asserts the impossibility of a sexual relationship, calling Xander "big brother"; Giles insults his intelligence by rejecting him in favor of the vampire Spike, who Giles is training as a Watcher. Feeling excluded and replaced, Xander tells himself he has "other stuff going on," and that it is important to "be moving forward," even though his life consists of manning a usually stationary ice cream truck. As a means of denying his stasis, Xander leaves his friends and takes off in the ice cream truck, stressing the idea that although careers are meant to move us forward in life, Xander's job is not moving him forward, but ultimately keeping him in place.

The sexual inferiority felt by Xander is highlighted again when Willow and Tara appear in his dream, inviting him to join them in a ménage-a-trois. Throughout the series narrative, as has been noted, the character of Xander has been constructed as other to the heteronormative male, and so his dream-state agreement to join the girls represents the re-surfacing of his repressed desire to be "normal." Though Willow once pined for Xander, she has moved on, and to a place where Xander cannot follow; this is emphasized in that Xander is unable to reach the couple, though they are only feet away from him. Instead, he crawls back into his basement cell, where he finds that he is still haunted by his ideal-I.

Like Willow's dream before him, Xander's truly enters nightmare territory in its third act. While Willow's nightmare took place in high school, for Xander, the ultimate symbol of his inferiority is the university which he has failed to move on to. Here, he finds himself unable to understand what even his lover Anya says to him; in the dream, she and Giles have been dubbed in French, pointing to Xander's lack of intellectualism and sophistication.

For Xander, the disconnect that has been developing throughout the dream between himself and those closest to him reaches its climax in this moment, and marks his ultimate failure. This failure results in his capture by the Initiative, and he is literally torn away from those he strives to emulate.

The fourth act of Xander's dream finds us again in his basement abode, which has now been breached by the unknown entity that has been stalking him. We find that, far from being a physical manifestation of his ideal-I, the intruder is Xander's father, who is instead the antithesis of what Xander considers to be his ideal. Thus, we can see that rather than being driven by the desire to become something more, Xander is running from that which he desires to be more than. As he is caught in stasis, he is caught between opposite ends of a spectrum, with the purpose, acceptance, and love of the Scooby Gang on one end, and the arguments, disappointment, and perceived failure of his parents on another. The final moments of his dream feature his father literally ripping Xander's heart out. Given that Xander is often cited as the heart of the Scooby Gang (Wilcox 142) this is a violent physical representation of Xander's repressed fear of being torn away from Anya, Willow, Buffy, and Giles by his inability to live up to what he perceives as their expectations for him.

GILES'S DREAM

If Xander is the heart of the Scooby Gang, then Rupert Giles is the brain. As Buffy's Watcher, he is the primary adult influence upon the young characters in *Buffy the Vampire Slayer*. Generally speaking, Giles's dream is a meditation on his inability to live up to any facet of his ideal self. Struggling to be both Watcher and father figure to Buffy, he can succeed at neither, and in the same way, in his devotion to Buffy's training, he is unable to live a "normal" life outside of his work.

In the first scene of Giles's dream, he is holding a pocket watch, which, as a dream symbol, has various meanings. First, the watch obviously symbolizes time: Giles is literally watching time pass him by. He is middle-aged and has yet to become the man he is "supposed" to be, the kind of "grown-up" he imagined he would become. He has not accomplished the rock stardom he pursued in his youth, and he is no longer Buffy's official Watcher. The clock is a barometer of his progress, or more specifically, a reminder of his lack of progress, and thus, his failure. The watch also connotes Giles's post as Buffy's *Watcher*. Cynthia Bowers observes that Giles "seem[s] convinced that the younger generation is out-of-control, in need of Watching, correcting, and policing" (10). As such, we see him, in the opening scene of his dream, attempting to exert his will upon Buffy, directing her into a state where he can more effectively control, correct, and police her. Joss Whedon acknowledges that "Buffy is Giles's little girl, in a sense, particularly because Buffy's biological father is absent" (Commentary). Giles tries to fulfill the role of father figure and Watcher simultaneously, but in trying to accomplish both he fails to achieve success in either role. He is overextending himself, trying to be everything for everyone, and subconsciously he fears that he is disappointing the most important people in his life: Buffy, his girlfriend, the Scooby Gang, and of course, himself.

The dream transitions to Giles and his girlfriend Olivia taking Buffy to a carnival; the rides and games are located in the cemetery, and all of the attractions are vampire-related. Buffy is dressed in overalls and her hair is in pigtails. Buffy, depicted as a child in her ordinary adult surroundings, stresses Giles's conflicted feelings about simultaneously being Buffy's Watcher and her substitute father. Rather than sheltering Buffy from trauma and danger, he thrust her into it, and now feels guilt for his role in robbing Buffy of her adolescence. Buffy's teenage years have been like a carnival of supernatural elements, and Giles was the one who hoisted her onto this merry-go-round of dark forces, an endless cycle of horror. The mingling of purity and decay in this scene illustrates that Buffy's innocence has been sacrificed, and Giles feels that he has been the one to sacrifice it. He cannot spare Buffy pain the way a father "should": he cannot take the weight of the world from her. He can only hope to prepare her to bear that weight. This is again illustrated when Buffy plays a game where she throws objects at vampires. When she successfully knocks the figure over, she excitedly grins at Giles, clearly waiting for him to voice his approval. He impatiently says, "I haven't got any treats." He cannot give her the encouragement she craves: he has to push her to be better because she constantly needs to improve if she is to have any hope for survival: the only "treat" he can give her is keeping her alive. His dual role in Buffy's life ensures that he cannot be fully successful as either a father or a Watcher. As such, he sees himself as a failure in both regards, amounting to his being unable to reach the expectations placed upon him by his ideal-I.

When Olivia tells him to be less harsh with Buffy, Giles explains that "[T]his is my business. Blood of the lamb and all that." As Wilcox notes, the blood of the lamb is an allusion "to the sacrifice of the innocent... Buffy is often a Christ-like figure. Giles's life is absorbed by guiding the saviour of the world" (Wilcox 170). Even if Giles feels that he is an ideal Watcher, he is still failing to become his ideal-I, for he cannot be the ideal Watcher and a responsible father; he cannot guarantee Buffy's safety or success, as it is Buffy who acts. Giles instructs her, and prepares her to the best of his abilities, but he is helpless. He is one of the primary influences on Buffy's super-ego, the internalization of the father figure: his presence, physical and mental, influences her decision making, but it is Buffy who makes the final decision.

Giles follows Spike into a crypt, and Olivia, who has been pushing an empty stroller for the duration of the dream, is crying on top of a casket. Wilcox argues that this is suggestive of unfulfilled elements in Giles life, noting that "a normal marriage with children seems unlikely" (170) for a man with the kind of responsibility Giles carries. Giles can be seen to have displaced his feelings about Buffy onto the empty stroller: Buffy cannot be his little girl, so he tries to fill this void with a phantom. When Giles appears confused and unsure of himself in the crypt, and does not know how to react, Spike reproaches him: "You gotta make up your mind… Haven't you figured it all out yet?" Again, time is of the essence for Giles. Will Giles start a "real" family of his own, and will he act in the capacity of Buffy's father or her Watcher? Can he handle the precarious balance, or will he sabotage Buffy's safety or emotional well-being on account of their mixing? Giles's expansive intellect does not hold the answer to these questions; no matter how much knowledge he acquires through studying, none of the pages in his innumerable tomes contain the answer on how to manipulate his life circumstances in order to come closer his ideal-I.

The final scene in Giles's dream takes place in the Bronze, a club that Buffy and her friends frequent. When Xander and Willow demand explanations from Giles for why they are being stalked by a primordial creature, Giles takes the stage and sings his theories, referencing his history as a musician. Before he can sing a solution to either his own existential crisis or the mysterious figure preying on the Scooby Gang, the sound system shorts out. Attempting to be the problem-solver he believes he should, Giles follows his microphone cord in search of the faulty wire, finding nothing but a mass of tangles. This unsalvageable mess is representative of the way Giles views his life: disorganized, broken, and without a clear path. And yet within the mess, we find something glittering: the pocket watch. Rather than a light in the dark, the watch tells Giles that time has wasted away without his having figured anything out.

In the mass of cords, Giles is finally confronted with the shadow that has haunted Willow and Xander before him. Similar to Xander's loss of heart, Giles is scalped and lobotomized; he loses his brain, that which he considers to be his primary use to Buffy. In the end, then, Giles's inability to make a decision as to whether he should serve as Buffy's Watcher or father leads to his destruction.

BUFFY'S DREAM

Buffy's dream, which is the fourth and final act of "Restless," offers perhaps the most complex exploration of the human desire to live up to imposed standards. Buffy considers herself to be a well-rounded Slayer in that she is still able to be engaged with life, and yet her dream tells another story, one in which she is unable to be a successful daughter or girlfriend while maintaining her position as the one and only Slayer.

The transition from teenager to adult is never an easy one to make, for it is a time when the bond between children and parents is tested. In Buffy's case, this inability to find common ground with her mother was evident even before her departure for college. As a teenage Slayer, Buffy chose to exclude Joyce from the Scooby circle, telling her friends about her role as the Slayer before confiding in her mother. Unlike Buffy's friends, who play very active supporting roles in her Slayer duties, Joyce is rarely even aware of impending apocalypses. Ultimately, Buffy erects walls to keep her family life completely separate from her life as a Slayer. In her dream, this is represented quite literally, as Joyce is living in the walls of Buffy's college. Though Buffy worries aloud the walls are an unsanitary dwelling place, she does not "break through the wall" as her mother suggests, but rather becomes distracted and leaves. As such, Buffy is sentencing Joyce to live on the outskirts of her life, neglecting even an attempt to break the partition that divides them. Though this is, to Buffy's conscious mind, in service of protecting her mother from the dangers that wait around every corner for Buffy, it ultimately serves to sever the only biological parental relationship she knows. Thus, Buffy's dream illuminates the ways in which she is unable to be an ideal (or even appropriate) daughter.

When Buffy first reveals her calling to her Mother, she criticizes Joyce for being in denial, for failing to notice how many times she had to wash blood out of Buffy's clothes. Whereas Giles spills blood at Buffy's side, Joyce bleaches its remnants out of her clothes. The male parent figure, Giles, is infinitely more involved with Buffy's missions than Joyce is: whereas Giles trains, educates, and fights alongside Buffy, Joyce is shown shopping, watching movies, and cooking with her. Buffy's "parents" thus conform to dominant gender roles. Buffy is unable to embody what is societally considered as an ideal daughter to Joyce partly because she is an atypical daughter with unusual circumstances, but also because she does not give Joyce a chance to adapt to her abnormalities.

While Buffy is recognized as "a radical reimagining of what a girl (and a woman) can do and be" (Byars 173), the show reveals the consequences of rejecting gender norms. These consequences are exposed in Buffy's scene with Riley, her boyfriend. Buffy finds Riley in a boardroom wearing a suit. He tells Buffy that his agency is in the midst of drawing up a plan for world domination; when Buffy questions whether that is a positive thing, Riley condescendingly responds, "Baby, we're the government. It's what we do." At that instant, the camera zooms in on a gun placed on the table which is pointed in Buffy's direction. Stevie Simkin observes that "the use of firearms—and especially pistols—can be seen as an important signifier of the wider issue of anxious masculinity" within *Buffy the Vampire Slayer* (2). Riley does not need to give Buffy an elaborate justification for world-domination: the gun communicates his message clearly. He and his male partners are dominating the world because they can.

Judith Butler notes that "one does not 'do' one's gender alone. One is always 'doing' with or for another, even if the other is only imaginary" (*Undoing Gender* 2). Riley is "performing" masculinity for Buffy and using the hyper-phallic symbol of a gun as a prop. Buffy is stronger than Riley, a fact which has been demonstrably difficult for him to come to terms with: he is compensating for his lack of strength by exaggerating his "masculine" power and displaying his gun. When Buffy enters the scene, Riley refers to her as "killer." Butler argues that "we regularly punish those who fail to do their gender right" (*Subversive Bodily Acts* 381), and as such, we can see that Riley is taking on the role of stereotypical male to punish Buffy for failing to perform femininity correctly; she is supposed to be weaker than he is, to require his protection. By referring to Buffy as "killer," Riley detracts from Buffy's honorable position as the Slayer, portraying her as a murderer rather than a hero as a punishment for her refusing to be the ideal woman to his ideal man. When under attack, Buffy does not need Riley and his gun to defend her: she has her own weapons. When her external weapons fail her, she can rely on her physical strength to conquer most opponents by embodying her Slayer persona, which is represented in Buffy's dream by what is akin to war paint. After Buffy's weapons turn into mud, Buffy paints herself with this earthy matter: she is returning to the Slayer's natural state, embracing her animalistic impulses. Now she is prepared for her quest for her deepest self.

Buffy heads to the open, expansive, and totally isolated desert: this contrasts with the polished interior of the government building Riley is working in. Buffy is turning away from civilization and as a result of this, she meets her primal counterpart: the first Slayer. Freud identifies two basic instincts in the mind: eros and the destruction instinct, the death drive (*The Mind and Its Workings* 5). The encounter between Buffy and the first Slayer juxtaposes eros and the destructive drive: in this scene Buffy represents the former, and the first Slayer the latter.

The first Slayer embodies the death drive: "I live in the action of death. The bloodcry. The penetrating wound. I am destruction. Absolute. Alone." Buffy resists this isolation: her supernatural lineage makes her different than other people, but she still manages to form meaningful social relations. She is not just the Slayer: she is Buffy, a person. She has friends, boyfriends, a mother. Joss Whedon explains that "the side of her that is Buffy is as important as the side of her that is the Slayer" (Commentary). The Slayer may have been, like Riley says, a "killer," but Buffy is a new Slayer: the kill is part of her duty, but she has an identity outside of her role as the Slayer. Buffy insists that she is not alone: she has loved ones, and her bonds to people make her more human than the first Slayer. When the first Slayer tells Buffy that the Slayer does not walk in this world, Buffy rejects this definition saying, "I walk. I talk. I shop. I sneeze." Buffy will not accept her destiny as the Slayer as a sentencing to be nothing more than a machine designed to kill. She is Buffy and she is a Slayer, and in this differentiating characteristic, this "abnormality," Buffy is whole. Smashing Lacan's mirror, Buffy ultimately refuses to be limited by an ideal (personal or societal) that no longer holds relevance for her.

The dreams of Willow, Xander, Giles, and Buffy in "Restless" each explore the ways in which none of us is able to live up to the multitude of pressures placed on the self from forces both internal and external. We are none of us perfect friends, lovers, or parents; no one can ever be the perfect man or woman. Like the forces of good and evil, the conscious self and the unconscious "murky shadow self of the dark" (Bacon-Smith) must co-exist, and ultimately need each other to exist. Without an image of ourselves, whether that image comes from within us or without, we would be locked in the stasis of our unconscious desires and fears forever. By allowing viewers a glimpse into the subconscious of *Buffy the Vampire Slayer*'s four main characters, creator Joss Whedon shows his audience that "Buffy's rejection of simple black and white" (Wilcox 52) broadens beyond conceptions of good and evil, extending into considerations of the grey area between self and self-image including that of gender identity.

Works Cited

Bacon-Smith, Camille. "The Colour of the Dark in *Buffy the Vampire Slayer*." Foreword. *Fighting the Forces: What's at Stake in* Buffy the Vampire Slayer. Ed. Rhonda Wilcox and David Lavery. Lanham, MD: Rowman, 2003. xi-xiii. Print.

Bowers, Cynthia. "Generation Lapse: The Problematic Parenting of Joyce Summers & Rupert Giles." *Slayage: The Online International Journal of Buffy Studies* 1.2 (2001). Web.

Buffy the Vampire Slayer: *The Complete Fourth Season*. Twentieth Century Fox Home

Entertainment, 2003. DVD.

Butler, Judith. "Subversive Bodily Acts." *ACS 500 Course Reader*. Comp. Andrew Hunter. U of Toronto: ACCESS, 2008. 371-82. Print.

Byars, Michele. "*Buffy the Vampire Slayer*: The Insurgence of Television as a Performance Text." Diss. U of Toronto, 2000. Print.

Eagleton, Terry. *Literary Theory: An Introduction*. Minneapolis: U of Minnesota P, 1983. Print.

Freud, Sigmund. "The Interpretation of Dreams." *ENG 931 Course Selection*. Comp. Stephen Voyce, 919-29. Print.

---. "Lecture XXXI: The Dissection of the Psychical Personality." *New Introductory Lectures on Psychoanalysis*. New York: Norton, 1933. 71-99. Print.

---. "The Mind and Its Workings." *ENG 931 Course Selection*. Comp. Stephen Voyce. 1-9. Print.

---. *The Unconscious*. Trans. Graham Frankland. New York: Penguin, 2005. Print.

Homer, Sean. *Jacques Lacan*. New York: Routledge, 2005. Print.

Jowett, Lorna. *Sex and the Slayer: A Gender Studies Primer for the* Buffy *Fan*. Middletown, CT: Wesleyan U P, 2005. Print.

Keller, Donald. "Spirit Guides and Shadow Selves: From the Dream Life of Buffy (and Faith)." *Fighting the Forces: What's at Stake in* Buffy the Vampire Slayer. Ed. Rhonda V. Wilcox and David Lavery. 165-77. Print.

Lacan, Jacques. "The Mirror Stage as Formative of the Function of the Eye as Revealed in Psychoanalytic Experience." *Ecrits, A Selection*. Trans. Alan Sheridan. New York: Norton, 1977. 1-7. Print.

Patemen, Matthew. *The Aesthetics of Culture in Buffy the Vampire Slayer*. Jefferson, NC: McFarland, 2006. Print.

The Pillow Book. Writ. Phillip Greenaway and Sei Shonagon. Based on the novel by Sei Shonagon. Dir. Phillip Greenaway. Alpha Films, 1996. Film.

"Restless." 4.22. Writ. and dir. Joss Whedon. *Buffy*.

Simkin, Stevie. "'You Hold Your Gun Like a Sissy Girl': Firearms and Anxious Masculinity in *Buffy the Vampire Slayer*." *Slayage: The Online International Journal of Buffy Studies* 3.3-4 (2004). Web.

Whedon, Joss. Commentary on "Restless." *Buffy*.

Wilcox, Rhonda. *Why Buffy Matters: The Art of* Buffy the Vampire Slayer. New York: Palgrave Macmillan, 2005. Print.

Winterson, Jeanette. *Written on the Body*. New York: Knopf Doubleday, 1994. Print. Vintage International Series.

1.13
"I'd Very Still":
Anthropology of a Lapsed Fan
Lily Rothman

Some things never die. For anyone who loves *Buffy the Vampire Slayer*, first on that list might be vampires. For true-blue fans of any stripe, it may be the love of a fictional person, place or thing. And even for the rest of the population, the category includes "things you said on the Internet."

Case in point: On November 7, 1999, I joined an e-mail list. It was a place for rabid fans of Oz, the werewolf played by Seth Green, to commiserate during his absence from *Buffy*. That list wasn't my first online *Buffy* hub, but it was the one to which I was most devoted and it remains first in my memory. Anyone who watched the show knows that Oz's absence became permanent—as did the mailing list; as did the community it formed; as did the virtual record of my adolescent identity: "I'm new and stuff, so here's me introducing myself. I'm Lily."

Other things do change. If not death, there's shrinking or aging or moving on. *Buffy the Vampire Slayer* went off the air in 2003. Not long after, I stopped checking the e-mail account that went with that mailing list. I now go days and often weeks without a thought of slayage, although a scone, official pastry of Gileses everywhere, can be to me as Proust's madeleine. And when that occurs, I wonder what happened to my fan family, and why I left them. Even more, I wonder how any fan community can survive for so long without the original object of its devotion.

Buffy fans are still out there, indisputably. Controversial plans for a non-Whedon *Buffy* movie were recently announced, and the 40th and last issue of the Season Eight series of the eponymous comic—which began production near the start of the show's third season—came out in January. I haven't bought one since 2007, but industry data consistently ranks *Buffy* among the best-selling independent comics out there; Season Nine is in the works. It was something about hearing that news that got me combing through the archives of that old mailing list. Among the flotsam of fandom, there were gripping reminders of what life had been like when the show was still on, the way we cared so much about actors and episodes and one another, and of what could have been if I hadn't let it go. Suddenly, I was 14 again, up too late on a school night, glued to the mid-'90s-model Power Macintosh in my family's living room, unable to make myself log off.

I had missed that.

So, in the interest of investigation, I let the nostalgia take over for a while.

"You need a thing, one thing nobody else has. What do I have?"

"An exciting new obsession. Which I feel makes you very special."
—Xander and Oz, "The Zeppo" (3.13)

While I confess that I stopped buying *Buffy* comics, I may as well come clean that I didn't start watching right from the first episode.

It was January 19, 1998. Halfway through its second season, the show moved from Mondays to Tuesdays; the romantic Buffy/Angel developments advertised in the commercials for the episodes that covered the switch, "Surprise" and "Innocence," were enough to get my friends who watched to tell me it would be worth checking out.

The battles! The baddies! The banter! I was hooked. I watched the next night and every week after for five years. Almost right away, I began compiling the collection of VHS recordings that still sit, meticulously labeled, in a box somewhere in my parents' basement. Before long, I was waking unsure whether my memories of what had happened on last week's episode were canon or my dreams. I even let myself be the anecdotal lead in a *New York Times* article about teenage television habits—a mention I've long tried in vain to get to sink in my personal Google hits.

And it turned out that "Surprise" was a serendipitous place to start. There, in the first few minutes of the episode, was Oz. He was sitting on the bleachers, strumming a guitar, and sweetly asking Buffy's friend Willow on a date. He had me at "Hey." More importantly, not starting at the beginning meant I had to catch up. I probably would have eventually done some sort of *Buffy*-related HotBotting anyway, but needing rerun schedules got me there faster. I had no idea what I would find, no concept of the world I could access via my AOL account, no clue that I wouldn't need reruns because other fans would gladly splice together a few of their own bootleg tapes and mail them to me.

Louisa Stein, a professor of film and media culture at Middlebury College who is an expert in fandom, says my experience is now common. She told me that the Internet has meant that being a fan has become "much more visible, and much less of a cult identity and more of a mode of mainstream engagement with media." In some ways, the Internet is just a quick and dirty shortcut—the comedian Patton Oswalt wrote a piece in the December 2010 issue of *Wired* magazine lamenting the ease with which anyone can quickly acquire fan-level knowledge of obscure bits of pop culture, claiming that the Internet has effectively destroyed geekdom—but, for better or worse, what Stein calls the "immense infrastructure of fandom" is readily accessible online. And it was, for me, a revelation. It wasn't long before I too was proficient with a pair of VCRs and a set of A/V cables.

By the end of the season, I more than knew my way around the online *Buffy* landscape, particularly the smaller Oz-centric community. I had overcome the nerves and embarrassment, the feeling that lurking on forums and mailing lists was somehow more respectable than getting involved, and I was talking about more than schedules and tapes. Which pop song of 1998 most applied to Willow's plot arc in the episode "Amends" (3.10)? We may never have an answer, but I'm sure I used all my high school debate team skills to fight for Edwin McCain's "I'll Be." The more I talked to those people—friends whose real names I didn't need to know, as long as they were willing to comb through the finer details of *Buffy* plots and characters—the more I wanted to watch carefully enough to contribute to the conversation. The more carefully I watched, the more I wanted to discuss it, and the time-consuming and passion-provoking spiral of fandom had begun.

"Well, we don't have cable, so we have to make our own fun." —Willow, *"Innocence" (2.14)*

From a very young age, if I had known to look, I could have found evidence that I was destined to be a fan. I was able to remember exact lines from my favorite movies on the first go-round, I had always felt strongly about reading long series of books consecutively and in order, and, at a Scholastic book fair, probably sometime in 1995, I purchased a *Saved by the Bell* novel. But, even though that book, the epic *Kelly's Hero*, should have been a clue that there were others out there, I was a fan of *Saved by the Bell* casually, happily, and alone.

Professor Stein acknowledges that personal engagement can be the defining aspect of some fans' relationship with their subject of choice—but, while she says that the definition of fandom is a debate among academics in the field, it's hard to be a fan by oneself. "It's very much about community authorship and shared values among these communities," she explains.

And those communities are a good thing. I learned the hard way that wanting to discuss the relationships of fictional characters with your friends who don't care is a good way to get the subject changed. Or, worse, to become that girl who always talks about *Buffy*.

(Years later, long after I had learned to bite my tongue, I stumbled across Nick Hornby's introduction to *Fever Pitch*, his memoir of soccer-fandom. In it, he describes being asked the age-old lovers' question of what he's thinking about, and the lies he provides in response. "If we told the truth every time," he writes, "then we would be unable to maintain relationships with anyone from the real world." This passage spoke to my heart.)

Whenever someone was unusually quiet on the mailing list, the inevitable reason was given as "real life," but the lines often blurred. The folks online were my release valve, a way to avoid talking about the Hellmouth the rest of the time. And as often happens when you tell people the truth, they become your friends.

"Buffy told me that sometimes what a girl makes has to be the first move." —Willow, "Phases" (2.15)

When Oz left for good in Season 4, our friendships peaked. We turned to each other in consolation and cautious hope, each of us crying in front of our consoles after the credits rolled. We held on through the end of the show, and then another year, and another. But at some point, it stopped. The core group made an effort to stay in touch, but lag time between messages grew. That was that.

Yet I didn't forget their personalities or their usernames. When I decided to find out what had happened to those friends, some of the e-mail addresses were readily accessible in my mind; others, especially some *grand dames* of that world with whom I had not had personal friendships, required combing through the Angelfire fossils of our fandom. I put together a brief paragraph introducing myself with both my old AOL handle and, in one sentence that revealed more about my non-fan life than I had told most of them in the course of years of regular conversation, my real identity. I asked them to get back to me. I waited.

The bounce-backs were immediate. I had barely hit send on my missive to that old crew, and already I was being told my friends no longer existed.

But not Karen. It had been Karen who had started that mailing list in 1999, bringing us all together after Oz left the show, transforming the erstwhile devotees of the werewolf into a new community. We were OzMIAns, after the "Oz: Missing In Action" website she had started. I had known more about her than about many of the other fans, and we had instant-messaged and e-mailed about non-*Buffy* topics. I didn't know if she still checked her old AOL e-mail address, and the possibility that I wouldn't be able to get in touch with her anymore made me sadder than I had thought it would.

My patience paid off: she did check that inbox, and she read my note. She wrote back, and she wanted to talk. A few days later, for the first time in the ten years I have known her, I called Karen on the phone.

I never really thought she was a robot or an old man, but you never know online.

"I bet you have a lot of groupies."—Willow, *"Surprise" (2.13)*

I never really thought she was a robot or an old man, but you never know online. I can now confirm that Karen Kalbacher, of Philadelphia, is a 33-year-old human woman.

This makes her, like me, more or less a prototypical fan of our species. In his 1992 book *Textual Poachers*, one of the seminal works of fan academia, media expert Henry Jenkins identifies the characteristics of those who inhabit the world of "media fandom," the category that encompasses television shows and movies: we are, according to him, "largely female, largely white, [and] largely middle class."

Which is not to say that there's a fan gene. "I don't know that I'd say that there's something essential in people that means they'll become a hardcore fan," Middlebury's Professor Stein explains. "Rather, there are people who discover the pleasures of fandom and then want more of it." And, she adds, because the Internet has normalized many fan behaviors, fan characteristics have also changed. Now media fans are, largely, anyone with a television and a computer.

But, while tweeting something about your favorite show may count as fan-type interaction, there's a missing part to that equation. A television habit and an Internet connection do not a Karen make. Karen told me that, at the height of her devotion to *Buffy* and Oz, she was spending about 20 hours a week on the topic. Those hours were mostly production, not consumption. She wasn't just watching and discussing, she was designing a website and writing fan-fiction and forming a community. Karen was good at being a fan.

A few days after speaking with her, I began to get responses from other OzMIAns. I found that all were long-time media junkies, all with the magic capacity for obsession. Jaime Vaughn, 29, of Cincinnati, summed it up nicely: "I fall in love with different [shows] very easily."

Those conversations confirmed that we were all good at whatever it takes to be a fan. They also reminded me of the fan's joy of shared passion, the recognition of a little of yourself in someone else. We shared a love of television and capacity for imagination, and we were serial monogamists, whether we fell in with *Buffy* after seeing Sarah Michelle Gellar on *All My Children* or turned to *Dollhouse* later because we knew and loved Whedon. I know there are people out there who watch the same television shows every week but leave those worlds behind when the TV goes off. For them, in the 167 hours between the end of an episode and next week's beginning, the storyline is frozen. I have often wondered what that's like. For us, head over heels, the story never stops.

"My whole life, I've never loved anything else." —Oz, *"Wild at Heart"* (4.6)

And there was something special about Sunnydale, at least for us. Despite a diverse slate of previous and subsequent obsessions, *Buffy* was the one that stuck. When I asked the women with whom I used to discuss the show, that sentiment was nearly unanimous. (There's one who prefers *Doctor Who*.) It's a self-selecting group, but a testament to the power of the Chosen One—and Whedon.

"I'm very much a square peg, so television was the best way to be out of that," said Karen. "Nothing hit me as as much fun as *Buffy*."

"There's no question," said Danielle DeLucia, a 36-year-old former OzMIAn who lives in Massachusetts. "A couple other shows I really enjoyed, and if I can catch reruns I still watch… but *Buffy* was my favorite."

"*Buffy the Vampire Slayer* definitely and absolutely has a special place in my heart, you know?" said Jaime, the television inamorata. "Even this long after it ended."

I do know, clearly. There was something there, instantly visible to those with the potential for fandom, something that made that first night in 1998 imprint itself on my memory the way big life moments have the tendency to do. I remember so well my classroom and the face of my friend when we discussed it the next day. I remember the couch my parents used to have. I remember the light in the room.

There's some method to our madness. Stein believes that media that attract big fan bases share a few key elements, and *Buffy* has them in spades: "One thing is an expansive universe or an expansive storyworld, the characters that inhabit it, and multiple entry-points and ways that people can invest… which *Buffy* absolutely has. You've got these archetypal characters and then you've got the expansive storyworld of the high school coming together with larger mythology."

Matt Hills, media scholar and author of *Fan Cultures*, adds that "extended narrative worlds that fans can imagine inhabiting" and "a structuring mystery or story-arc 'mythos'" can grab followers, as can links to established favorites (like Joss Whedon). But even they are never a guarantee. Much as I asked, he is adamant that there's never one reason a show succeeds with fans.

Maybe it's enough to know it when you see it. "The thing about *Buffy* for me," concluded Danielle, "was that it was the right place, the right time, the right show."

"I miss you. Like, every second. Almost like I lost an arm, or worse, a torso." —Oz, *"Amends"* (3.10)

I asked Karen whether she misses *Buffy*. She paused. "I miss what they had in the beginning," she said, referring to the time before Oz left the show. "I made some really great friends during that era, and I miss being in contact with them all the time." She's friends with some of them on Facebook, having graduated from Yahoo! Groups. It's strange to hear their names said out loud after all this time. ("I don't think you realize this," she told me, "but you live in a kind of Oz-centric area; a lot of our list members are probably in your neighborhood.")

Just as the community was responsible for the depth of Karen's devotion to the show, she cites other fans as the main source of her frustration with the second half of the show's run. It's bad enough when a favorite character leaves a show, but Karen remembers that many of her friendships in the non-Oz fan world quickly soured as well. For mourning his loss, something that went hand-in-hand with Willow's decision to date Tara, a character much loved in the rest of the fandom, she was called a homophobe. Samantha Warner, who is a friend of Karen's from well before *Buffy* hit the screen, said that her own experiences on that front had been enough to turn her off the show forever. (She's the *Doctor Who* devotee.)

Even within the Oz fandom, the community was to blame for our own falling apart. Karen described how OzMIA faded away within two years of the show going off the air. She tried to keep it going, but responses dwindled. I was among the guilty parties. She hasn't worked on the website for more than a year. Yes, it was sad. It felt inevitable. "People just stopped answering," she told me. "We ran out of things to talk about."

"I feel like some part of me will always be waiting for you." —Willow, "New Moon Rising" (4.19)

But I was right: moving on was normal. "People who want to maintain a sort of fan identity usually shift from one primary fandom to another when the source text is no longer new," Professor Stein confirms. "There are various ways to keep it feeling present, but at the same time they're also likely participating in other fandoms of shows that are on the air."

I did that, lurking on some *Alias* sites and falling for the wrong fictional guy with Charlie on *Lost*, but I also gave up some of my fan identity, and I'm okay with that. Being a real fan never interfered with my life, but it was incredibly time-consuming.

I wasn't the only one. "I had a lot more time on my hands then," said Karen. "I would be surprised if it happened again."

"My life changed after that," agreed Danielle.

Then again, both said they keep coming back to *Buffy*. Reruns, DVDs, daydreams—there's always the chance. It seems impossible to ever have enough time to be as active in any fandom as I once was in the Buffyverse, but maybe the real truth is just that nothing has ever been as good.

And, after all, the whole quest started because of a comic. I may have been an interloper when I revisited my local New York comic shop, Forbidden Planet, to see the latest issue in person, but the place is proof that at least some of us never abandoned or outgrew or forgot. Dani Lorrick, a *Buffy* fan and an employee at the store, told me that most of the people who buy the comic now were fans of the show—it's hard to catch up on all that back-story without watching—but those buyers, herself included, are more devoted to that part of the fandom now than ever before. "I pay more attention to comic books now than when it was on," she said. Now that the comics are the canon, with the ability to really change the story's universe, they mean more and they're better. It doesn't hurt that Whedon himself is directly involved in writing them.

David Glanzer, marketing director for Comic-Con, confirms that, even without studio presence to support the show, *Buffy* is alive and well at the annual fan convention. "Any Comic-Con attendee can tell you that when they find something they really love, it can live forever," he says. He hopes that the folks who come for *Buffy* but who don't buy any other titles will discover that they love the medium as well, and then come back for more than the Slayer. Not that she's going anywhere: a *Buffy* sing-along has been a closing event at the convention for the last few years.

A few weeks ago, I was cleaning out a cassette tape graveyard in my childhood bedroom. Between the Everclear and Elvis, I found a mix of my favorite lines from *Buffy*. I rustled up a working tape player and heard the distorted sound of a handheld recorder up against the TV speakers, the tinny echo of my obsession. I had forgotten about that part, some day—or night, more likely—when I had decided that I needed their voices Walkman-ready.

But I hadn't really forgotten, because it all came back. And I knew that, even if I didn't have a clue what was going on in the Season Eight comics and I had walked away from the online community that nourished and sustained my fan-ness, I was no less a fan than ever, as long as I was ready to remember. It was right there on that old cassette too, in a quote from "Earshot." Oz was talking about the girl, but it's no less true of the fandom: "Buffy is all of us. We think, therefore she is."

"I'd still if you'd still."
"I'd still. I'd very still." —Willow and Oz, "Phases" (2.15)

In media fan lingo, the idea of an OTP—the One True Pairing, a fan's absolute favorite fictional couple—can be tossed around rather casually. In terms of my history as a relationshipper, Willow and Oz will always be mine, but the real OTP in my fan identity is *Buffy* and me.

In an e-mail, Jaime mentioned a similar thought. "I've definitely mellowed out about aspects of the show," she wrote. "[But] I feel like that show will always be there, just because it was my first real fandom."

You may recognize the follies of your past self as just that, you may grow up and move away, you may lose touch—but you never forget your first love, your OTP, even after it's gone.

Or not so gone. I think I may go buy some comics.

1.14
Interview with Jane Espenson

Dr. Shathley Q

What Whedonite does not revere the work of Jane Espenson? After all, she wrote or co-wrote two dozen *Buffy* episodes—episodes like "Band Candy," "Earshot," "Superstar," "Intervention," "After Life," "Storyteller," "Conversations with Dead People," and "End of Days" —as well as *Angel*'s "Rm w/a Vu" and "Guise Will Be Guise" and *Firefly*'s "Shindig." On *Buffy* and *Dollhouse* she also served as a producer of many episodes. She wrote short stories for *Tales of the Slayer*, created the stories for one comic in *Buffy Season Eight* and a *Riley* one-shot, and edited companion books *Inside Joss' Dollhouse*, *Finding Serenity*, and *Serenity Found*. Outside the Whedonverse she has written/produced for a variety of shows: *Once Upon a Time, Husbands, Gilmore Girls, Game of Thrones, Battlestar Galactica, Caprica, Torchwood: Miracle Day, Warehouse 13, Tru Calling*, ad almost infinitum.

Our deepest appreciation goes to Jane Espenson for kindly taking time from her Fall 2011 schedule for a two-session interview by Shathley Q for *Joss Whedon: The Complete Companion*. The Whedonverse just would not be complete without her.

PopMatters: Jane, you're an incredibly accomplished screenwriter and television producer. Your work has simply captivated an entire generation of viewers. But before TV you found yourself in the entirely different environment. Just to kick off, I'd like to talk about your knowing George Lakoff, a preeminent researcher in the field of cognitive psychology and the use of metaphor. You were his teaching assistant, is that correct? Did you see yourself entering academia at that point?

Jane Espenson: George was my advisor in grad school, yes! He's a wonderful man. The doctoral project which I never finished was about metaphorical understandings of the concept of causation, and George guided all of that thought and research.

PM: At that point, how were you thinking about moving ahead in academia? Was it a question of moving ahead as a researcher? Were you interested working on your PhD first? And what was some of the allure of the field you were involved in? What were some of the core ideas and how did they transition back into the more creative aspects must already have been budding at the time. Actually maybe I'm jumping the gun, were those creative impulses already very strong at that point? And, not to push you to be too reductionist (I know Lakoff's work is rich), is there any way to give a concise example of the kind of work you were doing?

JE: The idea of the work was to examine how ordinary language reveals this whole structural underpinning of how we think about the world. In general, when concepts get too abstract, we have to come up with ways to translate them into more concrete physical stuff. So we understand the concept of CHANGING as MOVING, for example—so you "go from" one thing "to" another. Anyway I loved figuring out what that underpinning was, peeling back the complexity to reveal the way we really grapple with the world.

PM: Already, you being drawn to and engaged by the complexity is revealing of the kind of entertainment you later write and produce. But was it all smooth sailing? Did you find academic life was something that came easily to you? Or was it more the case that there was something of a struggle between your rationalist self and your creative self?

JE: But I didn't really care as much about the other stuff—about what this said about theories of cognition and how to write it all up for academic papers. I just wanted to solve the puzzles. So I felt a little trapped, but just by my own limitations—I knew I had to write a doctoral dissertation, but it just wasn't happening.

PM: Was this the key to get you moving towards screenwriting? The segue into the more creative phase of your professional path?

JE: And I knew that I'd always wanted to write for TV, so toward the end of my grad school career, I was applying myself a lot more to studying *Star Trek: The Next Generation* than I was to those metaphorical understandings of causation. George was very understanding when I left school, and it took years in Los Angeles before I finally threw away a number of large boxes with "dissertation work" written on them.

PM: What was your big break into the industry? You mention *Star Trek: The Next Generation* (*Star Trek: TNG*), and I know from your Wikipedia page that you sent off a script for an episode. How did this work? Was the show accepting scripts cold? And, were you thinking of yourself professionally as a writer at this time? Or was this more a labor of love? An advanced fan-fiction of sorts you hoped to leverage into a more permanent position?

JE: My college boyfriend had a friend whose girlfriend's father used to get the magazine put out by the WGA (Writers' Guild of America). And in the magazine it used to list all the shows in production and whether or not they accepted outside submissions. It was a very strange list because only *Star Trek: TNG* actually accepted outside submissions, and that had been true for a really long time. Anyway, I found out that you could submit scripts there and started writing like a madwoman.

PM: That's pretty amazing. It worked out well for you, but also, in a weird sense, it's your fans (and I'm speaking as one of them) that really benefited from *Star Trek: TNG's* policy. What happened next? After you wrote the scripts and then submitted them, did they all hit home? And was this the start of your professional career?

JE: I sent in three scripts and one of them struck the target. I was invited into their offices to pitch stories for the show. I was thrilled beyond belief. Every morning after that I would wake up afraid it had been a dream and then realize it was real. That was the start of my writing career and it's been a joy to me.

PM: And from there how'd your professional path go? I mean strictly in terms of genre. You started off with the science fiction of *Star Trek: TNG*, but what happened immediately after? And what happened after that? I know you've just wrapped on the phenomenal *Game of Thrones*, and that your new show, *Husbands* is debuting this season.

JE: So I started in sci-fi and then moved into comedy and then back to sci-fi and then into non-genre drama and then back to sci-fi.

PM: How do you respond to cynics who argue that genre-fiction occupies too much of the pop-culture mainstream? Who argue for more generalized drama, but don't acknowledge that level of drama when they see it in genre fiction like sci-fi or detective fiction? Do you think there's a double standard at play here? Or do you think writers of genre fiction can draw in antagonistic viewers with high quality material?

JE: There's maybe a tiny sense that sci-fi is "lesser than" because it doesn't win Emmys, but I don't know a writer who doesn't admire the work Ron Moore did on *Battlestar Galactica*. And shows like *Buffy the Vampire Slayer* and *Torchwood* and *Game of Thrones* get a lot of respect.

At this point the first session of our interview drew to a close. Some important motivations had already come to light, like Jane's attraction to the puzzle-making behind Professor Lakoff's work with metaphor and meaning. And also her determination and sheer grit to enter the entertainment industry as a writer, and her skill at harnessing known resources like a magazine editor with ties to the Writers' Guild of America. Writing for Star Trek: The Next Generation, *might scan as something of a fluke on the surface of it, but Jane's resilience in finding a science fiction show that accepted outside submissions speaks to a deeper truth. At a crucial moment in her evolution as a screenwriter, Jane made a decision about learning to write within the structure of genre fiction. She acknowledges the perceived limitations of genre fiction, particularly of science fiction. But at the same time she engages this dawning cynicism and demolishes it. Shows like* Buffy the Vampire Slayer *and* Game of Thrones *expand the accepted scope of science fiction shows. They become engaging dramas in their own right. Ahead, during our second and final session, I wanted to ask Jane about she came so flawlessly to "conceive of science fiction outside of science fiction". Did she have any other loves, other than science fiction? And of course, the on the focus of this interview, her time on* Buffy the Vampire Slayer *and her time working with Joss Whedon.*

PM: Picking up, we've discussed how you entered the industry, and the insights you brought with you from working under Professor Lakoff. Your move into science fiction early on in your career reads like a deliberate choice, but you've also focused on broadening the range and the depth of your average science fiction show. Do you have a particular passion for writing other kinds of material? And if so, what's your response to these impulses? Do you partition them? Do you actively seek them out?

JE: I love writing comedy, but I wasn't happy on most of the comedy shows I was on because I didn't feel I was contributing enough to the process—I just wasn't great at functioning in the rollicking room culture of half-hour comedy. I made a conscious choice to transition to hour-long and have been happier in the less room-intensive culture of the hour drama.

PM: Will you ever go back to comedy? Do you think there's a way of writing comedy without relying on the structure of needing to work in a room-intensive culture?

JE: I love variety, though—I've written for all kinds of shows and have even gone back to comedy now and then. I don't like to feel boxed into any particular kind of writing.

PM: So with this kind of intuitive pull towards multi-layered dramas and multifold storytelling, and a pull towards variety, what was your general experience of *Buffy the Vampire Slayer*? I know the conventional wisdom is "if you like the sausage never watch it being made," but I suspect (based on what you've been saying thus far) that your creative process would have mirrored the product you produced at the end of the process.

JE: *Buffy* was the perfect job because it had so many kinds of writing all folded in together.

PM: And what was the structure of the creative process itself? Did it mirror the process you encountered on other shows? What was show-runner Joss Whedon's role? Was he there in a supervisory capacity to oversee the work being done? Or did he have a more hands on approach?

JE: *Buffy* was a very top-down kind of show. It really was Joss's show. Almost every story came from him, and absolutely every theme did.

PM: And did you ever wrestle with putting in any themes of your own? Or did you focus more on the art of scripting out specific scenes and weaving themes into these scenes?

JE: If anyone was wrestling with having something to say, it was him. I was there to help him say it because there wasn't time for him to write every episode himself.

PM: Beside developing your skill-set as a writer, was there any emotional yield? Writing on *Buffy*, I mean.

JE: My work at *Buffy* gave me confidence in writing scenes with depth, scenes that had value other than being funny, confidence that I could take a very thin description of a story and turn it into producible pages quickly.

PM: What was it like working closely with Joss Whedon himself? Were there any particularly inspirational moments? And what was his creative process, how did it work? Did your and his creative processes synch up, or was there a shifting focus?

JE: Watching Joss work was also fascinating, but it could be hard to learn from because his process is so internal. It's like standing on the other side of the street watching a factory produce sports cars—they come driving out the doors at regular intervals, but that doesn't mean that you end up knowing how to make one.

PM: That's a beautiful image, standing outside a factory and watching the sports cars roll out the door. What happened after *Buffy the Vampire Slayer*? How did you enter the world after that experience?

JE: After *Buffy*, I went to lots of other shows and brought with me the main lesson of *Buffy*, which was "why are we telling this story"—Joss always insisted on stories that have a deep reason to be told, and that had a strong effect on the central character. That was a great gift that I have taken with me everywhere. I've also taken with me the great reputation that *Buffy* writers get—Joss's writing is so admired by other writers that his reputation got huge. So huge that we all got to pick up the pieces that fell off at the edges and take them with us!

1.15
How *Buffy* Changed Television

Robert Moore

When *Buffy the Vampire Slayer* debuted on the WB in March 1997 there was little suspicion that it might become not merely one of the most critically acclaimed series on television but would go on to exert considerable influence on television in general. When *TV Guide* senior critic Matt Roush was asked in an interview with NPR if he had ever been surprised by a show, his instantaneous reply was, "*Buffy the Vampire Slayer.*" Having started to watch the pilot out of sheer professional duty, he was instantly pulled in by the show's wit and intelligence. Roush's response is indicative of how little anticipation there was for *Buffy* in March 1997. People who knew of it at all knew it as a television series based on a rather unsuccessful 1992 film of the same name, which was little enough recommendation.

Despite the initial lack of anticipation, *Buffy* would go on to become one of the most critically acclaimed series on television, eventually gathering the support of high profile TV critics such as David Bianculli and Ken Tucker, in addition to Roush. It has clearly become one of television's canonical shows and almost certainly is the most widely studied series in TV Studies, spawning a veritable industry of serious essays, books, and academic conferences. Even so, the full impact that *Buffy* has had on subsequent television series is sometimes not fully appreciated. Sometimes the influence is explicit, sometimes less so. The show either initiated certain changes on TV or anticipated trends that were only beginning to overtake the industry as a whole. Certainly television is a different medium today than it was in the mid-nineties, and *Buffy* has played no small role in bringing that about. The aforementioned Matt Roush, in a response to a question asked in his column concerning *Buffy*'s influence ten years after its debut, acknowledged that it was a deeply influential show, but quickly added that *The Sopranos* was at least as influential, explaining that it paved the way for the gritty adult dramas that proliferated in the decade to come, such as *The Wire* (2002-2008), *The Shield* (2002-2008), *Deadwood* (2004-2006), *Dexter* (2006-), *Justified* (2010-), and *Boardwalk Empire* (2010-). There is, however, a distinction to be made between the kind of influence that *The Sopranos* has exerted and the kind that *Buffy the Vampire Slayer* has. While the influence of *The Sopranos* has indeed been very substantial—certainly the most influential series since *Buffy*—almost all of its influence has been in terms of *content*; it has, I would argue, exerted little or no *formal* influence. On the other hand, *Buffy* has had substantial impact on both *form* and *content*.

BUFFY AND THE RISE OF FEMALE HEROES ON TELEVISION

Of all the ways that *Buffy* has influenced television, the most important is unquestionably making the female hero an indelible part of television. Previous decades had seen female heroes in movies—though not nearly as many as one might think—and a significant number in comic books, but on television, at least, they remained disturbingly rare. One might take umbrage at my use of *female hero* instead of *heroine,* but the distinction is crucial. *Heroine* is a misnomer; too often *heroines* are in fact in need of *heroes*, and reflect the passive role that women were usually expected in action roles. "Heroine" has come to refer to a show's leading female character rather than to a brave and self-confident female. In order to grasp how profoundly Buffy altered the role of women on television, it is important to recount in some detail the history of female heroes on TV prior to 1997.

One assumes that there would be several heroic females in each decade, but a survey of the history of TV discloses far fewer than one would have anticipated. In the 1950s, for instance, there is Annie Oakley, portrayed by Gail Davis, who was not only beautiful but also a trick rider and trick shooter in rodeos. To the present day no lead actress on television has ever performed stunts with as high a level of difficulty as Davis did on *Annie Oakley* (1954-1956). She regularly performed such feats as riding a galloping horse while standing straight up on the saddle or leaping off a horse onto a speeding stagecoach or runaway wagon. But her Annie Oakley was, sadly, an exception rather than the rule during the decade.

In the 1960s a string of female secret agents partnered with John Steed (Patrick Macnee) on *The Avengers* (1961-1969), but far and away the most famous (so much so that many are not aware that Steed had other partners) was Mrs. Emma Peel (Diana Rigg), who was not merely beautiful in a cat suit but also was the first recurring character on television to demonstrate a knowledge of karate (though her martial arts skills leave something to be desired). Mrs. Peel was the iconic female hero of the 1960s, and arguably the most compelling female action hero prior to the 1990s, sadly apart from her predecessors and successors on *The Avengers*. There were few other equally powerful female characters in the decade.

Perhaps most emblematic of 1960s is that the two most powerful female characters of the decade were not only not allowed to be heroic, but were shown to be spectacularly submissive to the men to whom they were yoked (revealing something, perhaps, about male fears and anxieties in the face of increased opportunities for women in the real world). They were Jeannie (Barbara Eden) in *I Dream of Jeannie* (1965-1970) and Samantha (Elizabeth Montgomery) in *Bewitched* (1964-1972). While Jeannie was literally a genie (though not one who betrayed the Middle Eastern origin of the *djinn*) capable of doing virtually anything merely by thinking it—making her theoretically the most powerful character, male or female, in the history of TV—she completely and willingly subordinated her will to serving the whims of her master, Maj. Nelson (Larry Hagman), who was, of course, male. Samantha Stevens was very nearly as powerful as Jeannie, but after revealing on her wedding night to her husband Darren that she was a witch (considerable subtext there) and seeing his anger at being the less powerful of the two, she agrees not to practice witchcraft in the future, apparently so Darren's tender ego won't be bruised. The comic crux of the series is that situations inevitably arise in which she must—in every episode—engage in witchcraft and conceal her actions from Darren. Clearly, television wasn't yet ready for female heroes.

While the 1970s may look superficially better, deeper examination reveals an even bleaker situation. *Wonder Woman* (1975-1979) features one of the comics world's iconic superheroes, but in the Lynda Carter version she is more obsessed with making her love interest Steve Trevor look good than in taking credit for any heroics. When she does something extraordinary, that perhaps makes Trevor look less manly, she seems almost apologetic for it. Angie Dickinson's Pepper Anderson on *Police Woman* (1974-1978) got to wield a gun and subdue bad guys, but all too often her duty required her to dress up as a hooker or stripper; the point of the show seemed to be to create as many opportunities as possible for Angie Dickinson to show off her legs rather than to engage in heroics. *The Bionic Woman* (1976-1978), a spin-off of *The Six Million Dollar Man* (1974-1978), was hampered by the primitive state of special effects at the time, bland stunt work, and exceptionally weak writing. The various women on *Charlie's Angels* (1976-1981) were so clearly eye candy that they never could be taken seriously as action stars.

One exception to the rather lame run of weak collection of female heroes in the 1970s came in the character of Sarah Jane Smith (Elizabeth Sladen) on *Doctor Who*. From 1973 to 1976 Sarah Jane served as the companion to the Third (Jon Pertwee) and Fourth (Tom Baker) Doctors, and became so popular that thirty years later she was given her own series, *The Sarah Jane Adventures*, which ran from 2007 until her death in 2011. But Sarah Jane was a rare exception in a decade when heroic roles for women were few and far between.

Female heroes began to appear with some frequency in film in the

1980s, in particular Ripley in the *Alien* movies, but on television the situation remained bleak. Tasha Yar (Denise Crosby) lasted barely more than a season on *Star Trek: The Next Generation* (1987-1994), not being particularly convincing as the security chief for the *Enterprise*, and certainly captured the imagination of very few. Among the best in a bad decade for female heroes was perhaps Laura Holt (Stephanie Zimbalist) in *Remington Steele* (1982-1987). This character openly acknowledged and worked around the gender inequality of the time: Since the public would not accept a woman as head of a detective agency, trained detective Laura Holt hires a con man (Pierce Brosnan) who *looks* like a dashing detective to portray the mythical "Remington Steele" she created as figurehead of the company. Maddie (Cybill Shepherd) on *Moonlighting* (1985-1989) ran a detective agency, but her real function on the show was as David's (Bruce Willis) romantic foil. Perhaps the emblematic female of the 1980s was found on the series *Hunter and McCall*, which quickly saw the female half of the detective team, McCall (Stepfanie Kramer), relegated to a supporting role to Hunter (Fred Dreyer); the title of the show was quickly shortened simply to *Hunter* (1984-1991).

Mention should, however, be made of two female characters in the decade who indicated that there was a desire for a change in the role of women on TV: the protagonists on *Cagney and Lacey* (1981-1988). While not heroic in a traditional sense, they were rare female characters who were characterized by their extreme professionalism as police detectives, who struggled with a range of real life problems that reflected the experience of most women, including the difficulty of being women in a male-dominated occupation. As characters neither was primarily defined by her deference to men or her sex appeal. Despite a concerted lack of support by the studio and network for *Cagney and Lacey*, the show's significant critical acclaim as well as its popularity with fans nonetheless indicated that there was a hunger for strong, independent women on television. Susan Faludi in *Backlash: The Undeclared War Against American Woman* (New York: Crown, 1991: 149-152) contrasts the show's many critical and popular successes with the attempts on the other hand by the studio and network to shut it down because it portrayed women in a way that extended beyond the comfort level of the (male) network heads. Given the fate of *Cagney and Lacey* and the prevalence of other representations of women, such as those on *thirtysomething* (1987-1991) where women saw their lives as lacking in meaning unless they abandoned their working careers to "nest" and care for their family, Faludi saw little hope for better days for women on television. Little did she or anyone else suspect that things were about to change.

Strictly speaking, television from the 1950s through the 1980s was not devoid of strong women. *The Waltons* (1971-1981) had several strong women while a host of comedies and family dramas featured women who were the backbone of families. There were also spunky girls in a number of series, such as Penny in *Sky King* (1952-1959). But female action heroes were rare. One finds characters such as Mary Richards and Grandma Walton and Maude and similar strong women, but not female counterparts of the almost endless string of male action heroes found at any point in the history of television. The message was clear: it was the job of men to save the world; it was the job of women to hold their families together.

In the nineties everything changed. The first hint perhaps came on *The X-Files* (1993-2002) where FBI Special Agent Dana Scully (marvelously portrayed by Gillian Anderson) represented a new kind of female character. While attractive, her looks were not the primary facet of her character; she was instead portrayed as an exceptionally gifted FBI agent, intellectually brilliant with considerable courage and medical expertise. Dana was as competent an FBI agent as her male partner Fox Mulder, and even slightly more likely than Mulder to use her gun (though neither was particularly trigger happy over the course of the series). She was also the rational, sceptical half of the team, while he was the more credulous, emotional half, so that between them they subverted many traditional gender stereotypes.

Dana Scully was the first of three pivotal female heroes in the decade, the second being Xena (Lucy Lawless), the eponymous lead of *Xena: Warrior Princess* (1995-2001). Traveling with her companion Gabrielle (Renée O'Connor), the show was pure camp, a wonderfully absurd romp through the ancient world, essentially a female buddy show with mythical monsters and a pastiche of historical figures (in Xena's topsy-turvy world Goliath, Homer, and Julius Caesar were contemporaries). Although Gabrielle was initially little more than a poet and storyteller, she eventually became nearly as heroic as Xena herself, mastering a variety of hand-to-hand weapons. In Xena TV viewers were presented with the first female hero in the grand epic mode. In fact, although *Xena* was a spinoff of *Hercules: The Legendary Journeys* (1995-1999), Xena resonated more strongly with a majority of viewers than did Hercules.

The emergence of Dana Scully and Xena (along with Gabrielle) was a sign that times on TV were changing. The precise importance of Scully and Xena can be debated and perhaps no clear conclusion can be drawn. But it is difficult to believe that TV would have been permanently safe for female heroes even after Dana Scully; and Xena, though clearly a hero meant to rival Hercules, was too remote, too mythic, and too larger-than-life to provide a template for future female heroes. And, indeed, there have not been any female heroes after Xena who really resemble her.

With Buffy everything changed for good. She was clearly as heroic as Xena or Dana, yet provided a more viable model for further female heroes. Unlike Xena, who was heroic as a result of her semi-divine origin, Buffy was just a regular girl who suddenly found her destiny thrust upon her. Buffy's problems were a lot more like an average human being's than Xena's, who was constantly having to deal with the enmity of this or that Greek deity. While Buffy does deal with various supernaturally powerful beings and, eventually, her own hell goddess, a more typical problem would be needing to balance studying for a test and patrolling for vampires. Buffy, in other words, is like us, except for the superpowers and destiny.

The appearance of Buffy was a tipping point in the history of heroic women on TV. In the survey attempted above, the number of major female heroes prior to Buffy can be counted on the fingers of two hands, with perhaps several fingers unused. Take a quick inventory of female heroes *after* Buffy and you get Aeryn Sun on *Farscape* (1999-2003), Max Guevera on *Dark Angel* (2000-2002), Sydney Bristow on *Alias* (2001-2006), Veronica Mars on *Veronica Mars* (2004-2007), Kara "Starbuck" Thrace and Sharon Agathon from *Battlestar Galactica* (2004-2009), Sarah Connor and Cameron on *Terminator: The Sarah Connor Chronicles* (2008-2009), Kahlan on *Legend of the Seeker* (2008-2010), Olivia Dunham on *Fringe* (2008-), Sarah Walker on *Chuck* (2007-), Annie Walker on *Covert Affairs* (2010-), Nikita from *Nikita* (2009- ; who looks a lot more like Buffy than the Nikita from the earlier television series of 1997-2001, having started a few months after *Buffy*), and many others. In addition, a considerable number of women emerged who, if not quite action heroes, are nonetheless strong, brave, and capable, women like Kate Austen on *Lost* (2004-2009) or Laura Roslin on *Battlestar Galactica*.

Although Xena and Dana Scully demonstrated that TV viewers were both willing and eager for heroic women, it was post-*Buffy* that the entire culture of TV changed. Today it is inconceivable that a team of heroic individuals on a series would consist exclusively of males who are expected to take care of a group of helpless females. That this is the case is largely, though not entirely, due to *Buffy*. Joss Whedon has stated that in creating Buffy he had intended to create a powerful female character who would be an icon. Mission accomplished.

THE BODY COUNT

Joss Whedon was not the first TV creator to kill off one of his central characters, but he was the first to make a habit of it; certainly no previous showrunner had killed characters on anything like the scale that Whedon did. Previous TV series had occasionally seen a character die off, but in most cases this was either as a means to let a character out of a contract (such as when Denise Crosby's Lt. Tasha Yar was killed in *Star Trek: The Next Generation* or when Jean Stapleton's Edith Bunker passed away in *All in the Family*) or involved a relatively minor character on a show (such as Deepthroat or X on *The X-Files*). But on American television from its creation into the late-nineties, viewers could almost always take one thing for granted: no matter how dire their situation, no major recurring character on a series was going to die.

Starting with Angel's murder of Jenny Calendar in *Buffy*'s Season 2, however, Whedon embarked on a killing spree unlike anything ever seen before in TV. On any other series a character like Jenny would have somehow survived being chased by Angel, and, in fact, the first time one watches "Passion" (2.17) the natural assumption is that Jenny will indeed get away. But when Angel grabs Jenny and unceremoniously breaks her neck, television changed: danger became a part of the TV landscape. And Jenny's death was hardly unique on *Buffy* and its spinoff *Angel*. Kendra, Angel (even though his death by banishment to a hell dimension turned out not to be permanent), Principal Snyder (as well as his predecessor Principal Flutie), Joyce Summers, Tara, Warren, Jonathan, Anya, and Buffy (twice) all died on *Buffy*, while Doyle, Darla (who also died once on *Buffy*), Lilah Morgan, Cordelia, Fred, Lindsey McDonald, and Wesley failed to survive to the end of *Angel* and—for good measure—if the former hell god Illyria is correct, Charles Gunn died a few minutes after the end of the series.

While no previous series in the history of television had remotely approached the kind of slaughter of familiar characters seen on *Buffy* and *Angel*, a host of series post-*Buffy* have racked up substantial body counts, including *Farscape*, *Alias*, *Smallville* (2001-2011), *Veronica Mars*, *Lost*, *The Shield* (2002-2008—which was created by *Angel* alum Shawn Ryan), *Terminator: The Sarah Connor Chronicles*, *Primeval* (2007-), *Torchwood* (2006-), *Battlestar Galactica*, and many, many others. Knowing that beloved characters might die creates a heightened sense of tension, suspense, and danger lacking in pre-*Buffy* series, all thanks to the possibility that threats are real. On a "safe" series, there is no comparable tension, because a viewer knows that all the regular characters will return in the next episode. On shows willing and able to embrace the aesthetic, death suddenly mattered, even if on shows with a supernatural component some characters who die manage miraculous returns (e.g., Angel, Buffy, Darla, and Spike on *Buffy*/*Angel*).

BUFFY AND TV NARRATIVE, OR, THE END OF NARRATIVE WAFFLING

Buffy did not create long narrative on TV, but it did consolidate certain tendencies that had been emerging over the previous decade and a half. To understand the impact that *Buffy* had on narrative, it is once again necessary to look briefly at what had gone on before.

Beginning with *Hill Street Blues* (1981-1987), a number of series in the 1980s expanded what was possible with television narrative. Prior to *Hill Street*, virtually all prime time television series were committed to the episodic format, which meant that each episode contained an almost completely self-contained story. The major exception extended back to the beginnings of television: the soap opera. A host of daytime soaps and later primetime soaps such as *Peyton Place* (1964-1969), the vampire soap *Dark Shadows* (1966-1971), and *Dallas* (1978-1991), as well as *Soap* (1977-1981), a comedic parody of the soaps, had always embraced the serial rather than the episodic narrative format. More about soaps below.

The episodic format made a number of limiting demands on a series. One was that the events of one episode have no consequences for the next. Even if a character was shot, tortured, or otherwise physically—or emotionally—traumatized, the next episode offered a clean slate. If a character were tortured in one episode he showed no signs of it in the next. Actions, in other words, had no long-term consequences for any of the characters.

This lack of consequences was true to some degree even of the soap operas. Although there was narrative memory from one episode to the next, the character development was superficial—cartoonish even—and contained not a little self-parody. Soap opera narrative has many problems—not least that it isn't important that something significant happen but merely that *something* happen—and contains at its heart something of pure camp. Soap opera narratives almost make fun of themselves. But most significantly, the narrative arcs on soaps are inherently inconsequential. They represent supreme examples of narrative waffling, arcs moving here and there, but never anywhere definite. One character can rape a woman on one episode, and then marry her on a later one. It wasn't male violence against women! It was just his way of saying he cared—this very story line famously occurring on *General Hospital*. There is a Sisyphean quality to soap opera narrative; there is forever the sense that some significant conclusion is about to be reached, but that significant moment is never reached. The soaps, like much serial television, tell stories, but not a story.

Another consequence of the episodic format is that the order in which the episodes are seen is arbitrary. If you watch *Gunsmoke* (1955-1975) or *The Wild, Wild West* (1965-1969) or *It Takes a Thief* (1968-1970) or *Star*

Trek (1966-1969) or virtually any series made prior to 1981, you can jumble the order of the episodes with no real consequences. One may be able to date the approximate order of an episode by the loss or addition of a cast member—such as on *Bewitched* when the original Darrin (Dick York) was replaced by another actor (Dick Sargent) or Samantha and Darrin had their daughter Sabrina—not based on much else. In *The Fugitive* (1963-1967), it is really only the first and last episodes that are different from any of the others.

Hill Street Blues hit television like something of a bombshell; the new possibilities that it created for American TV narrative cannot be overstressed. *Hill Street Blues* broke through the single-episode narrative barrier, introducing as well a multi-arc format, with each episode containing perhaps five or six ongoing arcs. Unlike prior shows, *Hill Street Blues* had to be seen in the correct order to be understood. It brought a new level of narrative complexity to television, so much so that the network soon ordered the producers to allow few arcs to extend more than six weeks and to resolve at least one arc each week. Despite these network-imposed limitations the show revolutionized what was possible on American TV in telling a story.

Almost immediately other series like *St. Elsewhere* (1982-1988), *L.A. Law* (1986-1994), *Wise Guy* (1987-90), and *China Beach* (1988-91), continued the narrative revolution that *Hill Street Blues* began. Each of them took TV narrative to places only remotely imagined in previous decades. But even while these series broke down earlier narrative conventions, they remained constructed around relatively short-term narratives. Like the soaps, they all engaged in a degree of narrative waffling, telling a large number of small stories, but no overarching story. Even in aggregate, the collection of smaller narratives never led to a point where they all merged into one that created unity among diversity. An arc might last more than few episodes, but it was unlikely to last more than that, and never would a show be built around a dominant narrative. The stories in all of the shows of the 1980s were, viewed in the long run, rather directionless. Serial television had acquired a timeline, a show was no longer forced to resolve all conflict in a single episode, and events had consequences that continued into future episodes. All of these changes resulted in far deeper exploration of character and allowed more complex storytelling, but TV still did not attempt ambitious long-term narratives. This would change in 1990 with one of the most brilliant failures in the history of television.

Today it is heartbreaking to re-watch *Twin Peaks* (1990-1991) because while it promised so much and changed television so profoundly, it nonetheless failed on its own terms. The extraordinary first season can still generate awe at its originality, beauty, and surreal elegance. Even if Season 2 quickly degenerated into incoherent gobbledygook while losing narrative focus, one cannot overemphasize the importance of the show's absolutely stunning beginning. Leaving aside the pacing and timing that made the earlier episodes so gorgeous, the series was arguably the first ongoing series to be structured around a master narrative, excepting only various TV miniseries made either in Hollywood or by the BBC. "Who killed Laura Palmer?" presented itself as a question to be answered over the course of the series. Sadly, the "long run" turned out to be shockingly short. In the second season the narrative piled up mystery after mystery while resolving few of them, constructing a clumsy story that could not be sustained but which imploded due to its own silliness. Nonetheless, *Twin Peaks* gave both viewers and those within the television industry a vision of the possibilities of TV narrative. At its best, as in Season 1, *Twin Peaks* was better than anything else ever seen before on TV, and part of the reason was the promise of an ongoing story that was central to the series as a whole.

The X-Files was the first network television series that was not a soap opera that was able to sustain a long narrative over the course of several seasons. However, some points must be acknowledged: First, the show's master narrative was not clearly thought out ahead of time. The story of an alien colonization program that the governments of the world were intent upon covering up was, as creator Chris Carter acknowledged, made up as they went along. While the main arc would extend well over six seasons and a feature film, it was fraught with inconsistencies and self-corrections. Multiple answers were given to questions like "Who was Mulder's father?" and "What happened to Mulder's sister?" We were given a variety of explanations, only later to have contradictory answers provided. Second, the show's narratives focused on plot, not people. While Mulder and Scully were brilliant characters, the show strictly speaking was less about them than the conspiracy that they unearthed. Some character development took place despite this, but ultimately the show was less about Mulder and Scully than their adventures. Finally, *The X-Files* was not at its best in the so-called Mythology episodes, but instead in its standalone episodes. Its great innovation was constructing a very long narrative, but it excelled at episodic narrative. For many viewers, the show's highpoints were in standalone episodes like "Clyde Bruckman's Final Repose" (3.4) or "Home" (4.2) or "Jose Chung's *From Outer Space*" (3.20), the latter a brilliant parody of the show's own mythology. Even if the master narrative of *The X-Files* was less than completely successful, the series demonstrated that American TV viewers were not only open to but actively excited about a TV series that told a very long story.

What *Buffy the Vampire Slayer* did was jettison narrative waffling and provide the first completely successful template for long-term narrative on TV. Unlike *Hill Street Blues*, *Buffy* had a story to tell, though it did not cease to include shorter arcs as well, or even pure standalone episodes. Unlike *Twin Peaks* and *The X-Files*, it had a completely coherent narrative with a beginning, middle, and an end. Unfortunately, the stories had to be framed in one-season hunks, though not without some justification. Unlike many TV producers, Whedon has always feared cancellation and has planned his shows defensively and made sure that any season finale could also serve as a series finale. The one time that this didn't help him was with *Firefly* (2002), when cancellation occurred too quickly to produce a series finale as he did on *Angel* and *Dollhouse* (2009-2010) or that his colleague and *Firefly* co-creator Tim Minear was able to do on three shows on which he served as showrunner, *Wonderfalls* (2004), *Terriers* (2010), and *The Chicago Code* (2011). Though Whedon planned many elements of his shows two or more years ahead of time (such as embedding a reference in Season 3 to the eventual appearance of Buffy's sister Dawn, which occurred in Season 5), he was insistent that arcs occur during a time that he could reasonably count on having without cancellation. Thus he was unable to plan the kind of narrative that would run from the beginning until the end of a series, as with some shows that came afterward, such as *Lost* and *Battlestar Galactica*. The only seasons of his shows to end on a cliffhanger were those that had already been renewed, such as Season 3 of *Angel*.

Each season of both *Buffy* and its spin-off *Angel* told stories that were the longest self-contained and coherent narratives yet told on TV. Season 1 focused on Buffy's fight with The Master, a very ancient vampire who is struggling to get out of the underground cathedral in which he is trapped. Season 2 deals with Buffy and Angel's blossoming romance and then his losing his soul after gaining a moment of perfect happiness, all due to a pesky gypsy curse. Season 3 deals with the new Slayer Faith (Eliza Dushku) and the ascendance of Mayor Wilkins to full-fledged demon. Skipping ahead, Season 5 tells the story of the hell goddess Glory and her attempt to recover a mystical key that opens a portal to a hell dimension, a key that the monks who protected it have magically transformed into human form whose identity is Buffy's sister Dawn. These narratives were both deeply involving and for the most part successful, some season's narratives being more successful than others. But even the weaker long story arcs, such as Buffy's struggle to reconnect with being alive being brought back to life. This kind of storytelling was unique in American television at the time. It would not be unique today.

Did *Buffy* change TV narrative? This is impossible to answer with precision. There is no question that many TV creators have looked at Joss Whedon's shows in general and *Buffy* in particular as a guide to how to do long narrative on TV. Alan Ball has frequently spoken of *Buffy* with approval and admiration, as has many other producers. The truth is probably that while *Buffy* directly inspired some creators, it was at the vanguard of a particular change that was beginning to overtake writer-producers on television in the late 1990s. It may be that Joss Whedon merely anticipated the direction that TV narrative was already heading. As noted above, *Twin Peaks* and *The X-Files* had attempted very long narratives, as had the low budget SF drama *Babylon 5* (1994-1998; though the series proper was preceded by a 1993 TV movie). *Buffy*'s success at demonstrating the power of a long narrative arc cleared the way for others to attempt the same.

Post-*Buffy* a significant number of critically acclaimed series have been serial dramas, and most of these follow *Buffy* in building the shows around very long story arcs. Many creators or showrunners have explicitly credited *Buffy* as an influence, including Damon Lindelof (*Lost*), Amy Sherman-Palladino (*Gilmore Girls*), Alan Ball (*Six Feet Under* and *True Blood*), Bill Lawrence (*Scrubs* and *Cougar Town*), Shonda Rhimes (*Grey's Anatomy*), and Vince Gilligan (*Breaking Bad*). There is no question that *Buffy* was at the forefront of bringing a new approach to narrative on television.

BUFFY AND GENRE HYBRIDITY

In addition to these other forms of influence, *Buffy*, did perhaps more than any other show—with the possible exception of *The X-Files*—to popularize genre hybridity to television. *The X-Files* successfully shifted from gut-wrenching drama to outrageous comedy. One need only look at episodes like "Sein und Zeit" (7.10) and contrast it with "War of the Coprophages" (3.12)—I will admit to having cried while watching both, but tears of anguish at the first and tears of laughter at the second. But for the most part *The X-Files* maintained a consistent tone through a particular episode. "Gesthemane" remains tragic throughout while "War of the Coprophages" is comic. What *Buffy* did was shift from drama to comedy to tragedy to romance to action in the same episode, sometimes between one commercial break and the next.

BUFFY AND CHARACTER DEVELOPMENT

An entire book could be written about the new level of depth of character development. Even on very good shows—even most series since the end of

Buffy—virtually no television series have featured characters who changed to any significant degree over time. But on *Buffy*, every character on the series changed significantly over the course of the seasons. This was true not merely of well-rounded, in depth characters like Buffy, Willow, and Giles, but apparently one-dimensional, superficial characters like Cordelia (Charisma Carpenter). Cordy started off as the typical Queen Bitch in school, but evolved into a heroic character in her own right after she moved from Sunnydale to Los Angeles in *Angel*. On *Buffy* and *Angel* characters could mature and evolve to a degree that no previous series had allowed. Nor did villains stay evil or good characters necessarily remain so. Spike started off as a villain, but eventually became a member of the Scoobies and later even teamed with Angel in Los Angeles. Angel and Willow were fundamentally good, but at times they became less than virtuous. Wesley started off as an epically comic character on *Buffy* before moving over to *Angel*, where he evolved into a character that was anything but comic. In perhaps the most extreme instance, the character responsible for killing Fred, Illyria, ended up fighting on the side of the angels. Take any significant character on *Buffy* or *Angel*. Over the course of time he or she will have undergone remarkable and complex changes over time. Then take virtually any other series either before or after *Buffy* (except, interestingly, for some other SF or fantasy series like *Farscape*, *Lost*, and *Battlestar Galactica*) and one will discover that virtually all characters on it end up pretty much the same way that they started off.

CONCLUSION

Even noting *Buffy*'s influence in establishing the permanent presence of female heroes on TV, in creating the Body Count and making it a permanent feature of the genre, in changing the nature of serial narrative on TV, in creating new forms of genre hybridity, and in bringing a new level of depth to character development, the series was influential in other ways as well that can only be briefly noted. *Buffy* has had, for instance, substantial influence on series dealing with high school experience. It has helped popularize making pop cultural references in TV and it was key in bringing a new level of intelligence to genre television series. There is also a story to be told about *Buffy*'s role in expanding fan participation with the Internet, both with chat boards and file sharing (the *Buffy* episode "Earshot" [3.18] was the first file heavily shared on the Internet after the WB postponed it after the Columbine shootings; it was shown outside the U.S. first and uploaded to various early file sharing sites). Or the way that *Buffy* has become a part of our cultural landscape could be examined at length. Or the impact that *Buffy* has had on comic books could be examined, having become one of the first TV series to continue in comic book form under the direct guidance of its creator (plenty of shows had had comics based on them, but without the involvement of the creator). Or the deep influence that *Buffy* has had in transforming TV Studies, spawning numerous academic conferences, and generating a body of literature without precedent in the serious consideration of television.

There have been many shows that have helped change television over the course of its history. But perhaps no series has ever been quite as influential in so many ways as has *Buffy*. The debut of *Buffy* in March 1997, therefore, was not merely the debut of a new series, but the first vision of what television would look like in the future.

1.16
TV's Grim Reaper:
Why Joss Whedon Continually Kills the Characters We Love

Kristin M. Barton

In the world of primetime television and major motion pictures, killing off characters within the principal cast of a lucrative franchise has become impractical, especially when it is the popularity of those characters that drives ratings and box office revenues. But for writer and director Joss Whedon, who has developed properties such as *Buffy the Vampire Slayer*, *Angel*, *Firefly/Serenity*, *Dollhouse*, and *Dr. Horrible's Sing-Along Blog*, killing off members of his central cast has almost become standard operating procedure. As fans, we are not shocked when Whedon quietly introduces us to new characters only to have us form an emotional attachment that is ultimately shattered when their lives are seemingly thrown away in an act of casual violence. When the continued success and profitability of a franchise depends on viewers establishing connections with the characters they see, killing off those characters can prove to have costly and terminal consequences.

But in the world of TV and film, Whedon has gone against conventional thinking and killed off numerous beloved characters, and with great success.

The secret, perhaps, is in how he uses those deaths to promote the gritty reality his characters face and to help motivate characters and push the stories forward. While television has provided us with some memorable character deaths along the years (Detective Bobby Simone on *NYPD Blue* and Colonel Blake on *M*A*S*H*), many of these deaths only served short-term purposes for the story, and in some cases acted as the catalyst for a single emotional episode. Even contract negations and creative differences with actors can lead to the premature demise of popular characters (such as when Denise Crosby was unhappy with how her character Tasha Yar was utilized on *Star Trek: The Next Generation*). But rarely do these events have any real long-term ramifications for the series or the other characters. Seldom are characters killed off in their prime or at the height of popularity, especially when that is in contrast to what most viewers would expect or want to have happen.

With an unprecedented and unparalleled storytelling style, Whedon has become somewhat notorious for the seemingly indiscriminate killing of his leading characters without the usual pomp and circumstance that surrounds that kind of major TV event. Anya in the *Buffy* finale, Paul Ballard in the *Dollhouse* finale ("Epitaph Two: Return" 2.13), Wash in *Serenity*—all of them killed in an instant without warning and without the grandeur normally bestowed upon major characters. Although each is killed in an impersonal and seemingly random way (sliced in half, hit by stray bullet, and impaled by wooden missile, respectively), their passing serves to remind us that death is an inevitable part of life. While we would like to believe that the good guys will always walk away and live to fight another day, Whedon reminds us that casualties occur on both sides in a war. Perhaps Whedon articulated this sentiment best in an interview for *Serenity: The Official Visual Companion* when he noted regarding Wash's death, "Dramatically, the more I worked on [the screenplay], the more it became clear that in order to make people feel that this was real, a certain shocking thing is going to have to happen" (37). To think the protagonists will always come out victorious and unscathed would be unrealistic, and notwithstanding the fantastical worlds in which these stories take place, Whedon has strived to ensure that the societal and emotional situations faced by his characters are as true to life as possible. And while these examples all derive from events where the deceased were participants in active hostilities, innocent bystanders are not immune from Whedon's lethal plot twists either.

Despite the death and violence that permeate every other aspect of their lives, Buffy and her friends are unprepared for the impact it has when they must confront it on a more personal, non vampire-slaying-related level.

Highlighting the power and overwhelming effect of losing a loved one, the Season 5 episode of *Buffy the Vampire Slayer* titled "The Body" (5.16) shows what happens when Buffy arrives home to find her mother dead on the couch from a brain aneurysm. This episode departs from the traditional storytelling done in the series and largely excludes any reference to or mention of the occult world in which Buffy operates. Whedon spends the entire episode examining the impact of death, and carries that impact forward through the remainder of the series as Buffy realizes that she is no longer a child and quickly evolves into a mother-figure for her younger sister Dawn.

The primary difference here between Whedon's shows and others on television is that death in these cases has occurred in an instant, and is not some long or drawn-out event to capitalize on the emotional investment made by the audience. There is no heroic last stand where the heroes remain stalwart against the oncoming hordes of evil to save their companions. These deaths, like so many in real life, happen in an instant—almost so quick that we don't realize what has actually happened.

In no episode of television can this be better observed than in the *Buffy* Season 6 episode "Seeing Red." While confronting Buffy at her house, aspiring super-villain Warren blindly fires a gun in Buffy's direction as he scrambles to escape the gathering Scoobies in the backyard. Unknown to those below, an errant bullet has strayed through a second-floor window and hit Tara in the chest, who manages to say only, "Your shirt..." after seeing the blood spatter appear on Willow in front of her ("Seeing Red" 6.19). With those as her finals words, a principal character in the Buffyverse has passed.

No speeches.

No death scene.

Senseless violence randomly perpetrated against a bystander.

The result of this sequence of events is to produce a reaction in Willow that, under normal circumstances, would be entirely out of character and could quite possibly rip viewers out of the reality created by the show. But because of Whedon's slow progression towards reuniting the couple over the course of many episodes and the sudden shock of Tara's death, Willow's unimaginable rampage climaxing in an attempt to destroy the world resonates as believable for that character.

Similar to Willow's rage, Malcolm Reynolds's reaction to the death of a crew member sets in motion a sequence of events that can easily be perceived as suicidal. In the film *Serenity*, Mal finds Shepherd Book slowly dying after an Alliance attack wipes out the settlement where he has been living. In response, Mal goes through what can best be described as a moment of bloodlust, looking to get revenge on those who have cost him and his crew so much. While certainly not a coward, Mal was shown throughout the television series as making what he would call practical, measured decisions that, while certainly dangerous, ultimately afforded him the ability to keep his crew together and his ship in the air. Once again, Whedon uses a primary character's death to motivate another to act irrationally, sending Mal on a mission to traverse Reaver space. Certainly a desperate action, but one that Mal sees as the only option left given the circumstances.

Just as these deaths faced by so many characters in Whedon's world may seem senseless and be heart-wrenching for the viewer, it is clear that the torment brought about by death continues even for those who manage to return from the dead. In worlds populated with vampires, demons, and demigods, nothing is beyond the realm of possibility. For a few characters, resurrection becomes a second chance at life filled with new pain and torments that only Whedon would inflict on his beloved characters.

At the beginning of Season 5 of *Buffy*, Buffy learns that the person she thinks is her sister Dawn is actually the embodiment of a magical key. In the season finale Buffy comes to realize that only her blood (and thereby death) can prevent the oncoming apocalypse. In a classic moment of heroic sacrifice, Buffy leaps to her death and saves the world once again, leaving her friends behind to mourn and endure without her ("The Gift" 5.22). Not long into Season 6, her friends have discovered a way to bring her back and soon Buffy has returned to Sunnydale and the land of the living ("Bargaining" Part 2, 6.2). But rather than allow Buffy, her friends, and the audience to enjoy this moment of triumph and exalt in what can easily be described as a miracle, Whedon instead chooses to incorporate the consequences of her death (and rebirth) into her new life.

What we quickly learn (and the Scoobies learn in the musical episode, "Once More with Feeling" 6.7), is that in bringing Buffy back from the dead they had inadvertently ripped her out of a peaceful and serene existence where her problems and worries didn't exist: Heaven. In doing this, Whedon has taken his perception of death as the final transition and carried it forward through to the next evolution. Buffy has been inherently changed by her experience, and Whedon doesn't give the audience an opportunity to revel in her return before reminding them that death affects everything, and nothing is the same afterwards. Her life, her actions, and her interactions with her friends are changed as a result of her reappearance and this moves the story forward in a direction that would have seemed out of character for Buffy prior to the events surrounding her death and return to life.

Like Buffy, Spike's return to life in the Season 5 *Angel* episode "Conviction" (5.1) turns his noble sacrifice at the end of *Buffy* ("Chosen" 7.22) into a return to the life he'd chosen to give up. Choosing to sacrifice himself so Buffy and others might live, Spike's rebirth in the Wolfram & Hart offices in Los Angeles brings with it consequences no one could have foreseen. While certainly the character of Spike had evolved significantly since obtaining a soul at the end of Season 6 of *Buffy* ("The Grave" 6.22), the change in Spike prompted by his return from the amulet (where he was, for all intents and purposes, dead) in *Angel* brought about more change that would result in pain and emotional distress for the vampire. Upon getting a soul, Spike dealt with issues that could be seen as selfish and centered largely on himself; his feelings for Buffy, whether people liked him, sacrificing himself to save Buffy (would he have done the same for Xander? Probably not). But upon his rebirth from the amulet, Spike begins making choices that are about others, looking at the bigger picture and considering the welfare of others he may not know or even care about.

Spending the first seven episodes of his return incorporeal, Spike realizes that he is quickly fading away from the living world and is being drawn into Hell. After regaining his physical form ("Destiny" 5.8), Spike's behavior and attitude appear to change, even more so than the change that took place after his re-souling in the final season on *Buffy*. Spike becomes close with Fred, taking on the role of her big brother and protector. When Fred is killed, it becomes clear that Spike has evolved into a much more complete person that his near-descent into Hell helped prompt. The downside for Spike, at least from one perspective, is that in his new life filled with moral choices and putting others before himself, Spike is faced with heartache and emotional pain that he'd possibly never experienced before.

For all the hardship that death brings to the characters of Joss Whedon's worlds, it also serves as the impetus to push characters towards being more than they thought they could. Without Doyle's death in the first season of *Angel* ("Hero" 1.9), Cordelia could have very easily become a stagnant character who continued through life as she had in high school. But through Doyle's death and his imparting his gift to her, she became a better person (and a more complete character) as a result.

In the series finale of *Angel*, Wesley's death brings about a turn in Illyria, where for the first time we see her act out of compassion and caring for someone else. In asking Wes, "Would you like me to lie to you now?" ("Not Fade Away" 5.22) and shifting her form to appear as Fred, she shows that she has moved beyond the self-centered being who took over Fred's body and has come to appreciate more fully the importance of having others in her life she cares about and that care about her.

In *Dr. Horrible's Sing-Along Blog* as Billy/Dr. Horrible half-heartedly points his death ray at the cowering denizens of the bank, we're given insight into just how profoundly Penny's death has affected this would-be super-villain. It becomes clear (though not explicitly stated) that what he thought he'd wanted out of life is now a distant second to what he might have had. As he enters the Evil League of Evil's boardroom and meekly stares into the camera to eke out his final line, we can appreciate how unprepared he was for the consequences of the life he's chosen and how completely the reality of his situation and Penny's death has affected him.

In the past, Whedon has suggested that no characters are ever truly safe on his shows; that unless your name is in the title, you're fair game for an early demise (and even Buffy was killed twice during her series run). Maybe this is what makes Whedon such an exciting writer: his unpredictability. Most people would consider characters like Fred, Wash, and Tara indispensable fan favorites, sure to cause uprising and revolt should anything happen to them. But using their deaths to advance the story, Whedon provides justification for changing the essence of his characters and progressing storylines to places that they could not have otherwise gone.

Works Cited

Angel *Collector's Set: Seasons 1-5*. Box Set. Twentieth Century Fox Home Entertainment, 2007. DVD.

"Bargaining," Part 2. 6.2. Writ. David Fury. Dir. David Grossman. *Buffy*.

"The Body." 5.16. Writ. and dir. Joss Whedon. *Buffy*.

Buffy the Vampire Slayer: *The Chosen Collection*. Box Set. Twentieth Century Fox Home Entertainment, 2006. DVD.

"Chosen." 7.22. Writ. and dir. by Joss Whedon. *Buffy*.

"Conviction." 5.1. Writ. and dir. Joss Whedon. *Angel*.

"Destiny." 5.8. Writ. David Fury and Steven S. DeKnight. Dir. Skip Schoolnik. *Angel*.

Dr. Horrible's Sing-Along Blog. Writ. Maurissa Tancharoen, Jed Whedon, Joss Whedon, and Zack Whedon. Dir. Joss Whedon. Mutant Enemy 2008. DVD.

"Epitaph Two: Return." 2.13. Writ. Maurissa Tancharoen, Jed Whedon, and Andrew Chambliss. Dir. David Solomon. Dollhouse: *The Complete Season* 2. Twentieth Century Fox Home Entertainment, 2010. DVD.

Firefly: *The Complete Series*. Twentieth Century Fox Home Entertainment, 2002. DVD.

"The Gift." 5.22. Writ. and dir. Joss Whedon. *Buffy*.

"The Grave." 6.22. Writ. David Fury. Dir. James A. Contner. *Buffy*.

"Hero." 1.9. Writ. Howard Gordon and Tim Minear. Dir. Tucker Gates. *Angel*.

"Not Fade Away." 5.22. Writ. Jeffrey Bell and Joss Whedon. Dir. Jeffrey Bell. *Angel*

"Once More, With Feeling." 6.7. Writ., dir., and music by Joss Whedon. *Buffy*.

Serenity. Writ. and dir. Joss Whedon. Universal, 2005. DVD.

Serenity: *The Official Visual Companion*. London: Titan, 2005. Print.

CHAPTER 2

ANGEL

2.01
Joss Whedon 101:
Angel
Stacey Abbott

While the character Angel, the vampire with a soul, was introduced in the first season of *Buffy the Vampire Slayer* (WB/UPN, 1997-2003), the origins of the TV series *Angel* (WB, 1999-2004) stem from Season 2 of *Buffy* when Angel loses his soul after experiencing one moment of perfect happiness when sleeping with Buffy ("Surprise"/"Innocence" 2.13/14). At this moment, Angel's deliciously sadistic and cruel alter ego, Angelus, emerges and no one would ever be able to look at Angel in quite the same way again. This character transformation served both to showcase David Boreanaz's acting ability—he is never better than when he plays Angelus (except maybe when he is a puppet)—and the underlying complexity of Angel, a vampire cursed with a soul, haunted by his past actions and looking for atonement. This brief glimpse of Angelus made Angel's struggle with his literal inner demon all the more tangible and moving.

It was while shooting Season 2 that Joss Whedon approached *Buffy* co-producer David Greenwalt and David Boreanaz about potentially spinning Angel off into his own series. Angel would stay on *Buffy* for a third season, the point of which was to build to his and Buffy's painful breakup and Angel's departure for Los Angeles.

In creating a spin-off from *Buffy*, Whedon and Greenwalt had to consider how to construct a new series that was distinct in its own right. Their desire was to aim *Angel* at a slightly older audience and to achieve this, they broke away from *Buffy*'s high school location, sunny atmosphere, and bright colors. In contrast, *Angel* draws upon the legacy of film noir associated with Los Angeles by filming primarily at night in typically noir-style locations such as seedy bars, nightclubs, back alleys, and sewers. This may seem like an obvious move for a series based around a vampire who cannot go out in the day, but compare the visual style of *Angel* with more recent vampire series such as *Moonlight* (2007-2008) and *The Vampire Diaries* (2009-) and you will see the difference. While these shows come up with narrative means of shooting during the day, *Angel* is primarily shot at night (until its fifth season when budget cuts made it necessary to shoot during the day and so UV-resistant windows were introduced). As a result, Whedon and Greenwalt, through their highly skilled Directors of Photography Herb Davis and Ross Berryman, match the show's brooding and existential storyline and themes with what Rhonda Wilcox and David Lavery describe as repeated "moments of beautiful dark" (225). The cinematography on *Angel* emphasizes deep shadows, expressionist lighting, and isolated compositions. This noir legacy is never more apparent than in the opening montage of bright urban lights of Los Angeles accompanied by the following voiceover:

"Los Angeles. You see it at night and it shines. A beacon. People are drawn to it. People and other things. They come for all sorts of reasons. My reason? No surprise there. It started with a girl" ("City Of" 1.1).

With this opening, *Angel* acknowledges its association with *Buffy* but also transforms Angel from a teenage girl's first love into a noir detective, losing himself in L.A. to escape the pain of the past. A past that includes Buffy but also, as the series would go on to explore, a long history of obsession, sadism, and violence. Angel's path to redemption was just beginning.

It is the theme of redemption through action that came to define the series, first through Angel and then the family he builds around him: Doyle, Cordelia Chase, Wesley Wyndam-Pryce, Faith, Charles Gunn, Lorne, Winifred "Fred" Burkle, Connor, Illyria, and finally Spike—resurrected from his fiery death on *Buffy* to appear in *Angel*'s final season. Each of these characters is damaged in one form or another, looking to find redemption for past failings by "helping the helpless" one soul at a time. They are also looking to make sense of who they are and how they fit into the world around them. While *Buffy* offered insight into the pains of growing up, *Angel* explored the painful challenges of adulthood. But that was just the start for *Angel*. There is no one way to read *Angel*.

Over the five seasons, *Angel* offered its audience countless moments of aesthetic pleasure (the *Angel* theme and credits give the show a brooding sensibility while the action scenes offer kinetic energy), provocative storylines (two vampires give birth to a human baby), transgressive representation of gender (vampires Darla and Drusilla go on a shopping spree), heartbreaking moments (Fred and Wesley's death scenes), great comedy (Wesley fantasizing about dancing the ballet with Fred), and televisual innovation (Angel as a puppet, anyone?). The following discussion will highlight some significant ways of approaching *Angel*, but they aren't the only ways. The more you watch *Angel* the more there is to discover and this is just the beginning.

While *Angel* began as film noir detective series, with a touch of *Batman* thrown in for good measure—particularly through the repeated shots of

Angel standing on high overlooking the city not to mention his use of Batman-style gadgets ("City Of")—the show increasingly demonstrated a playful engagement with genre which is characteristic of Joss Whedon's work. The series infused into its noir matrix conventions of horror, as in the *Dawn of the Dead* style episode when all of the staff of evil law firm, and Angel's primary nemesis, Wolfram & Hart are killed by The Beast and then rise again as zombies ("Habeas Corpses" 4.8). Later in one of the show's most graphic episodes, Spike staves off being pulled into hell as he is haunted by the ghosts of Wolfram & Hart who threaten him with physical dismemberment and mutilation ("Hellbound" 5:4). In "Billy", Wesley becomes infected with demon blood that brings forth "a primordial misogyny" inherent in men (3.6) and stalks Fred through the corridors of their hotel office, The Hyperion, calling to mind Stanley Kubrick's *The Shining* (1980). Wesley's quiet reserve and twisted humor as he taunts Fred makes this one of the most disturbing and frightening episodes of the series.

Horror is, however, just the beginning of the show's genre hybridity. The introduction of Caritas, a demon karaoke bar in Season 2 brought the musical into the mix with repeated episodes featuring cast members singing in order to receive guidance from the bar's empathic Host, eventually known as Lorne. Memorable renditions include: Wesley, Gunn, and Cordelia singing "We are the Champions"; Darla's femme fatale rendition of "Ill Wind"; Fred ironically choosing to sing "Crazy" as she recovers from her five-year ordeal as a slave in a demon dimension; and of course no one will ever forget Angel's painful version of "Mandy"—which was so wonderfully comic in its badness that they repeated it over the episode's end credits and it has become a signature tune associated with the show.

The Season 3 storyline focusing upon the return of a now pregnant Darla and the birth of her and Angel's son Connor is pure family melodrama, culminating in Darla's self-sacrifice in the alley behind Caritas ("Lullaby" 3.9). Cradled in Fred's lap as Angel watches helplessly and the rain pours down, Darla tells Angel that this baby is the "one good thing they did together" before staking herself in the heart, bursting into dust and leaving a wailing human(ish) baby behind. This scene brings Darla and Angel's relationship full circle as its alley setting is designed deliberately to echo the place of Darla's transformation of the human Liam into the vampiric Angelus, and it reminds us that no matter how evil a character can be, on *Angel* everyone is capable of tenderness, self-sacrifice, and redemption through action. It is one of the most beautifully staged and moving moments in the series.

More than any genre, however, *Angel* is at its best when it mixes comedy within its horror/noir aesthetic. These can be isolated moments designed to undercut the brooding quality to the show such as Angel's horrified vision of himself dancing at Cordelia's house party, before declaring "I don't dance" ("She" 1.13) or Doyle in "City Of" working up the courage to drive through Russell Winters's main gates in order to rescue Angel, only to have the car bounce back on impact as Doyle responds "Good gate." Comedy is also used more broadly in certain episodes to deconstruct notions of masculinity and heroism. In "Guise will be Guise" (2.6) Angel goes to see a swami in order to help him control his growing obsession with his sire Darla, while Wesley poses as Angel when Cordelia is threatened by gangsters. Wesley's masquerade serves as a parody of Angel's affected mannerisms, as he dons Angel's iconic black coat and sweeps confidently into the office only to stumble at the entrance. At the same time Angel's self-image comes under direct comic attack when meeting the swami who questions Angel's choice of clothes, car, and hair product: "Don't get me wrong, if you are out there fighting ultimate evil. You're gonna want something with hold." If "Guise Will Be Guise" serves as a critique of the image of the superhero, then the comedy episode "Smile Time" (5.14) where Angel, our superhero, is turned into a puppet, completely shatters it. In this episode, Angel must suffer the indignities of being described as "cute" by Fred, called a "wee-little puppet man" by Spike and being almost eaten alive by his would-be girlfriend, Nina. These comedy episodes don't undermine Angel's actions or his position as a hero, but do challenge the traditional image of the hero, replacing it with an all too human vision of heroism, replete with insecurities, weaknesses and self-doubt.

As such comedy episodes demonstrate, one of the primary preoccupations of *Angel* is its focus upon the shifting representation of masculinity. David Greenwalt makes this clear in a statement that is fast becoming the calling card of the series, "*Buffy* is about how hard it is to be a woman and *Angel* is about how hard it is to be a man" (cited by Nazzaro, 158). In trying to show how "hard it is to be a man," however, the series raises questions about what it means to be a man and it does this through the characterization of not only Angel but also the men who surround him: Doyle, Wesley, Gunn, Lorne, Lindsey, Connor, and Spike. Each of these men offers distinct representations of masculinity that if taken alone might be considered stereotypical (Connor the annoying teenage boy, Gunn the black gang member, Lorne the camp nightclub host, Wesley the uptight British intellectual), but when considered together offer a complex image of modern masculinity. More importantly, the serial nature of *Angel*'s storytelling allows these characters to grow and evolve, never offering one image of masculinity but rather presenting masculinity constantly in transformation and evolution.

This is nowhere more apparent than in the characterization of Wesley who, between his first appearance on *Buffy* and his death on *Angel* in "Not Fade Away" (5.22), undergoes the most dramatic character development of any character in the Buffy/Angelverse (except possibly for Cordelia). This is highlighted in the aforementioned "Billy," where Wesley undergoes a crisis of masculinity that serves as a key pivot point for his transformation from buffoonish sidekick to dark and brooding anti-hero. This is an episode that overtly and controversially addresses gender issues and is described by writers Tim Minear and Jeff Bell as "widely acclaimed and much loathed" (Commentary). They further state that those who hated the episode either hated it because "it was accused of being anti-woman, or it's accused of being anti-man." Presumably much of the criticism leveled at the episode for being anti-man comes from the suggestion that misogyny is inherent in men rather than learned social behavior. The "anti-woman" sentiment is based upon the fact that the episode features strong images of violence against women including Wolfram & Hart lawyer Lilah Morgan being graphically beaten by colleague Gavin Park and Fred's physical and psychological abuse at the hands of Wesley in the third and fourth acts of the episode, drawing upon the generic trope of the "woman in peril." The episode, like *Buffy*, however, also works along the lines of much postmodern horror as it knowingly subverts the classic conventions of the genre that present women as victims by having the women save themselves. Cordelia takes it upon herself to hunt Billy—the demon whose blood incites masculine aggression—and it is Lilah who shoots and destroys him. Furthermore, in true final girl fashion, Fred saves herself from Wesley through her own ingenuity and mechanical mindedness—she builds a trap for him that knocks him out until Billy's effect has worn off—and in so doing she also saves Wesley. This is all a very familiar aspect of modern horror.

The episode also introduces another discourse, this time about masculinity, into the gender dynamic of modern horror. What is significant is the manner in which the episode is deliberately ambiguous about the nature of Billy's effect on men. Lilah may describe this effect as bringing out a "primordial misogyny," an interpretation supported by Angel who equally describes Billy's affect as *bringing out* "hatred and anger" from his victims, but Fred specifically tells Wesley that "it wasn't something in you, Wesley. It was something that was *done to you*." It is therefore unclear whether Billy's touch changed the men or brought out something innate within them and this ambiguity is central to the episode. It raises questions about masculinity rather than answers them. Furthermore, the implication of the episode is that it is Wesley who is victimized by Billy. His body is penetrated by Billy's blood and he is transformed, against his will, from his usually gentle persona into a violent attacker. As a result, at the end of the episode it is Wesley, not Fred, who is traumatized by the preceding events.

When Fred comes to Wesley's apartment to encourage him to come back to work, he is presented as sitting alone in his dark apartment, isolated and cut off from the rest of the team as he stares at the wall. When he answers the door he can't face Fred and averts his eyes where possible. The episode ends with him breaking down, unable to contain his emotions. What this scene demonstrates is that he is not simply traumatized by the invasion of his body/personality by Billy but by the questions the experience has raised about who he is, telling Fred, "I don't know what kind of man I am anymore." Wesley, the gentle buffoon who has gradually been learning how to become a commanding leader, has had violent, masculine aggression forced upon or out of him. Either way for the sensitive "new man," this is a horrible violation and causes Wesley to question his identity.

Wesley is not the only man on *Angel* to question his identity. Gunn undergoes an equally traumatic and unsettling crisis of identity throughout the series as he seeks to understand his place within the gender and class dynamics of Angel Investigations, seeing himself as having little to offer but muscle; and as a result he risks losing his soul to Wolfram & Hart in order to improve his position. W&H lawyer Lindsey McDonald becomes the epitome of damaged masculinity struggling with his own identity in "Dead End" (2.18) when he questions the paternal hold that W&H have over him and then later comes back to reassert his authority over both W&H and Angel. Lorne is initially scarred by Fred's death (as they all are) and then finally and ultimately damaged by Angel's request that he be the one to shoot Lindsey in "Not Fade Away." Like Wesley in "Billy" Lorne suffers for having violent aggression forced upon him and out of him through this act. He tells Angel that "he'll do this last thing for you… for us… but then I'm out."

The last we see of Lorne (until the *Angel After the Fall* comics, that is) is him leaving the murder scene in an uncharacteristically noir-style leather coat with the departing line "goodnight folks." Finally, Connor is initially the most damaged of all the characters, born of two vampires and raised in a hell dimension, but ironically is the only one that seems to find some form of reconciliation to his identity when he is first given false memories of an alternative *normal* life which later collapse forcing his new and old memories to co-exist. As a result, he is able to reconcile his action and new man existence and find the peace that the others never find. Through all of these multiple struggles with identity, *Angel* raises exploratory questions about the nature of masculinity. It doesn't try to answer them. The questioning is what matters.

To conclude, *Angel* explores the problems of being an adult in an increasingly complicated and morally ambiguous world. It does not suggest that these problems are solvable, any more than discourses around masculinity can be easily reconciled. Instead *Angel* simply highlights the importance of trying. As Angel tells Connor, "We live as if the world were as it should be to show it what it can be" ("Deep Down" 4.1). The final moments of the series are a testament to this philosophy, as the remaining members of Angel Investigations face, in yet another rainy dark alley, the demonic hordes unleashed by Wolfram & Hart. When asked about his plan, Angel responds: "Well personally, I kinda want to slay the dragon. Let's go to work"—to cut to black with Angel in mid-swing. What matters is not what happens to Angel and his team but simply that they keep fighting.

Works Cited

Angel: The Complete DVD Collection. Region 2. Cr. Joss Whedon and David Greenwalt. Perf. David Boreanaz, Charisma Carpenter, Alexis Denisof, J. August Richards, and Amy Acker. Twentieth Century Fox, 2007. DVD.

"Billy." 3.6. Writ. David Greenwalt. Dir. Turi Meyer. *Angel*.

Buffy the Vampire Slayer: The Complete DVD Collection. Region 2. Twentieth Century Fox. 2004. DVD.

"City Of." 1.1. Writ. David Greenwalt and Joss Whedon. Dir. Joss Whedon. *Angel*.

"Dead End." 2.18. Writ. David Greenwalt. Dir. James A. Contner. *Angel*.

"Deep Down." 4.1. Writ. Steven S. DeKnight. Dir. Terrence O'Hara. *Angel*.

"Guise Will Be Guise." 2.6. Writ. Jane Espenson. Dir. Krishna Rao. *Angel*.

"Habeas Corpses." 4.8. Writ. Jeffrey Bell. Dir. Skip Schoolnik. *Angel*.

"Hellbound." 5.4. Writ. and dir. Steven S. DeKnight. *Angel*.

"Innocence" (part 2 of 2). 2.14. Writ. and dir. Joss Whedon. *Buffy*.

"Lullaby." 3.9. Writ. and dir. Tim Minear. *Angel*.

Minear, Tim, and Jeffrey Bell. Commentary. *Angel*.

Nazzaro, Joe. *Writing Science Fiction and Fantasy Television*. London: Titan Books, 2002.

"Not Fade Away." 5.22. Writ. Jeffrey Bell and Joss Whedon. Dir. Jeffrey Bell. *Angel*.

"She." 1.13. Writ. David Greenwalt and Marti Noxon. Dir. David Greenwalt. *Angel*.

"Smile Time." 5.14. Writ. Joss Whedon and Ben Edlund. Dir. Ben Edlund. *Angel*.

"Surprise" (part 1 of 2). 2.13. Writ. Marti Noxon. Dir. Michael Lange. *Buffy*.

Wilcox, Rhonda V., and David Lavery. "Afterword: The Depths of *Angel* and the Birth of *Angel* Studies." *Reading* Angel: *The Spin-off with a Soul*. Stacey Abbott, ed. London: Tauris, 2005.

2.02
Lindsey and Angel:
Reflecting Masculinity

Lorna Jowett

Wolfram & Hart lawyer, Lindsey McDonald is the only character who appears in the first and last episodes of *Angel* apart from its title character, and his long-term development makes him an interesting parallel to Angel. While vampires like Angel and Spike are sired, Lindsey is self-made and his character is reinvented more than once. Roz Kaveney suggests that one of *Angel*'s themes is "that self-reinvention is both necessary and morally dangerous" and she notes that "Lindsey... has always been another of Angel's shadows" (66). While Lindsey is introduced as a professional, the focus soon shifts to his body and the physical, something that allows his character to more effectively shadow, or reflect, Angel. In his first two seasons, the vehicle for this is the loss of Lindsey's hand and its artificial replacements. Kaveney notes that this "reinvents [Lindsey] as a liminal being" (66) and Lindsey's representation is part of a larger concern in the show with the body as a site of vulnerability, excess, and humanity, as well as liminality. His later Season 5 appearances see him attempt to reinvent himself as a worthy adversary or partner for Angel, via his acquisition of or bid for power (magical, physical, and material). Throughout, the ongoing homoeroticism of this antagonistic relationship is matched with superficial heterosexuality and this adds further complexity to their respective versions of masculinity. In "Underneath" Lindsey greets Angel's appearance with a flippant, "Oh look, it's the hero of the hour." When Angel corrects him, saying, "I'm not your hero. I'm your warden," he merely responds, "It's all how you look at the glass." Lindsey and Angel constantly function as reflections of each other, and of the ways masculinity, as well as characters, are reinvented by the show.

Identity on *Angel* is fluid and contingent, not fixed. This is partly the nature of serial television: story requires change and development. The construction of identity on *Angel* is informed by its genre mix too. Characters change and identity is fluid because this is how we currently understand the ways subjectivity is constructed and reconstructed (a kind of realism); characters on *Angel* often have to reconstruct their identity, to reinvent themselves, because of fantastic events, however. The transformations common to horror are perhaps the most obvious factor here: when Liam is sired as a vampire he is forced to reinvent himself and eventually becomes Angelus, who in turn becomes Angel. Many other characters change or develop because of supernatural transformations (Cordelia, Fred), others simply because of the nature of their fight against evil. All key characters are transformed by their search for redemption. As a vampire fiction, *Angel* also negotiates time, and the use of flashback and backstory in particular emphasise the importance of the past to character development. The physical and moral places they came from create characters in particular ways and this is partly why there is no clear binary structuring identity: Angel and Angelus are not alter egos but points on a fluid continuum and other characters encompass similar range. *Angel*'s fascination with the body, an aspect of horror as well as other constituent genres, also inspires change or reinvention.

"YOU SOLD YOUR SOUL FOR A FIFTH-FLOOR OFFICE AND A COMPANY CAR"

Lindsey appears to be a self-made man in the traditional sense of the term. In "Blind Date" when he asks for Angel's help saving three seer children from assassination, he reveals part of his history:

"I guess it's fair to say that you've never seen anything like real poverty. I'm talking dirt poor: no shoes, no toilet. Six of us kids in a room, and come flu' season it went down to four. I was seven when they took the house. They just came right in and took it. And my daddy's being nice, you know? Joking with the bastards while he signs the deed. Yeah, so we had a choice. Either you got stepped on or you got to stepping and I swore to myself that I was not going to be the guy standing there with a stupid grin on my face while my life got dribbled out" ("Blind Date" 1.21).

It is worth noting that while Lindsey, like other characters, is defined by his past (in the remarks just prior to this speech he refers to both Liam and Angelus), that past is not made concrete for the viewer. We never see flashbacks of Lindsey; he exists only in the present. Later in the episode we discover that he was picked out by Holland Manners while at Law School and Holland describes Lindsey's drive as partly being based in a sense of having to do better, to achieve more because of his background, a demonstration of the way his past is *used* by Wolfram & Hart, rather than valued as what makes him an individual ("Blind Date"). In this way Lindsey fits the American model of the self-made man from a lower class family who works hard and achieves material and professional success, reinventing himself in the process, a trope closely aligned with the American Dream.

Benjamin Franklin is one of the earliest examples of (and a template for) this figure, which features prominently in popular fiction of the nineteenth century and beyond. That Lindsey has moved from "dirt poor" kid to hotshot L.A. lawyer seems to describe this arc. The avuncular Holland tells him that he has "everything it takes to go all the way here—drive, ambition, excellence" but also observes that Lindsey needs to develop "that sharp, clear sense of self a man gains once he's truly found his place in the world" to distinguish himself rather than just "mov[ing] with the crowd." Lindsey, however, exhibits divided loyalties to the firm which inhibit this "sense of self" ("Blind Date").

John Cawelti distinguishes among three types of self-made men: those who act as examples of moral values such as "piety, frugality, and diligence;" those who seek economic success, embodying capitalist values such as individualism and competition, and those who measure their success by "individual fulfilment and social progress" (in Geraghty 70). Thus in some representations the self-made man rises not simply through hard work but because his convictions rest on a solid moral foundation. F. Scott Fitzgerald's classic novel *The Great Gatsby* demonstrates the tragedy that can ensue from taking an easier route to wealth and success: Gatsby fails partly because his gains are ill-gotten. Thus when Kaveney describes Lindsey as a "poor boy made good by doing bad" (66), this also describes a recognisable type in American culture. Lindsey's morality is not clear cut: much of the interest in his character comes from his moral ambivalence as he swings between condoning evil at Wolfram & Hart, and resisting it by working with Angel. This ambivalence persists through to Season 5, where he returns apparently determined to kill Angel, but ends by working alongside him to bring down the Circle of the Black Thorn (albeit potentially to take over Wolfram & Hart if they succeed). As his "working-class kid with a chip" speech (Kaveney 66) indicates, Lindsey is less concerned with right and wrong than with taking control of his life by accumulating power: in order not to be stepped on, he must rise far enough to do the stepping. "It's not about good or evil, it's about who wields the power," as Holland tells him in "Blind Date." Furthermore, like many morally dubious characters (Jayne from *Firefly*, for instance), Lindsey does not see himself as a villain, and the focus on power allows him to sidestep that issue. When he returns in Season 5, he seems to have become more like Cawelti's third type of self-made man, the one seeking self-fulfilment, though this is to be measured in personal terms rather than social progress and perhaps comes closest to Holland's "sense of self."

Reading the self-made man according to the philosophy of Frederick Douglass, another historical example of the trope, offers further interesting angles. In a lecture from 1872 Douglass suggests that, "Properly speaking, there are in the world no such men as self-made men"; rather he suggests that men are made in relation to others. This is partly down to, in Douglass' view, the impossibility of evading influence or inspiration from the past: "We have all either begged, borrowed, or stolen," he says. In Douglass' conception, men are also made in relation to each other as a means of maintaining a balance of power through complementary qualities. This fits perfectly with the ensemble cast of a serial TV show, since character development is often managed via contrast and comparison, and the notion of power is interesting with regards to *Angel*'s negotiations of morality, heroism, and masculinity. Lindsey, like many other male characters, functions as a shadow for or reflection of Angel: he is a conventional self-made man via his backstory, but he is also re-made in relation to Angel, and vice versa. *Angel*'s male characters are all made men in relation to each other, in the sense that the show offers a range of contrasting masculinities.

The duality that Lindsey and Angel create is undeniable and while it may seem to be about morality, the connection between them is frequently about physicality. This is another play on Lindsey's self-made man status: his working class roots facilitate an emphasis on the body, physicality, and control. Stereotypes of class often locate working class identity in the physical, middle or upper class identity in the intellect. The social status of a character is defined as much by how they speak, what they wear, what they do, and how they do it, as by their employment or birth, and this is certainly true of characters in *Angel*, as Wesley and Gunn immediately demonstrate (Gunn also makes a "chip" speech to Angel in "War Zone," 1.20) and as seen with Lindsey in "Dead End" (2.18, see below). Lindsey's position as a lawyer and professional, therefore, does not prevent him from being part of *Angel*'s fascination with the body, and he works successfully to reflect Angel because of this.

"EVIL HAND ISSUES"

Stacey Abbott suggests that because *Angel* operates "within horror conventions" it is "able to openly address the indeterminacy and liminality of the human body" (*Angel* 48). The body in *Angel* is often uncanny, even when human characters are in the frame. Discussing other genres that focus on the body, Abbott notes, "While the body in *ER* is something to be fixed or cured, and in *CSI* it is a 'speaking witness' to crime, on *Angel* it is something that is always under attack, redefining its boundaries or undergoing processes of transformation" (*Angel* 48). In this sense *Angel*'s characters undergo a different kind of self-reinvention via the tropes of horror.

The most obvious way in which Lindsey is used to further *Angel*'s negotiation of the uncanny body is through his lost hand and its replacements. In the Season 1 finale, "To Shanshu in L.A.," Angel cuts off Lindsey's hand, an act that evokes immediate physical pain and leaves a lasting (physical) reminder of its violence. (A later example with some resonance here is when Spike has both hands cut off by a psychotic Slayer in "Damage" (5.11), an event designed to examine the consequences of Spike and Angel's past as vampires and also presented in body horror terms). During Season 2, Lindsey has first a plastic prosthetic and then a "real" hand to replace his amputated one. Kaveney notes that "The loss of his hand reinvents him as a liminal being, since part of him is alive and part dead, and this does not cease to be the case when he is given new hands" (66). Thus not only is Lindsey reinvented as someone whose body is shown to be at the least problematic, and at most uncannily out of control; he is also reinvented as not quite human, a quality exacerbated by his reappearance in Season 5.

As Season 2 begins, Lindsey's smooth professional exterior and physical perfection are marred by the loss of his hand and the presence of an obviously plastic replacement. This prosthetic is often referred to as "plastic," underlining its artificiality, and it consistently undermines Lindsey's control. In "Judgement" (2.1) when he is having trouble opening a CD case Lilah comments, "You're not handicapped, you're handi-capable." (Compare puppet Angel having trouble with the TV remote in "Smile Time" 5.14, another reinvention of familiar notions of control and masculinity). That this happens in front of the resurrected Darla, for whom Lindsey develops an emotional attachment, simply humiliates him the more. The hand becomes a symbol of what Angel has taken from Lindsey. In "Blood Money" (2.12) he comments on the possibility of demon Boone killing Angel against the Senior Partners' wishes, "Boo hoo. Let me wipe away my tears with my plastic hand." In an even more loaded exchange, Darla comments in "Dear Boy" on Angel's actions. Indicating the hand, she says, "He did that to you. What's it feel like?" Lindsey responds, "Doesn't feel like anything." When Darla strokes his plastic hand, she observes first, "It's very smooth," and then, "You don't feel anything." "Not in my hand," returns Lindsey ("Dear Boy" 2.5). This comes as a sexual triangle is established involving Lindsey, Darla and Angel, discussed in more detail later. For now, it's sufficient to notice the way the plastic hand is used to draw attention to (lack of) physical feeling and to sexuality. The hand represents a "sacrifice" made for Wolfram & Hart (who eventually reward

Lindsey with a different replacement) and therefore also functions as a reminder of Lindsey's dubious loyalties.

To reinforce the loss of control, Lindsey's plastic hand is smashed by Angel during a fight (over Darla) in "Epiphany" (2.16). This fight, of course, is motivated by sexual jealousy. Following this, in "Dead End" Lindsey is rewarded with a new, human, fully-functioning replacement hand via a mixture of medical and mystical procedures, paid for and provided by Wolfram & Hart (see Jowett for more on this mixture). The difference this makes to Lindsey is emphasized by the repeated morning routine sequence in this episode. The first time Lindsey wakes up he stretches with his remaining hand to switch off his alarm clock, chooses from a selection of pre-knotted ties, and looks at his guitar, now relegated to the back of the closet. The second time around, he easily disengages the alarm clock, shaves using both hands, and lifts out the guitar, leading to a subsequent scene of him playing and singing at Caritas ("Dead End"). Apparently his physical perfection, and therefore control of his body, has been restored and he is back to normal.

Of course, this is far from the case. Lindsey's new hand might appear more natural, yet it is even more uncanny than the last. During a meeting with clients he looks down to see it has written "kill" repeatedly on his notepad. This retreads a familiar horror plot in which a replacement limb has a life of its own, and may even commit evil deeds without the subject's volition, as seen in films like *The Hands of Orlac* (1960) or *Evil Dead II* (1987). A later scene shows Lindsey sitting at home, pen in hand, attempting to regain control. He tries to see if the hand will write again, then pokes and stabs it to try and elicit some response. Although he draws blood, this scene demonstrates how the hand is now alienated from the rest of his body, not part of him. Finally he asks it, "Who are you?" ("Dead End"). (Again similar scenarios recur throughout the show, notably in "Carpe Noctem," 3.4, and "Smile Time," 5.14, where whole bodies are changed. That it is usually Angel who loses control in this way demonstrates how closely Lindsey and he reflect each other.)

The revelation of Wolfram & Hart's cryogenic lab again foregrounds the uncanny body, as Angel and Lindsey, now working together, discover bodies being harvested for parts, a typical scenario from both science fiction and horror that evokes mad, bad science and its disregard for humanity, as well as corporate commodification of humans, and a freak show spectacle of dismembered bodies in one neat package. Lindsey discovers that "his" new hand came from Wolfram & Hart mail room employee Bradley Scott, who completes the automatic writing when he begs Lindsey, "Kill me." Lindsey's emotional response is disgust and the provenance of his new hand is a literal and physical example of the ways in which reinvention can be morally dangerous: "Your firm in action, Lindsey," Angel comments, "lots to be proud of." Destroying the lab strikes at Wolfram & Hart and demonstrates how the loyalty that led Lindsey to lose his hand in the first place has been reversed. Lindsey then not only rejects another promotion from Wolfram & Hart but uses his "evil hand" to make a striking exit. Interrupting an important "re-evaluation" meeting, he punches a security guard, then takes his gun and shoots the guard in the foot, threatening superior Nathan Reed while saying, "Stop, evil hand, stop it." Finally, he recommends Lilah for promotion, telling the assembled employees that he is "unreliable" and has "these evil hand issues," as well as being "bored with this crap." On his way out, he wishes Lilah good luck, then (apparently) gooses her with his "evil hand" ("Dead End"). The excess of horror is here combined with the excess of comedy to great effect (as in the famous scene from *Evil Dead II*): Lindsey performs being out of control ("unreliable") in order to take back control from Wolfram & Hart. They are responsible for Lindsey's evil hand, as he points out to Nathan, and Lindsey, like the other corporate drones, may claim that he is not acting of his own accord when he carries out their work. (This chimes with many other comments about corporate puppets in Season 5). Here Lindsey abdicates power/status within the firm in order to control his life in a different way, moving away from material success and capitalist competition to pursue self-fulfilment.

In Season 5, Lindsey reinvents himself again, reappearing, bulked up and with new powers (mystical as well as physical). Magical tattoos work to keep him "off Wolfram & Hart's radar" (in "Soul Purpose" 5.10), deflecting the Senior Partners' ability to "see" him acting in and around their L.A. branch. The scene from "You're Welcome" where Lindsey moves through unbroken lines of laser light produced by a security system is a key visualisation of how his body has changed again. The tattoos, like his replacement hand, make him more than a man: he is invisible to the lasers as well as the more mystical elements of the security, as demonstrated when Angel, Spike, and Cordelia take the same route, triggering all the booby traps ("You're Welcome" 5.12). The visual image here draws attention to the body, as so often with Lindsey in this season. This scene also echoes the infiltration of Wolfram & Hart in "Blind Date," the first time Angel and Lindsey worked together, and, since "You're Welcome" is the 100th episode, it contains several references to the history of the show and its characters.

The device of the tattoos allows the show to overtly display Lindsey's body, sometimes in bedroom scenes with Eve, sometimes in action scenes.

When Eve fondles the tattoos, Lindsey tells her "These aren't for playing," and covers himself, but she responds "Doesn't mean I can't think they're sexy" ("Soul Purpose"). On the verge of defeating Angel in the showdown fight of "You're Welcome," Lindsey strips off his shirt and postures, before being beaten by the re-energised Angel and losing his magical protection through a joint effort from the team (Wesley and the others perform a ritual to negate the tattoos). Thus something narratively intended to hide and protect his body not only draws attention to it visually but also, in the end, emphasises its vulnerability. Cordelia tells him, "Sweetie, your epidermis is showing," as the tattoos literally float off Lindsey's skin and disappear, naked skin visualising his new weakness ("You're Welcome"). (In fact, Allison McCracken notes of Angel's own tattoo in *Buffy the Vampire Slayer*, that "the dominant cultural connotation of body armor is here reconfigured to serve as an early and enticing indication that Angel's body is one on which impressions can be made" [122], so that even the tattoos themselves can signify permeability). His violent exit via the portal opened by the Senior Partners again offers a spectacle that presents the body as vulnerable and easily controlled. Using conventions familiar from the action genre, this confrontation has Angel re-establish his masculine identity through physical combat and through his (moral and physical) integrity, as contrasted with the penetration, disintegration, and consumption of Lindsey's body.

The next we see of Lindsey, in "Underneath," he is trapped in a prison dimension being tortured daily, presumably his punishment for betraying the Senior Partners. Since Lindsey's new powers combine the mystical and physical, his punishment does too. He believes he is living a perfect life in the suburbs but every time he enters the cellar, he is eviscerated by a demon. When Angel, Spike, and Gunn come to rescue him and take refuge in the cellar we see a pile of bloody organs lying to one side. Spike picks one up and asks whose hearts they are and Lindsey replies, "Mine." Spike's revulsion heightens the visceral body horror in this spectacle, playing on the extreme vulnerability of the human body. Yet, the multiple hearts simultaneously emphasize Lindsey's liminality as existing in more than a human plane: his heart must magically grow back in order to be removed all over again ("Underneath"). Given how often Angel himself is tortured and physically beaten in both *Buffy* and *Angel*, this further parallels Lindsey and Angel. McCracken describes how "Because Angel is immortal and will not die in a single narrative climax, his beauty and body can survive repeated torture and thus be enjoyed multiple times" (123) and here this is equally applicable to Lindsey, another indication of his liminal status. In contrast, Abbott notes that when Gunn takes Lindsey's place he is on a road to redemption that involves getting back in touch with physical humanity (*Angel* 57). Lindsey's ordeal reinscribes both his vulnerable humanity and the new physical toughness (partly mystical) that backs up his reinvented sense of self. When Angel comments, "I thought a few months of torture at the hands of the senior partners would have dug a little deeper," he simply replies, "Just scratched the surface. Turns out they can only undo you as far as you think you deserve to be undone" ("Underneath"). Earlier, in Season 2's "Reunion," Angel comments to Holland Manners, "I'd be careful who you offer that hand to, Mr. Manners. You might just lose it, isn't that right, Lindsey?" Lindsey, refusing to be baited, responds, "There's worse things to lose, aren't there?" ("Reunion" 2.10). Both Angel and Lindsey undergo bodily suffering, believing that the stakes are higher. Here, Lindsey has remade himself so that physical torture, far worse than losing a hand, cannot touch his core identity. This is still largely defined in relation to Angel, however, and to Wolfram & Hart.

"I WANT YOU, LINDSEY"

Both Season 2 and Season 5 also highlight sexuality as a problematic area for Lindsey, something that forges a further affinity with Angel. When Darla is resurrected by Wolfram & Hart, Lindsey begins to form an "unhealthy" attachment to her (according to Holland in "Reunion"), something that undermines his usual cool behaviour, and that brings about both tension and cooperation with Angel. Like Gatsby, success to self-made man Lindsey is not simply a matter of material wealth or status. It is also about getting the girl, another form of measuring success through personal fulfilment as well as through competition. Both Lindsey and Angel are obsessed with Darla but as Kaveney notes, Lindsey's feelings are also inflected with "a struggle to possess something which is Angel's" (66). Lindsey persistently defies Wolfram & Hart to help Darla, even after she is turned into a vampire again. Unrequited love is always about exposing a vulnerability, and Lindsey becomes more sympathetic as this lack of control over his desires is revealed. Holland comments, "You allowed yourself to be ruled by your emotions" ("Darla" 2.7) but when Lindsey sings his song of loss in Caritas on gaining his second new hand, the lyrics proclaim that he does not feel a thing ("Dead End"). Feeling works emotionally *and* physically, as demonstrated by the already-quoted exchange over Lindsey's lack of feeling in his plastic hand.

Both Lindsey and Angel suffer unfulfilled love as well as physical abuse. Darla's own obsession and her history with Angel/us make it unlikely she will ever accept Lindsey, despite his liminal status. Meanwhile, Angel believes he can never consummate love physically for fear of losing his soul, as happened with Buffy in Season 2 of *Buffy the Vampire Slayer*. This ends in an ironic reversal. Wolfram & Hart's plan may be to play on Angel's weakness by having Darla seduce him and bring back Angelus, but in this case Angel gets to have sex *without* losing control of who he is, while Lindsey never gets the girl and *his* identity is thrown into crisis. When Lindsey finds out that Darla and Angel have had sex, he is consumed by jealousy and takes it out on Angel physically, distancing himself from his lawyer self and becoming, as Michelle West puts it, "primal Lindsey... the man beneath the suit, the man beneath the ambition, the person that Wolfram & Hart can't—quite—obliterate" (99). Stereotypes of the working class usually include unbridled sexuality and violence, both physical appetites (see Spike's performance of these, for example); here one stands in for the other.

Lindsey wears a white sleeveless undershirt (the type often referred to as a wifebeater) under his lumberjack shirt, a visual allusion not only to other blue collar American heroes like *Die Hard*'s John McClane (1988), but also to Angel himself, who wears a white singlet in training scenes that focus on his body. Clothes combine with the vintage pick-up truck to show Lindsey's "roots" here, presenting him as the "urban cowboy" he reappears as in Season 5. The cowboy/country element, while loosely implied rather than concretely defined, invokes a rugged and physical masculinity. Lindsey's brand of country music, likewise, connotes raw emotional expression, again a more primal state usually concealed behind the slick lawyer's game face. In one sense both physicality and emotional expression (through violence or song) work to suggest that this is the "real" Lindsey, authenticating this version of subjectivity and masculinity. In Caritas, as Janet Halfyard notes, "Lindsey is the only character who does not sing karaoke" rather "he brings his guitar along and sings a song apparently of his own composition... enhancing the sense that what he sings is genuinely felt" (par. 12). Lindsey's unrequited desire for Darla (who leaves both him and Angel), as much as his evil hand issues, are what cause him to leave Wolfram & Hart and L.A. to try to "find himself" again.

The triangle with Darla and Angel, of course, fulfils another function. It displaces the homoerotic tension between Angel and Lindsey onto an outwardly heterosexual relationship that allows them to interact closely, a frequently adopted narrative structure, as Eve Kosofksy Sedgwick has noted of many narrative structures. Alyson R. Buckman applies this model and explains how "the conquest of Darla is just one more example of their homoerotic competition with each other," observing that the triangle is "a displacement of Lindsey's potential desire for Angel" (71), so that Lindsey's obsession with Darla derives from his obsession with Angel. When the two plot strands of "Dead End" converge, Lorne's description of it "all coming together in a beautiful buddy movie kind of way" underlines how Lindsey and Angel are positioned as an odd couple, leading us to expect the conventional resistance then acceptance arc, as well as sublimating homoeroticism in homosociality. That this happens in Caritas, identified by Stan Beeler as queer space, further underlines the homoerotic element. McCracken notes how Angel himself is "reposition[ed] as a homoerotic object in his own series" (117) and Lindsey plays a key role in doing so.

In Season 5 this is raised a power. Lindsey positions himself as a worthy adversary for Angel in "You're Welcome": "You, me, fight to the death." However, Angel identifies this as just a performance (of masculinity, of heroism), "First time we ever met, you put on a show," discounting the authenticity of Lindsey's position. Physical contact via fighting is accompanied by constant banter typical of an antagonistic flirtation. Lindsey visibly compares Angel's sword with his own knife and jokes, "Oh well, it's not the size that matters, big guy. It's how you use it," and transforms the knife into a sword to match ("You're Welcome"). Eve is Lindsey's sexual partner, though she is well aware that she is not the center of his attention. (As Buckman also notes, Eve functions as the female point in another homoerotic triangle). "It all comes back to Angel, doesn't it?" she asks plaintively in "You're Welcome," "He's still the center of your universe." Lindsey's "No, baby, you are," is as unconvincing to her as it is to the audience ("You're Welcome"). However, while Lindsey is confident that Eve is "one of the few things in [his] life [Angel] didn't get his mitts on" ("Not Fade Away" 5.22), regular viewers know that she conceals her own magic-induced sexual fling with Angel (in "Life of the Party" 5.5) and it is possible that Lindsey is only using Eve as his insider in Wolfram & Hart. Initially on his return, Lindsey calls himself "Doyle" and makes contact with Spike, hoping to engineer rivalry between the two vampires with souls. He picks Spike up in a bar and sets him up with a small apartment. Here, too, Angel is part of the triangle, but this time the triangle overtly comprises three males and while Doyle is invoked as a dead hero, his name also reminds us of another male bond, one that Doyle openly admitted sometimes verged on sexual attraction ("I Fall to Pieces" 1.4). The sexual tension between Angel and Lindsey culminates in a memorable exchange from "Not Fade Away" when Angel persuades Lindsey to fight against the Circle of the Black Thorn. Lindsey concludes, "If you want me, I'm on your team," only to have Angel reply, "I want you, Lindsey," pause and admit, "I'm thinking about rephrasing that" ("Not Fade Away").

"YOUR COMPETITION HAS BEEN VICIOUS, DESTRUCTIVE AND—HEALTHY"

At the end of "Blind Date" Lindsey and Angel are visually conflated (see Abbott, *Angel* 30): Lindsey looks out over L.A. from his new office at Wolfram & Hart and the shot dissolves into Angel looking out over the city. Lindsey spends most of his time on the show remaking himself in relation to Angel, trying to forge a relationship between them, either as a worthy adversary or a perfect partner. He is slightly redundant in both these roles by the end of Season 5 because Spike takes them on and the attraction-repulsion dynamic of both their relationships with Angel is similar. In the end, Lindsey nominally becomes part of the team but he is still an outsider. While we see Angel, Spike, Gunn, and even Lorne returning to the past that made them who they are and taking strength from it in "Not Fade Away," Lindsey's and Wesley's last hours are stuck in the present. The death of Fred leaves Wesley with little hope and, until the last moment, he refuses to revisit the past, seeing in it only the future he has lost. Lindsey spends his time with Eve, who lies to him, and his past has failed to make him what he wants to be: someone important to Angel. When the two fight during "You're Welcome," both reminisce about their previous encounters and in this final stage Lindsey's past with Angel is the only thing he values, demonstrating his inability to define himself any other way (rather like Holtz). When Lorne shoots him in the series finale, his last words are disappointment that he still means nothing: "You kill me? A flunky? I'm not just—Angel—kills me. You don't—Angel—" ("Not Fade Away").

Both Spike and Angel/us were Big Bads in *Buffy*; Lindsey is described by Kaveney as a Little Bad in *Angel* (67). In one sense, Lindsey is belittled by his arc; Angel even remarks to Cordelia that all he has done in "You're Welcome" is beaten a "Tiny Texan." Yet, without Angel, Lindsey would not be a villain; without Lindsey, Angel would not be a hero. Each reflects the other. This is often articulated explicitly, as during Season 2 when Angel himself slides into amorality while Lindsey tries to do right because of his attraction to Darla. It is assumed that working for Wolfram & Hart makes Lindsey evil, but Angel and the others end up *being* Wolfram & Hart in Season 5. In this sense, as Kaveney suggests, reinvention is always morally dangerous because it unsettles any lasting definition of a character as good or evil (as almost all the regular characters attest). Wolfram & Hart's management believes that Lindsey and Lilah's competition is good for the firm (in the section title above, "Dead End" 2.18); likewise, Angel and Lindsey's competition, like Spike and Angel's, is "healthy" because it reinforces and extends the show's negotiation of masculinity and its challenges to conventional notions of the male hero. Lindsey/Doyle makes Spike a hero in "Soul Purpose"; Angel recovers his sense of himself as a hero by (physically) beating Lindsey in "You're Welcome," and then is brought back to heroic action by Lindsey's wake-up call in "Underneath." Lindsey dies a villain's death so Angel can continue to "go to work" as a hero.

Works Cited

Abbott, Stacey. *Angel*. Detroit, MI: Wayne State U P, 2009. Print. TV Milestones Series.

---, ed. *Reading* Angel: *The TV Spin-off with a Soul*. London: Tauris, 2005. Print.

Angel: *The Complete DVD Collection*. Region 2. Twentieth Century Fox, 2007. DVD.

Beeler, Stan. "Outing Lorne: Performance for the Performers." Abbott, *Reading* Angel 88-100. Print.

"Blind Date." 1.21. Writ. Jeannine Renshaw. Dir. R. D. Price. *Angel*.

"Blood Money." 2.12. Writ. Shawn Ryan and Mere Smith. Dir. R. D. Price. *Angel*.

Buckman, Alyson R. "Triangulated Desire in Angel and Buffy." *Sexual Rhetoric in the Works of Joss Whedon*. Ed. Erin B. Waggoner. Jefferson, NC: McFarland, 2010. 48-92. Print.

"Carpe Noctem." 3.4. Writ. Scott Murphy. Dir. James A. Contner. *Angel*.

"Darla." 2.7. Writ., dir. Tim Minear. *Angel*.

"Dead End." 2.18. Writ. David Greenwalt. Dir. James A. Contner. *Angel*.

"Dear Boy." 2.5. Writ., dir. David Greenwalt. *Angel*.

"Damage." 5.11. Writ., dir. Steven S. DeKnight. *Angel*.

Douglass, Frederick. "Self-Made Men." Lecture. 1872. <http://www.monadnock.net/douglass/self-made-men.html> Web. 13 May 2010.

"Epiphany." 2.16. Writ. Tim Minear. Dir. Tim Wright. *Angel*.

Geraghty, Lincoln. *Living With Star Trek: American Culture and the Star Trek Universe*. London: Tauris, 2007. Print.

Jowett, Lorna. "Plastic Fantastic: Genre, Technology, Science and Magic in *Angel*." *Channeling the Future*. Ed. Lincoln Geraghty. Lanham, MD: Scarecrow Press, 2009: 167-81. Print.

"Judgment." 2.1. Story by Joss Whedon and David Greenwalt, teleplay by David Greenwalt. *Angel*.

Kaveney, Roz. "A Sense of the Ending: Schrodinger's *Angel*." Abbott, *Reading* Angel 57-72. Print.

Halfyard, Janet K. "Singing Their Hearts Out: The Problem of Performance in *Buffy the Vampire Slayer* and *Angel*." *Slayage: The Online International Journal of Buffy Studies* 5.1 (2005): 45 pars. Web. 13 May 2010.

"Life of the Party." 5.5. Writ. Ben Edlund. Dir. Bill Norton. *Angel*.

McCracken, Allison. "At Stake: Angel's Body, Fantasy Masculinity, and Queer Desire in Teen Television." *Undead TV: Essays on Buffy the Vampire Slayer*. Ed. Elana Levine and Lisa Parks. Durham, NC: Durham U P, 2007. 116-144. Print.

"Not Fade Away." 5.22. Writ. Jeffrey Bell and Joss Whedon. Dir. Jeffrey Bell. *Angel*.

"Reunion." 2.10. Writ. Tim Minear and Shawn Ryan. Dir. James A. Contner. *Angel*.

"Smile Time." 5.14. Writ. Joss Whedon and Ben Edlund. Dir. Ben Edlund. *Angel*.

"Soul Purpose." 5.10. Writ. Brent Fletcher. Dir. David Boreanaz. *Angel*.

"To Shanshu in LA." 1.22. Writ., dir. David Greenwalt. *Angel*.

"Underneath." 5.17. Writ. Sarah Fain and Elizabeth Craft. Dir. Skip Schoolnik. *Angel*.

"War Zone." 1.20. Writ. Garry Campbell. Dir. David Straiton. *Angel*.

West, Michelle Sagara. "Why We Love Lindsey." *Five Seasons of* Angel. Ed. Glen Yeffeth. Dallas, TX: BenBella, 2004. 93-101. Print.

2.03
"The Shell I'm In":
Illyria and Monstrous Embodiment
Bronwen Calvert

Ideas and images of monstrous embodiment are strong in *Angel*, with its vampire hero and, as the series progresses, its variously "monstrous" supporting characters who occupy key places in the narrative (for instance, Doyle, Lorne, and Spike). Throughout the series, there is also a strong emphasis on monstrosity "embodied," in various ways, through female characters, most significantly with Darla (in Season 3) and Cordelia (in Season 4), and it is here that I situate Illyria. Although Illyria appears in just seven episodes (eight if the brief appearance at the very end of "A Hole in the World" [5.15] is included), this character creates a great deal of resonance and fascination for viewers and critics alike. Despite the fact that Illyria literally takes the place of beloved long-term regular Fred, viewer reaction to Illyria was very positive (see, e.g. City of Angel, Whedonesque discussions). That Illyria appeared only as the show was coming to a close seemed to add to viewers' fascination and speculation about aspects of the character,[1] and the character also immediately attracted critical comment (see Battis, Hudson). This character brings to the fore questions regarding monstrosity, the feminine/female, and aspects of embodiment; Illyria can be read as moving through different versions of monstrosity in an attempt to achieve a sustainable embodied self.

Barbara Creed's theories on what she calls "the monstrous-feminine" provide a useful starting point for an examination of Illyria, as Creed notes that:

"[D]efinitions of the monstrous as constructed in the modern horror text are grounded in ancient religious and historical notions of abjection—particularly in relation to the following religious 'abominations': sexual immorality and perversion; corporeal alteration; decay and death; human sacrifice; murder; the corpse; bodily wastes; the feminine body and incest" (8-9).

Certainly, we can begin to look at Illyria as a version of the monstrous-feminine, and the eruption of this monster into the narrative of *Angel* could be viewed as a kind of "murder" or "human sacrifice" involving "decay and death," "the corpse," "the feminine body," and "corporeal alteration." However, I see Elisabeth Grosz's work on female embodiment as particularly useful to a reading of Illyria's monstrous embodiment. In her "Notes towards a Corporeal Feminism" Grosz states that "the body is not inert or fixed. It is pliable and plastic material…" (3). Grosz puts forward two views of what she calls "corporeal subjectivities." Firstly, an *interior* view: she says, "the body can be approached, not simply as an external object, but from the point of view of its being lived or experienced by the subject" (Grosz, "Notes" 9). But there is also an *exterior* view, as she describes, "the corporeal… can be seen as a surface, an externality that presents itself to others and to culture as a *writing* or inscriptive surface" (Grosz, "Notes" 10). In *Angel,* the body that Illyria inhabits can be seen as (as Grosz puts it), a "site of struggle and resistance" (*Space, Time* 36) or "as a kind of *hinge* or threshold" (*Space, Time* 33). It can also be seen in terms like Rosi Braidotti's "teratological imaginary," which she defines as "[t]he monstrous, the grotesque, the mutant and the downright freakish" (156). As she explains, "the monstrous signifies the difficulty in keeping manageable margins of differentiation of the boundaries between self and other" (Braidotti 167); this is certainly relevant if we consider the way Illyria's existence is dependent on the body of an "other," Fred.

I concentrate here on some particular aspects of Illyria's monstrosity, beginning with Illyria's embodiment and with the powerful embodiment seen at first, particularly in "Shells" (5.16) and "Time Bomb" (5.19). I shall consider further developments in Illyria's monstrosity, first the notion of Illyria as an "essence" that inhabits a "shell," and then the ability to metamorphose into Fred. In many ways I am thinking of the initial version of Illyria as the more conventionally "monstrous," and of Illyria-as-Fred as a different kind of monstrous embodiment. So, I shall explore Illyria's monstrous embodiment as "site of struggle," as "threshold," and, finally, as a body that is "lived and experienced by the subject."

MONSTROUS BIRTH: INFECTION AND GESTATION

To begin with, the "site of struggle" for Illyria is Fred's body. Illyria's monstrous embodiment is a process described in terms suggesting both birth—"hatching" and "gestating"—and infection so that birth becomes conflated with sickness; for example, Fred describes her infection as "monster flu" and Lorna Jowett notes the way Fred's "transformation is medicalised" in the hospital room and the lab (26). In a process that recalls the primal scenes of *Alien* when Kane is fertilized by the alien egg inside a womb-like chamber, discussed by Barbara Creed as a version of horror dominated by the monstrous-feminine (18), Fred is "infected" by Illyria after touching the round, organic-looking carving on the top of the sarcophagus. Fred's "transgression"—touching something she shouldn't—opens her up to abjection, as her body decays, her skin "harden[s] like a shell," and she is "hollowed out"—made empty, recalling the "vessel" that Cordelia became to give birth to Jasmine ("A Hole in the World" 5.15). This parallel between Fred and Cordelia is made explicit in Angel's words: "I lost Cordelia because some thing violated her, crawled inside, used her up. No way in hell am I letting that happen again" ("Shells" 5.16).

Illyria is "born" after scenes in which death, birth, and femininity are linked. A large proportion of "A Hole in the World" features what Stacey Abbott has called Fred's "Victorian death" ("Death Becomes Her")—tucked up in bed listening to Wesley read from the children's book *A Little Princess*. During these scenes we are in Fred's own bedroom; the setting emphasizes Fred's "down-home" image and there are many signs of female domesticity in this environment, with its homely objects including piles of laundry, photographs, floral-patterned furniture, Fred's patchwork quilt and old toy rabbit. This room also appears softly lit (although the scenes commence in daylight hours), and the red walls set up some womb-like imagery which chimes, in a disturbing fashion, with the images of "hatching" and monstrous birth that have already been evoked. When Illyria finally succeeds in cracking out of this "shell" (metaphorically speaking) there are some definite changes, both in the room itself (where the soft light and red color slowly fade away as Fred comes closer to death) and in Fred's now-dead, but not lifeless, body, which becomes overlaid with the blue tints that are characteristic of Illyria. [2]

MONSTROUS EMBODIMENT 1: "I AM MY POWER"

However, perhaps contrary to expectation, Illyria's "birth" does not mean that a demonic entity emerges *from* Fred's body. Rather, Illyria puts on Fred's form in order to gain existence as a new being that is described by Joss Whedon as "regal and scary and different" (Commentary). There is an exaggerated *performance* of embodiment in the initial stages of Illyria's new life. Illyria's is an impervious body that does not even react when Wesley hits it with an axe; yet this is also a body that is not quite in control of itself.

Illyria's movements, at first, are awkward and tentative, quite puppet-like, accentuating the otherness of this re-animated body, as though Illyria is now wearing Fred's body like a kind of suit or structure. Paradoxically, this body is also incredibly strong and is further strengthened when Illyria sucks power out of the sarcophagus.

This moment with the sarcophagus is interesting to me in how it sets up Illyria's embodied portrayal for the rest of the season, and here I also see gender problematised in the appearance of a nominally masculine or even genderless character (a "god") as a leather-clad female. Throughout Team Angel's attempts to stop Illyria's rebirth in "A Hole in the World" (5.15) this particular monster is consistently called "a god" and referred to as "it." This continues into "Shells" when Wesley shows the team a picture of Illyria "in *its* native form." Yet in his next sentence he refers to "*her* army of doom" (my emphasis) and very quickly Illyria is consistently "she" and "her," not "it" or "him." The exception is Knox who insists, "I'm with the King" towards the end of "Shells" (5.16) (and it is Knox's slip when he says "it" instead of "her" that tells Gunn something is wrong in "A Hole in the World" 5.15). When I began working on these episodes, I was determined to call Illyria "it," as I believed that this reflected Illyria's monstrosity and god-status most accurately. However, as I have examined the character's state more closely I am persuaded to put forward a reading of Illyria as "she," as I shall explain.

When Illyria draws power out of the sarcophagus, the body that is displayed is, at the same time, ungendered (now inhabited by the god-essence) *and* excessively feminine. To prepare to draw out this power, Illyria rips off the skirt and blouse that Fred's body was wearing and this naked body is then clothed or coated in a leather-like armor or carapace that covers it completely except for throat, face and head. So, this god-like "it" is now wearing extremely body-revealing clothing; this tight-fitting armor is even more revealing than Fred's often-skimpy outfits. Despite the fact that the front of this "suit" or "armor" can be viewed as a breastplate, and so adds to Illyria's impervious power, it also manages to accentuate the breasts, and recalls the similar revealing-yet-concealing suit worn by Seven of Nine in *Star Trek: Voyager*. I note that as Illyria alters the physical appearance of Fred, with a leather-covered and blue body, Amy Acker likewise alters the viewer's perception of this character as she transforms Fred's light, perky Southern tones into Illyria's stern and low-pitched vocal register. However, the version of embodiment that is demonstrated here is a specifically *female* embodiment, and it seems to me that calling Illyria "she" further emphasises the monstrosity of this embodiment. Illyria can only exist because "it" inhabits Fred's body. "It" has become "she," although "she" is no longer *Fred*.

There are some subtle and not-so-subtle links between Illyria's god-like power and the feminized or sexual power of *her* appearance in Fred's body. Many of these links come through Knox, who calls Fred "the most beautiful, perfect woman I ever met" but says that Illyria is "beyond flesh, beyond perfection" ("Shells" 5.16). As he introduces himself as Illyria's "Kwa Hazan," "priest, servant and guide in the world," Knox recalls his early sightings of Illyria portrayed in the "forbidden texts," adding, "my mom thought I was looking at porn" ("Shells" 5.16). And this link becomes far more prominent in his appreciative reaction as the naked Illyria draws power out of the sarcophagus. (It is worth nothing, I think, that Knox's connection with Illyria is also through the body; she is able to locate him because he has sewn "the sacraments" under his own skin ("Shells" 5.16).

Illyria's "monstrosity" is initially demonstrated through her embodied strength, the great physical power that is now animating Fred's body. Illyria beats Team Angel in more than one fight—most spectacularly killing the entire team in one version of the future presented in "Time Bomb" (5.19). "Shells," the first episode in which she appears, includes spectacular fight scenes together with special effects, which allow Illyria to show her powerful superiority. The first encounter sees her facing down an armed response unit and throwing Angel out of the building for good measure.[3] Later, she takes on and beats Angel, Spike, and Wes despite the guns and swords they attack with. This particular scene shows Illyria at the height of her powers. The way she fights displays her "monstrosity" and shows the difference between her abilities and those of Team Angel. We can note that, throughout this scene, her face remains expressionless and her breathing is inaudible—these small factors further emphasise her inhuman nature. Moreover, she is able to beat Angel, Spike, and Wes with no weapons except her body, which she is now able to move fluidly and sparingly, gaining most effect from minimal movement. This is a long way from the puppetlike movements shown when Illyria first emerges. I see this as an early stage of the process by which Illyria's monstrous embodiment begins to shift away from the idea that she occupies a "shell" towards a different, lived embodiment that, finally, creates a hybrid identity.

MONSTROUS EMBODIMENT 2: "WHO IS WINIFRED BURKLE?"

The idea of body as shell is strongly emphasized in early scenes of Illyria's existence. This serves to highlight the separation of the "inside" and the "outside" of Illyria's body—the essence that is Illyria is distinct from the body that was Fred. As Illyria continues in her monstrously embodied existence, however, we can see in her struggles, as Braidotti puts it, "the difficulty in keeping manageable margins of differentiation of the boundaries between self and other" (167). For Illyria, at first, Fred's body is emphatically "other"; it is empty, or, as Illyria puts it, "Winifred Burkle is the shell I'm in" ("Shells" 5.16).

Illyria *itself* is only once seen as embodied, in the drawing Wes shows the team of "Illyria in its native form" which shows a large, tentacled monster ("Shells" 5.16). Otherwise, Illyria is referred to as an "entity" or an "essence." At this stage, we might see Illyria as representing a version of Cartesianism, summarized by Elisabeth Grosz as the idea of the body as "an instrument, a tool, or a machine at the disposal of consciousness," and as a passive "conduit" of information, "a circuit for the transmission of information from outside… a vehicle for the expression of an otherwise sealed and self-contained, incommunicable psyche" (*Volatile Bodies* 8). This seems close to Illyria's own notion of how her embodiment works. Illyria sees the body she inhabits as a "vessel" ("The Girl In Question" 5.20), a "shell," "this bag of sticks" ("Time Bomb" 5.19): something that imprisons her. She rages that, "It's too small, I can't breathe… There's not enough space to open my jaws. My face is not my face, I don't know what it will say" ("Underneath" 5.17), and after her power has been diminished she declares, "This fate is worse than death—condemned to live out this existence in a vessel incapable of sustaining my true glory. How am I to function with such limitations?" ("The Girl In Question" 5.20). Yet despite Illyria's insistence on the separation of her "essence" from the body or shell that is Fred, the two are fused and cannot exist otherwise. Illyria herself states quite early on that "I exist here"; although "here" would normally refer to a place, e.g. Los Angeles, Illyria's usage links to the body she inhabits ("Shells" 5.16).

Her timeshifting in "Time Bomb" (5.19) represents a breakdown between inside and outside, as Wes explains: "The fusion between her demon essence and her host's body seems to be deteriorating. It's as if the human part of her can no longer contain the demonic power within." This excess of power is also represented as embodied, however—Illyria feels the deterioration Wes describes as a physical spasm that seems to be located in her stomach. Illyria as "essence" is excessive, too much for a human body, and must be contained, controlled, and drained; this changes her physical power and means that her body is more firmly anchored in time and space. This "containment" or "domestication" can be read as a diminishing of her powers, (see Buckman 70), but I see this as a movement towards a different kind of monstrous embodiment. It appears that Illyria's essence and Fred's physical body are able to achieve a kind of balance and begin a new process of integration. This, I think, is signalled in "Time Bomb" (5.19) when Angel tells her to "be what you are" and to recognise that her continued existence must take a differently embodied form.

MONSTROUS EMBODIMENT 3: "IT'S A SIMPLE MODULATION OF MY FORM"

This new aspect of Illyria's monstrosity appears *after* her physical power has been lessened, and this suggests that it is a development related to her new and different monstrous embodiment. Although Illyria states early on that elements of Fred persist within her body—as what she calls "fragments of memory channeled into my function systems" ("Shells" 5.16)—and reveals one of these fragments at the end of "Shells," there is no hint in other episodes that Illyria can also metamorphose into a version of Fred. In "The Girl in Question," however, Illyria suddenly and startlingly "becomes" Fred to Fred's own parents, and this raises many questions about how, exactly, Illyria is animating Fred's body. With this metamorphosis, we see a complete physical transformation, including clothing, voice, and mannerisms: instead of the leather covering, this version of "Fred" wears a close-fitting top and short, rather schoolgirlish skirt; Illyria-as-Fred also adopts Fred's more high-pitched voice, her accent, and a more relaxed posture that includes casual hand gestures, and more mobile facial expressions. However, Illyria-as-Fred can also speak with Illyria's deeper voice and move in Illyria's more stilted fashion; the head-tilt is immediately characteristic ("The Girl in Question" 5.20). While Illyria apparently has access to Fred's "essence"—her memories, personality, and behaviour—in order to achieve this (see Masson 170, n. 46), the result is a kind of monstrously split *embodiment*.

Here, I think, we have a clear demonstration of what Grosz describes as the "pliable and plastic" body. Jes Battis calls Illyria "a living absence" (42) but this newer version of Illyria is also about *presence*. While Illyria-as-Fred strongly emphasizes the absence of the "real" body, this also demonstrates the monstrosity of the body that has replaced it and that continues to exist. As Spike tells Illyria, "Looking like Fred, for some of us, is the most devastating power you have" ("Power Play" 5.21). The monstrosity of Illyria-as-Fred is emphasized in the complex relationship that develops between Illyria and Wesley. Initially, Wes agrees when Illyria asks for his help in "learn[ing] to walk in this world" at the end of "Shells," and it is obvious from the succeeding narrative that his motives for doing so are largely owing to his love for Fred and his wish to keep even this imitation of Fred close to him. Wes is horrified, however, by the appearance of Illyria-as-

Fred and he flatly rejects her when she proposes to continue to explore this version of embodiment—"Be blue. Be anything. Just don't be her" ("Girl in Question" 5.20). However, Illyria-as-Fred begins to shift away from the early embodiment as "shell" plus "essence."

When Illyria first becomes embodied, her "essence" is clearly *not* human and not able to comprehend human emotions—so that, for example, Battis' reading of Illyria as "depressed" is almost impossible to reconcile with the evidence of Illyria's initial separation from human emotion. Yet Illyria herself says that she returns to Wes in "Not Fade Away" (5.22) "because I was concerned," naming an emotion that would have been completely alien to the Illyria of "Shells." And the shift in Illyria's being is neatly summed up by Jeffrey Bell's remark that "Illyria is finding herself falling for Wesley because it used to be inhabited by Fred" ("Not Fade Away" Commentary), a sentence that is fascinating in its gender-specificity for both Fred and Illyria. Critical writing on Illyria has insisted that Fred is the cause of this change, yet many critics locate Fred's influence in a purely spiritual realm. Battis states that, "There is something of Fred still inside of Illyria" (44) and Jennifer Hudson concludes that Illyria is "influenced by Fred's lingering psychical energy and humanity" ("She's Unpredictable"). Cynthea Masson focuses on Illyria's use of Fred's "essence," which is non-corporeal, linked to memory and consciousness. However, I disagree. What I see as key here is not a "spirit" or "essence" of Fred but a very concrete and present thing, her body. As Illyria herself states, she alters by means of "a simple modulation of my form"; in other words, this change is to do with her embodiment. It is through the body that Illyria is able to metamorphose into Fred, and through the experience of being embodied that she comes to manifest some recognizably *human* emotions (for example, concern and grief, most spectacularly in Wes's death scene in "Not Fade Away" 5.22). Illyria's transformation is intimately connected with her monstrous embodiment.

We can see this process of transformation very clearly through the different ways she experiences grief, which is, after all, a physical emotion, experienced through the body. When she first takes control of Fred's body, she insists she can feel Wesley's grief: "It's like offal in my mouth." This is echoed when she begins to need his help and asks, "Is there anything in this world but grief?" ("Shells" 5.16). Her excuse for appearing as Fred to the Burkles is also connected to the way she experiences grief. As she tells Wes, "Your grief hangs off you like rotted flesh. I couldn't tolerate it from them as well" ("Girl in Question" 5.20). But finally, after Wes's death she is able to say, "I am feeling grief for him… I wish to do more violence" ("Not

Fade Away" 5.22) and with this she demonstrates how much her monstrous embodiment has shifted over time.

Perhaps the best demonstration of this, and certainly the most satisfying from a viewer's perspective, is her final on-screen transformation from Fred into Illyria, when she defeats Cyvus Vail and avenges Wes's death. Here all the aspects of her embodied self are brought into play—including Fred, which, in a sense, allows Fred to be present in a defining moment of the series. So, we can see that Illyria has moved through stages in her monstrous embodiment. She has moved from the "King" Illyria that first emerged; she has struggled with the "boundaries between self and other" (Braidotti 167) and come to a version of embodiment that transforms "the corporeal... [into] a writing or inscriptive surface" (Grosz, "Notes" 10), presenting a hybrid identity,[4] somewhere between Illyria and Fred but not completely either. By the end of the series, she is firmly embodied, no longer inhabiting a "shell" but experiencing all facets of being within a body, and, finally, is accepted as a vital part of Team Angel.

Notes

1. Development of the character has continued in graphic novel form (*Angel: After the Fall* and *Spotlight: Illyria*), but these sources will not be covered here.

2. This red-to-blue shift also occurs in "Underneath" (5.17), where Wes' dream of Fred is filmed in red tones, but his awakening with Illyria is starkly and coldly blue.

3. This is available in the *Angel: Season 5 DVD Collection* as a featurette entitled "Choreography of a Stunt," highlighting both the visual impact of such scenes and the physicality involved in creating them.

4. As Robert Moore notes, this is a facet of the character that might have been further developed if the series had gone to a sixth season.

Works Cited

Abbott, Stacey. "Death Becomes Her: The Afterlives of *Angel*'s Women." Paper presented at Bring Your Own Subtext, University of Huddersfield. 29 June—1 July 2005.

Angel: *Season 5 DVD Collection*. Twentieth Century Fox Home Entertainment, 2006. DVD.

Battis, Jes. "Demonic Maternities, Complex Motherhoods: Cordelia, Fred, and the Puzzle of Illyria." *Slayage: The Online International Journal of Buffy Studies* 5.2 (2005). Web.

Bell, Jeffrey. "Not Fade Away" Commentary. *Angel*.

Braidotti, Rosi. "Teratologies." *Deleuze and Feminist Theory*. Ed. Ian Buchanan and Claire Colebrook. Edinburgh: Edinburgh UP, 2000. 156-72. Print.

Buckman, Alyson R. "Triangulated Desire in *Angel* and *Buffy*." *Sexual Rhetoric in the Works of Joss Whedon*. Ed. Erin B. Waggoner. Jefferson, NC: McFarland, 2010. 48-92. Print.

Creed, Barbara. *The Monstrous-Feminine: Film, Feminism, Psychoanalysis*. London: Routledge, 1993. Print.

Fuller, Nikki Faith. "Touch Me and Die, Vermin: The Psychoanalysis of Illyria." *PopMatters* Spotlight: Joss Whedon. 17 Mar. 2011. Web. 22 July 2011. Rpt. *Joss Whedon: The Complete Companion*, 199-205

"The Girl in Question." 5.20. Writ. Steven S. DeKnight and Drew Goddard. Dir. David Greenwalt. *Angel*.

Grosz, Elizabeth. "Notes towards a Corporeal Feminism." *Australian Feminist Studies* 5 (1987): 1-16. Print.

---, *Space, Time and Perversion: Essays on the Politics of Bodies*. London: Routledge, 1995. Print.

---, *Volatile Bodies: Toward a Corporeal Feminism*. Bloomington: Indiana UP, 1994. Print.

Haraway, Donna. "The Promises of Monsters: A Regenerative Politics for Inappropriate/d Others." *Cultural Studies*. Ed. Lawrence Grossberg, Cary Nelson, and Paula Treichler. London: Routledge, 1992. 295-337. Print.

"A Hole in the World." 5.15. Writ. and Dir. Joss Whedon. *Angel*.

Hudson, Jennifer A. "She's Unpredictable": Illyria and the Liberating Potential of chaotic Postmodern Identity." *American Popular Culture* (Mar. 2005): n. pag. Web. July 2007; Aug. 2011.

Jowett, Lorna. "Lab Coats and Lipstick: Smart Women Reshape Science on Television." *Geek Chic: Smart Women in Popular Culture*. Ed. Sherrie A. Inness. New York: Palgrave, 2007. 11-30. Print.

Masson, Cynthea. "'It's a Play on Perspective': A Reading of Whedon's Illyria through Sartre's *Nausea*." *The Literary* Angel: *Essays on Influences and Traditions Reflected in the Joss Whedon Series*. Ed. AmiJo Comeford and Tamy Burnett. Jefferson, NC: McFarland, 2010. 159-72. Print.

Moore, Robert. "Angel Goes Out in Style with a Marvelous Final Season." *Angel: Season Five* Amazon Review. Amazon.com 3 Nov 2004. Web. July 2007.

"Not Fade Away." 5.22. Writ. Jeffrey Bell and Joss Whedon. Dir. Jeffrey Bell. *Angel*.

"Power Play." Writ. David Fury. Dir. James A. Contner. *Angel: Season 5 DVD Collection*. Episode 21.

"Shells." 5.16. Writ. and dir. Steven S. DeKnight. *Angel*.

"Shells" review, City of Angel.com n.d. Web. 18 Apr. 2006.

"Time Bomb." 5.19. Writ. Ben Edlund. Dir. Vern Gillum. *Angel*.

"Underneath." 5.17. Writ. Elizabeth Craft and Sarah Fain. Dir. Skip Schoolnik. *Angel*.

Whedon, Joss. Commentary. *Angel: Season 5 DVD Collection*.

Whedonesque: Preview of *Angel Spotlight: Illyria* Comic Book Discussion Thread. Whedonesque.com 31 March 2007. Web. 25 July 2007.

2.04
The Three Faces of Anne:
Identity Formation in *Buffy the Vampire Slayer* and *Angel*
Don Tresca

Of all the characters that have appeared throughout the twelve seasons that make up *Buffy the Vampire Slayer* and *Angel* combined, one of the least understood and examined characters is Anne Steele. As far as screen time goes, she was a relatively minor character, appearing in only five total episodes, two on *Buffy* ("Lie to Me" 2.7 and "Anne" 3.1) and three on *Angel* ("Blood Money" 2.12, "The Thin Dead Line" 2.14, and "Not Fade Away" 5.22) scattered across four seasons of the two shows. Such a minor character can easily be dismissed on most shows, but the fact that the writers kept returning to the character of Anne, even years after her original appearance, demonstrates that something about the character continued to fascinate both the writers and the audience. For me, Anne is a fascinating character because, although she is tangentially touched by the supernatural occurrences that are regular events on both programs, she maintains her identity as a "regular" individual throughout. This ability to live a "normal" life (despite her first-hand knowledge of the existence of vampires, demons, and zombies) demonstrates her strength of character and also allows the writers to explore the elements of an important psychological concept outside the supernatural realm that permeates both series: the concept of identity formation. Naturally, all of the characters in both programs have strong identities that form as the shows progress, but Anne is different in that, while many of the other characters develop identities that are very much determined by their experiences with the supernatural, Anne's identity develops outside the supernatural realm: the way the identities of those young people watching the show develop.

Anne's experiments with various identities reflect the theories of three modern psychologists: Erik Erickson, James Marcia, and Raymond Lloyd Richmond. Modern theories about identity formation began in 1963 with Erik Erickson's groundbreaking work *Childhood and Society* in which he first coined the phrase "identity crisis." According to Erickson, identity is "a subjective sense as well as an observable quality of personal sameness and continuity, paired with some belief in the sameness and continuity of some shared world image" (qtd. in Cherry 3). For Erickson, an identity crisis frequently emerged during the teenage years as a "time of intensive analysis and exploration of different ways of looking at oneself" (qtd. in Cherry 2) during which individuals struggle between feelings of identity and role confusion.

In 1966, James Marcia expanded on Erickson's initial theories. He posited that the identity crisis discussed by Erickson eventually leads to an identity commitment, which occurs when the individual makes a firm commitment to an identity (social role or value) that he or she has chosen for himself or herself. After interviewing numerous adolescents and young adults for his study, he concluded that there are four separate "identity statuses" which make up psychological identity development (Marcia 551-58).

In *Helium* Jarred James Breaux briefly summarizes Marcia's four identity statuses. Marcia's **Identity Diffusion** is the status in which the adolescent has not yet experienced the identity crisis, explored any meaningful identity alternatives, or made any commitments to identity. Marcia describes **Identity Foreclosure** as the status in which the adolescent has chosen a commitment without undergoing an identity crisis or even having the opportunity to experience alternatives. The adolescent accepts what has been chosen for her or him by parental figure(s), and often identifies with and emulates the choices of the same-sex parent. Thus, the mechanic's son becomes a mechanic and inherits his father's garage; the pediatrician's daughter becomes a medical doctor. Marcia explains the **Identity Moratorium** status as a brief period of delay in which the adolescent is on the verge of his or her identity crisis but still cannot decide to make a commitment. He or she experiments with different identities, roles, and life philosophies, searching for a compatible identity on which to commit. Finally, Marcia posits that many—but not all—reach **Identity Achievement**. This status occurs after the period of identity moratorium and after the adolescent has undergone the identity crisis. After exploring various roles, the adolescent decides on a life identity for himself/herself (Breaux pars. 2-6).

Marcia was very adamant that these four statuses were not stages that every individual went through in a strictly sequential process and that people throughout their lifetime would fluctuate within the statuses as new circumstances arose to challenge the commitments they have made in their lives. Numerous decisions and commitments are made throughout an individual's life to help determine who that individual will be (Breaux pars. 2-6).

A third psychological researcher, Raymond Lloyd Richmond, challenged both Erickson's and Marcia's claims about identity formation in a 1997 article in *Psychology Guide* in which he argues that all identity is a "fraud" (7), that an individual's identity is only "whatever you 'think' you are [but] is, ultimately, nothing but a vague approximation of what you really are. And what you really are is revealed [only] in discrete moments of genuine encounter with your inner life" (Richmond 9). Richmond stated that people reveal their true identities only during moments of the "unexpected," when they are less concerned with what will "look good" than what is truly in accordance with the nature of the individual's "inner identity" (13). Richmond believed that individuals created "false public identities" to avoid facing their "inner identities" which are frequently dark and ugly and that many psychological conditions (such as depression and phobias) were nothing more than symptoms of individuals' fear and rejection of their true identities (14).

The character of Anne demonstrates all of these psychologists' theories of phases of identity in her five appearances in *Buffy* and *Angel*, and finally achieves a life identity all her own. Anne's first appearance on *Buffy* is in the episode "Lie to Me" (2.7) in the show's second season. At the time of this episode, she is known as Chanterelle (thus referring to herself as an elegant type of mushroom, a fungus). Here, Chanterelle is trapped between two different identity statuses, foreclosure and moratorium. Although we in the audience do not know it at the time of the episode "Lie to Me," clearly the "Chanterelle" identity represents, for Anne, one in a long series of identities that she is experimenting with in an attempt to find an identity to which she can commit. "Lily" (as Anne identifies herself in a later episode) tells Buffy that "Chanterelle" was part of her "exotic phase" and before that she was known as "Sister Sunshine" (thus a beautiful but non-corporeal light) while following "this loser preacher." The audience never learns her true name since she refuses to answer Buffy's question of "What do they call you at home?" (*Buffy*, "Lie to Me").[1] Her trying-on of identities is a clear sign of identity moratorium. But this particular identity is also one of foreclosure, as described by Marcia, one which she does not choose so much as desperately seize in the hopes of gaining a permanent identity commitment and of finding an identity that will make her part of a larger social group rather than a lonely, isolated individual. Here she is concerned more with what will look good to the others (the very definition of a "fraud" identity, as described by Richmond) than in making an informed decision. Even when Angel attempts to force her into seeing the true nature of the identity she is seeking, she refuses to listen, telling Angel he "doesn't have to be so confrontational about it. Other viewpoints other than yours may be valid, you know" (*Buffy*, "Lie to Me"). In the aftermath of Angel's conversation with Chanterelle, Willow seems to parrot Richmond's theory about identity choice in her response to Angel's comment about the vampire wanna-bes ("they're children making up bedtime stories of friendly vampires to comfort themselves in the dark"), saying, "Is that so bad? I mean, the dark can get pretty dark. Sometimes you need a story" (*Buffy*, "Lie to Me").

The subsequent vampire attack on the Sunset Club at the end of "Lie to Me" and Chanterelle's near-death at the hands of Spike (only to be saved by Buffy) breaks her free from the foreclosed identity of vampire-wannabe, and she runs as far away from Sunnydale as she can, to the streets of Los Angeles. When Buffy next meets her in "Anne," the first episode of Season 3, Chanterelle has changed her name to Lily (the name of a flower, but again a name/identity that was chosen for her, this time by her boyfriend Rickie). She is still floundering in search of a committed identity (her homelessness is symbolic of this lack of direction in this regard), but she is beginning to show signs of committing. The tattoos she and Rickie get indicate her willingness to commit and connect with another individual—one of the key components of Marcia's functional identity, along with the occupational role and fundamental beliefs and values (Cherry 4). When she loses Rickie, she seeks out the one person she knows that helped her through her previous "identity crisis," Buffy. However, Buffy, during this time, is undergoing an identity crisis of her own. Having recently killed the man/vampire she loved, Angel, she abandons her identity as Slayer and takes on a new identity, Anne.[2] Since "Anne" is actually Buffy's middle name, however, it indicates that her new identity and old identity are still tied together; therefore, "Anne" represents, for Buffy, a return to the diffuse identity. As Anne, Buffy spends her days drifting between working her menial job as a coffee-shop waitress and moping in her apartment. When Lily eventually confronts her, she denies her former identity and seeks to avoid Lily since she serves as a constant reminder of the life she has tried to escape. But when Buffy finds herself trapped in a hell dimension and confronted by a demon threatening to strip her of any identity whatsoever, she makes a choice. Buffy chooses to fully accept her identity as the Slayer and refers to herself, for the first time, as "Buffy the Vampire Slayer" (*Buffy*, "Anne" 3.1). Unlike earlier in the series when Giles forces her to accept the Slayer identity (a clear indication of a foreclosed identity), here Buffy herself makes the choice during the moment of crisis, moving her identity as "Slayer" from a foreclosed identity to a committed identity.

Lily also makes a choice at the conclusion of the episode. She chooses to take on the identity of "Anne" (even if borrowed, a traditional personal name and not an abstraction, a fungus, or a flower). However, she does ask Buffy's permission, indicating her continued search for validation in her latest identity. The identity of Anne offers Lily another element of functional identity, as described by Marcia, that of an "occupational role": Buffy's job at the diner. For the first time (apparently, since we are never given a complete view of Anne's background prior to "Lie to Me"), she has an identity that she has chosen for herself. How well she commits to that new identity will be seen in subsequent episodes of *Angel*.

In "Blood Money" (*Angel* 2.12), the audience learns that Anne is now Anne Steele (her self-chosen name of strength) and is running a homeless shelter, the East Hills Town Center. This new incarnation of the character is much stronger and more forceful than the character initially seen on *Buffy*. Anne has now found something to commit to, an ideal, the protection of the runaway teens of Los Angeles. This commitment to an ideal is the final functional aspect of the committed identity (Cherry 4). Anne's commitment to this new identity and all that it entails is evident throughout the episode. The first scene showing her in the shelter shows the strength of her character. Unlike the meek girl of "Anne," here she is confrontational, refusing to jeopardize the safety of her charges by allowing a drunk teen into the center. However, her identity is not yet as fully established as she would believe. When Angel confronts her with his accusation about Wolfram & Hart's plans to steal the fundraising money from the charity ball they are organizing for the shelter, Anne reacts in much the same way she did to his accusations against the vampires in "Lie to Me." She is so naïve (despite her claim to Lindsey that she is not) that she initially believes in the good nature of those using her, even when confronted with evidence to the contrary. Unlike in "Lie to Me," when she almost literally has to die before her eyes are opened to the darkness of the world around her, here she makes a conscious decision not to blindly trust but rather to accept that people may not always have her best interests at heart.

In this episode, we see the conflict between Marcia's theory of identity (with Anne being representative of that theory) and Richmond's theory of fraudulent identity (with Lindsey and Wolfram & Hart being representative of that theory). Despite Wolfram & Hart's best efforts to keep the dark nature of their identity secret from Anne, she is able to see through their deception and do the right thing, despite the inherent danger to both herself and her committed identity as operator of the homeless shelter. This seems to indicate the strength of Marcia's theory of committed identity over Richmond's theory. Anne has her commitment tested further when she discovers that Angel has betrayed her as well, having forced her to make the choice to risk herself and her shelter in his own personal vendetta against

Wolfram & Hart. Their confrontation directly after the charity ball is revealing: her anger with him over his willingness to destroy her identity and the well-being of those in her care shows how committed she is to her chosen identity. His comment to her that "that's the difference between us—you still care" indicates that he knows that she will continue to remain committed to her ideals despite all that has happened to her. The final scene of the episode, where Angel delivers the "blood money" to Anne, reinforces this notion. When she notices the actual blood on the money, she tells him, "It'll wash," showing that she has come to accept the darkness that comes with her committed identity (*Angel*, "Blood Money"). She is fully dedicated.

Two episodes later, in "The Thin Dead Line" (*Angel* 2.14.), Anne's commitment to her new identity is complete. She refers to the teens in the shelter as "my kids" and the staff of the shelter as "my regular staffers." She demonstrates her "true identity" (according to Richmond) when she engages in a "genuine encounter" with dangerous outside forces. As stated earlier, Richmond argues, that an individual's "true identity" is revealed during when the individual faces a confrontation during which he or she is more concerned with personal safety and life preservation than what "looks good" to others. Anne confronts the street gangster Jackson when he muscles his way into the shelter without any concern for personal safety, only backing down for fear of his starting trouble within the residence. She later uses a baseball bat to beat off the zombie cops attempting to enter the shelter, despite the inherent danger of the situation; only a timely intervention from Cordelia saves her. Clearly, Anne is now much more concerned with the safety and well-being of her charges than with her own personal safety.

Richmond also discusses what he calls "the pride-love dichotomy." He states that many individuals in the helping professions (medical, teaching, social work, psychology, etc.) are motivated less by the need to help those less fortunate and more by the:

"need to project a certain image of oneself into the world, an image such as a "peacekeeper" that in itself might derive from a childhood role within a family system of conflict. In such cases, the caretaking becomes not much more than *an exercise of authority and power over the patient… In other words, many persons "give" in order to advertise an identity and to maintain a position of power.* This is pride, not love, because love empties itself of worldly desires through service, in order to give selflessly. Pride, however, makes giving into a form of bribery, in order to get something bigger in return" (Richmond 18-19, italics in original).

Clearly we see in Anne's willingness to put herself in harm's way to protect the teens in her shelter that she is acting from a vantage point of love and not pride. She, in fact, acts more heroically in this episode than the show's supposed hero, Angel, does in "Blood Money," when he acts more with pride than love. It is obvious that Angel is helping Anne not out of compassion or a desire to "help the helpless" but instead simply because helping Anne would allow him to gain some measure of revenge against Wolfram & Hart. Anne even references his motivation in her comment to the Angel Investigations team at the beginning of this episode when she tells them that Angel tried to help her a few weeks earlier although it turned out he was only doing it "to screw over this law firm" ("The Thin Dead Line").

Anne's strength of identity is further intensified in the final episode of *Angel*, "Not Fade Away" (5.22), when Gunn seeks her out on what he believes will be his final day. During the final season of the show, Gunn has literally sold his soul to the dark forces by allowing Wolfram & Hart to manipulate his mind/his identity in order to gain advanced legal knowledge and prove himself to be more than just "the muscle" of the team. Unlike Anne, whose identity is governed by love, Gunn has allowed himself to be ruled by pride. In his mistaken belief that his role as protector is not enough to validate his existence, he hopes to get more recognition as a valued member of the team if he is viewed by others in a more "respectable" position. This pride, and then the fear of losing this new "identity," leads inevitably to Fred's death.

In the scene with Anne, Gunn tests her commitment to her "identity" by suggesting a scenario that reflects psychologist J. B. Rotter's concept of "locus of control." Rotter defines the term as the psychological "place" in which a person puts responsibility for the outcomes of various life situations. A person's "locus of control" may be external (determined by forces outside of her control) or internal (determined by her own personal actions and life philosophies) (Richmond 20). Gunn asks Anne, "What if I told you it doesn't help? What would you do if you found out that none of it matters? That it's all controlled by forces more powerful and uncaring than we can conceive, and they will never let it get better down here. What would you do?" Without skipping a beat, Anne replies, "I'd get this truck packed before the new stuff gets here." ("Not Fade Away" 5.22)

Anne does not allow an external locus of control to determine her life, for those who have an external locus of control "live in a perpetual feeling of victimization, always blown about by the whims of the world around you" and instead lives by an internal locus of control in which "you love [and] you lay down your life for others" (Richmond 21). Anne has now fully committed to her identity. She is no longer dependent on others (as she was in the *Buffy* episodes) to determine her value and is not willing to be downtrodden and victimized by others. She is fully her own person now. The development of Anne's character from "Lie to Me" to "Not Fade Away" represents an everyday, non-supernatural identity formation not unlike that of many of the show's more supernaturally-related characters, such as Buffy, Angel, Spike, and Wesley. Each of them moves away from identities largely defined by others towards identities forged by their own beliefs, personalities, and life philosophies. The character of Anne shows those young people in the audience that they each have the strength of character to form their own identities and become committed to those identities fully in their own lives. Anne's chosen surname, Steele, symbolizes the power and strength of that commitment. And with that powerful and strong commitment to identity should come an equally powerful and strong commitment to your fellow man, to a love of humanity unblemished by personal pride. In that way, and many others, Anne Steele becomes Joss Whedon's prime example of humanity at its very best.

Notes

1. However, the shooting script of "Lie to Me" lists her original name as "Joan Appleby" (Ozzman 2).
2. Ironically, not only did Anne take her name from Buffy, but also in the episode "Tabula Rasa," 6.8 in *Buffy*, Buffy briefly and unwittingly took Anne's original name: Joan (from the "Lie to Me" shooting script) (Ozzman 10).

Works Cited

Angel *Collector's Set: Seasons 1-5*. Twentieth Century Fox Home Entertainment, 2007. DVD.

"Anne." 3.1. Writ. and dir. Joss Whedon. *Buffy*.

"Blood Money." 2.12. Writ. Shawn Ryan and Mere Smith. Dir. R.D. Price. *Angel*.

Breaux, Jarred James. "James Marcia and the Four Identity Statuses Theory." *Helium* (20 Aug. 2009). Web. 15 Jan. 2011.

Buffy the Vampire Slayer: *The Chosen Collection: Seasons 1-7*. Twentieth Century Fox Home Entertainment, 2005. DVD.

Cherry, Kendra. "Identity Crisis—Theory and Research." *About Psychology* (2005). Web. 15 Jan. 2011.

"Lie to Me." 2.7. Writ. and dir. Joss Whedon. *Buffy*.

Marcia, James. "Development and Validation of Ego Identity Status." *Journal of Personality and Social Psychology* 3 (1966): 551-58. Print.

"Not Fade Away." 5.22. Writ. Jeffrey Bell and Joss Whedon. Dir. Jeffrey Bell. *Angel*.

Ozzman. "Anne Steele." *Buffywiki* 30 Dec. 2010. Web. 15 Jan. 2011.

Richmond, Raymond Lloyd. "Personality and Identity: Identity and Loneliness." *Guide to Psychology.com* (1997). Web. 14 Jan. 2011.

"The Thin Dead Line." 2.14. Writ. Shawn Ryan and Jim Kouf. Dr. Scott McGinnis. *Angel*.

2.05
"Touch Me and Die, Vermin!":
The Psychoanalysis of Illyria

Nikki Faith Fuller

The events in the *Angel* Season 5 episode "Time Bomb" (5.19) unveil former hell goddess Illyria's humanistic development. Her path toward becoming more human is tedious, much like the path humans face in their daily struggles. While her dreams are more grandiose than those of *mere* humans, she becomes a relatable character experiencing a very humanlike existence. *Angel*, which captures the culture and language of present day Los Angeles, meets the important criterion for using psychoanalysis (the study of psychological behavior) to evaluate a text: it conveys the sense of a lived experience (Parker 314). The psychoanalytic theory developed by psychoanalyst Jacques Lacan offers a framework for understanding the process Illyria undergoes. Lacan posits that "all individuals are fragmented: No one is whole" (Bressler 129). His theory focuses on "understanding the human psyche" by looking at the individual's "divided self" (Bressler 131).

Lacan's theory is specifically relevant to Illyria's experiences as she endures the two key elements to his theory, lack and fragmentation. According to Lacan, lack stems from a desire to return to the Imaginary Order. In fiction, the Imaginary Order is typically represented as a place where an individual feels whole. Illyria's Imaginary Order is the world as it once was when she ruled it eons ago. The desire for the unattainable Imaginary Order results in fragmentation (a breakdown of the psyche) in the Real Order, which consists of the physical universe and all the things within it (Bressler 129). The Real Order is the reality in which any person exists, whether he or she wants to or not. For Illyria, the Real Order is modern day Los Angeles, which to her is both limiting and suffocating. She must reconcile her loss in order to overcome lack and fragmentation in the Real Order.

In literature, both language and profound experiences such as death are often used to depict fragmentation. Both of these devices illustrate Illyria's fragmentation throughout the episode "Time Bomb." Language is used as a "symbolic system which provide[s] a communicational bridge" between individuals, allowing them to make sense of things after events have occurred (Parker 307). This helps the characters and the viewers process the events around them as the actions in the episode force Illyria through a painful physical and mental fragmentation that will lead to her death.

In the earlier episode "Shells" (5.16) Illyria initially sought her Imaginary Order by visiting her ancient temple, which is now empty and desolate. With her army gone, she resides at Wolfram & Hart as a lost god without a kingdom or followers. Wesley Wyndam-Pryce has accepted the task of being Illyria's guide to this world, the Real Order. As author Jes Battis discusses in his book *Chosen Families in* Buffy the Vampire Slayer *and* Angel, when Illyria first asks Wesley to be her guide, she is not concerned about "human attachments." Her initial interests are "entirely clinical" (Battis 127). However, in "Time Bomb" Illyria's powers become unstable, and she is on the brink of destruction. As she enters the state of mind that Lacan identifies as fragmentation, she starts to demonstrate human emotions.

In the opening of "Time Bomb," Illyria has left this dimension to retrieve Angel's colleague Charles Gunn, imprisoned in another dimension. When Wesley informs Angel of her act, they agree she is unpredictable, and Angel concludes she is not doing this for the benefit of their team. As they argue over their attitudes toward Illyria, Wesley explains that she has the "power of a god" while Angel claims all she has now is the "ego of a god." Wesley reminds him that she was once ruler of the world, and acknowledges that she will never accept any of them as peers. Angel concludes that Illyria remains at Wolfram & Hart only because it "reeks of influence" ("Time Bomb").

The statements both men make reflect the very struggle Illyria is experiencing in her divided self: she is forced to live in the Real Order while longing to return to the Imaginary Order. Upon her return with Gunn, Illyria calmly holds him by the throat, acknowledging that he is precious to the others. Considering her understanding of the world, Wesley agrees they owe her a debt for returning him safely. Illyria accepts this and releases Gunn from her deathly grip. She never requests repayment, as she is satisfied by the power she holds in attaining indebtedness. Despite the fact that she has no kingdom to rule, she is still a god demanding authority. As Wesley reflects, everyone looks "so tiny to her" and she is "monumentally self-possessed" ("Time Bomb").

During a sparring session with Spike, Illyria reflects on the powers she once held and believes she still holds. In theory, Spike is testing her skills, though Angel later comments that she is testing all of them. As they spar, Illyria tells Spike "adaptation is compromise." Reflecting on her ancient history, she tells Spike that the world "shuddered, groaned, [and] knelt at [her] feet" when it met her. She concludes that "to never die and conquer all" is winning ("Time Bomb"). Illyria's desire to return to the Imaginary Order is fierce. She refuses to accept her fate of existing as a lesser being in a world so changed. However, the dialogue Illyria continuously uses to voice her purported power clearly shows how she is desperately struggling to hold onto it. If she still had such power, it would be unnecessary to remind people of it. Her language demonstrates how adamant she is against adapting.

The stage Illyria is experiencing is much like the mirror stage children reach when they begin to identify parts of themselves with what is reflected in a mirror (Olivier 3). Though Illyria is centuries old, her human development is in very early stages. This mirror stage is representative of a promise of wholeness and unity, though it actually has the effects of alienation (Olibier 4). Metaphorically, Illyria's memory of the power she used to have is her mirror, and the only way she sees herself. Individuals lack improvement beyond the mirror stage until they grasp the Real Order and no longer seek the Imaginary Order (Olivier 6, 15). In order for Illyria to avoid fragmentation and fulfill the lack she is experiencing, she must accept the Real Order.

As Spike and Angel discuss Illyria after the sparring session, she suddenly experiences her first shift in time. Initially, the other characters are unaware of this occurrence, and neither Illyria nor the viewers understand what is happening. In a later conversation, Wesley explains to Spike and Angel that Illyria is unstable and overloading. The fusion that exists between her demon essence and her host body is deteriorating. The human part cannot hold the power of the god within and will cause her to self-destruct violently and soon. Illyria continues shifting out of linear progression, becoming more uncertain and concerned about her future. By Lacan's principles, the future is based on human interaction. If an individual "loses the capacity to make sense of the past and future," he or she faces a symbolic life or death situation, potentially leading to inner fragmentation (De Grave 436). The events in "Time Bomb" illustrate Illyria's mental (inner) and physical (outer) fragmentation as she shifts through time and begins to destruct physically. She is trying to make sense of events and hold onto her ancient power as she literally faces death.

Relying on dialogue to make sense of what is occurring, Illyria questions Wesley about some of the constructs of this world such as days and time. Battis describes Illyria as "coldly analytical" with "a strange curiosity for human affairs" (113). However, Illyria's curiosity begins to demonstrate that she slowly is developing human emotions and attachments. As Wesley explains time to her, she suddenly accuses him of being her betrayer. In the previous episode, "Origin," Wesley shattered the Window of Orlon, a mystical orb that contained altered elements of the past, in hopes of undoing Illyria's infection of Fred.

The distinction that Illyria did not viciously murder Fred is important to remember in understanding her character structure. She infected a body, as a virus does, for her own preservation. In "Origin," Wesley too acted out of self-interest and a sense of emotional preservation: he explains he was willing to destroy Illyria if it would bring back Fred. When he questions Illyria on whether or not his betrayal stings her, she explains that "betrayal" was once a neutral word that was "as unjudged as water or breeze". After a pause, she explains that what bothers her is the fact that she is bothered. Wesley explains that her statement "sounds very close to human" ("Origin").

ILLYRIA IS DEFENSIVE WHEN WESLEY COMPARES HER TO A HUMAN.

Illyria is defensive when Wesley compares her to a human. She reflects that humans are merely "motes of dust" that die so quickly after their birth that they might as well have not lived. Battis explains that Illyria's "outsiderness" concerning humans is not simply a function of her being "icy," but stems from a sense of "loneliness" (115). Without anything bowing down before her, Illyria is confused and isolated. This cynical moment with Wesley is representative of that hidden feeling. According to Lacan, people find their identities based upon their interactions with others (De Grave 437). Her coldness toward Wesley here is an expression of her inner frustration at developing human traits. She despises the change she recognizes in herself and denies it for some time, still fixated upon her Imaginary Order and previous state of being.

As the conversation between Illyria and Wesley continues, she informs him that his opinion of her "weighs less than sunlight" ("Origin"). It's clear by her tone that his betrayal has greatly upset her. When she ruled the world, she would have never considered the opinion of a lesser being. In telling Wesley that his opinion means nothing to her, she is ultimately trying to convince herself of that fact. Her desire for the Imaginary Order is so strong that she continues denying herself any attachment to the Real Order.

Illyria experiences another time shift during this conversation. First, she moves forward to a moment when Wesley and other members of Angel's team appear to be killing her. Then she moves backward to a conversation with Angel and Spike. Upon returning to the present moment, she angrily tells Wesley that he tried to murder her again and storms out of his office. ("Origin"). Her dramatic exit assures viewers of her growing emotional attachment toward Wesley. She is not merely upset that there seems to be a scheme to plot her murder, but that Wesley specifically is a part of it. He has disappointed her again. Lacan's theory indicates that any expectations of behavior between individuals are grounded in relations that are a distinct characteristic of human interaction. Illyria is closer to human in this moment of anger than she would ever want to admit.

Illyria had never experienced any emotions toward anyone before she met Wesley. As Battis points out, this sense of being bothered is a part of being connected to something. Though it seems Wesley is guiding Illyria through this world by teaching her about humans, he is actually showing her how to become human. For reasons neither of them can articulate, he continues to teach her, and she continues to learn (Battis 130). This relationship, which continues through Wesley's death in the series finale, is pivotal to her development.

After experiencing her first two shifts in time, Illyria believes Angel is doing something to her and confronts him about it. She explains to him that it is absurd to do anything besides bow to her will. Her verbal attack on Angel differs from the one she just had with Wesley. When she accuses Wesley of betraying her, she takes it very personally. Yet when she believes Angel is trying to kill her, she demands authority by defending her position as a god. With Angel, she is only concerned about her own preservation and displays no concern whatsoever for his attitude or actions toward her on a personal level.

In the final events of "Time Bomb," Angel, Wesley, Spike, and Lorne meet in order to destroy Illyria before her unavoidable physical self-destruction annihilates all of them and a large part of Los Angeles. Wesley has a generator designed to draw out Illyria's essence and has falsely informed Angel it will kill her. Illyria and Angel then begin shifting through time together, and she continues to accuse him of being responsible for what is happening and continues to try to assert her power over him. Though Angel is not responsible for the time shifts, he is tired of hearing her ranting about the days when she ruled, and he definitively declares that this is now his kingdom. Illyria claims that she is "the god-king of the Primordium, Shaper of Things." As they argue about power, Illyria assuredly declares that "reign persists from victory" and "if you want to win a war you must serve no master but your ambition" ("Time Bomb"), giving Angel something to consider in his war with Wolfram & Hart.

After this series of time shifts, Illyria comes back to the present several times. When Wesley is finally able to explain to Illyria that he is not trying to kill her, she objects to his use of the generator, claiming that she "would rather be [the] titanic crater" that her explosive destruction would cause than be similar to human. She states that she possesses so much grace and "was the immaculate embodiment of rule," when her body overloads and she again begins to fragment and die. Angel tells her that holding onto what she used to be, her Imaginary Order, is destroying her. Her final statement through her breaking body is that she blames it on the "weakness" of the human species.

Before Illyria can die, Wesley uses the generator to draw out some of her power. She collapses to the floor, and when Wesley offers her a hand she harshly replies, "Touch me and die, vermin" ("Time Bomb"). Confused and terrified, Illyria unwillingly completes her transformation from a higher being into one resembling human (Battis). She is now forced to endure in the Real Order after struggling so greatly against its confines in pursuit of her Imaginary Order. Her physical fragmentation is prevented, but she is left to contend with her newly developing emotional view of the world in a diminished physical form.

As Wesley and Angel discuss Illyria outside of the training room, she lies on the floor motionless where she has collapsed. Through the remaining moments of the episode, she never gets up. Angel decides to let her to live in this less powerful form, telling Wesley that he realizes she may be a resource after all. The comments that Illyria made to Angel as they moved through time together helped him to recognize his position as leader of his team; he begins to see how he must use his own power in order to avert the upcoming Apocalypse (Abbott 68).

After "Time Bomb," Illyria continues to explore and experience the world around her. Though she will never lose her desire to rule the universe and be treated like a god, she embraces the Real Order and recognizes she will never ascertain her Imaginary Order. In different social interactions, an individual can become anything ranging from a mother to an enemy or even to a goddess (De Grave 443). The ability to shift personas is part of what makes people human. This ability is demonstrated with Illyria when she takes on the personality of Fred to explore the relationship with her parents, who do not know their daughter is gone. Until we die, we are always in the process of "becoming" ("The Girl in Question" 5.20). While Illyria has an understanding of who (or *what*) she was and wants to remain, she finally accepts change under new circumstances. Operating within the Real Order offers her the opportunity to become, and not remain simply what she is.

All of these events culminate into what become the final actions of the *Angel* series. The significant change and development in Illyria is powerful not just for her as a character, but in the ripple effect it has for the closure of the series. Throughout "Time Bomb" and the following episodes, Wesley continues to help Illyria adjust to this world, ultimately instilling a sense of humanity in her. Illyria's emotional tie to Wesley compels her to fight on Angel's side in the final battle where she proves a valuable asset.

Works Cited

Abbott, Stacey, ed. *Reading* Angel: *The TV Spin-off with a Soul*. London: Tauris, 2005. Print.

Angel *Collector's Set: Seasons 1-5*. Boxed set. Twentieth Century Fox Home Entertainment, 2007. DVD.

Battis, Jes. *Blood Relations: Chosen Families in* Buffy the Vampire Slayer *and* Angel. Jefferson, NC: McFarland, 2005. Print.

Bressler, Charles E. *Literary Criticism: An Introduction to Theory and Practice*. 3rd ed. Upper Saddle River, NJ: Prentice Hall, 2003. Print.

De Grave, Dieter. "Time to Separate the Men from the Beasts: Symbolic Anticipation as the Typically *Human* Subjective Dimension." *AIP Conference Proceedings* 718 (2004): 435-44. Print.

"The Girl in Question." 5.20. Writ. Steven S. DeKnight. Dir. David Greenwalt. *Angel*.

Olivier, Bert. "Lacan's Subject: The Imaginary, Language, The Real, and Philosophy." *South African Journal of Philosophy* 23 (2004): 1-19. Print.

"Origin." 5.18. Writ. Drew Goddard. Dir. Terrence O'Hara. *Angel*.

Parker, Ian. "Psychoanalytic Narratives: Writing the Self into Contemporary Cultural Phenomenon." *Narrative Inquiry* 13.1 (2002): 301-15. Print.

"Shells." 5.16. Writ. and dir. Steven S. DeKnight. *Angel*.

"Time Bomb." 5.19. Writ. Ben Edlund. Dir. Vern Gillum. *Angel*.

2.06
Interview with Alexis Denisof

Laura Berger

You might have first met Alexis Denisof as the bumbling Watcher Wesley Wyndam-Pryce in *Buffy the Vampire Slayer*, or as the self-proclaimed "rogue demon-hunter" in *Angel*, or later in *Angel* as the hero manqué (and if you didn't shed tears during "Not Fade Away," well, you just aren't properly ensouled), or in *Dollhouse* as Senator Daniel Perrin who wanted to save all the dolls, or in *How I Met Your Mother* as that woman-chasing news anchor, or you might meet him as Benedict in Joss Whedon's *Much Ado*. Wherever you see him, he is a memorable actor. Just before Christmas 2011, Laura Berger interviewed him in a telephone conversation about these and other roles.

PopMatters: When asked to identify your favorite moments on *Angel*, your answer was "Pretty much every time Wesley fell over in Season 1," explaining that you loved the "physical humor." Obviously Wesley undergoes a dramatic transformation in the course of the series and goes to some very dark places. In your own words, he was "a temporary character" and, as such, you "weren't expected to go deeply into this human being." As Wesley became more complex, you had the opportunity to dig deeper. That being said, did you ever miss Old Wesley?

Alexis Denisof: I did miss the Old Wesley, which is why it was so much fun to return to the old Wesley in "Spin the Bottle," the episode [*Angel* 4.6] that Joss [wrote and] directed where we're all affected by a spell and revert to our teenaged selves, or late teenaged selves. I think all the actors enjoyed retreading some of the naïve and awkward ground of our characters' early years. The progression and development of Wesley was one of the things that I most enjoyed about playing the character. Because of its long time span, we were able to progress slowly with his evolution—never knowing exactly where it would end up, but feeling that it was moving in an interesting and organic way. That made it exciting for me as a performer and I think interesting for the writers as storytellers.

PM: When Wesley shifts from light to dark, his behavior changes, but his physicality seems to as well. He's obviously a more competent fighter, but did you consciously alter his body language in less overt ways?

AD: I did adjust his body language, yes. I felt that some of his emotional insecurities were being resolved as he grew up and grew older. As he put things behind him, he developed a different relationship with his body. As he changed internally the manner in which his body expressed his being changed too, in some subtle and some not-so-subtle ways, just as all of ours do. I'm sure that if you were to look back at your high school photo you would cringe a little bit: you see that old hairstyle or that old outfit. That was sort of the task—to keep him alive in the process of growing. His body language changed, his appearance changed, and at some point I think he got laser surgery because the glasses disappeared. [Laughs] We probably should have done a funny bit with contact lenses.

PM: Did you do any of the stuntwork?

AD: Yeah, I did—the stuff that I was capable of doing. We had a great stunt team led by Mike Massa, who is a fantastic coordinator, stunt man, and one of the nicest guys. We all had fantastic stunt doubles. For most of the run of the show, Mike Gaines doubled me. He really nailed Wesley's physicality. There were times when for safety reasons, or level of complexity, that the stunt team executed the stunts. I did some of the more basic and straightforward stuff: most of the gun stuff, and the close hand-to-hand. But falls, jumps, big stunts, car crashes, etc. that's all Mike. That dude is tough as nails!

PM: Did fans react differently to you according to your present incarnation on *Buffy* or *Angel*?

AD: I think that their reaction seemed to change, yes. In the early days of Wesley from *Buffy*, I would get some pretty funny and irritable reactions from fans. That show had a fan base by then, and there was a long list of favorite characters, and of course when Wesley came into that show, he wasn't designed to be entirely loveable. I had some pretty funny encounters with people in those days. Some fans enjoyed him and got the humor of him, and some didn't. As we got further into *Angel*, and the longer people had time to get to know him and become involved in the show, there was much greater affection and interest in the character and therefore, I suppose, greater affection for me by association.

PM: When you say that there was initially a negative reaction, did people actually approach you on the street and say nasty things, or…?

AD: There's one experience in particular that sticks out in my mind. We were shooting at the high school late in Season 3 of *Buffy*. There were a lot of kids still around, in and out of their classes. There was a corner of the school blocked off for us but we had to pass through some of the school ground to get to our base camp. I think I was with my future wife [Alyson Hannigan, who played Willow] at the time, walking to the trailers when some kids passed and recognized her. They were so excited to see Willow, then noticed me and said, "Oh, oh my God. You're that guy." Then, lost for words, they let out a sound that went something like "Ewwwww! You're just ewwwww!" by which it was clear they meant "Yuck."

PM: Joss Whedon fans are widely recognized as being deeply passionate about his work. Are you now, or have you ever been an avid fan of a particular cultural text—perhaps a geeky one?

AD: I'm a little older than a lot of fans of the shows, so my generation was watching *Star Trek* on TV in syndication. I was certainly obsessed with that. When *Star Wars* came along I was equally obsessed with that. *Blade Runner* is definitely on my top 5-movie list, maybe top 3. In terms of literature, I don't know if it's geeky, but I was deeply into *The Lord of the Rings* trilogy. I devoured Philip Pullman's *His Dark Materials*. And I remember way back that I had a phase where I read anything by Ursula K. Le Guin. As I got a little older and was watching later night TV, although it's kind of cheesy, I always got a kick out of *The Twilight Zone* and *Outer Limits*.

PM: Who other than Joss influenced your work on his series the most?

AD: David Greenwalt, for sure, and later on Tim Minear and Drew Goddard. I had close relationships with them. Joss and David were the main people I would have conversations with about Wesley: the evolution of the character, and the choices that we were making about him.

PM: Wesley's kiss with Cordelia in the Season 3 finale of Buffy has to be the one of the most awkward kisses in television history. How did you and Charisma Carpenter do such a good bad job?

AD: It's either good luck or good talent: take your pick. Charisma is a beautiful and attractive woman so it was a cruel irony that I had to perform a bad kiss with her. I think we sort of found the key when we started clashing teeth, which I can still feel in the sense memory of my dental bridge as I think about it, and it sends a shiver through me. We laughed at that kiss and had a lot of fun.

PM: You appeared as a series regular or recurring character in three of Joss's shows: *Buffy*, *Angel*, and most recently, *Dollhouse*. Your involvement in these series spanned from 1999 to 2009. What do you make of the evolution of Joss's work?

AD: That's a big question! I think as Joss matures in his own life, that allows for his storytelling to be broader, richer, and deeper. He is an incredible talent, and Joss on his worst day at age 14 is still a writer, director, and producer that I'd love to work for. When you're talking about Joss Whedon, you're talking about a titan in the creative arts. It's been a great pleasure to be near him through these years of his growth, both on TV and in film, and I certainly count myself as hugely fortunate to have had the chance to watch him work and benefit from him including me in his work.

PM: You have said that your "respect for educational institutions was kind of ground into you by virtue of going to an Ivy League boarding school." Are you aware of the fact that Joss's narratives have been the subject of countless scholarly articles and books? There's even a biannual Whedon academic conference.

AD: Yes, I had heard that there were college level classes that were giving credit for studying Joss's work. Sign me up! I'd like to go to that class.

PM: My Master's thesis was on *Buffy*!

AD: The truth is, you guys probably know way more about it than I do.

PM: You were involved in it! You created it. We can only interpret. You're a part of it. That's magical!

AD: My job was just to put my coffee cup down, and say the lines in the right order, and fall over in a funny manner.

PM: No, no, no! The editor of this book, Mary Alice Money, paid you a better compliment than I will be able to come up with on the spot, so I'll read what she wrote about you in an email she sent me: "I can't think of another actor who has morphed from naively dangerous doofus all the way to sexy sinister hero—all in the same role and all believable."

AD: Thank you. That's a beautiful compliment. I was very lucky to have the chance to play Wesley and be part of the journey that he took. And it's very gratifying that viewers also enjoyed that journey. I know Joss and everyone else that worked on those shows is very gratified by the interest and passion of the fans; all of his projects are exciting and interesting to work on, but that isn't where it ends for us or him. He cares so deeply about what his fans feel about the material he's creating. It means a lot to all of us that there is this passion, and love, for his work.

PM: To return to your own schooling, I'm assuming that your education focused on much more traditional texts than Joss's. How do you feel about the relationship between educational institutions and popular culture, and more specifically Joss's work?

AD: Well I can only speculate, because at the time I was in the education system it was before Joss was being studied. In principle, I totally and entirely approve of popular culture being examined and considered and discussed by intellectuals and by non-intellectuals. Culture is a link that binds us all. It's a common thread through our society. Differences from one culture to another, or within a single culture, those are all fascinating similarities and differences. To find the voices that are shaping culture, and dig deeply into the message that those voices are carrying, is, I think, a worthy endeavor. As a consumer we each are responsible for what messages we are consuming and re-broadcasting. So it is important to look deeply and consider the kind of culture you want to support.

PM: You were deprived the opportunity to study *Star Trek* in high school.

AD: [Laughs] Well, I studied it after hours. But seriously, as I'm sure you know, that show broke a lot of boundaries culturally. Its sci-fi genre allowed it to cloak some challenging messages.

PM: You recently filmed *Much Ado About Nothing*, a modern retelling of Shakespeare's comedy, written and directed by Joss. The movie was filmed in a very short period of time in Joss's backyard, if I'm not mistaken. Did it feel like a summer camp, or even a reunion because you had previously worked with a number of the other actors and crew?

AD: It did have that feel, yes. But it also was hard, fast work. As enjoyable as it was to be in that atmosphere with friends and old colleagues, there was still a lot to do in a short amount of time. I think it was a joy for everyone involved. Yes, Joss's backyard was one of the primary locations, but so was the rest of the house, inside and out. In fact, I hope that the house is on the cast list because it's certainly a very important character in our version.

PM: Can you tell us a little bit about *Little Women, Big Cars* and other future projects?

AD: I've done a couple of web-series that I found interesting and exciting. One from Warner Digital called *H+*. This series will particularly appeal to fans of the sci-fi and fantasy genre. It's set slightly in the future and it follows the aftermath of a partial population annihilation due to a computer virus. I have a small but significant role in the series. I loved the story and liked the people involved. We shot it in Chile. I hope it turns out to be something we're all proud of. I haven't seen any of it yet other than the trailer. The other web series is called *Little Women, Big Cars*. In this instance, it was a role and a relationship that interested me. The series revolves around four women trying to balance home life and their friendships with each other. It weaves in and out of the friendships and romances of four female characters, and I'm the husband to one of the primary characters. There are a lot of gently humorous—I hope humorous—and also real domestic scenes that I think people will relate to. Again, that's another project I haven't seen edited together yet. I think there's a screening coming up so I'll be able to talk about it more after that. My lascivious news anchor, Sandy Rivers has been back in action on Aly's show [*How I Met Your Mother*] this season too. And that has been huge fun. It's rare to play a character that has no filter.

PM: You met your wife, Alyson Hannigan on the set of *Buffy*. Were your co-workers surprised when you told them about your relationship? Did anyone have a particularly memorable reaction?

AD: I don't know if people were that surprised. They could see that we were having a lot of fun together and developing a friendship, and we were certainly flirting. I think the only person that was concerned was my friend Tony [Anthony Stewart Head, Giles] who I had known for quite a few years before *Buffy*; he's the only person I knew going into that job. He was also very close friends with Aly. So I think he was…

PM: Protective?

AD: He was protective of both of us, and selfishly concerned: "If my two friends fall in love with each other and it all goes wrong, what do I do?" He was the only one who spoke up. I think he told one, or both of us, not to date each other We've been teasing him about it ever since.

PM: I assume that when you see casual fans of the series, ones who might not realize that you and Aly are married, they are totally shocked and delighted that the actors who play Wesley and Willow are married in real life and have a child.

AD: There are three categories. There are those who approach us, knowing we are married, and are thrilled to get a two for one; they're delighted to meet and talk to Willow and Wesley. Then there are those who are thrilled to have spotted Aly, and in the middle of asking her to take a picture, they notice me say, "Oh, it's you too!" and then they say, "Well then, can I take a picture with both of you?" Then there's the third category, they recognize Aly, have no idea who I am, and ask me "Would you mind taking a picture of me with her?"

PM: I must say, I love your family Halloween costumes. [For some examples, Google "Alyson Hannigan Alexis Denisof Halloween."] They are amazing!

AD: Well, I can't take any credit for that. The only credit I can take is for agreeing to do it. My wife is passionate about Halloween—every aspect of it, including dressing up. I'm actually starting to like it too, I must say. It's rubbing off on me. It's a lot of fun.

PM: This book offers a comprehensive survey and analysis of Joss's career as a whole. You've referred to Joss as a "brave storyteller and brave writer." Can you expand on that?

AD: I think he's willing to take on personally difficult issues, both for himself and human beings at large, and face them with honesty and humor. I think he makes hard choices as a writer. He'll sacrifice some of his favorite pieces of the story for the overall good of the story, and I think that takes courage. He will fight for the story and the people in it. He will justify everyone as much as possible in his story, and make them real, and poignant. He has a way of making you care about everybody that he's writing. He will go to the mat against the studio or the Powers That Be in order to preserve as much of his original intention as is possible, and in his line of work, that's not easy. I think that he makes brave casting choices. He's loyal, obviously; I would be the first to say that because I've benefitted so much from his loyalty. Whether I had worked with him or knew him as a friend or not, I'd be a fan of his work, but knowing him, having worked with him, makes me an even bigger fan.

PM: That's a lovely compliment.

AD: Well, it's just true.

2.07

"The Strength and Conviction to Lose So Relentlessly":
Heroism in *Angel*

Ian Mathers

"Evil happens without effort, naturally, fatally; Good is always the product of some art." —Charles Baudelaire, "The Painter of Modern Life"

"In a fight between you and the world, bet on the world."
—Franz Kafka, "Aphorism 52"

"Not Fade Away," the final episode of *Angel*, ends the show with (most of) the Angel Investigations (A.I.) team facing down a literal army of demons. They have succeeded in their master plan, described by other-reformed-vampire Spike as "Kill 'em all. Burn the house down while we're still in it" ("Power Play" 5.21). They have eliminated the Circle of the Black Thorn, and dealt a serious blow to the Wolf, the Ram, and the Hart. Crucially, this army turning up on their doorstep isn't a sudden reversal of fortune; Angel and his team were fully aware that their plan carried with it this kind of retribution.[1] Everyone there knew exactly what they were getting into when they helped temporarily curtail the evil that they had been struggling against for so long. But their impact is just that, temporary. And these are the lines that end the series:

Spike: And in terms of a plan?
Angel: We fight.
Spike: Bit more specific?
Angel: Well, personally, I kinda wanna slay the dragon. Let's go to work. ("Not Fade Away" 5.22)

Bravado is bravado, of course (that's a literal dragon Angel is referring to), and last stands have a rich history in heroic tales; but you will struggle to find a last stand in recent pop culture that's as Quixotic as the one at the end of *Angel*, which is practically willed into being by our protagonists. As with most plot and character developments on TV shows, there's an element of real-world practicality to the decision—this particular plot probably happened when it did because the show was ending—but it's fully in keeping with the character of the members of A.I. and the way heroism is presented on *Angel*. So far, all of Joss Whedon's series follow to some extent the same set of ideals and ethics, but *Angel* takes those ideals further than on *Buffy the Vampire Slayer*, *Firefly*, or even the grimly pre-apocalyptic *Dollhouse*. Here, heroism is presented as something that you do, not despite the possibility of failure, but because of the certainty of it, to scorn that certainty.

Now, obviously any portrayal of goodness or heroism that states that one should only be good or heroic when one is rewarded for it (or, in a more basic sense, when one will not be punished for it) is lacking, but what *Angel* does is present the converse case in the starkest possible sense. Not only is hero-ing a generally thankless job, one that seems doomed to fail on the larger scale of existence, but the universe doesn't give you any credit for it. If one were to appeal to the Higher Powers that apparently exist in *Angel*'s universe in the face of some disaster that one was good, had done good, had helped others, one would receive the same answer the Higher Powers give to every question and plea in the series: silence.

Over the course of the series Angel and his team win many times on a smaller scale, and just before the armies of Hell engulf them[2] they win a fairly major victory. But it would be hard to argue that they've actually made that much of a difference. As Angel himself puts it in "Power Play," the penultimate episode of the series, "We're in a machine and that machine is going to be here long after our bodies are dust. The senior partners will always exist in one form or another because mankind is weak" (5.21). Again, this pessimistic worldview is *part* of his pitch to his friends and comrades to, essentially, give up their lives in the service of one last stab at the heart of evil. Whenever I watch that speech, I think about Grant Morrison and Frank Quitely's *JLA: Earth 2*, where Morrison posits that the regular DC Comics universe is metaphysically predisposed towards good, and Earth 2, where only the heroic Alexander Luthor opposes the Crime Syndicate, is similarly predisposed to evil. Ultimately, to save both universes, the JLA has to let evil win, at least on Earth 2. After they send Luthor back to a universe where he can never truly succeed, there's a moment of conversation:

Wonder Woman: I keep thinking about Luthor. Alone, doomed to fail. I don't know if I could have the strength and conviction to lose so relentlessly. Do I try too hard sometimes?

Batman: No one tries too hard to make the world better, Diana. (Morrison and Quitely)

The members in A.I. don't have the deck stacked against them quite as unfairly as Luthor, but enough is set against them that it's not wrong to think that one of their major heroic qualities is simply their refusal to give up. And that refusal is not based around a belief that they will be rewarded, so much as a faith in the rightness of the attempt, regardless of result. Earlier in the series, Angel manages to save recently-ex-cop Kate Lockley from her suicide attempt, prompting them to talk about what really matters:

Kate: I just couldn't... My whole life has been about being a cop. If I'm not a part of the force, it's like nothing I do means anything.

Angel: It doesn't.

Kate: It doesn't what?

Angel: Mean anything. The greater scheme. The big picture. Nothing we do matters. There's no grand plan, no big win.

Kate: You seem kind of chipper about that.

Angel: Well, I guess I kinda... worked it out. If there's no great, glorious end to all this, if nothing we do matters, then all that matters is what we do, because that's all there is, what we do. Now. Today. I fought for so long. For redemption, for a reward, and finally just to beat the other guy, but I never got it.

Kate: Now you do?

Angel: Not all of it. All I want to do is help. I want to help, because I don't think people should suffer as they do. Because if there's no bigger meaning, then the smallest act of kindness is the greatest thing in the world. ("Epiphany" 2.16)

Crucially, this conversation takes place in an episode where Angel pulls himself out of a tail spin. Before "Epiphany," he had been attempting to fight evil through becoming more evil himself, culminating in the end of the previous episode, "Reprise," where he sleeps with his sire Darla, thinking that the sex will turn him back into the soulless Angelus. When he wakes up with soul intact, it instead triggers him into changing his ways; he gave in as much as he possibly could to the undertow of evil, and all it did was make him feel horrible, alienate him from his friends, and eventually wake him up to the necessity of action. That this course of action leads to Angel revoking, in "Not Fade Away," his claim to the Shanshu Prophecy that would reward him with humanity again, the ultimate example of putting his money where his mouth is, is only fitting. That the sacrifice is in service of an effort that he knows will bring the forces of evil, the same ones he could get away with defying in a less major way for years longer, immediately and crushingly down on himself and his friends, is what really makes that last stand striking. Angel and company *could* exist in this world and do good in a smaller way; they just *won't*.

In *Angel*'s universe, the belief that people shouldn't suffer as they do is a necessary and sufficient criterion for actual heroism. As both Angel and theoretically evil but human ex-attorney Lindsey MacDonald say in "Power Play," "Heroes don't accept the world the way it is."[3] One of the elements that makes the final season of *Angel* so thematically rich and dramatically compelling is that A.I. throws its lot in with demonic law firm/bringers of the apocalypse Wolfram & Hart (a move that all of the members of the team have their reservations about, of course). When they do so, they come perilously close to accepting the world the way it is. Their arguments are the arguments that pragmatism always makes: Someone is going to get Wolfram & Hart's resources, why not the good guys? If they join Wolfram & Hart, can't they work to mitigate the evil of the firm and maybe even influence it towards some form of good? Wouldn't the best way to counter Wolfram & Hart's plans be to be present on the inside?

Interestingly enough, this plotline comes right after the A.I. team narrowly defeated Jasmine, the evil god who wanted to take over the world and bring... world peace. Yes, Jasmine's true form was rather more "evil" looking than the face she presented the world, and that world peace was going to be enforced by mind control, but having Wolfram & Hart congratulate you for averting it is going to give most heroes pause. But ultimately, our heroes had to choose free will over tranquilized happiness,[4] just as they have to choose rebellion against accommodation. Past a certain point, staying with Wolfram & Hart is making things worse, not better. And that slide from resistance to accommodation is subtle; as Lindsey says about the apocalypse, "What'd you think, a gong was gonna sound? Time to jump on your horses and fight the big fight? Starting pistol went off a long time ago, boys. You're playin' for the bad guys. Every day you sit behind your desk and you learn a little more how to accept the world the way it is" ("Underneath" 5.17). In a sense, that acceptance is also a slide towards the idea that there should be some reward for heroism. Don't Angel and his friends deserve some support in their fight? They've worked so hard for so long, shouldn't things be getting *easier*, not harder? Don't they deserve the resources, the relative rest, that Wolfram & Hart provide?

Sure they do, but deserve has nothing to do with it. That's Connor's problem. Well, actually his problem is that he's the kind-of son of two vampires, who was raised in a hell dimension by one of Angel's most intractable, implacable, and unreasonable enemies, then brought to L.A. to meet/kill his father, which he almost does, and is then seduced by his surrogate mother-figure when she's possessed by an evil god, in order to father the body that evil god will use to take over the world. So certainly he's got some reasons for what he does in the series. But it's not coincidence that so many different forces in *Angel* are able to use and abuse Connor by playing into his belief that he's special. On some level, Connor thinks he's destined for great things, and that he deserves commensurate rewards. Angel, his father, doesn't buy into or tolerate that mindset and tries to talk sense into Connor after being rescued from his son's attempt to bury him forever at the bottom of the ocean:

"Nothing in the world is the way it ought to be. It's harsh and cruel, but that's why there's us. Champions. It doesn't matter where we've come from, what we've done or suffered or even if we make a difference. We live as if the world were as it should be, to show it what it can be. You're not a part of that yet. I hope you will be. I love you, Connor. Now get out of my house" ("Deep Down" 4.1).

It's questionable whether what Angel says to Connor ever really sinks in. Even when Connor manages to stay on the side of the, ahem, angels and not be a petulant jerk to everyone, he never really seems to get into the spirit of what comes to Angel, Wesley, Gunn, Fred, Cordelia, and even Lorne so effortlessly. To be sure, most of the reason that Angel sends Connor away at the end of "Not Fade Away" is that Connor is his son; but if Connor really was a hero, rather than just a boy trying his best to be heroic, I'm not sure things would have played out the same way.

And of course, it's not just Angel who suffers. Whedon has a reputation not just for killing characters, but for killing them in the most painful way possible. Generally speaking, when one of his shows decides to kill off one of the heroes, it's going to *hurt*. In all of his work, though, the death of Winifred "Fred" Burkle might hurt the most. It's just so *unfair*. Unfair in the sense that Fred certainly didn't deserve it; unfair in its arbitrariness (some dust from an artifact, and that's it); unfair in the way that the heroes are implicated in it (Fred might have lived if the A.I. team hadn't joined Wolfram & Hart) and of course Angel and Spike have to make the necessary, horrible decision to let Fred die in order to save the lives of hundreds of thousands more; unfair in that she and Wesley had just finally begun their long-gestating romance. Fred was never a victim, even when she knew she was dying:

Fred: I am not—I am not the damsel in distress. I am not some *case*. I have to work this. I lived in a cave for five years in a world where they killed my kind like cattle. I am not going to be cut down by some monster flu. I am better than that! ("A Hole in the World" 5.15).

Fred's right; she *is* better than that, having displayed tremendous smarts, guts, compassion, and other heroic qualities since Angel found her in that cave. Being better than that, being a hero, doing an enormous amount of good for others; it doesn't help at all, even if it should. But *Angel* is hopeful rather than depressive; in addition to being marvelous entertainment it's something we can draw guidance from in our own struggle with a world that, if not actively under siege from the forces of hell, certainly is so much bigger than us that it seems futile to fight for what we believe in. That's because, as Angel said to Kate, realizing that the universe isn't going to give us any credit for our heroism, that there is no big final battle or reward, should galvanize us to act now, in whatever ways we can. To be unsatisfied with the world the way it is, and to live as if the world were as it should be.

During "Not Fade Away," Angel tells his team to go off and live the day as if it's their last (because it almost certainly will be). This leads to a series of scenes both touching and funny, but the key one, maybe the key to the entire series, is Gunn's visit to his friend Anne's[5] homeless shelter. Gunn's there to help, but also to catch up, and maybe to hear what he needs to hear:

Gunn: What if I told you it doesn't help? What would you do if you found out that none of it matters? That it's all controlled by forces more powerful and uncaring than we can conceive and they will never let it get better down here? What would you do?

Anne: I'd get this truck packed before the new stuff gets here. Wanna give me a hand?

Gunn: I do. ("Not Fade Away" 5.22)

The thing about a dragon is, it's probably going to kill you. But if you don't get in front of it, it's definitely going to kill the rest of the village. What makes Angel and his team heroes, real heroes, is that they've always wanted to take one on, and when they get the opportunity, they get in front of the dragon.

Notes

1. Angel even says to his team "We can't bring down the senior partners" ("Power Play" 5.21) in the course of recruiting them for his plan. The plan is explicitly described as one that *cannot* succeed, at least in the sense of the grand heroic triumph that most shows would use for their climax.

2. Those armies don't engulf the A.I. team until after the show ends; even Whedon isn't quite that cruel. You can contrast that ending to the final shot of *Buffy*; in that series, the last shot is of the ensemble standing in daylight, just having finished defeating the ultimate evil. The last shot of *Angel* is also of the ensemble, albeit in the rain, about to face near-certain death. Much as in the end of *Butch Cassidy and the Sundance Kid*, they end in a freeze frame; you don't have to see them gunned down, they (technically) finish still fighting (my thanks to Mary Alice Money for reminding me about the latter point).

3. I am writing this essay in mid-October, 2011; any contemporary political resonances are

both noted and tantalizing, but fall outside of the scope of this essay.

4. This choice also comes up rather strikingly in *Serenity*; the conflict there between Malcolm Reynolds' ethics and the Operative's ethics is a very clear example of what Whedon tends to value in his work. The Operative, a villain that we nevertheless sympathize with, is a perfect example of the kind of pragmatic, accommodating desire to do the right thing that can lead to monstrous evil in Whedon's view. Thanks again to Mary Alice Money for helping me develop this point.

5. Although it's too complicated to detail here, it's worth looking up Anne Steele; her history before she showed up on *Angel* is one of the unexpected delights Whedon and company have put into the background of *Buffy* and *Angel*, and her character arc is an excellent example of the kind of heroism Whedon's work extols.

Works Cited

Angel: *Collector's Set: Seasons 1-5*. Box set. Twentieth Century Fox Home Entertainment, 2007. DVD.

Baudelaire, Charles. *The Painter of Modern Life and Other Essays*. Trans. Jonathan Mayne. London: Phaidon Press, 1995. Print.

"Deep Down." 4.1. Writ. Stephen S. DeKnight. Dir. Terrence O'Hara. *Angel*.

"Epiphany." 2.16. Writ. Tim Minear. Dir. Tim Wright. *Angel*.

"A Hole in the World." 5.15. Writ., dir. Joss Whedon. *Angel*.

Kafka, Franz. "Aphorismen" in Unpublished Works 1916-1918. www.kafka.org Web. 13 Oct. 2011.

Morrison, Grant, and Frank Quitely. JLA: Earth 2. New York: DC Comics, 2000. Print.

"Not Fade Away." 5.22. Writ. Jeffrey Bell and Joss Whedon. Dir. Jeffrey Bell. *Angel*.

"Power Play." 5.21. Writ. David Fury. Dir. James A. Contner. *Angel*.

"Reprise." 2.15. Writ. Tim Minear. Dir. James Whitmore, Jr. *Angel*.

"Underneath." 5.17. Writ. Sarah Fain and Elizabeth Craft. Dir. Skip Schoolnik. *Angel*.

CHAPTER 3

FIREFLY and SERENITY

3.01
Joss Whedon 101:
Firefly
Ian Chant

The thing about *Firefly* is that it's classic.

Not necessarily "a classic," though plenty might argue for that status, your author among them. But what *Firefly* inarguably is, is classic. In just one season, the show managed a maturity far beyond what some programs achieve in lengthy runs. It demonstrated an age beyond its years. And it did it all by shamelessly cribbing and paying homage to a generation of brilliant but largely disregarded Westerns, doing more than its part in ushering in the current renaissance of the genre.

Firefly is not, at the end of the day, an utterly original work. That's not said to take anything away from it—just to call a thing what it is. Before *Firefly*, Whedon did some serious genre bending with *Buffy*, taking elements from horror, comedy, and teen melodrama, mixing well, and producing through alchemical means an utterly new creature. Not so with *Firefly*. The show begs the question "what if instead of horses, cowboys had spaceships?" and pretty much stops when it gets to the answer. Considering the answer is "they would pretty much still be cowboys," this is the exact right thing to do.

For all its snappy one-liners and rousing chases through deep space, *Firefly* is most beautiful—and most effective—in its simplicity. The show envisions the depths of outer space and humankind's very future into the classic setting of for any Western, and does so it with the utmost elegance. *Firefly*'s space is the space of an untamed frontier, shattered by the repercussions of war and peopled in seemingly equal parts by ranchers and outlaws, vigilantes and lawmen. It's a rough and tumble place, a future made primitive, where the progress of mankind means trudging through plenty of cow flops, and making victims out of whole societies of innocent people. It's the American Old West writ large, and there's perhaps no surprise in the fact that every planet that the motley crew of the *Serenity* touches down upon looks like it could have been pulled from Monument Valley or the scrub plains of Oklahoma.

From our first introductions to the crew, it's made clear that we're not going to meet anyone new. We know all of these characters—all we need to do is remember how great they can be. The Honorable Outlaw. The Loyal Sidekick. The Goofy Getaway Man. The Hooker with a Heart of Gold. The Wandering Priest. The Kid. The Dandy. The Doltish Mercenary. There's a bit of an X-factor in River, but beyond that, these archetypes are comforting and familiar. That they're brought to life by a cast with what can only be described as utterly remarkable chemistry is a credit to the entire ensemble, but as far as the types of people they're portraying are concerned, we've been down this road before. By and large they don't surprise us. But that's the whole point. They don't have to surprise us. We don't want them to be more complicated than they are. We want Jayne to be a lovable sonuvabitch because he's already a lovable sonuvabitch. We want Kaylee to be adorable because Kaylee is adorable.

Firefly borrows not only the physical space and group dynamic of Westerns, but even the story structure, which will be familiar to anyone who grew up on late night reruns of *Kung Fu* or Sunday morning marathons of *Have Gun–Will Travel*. The crew blows into an out of the way town looking for work, only to find trouble. They topple the local petty tyrant or scam the thuggish bureaucracy, and they jet off into the sunset and over the horizon. There's snappy dialogue and out of nowhere bits of brilliant storytelling. But the frame remains a sparse one, and less than complex.

The great shame of *Firefly* is that it got just one season, shining brightly but all too briefly. But that brevity may also be the thing most responsible for keeping its legacy untarnished. *Firefly* didn't last long enough to go south on us. Where *Buffy* is fondly remembered, it also bears the weight of two— now three, depending on whether you're counting the canonical *Season Eight* comics published by Dark Horse—seasons of what can generously be termed mediocrity. *Buffy* is a significant other; there were good times and bad times, spats and lovers' quarrels. *Firefly* gets to be the passionate fling; that last week before one party leaves town, the month of embracing some crazy thing that isn't built to last and riding it for all it's worth. It's easier to be nostalgic about this sort of thing. It's natural to remember it fondly.

But maybe not *Firefly*. Because it never quite goes away. Not ever, not really. Even when it's gone for years, someone picks it up. Someone does something new with it, like movies or comics or commentaries on the science. Or it hangs on in different ways, in little things we do—a public marathon screening, a trivia night, an at this point fairly regular chorus of "we'd love to bring the show back" from everyone involved. At some point it feels like the show is bound to make a comeback, somewhere, somehow… and why that's not a Kickstarter project by now is just beyond me. But every year it doesn't happen, one has to assume that it gets less likely that it ever will.

Except that no one who's a fan of the show will actually admit that. I just wrote it down and I don't believe it. Objectively, I mean, it seems true. It's the course I see things taking if I'm being rational. But in that place where believing things really matters? I don't buy it. Neither does any other Browncoat.

What is it about a show that only lasted one season that inspires such devotion and loyalty among fans? It's because *Firefly* was the Underdog. The show that got shuffled around, picked on and picked apart by management. It got shoved in lockers by antagonistic forces outside of its control. It was never really given a fair shake. And people have an underdog's love for it.

That's a very strong love to be on the right side of. And it might be the reason that it's held so dear; it lives in that sympathetic place in the hearts of fans. The place we hold for someone playing against a rigged deck. We get to love *Firefly* for what it was, sure. That's worthy. But we also get to love it for what it could have been. And that's powerful. It skews perceptions, as looking in any rearview is bound to. It makes a thing seem better than it was, even if it was already pretty brilliant.

After all, at the end of the day, *Firefly* is just one more Western. One more tale of heroes living on the wrong side of the law and villains who hold all the cards. One more round of glorious gunfights, barroom brawls and pulse pounding chase scenes. That's all it is. But what more can one ask for?

3.02
Still Flying:
An Interview with Tim Minear

Tanya R. Cochran

First published in "Spotlight on Joss Whedon" on PopMatters.com, 18 and 21 March 2011.

At just 23 years old, Tim Minear was working side-by-side with Oliver Stone as an (uncredited) assistant director on *Platoon* (1986) and beginning a thus-far full career of mostly short-lived television series. So short-lived, in fact, that when he signed up for a Twitter account, he chose "CancelledAgain" as his handle. Yet he swears he's neither bitter nor defeated, having had, among his writer/director/producer peers, a unique experience of working on many and varied series, series that though fleeting are also some of the sharpest around: *Firefly* (2002–2003), *Wonderfalls* (2004), *The Inside* (2005), *Dollhouse* (2009–2010), and *Terriers* (2010), among others. In fact, much of his work could be described as small-screen poetry—condensed, potent.

When I had the pleasure of speaking with Minear via phone on January 12, 2011, we casually yet seriously reasoned that he might be a better fit for the British model of television. Though our conversation came soon after he had learned of *Terriers'* cancellation, Minear was hopeful about his new series *The Chicago Code*, which premiered on Fox at the beginning of February. Unfortunately, it was canceled several months later on May 10, 2011, after thirteen episodes. What Minear did not know when we spoke was that he would be involved in the success of *American Horror Story* (2011–), currently in its fourth iteration, as an executive producer as well as a writer. So in this interview, we talk about his work with Joss Whedon, work he was happily reminiscent about, among many other topics: *Firefly* and *Angel* (1999–2004), the role socio-political and cultural issues play in his creative work, writing strong female characters, and what he learned while working alongside Whedon.

We also talk about the rise of reality television and how Minear sees his own work in relation to the phenomenon. He considers whether or not Whedon's *Dr. Horrible's Sing-Along Blog* is a viable model for the future of small-screen narratives, especially in light of Whedon's talent and very loyal fan base, then notes the succession of canceled shows he has experienced over the last decade. We spend a little time on his personal writing habits and what he enjoys about conducting writers' workshops, before Minear offers his perspective on fandom and how he feels about having his work studied and taught by academics. Next I invite Minear to comment on his unrealized project *Miracle Man* and how the Writers Guild of America Strike derailed the penning and filming of the pilot. To close, Minear discusses *The Chicago Code* and what excites him about the series.

POPMATTERS (PM): Readers of the *Firefly* comic books have recently learned some much-coveted information about Shepherd Book's past. What deeper insight into the character Inara Serra can or will you share?

TIM MINEAR (TM): Well I could, but I won't. I don't feel like I have the freedom to reveal that.

PM: Well, it was worth asking [both laugh].

TM: Yeah, I just don't feel like I have the freedom to reveal that.

PM: Moving on then… Whedon has participated in politics in ways that can be directly connected to his creative work. He sponsored the "High Stakes" fundraising parties for John Kerry; he supports the non-profit organization Equality Now. In particular, he himself—as well as fans, journalists, and scholars—have described Whedon as a feminist. What role, if any, do you find social, cultural, or political issues playing in your own work?

TM: I suppose on some level. And all that is definitely true about Joss. I remember in the last season of *Buffy* he came in once and said, "Buffy has become like George W. Bush… forming an army." The truth is that sometimes art may not exactly reflect one's personal politics, but the story, the drama, the thing you're trying to say might want to go in a certain direction, and while it may seem like it has resonance with things that are happening topically, you kind of want the world you're creating to have its own internal logic. Above all, you want it to track, make sense, and resonate emotionally. So I actually don't know if I do that consciously or not. That's probably not the answer you want; it's not a very interesting answer, but that's the answer.

PM: No. Actually, it *is* interesting. Because those who study popular culture—and those of us who are scholars of Whedon's series, including your work—are particularly interested in how consciously you're thinking about these real-world issues when you're writing. So to have your answer is illuminating.

TM: Joss is more center-left, and I'm more center-right. I'm more of a libertarian. Joss would tell me that his sympathies were often with the Alliance—universal health care and that sort of thing. But when you're doing a Western like *Firefly*, the drama is really with the iconoclast—I don't want to say a libertarian with a big L, but you know, the guy who's out there searching for his own freedom. So, I don't know that Joss was particularly making a libertarian statement, but I know from what I've read on the web that a lot of libertarians embrace *Firefly* in particular as a libertarian ideal.

Kind of backtracking a little bit on your original question… one cannot divorce oneself from sitting down and closely examining one's work. You're always trying to tell a story and make it interesting, yet you might also realize a scene says something offensive about women or some other group. Then you might go in and adjust it accordingly. I did this recently with *Terriers*. We had this story thread with a character who cheated on her boyfriend. She had a drunken night and ended up in bed with her professor.

When we were breaking that story, there were all sorts of reasons why we wrote the thread like we did. We wanted to give the character agency of her own; we didn't want her to feel like some appendage to the male character, so she had her own life and her own stuff to work out. On the other hand, we had to be very careful not to make it seem like she was date-raped. So how do you do that and not give the audience the idea that you're trying to say something when you're really not? I think often it's more about being careful that you're *not* saying something that you didn't intend, as opposed to trying to infuse your work with things that you want to say. Joss would probably have a completely different take on this question.

PM: Well, that's why I'm interviewing you [both laugh]. In a similar but slightly different vein, when Joss Whedon accepted an award during Equality Now's "Men on the Front Lines" event in 2006, he organized his remarks around an imaginary press junket during which reporters repeatedly ask him the same question: "Why do you write these strong women characters?" After many other responses—some funny, some not, all of them serious— Whedon ultimately answers, "Because you're still asking me that question." Is there a recurring question that you get asked that makes you wonder about the sanity of our culture? Or one that simply drives you crazy?

TM: Nothing's leaping to mind. It's interesting, though. I totally understand his frustration with *that* question. When I first started working with Joss, I did *Angel*, which was sort of the boy version of *Buffy*, so it wasn't about the empowered female necessarily. It was more about the empowered male. But after I left that show, I went and did *Wonderfalls*, which was absolutely about this young woman at the center of the story.

PM: A story I love, by the way.

TM: Thank you. And then after *Wonderfalls* I did *The Inside*, which was also about a female character doing things that are more male-oriented—on television at any rate—sort of an action hero. She wasn't using stereotypical feminine intuition to solve cases; she was much more attuned to the masculine side of her brain. I never really planned to sit down and write shows that have young women at the center of them because I often feel foolish. Actually, I don't. I'll take that back because when I actually sit down and write, I just try to get in her head and be as honest as I can about what the character would be doing or thinking in a particular situation. I think female characters on TV are often more interesting than male characters... or can be.

PM: I know you have Jennifer Beals at the heart of *The Chicago Code*, which premieres soon.

TM: Yep. That's exactly right.

PM: Fans are already commenting on her casting and the character she plays.

TM: Yes, she's awesome, really great.

PM: We'll come back to the topic of *The Chicago Code* a little later. For now, let me finish asking you about your work with Whedon. What is the greatest lesson, professional or personal, you've learned from Joss Whedon?

TM: That's a good question because there's not just one thing. The thing about my experience with Joss [laughs]… it's actually kind of a funny story. About ten years ago, I was working on a show with Howard Gordon called *Strange World*. I had just come off of *The X-Files*, but while I was on that show—I'm going to ramble for just a second if it's okay with you—there was a woman there, Kim Metcalf, who was the assistant of Ken Horton, the president of Chris Carter's company. By the time I came on to *The X-Files* in season five, Ken was putting most of his attention on *Millennium*. So I would go over [to their set] and hang out with Kim because she was awesome. Once she took me into a room and said, "I want to show you something." I absolutely remember what she put into the VCR (it wasn't a DVD player at the time): she put in "Surprise," the episode where Buffy sleeps with Angel. She said, "You have to see this." I'd never seen *Buffy*. And for whatever prescient reason, Kim said, "You should be working with Joss Whedon. You shouldn't be here; you should be off working with Joss Whedon." I thought, *She's a cheerleader; I just don't get the show*.

Fast-forward a year or two later. I'm working on *Strange World*, and my agent tells me that Joss Whedon wants to have a meet-and-greet. That's pretty normal; you have these meet-and-greets when you're a writer in Hollywood. You go, you meet people, you talk, and you hope that means you'll get work later. So I go in and meet with Joss and David Greenwalt. But right before I went in, my agent told me I was supposed to have four or five episode pitches. So I'm thinking, *Okay, so it's not a meet-and-greet. It's a pitch!* That means I have to search out some college girl I know who's got all the *Buffy* episodes on tape and borrow them. So I borrowed the videotapes and watched them. And I said, "Okay. That's pretty good. That's pretty good."

I came up with five ideas. I was also told that Joss likes a scene, a teaser, what the story's about, certain elements. I walked in with these sort-of-worked-out pitches. Now I don't remember what most of them were. I remember one—this was back before Xander [had had sex for the first time]—I think the pitch was: druids come to Sunnydale and they're searching for a virgin to sacrifice. Xander, who is a virgin, is running around to all the girls he knows saying, "You have to sleep with me or I will die!"… I pitched all this stuff to Joss, and the report I got back was that "those were the best pitches Joss has ever heard; *however*, he thinks you're the angriest man he's ever met and can't bear to be in the same room with you." I said, "Okay, whatever." When *Angel* was spun off, David Greenwalt said, "What about that 'mountaineer' guy who came in here and pitched?" Joss said, "Fine, as long as I don't have to be in a room with him." So I went to *Angel*, and then of course, fast-forward, it all worked out great. We became "besties" and sat around French-braiding each other's hair and knitting booties [both laugh].

So the thing I learned from Joss? There were things I understood before I got to *Angel* because I had been doing this for a while. I had been with a couple of shows, and beyond that I had been writing syndicated television for a couple of years. I had probably 50 produced hours of television under my belt, which is kind of unusual for someone who has just started working in network TV. When I went in there, I had an understanding of what I was doing, but Joss gave me the language to articulate what it was that I was doing. When he talked about a story that we were breaking and putting up on a board being just a bunch of plot moves as opposed to being about something, getting to the heart of what's the *Angel* of it, what's the *Buffy* of it, what's the emotional center of this story, and what're we trying to say about these characters, that process gave me language to articulate what it was I had already been doing. Once I knew what to call things, I got better at it. That's one thing he gave me.

The other thing he gave me was—and this is hard to quantify—but he has a kind of enthusiasm for what he does that translates. In other words, when I produced something for him that he loved, he expressed his delight. He had no ego in terms of wanting the people who worked for and with him to succeed. I know a lot of these big-name guys who have to make sure you know that it's really their genius that's running everything. Joss, on the other hand, would go out in print… like when I got my deal with Twentieth Century Fox and there was a pretty big piece in *Variety* the next day. In the article, he basically said, "Without Tim Minear, there would be no *Angel*." He is very quick to give credit where it is due. Now, he doesn't just give you empty praise; you need to perform. It's really nice to be recognized because I've been on a couple of [projects] that were unpleasant. I also learned technical things from Joss. When someone as good at what they do as Joss is expresses admiration for the work you're doing, it makes you want to be better, and then you can actually get better.

PM: What's the greatest lesson you've taught Whedon?

TM: You'd have to ask him that [both laugh].

PM: In a 2004 Q&A for the Buffistas, you commented, in reference to reality TV, "It devours you from your bottom." [Both laugh.] Great quote, by the way. Seven years later, has your opinion changed? Do you ever feel the burgeoning of the genre as a threat to your own work or to the art of television in general?

TM: Wow. I think I was probably going for a cheap laugh. So has my opinion of reality TV altered? Yes. Probably because I've seen some of it. But I still wonder, *What social good is* Jersey Shore? [Both laugh.] On the other hand, I don't watch it; I've never seen it. So it's sort of asshole-ury for me to make fun of it. However, I will say I have watched *The Amazing Race* and *Survivor*. I enjoy shows like *What Not to Wear* and *American Idol*. And yes, reality TV does encroach because there is only so much real estate on network TV. With the advent of cable TV, the Internet, and everything else, though, the idea that someone can't do the thing they're doing because it will take away from me is probably false. I think that's false.

PM: Actually, your answer leads me to the next question, one about how contemporary viewers receive small-screen narratives. In some past interviews, you've talked about the various media platforms that provide television to audiences. Do you think Whedon's *Dr. Horrible's Sing-Along Blog*, for example, is a good model for present and future visual storytelling?

TM: It probably is. It's a sort of creative disruption of the market. Things will shake out in some way, but they also move so fast that you can't really predict what the models are going to be. That's what the whole writers' strike was about on some level. Nobody can agree on what the ancillary value of the Internet is. Even by the time I got into writing network television—the first thing I did was *Lois and Clark* and then I had come to *Angel* by 1999. Since *Angel*—and this has something to do with the fact that nothing I ever do lasts more than 13 episodes—summer re-runs have never really happened for the things I've worked on. Take *Firefly*. Whatever success *Firefly* achieved happened in its afterlife. It happened through iTunes, DVDs, the Internet, and all that stuff. People have been paying for downloads and buying the DVDs, and that put it into the success category after it had failed. Probably five years before that, however, [*Firefly*'s rebirth] may not have happened. The notion that a TV series that never even had a full season would have some kind of an afterlife was absurd! Everything has sort of changed between *Firefly*'s cancellation and the writers' strike.

In terms of *Dr. Horrible*, I know that was a huge success for Joss. I think he made some money off of that.

PM: I hope he did. I supported it by buying multiple copies.

TM: Yes, he did. He definitely made his money back and then some. The beauty of it was, of course, he was in complete control. There was no studio. There was nobody taking a piece of it. He paid for it, he produced it, he worked out how to distribute it, and he created the commentary tracks for the DVD and everything else. When it was released on the Internet, there was no middleman. As Joss likes to say, "*Dr. Horrible* broke the interweb" because there were so many hits when it was being released online.

But I would not use that particular example to point the way to the future of producing pieces for the Internet, and the reason I say that is there are a couple of things that make *Dr. Horrible* unique. Actually, there's one thing that makes *Dr. Horrible* unique, and that's Joss. I mean, not only the talent, but the fact that he has the geeky fan base that is Internet-savvy. He chose actors from his projects who were already beloved by this particular audience. As an audience, they were ready to buy this thing on the Internet. I'm just not sure that that kind of lightning is going to strike a whole bunch of people. Do you know what I mean? If I made something for the interweb and spent $100,000 on it, it's just not going to have the same... yeah [laughs]. There are actually many things like *Dr. Horrible* that have been produced in a similar way for the net. You can find examples all over the place that are of comparable quality—production-wise, writing-wise. But I'm not sure those people are buying houses based on their work.

PM: Speaking of cancellation, I'm sure you knew that was going to come up. In fact, you talk quite a bit about it in interviews.

TM: Of course!

PM: I'm trying not to repeat questions you've been asked before, but I am interested in your Twitter handle "CancelledAgain." One of your own tweets says, "I really need to change this twitter name." What do that statement and your handle have to do with each other? Do I detect sadness, bitterness, resignation, superstition?

TM: It's just a joke. I have no bitterness. I mean, please, how could I be bitter? I have no bitterness. I'm not bitter. Actually, in a weird way, being canceled has kind of worked out for me. Let's say *The Inside* had become a big hit like *Criminal Minds*. I'd still be writing serial killers to this day. Instead, I got to do 13 episodes of a really cool thing. I got to do 13 episodes of *Wonderfalls*, which was a really cool thing. And I got to do cowboys in space, and that was a really cool thing. And *Terriers*—which is as good as anything I've done and was also completely different. I would have loved for *Terriers* to have been picked up again. I'm not saying I love to be canceled all the time, but I *am* saying, how many people get to do that many different things? And most of these [projects] are pretty well received by the people who actually watch them.

PM: Yes, they are. Actually, the way you've had to work with these involuntarily short series is not unlike how British television works on purpose.

TM: I've said that myself. I'm my own little BBC [both laugh]. Even if I look back at *Strange World*—which nobody's ever heard of—the show I did with Howard Gordon before I went to *Angel*... Howard and I saw the writing on the wall, so there are 13 episodes of that show *with* an ending. I've gone into most of these series thinking—and maybe that's the problem—even if this thing only lasts for 13 episodes and there's a DVD release, I want people to go out and buy it and feel satisfied on some level when they're done with it. Maybe that's my mistake: I'm sort of planning for failure [both laugh]. I always try to bring it to some kind of arc around the third or sixth episode and to give that arc some sort of resolution by the end of episode 13, but never in such a way that I'm planning on the show not coming back.

PM: In addition to being very much like the British television broadcast model, those of us who study and teach television—your work, Whedon's work, the work of many others—those succinct series and completed texts help us out when we're trying to make sense of them, to answer questions about what a series does, how it works, how it's received, what it means to and for viewers or cultural (re)production more broadly.

TM: Well, I'm certainly glad that my abject failure can be convenient for you [both laugh heartily]!

PM: In the many interviews you've given, you talk about your habit of procrastinating when it comes to writing. Do you truly procrastinate, as in do absolutely nothing (other than eating ice cream and cereal, as I've read), or do you practice what my graduate school professor called "active waiting," another way of saying that rather than putting pen to paper or fingers to keyboard you're working inside your head?

TM: It's both of those things. I think the trick is… [chuckles] being able to differentiate. It's easy to *say* you're doing the active waiting when really you're just like, "Oh look, porn. Porn, porn, porn." [Both laugh.] Really, both. It's both.

PM: I also understand you do quite a few writers' workshops. What do you enjoy most about teaching others to write?

TM: Boy, that's a good question. There are probably a couple of things. One is that it's kind of fun to be in a room with a bunch of fans who think you're awesome, and then you get to act like you know a bunch of stuff and they are all impressed. There's certainly the "Oh, look, I get to be worshipped… and get paid!" [Both laugh.] So there's that. But other than that, there's something exciting about being able to unlock what seems impenetrable for people, and then—I don't need to tell you this [because you're a teacher]— there's something satisfying about having discovered something and then sharing it with somebody else so that they can discover it too.

PM: Yes, that's what's wonderful about teaching. I love that part.

TM: Yeah, that's really what it is. Also when you talk about writing, when you have to articulate what you know about it to somebody else, doing so helps *you* understand it more. Teaching others makes you better at what you're doing because you're really teaching yourself at some level.

PM: You've been in the business long enough to have a tangible sense of the power of fandom. What do you think is the healthiest kind of relationship between yourself as a writer/director/producer and the fans of a project you're working on?

TM: I think the healthiest relationship is when they write things that praise me [both laugh heartily]! I think I mentioned that the first thing I did was *Lois and Clark*. At that time, Internet fandom was in its infancy. Well, more of a toddler than an infant. There was definitely immediate response during an episode and after an episode aired. It can be pretty [intimidating] at first because your ego's out there. You go on the Internet, you're waiting for the praise, and then some fans begin to criticize you, talk about how you're ruining the show or how could you have done this or that better. I'm way beyond all that stuff now, but it can be harsh. For the most part, I don't go to those places if I can avoid them. I think fandom is healthy so long as fans aren't armed [both laugh]. It's really positive in a way. You don't want to have to create things in a vacuum. I can't imagine what it was like—I mean TV is so different now than how it was in the 1970s—because you really do have interaction with the audience. I'm not saying it's like being on stage. On the other hand, it's weird for me because I come from fandom. I was one of those kids growing up in southern California who dressed up as Captain Kirk and went to *Star Trek* conventions when I was 14. So I've always been one of those people. I still consider myself one of those people, so it doesn't feel as if the line of demarcation is all that clear for me. I'm just the lucky fan who gets to make this shit!

PM: You *are* lucky. And those of us on the other side of the screen are glad you're lucky.

TM: Thank you.

PM: As you've just suggested, we're all fans in some way. You probably understand, then, that fans can become really upset, even distraught, when a series they love is canceled. In fact, fans' mourning process has lately become quite public and organized, with the *Firefly* Browncoats being a now classic example. You've recently shared a little of what it's like to be on the creator side of a cancellation. What advice might you offer to those on the other side of the camera, to the fans whose favorite show has just been terminated?

TM: Boy, I don't know. I'm not sure I have advice. I don't want to make it more important than it is. I understand there's a grieving process because fans get involved, characters become real to them on some level, and they feel like they're losing a friend. Those friends will reemerge in different permutations, though. I brought Nathan [Fillion] onto *Drive*, for instance. Or think *Dr. Horrible*. Joss is going to make other stuff, and the actors fans love are going to appear in other things. [The death of a series] allows the actors to go off and create the next thing. I see these fan campaigns: we're going to send TABASCO® sauce to the network, or whatever it is. I worry that sometimes people are wasting their money, and I don't want to see them put a lot of effort into trying to save a show that's already been canceled. If the creator comes out and says, "Yes, please send those things," that's fine. Do what you're going to do. However, perhaps that energy would be better spent volunteering for a charity or something.

PM: In a 2006 podcast with Glenn Reynolds and Helen Smith, you joke that the reason for your King of Cancellations title is, and I quote, "I suck." [Minear laughs.] Helen Smith asks if you think part of the cancellation problem is related to making shows that appeal to, in her words, "the weird and the intellectual." You reply, "The weird certainly; I don't know about the intellectual." [Both laugh.] Are you aware that your work is studied (and often highly praised) by scholars? Do you read academic scholarship on your work?

TM: Vaguely aware? I've seen some things online, for instance. I don't sit around googling my name *obsessively*, but I have seen that there are courses on the works of Joss Whedon and that those courses have me listed also. So I'm kind of aware.

PM: How does it feel to know that academics are not only noticing your work but sometimes teaching it to their students?

TM: It's kind of surreal, but it's flattering. And I don't understand why they're not emailing me and asking me to come speak [both laugh]!

PM: Are you willing to share a little bit about your American Broadcasting Company (ABC) project *Miracle Man*? Both fans and scholars were anxiously anticipating the series. What happened to it? Did the writer's strike play a role? Does it still have a future?

TM: That's an interesting question that you raise. I will try to speak about this as delicately as possible. What happens in television is that there's a sort of frenzy of selling around pilot season. You take your ideas out and pitch them to a network, and they say, "Yes, we want that idea," and they pay you or the studio to write a pilot script. Then the networks get in this pile of scripts that they have commissioned, and from that pile they decide which scripts they're going to green-light to pilot, which ones they're going to spend millions of dollars on to make into a pilot. From those pilots, which they spend millions and millions of dollars on, they have a screening, and then they pick those pilots that they want to green-light to series. This [process] means that they may make many pilots, but only a small percentage of them actually get born into series. This is the only business I know that does something so dumb. They spend so much money going through six months of casting and building sets and more to shoot an hour of television so they can screen it and then say, "Nah, we don't think so." They can't tell from the script whether they want to go with it. That business model has got to change.

What happened with *Miracle Man* was... yes, the writers' strike really screwed that whole thing up. I sold it. I was given the green light to go to an outline and from an outline to a script, but then the writers' strike happened. Right after that happened, the networks cried, "Where are our pilot scripts?" We were on strike! I guess they expected us to be off writing our pilots during a strike. I don't know anyone who did that. I certainly didn't. Partially [*Miracle Man* never materialized] because of the strike, partially because I said to myself, "I'm on strike; I don't have to work." Obviously, I wasn't going to write during a writers' strike. After the strike, everyone was in a frenzy to get their pilot scripts written. I ended up writing a couple versions of the pilot for that idea, and I never felt like it was the right direction for that story. However, because of the strikes, and because of the accelerated period in which ABC was demanding to have a draft on their desk, I never had the normal development relationship with the network that I would usually have had. We never had meetings; I was just never really partnered with that network.

To make a long story short, *Miracle Man* was just one of those projects that they decided not to do. That being said, I believe there may be some life in the old boy yet. I just think we went down the wrong track with that particular project. I feel strongly that I know now what it should have been, and maybe I'll get a chance to do that.

PM: Well, I suppose the beauty of a good story is that it never really goes out of style.

TM: You would think that. In this particular town, though, there are things people are incredibly excited about one minute, but if it's on a shelf for a certain amount of time, it gets stale to them. This is the way they are a lot. It's like they go into a restaurant and see something on the menu—"Oh that looks good!"—but by the time it comes out of the kitchen, they've decided they want the chicken.

PM: In your recent interview with *Assignment X*, you mention that the city of Chicago should be understood not just as a setting but even more so as a character in your soon-to-premiere series *The Chicago Code*. That reminded me of Malcolm Reynold's spaceship *Serenity*, which was a central character in *Firefly*. How will the writers, directors, and producers give Chicago the depth of personality you, Whedon, and the *Firefly* creative team gave Mal's "boat"? What are the challenges of doing so with a landscape versus an enclosed space?

TM: It's easy with Chicago, interestingly enough. I don't think it's going to be intimate like *Serenity*. The one thing all my favorite television series have in common is that they create these very specific worlds. No matter what show you're talking about—*Mad Men, Firefly, Deadwood, Rome*, or *The Wire*—all of these shows, though they're completely different, are not generic. They take you to a specific world and allow you to experience one you might not otherwise have any familiarity with. For instance, *The Wire* may seem impenetrable to you at first, but by the time you're well into the first season, you're starting to understand it. Same with *Firefly* and the weird amalgam of English and Chinese and Western-ism that we created for that show. So in terms of *The Chicago Code*, with a city like Chicago that is so specific and has its own personality... you can set some generic cop show in Chicago or you could do *The Untouchables* or you could do something that is a little bit more modern.

The show captures the corruption of Chicago in City Hall and the racism on the streets, but we're not bad-mouthing Chicago, saying that it's some cesspool. We're saying something entirely different. We're saying that it's a city that works in spite of itself. While there has always been epic corruption, there have always been those—like Jennifer Beal's character [Teresa Colvin]—who have been determined to reform it. And that's specific to that city. It's very hot in the summer, it's very cold in the winter, it's a city of extremes. That's different to setting some show in Los Angeles (like we did with *The Inside*), San Francisco, or Miami. There's a reason the series takes place in Chicago. You couldn't tell the particular stories we tell in another setting. We were trying to make every story a Chicago story, not just some cop show. That's really what our goal was.

PM: What are you most excited about in regards to *The Chicago Code*? And what should viewers be most excited about?

TM: What I just spoke of is the most exciting part for me: the city. Viewers should be excited about the characters' world. The world is interesting. Midwestern people are interesting. The one thing the show is not is a procedural. This is not *Adam-12* writ large. It's less about following the clues to catch the bad guy each week and more about the interesting emotional and political cauldron that is at the heart of the show. It's more an operatic story than a crime story, although there are also great crime stories, chases, and gunfire too.

I couldn't help but be reminded of *Firefly* and *Serenity*'s Malcolm Reynolds while interviewing Minear. Conjuring images from the final moments of the film, I envisioned Captain Mal at the helm of his patched up space boat explaining to River Tam that "love keeps her in the air when she oughta fall down." The same can be said of Minear. Over the years, the writer/director/producer has suffered some blows, but there's no doubt that he's good at what he does and loves doing it. After so many cancellations, others might have given up. Not Minear. He's still flying.

Notes

I wish to thank Tim Minear for generously sharing his time and responses and John J. Gray for helpfully arranging the interview.

3.03
Joss Whedon 101:
Serenity
Kristin M. Barton

On September 30, 2005, Joss Whedon made his feature-film directorial debut with *Serenity*, the much-anticipated follow-up to his canceled Fox TV series *Firefly* (2002). Despite a number of positive reviews and a groundswell of fan support, Fox pulled the plug on *Firefly* after airing only eleven of the original fourteen episodes produced. Cast, crew, and fans alike were devastated that a show so beloved could be taken so quickly away from them, and Joss Whedon, the show's creator and producer, vowed to find it a new home. With the help of Universal executive Mary Parent, *Firefly* was re-launched three years later as the film *Serenity*. *Serenity* follows the story that Whedon had initially mapped out for Season 2 of the show, but was never able to air because of Fox's decision to cancel it before its time. Although the storyline was obviously condensed to fit a two-hour film, Whedon's vision of how the story would unfold remained intact.

Taking place approximately six months after the events of *Firefly*, Captain Malcolm Reynolds (Nathan Fillion) and his crew are still flying and still making their way by finding jobs that keep them on the fringe of civilized society. The differences between the show and the film are few, but one that fans are quick to notice is the absence of two crew members who are no longer on board *Serenity*: Shepherd Book (Ron Glass) has left to carry on a life preaching to those that need it, while Inara (Morena Baccarin) has left to become an instructor at a companion training house, something she had hinted at doing in the unaired *Firefly* episode "Heart of Gold" (13).

But unbeknownst to the crew, forces are at work to track down and capture the young and seemingly innocuous River Tam (Summer Glau). An Operative (Chiwetel Ejiofor), one of the Alliance's most lethal assets, has been tasked with finding River and bringing her in. It is from the Operative that the audience learns River's importance to the Alliance and what she was put through at their hands. As had been strongly suggested during *Firefly*, River is psychic (or in Malcolm Reynold's words, "a reader"), and as such has been experimented on by the Alliance in an effort to turn her into a living weapon. But the Alliance fears she may have learned a dangerous secret, one that could bring the Alliance to its knees. Before the Alliance is able to silence River, her brother, Simon (Sean Maher), orchestrates her escape from an Alliance facility, which shortly leads them to their inevitable convergence with *Serenity*'s crew.

The film also brings back from the series one of the most frightening and gruesome varieties of villains Whedon has created thus far: Reavers. Savages on the edge of space, Reavers serve as subjects of ghost stories for some and nightmares for those who encounter them. Zombie-like in both appearance and demeanor, Reavers sail across the 'verse in scavenged ships looking for victims to, as Zoe (Gina Torres) describes it in the pilot episode of *Firefly*, "rape us to death, eat our flesh, and sew our skins into their clothing. And if we're very, very lucky, they'll do it in that order" ("Serenity").

With these elements in place, the film tells the story of the crew's attempt to prevent the Alliance from capturing Simon and River, while also uncovering the secret that makes River so valuable. Determined to learn the truth, the crew navigates through the heart of Reaver territory to find the proscribed planet Miranda. Once there, the crew discovers the unspeakable evil that the Alliance has perpetrated, in a scientific experiment intended merely to pacify the planet. Armed with these revelations and with the intent to end this conflict once and for all, Mal and his crew navigate their way through a maze of Alliance and Reaver ships with catastrophic results, including the near-destruction of *Serenity* herself. In desperate straits and with little choice, the crew mounts a last stand against a horde of attacking Reavers in order to buy time for Mal to fight his way past the Operative in a bloody showdown and broadcast Miranda's secret to the entire 'verse.

But for all the terrible adversaries Whedon included devised to oppose the crew, this film (even more so than the preceding series) is the story of River Tam. It is ultimately through River's story that we understand how her fate and the fate of the crew are tied to the secrets she knows, and precisely how far the Alliance is willing to go to stop her. The connection between River, the Alliance, and the Reavers ties the series and film together in a way that leaves fans with a better understanding of the overall story Whedon set out to tell.

As much as the film serves to answer some lingering questions left by the series, fans were disappointed when Whedon failed to reveal some of the most intriguing mysteries left during the show's short run. In more than one instance, mention had been made of Book's past and more than once it was suggested that despite his current station in life, he wasn't always a man of the cloth. Ultimately, the film ends with only more speculation on Book's secret life. In a move suggesting that future sequels may not be coming, Whedon decided to reveal Book's back story in the Dark Horse graphic novel *A Shepherd's Tale*, released in November 2010.

Another mystery left unanswered by the film concerns Inara's illness. Casual watchers of the show may not be aware, but serious fans of *Firefly* (also known as Browncoats) are probably familiar with the undeveloped plot detail leaked by Morena Baccarin (who played Inara) in answer to a fan's question at a DragonCon 2008 panel. In one hint, during the series' pilot ("Serenity"), Inara is seen opening a box containing a syringe that she considers using when Reavers appear and the crew fears capture. While many viewers originally thought Inara was considering suicide to escape torture at the hands of the Reavers, Baccarin confirmed that Inara is actually dying. The nature of her character's illness has never been explained, but fans hold out hope that the secret may eventually be revealed in some format.

As with any tale Whedon tells, death plays an intricate role in moving the story forward and inciting the characters to take action they might otherwise rationally avoid. While many fans were initially heartbroken over the loss of some of their beloved crew members, the finality of their deaths serves the story in more ways than one. But perhaps most importantly, it gives the film more emotional weight to know that the characters operate in actual danger, unlike the danger faced by primary characters in other film franchises. While many enjoy watching Captain Kirk and the *Enterprise* crew battle and defeat foes in supposedly no-win scenarios, the audience understands that their lives are too vital to the franchise to lose. Even when Spock's life was sacrificed in *Star Trek II: The Wrath of Khan*, it wasn't far into the next film before he was back on screen with his crew mates. Whedon has the more realistic approach to his storytelling: To bring a believable character to life on the screen requires that the character deal with pain and loss like everyone else, whether she is a teenage vampire hunter or he is the captain of a spaceship. The constant threat of losing a character who is loved by the fans makes watching the space battles and shoot-outs much more intense and emotional.

Despite the tragedy and loss suffered by the crew, Whedon does offer some hope at the end of the film that things may be looking better on the *Serenity*. River, no longer burdened by the secret she's been keeping, appears to have regained her sanity and found her place within the crew. *Serenity* is rebuilt and returned to her original glory—although occasionally a part might still fall off. Inara decides not to return to the companion training house, but instead stay aboard the ship, subtly hinting that her unresolved feelings for the captain might be a strong motivating factor. And in a moment Browncoats knew was inevitable, Simon and Kaylee (Jewel Staite) finally shared a kiss and consummated a relationship that had been building since the show began.

Shortly after *Serenity*'s release, Whedon continued his grassroots approach to marketing by calling on fans to go out and promote the film to people who hadn't seen it. As incentive, he teased that a possible sequel to *Serenity* might feature the return of Jubal Early, the antagonist portrayed by Richard Brooks in the *Firefly* episode "Objects in Space" (14). But for now, with no sequel on the horizon and Whedon having moved on to *The Avengers*, fans must be grateful that a show, canceled after completing only fourteen episodes, made it to the big screen. By creating the demand for this film, the Browncoats can truly hold claim that they have done the impossible.

Works Cited

Firefly: *The Complete Series*. Cr. Joss Whedon. Perf. Nathan Fillion, Gina Torres, Adam Baldwin, Jewel Staite, and Summer Glau. Twentieth Century Fox Home Entertainment, 2003. DVD.

"Heart of Gold." 13. Writ. Brett Mathews. Dir. Thomas J. Wright. *Firefly*.

"Objects in Space." 14. Writ. and dir. Joss Whedon. *Firefly*.

Serenity. Writ. and dir. Joss Whedon. Perf. Nathan Fillion, Gina Torres, Adam Baldwin, Jewel Staite, and Summer Glau. Universal Studios Home Entertainment, 2005. DVD.

"Serenity" (Parts 1 and 2). 1. Writ. and dir. Joss Whedon. *Firefly*.

A *Shepherd's Tale*. Story by Joss Whedon and Zack Whedon. Pencils by Chris Samnee. Portland: Dark Horse, 2010. Print.

3.04
A Postcolonial Provocation:
Serenity
Leanne McRae

"As far as *Firefly* is concerned, that will always be unfinished business. *Serenity* was a Band-Aid on a sucking flesh wound. I think every day about the scenes that I'll never get to shoot and how badass they were. It's nice to know that people still care about *Firefly* but it's actual grief that I feel. It's not something you get over, it's just something you learn to live with."
—Joss Whedon, quoted in *SFX World of Whedon*, 2010

Joss Whedon evocatively conveys the mourning he still experiences as a result of his short-lived series *Firefly* being canceled by network executives in 2002. The demise of this program created a special moment in popular culture when something unexpected emerged from the crisis. What was created activated a transformative dialogue between the postcolonial and the popular that generated space for questioning and representing processes of power that normally remain unseen. *Serenity* operates in unclear spaces of meaning as it was conceived as a brokered attempt to extend the life of a severely curtailed plot envisioned for *Firefly*.

If the series had continued on television, Whedon would have been able to map out the complexities of characters and plot trajectories to provide challenging televisual terrain for a new generation of TV fans post-*Buffy* and -*Angel*. Instead, Whedon had to make do with the temporal compressions of cinematic viewing to do justice both to the narrative and to the characters. As a result, *Serenity* was composed of half-truths and conflicted contexts where the spaces for unconventional and unruly meanings were able to emerge from the diegesis. These meanings offer insight into the political trajectories of colonization and the creation of Empire that are difficult to control.

Serenity is a hybrid film straddling the worlds of two viewerships that were invested in the film. For the fans of *Firefly*, their viewership held different requirements than those of individuals unfamiliar with the text. In order to gather up a wholly unfamiliar audience of cinema viewers with little knowledge of the *Firefly* universe and its key actors, Whedon had to provide a filmic structure to reveal the characters' motivation and reasoning. As a result, *Serenity* is an odd film that sits uncomfortably in terrain between *Firefly* fans and newer audiences with competing and contrasting story needs. The postcolonial potential of the plot provided unstable terrain through which this matrix of meaning could be knitted together in a playful and perverse representation of a future universe where power asserts itself and is re-encoded and reinscribed by individuals and communities from within and on the border of this system.

Differences between the Whedonesque universes of *Firefly* and *Serenity* are revealed in plotting inconsistencies that would be known to fans of *Firefly*, but not necessarily identified by viewers with no knowledge of the series. For example, *Serenity* is structured as a continuation of the *Firefly* narrative, but it does not begin exactly where the series ended or explain all intervening events. For new viewers, important time markers include dialogue indicating Simon and River Tam's tenure on *Serenity* as eight months, and stating that Inara—the captain's love interest who is a "companion" (not unlike a geisha but also a high-class prostitute)—has left the ship and now resides as an instructor at a companion training house. Fans would recognize this narrative development introduced in the last two episodes of *Firefly*, when Inara decided to leave *Serenity*. In a new development, Shepherd Book has also—between the end of the television series and the start of the film—elected to leave the ship and now lives on the planet of Haven. However, in the series Simon Tam and the crew of *Serenity* become fully aware of River's true abilities only in the final few episodes. Yet the film reveals that Simon had this knowledge all along. If this was the case, the series is very ambiguous on this point. In "Safe" (5), for example, Simon states that his sister is highly intuitive as if he suspects there may be something more to her ability to discern what people are thinking and feeling, but it is never made clear to the viewers that he definitely knows—or admits to himself—that she is psychic.

Such moments of continuity and discontinuity with the *Firefly* series make *Serenity* a hybrid text moving between worlds and readerships in a complex dance of the familiar and unfamiliar. The history of *Firefly* combined with the need to make *Serenity* a commercial success—to gather up viewers who may not have seen the series—creates a carnivalesque text that generates hybrid viewing strategies by audiences. These thematics are encoded and deployed within the narrative strategies of *Serenity* as a postcolonial text of the experiences of the colonial and the imperial, to create a narrative perversion of sense making in the post-*Firefly* Whedon universe.

Serenity is postcolonial science fiction. It is a text that embodies in its structure and intention an engagement and dialogue with imperial themes involving the colonization of other worlds. Many science fiction films possess these tropes. Indeed, "The history of space representation is full of versions of settler colonization" (Redfield 799). The archetype of late 20th century science fiction cinematic success, *Star Wars*, has its evil Empire of colonialists constructing death stars and using "the dark side" to annihilate rebellions on multiple conquered and unconquered worlds. This is just one of many science fiction films relying on and deploying the colonial context as setting for conflict, climax, and resolution. The relationships between science fiction and the colonial trope have been intertwined with popular imaginings of the rationalized project of "western" enlightenment. Indeed, the thematics of "SF [science fiction] came into being as a popular genre during a specific period in European history, the high age of empire" (Alessio 11). The ideas and ideologies of science fiction are exceptionally reliant on the conditions that stimulated the global and local shifts embedded in empire formation and maintenance. More recently, *Avatar* has explored the consequences of imperial greed and hyper-capitalist rationales that motivate the conquering of land and indigenous peoples for profit. The postcolonial potential in science fiction resonates in contemporary texts conveying conflict between disempowered communities and a significant state or corporate entity seeking control over land, resources, solar systems, and people.

Serenity offers punctuation to the postcolonial diegesis in that the colonialists are not represented taking land from indigenes, but rather terraforming unpopulated planets for human settlement. These populations are left with few supplies and are expected to craft their own livelihoods from the land or raw materials native to the landscape. These populations suffer all sorts of difficulties ranging from illness created by side effects of the terraforming process to unlawfulness and poverty due to their geographical distance from the "core" planets of the Alliance that are technologically advanced and "civilized." A key motivation for the life choices of Malcolm Reynolds and his crew is to remain, nomads drifting through the outer planets on the border and keep their distance from the centralized and colonial power of the Alliance. Malcolm Reynolds and his first mate Zoë were soldiers in the war for independence fought by the populations of the border planets against the imperial rule of the Alliance. The independents lost and Malcolm and Zoë now make their living in a way that resists the imposition of imperial "civilization" and subjugation by the core planets. This inside rebellion is what makes *Serenity* and its predecessor *Firefly* so volatile. These characters are not unruly natives opposing the civilizing force of the empire; they are themselves subjects of the empire, those who from the inside are resisting the ideals of technological advancement and enlightenment that coerce populations to the will of the Alliance. They prefer to live at and on the "border" rather than be manipulated to the will and power of Alliance interests. It is a tense and conflicted relationship that River Tam keenly observes in *Serenity*:

Teacher: With so many social and medical advances, why would the independents fight so hard against us?

Young River: We meddle.

Teacher: River?

Young River: People don't like to be meddled with. We tell them what to do, what to think. Don't run. Don't walk. We're in their homes and in their heads and we haven't the right. We're meddlesome.

Teacher: River, we're not telling people what to think, we're just trying to show them how.

THE ALLIANCE SEEKS TO CONTROL AND CONTAIN OPPOSING AND DIFFICULT IDEAS IN ORDER TO ALIGN POPULATIONS UNDER THEIR AUTHORITY

The Alliance seeks to control and contain opposing and difficult ideas in order to align populations under its authority. In both *Firefly* and *Serenity* the processes by which it achieves this assertion is represented as multifaceted, involving both military force and the manipulation of information via news media or "the puppet theatre" as it is referred to in *Serenity*.

These structures are embedded and potent, making the oppressive power structures implicit and conventional instead of strange and perverse. The parallels by which the social media, military force, government, and corporate interests are aligned in *Serenity* offer a sinister insight into the world of rule and regulation as well as the irreverent practices of resistance to them. It is a double vision—a way of seeing into the fictional and "real world" methods by which control and power are asserted and inserted into everyday lives. *Serenity* operates as a "looking glass"—a way to look back at ourselves and examine the meanings by which we live our own lives and the systems through which we make sense of power, authority, and resistance. The two-way mirror offered in *Serenity* operates in the space left vacant by *Firefly*, but its image is less acute and slightly blurred. It is an incomplete vision and a limited glimpse into the scenes and situations that seduce citizens, offering a space for the reimagining of rebellion that is contained and controlled, but also messy and mesmerizing.

These ideas are unruly, and they filter through *Serenity* in ways that are subtle and seductive, implanted in the narrative context as simultaneously normative and deviant. They slice through the facades of meaning-making offering a troublesome text that re-imagines the everyday through future tropes that connect and cauterize senses of the self via the (post)colonial. This makes *Firefly* dangerous and *Serenity* seductive. The film and series peeled open spaces of critique through a perverse potlatch of plotting that knitted together desire and deviance, consumption and colonization, the lawful and unlawful.

Whedon managed to translate many of the ideas at the core of *Firefly* into *Serenity*, by maintaining the key relationships between the Alliance and the border planets as well as depicting the hedonistic and uncompromising values of thievery among the *Serenity* crew. Audiences are left with an unruly and fragmented text that walks the lines between the popular and the unpopular. The glimpses of insightful dialogue that slice through the clichés of meaning embedded in the imperial intention sit uncomfortably beside the action sequences designed for spectacle and easy consumption, and character traits circumscribing narrative conventions. *Serenity* embodies postcolonial politics because it revels in the fractures of meaning systems where there are unclear meetings between imperial ideals, ordinary citizens, and their everyday lives. It is not postcolonial science fiction only because it deals with the themes of colonization and resistance in the future, but rather because it provides a mechanism by which the diegesis as well as the conditions which created *Serenity* as a cultural text coincide and are embedded in the tensions between authority and rebellion, the inside and the outside, the popular and the unpopular.

Both the content and the means of production of *Serenity* interface with postcolonial meanings and moments. These moments are insightful and challenging as they convey the complexities of the ambiguous and what it means to walk between contradictions—in meanings, identities, and representations. Malcolm Reynolds is the key contradictory character in the film, giving voice to the unconventional, whereas in the series the ensemble cast creates a volatile network of contradictory characterization to provide a nexus through which these unpredictable meanings manifest. As Mal explains:

"I look out for me and mine. That don't include you unless I conjure it does. Now, you stuck a thorn in the Alliance's paw. That tickles me up here. But it also means that I gotta step twice as fast and that means turning down plenty of jobs, even honest ones. Put this crew together with the promise of work which the Alliance makes harder every year. Come a day there won't be room for naughty men like us to sneak about at all. This job goes south, there may not be any. So here's us. On the raggedy edge" (*Serenity*).

Malcolm Reynolds and his crew are unruly. They desire the untamed frontier of the outer-world planets and the space in-between where they can operate outside of the imperial gaze of the Alliance. They are nomads who are always just passing through, and they, like consumers of the film (and series) are playing in the spaces between the sanctioned and the unsanctioned.

The border planets are depicted as lawless, savage, and barbaric. At the very fringes of this space exist the mythologized (for those on the central planets) Reavers—beings outside the power and imposition of the Alliance. While Reynolds and his crew are part of the empire and resist from within— by stealing, smuggling, and harboring fugitives—the Reavers are banished to the imaginary excesses for core planet populations. They are real only to those on the border where the excessive and the grotesque can exist. Reavers rape, tear the flesh from live humans, and disfigure themselves in their madness. The Reavers are the extremes of resistance. They cannot be colonized and are beyond the meanings of imperialism. Moving from the irrational to the rational is a colonial trope subverted by the Reavers. In *Serenity*, reason, enlightenment, and the civilized development of humanity, economically, politically, and culturally through colonization is corrupted by these creatures. They are irrational and cannot be brought to the rational—advanced and civilized—ideals of the colonizers. The Reavers are the embodiment of madness—of the colonial project gone wrong and the perversions that result from imperialism. In *Serenity* it is discovered that the Reavers were created by the Alliance as a result of a population experiment gone wrong on the planet of Miranda.

The planet name "Miranda" is a clear allusion to *The Tempest* by William Shakespeare. His Miranda is a girl of intense emotion, loved by her father and raised on an isolated island. This analogy is used in *Serenity* when

River's knowledge of Miranda draws the crew to the planet and its secret. The Alliance experiment there was to use an air-born medication known as "the Pax" to subdue the population and weed out aggressive attitudes and intentions—to colonize hearts and minds and force compliance. The experiment failed, causing most of the citizens of Miranda simply to lie down and die, lacking the motivation to rise, eat, wash, or even breathe. But a small minority of the population experienced an extreme increase in aggression, thus creating the Reavers.

The desire to keep Miranda a secret motivates the Alliance to pursue River Tam and the crew of *Serenity*. River is also mad but not irrational like the Reavers and is therefore able to access some of her knowledge and information that is "outside" the Alliance's approved archive. Her tenuous position within these spaces of knowledge means she must be silenced as she is able to translate between the irrationalities of imperialism and reveal the embedded structures of resistance. In *Firefly* the relationships between River, *Serenity*'s crew, and the Alliance are more complexly depicted as the Blue Sun Corporation is responsible for River's abduction, torture, and pursuit. In the series, the pursuers are not simply the Alliance, but a sinister sector of this complex driven by greed and pathology. As the narrative shifts into *Serenity*, the potency of the pathological is unraveled as the unintended consequences of the colonial project are revealed.

In *Serenity* the emphasis of empire is shifted to the Parliament—the faceless ruling body of the Alliance—as the key entity pursuing the Tams and that which sends a nameless Operative as opposed to the psychotic but named bounty hunter Jubal Early in the "Objects in Space" episode of *Firefly*. This nameless Operative embodies the unknowable cortex of imperialism and the interface of ruthless and institutional ideologies that motivate the meanings created in this center. As these ideas about power, governance, and greed move toward the fringe, the meanings become unstuck and are able to be rewritten by Reynolds and the crew. Malcolm defeats but does not kill the Operative. When Mal shows the Operative the "world without sin" that the Alliance created on Miranda, he stops the imperial troops from killing the crew and even allows Serenity to be repaired at facilities he has authority over—demonstrating the unraveling of meanings that spiral out from the centers of authority to the edges of empire and back into the core. At his defeat and the revelation of government secrets, the Operative no longer can fulfil his function—he is stripped of his power and imperialism is emptied. The ideologies of the Alliance have been exposed, re-encoding the Operative and nullifying his monstrousness.

IT IS THE UNINTENDED CONSEQUENCES OF EMPIRE THAT ARE ULTIMATELY DANGEROUS

It is the unintended consequences of Empire that are ultimately dangerous, and not the cultivated contexts of power maintenance and monitoring at the heart of the colonies. The Operative admits to his monstrousness in the narrative, but is ultimately neutralized as the spaces of postcoloniality extend. The Reavers are the real monsters as their creation and containment are unpredictable—an unintended consequence of the corrupt colonial project. They exist at the edges of meaning and are therefore the most dangerous threat to Empire. The crew of *Serenity* operate between these spheres, where the controlled and cultivated monsters of the Alliance and the spontaneous and sinister monsters at the border are always threatening to undo the codes and contexts of reality. *Serenity*'s crew succeeds in harnessing these entities to further their own agenda to declaw the Alliance and visualize the in-between spaces of sense making that are functional, measured and sensible.

These subtle shifts streamline the narrative, making the bad guys easily cohered and constructed within the imposing power bloc of the Alliance and assisting with the audience's attraction to the irreverent resistance of the *Serenity* crew. Key paradigms are being drawn between the power of the Alliance, the resistive thievery of Malcolm Reynolds and the oppositional barbaric savagery of the Reavers. The crew of *Serenity* are unknowingly part of a much larger political and social conspiracy involving ideologies at the core of the rhetoric of Empire. This trinity of power blocs creates a moving vortex of meanings that provide space for multiple strategies of understanding resistance. River is an imperial aberrance, simultaneously inside and outside of empire—able to reveal Reavers and (re)encode the resistance of *Serenity* and her crew as essential and ethical instead of deviant or unlawful. Through her knowledge of Miranda, their actions are not simply rebellious or criminal, but part of an ethical project of reinscription, reconstruction, and rewriting of imperial histories.

It is the Reavers that provide the ultimate uncontrollable variable within the narrative and it is also Malcolm Reynolds's ability to move between the convoluted meaning systems that enables him to harness their unruliness for his purposes. In *Firefly*, the power structures were conveyed as an intricate network with local warlords on outer rim planets holding sway, along with petty thieves, corrupt Alliance officials and lawmen, and brutal organized crime bosses. Reavers only make one appearance in the series when one of their ships is seen in "Serenity," the first episode. When they play a much greater role in *Serenity*, they provide a counterbalance to the Alliance and construct the provocative postcolonial potential of the film. They are the monster in the closet—the warning about the consequences of perverting populations. This lesson is encoded into the ideologies of empire and activated in the manipulations of people genetically and politically, not in some abstract scientific leap or morally corrupt future context, but in the conditions of imperialism that were and are used to motivate the discoverer ideals of "adventure," "exploration," and "discovery."

These are not future ideas, but those of our immediate colonial past and present. These are concepts with us in the contemporary where "advocates of space exploration constitute perhaps the last unabashed enthusiasts of imperialism, cheerfully describing conquest, settlement and expansion, and hesitating not a whit before employing the term 'colony'" (Redfield 797). The implicit and expected imperial ideologies that are embedded within the language we use to speak about space and even think about an off-world future are revealed in the subtleties of *Serenity*. This also represents our failure to adequately understand the impacts and tragedies of colonization in our historical proximity. The pasts of colonial exploitation are encoded in the power structures of indoctrination, resistance, and rebellion within the filmic narrative. *Serenity* walks these lines where the conventions of the colonial are spotlighted and questioned. The spaces between the colonial and the postcolonial are presented as dangerous and playful—where new languages and grammars are revealed. The potential for perversion is always simmering just below the surface in *Serenity*. Mal tells his crew:

"This report is maybe 12 years old. Parliament buried it and it stayed buried until River dug it up. This is what they feared she knew and they were right to fear, coz there's a whole universe of folk who are gonna know it too. They're gonna see it. Somebody has to speak for these people. You all got on this boat for different reasons. But you've all come to the same place. So now I'm asking more of you than I have before. Maybe all. Sure as I know anything I know this. They will try again. Maybe on another world. Maybe on this very ground swept clean. A year from now—ten— they'll swing back to the belief that they can make people... better. And I don't hold to that. So no more running. I aim to misbehave" (*Serenity*).

The motivations of empire—to civilize other peoples, to bring enlightenment where little exists, to develop culturally, politically, technologically and socially, and to extend geographical boundaries—are all encoded as corruptions within *Serenity*. The power of the Alliance does not hold sway—it is unsteady and poisonous. There are other spaces for resistance activated and visualized. The importance and significance of the fringe expanding the roles and rules of colonization are embodied in the crew of *Serenity* and in the Reavers that haunt the edges of empire.

The potential for the finely crafted colonial context to come tumbling down is ever present in these spaces. The postcolonial potential is present not in a cosmopolitan togetherness as outlined by Lindy Orthia in her argument involving *Doctor Who* where the future is composed of "a multi-racial cosmopolitanism" (Orthia 208)—there are no aliens in *Serenity*—but instead in a tenuous and savage interface between the ideologies of colonization, human evolution and mutation, war, civilization, and lawlessness.

In *Serenity* the future is unstable—in the process of being made and constantly being torn down. The postcolonial problematic of the fringe always and implicitly influencing the core is represented by the Alliance's relentless pursuit of the Tams, and in their desire to control information, emotions, and embodiment. Simon Gikandi's argument about the "incomplete project of colonization" (Gikandi 9) is realized when we can visualize through *Serenity* the spaces for rebellion against imperial ideas and their influence on the shifting meanings of our present, as well as the fundamental corruption of the project embodied by Reavers.

Serenity plays in the spaces offered by the tropes and tones of the *Firefly* template, but it cannot capture the depth of Whedon's *Firefly* vision. Instead, it is a half-life for the story—a moment of survival for an idea beyond realization. But, perhaps it is this tenuousness that makes *Serenity* inherently and powerfully postcolonial. In *Serenity*, we find the archetypal postcolonial moment—the grief for what could have been—for who we could be if the colonizers had never come.

The postcolonial landscape of the 'Verse is palpable as the begrudging submission of the Outer World Independents to the Central Alliance frames the narrative arc of Captain Malcolm Reynolds and his *Firefly* crew. *Serenity* is postcolonial science fiction through which Whedon is activating a space for the engagement of rebellious and resistive ideas about government, crime, sexuality, and belonging that struggle for popular articulation in an era highlighted by compliant consumer consciousness and rigorous retail sales. Yet the strength of these ideas—their subtleties and subversions—has seen them survive network cancellations and mismanagement, to re-emerge in *Serenity*. This struggle between power and resistance in the metamorphosis of *Firefly* into *Serenity* paralleling the diegetic intentions of the story arc creates an engaging and insightful exposition on postcoloniality and its manifestations in popular culture.

Works Cited

Alessio, Dominic. "From Body Snatchers to Mind Snatchers: Indigenous Science Fiction, Postcolonialism, and Aotearoa/New Zealand History." *Journal of Postcolonial Writing* 47.3 (July 2011): 257-69. Web. 10 Dec. 2010. (Available online before print issue).

Firefly: The Complete Series. Twentieth Century Fox Home Entertainment, 2003. DVD.

Gikandi, Simon. *Maps of Englishness: Writing Identity in the Culture of Colonialism.* New York: Columbia U P, 1996. Print.

"Objects in Space." 14. Writ. and dir. Joss Whedon. *Firefly.*

Orthia, Lindy. "'Sociopathetic Abscess' or 'Yawning Chasm'? The Absent Postcolonial Transition in *Doctor Who.*" *Journal of Commonwealth Literature* 45.2 (2010): 207-25. Print.

Redfield, Peter. "The Half-life of Empire in Outer Space." *Social Studies of Science* 32.5-6 (2002): 791-825. Print.

"Safe." 5. Writ. Drew Z. Greenberg. Dir. Michael Grossman. *Firefly.*

"Serenity." 1. Writ. and dir. Joss Whedon. *Firefly.*

Serenity. Writ. and dir. Joss Whedon. Universal, 2005. DVD.

"SFX Special Preview: *Serenity* 2 Painful to Think About, Says Joss." *SFX World of Whedon* 26 Sep. 2010. Web. 6 Jan. 2011.

3.05
The Death of Utopia:
Firefly and the Return to Human Realism in TV Sci-Fi
Chris Colgan

Science fiction television before the year 2000 was remarkably uniform in its view of humanity becoming a somewhat idyllic society in the future. True, wars still existed, but most other problems that plague mankind in the current era had disappeared from these universes. *Star Wars*, *Star Trek*, *Stargate*, *Babylon 5*, and even *SeaQuest DSV* all showed a future where mankind had, for the most part, eliminated poverty and disease from the social structure and people lived in a clean, almost utopian environment, as long as war was not in the picture. Consequently, most of the television franchises during the 1990s, *Star Trek* chief among them, also showed a future where social classes had disappeared, and the baser desires of people for acquisition and wealth had been suppressed.

While this vision did help represent a better future and gave people aspirations for such a future, many of these series omitted the human struggle against one's own environment and the desire to improve one's standing through possessions and material worth. This is one reason the *Star Trek* franchise has received some criticism in the past, for having human characters that are nearly devoid of current-day motivations, and for depicting characters that did have such motivations as either wholly evil, comic relief, or inconsequentially minor.

Joss Whedon, however, changed all of this with *Firefly*. In one fell swoop in 2002, he took the concept of the human utopia in science fiction, tossed it aside, and revolutionized the view of the human future on television. Whedon did not want a future without struggle against environment, nor did he want humanity to be without social classes and the allure of the almighty dollar. Thus, he created *Firefly* as an antithetical foil to *Star Trek*—a universe where power was still in one's wallet, where corruption and deception retained their strongholds in the highest levels of society, and a man would (and actually could) still bleed to achieve his dreams. Science fiction was forever changed by this, and it is why *Firefly* should be one of the names listed among the greatest science fiction series of all time.

The cultural diversity and simultaneous uniformity of *Firefly* is one of its greatest strengths and one of its most innovative achievements. Creating a society dominated exclusively by American and Chinese culture not only allowed for a richer linguistic palette but also let viewers indulge in a multitude of new visual and sensory experiences on how common culture could be displayed and participated in. However, the variety of settings shown on the various worlds in the *Firefly* universe created a realistic atmosphere of humanity still leading an individualistic society, as each world had its own distinct flavor and biodiversity. In a sense, each world in *Firefly* represented a different piece of Earth's own environmental mixture, and these worlds also reflected the ethnic and cultural choices of different groups within modern-day humanity. From the low-class urban areas of Persephone seen in the pilot episode and the backwater rural community of Paradiso in "The Train Job" (2), all the way to the hyper-civilized cityscape of the core in "Ariel" (9) and the ultra-rich floating islands of Bellerophon in "Trash" (11), *Firefly* ran the gamut of cultural possibilities, just in its settings.

Of equal significance, though, are the goals and aspirations of the main characters in *Firefly*, and none of these are more important than the star of the show, Captain Malcolm Reynolds. In many ways, Mal is *Firefly*'s answer to Han Solo of *Star Wars*. The two share many of the same character traits: nobility, brashness, charm, and a certain degree of selfishness. However, Mal's goals are more centralized on himself. He sees the Alliance as evil, but he has given up fighting them in order to serve his own needs. His is a cautionary tale of what Han Solo could have become if the Rebellion had lost in *Star Wars*. On the flipside, Mal exhibits the positive aspects of the aforementioned character traits at greater levels than Han Solo does, and it's easy to see that Mal's sense of justice is broader than Han's.

The episodes "The Train Job" and "Safe" (5) are the best examples of this, where Mal risks his life to help people that he could have very easily left behind without consequence to himself or his crew. The fact that he gave of himself without question and put the well-being of others ahead of himself without any personal stake makes Mal a better version of the "lovable rogue" than Han Solo could ever hope to be. But Mal also has some dark qualities, most stemming from the crushing defeat he and his comrades in the Independents suffered in the pilot episode. These losses are what ultimately give rise to his selfishness, his principle that elevates the safety of himself and his crew over helping absolutely everyone in need. The basic human desires for security and freedom are the divining rod for Mal, which make him a positive character despite some of his less virtuous choices.

However, while Mal does show a lack of altruism on several occasions, he isn't the foremost example of a character motivated strictly by self-interest. For that, one only needs to look at Jayne Cobb, Mal's hired gun and the most selfish character in *Firefly*. Truly, no character has ever embraced and extended Maslow's hierarchy of needs more than Jayne. He is a paragon of selfishness, desiring first to be able to eat, then to have protection, and finally to have his creature comforts. Indulging in every vice and excess that is presented to him, Jayne's sense of restraint is nonexistent, and his nobility is severely limited, although it does exist. Before Jayne, no major "heroic" character in any science fiction series possessed such moral ambiguity. While Jayne's greed and unenlightened self-interest can sometimes turn him into a source of comic relief, his questionable nature is the biggest reason why he is so well-liked among *Firefly* fans. Jayne is the man of the future still in search of the twenty-first century American dream: get rich quick, live hedonistically, and die before the money runs out. What member of a Western capitalist society wouldn't love a man embracing such character traits? Nearly every viewer can identify and agree with Jayne at some point in the series for some reason, even if they all think he is scum for the rest of the time.

What *Firefly* changed most in science fiction, though, was the realism in the lives of the characters. As Joss Whedon put so eloquently in the bonus features of the *Firefly* DVD collection, the show dealt with the people that *Star Trek* would have just flown past without a second glance. *Firefly* was one of the few science fiction shows up to that point that displayed poor, homeless, diseased, and destitute people with any regularity. The aforementioned struggle against environment was visible in every major character in the show, as well as the majority of the minor characters that appeared in the show. And while *Serenity* minimized this aspect of the show to focus on the storyline centered on River, these elements still were part of the overarching plotline of the movie as it related to the goals of Mal and the crew. Everyone wanted to attain something that would give a greater sense of independence, security, comfort, freedom, and ultimately of self. The depiction of these desires and the trials associated with them are the greatest success of *Firefly*.

The realism of the show covered not only the mental and emotional aspects of the characters, but the physical and biological realities as well. On *Star Trek*'s television incarnations, when a character was hit by a phaser blast or even stabbed, the victim was rarely seen to bleed. Even in the movies, when bleeding occurred, it rarely looked realistic (see the almost-comical bleeding effects of *Star Trek VI* for reference). On *Firefly*, characters bled frequently and profusely, and when someone got hit with a bullet, there were no dermal regenerators, nano-probes, or other techno-babble devices to provide instant fixes. Gunshots, stab wounds, and other physical injuries are just as serious in *Firefly*'s future as they are today. Furthermore, no one on the crew of *Firefly* was seen doing impossible physical tasks or remarkable feats of strength well beyond human abilities, with the obvious exception of River, whose physical enhancements were, arguably, still within the limits of human normalcy. Staying outside these realms of fantasy is what makes the *Firefly* universe seem like a possible future for humanity, and is an enormous contribution to its appeal.

The impact of these changes on traditional science fiction archetypes not only added a great deal to *Firefly*'s success over time but also influenced future science fiction shows and franchises. The revamped *Battlestar Galactica* franchise, launched just a year after *Firefly*'s television run, was successful in part because of a similar approach to that of *Firefly*, adding a great deal of human realism to the classic story. Thus, the new *Battlestar Galactica* created a more plausible future for humanity than its original incarnation portrayed and also made the human characters more accessible and the ominous Cylons even more terrifying. Additionally, the television incarnation of *Stargate*, entitled *Stargate SG-1*, made subtle changes in its characters that made them seem more human and realistic, although not to the level that *Battlestar Galactica* did. These elements of increased humanity also became integral parts of the writing in the spin-off series *Stargate Atlantis* and *Stargate Universe*. Even the 2005 resurrection of

Doctor Who and the subsequent seasons have taken a much more serious tone and attempted to be more realistic than their predecessors, although the differences between American and British science fiction television will always make that discussion a matter of perspective.

Newer shows outside of existing franchises have also used the *Firefly* model of character portrayal, especially shows that deal with people on Earth. Both *Supernatural* and *Warehouse 13* created characters with believably strong human desires, grounded in emotion and immediacy rather than logic and virtue. Meanwhile, traditional science fiction shows that adhered to the characterization models of old space operas lost public favor, such as the ill-timed *Andromeda*. There were also shows, such as the *Battlestar Galactica* spin-off *Caprica*, that took the elements of realism too far, resulting in their swift demise for lacking the inherent fantastical elements of science fiction in the storyline.

In the end, only one conclusion can be drawn from this: Joss Whedon and *Firefly* have helped kill the old model of the "space opera" as we know it. The grand epics of superhuman, hyper-virtuous, and utopian people are a relic of the past now. Modern science fiction meant for mature audiences will focus on the human mind, the capacities for good, evil, virtue, and vice that exist within it, and the struggles against environment that occur to attain success and self-actualization. While other franchises and series have received similar acclaim for their own use of these changes, *Firefly* was the first to do it successfully without losing its science fiction core. The universe of *Firefly* is a future that every person alive today can relate to in some way, which is ultimately the deciding factor in the success or failure of any science fiction franchise in the modern day. Thus, even without the television ratings, merchandising sales, or international renown of its other series, *Firefly* will always be one of the greatest successes of science fiction.

Works Cited

Firefly: *The Complete Series*. Twentieth Century Fox Home Entertainment, 2002. DVD.
"Safe." 5. Writ. Drew Z. Greenberg. Dir. Michael Grossman. *Firefly*.
Serenity. Writ. and dir. Joss Whedon. Universal, 2005. DVD.
"The Train Job." 2. Writ. Joss Whedon and Tim Minear. Dir. Joss Whedon. *Firefly*.
"Trash." 11. Writ. Ben Edlund. Dir. Marita Grabiak. *Firefly*.

3.06
Can't Stop the Serenity:
Joss Whedon's Shows and Fan Activism
Lisa Anderson

By now, the pop culture world knows the story of how Joss Whedon overcame the cancellation of *Firefly* to tie up many of the loose ends in the movie *Serenity*. What's less widely known is how Whedon's fans, who bolstered him in this effort, turned *Serenity* into a movement, and in the process became real-life heroes.

In 2006, the year after *Serenity* came out, a fan in Portland, Oregon, decided to hold a charity screening of *Serenity* on Joss's birthday, June 23. The money would go to Equality Now, a women's rights organization with which Joss is involved. The idea quickly mushroomed to events in forty-six cities in the US, UK, Canada, Australia, and New Zealand. Some events were simple screenings of the movies, while others included events like costume contests, dances, and banquets. There have been Can't Stop the Serenity (CSTS) events every year since then, in a "season" running from June to September. In 2010 alone, there were fifty-two events worldwide. The all-volunteer CSTS Global team coordinates and provides technical support for the local events, as well as providing auction and sale items and official memorabilia. Seventy-five percent of each event's profits must go to Equality Now, and crews of the individual events chose which charities receive the rest. Since 2006, over half a million dollars have been raised for Equality Now. The CSTS Global team and the local event crews are, of course, volunteers ("History").

I am on the crew for one event, Nashville's WhedonFest, which is in its third year. So what does the Can't Stop the Serenity movement mean to me? I've found that there is a surprising overlap between fan activism and the themes in Whedon's work. Specifically, those themes are Women's Empowerment, Chosen Families, and Boosting the Signal.

WOMEN'S EMPOWERMENT

One doesn't have to know much about Joss to know that women's issues are important to him. His work is filled with strong, three-dimensional female characters. From a feminist perspective, he occasionally stumbles, but his respect and empathy for women are obvious and consistent. He does more than pay lip service to equality; he also shows respect for women behind the scenes. Many important writing and production roles on his projects have long been given to talented women. Simply checking the episode lists of Whedon's four television series will yield the names of writers and directors as Jane Espenson, Marti Noxon, Marissa Tancharoen, Rebecca Rand Kirshner, Sarah Fain, Elizabeth Craft, Jeannine Renshaw, and more.

Joss traces this respect for women in large part back to his late mother, Lea Stearns, who was a strong person and a profound influence on him, as he has said in countless interviews. It is not surprising then, that one of her high school students, Jessica Neuwirth, went on to co-found Equality Now ("About"). Equality Now was founded in 1992, by Neuwirth and two other attorneys, Navanethem Pillay from South Africa and Feryal Garahi from Iran. Their mission is to promote and protect the human rights of women around the world. This is done by bringing the public's attention to human rights violations against women and taking action to protest them. Their issues include, but are not limited to, human trafficking, economic participation, and domestic violence ("Our Work").

Whedon was honored by Equality Now in 2006 at their benefit dinner honoring Men on the Front Lines. In his speech, he played the dual roles of himself and the press, giving various answers to a question posed numerous times: "Why do you write these strong women characters?" In the end, the answer was simple: "Because you're still asking me that question" (Whedon). His speech quickly spread across the Internet and is still available on sites from YouTube to Equality Now.

CHOSEN FAMILIES

The significance of chosen families is a recurring theme in Whedon's work. From the crew of *Serenity* to the Scooby Gang on *Buffy*, Whedon's protagonists survive and succeed by banding together. Even if they do so just to survive initially (as in *Firefly*), they end up in the service of something more important than themselves. Dr. Horrible alone stands in contrast to this, and his aspirations to change the world take a tragic turn.

Whedonites United, the organization that puts on WhedonFest, is more than just a fan group or a CSTS crew. We're friends who share in each other's troubles and concerns as well as our joys and successes. What's more, we all bring something different to the table to make our event happen. We have people who are good at getting sponsors, people who are good with technology, those who are good with money, and so on. Many of us are good cooks, and attendants at WhedonFest benefit from that every year. Like the crew of *Firefly*, CSTS crews "aim to misbehave"—but only in the best possible way. There's no Alliance to fight, but CSTS challenges negative aspects of the status quo. In the case of Whedonites United, we fight women's oppression by supporting Equality Now, we help get children's books into libraries through Kids Need to Read, and address the plight of stray animals through New Leash on Life of Lebanon, Tennessee ("About").

If you look at Joss's work, he *doesn't* seem to believe that one person can save the world. But if you work together with like-minded people? Then no power in the 'Verse can stop you.

BOOSTING THE SIGNAL

Here's the thing about empowerment, though: once you're empowered, you can't keep it to yourself. You have to share that power for the good of the world. Taking a page straight from Joseph Campbell, the conclusions of *Serenity*, *Buffy*, and *Dollhouse* all involve the sharing of power with the wider world. I suspect that *Serenity* is the reason why people refer to "boosting the signal" when spreading news through online social networks. The line also occurs in the episode of *Firefly* when Wash rigs a way to boost the dying ship's signal to call for help and save the crew ("Out of Gas"). When CSTS crews look for sponsors, they're inviting people to get empowered by participating in the change we seek to create. Some sponsors will be motivated by the specific charities. Others only need to know that it's for charity, or that someone they know is involved... or that it's about Joss.

The same invitation is extended to people attending CSTS events. Our charities need money, that's true, but this movement also needs fans. It needs their opinions and discussions, their cosplay and their fanfiction, their parody songs and their scholarship. Fans share these things at other conventions, but fan activism like CSTS gives people the opportunity to create change with the truths that they've learned from the stories they love.

This is what the Can't Stop the Serenity movement means to me. I hope that I've inspired some of you to attend a CSTS event... or even to join your local crew!

Works Cited

"About the Organizations You'll Be Supporting." *Whedonites United*. Web. 18 Oct. 2011.
"History." *Can't Stop the Serenity*. Web. 18 Oct. 2011.

"Our Work." *Equality Now*. Web. 18 Oct. 2011.

"Out of Gas." 8. Writ. Tim Minear. Dir. David Solomon. Firefly: *The Complete Series.* Twentieth Century Fox, 2003. DVD.

Whedon, Joss. The Equality Now Speech. *Equality Now*. 5 May 2006. Web. 18 Oct. 2011.

3.07
The Ethics of Malcolm Reynolds

Mike Bailey

In the episode entitled "The Train Job," Mal and crew take on a job stealing cargo from a train on the frontier colony of Paradiso. When asked by Niska, who had hired them, whether they wanted to know what it was they were stealing, Mal answered that it didn't matter. When the job goes wrong later, Mal discovers that it was, in fact, medicine that they were stealing—medicine which was desperately needed by the colonists. This revelation leads Mal to return the medicine, which ends in a confrontation with the local sheriff. The sheriff explains, "These are tough times. A man can get a job, he might not look too close at what that job is. But when a man learns all the details about a situation like ours, well then he has a choice." Mal replies quite succinctly, "I don't believe he does." For Mal there is no choice.

This is evidence that Mal follows a deontological, or duty-based, system of ethics. Perhaps the best-known ethical system of this type is that of eighteenth century philosopher Immanuel Kant. In the first formulation of his categorical imperative, Kant argued that one should "Act only according to that maxim by which you can at the same time will that it would become a universal law." In other words, an action is right only if it can apply to all people at all times with no exceptions. To formulate Mal's decision as a maxim: *one should never steal medicine from sick people who need it*. It was his duty to return the medicine, even though it would mean making a very powerful enemy out of Niska.

Another example of Mal following the categorical imperative is in "Safe" (5), when Simon and River are abducted by villagers. Mal takes the ship and crew to rescue them. This surprises everyone, including Simon, who confronts Mal and wants to know why he would rescue them if he doesn't even like them. Once again, Mal answers simply, with "you're on my crew": thus following the maxim *a captain always rescues a member of his crew.*

A duty-based ethic also addresses how one should treat other people. Mal is against slavery, which apparently still rears its ugly head in Whedon's version of our future. Whether it is picking a fight with a slaver in the bar at the beginning of "Shindig" (4) or looking disgusted at the conditions of the indentured "mudders" in "Jaynestown" (7), Mal does not think well of the idea of someone owning another person. Slavery and indentured servitude are both violations of the second formulation of Kant's categorical imperative which is, "Act in such a way that you always treat humanity, never simply as a means, but always at the same time as an end." Simply put, it is not acceptable to use a person only as a means to an end. One should not use, without consent, another person to pursue one's own ends, or coerce that person to do something only for one's own benefit or self-interest; to do so would deny that person the freedom to do what he/she wishes to do.

This explains one reason that Mal is so opposed to Inara's profession. He likely sees it as simply another form of person ownership. Mal would view Inara's clients as having purchased her, and that they are looking at her as little more than property. As he tells Inara in "Shindig," her client Atherton Wing "treats you like an ornament." Similarly, when Mal is told he has been "given" a wife as payment for helping the settlers at the beginning of "Our Mrs. Reynolds" (6), he is appalled. "You are no one's property" is his reply to Saffron's insistence that she had been given to him. He is later disgusted by Jayne's offer to trade Saffron for something Jayne values—a gun that Jayne has personified with a woman's name, Vera, further equating a person with an object to be owned. However, Mal points out that Saffron is not an object (like the gun), but a person who is "not to be traded, borrowed, or lent" ("Our Mrs. Reynolds"). To treat another person as property is to use her or him only as a means and not as an end.

At the core of Mal's ethical system is his belief that all people should be free. This is clear in his views concerning slavery, but also in his opposition to the Alliance whose views are personified in the movie *Serenity* in the character of the Operative. Just before he forces a scientist to fall on his sword in the opening of the film, the Operative says, "We are making a better world—all of them." We find out through the course of the movie that the Alliance had, in fact, literally tried to create a better world on the planet Miranda. This was done by introducing a drug, called the Pax—or *peace* in Latin—to end all conflict and control the population. The drug did remove people's aggressive natures. Unfortunately, it also caused them to lose their desire to do anything. The majority of the people simply lay down and died, but it had the opposite reaction with a small number of people who were transformed into the much-feared Reavers.

The Alliance continually tries to make the 'verse better. It first waged a lengthy and costly war in order to unify and bring "civilization" to all human worlds. Now that all worlds were unified under one central authority, the Alliance had to find ways to control them. One attempt at that control was the experiment on Miranda. However, there is no hint in the film that the planet had been particularly disorderly or on the brink of rebellion or civil war. The impression is that Miranda was simply a convenient place—because of its isolation or some other reason or no reason—to test the new drug. So an entire population unknowingly became lab rats in the Alliance's "meddlesome" attempt to find a better way to control people for their own good.

One common goal of moral philosophy is to define what is known as "the good." The Alliance's answer to this goal is that in order to achieve the good; you have to make people better. However, as Voltaire famously pointed out, "better is the enemy of the good." Often, the more one tries to improve on something, the worse one makes it.

For Mal, the ultimate good for human beings is freedom. Mal understands that there is a price to pay for freedom. One has to protect oneself and one's property, without having a government authority to call when someone threatens you. Or, to translate it into a Mal maxim, "*If someone tries to kill you, you try to kill 'em right back.*" Mal believes that the more we rely on government, the more it tries to take over our lives.

However, Mal does not agree with simply using violence to obtain what you want—at least, not from innocent individuals. He has no qualms about stealing from the government, whether an Alliance security firm (*Serenity*) or an Alliance-run hospital ("Ariel" 9). He may be a smuggler, but Mal is no ordinary thief or cheat. When he tries to reimburse Niska's money after returning the medicine Niska paid him to steal, Mal says, "We're not thieves—well, we are, but the point is, we're not taking what's his" ("The Train Job" 2). The pirate ship's captain that shoots Mal and attempts to steal *Serenity* in "Out of Gas" tells Mal that he would have "done the same." However, Mal makes it clear that he would not have done so; he lets the pirates leave alive ("Out of Gas" 8).

True, Mal does not always hold up to even his own ideals. For example, he makes it clear to Simon that he would never shoot an unarmed man. Yet he does this very thing in *Serenity* when he takes out the pilot who attacked Haven, a pilot who clearly had his hands up. Of course, this unarmed, wounded man had just piloted the craft that attacked and murdered an entire colony of unarmed civilians. Those categorical imperatives do not quite cover every ethical situation. But this is the very thing that makes

Whedon's characters interesting and compelling. The characters are like real people, not just tired clichés, and those of us trying to follow our own moral standards in the so-called real world sometimes fail to live up to them as well. All we can do is keep trying, much like our captain, Malcolm Reynolds.

Works Cited

"Ariel." 9. Writ. Jose Molina. Dir. Allan Kroeker. *Firefly*.

Firefly:*The Complete Series*. Twentieth Century Fox Home Entertainment, 2003. DVD.

"Jaynestown." 7. Writ. Ben Edlund. Dir. Marita Grabiak. *Firefly*.

"Our Mrs. Reynolds." 6. Writ. Joss Whedon. Dir. Vondie Curtis Hall. *Firefly*.

"Out of Gas." 8. Writ. Tim Minear. Dir. David Solomon. *Firefly*.

"Safe." 5. Writ. Drew Z. Greenberg. Dir. Michael Grossman. *Firefly*.

"Serenity." 1. Writ. and dir. Joss Whedon. *Firefly*.

Serenity. Writ. and dir. Joss Whedon. Universal, 2005. DVD.

"Shindig." 4. Writ. Jane Espenson. Dir. Vern Gillum. *Firefly*.

"The Train Job." 2. Writ. Joss Whedon and Tim Minear. Dir. Joss Whedon. *Firefly*.

3.08
Heroic Humanism and Humanistic Heroism in Joss Whedon's Shows
Candace E. West

"That's why we write in the first place. To find our darkest place and lift it up into the light where we wish we were standing." —Joss Whedon, "2009 Outstanding Lifetime Achievement Award in Cultural Humanism"

For those who believe that popular culture, and especially popular narratives, can be an important place to explore meaningful ideas, Joss Whedon has been something of a patron saint. Whedon's focus on female strength tends to be the most visible part of his work—this has much to do with his self-professed feminism. In what follows, I'll be looking at a set of somewhat different, though not wholly unrelated aspects of his life and work. The first is his humanism, which I will then relate to his ideas of heroism. Given the breadth of his creative output, I'll focus on two examples, *Firefly/Serenity* and *Buffy the Vampire Slayer*, and I'll suggest that in addition to telling good stories that raise important issues about gender, they're both also thoughtful considerations of heroism in contemporary humanistic terms; specifically, both re-examine the relationship between the hero and the larger community. (For the purposes of this piece I'm taking *Firefly* and *Serenity* as a continuous narrative whole, thus the *Firefly/Serenity* notation. When I am speaking specifically of an episode of the show or of the film, I will note each separately.)

Remember that amazing moment when the Sunnydale High School students acknowledge Buffy's place as class protector and then give her an umbrella, a moment that should be cheesy, but is somehow perfect? Or when the townspeople want to burn River as a witch and Mal says, "Yeah, but she's our witch"? Those moments feel good because they're nice, but I'll be suggesting that there's more to them than that.

It's true that Whedon often reshapes the hero most noticeably by changing her gender, but his versatility as a storyteller has allowed him to speak with insight and nuance on a range of important ideas. Alongside his intentional focus on girls with killer roundhouse kicks, his work has repeatedly taken up a network of ethical concerns. Who are we? How should we live, act, choose, love, fight, die, value? *Buffy the Vampire Slayer* and *Firefly/Serenity* take up these questions from different angles, and the most reliable constants seem to be that the questions are difficult, that the answers will shift just as the characters in question (and, by extension, the viewers) become comfortable with them, and that the odds are not usually in our hero's favor. These dark odds do not, however, lead to a fatalistic viewpoint; there is usually a glimmer of hope, though it may be a faint one.

Given the recurrence of these ethical concerns, we might wonder what sort of worldview underlies them. Without delving too deeply into theories of authorial intent, a glance at outside events and relatively recent history may provide some useful context. In 2007, Harvard University's Humanist Chaplaincy sponsored a three-day conference called "The New Humanism." The Harvard Humanist Chaplaincy refers to many definitions in its online literature, including this one from the American Humanist Association: "Humanism is a progressive philosophy of life that, without supernaturalism, affirms our ability and responsibility to lead ethical lives of personal fulfillment that aspire to the greater good of humanity" ("Humanism and Its Aspirants: Humanist Manifesto III, a successor to the Humanist Manifesto of 1933"). Their goal was to highlight humanism as the philosophy most representative of the majority of people around the world who self-identify as having no religion, and, in the words of Harvard's Humanist Chaplain Gregory M. Epstein, to show that this can be a "diverse, inclusive, inspiring way to live… a way of uniting those [nonreligious] people into a positive community that can make a major contribution to a more peaceful, more stable world" (qtd. in Markel). At that conference in 2007, the first annual Outstanding Lifetime Achievement Award in Cultural Humanism went to Salmon Rushdie. In 2009, their third went to Joss Whedon. In his acceptance speech, Whedon spoke very little about his creative work, focusing mainly on his understanding of humanism, and its relationship to religion and faith. He described religion as a tool created by human beings to answer a need that is not going away, then differentiated religion from faith, saying that neither, especially the latter, is the opposite, or in his language "the enemy," of humanism:

"The enemy of humanism is not faith. The enemy of humanism is hate, is fear, is ignorance, is the darker part of man that is in every humanist, every person in the world. That is the thing we have to fight. Faith is something we have to embrace. Faith in God means believing absolutely in something with no proof whatsoever. Faith in humanity means believing absolutely in something with a huge amount of proof to the contrary. We are, in point of fact, the most cockeyed optimists, and we deserve to take our place as such" (Whedon, "2009").

At the core of Whedon's worldview, then, is actually an act of faith, not in God, but in humanity. And, this faith is necessary in the face of the enemies of humanism, most notably the darkness in everyone, which must be fought. Put in these terms, the "ism" brought most strongly to mind by the rhetorical cues of the quote is not optimism, as stated, but heroism (though I'd argue that the two are not unrelated). This returns us, then, to the question of reshaping the hero.

In strictly humanist terms, one needs no special *chosenness* for this type of heroism, though it seems clear from the rest of his comments that there are weapons—education, community, courage—that make the battle somewhat less overwhelming, if not necessarily easier. You don't get any super powers, but neither does the enemy. And the heroic act itself is the deceptively simple task of embracing humanity. "There's a case to be made for hating people," Whedon says, "called history" ("2009") but the humanist has the difficult task of resisting seemingly justified anger, keeping an open mind and not only passively refraining from harming others, but actively embracing a faith in humanity.

So, this is a way of understanding humanism, which turns out to be a rather heroic stance towards the world. What I'm suggesting is that we can see this humanism reflected in Whedon's narratives, in which the real acts of heroism are often acts of humanism: to become truly a part of a community, to believe in the potential goodness of humanity itself, to take personal responsibility, and to allow others the power that will enable them to do the same. These humanistic values exist in different relationships to the more traditional heroic narrative expected by the audience (or perhaps by the network).

Take *Firefly*, for example. In Whedon's choice for an introduction to the characters we begin with a scene that unequivocally sets Mal and Zoë up as a particular type of war hero: both are brave, and outgunned, Mal is slightly rash, Zoë is competent and loyal. During the battle scene, Mal speaks of the "angels" (metaphorically; *these* angels are warplanes) that will come to their rescue, and the God who will not let his men die; he is disappointed on both counts. Later, it is made absolutely clear that they are now criminals—scavengers, they're called—and that winning and losing will be contested vocabulary. This introduction raises a host of questions about their heroism. Are they heroes if they lose? How do they think about their moral framework now that the rules have changed so dramatically? And who is the weird guy with the dinosaurs?

In the first episode that actually aired ("The Train Job," *Firefly* 2), we meet Mal and Zoë in a way that only hints at this complexity. We open on what feels like a saloon, calling up vague images of the Wild West, and segue into a good old Western style brawl. We still see Mal, slightly rash, Zoë loyal and competent, and we get the information that they were on the losing side of a big war. But the tone here leans more towards bolstering the audience's positive identification with a different heroic myth, that of the American West and the cowboy (generally a loner with a strong moral compass, also often outgunned, brave, and potentially rash, tied to a largely imagined history and a misunderstood sense of pride) than towards a consideration of the murkier questions raised in the original pilot. (There is also the problematic, at least for this viewer, identification with the Confederacy, further complicating things.)

As the series progresses, however, these two threads begin to come together: the defeat in Serenity Valley is both military and moral, and it estranges Mal from both God and other people. It is only through a series of interactions with others—especially those interactions that force him truly to expand his crew, taking new people into his "family" and admitting that he has done so—that he overcomes one side of this, and begins truly to participate in his community. This is where his mythically resonant hero and his humanistic hero can converge: in taking up the humanistic challenge to aspire once more to the greater good, he cannot help but take up River's cause. "No more running," he says in *Serenity*. Or, as Whedon has said,

"What Mal needs is to care, to care about what he's doing, to admit that he cares about what he's doing, and the good works will follow from there" ("2009").

In *Buffy the Vampire Slayer*, the types of heroism were always in greater tension, and I would argue that the humanistic hero won out in a big way. (I should clarify, just in case that I'm only talking about the run of the television series, and I'm not including anything from the timeline or narrative continuity of the *Season Eight* comic.) If we look at the classical hero that *Buffy* so often parallels and parodies, there is the obvious gender difference, but also the position in which the hero stands between the normal realm and the realm of higher powers. That hero is often descended from or in some sense chosen by the gods. In the latter case, this is usually seen as a sign of favor. That doesn't mean that the hero's relationship with the gods is uncomplicated, but it does mean that the classical heroic posture is usually one of honor, and also of being set apart from mere mortals, marked out as special. This obviously describes Buffy, to an extent: "In every generation, there is a Chosen One. She alone will stand against the vampires, the demons, and the forces of darkness. She is the Slayer." But from the beginning, Buffy herself fights this chosenness, wanting no part of it.

Giles: Into each generation, a slayer is born. One girl in all the world—a chosen one. One born with the strength and skill…

Buffy: …to hunt the vampires. To stop the spread of their evil blah blah blah ("Welcome to the Hellmouth [Part 1 of 2]," *Buffy* 1.1)

This back and forth, between Buffy's "divine" calling as the Slayer (we find later, of course, that it was man-made, and from demonic power)—an elevated but isolated place in the community—and her desire to be a normal girl, perhaps to hold a place in society less but also less separate, will be one of the prevailing narrative tensions of the show. She will save the world (a lot), but she will repeatedly do so in ways that increasingly undermine the very separateness of her Slayerhood, from the immediate formation of the Scoobies to the ultimate arc of the Potentials, placing a humanistic model of fighting for the greater good from within a community (as opposed to on behalf of one) on top at almost every turn. It is, in fact, arguable that Buffy makes her worst decisions when she does not follow this model, as when she runs away at the end of Season 2, draws too close to Faith's reckless disregard for the good of others in Season 3, or abuses her power from the leadership position she is forced to take on in Season 7. At each of these moments, there seems to be a different sort of reconnection with her community that must take place—the turn to them for comfort, the reminder that she does, in fact, have moral duties to them, and figuring out "that power is something you share, that being a chosen one is not nearly as interesting as being one of the many" (Whedon, "2009").

Thus far, I have tried to show a connection between Whedon's heroically characterized humanism and his humanistically characterized heroism by examining the relationship between heroes and their respective communities in two of his previous works, *Firefly/Serenity* and *Buffy the Vampire Slayer*. In closing, I turn momentarily to his most recent work, *The Avengers*. In this film we see the same sort of interplay between the separate specialness of these heroes and whatever mission is laid out for them and the humanistic demands of communal existence and responsibility. Or, as Whedon put it in an *io9* interview at Comic-Con 2010:

"The whole movie is about the idea of finding yourself through community, and finding that you not only belong together, but you need each other very much. Obviously, this will be expressed through punching, but it will be the heart of the film" (Interview).

Humanistic heroism. Avengers assemble!

Works Cited

Buffy the Vampire Slayer: The Chosen Collection. DVD Boxed Set. Twentieth Century Fox Home Entertainment, 2006. DVD.

Firefly: The Complete Series. Twentieth Century Fox Home Entertainment, 2002. DVD.

"Humanism and Its Aspirants: Humanist Manifesto III, a Successor to the Humanist Manifesto of 1933." *American Humanist.org* 2003. Web. 4 Jan. 2012.

Markel, Arianna. "Humanist Forum Hosts Rushdie." *The Harvard Crimson* 23 Apr. 2007. Web. 29 Dec. 2011.

Serenity. Writ. and dir. Joss Whedon. Universal, 2005. DVD.

"The Train Job." 2. Writ. Joss Whedon and Tim Minear. Dir. Joss Whedon. *Firefly*.

"Welcome to the Hellmouth (Part 1 of 2)." 1.1. Writ. Joss Whedon. Dir. Charles Martin Smith. *Buffy*.

Whedon, Joss. "2009 Outstanding Lifetime Achievement Award in Cultural Humanism." The Humanist Chaplaincy at Harvard University. The Memorial Church, Harvard Yard, Cambridge, MA. 10 Apr. 2009. Speech. *Forum Network: Fee Lecture Videos*. Web. 29 Dec. 2011.

---. Interview by Meredith Woerner at Comic-Con 2010. "Joss Whedon Says Captain America and Iron Man Won't Be Pals in His *Avengers*." *io9.com* 24 July 2010. Web. 29 Dec. 2011.

3.09
The Power of Fandom in the Whedonverse
Jack Milson

Joss Whedon, critically acclaimed television auteur and creator of the hit television show *Buffy the Vampire Slayer* (1997), is not only a master of storytelling, but also an excellent catalyst to investigate the internal workings and politics of the television and film industry. Within the film and television industry there are a number of key struggles and relationships involving power. The internal politics of the industry warrants much discussion and analysis in its own right, as do issues of production, financing, distribution, and marketing. Whedon's career and body of work provide a constant for us to look at during a period when the industry moves into an arena completely changed by the arrival of new media like the Internet. The Internet has changed the way people live and work and, without doubt, the internal politics of the film and television industry. The changing face of the industry has also brought to the forefront the value of creators such as Whedon, the auteur's role within the television industry, and, arguably most importantly, the audience, the latter being the fans who watch and support the shows that ultimately give the creators their power.

Although the creators and the mass media companies/networks both fall under the same umbrella of production within the industry, they do not always share the same values and interests. One such power struggle is between commercial and creative control over a property, involving issues of auteurism. In television, it's widely accepted that the director isn't necessarily the auteur; the role of auteur is instead embodied by producer(s), executive producer(s), or show runner(s). The producers or show runners are the ones who have to make the day-to-day decisions, both large and small, and it is these decisions that ultimately lead to the power struggles between creator and media companies.

My aim here is to examine how these relationships have changed, including how the audience's relationship with the creator has altered; how the audience's relationship with the media companies has evolved because of new media; and how these changes have affected the relationship between media companies and creators. The causes and effects of many of these changes are revealed in the works in Joss Whedon.

In 1992 the motion picture *Buffy the Vampire Slayer* was released in cinemas across the US, directed by Fran Rubel Kuzui and written by an up-and-coming, yet relatively unknown television writer, Joss Whedon. Whedon would go on to create a number of critically acclaimed works including the television series based on the *Buffy* movie, and the Internet sensation *Dr. Horrible's Sing-Along Blog*. It would be *Dr. Horrible* that would earn Whedon a Vanguard Award from the Producers Guild of America. The award saw Whedon join the ranks of previous winners James Cameron and George Lucas as he was recognized for his achievements in new media and technology. Of course, the original *Buffy* film and *Dr. Horrible* don't mark the totality of Whedon's work, nor do they mark the beginning or end of his career. What they do show is how a creator's control has changed.

Instead of making a strict comparison between the two products, I will examine chronologically the evolution of the differences, using Whedon's work and career as a catalyst to understand how the varying relationships within the television industry operate, and how the changing context led to the creation of *Dr. Horrible*.

While serving as a staff writer on *Roseanne* and *Parenthood*, Whedon wrote the script for the original *Buffy*. After he tried and failed to sell his script to any of the major studios, it was finally picked up by Fran Kubel and Kaz Kuzui (she directed; both produced). Here, it seems, Whedon ceased to have creative control over the film, with rumors that he eventually left the set and never returned when he saw how his script was being interpreted. Whedon openly acknowledges that the film was not what he had in mind and makes a sharp distinction between the script and the film. As a writer selling a script, Whedon had surrendered his creative control to the Kuzuis, something he would actively rectify when given his second chance with *Buffy* on television. Although having no involvement with the show, the Kuzuis would continue to receive royalties from *Buffy* and the merchandise surrounding the property. The political economy of the film and television industry means they would continue to reap the rewards. These rights would later be exercised in May 2009 when the Kuzuis announced their intention to relaunch the franchise without the involvement of Whedon. This news was met with a substantially negative response and, though rumors of casting and production continued into 2010, no such film was in production by the end of 2011.

Filming *Buffy* wasn't the only time Whedon felt a script of his had been misunderstood and wrongly interpreted. In 1997 *Alien Resurrection* was released, with Whedon and two other writers credited for the screenplay. Critically and financially *Resurrection* wasn't a failure, yet Whedon was still unhappy with the treatment of his script. It was this disappointment that led Whedon to proclaim, "The next person who ruins one of my scripts is going to be me" ("JoBlo.com Visits the Set of *Serenity*"). Whedon wanted more control. Though the *Buffy* film would be one of Whedon's most disappointing ventures, it would also ultimately offer him the opportunity to have creative control over his later work.

On March 10, 1997, *Buffy the Vampire Slayer* debuted on the WB network. Gail Berman of Sandollar Production saw the potential in the premise of the film and approached Whedon about adapting it for television As showrunner he would have principal responsibility if the show failed. Academics have labeled Whedon a *hyphenate*; this term is used not only to encompass Whedon's role as creator and writer but also that of executive producer (Pearson 11-16). This creator-writer-producer's responsibilities would also include hiring writers and directors and casting actors, as well as interacting with network and studio.

Buffy would go on to be a critical success, among a host of honors making *Time*'s list of "The 100 Best TV Shows of All-Time" (Poniewozick). The quality of the show was widely acknowledged as was Whedon's role. For the most part Whedon had a healthy relationship with the WB. In the fifth season of *Buffy*, however, Whedon was to witness his first real difficulty in terms of the political economy of the television industry. Although *Buffy* aired on the WB, it was produced and distributed by the studio Twentieth-Century Fox. *Buffy* and Whedon would be in the middle of a multi-entity disagreement over finances that would put the future of the show in jeopardy. Fox produced *Buffy* at a cost of $2 million per episode; the episode would then be sold to the WB at a cost of $1 million per episode. Fox would produce the show at an initial loss, with the balance recovered through reruns and merchandising. It would be this arrangement that would later fuel the disagreement between network and studio (Havens 77).

With the WB's five-year contract for *Buffy* coming to a close, Twentieth-Century Fox was expecting a large increase in the amount that it received from the WB in the new contract. Jamie Kellner CEO of the WB, however, took a hard line stance in the negotiations, refusing to pay Twentieth-Century Fox the $1.8 million an episode it demanded and playing down the importance of the show to the network. These negotiations would ultimately lead to what is arguably one of the biggest coups ever seen in the television industry, as *Buffy* would switch to one of the WB's biggest rivals, UPN (Havens 77-78).

The dispute was settled when UPN signed a two-year deal for *Buffy* with Twentieth-Century Fox. The *Chicago Tribune* reported that the deal would be worth "$2.3 million per episode the first year and $2.35 million the second" (Pearson 19). What this decision brings to the forefront is the value of audience. UPN had a predominately young male audience and hoped to expand its audience and re-brand its image by capturing *Buffy*, which was known for having a strong female demographic. It was hoped this move would ultimately improve UPN's overall performance. What *Buffy* also had was an established fanbase, one that was vocal, active, devoted, and enthusiastic.

Although there would be some individuals who self-identified as *Buffy* fans, there were others who self-identified as fans of Whedon in general rather than any of his works in particular. This would be supported by the existence and prominence of fan sites such as www.whedonesque.com. The site is run by fans, although Whedon and other writers have been known to visit and post on the site. The site offers a direct interaction between fans and creator. Although it would seem naive to use a single website as an example of the mass, it is noteworthy that the site was listed in 2007 by *Entertainment Weekly* as one of the 100 greatest websites ("The 100 Greatest Websites").

Although I set out to discuss how the relationships involving creator, mass media, and audience have changed, I will look at audience instead under the classification of fandom. Some would claim that "fandom" and the "general audience" are not representative of each other. True, it would be wrong to assume that every member of an audience is a fan; however, it can definitely be argued that the lines between the two types of audience are becoming blurred: the mainstream market or viewer is increasingly resembling that of fandom.

BEFORE THE 1990S, ONLY A MINORITY OF AN AUDIENCE COULD BE CONSIDERED FANS

Before the 1990s, it could be argued that only a minority of an audience could be considered fans, with an even smaller number being considered fans in terms of participation and engagement. The definition of the word *fan* simply is, however, "an ardent devotee; an enthusiast." I do agree with the academics who in the early studies in fandom note that rarely do fans merely love a show, watch it religiously, and talk about it, but engage in no other fan practices or activities. It is fan participation and consumption that make fan communities and fandom so interesting. Fans can now communicate with other fans who are located thousands of miles away and chat about the newest episode of the show. The "Internet Fan" is a very different animal, compared to both the casual audience and a casual "ordinary" fan. What is relevant to this study is how a fan operates within the community, specifically how a fan participates.

Like most fandom surrounding television shows/films/books or other texts with narrative structure, fandom surrounding the works of Whedon has spawned a large number of news sites, fan sites, fan fiction, fan art, fan video, and fan film. These examples of fan participation exist in a gray area between legal and illegal with regard to copyright and intellectual property laws. Twentieth Century Fox, the copyright owner of *Buffy*, would be wary of any productions involving the series that could damage the intellectual property, or any profits made from the exploitation and use of their property and characters. Whedon, however, has a different stance: "I love it. I absolutely love it. I wish I had grown up in the era of fan fiction," only stipulating that such productions be true to his characters (qtd. in Airawyn). Fan-made texts are not a phenomenon original to the age of new media; fan texts existed prior to the rise of the Internet. New technologies have, however, made it easier to create, disseminate (now by posting), and find these texts. From being circulated among a small group of fans or posted in a fanzine or screened at conventions, fan texts now have an almost unlimited audience. The creation of fan texts opens up a wealth of tricky questions, including those touching on morality and legality. It would be PR suicide for studios or networks to ban outright the use of copyrighted text or to take action against that which was already created; although the legal owners would protect their property, they would inevitably antagonize the fanbase. By alienating the fans, they would also be alienating the audience the industry depends upon to purchase merchandise based upon the original text. Here the importance of keeping fans happy can best be seen; the most active audience is also the most enthusiastic.

A more interesting facet of fan participation is its evolution and mobilization into social movements, of which the fan community surrounding Whedon's work is a superb example, with well-organized campaigns to save both *Firefly* (2002) and *Angel* (1999). The *Firefly* campaign had substantial influence on the future of the franchise and fandom's involvement with the 2007-2008 Writers Guild of America Strike (itself in part a strike demanding that writers receive acceptable remuneration for work posted online), and a number of charitable ventures. The mobilization of fan communities alters the triangular relationship in profound ways.

In order to understand the reason for the intense fan participation with *Firefly*, it is important to take a look at the political economy and problems surrounding the show and its cancellation. Whedon's first show on a major network, *Firefly* debuted in the fall of 2002 on Fox, to be canceled after only 11 of its 14 produced episodes had been broadcast.

Whedon's relationship with the network was not smooth from the start. Fox asked Joss to reshoot scenes of the two-hour pilot because it wanted more action and humor. Whedon eventually made a standard one-hour pilot to launch the series. As well as asking for a new pilot, the network also asked for a number of creative changes. It is here we can see again the struggles between an auteur and network for creative control. Whedon spoke contentedly at the time of the changes that Fox demanded: "Your initial vision is always there but you have to make it work within the context of what you are doing, and within a budget" (qtd. in Havens 144-46). It is, however, widely accepted throughout the fan community that Fox's creative interference was one of the factors that led to the show's cancellation. A second factor was Fox choosing not to air the episodes in their intended order. This reordering led to plot holes and an incoherent narrative flow that some would argue alienated viewers, even those who had tuned in every week. Fox's broadcasting of the show clashed with Whedon's narrative and the way he intended fans to experience the series. A third factor leading to cancellation involved the actual content of the show. Comparing it to other programming in the fall of 2002, *TV Guide* commented: "Bucking the timidity of a TV season lacking in originality, Fox's funky *Firefly* may be guilty of overcompensating. You don't get more offbeat that this" (Roush). In a media industry already operating in the vein of "narrowcasting," the appeal and audience surrounding *Firefly* was almost too narrow. Whedon had captured an audience that was small albeit enthusiastic, but for Fox this was not good enough.

Whedon's experience on *Firefly* would be one of the reasons he would begin looking for another medium in which to express himself. The film industry had, up to this point, failed him as a platform of expression, and Whedon's television productions had failed to capture a broad mainstream audience. *Firefly* and later *Dollhouse* (2009-2010) would have only limited runs. Through new media Whedon would in two different ways express himself creatively. He would later go on to utilize a different medium with the release of *Dr. Horrible's Sing-Along Blog*, but first he would take another crack at *Firefly* thanks to the film industry. In 2005 *Serenity* was released, a major motion picture sequel to *Firefly* produced by Universal Pictures. But how exactly did this happen, after the series had survived for only eleven episodes?

Not just Whedon, but also the fans who took the name of "Browncoats" were responsible. Taken from within the show's narrative universe, "Browncoats" was a nickname for the "Independents" (among whom were two of the show's main characters, Mal Reynolds and his second in command Zoë) who resisted rule by the Alliance. Many fans of the show began to identify themselves as Browncoats. Some Browncoats would argue they are much more than just fans and identify themselves as fan activists. Fan activism is not a new phenomenon; during the 1960s Trekkers protested the cancellation of *Star Trek*, and there have been more recent campaigns, such as that to try to save *Jericho* and *Eureka*.

When *Firefly* was canceled in December 2002, the full potential of fandom was realized. Fans of the show transcended existence as a participatory audience and moved into the realm of a social movement. This is not the only example of fandom surrounding Whedon emerging as a social movement, as will be shown in looking at the Writers Strike. Obviously, social movements are not a phenomenon created in the age of the Internet. A more accurate term would be *e-mobilization*: a social movement in which members of a common interest group use the Internet to organize and recruit others to campaign for a cause.

Browncoats engaged in a number of strategies to campaign for the renewal or continuation of *Firefly*. There was, for instance, a campaign to raise money to put ad in the television and film trade magazine *Variety*. Its purpose was to market the show, something Fox was doing wrongly, if at all. This effort by fans is especially interesting in terms of the political economy of the Internet in which the fans often bypass the media industry and work directly with the creator and his production company. In this case the Browncoats were in direct contact with Joss Whedon and his production company Mutant Enemy. The campaigns were not enough and *Firefly* was canceled. The fandom, however, refused to accept the cancellation but instead challenged it. They began their campaigning once again. Mobilizing on forums and message boards, the Browncoats began campaigning with hope that another network would pick up the show, much like the UPN picked up *Buffy*. Instead of an ad the Browncoats' aim was to show that an audience existed for the show by sending postcards to UPN. They wanted more than just a petition; their actions could be more accurately described as guerrilla marketing. Their campaign towards UPN also failed, so they redirected their letters to Universal Pictures (*Done the Impossible*).

The Browncoats' campaign had led to the DVD release of *Firefly*, which became number one on the DVD presale chart on Amazon.com and was, along with *Family Guy*, the first failed TV series to become a popular hit thanks to DVD. The marketing finally caught the eye of producer Mary Parent of Universal Studios. As Joss Whedon notes in the fan documentary *Done the Impossible* (2006), the fans were marketing a film that had not even been made yet. The marketing and DVD sales numbers, Mary Parent admits, were part of the reason she wanted to be involved with the movie; fan efforts had shown the studio that the property could make money. On September 30, 2005, *Serenity* was released. The fans had got their film. Parent, although influential in release of the film, acknowledges that *Serenity* is "a movie by the fans" (qtd. in *Done the Impossible*).

THE BROWNCOATS, MUCH LIKE WHEDON, ARE HYPHENATE PRODUCERS

The Browncoats, much like Whedon, are hyphenate producers, and are in fact a hyphenate audience. Just as Whedon is a writer-producer, the Browncoats are audience-marketers or audience-producers. Although they were not the actual marketing team or producers, they had effectively engaged in the sphere of production. Their influence in the relighting of the project cannot be denied; neither can their efforts to publicize and market the film. To paraphrase, "[They had] done the impossible, and that makes [them] mighty." Just as the "Independents" attempted to fend off the Alliance in the show, the fans stood their ground against the political economy of the media industry, in particular, the Fox television network. They succeeded, and the "might" of fandom became ever more visible. In terms of fan activism and social movements surrounding the birth of *Serenity*, there was no conflict with the media companies; Universal was happy with the free marketing the fans offered, and the fans and Whedon were happy they got their movie. What is extremely interesting is what would have happened if the three factors had not aligned ideologically.

On November 5, 2007, the television and film industry came to a standstill as the Writers Guild of America strike began. The strike was to last for 100 days and would cost Los Angeles an estimated $2.1 billion dollars. The strike also cost the striking writers an estimated $285 million in wages (Cieply). This begs the question: what meant so much to these writers that they were willing to put their financial stability on the line? And more importantly, what did the strikes have to do with new media and the triangular relationship involving the media industry, the creators (including writers), and the audience (or fandom)?

First, one should look at who was involved. The parties on strike were the trade unions for television, film, and radio writers, represented by the Writers Guild of America East (WGAE) and Writers Guild of America West (WGAW), who were striking against the Alliance of Motion Picture and Television Producers (AMPTP). The two parties, the WGA (both East and West) and AMPTP, were gridlocked in renegotiating the renewal of the

MBA, Minimum Basic Agreement. The parties had differing opinions on a number of matters, but it was the issue of residual payments over the distribution of texts through DVDs and new media that was the cornerstone of the disagreement. This is a clear example of the economic conflict between the media industry (AMPTP) and the creators (WGA). Despite being the author of the scripts, the writers take only a small percentage of the profit a series makes from distribution through new media and DVDs. Although it would be easy to discuss DVDs and new media separately, they are governed by the same agreement. So because of the relevance to this essay, it is appropriate to look at the strike itself and the mobilization surrounding it, as well as the reasons for the strike, looking specifically at the issues surrounding new media (Cieply and Barnes).

Before looking more closely at the reasons for the strike it must be acknowledged that although neither Whedon nor his fans created the strike, they both were actors within the strike. Their actions are a perfect example of the triangular relationship between the media, creator, and audience.

Since the dawn of the VCR, a television show (or film) has not been limited exclusively to its original broadcast. The birth of home videos had created a new market through which to profit by selling a text. This led to a debate about what the writers/creators who had created the script for the original broadcast should be paid for additional sales in the home entertainment market. A minuscule 0.3%-0.36% residual payment was agreed to, due to the untested nature of market. The intent was to renegotiate the agreement when the industry had a more informed understanding of what was at the time a new market. This level was maintained with the advent of DVDs, and the industry was intending to maintain this with a 0.3% residual payment for new media as well. Although the intent was to revisit the level of payment, it never was, with the result that the striking writers were asking for a residual payment of 0.6%-0.72% (Fans4Writers, "Strike FAQ"). Residual payments were of profound importance to writers, who often spend considerable time between jobs. The residual payments offered a level of financial support.

Creators were asking for 2.5% of the receipts received when a text is rewatched not just on the Internet, but via other forms of delivery systems such as mobile phones, iPods, and other handheld devices. But as mentioned before, the AMPTP had only offered the 0.3% that had been established for the video and DVD market. Under the current contract the writers were entitled to 1.5% for texts for which the audience had to pay, with 2.0% being paid for post-1984 work and 2.5% paid for pre-1984 scripts for texts that were available for free. The media companies were not willing to offer any residual payment for texts that were being offered for free, because they argued no profit was being made. The writers argued a profit was in fact being made from advertisements either present on the website or preceding the streaming of a show. This is similar to the financial structure of the television industry, where advertisements constitute a high percentage of the networks' profit (Fans4Writers, "Strike FAQ"). The clearest example is the advertisement space sold during the Super Bowl. A 30-second spot in 2010 cost $2.5-$2.8 million (Foley). The climate of broadcasting was changing and this had brought the industry to a standstill.

The Writers Strike was just like any other strike; as in any other industry, the writers put down their pencils (or laptops) and took to the picket line. With all WGA members on strike, only unregistered writers and those writing for sports and reality television were at work, which shut down many shows. New episodes of scripted series began to dry up and many shows went temporarily off the air. The strikes created seriously disgruntled audiences, especially fans, whose favorite shows were threatened. As seen with the Browncoats, fans are not a passive community.

Many fans of Joss Whedon's shows, although identifying themselves as fans of particular works, also identify themselves as "Whedon" fans. What this reveals is the understanding the audience has about the creation of the shows of which they are fans, and the role of creators/writers within that. This understanding is a result of the rise of the Internet, which made possible a more direct relationship between creator and audience; the creator is no longer just a name on the credits or a special guest at a convention. Creators nowadays are often as involved in the fandom community as the fans themselves. This partly explains why fan organizations such as "Fans4Writers" were formed in support of the writers during the strikes.

Fans4Writers was a group of fans of TV shows, movies, actors, directors, producers, and anyone involved in the team effort of crafting media. Fans4Writers, although not directly related to Whedon and his fandom, is a movement in support of all writers and for all fandoms. What is interesting in terms of Whedon's fandom, however, is that the Fans4Writers campaign was set up by the people behind www.whedonesque.com, a number of Browncoats and people who had run the "Can't Stop Serenity" events and various Whedon-related charity events.

Fans4Writers could have used new media and forms of e-governance such as petitioning in order to show their support. E-mobilization has, however, been criticized for its lack of effectiveness and authenticity. Even those inside the Browncoats' campaign realized that to be noticed, the online fandom community needed to be more than an online presence; the members needed to engage in grassroots activities. The Fans4Writers campaign was a perfect example of media convergence, between new and old media, online and offline. Fans not only took to the picket lines themselves, but through a number of other campaigns, utilized the Internet to "capitalize on [the] potential for recruitment, fund-raising, organizational flexibility and efficiency" (Chadwick 115).

Fans4Writers split their efforts into three categories: educating, protesting, and morale boosting. "Educating" means simply that, educating those who were unaware of the inner workings and rationale for the strike, protesting to both networks and advertisers. Fans4Writers most publicized activities fall under the classification of morale boosting. Food4Thought used donations to keep morale high on the picket lines by providing food drops (Fans4Writers, "Morale Boosters"). On February 12, 2008, 92.5% of the WGA voted to end the strike after agreeing on a three-year deal. Although exact figures of the negotiated deal are not widely known, Michael Winship of WGA East describes the deal as "We're receiving a percentage of the distributor's gross... which is very real money, as opposed to what people refer to as creative or Hollywood accounting" (Littleton and McNary). Although some would consider this new and seemingly improved deal as the successful outcome of strike, it was not its only success. On July 15, 2008, Joss Whedon and his production company Mutant Enemy released the web series *Dr. Horrible's Sing-Along Blog*. It was a critical and commercial success, winning "Best Internet Phenomenon Award" at the 2009 People's Choice Awards and "Outstanding Special Class—Short-Format Live-Action Entertainment Programs" at the 2009 Primetime Emmy Awards. What did the venture mean for the television industry, the Internet, and social media, and what would it mean for the future?

DR. HORRIBLE'S SING-ALONG BLOG

Dr. Horrible was a three-part series released at first for free on Hulu.com and later on iTunes at a price of $1.99 per episode and $3.99 for a "season pass." *Dr. Horrible* was for a time the number one video on iTunes, and its initial release saw the site crash of both its distribution service Hulu and of Whedonesque.com. Beth Negus Viveiros on the market industry blog, Chief Marketer, poses that marketers launching a campaign could learn a lot from the mantra "WWJWD. What Would Joss Whedon Do" (Viveiros). Besides using media establishments such as iTunes and Hulu, *Dr. Horrible* was an independent venture with no involvement from any mass media networks. Filmed in six days, the production cost $200,000 with many of the cast and crew working for free, to be reimbursed when the project became profitable. Whedon had struck deals with both the WGA and the Screen Actors Guild (SGA), and both the writers and actors were positioned as profit participants, with Whedon serving as studio (Rosen).

As Whedon points out, the success of this production model was in direct opposition to the model the AMPTP was taking. He explains, "After I make back my production costs and everything's paid out, when we're into pure profit, which at this point we are, I win. So—and this was the whole thing during the strike—why try to offer us nothing, when all we're asking for is a percentage? You can't say that 99 percent is ever a bad number" (Whedon, qtd. in Rosen). The model of production had created a buzz of interest within the industry. Web-based products were grabbing the interest of the industry, and with *Dr. Horrible* making an estimated $2.4 million within a year, the project was being cited as proof of the potential of such distribution.

Arguably one of the reasons *Dr. Horrible* was such a breakthrough success was Whedon himself. Although other web-based products have been successful (as will be explained in the concluding section), none were as high profile as *Dr. Horrible*. Lisa Rosen poses the question whether the success can be repeated by others, or if the success of *Dr. Horrible* can be put down to Whedon's fan base, his critical support, and his recognition as writer and creator.

A creator's relationship with the media can be limited; however, we have seen that new media can offer creators almost total freedom, *Dr. Horrible* being a clear example. *Dr. Horrible* can be seen as a new industry model and form of broadcasting, one posing the question where does the industry go from here.

Thus, it is clear that since the deregulation of the media, the mass audience has fragmented. The 1970s saw the three major U.S networks taking 90% of prime-time viewership; by 2002 their share had fallen to 40%. Cable television offered much more variety and diversity; by 2002 cable had 60% of prime-time viewers. Television production now existed in an age of demographics and narrowcasting, the creation and marketing of shows had to attract a much more specific, niche audience (Pearson 14-15). I would also argue that audience appeal and fans of genres and the understanding of audience is equal to the understanding of demographics. The existence of the Sci Fi (later SyFy) Channel, aimed at fans of science fiction stands next to the BET network aimed at the demographic of African-Americans (Ross, *Beyond the Box* 19).

With the rise of a participatory and enthusiastic fan community, the power now lies in balance and flux between industry and audience. *Dr. Horrible* and *Firefly/Serenity* are prime examples of off kilter works succeeding in an environment flooded with reality television, mainly because of the devotion of their audience, however small. The rise of the hyphenate producer, the rise of the Internet, and the transition of fan communities into the virtual world have all brought creator and his audience closer together. The Browncoat and Writers Strike showed us that fans were in direct contact with the creators, just as we can see the creators participating online too, including posts on *Whedonesque.com*. The Internet has created a vast range of ways for an audience to participate with and experience television.

The Internet has moved the fan communities from the margins of the television industry into the center, and now the industry is taking notice; consumer power has become a discussion point at industry conferences in recent years. The rise of fandom and audiences on the Internet has allowed a creator more creative freedom. Niche television is able to survive because the power of a participatory audience is clear for all to see. *Newsweek* points out that Universal Pictures green-lighting *Serenity* is a perfect example of the studio understanding the value of the audience (cited in Jenkins 257). One could argue that social media have altered the way in which fandom operates, from an audience to a community. It is therefore interesting to point out in the TVAddict's 5 *Things that Transformed Television this Decade*, at number three listed along with the likes of Twitter, YouTube, and Facebook is *Whedonesque.com* (The TV Addict).

Whedonesque.com, though not the source of all Whedon-related web activity and participation, is dominant within the community, having been involved with a number of campaigns and efforts of fan participation. Those involved with *Whedonesque.com* are prime examples of what I describe as a hyphenate audience. The creation of fan texts and fandom's participation in the marketing and production of texts means the lines are becoming blurred between amateur and professional. Academics have struggled to provide an accurate name to describe this type of audience, some choosing "prosumer," others "inspirational consumers" or "influences."

Dr. Horrible showed that a production, marketing, and distribution model can survive outside of the networks and the media industry. The problem, however, lies in the reason for its success, which is arguably Whedon himself. Many put the success down to Whedon's ardent fan base, arguing that although web-based, On Demand, direct-to-DVD products are viable outside of the industry, Whedon is only one of a very small number who could succeed because of his niche yet loyal audience. The likelihood of successful web-based product without a big name creator or actor is yet to be fully realized. Other online successes, *The Guild* and *Sanctuary*, both have the anchorage of known stars, Felicia Day (*Buffy*, *Dr. Horrible*, and

Dollhouse) and Amanda Tapping (*Stargate SG-1*) respectively. One could argue that without a pre-existing fan base, be it of the star or creator, a web-based product could easily be lost within the plurality of the Internet, and fail to capture an audience.

Although not the basis for this essay, the use of the Internet to market a text has been touched upon. Most shows currently airing have at least a minimal advertising presence online. One would assume shows that have limited appeal would have a greater presence online in order to create and maintain an audience. This, however, is not always the case, and some would argue the lack of advertising and marketing on Web 2.0 and social networking could have an effect on the success of shows. *Dr. Horrible*, like *Serenity*, was able to become a success partly due to fan marketing, so the marketing of niche products cannot be discounted. Fox's lack of advertising for Whedon's most recent television venture *Dollhouse* was arguably one of the major factors that led to the shows cancellation. While Fox had accounts on social networking/media sites for all its shows, efforts to advertise and promote *Dollhouse* paled in comparison to the efforts to promote *Glee* and *House*. Now that the importance of the audiences, especially fandom and demographics, has been understood, the mass media must now improve their efforts in order to capture these audiences.

The success of web-based products could lead some to believe that eventually the Internet would replace television as a means of broadcasting; however, it would seem that web-based products are in fact reinforcing television as a broadcasting model, the Internet purely acting as a gateway. Web shows *Quarterlife* and *Sanctuary* made transition from the web to television, and because of the success of these ventures, Hollywood is moving to support such projects, increasing their budgets and raising their quality. Recent reports suggest that the sequel to *Dr. Horrible* may not be web-based, but instead may debut on television or film.

In conclusion we can see that with the gap closing between viewer and television and television and the Internet, the environment is changing. *Re-configuration* is a good term, as television as we can see is not being replaced but is more accurately having to reassess the way it interacts with its audience and the creators. The industry must respect the power and influence of the audience; now that audience is much more fragmented, viewers are becoming used to having television on their terms. As we have seen through fan mobilization: upset them, and they will respond. In terms of our triangular relationship, creators have gained even more creative freedom, partly because of fan support and secondly they have alternative outlets if the industry does not satisfy their creative needs, through the new models offered by new media. What is clear is the potential for both the fandom and the creator to employ their power to satisfy their own needs, and if the industry is to maintain its presence, it must be willing to allow both these actors to participate, while utilizing new media themselves to strengthen their own position.

Works Cited

Airawyn (User name). *Lost in a Story: Fan Fiction Supporters*. Web. 22 Mar. 2010. <http://airawyn.fiddlergirl.com/fanficsupport.shtml>

Chadwick, Andrew. *Internet Politics: States, Citizens, and New Communication Technologies*. Oxford: Oxford U P, 2006. Print.

Cieply, Michael. "Writers Vote to End Strike." *NewYorkTimes.com* 12 Feb. 2008. Web. 15 Apr. 2010.

--- and Brooke Barnes. "Writers Say Strike to Start Monday." *NewYorkTimes.com* 2 Nov. 2007. Web. 15 Apr. 2010.

Done the Impossible: *The Fans' Tale of* Firefly *and* Serenity. Dir. and prod. Brian Wiser et al. Donetheimpossible, 2006. DVD.

Fans4Writers. "Morale Boosters." *fans4writers.com*. [2007] Web. 19 Apr. 2010.

Fans4Writers. "Strike FAQ." *fans4writers.com*[2007] Web. 17 Apr. 2010.

Foley, Stephen. "Super Bowl Ad Price Falls in Commercial Slowdown." *TheIndependent.co.uk* 11 Jan. 2010. Web. 17 Apr. 2010.

Havens, Candace. *Joss Whedon, The Genius Behind Buffy*. London: Titan Books, 2003. Print.

Jenkins, Henry. Afterword. "The Future of Fandom." *Fandom: Identities and Communities in a Mediated World*. Ed Jonathan Gray, Cornel Sandvoss, and C. Lee Harrington. New York: New York U P, 2007. Print.

"Joblo.com Visits the Set of *Serenity*." *Joblo.com* 8 Nov. 2004. Web.

Littleton, Cynthia, and Dave McNary. "It's Official: WGA Strike Is Over." *Variety.com*. 12 Feb. 2008. Web. 22 Apr. 2010.

"The 100 Greatest Websites--New and Improved!" *EntertainmentWeekly.com* 20 Dec. 2007. Web.

Pearson, Roberta. "The Writer/Producer in American Television." *The Contemporary Television Series*. Ed. Michael Hammond and Lucy Mazdon. Edinburgh: Edinburgh U P, 2005. 11-26.

Poniewozik, James. "The 100 Best TV Shows of All-Time." *Time.com* 6 Sep. 2007. Web.

Rosen, Lisa. "New Media Guru." *Written By* Jan. 2009. Web. 25 Apr. 2010.

Roush, Matt. "Out (or Up) Yonder *Firefly* Puts Wild West in Outer Space." *TVGuide.com* 4 Nov. 2002. Web. 15 Apr. 2010.

The TV Addict. "5 Things that Transformed TV this Decade." *Thetvaddict.com* 29 Dec. 2009. Web. 25 Apr. 2010.

Viveiros, Beth Negus. "Dr Horrible's Sing-Along Social Media Blitz." *chiefmarketer.com* 23 July 2008. Web. 22 Apr. 2010.

Whedon, Joss. Post. *Whedonesque.com* 12 Dec. 2009. Web. 18 Mar. 2010.

3.10
Zombies, Reavers, Butchers, and Actuals in Joss Whedon's Work
Gerry Canavan

For all the standard horror movie monsters Joss Whedon took up in *Buffy* and *Angel*—vampires, of course, but also ghosts, demons, werewolves, witches, Frankenstein's monster, the Devil, mummies, haunted puppets, the Creature from the Black Lagoon, the "bad boyfriend," and so on—you'd think there would have been more zombies. In twelve years of television across both series zombies appear in only a handful of episodes. They attack almost as an afterthought at Buffy's drama-laden homecoming party early in *Buffy* Season 3 ("Dead Man's Party" 3.2); they completely ruin Xander's evening in "The Zeppo" (3.13) later that same season; they patrol *Angel*'s Los Angeles neighborhood in "The Thin Dead Line" (2.14) in *Angel* Season 2; they stalk the halls of Wolfram & Hart in "Habeas Corpses" (4.8) in *Angel* Season 4. A single zombie comes back from the dead to work things out with the girlfriend who poisoned him in a subplot in "Provider" (3.12) in *Angel* Season 3; Adam uses science to reanimate dead bodies to make his lab assistants near the end of *Buffy* Season 4 ("Primeval" 4.21); zombies guard a fail-safe device in the basement of Wolfram & Hart in "You're Welcome" (3.12) in *Angel* Season 5.

That's about it—and most of these don't even *really* count as zombies at all. Many can talk, and most exhibit a capacity for complex reasoning and decision-making that is totally antithetical to the zombie myth. Not a one of these so-called zombies seems especially interested in devouring our heroes' delicious flesh. Of the aforementioned episodes only "Dead Man's Party" (*Buffy* 3.2) and "Habeas Corpses" (*Angel* 4.8) really come close to evoking the wonderfully claustrophobic adrenaline rush of the shambling, groaning zombie horde that has become so popular in American horror since George Romero's genre-establishing *Night of the Living Dead* series: a small group of people, desperately hiding within a confined, fortified space, with nowhere to run and no hope for survival when the zombies finally penetrate their defenses.

In interviews Whedon frequently cites Romero as a major influence on his work. In one he describes his early ambition to become "a brilliant, independent filmmaker who then went on to make giant, major box office summer movies" as "Spielberg by way of George Romero" (Whedon, "The *Buffy* Writer"); in another he credits Romero with writing strong, complex female characters long before either James Cameron or Whedon himself came around (Whedon, "Sci-Fi-Online Interview"). In a video interview with Fear.Net Whedon describes Romero as "a huge influence," adding that Romero "is the only really ambitiously political filmmaker in that genre—and the *Night of the Living Dead* trilogy is just an incredible example of what can be done with gut-wrenching terror" (*Fear.Net*).

Why then are there so few (and such poor) zombies in the early Whedon canon? We might speculate that filming a properly immense zombie horde would have risked busting the budget for any show, an ever-present concern for supernatural and science fiction series on television, especially on UPN and the WB. A properly ravenous horde, too, might have made Broadcast Standards and Practices rather nervous; American television's very first zombie-themed series, AMC's gory hit *The Walking Dead*, only made it to cable in 2010. When cost and potential censorship are not a factor, Mutant Enemy turns to zombies almost immediately; Whedon wrote a zombie horde attack on the Slayer castle in the first arc of the *Buffy Season Eight* comic, *The Long Way Home*, and zombies have been a common fixture in *Buffy* video games as well.

But let me suggest there's something more at work. First, despite his admiration for Romero, Whedon seems to exhibit a strong preference for the original Haitian *zombi*—a nightmarish transfiguration of slavery into a curse that continues even after death—over George Romero's mindless, ravenous consumer of flesh. The American horror zombie is a corpse without a mind, wandering aimlessly in search of food and governed by pure instinct; the *zombi*, in contrast, is only sometimes a revivified corpse, and is more commonly a traumatized but still living person whose will has been replaced with the will of the zombie master and whose body has been put to work. Whedon fairly frequently makes his characters pedants on this point; in "Some Assembly Required" (*Buffy* 2.2) Giles scolds Xander when he suggests that zombies might feed on the living, and Wesley does the same thing to Gunn in *Angel*'s "Provider," dismissing flesh-eating as a myth (though Wesley's zombies still "mangle, mutilate, and occasionally wear human flesh"). Anya says it again in *Buffy* Season 6's "Bargaining, Part I" (6.1), when Xander speculates that their resurrection spell might have accidentally turned Buffy into a zombie who will attempt to eat their brains: "Zombies don't eat brains, anyway, unless instructed to by their zombie masters. Lotta people get that wrong" (Alas, Romero!).

Remembering Whedon's oft-stated political ambitions for the *Buffy* franchise, a second reason why zombies receive so little attention emerges.

"The first thing I ever thought of when I thought of *Buffy: The Movie*," he explains on the DVD commentary track for the first episode of *Buffy*, "Welcome to the Hellmouth," "was the little blonde girl who goes into a dark alley and gets killed in every horror movie. The idea of *Buffy* was to subvert that idea, that image, and create someone who was a hero where she had always been a victim" (Whedon, Commentary). As he says this he's talking, interestingly enough, over the very first scene of the series, which features not Buffy but Darla, playing the part of a misleadingly naïve high school girl who lures an unsuspecting boy into a deserted classroom before unexpectedly revealing herself as a vampire and going for his throat. The scene subverts and reverses the horror movie cliché; the sketchy football player turns out to be the victim, while the blond ingénue turns out to be a killer.

That scene—like countless later scenes featuring such lovable and charismatic vampires as Angel, Spike, Drusilla, Dracula, The Master, Harmony, Mister Trick, and Holden—just wouldn't work if a dead-eyed, lurching Darla were groaning incoherently, covered in pus and blood, her skin falling off. This is the difference between vampires and zombies: despite superficial similarities in appetite, bad skin, and ghastly undeath, vampires are characters, they are agents, they are (despite everything else) *people*. The popularity of the vampire as a figure for both transgressive heterosexual lust and queer sexuality—both on *Buffy* and in popular successors like *True Blood*—could never be located in the zombie, as the zombie is never a possible point of identification or romance but is always hopelessly, permanently, intractably Other. The Hollywood zombie popularized by Romero is not a person but a force of nature: it can't be reasoned with, it certainly can't seduce us, and it cannot ever be redeemed. It doesn't want anything but to gnaw on your bones.

Of course, most vampires in the Buffyverse never get the sort of elaborate backstory of Angel, Spike, or Darla; most are actually so much like zombies that to include both might have seemed frankly redundant. The random monster-of-the-minute vampires who jump out snarling in dark alleyways are zombielike in their hunger, apparently slaves to their impulses and just as fundamentally disposable as any individual zombie in a horde. Giles lays out this proposition early in *Buffy* when he insists that "A vampire isn't a person at all. It may have the movements, the memories, even the personality of the person it took over, but it's still a demon at the core. There is no halfway" ("Angel" 1.7). But Whedon can't seem to stick to this edict over the course of the series; where in the beginning all vampires must be killed, with Angel as the sole exception only because of the infamous Gypsy curse that re-ensouled him, by the end of the series Spike is able to choose to seek out the return of his soul out a desire to be a better man, and even as vapid a vampire as Harmony is, by the end of *Angel*, able to voluntarily give up human blood altogether without much difficulty at all. Central to Whedon's vision of postmodern horror is a layering of complication and contradiction in his characters that presents itself, especially as the series goes on, as a kind of mania for addition: Buffy is a ditzy cheerleader who is also a Slayer; Angel is a vampire with a soul *and* a soul-loophole; Willow is a nerd who becomes a witch and becomes a junkie and then gets better; Spike is a nebbish poet who becomes a vampire and falls in love and gets chipped by the government but remains fundamentally evil until he eventually goes off to win back his soul, and that's not even counting the post-hypnotic suggestions implanted in his mind by the First Evil or the time he briefly becomes a ghost after sacrificing himself to save the world...

Vampires and the other creatures Joss favors in *Buffy* and *Angel* are about all addition; they're humans, plus a little something more. But zombies are typically about subtraction, about the expression of a fundamental, irrecoverable lack. As Marina Warner notes in her essay "Our Zombies, Our Selves," the difference between vampires and zombies originates in the problem of will: "Unlike phantoms, who have a soul but no body, zombies and vampires are all body—but unlike the vampire who has will and desire and an appetite for life (literally), a zombie is a body which has been hollowed out, emptied of selfhood" (*Phantasmagoria* 357). Warner's definition points at the common thematic thread linking the Romero-style consumer-zombie with the original Haitian producer-zombie: both are stories of "soul-theft" (357), the evacuation of individual will in favor of either mindless herd instinct or whims of the enslaving zombie master. This soul-theft manifests itself in myriad ways; most relevant to the Buffyverse zombie is the fact that unlike vampires (who as Warner notes sometimes even dictate their own autobiographies, as in Anne Rice's *Interview with a Vampire*), the zombie cannot speak at all, replicating the tongue-mutilating punishment sometimes inflicted on slaves (358). (Perhaps this is still another reason Whedon shied away from vampires in *Buffy*; zombies offer little opportunity for his famous Buffyspeak.)

Whedon and the Mutant Enemy writing stable ruin nearly every one of their early attempts at zombie stories by refusing to let this fundamental lack remain unfilled. They can't let zombies just stay zombies. In the Marti Noxon-penned "Dead Man's Party," for instance, which condenses the typical zombie home invasion plot to about twenty minutes, the instinct driving the zombies is not the desire for food but to reacquire a mask Joyce has foolishly hung in the Summers' home. When one of the zombies is able to acquire this object, the mask turns the character into a kind of zombie god—which among other things grants it that power zombies never have, the power of speech. "I live, you die," the zombie god asserts, just before things devolve into the usual fistfight.

Similar problems abound in most of the other Buffyverse zombie episodes I've mentioned. None of them really scratches the zombie itch, in part because none of them are really about *zombies* at all; they're just about dead people who come back to life. To tackle the zombie, Whedon has to move from horror to the realm of science fiction, a place where the contemporary zombie of *28 Days Later*, *I Am Legend*, and *The Walking Dead* is a little more at home. In distinction from the original Romero zombie—which is generally a universal condition, cause unknown, affecting every dead body on the planet whether they've been bit by a zombie or not—the contemporary zombie is generally a biological contagion, very commonly a disease that has escaped from a government laboratory. The new, science fictional zombie reflects Vivian Sobchack's observation in *Screening Space: The American Science Fiction Film* that "the horror film is primarily concerned with the individual in conflict with society or with some extension of himself, the science fiction film with society and its institutions in conflict with each other or with some alien other" (30); the old-style horror zombie reflected (as in Romero's *Dawn of the Dead*) a monstrous emptiness at the core of everyday American life, while the new zombie is something that's been done to us, something foreign that's invaded from outside. (Sobchack puts this in terms of the sort of chaos created by the monster; the horror monster generates "moral chaos," while the science fictional monster generates "social chaos.") This difference in scale is certainly reflected in Whedon's shift from horror to science fiction; Tracy Little's four-word summary of basically every *Buffy* plot—"high school is hell" (Little)—reminds us just how local that show remained over the course of its seven seasons, almost never leaving its tiny California suburb. *Firefly* and *Dollhouse*, in contrast, take place at the margins of worlds are so vast we only ever see the tiniest sliver of what's really going on.

If in horror zombies are scary, in science fiction they become utterly apocalyptic. And both *Firefly* and *Dollhouse* turn out somewhat unexpectedly to be centered on this aspect of the zombie; on these narratives the zombie becomes a limit for society, its final destination. In creating this bleak vision of a zombie future Joss, true to form, finds a way to transform the zombie lack into a new type of excess—performing a clever kind of subtraction by addition that allows him to make the zombie function as something more than just a hole where a character used to be.

ZOMBIES IN SPACE: *FIREFLY/SERENITY*

In *Firefly*—Whedon's gone-much-too-soon "space Western" from 2002—Romero-style zombies appear as rampaging space maniacs called Reavers. In the television series we never actually *see* a Reaver; they appear only in the form of rumors, whispers, and threats, and occasionally in the form of a distant spaceship on the viewscreen. But we can be certain that they're zombies. Described both as "men gone savage on the edge of space" and "men too long removed from civilization," Reavers will "rape us to death, eat our flesh, and sew our skins into their clothing; and if we're very very lucky they'll do it in that order," as Zoë memorably warns Simon in the show's original pilot ("Serenity" 1). The mere mention of Reavers brings panic to everyone on board, causing Inara to bring out what appears to be a suicide kit and causing even resident tough-guy Jayne to abandon any hint of machismo. Human beings transformed into monsters, Reavers are now simply outside the family of the human altogether: "Reavers ain't men. Or they forgot how to be. Now they're just nothing. They got out to the edge of the galaxy, to that place of nothing, and that's what they became" ("Bushwhacked" 1.3). They likewise exist beyond life and death. The crew's first close-up vision of a Reaver vessel directly suggests a kind of undead status; they figure out it is a Reaver ship because it is operating suicidally without radioactive core containment.

Over the course of the television series neither the audience nor the crew ever actually sees a real Reaver; the closest we come is the survivor of the Reaver attack in "Bushwhacked," who has been so traumatized by what he has witnessed that he begins to associate, transforming into a Reaver himself. This is the first way Whedon makes the zombie's lack into an excess; as Mal explains, it becomes trauma:

"They made him watch. He probably tried to turn away—they wouldn't let him. You call him a "survivor?" He's not. A man comes up against that kind of will, only way to deal with it, I suspect... is to become it. He's following the only course that's left to him. First he'll try to make himself look like one... cut on himself, desecrate his own flesh...then he'll start acting like one" ("Bushwhacked" 1.3).

Sure enough, this is exactly what happens: he tattoos himself, splits *his own tongue* down the middle (giving himself the zombie's muteness), and soon after begins to run violently amuck.

We only finally *see* Reavers in *Serenity* (2005), which begins when a bank heist the crew is engaged in is unexpectedly interrupted by a Reaver attack on the planet. The animalistic sound effects that accompany Reavers in the film—as well as the quick-cut flashes that represent River's psychic flashes of the violence in their minds—have been borrowed directly from zombie cinema, most directly the various "fast zombie" films that came in the wake of *28 Days Later*. The Reavers' actions, as much as the cinematography, suggest the extent to which they have been modeled on zombies; when they capture a man during the crew's escape, they begin to eat him, and when Mal takes pity on the man and shoots him through the skull, the Reavers immediately drop the corpse. River understands why: "They want us alive when they eat us."

For much of the film the early Reaver attack seems to be an entirely gratuitous action sequence for a film that is otherwise about the attempts of the crew of *Serenity* to evade an uncannily serene government agent, known only as The Operative, dedicated to retrieving the fugitive River. But near the end of the film the central importance of the Reavers reemerges with newfound clarity; the "campfire stories" about men driven mad by the blackness of space turn out to have just been just fairy tales, obscuring the more disturbing truth that Reavers are actually the accidental byproduct of deliberate Alliance governmental experiments with behavior-modifying drugs intended to pacify the population. The Reavers aren't killers at all; they're victims too. Recalling the concept of "blowback" coined by the Central Intelligence Agency to denote euphemistically the inevitable unintended consequences that result from its efforts, the Alliance state has become a monster itself in a doomed effort to perfect the human. Like colonial powers and imperial militaries right here on the Earth-That-Was, the Alliance outlives its usefulness to become itself the greatest impediment to its self-proclaimed mission of civilizing the Outer Planets and bringing light to darkness. This is the peril that political theorist Achille Mbembe has called "the mutual 'zombification' of both the dominant and the apparently dominated" (104); in the structures of domination that arise in of the colonial system and survive into the postcolonial era, both parties are ultimately sapped of their vitality.

In her essay for the Jane-Espenson-edited anthology *Finding Serenity*, Mercedes Lackey argues that this is why the 'verse, despite its futuristic trappings, feels so real to us:

"...the rules by which this dystopia operates are familiar. The Alliance uses a lot of the same psychological weapons on its own people that all the major governments of the world used back when I was growing up and are still using today. Demonization of the enemy, even the construction of enemies that don't exist, create the fear of nebulous threats and the willingness to sacrifice freedoms for security" (Lackey 63-64).

Taking up where Romero's politicization of the zombie left off, Whedon again transforms the zombie's lack into an excess—not of any individual person but of the very notion of Homeland Security, its unacknowledged dark side and its secret truth. Reavers terrorize the Alliance at the edge of civilized space—but it was the Alliance that put them there.

But this critique of state power is still not Whedon's final turn of the screw. Where Whedon ultimately takes the zombie mythos is in the discovery that the only way to defeat zombies—whether ravenous Reavers or zombie governmental institutions that now exist only to perpetuate themselves and their own power—is not to be more alive than they are, but to be more dead. This strategy of judo-like reversal mimics the logic of the original Haitian *zombi* myth, where the flipside of the *zombi*'s enslavement is his capacity to defy the limits of both death and pain. Alongside the legend of the enslaved *zombi*, then, we have from controversial anthropologist Wade Davis a description of the related legend of the Bizango, a zombified outcast who functions not as a ghoul but as a protective spirit for the community (*The Serpent and the Rainbow*), as well as the importance David Cohen and C.L.R James (*The Black Jacobins*) have placed on voodoo rituals as a means of communication, military coordination, and morale-building during the 1791 Haitian revolution. In their recent "Zombie Manifesto" Sarah Juliet Lauro and Karen Embry point to this history to suggest that the zombie, in its position at the boundary between subject and object, rebel and slave, life and death, is still the best metaphor we have for what it means to resist power (86).

In accordance with this political prehistory of the zombie, the last hour of *Serenity* is one long, continuous reprisal of that ubiquitous scene in zombie cinema in which a live human must attempt to pass for a dead one in order to escape an otherwise hopeless situation—only our characters aren't exactly pretending. First Mal orders his crew to retrofit *Serenity* as a Reaver vessel, complete with a leaking containment core and corpses lashed to its exterior, so they might pass safely through Reaver space. By the time they arrive at the site of the final confrontation with the Alliance, most of the crew has by now accepted that this is a suicide mission and that they are all already dead: "Do you really think any of us are gonna get through this?" In the midst of all this hopelessness, with much of the crew seriously injured or already killed, River is finally able to access consciously her super solider training and dives headlong into a battle with a group of Reavers that has also made landfall on the planet, singlehandedly killing them all. The shot that lingers on River after this battle is over makes it clear: animal-like, uncannily unfeeling, and completely covered in blood, River has essentially become a Reaver herself.

The same happens to Mal. In his fistfight with the Operative at Mr. Universe's mainframe, the Operative is winning as always—until the Operative punches Mal in the back and appears to disable him. (The Operative is using his own super solider training here: the targeted punch, like the "touch of death" from a kung-fu film, is intended to temporarily paralyze one's opponent by overwhelming his muscles' ability to move.) The Operative takes a moment to gloat: "You should know there's no shame in this. You've done remarkable things. But you're fighting a war you've already lost." He turns his back—allowing Mal to strike. He'd had that particular nerve cluster removed as a result of an injury he'd received during the war. Already metaphorically dead—his nerve cluster literally so—and with nothing left to lose, Mal is just enough of a zombie to finally win the fight.

ZOMBIES IN CYBERSPACE: *DOLLHOUSE*

In *Dollhouse* Whedon takes this twist on the zombie myth still further, focusing more directly on the original myth of an immortalized slave that stands behind Romero's ghouls to explore the unexpected agency to be found even in positions of extreme powerlessness. *Dollhouse* depicts a world in which (mostly female) human bodies might be fully stripped of their autonomy and be made *zombis*, subject entirely to the whims of the computer programmers who can now write and rewrite the human brain as well as any hard drive. "Dolls" are programmed with new personalities in order to fulfil various one-off jobs that almost always involve satisfying the sexual fantasies of the extremely rich and powerful. The Dolls themselves are nominally volunteers, having signed a contract (if, in some cases, under duress) in exchange for a large cash payout at the end of their tenure and (often) a promise that some aspect of their personal psychology will be reprogrammed to make them happier people afterwards—but real questions linger about the extent to which you decide to can sign away the very power to make decisions.

In an episode that features in-universe news reporting on "urban legends" about the Dollhouse, "Man on the Street" (1.6), one woman, dressed as a Wal-Mart employee, suggests she would be quite happy to work as a Doll even without this payment: "So being a Doll, you do whatever, and you don't gotta remember nothing, or study, or pay rent, and you just party with rich people all the time. Where's the dotted line?" This woman's eagerness reinforces the wisdom of another interviewee, an African-American woman who angrily denounces the very idea that workers in the Dollhouse are "volunteers": "There's only one reason why a person would volunteer to be a slave: if they is one already. Volunteers. You must be out of your fucking mind." When the newscaster interviews a college professor, perhaps a teacher of biology or cognitive science, he takes a much more aggressively nightmarish view of the possibility of the Dollhouse:

"Forget morality. Imagine it's true. Imagine this technology being used. Now imagine it being used on you. Everything you believe, gone. Everyone you love, strangers. Maybe enemies. Every part of you that makes you more than a walking cluster of neurons dissolved at someone else's whim. If that technology exists, it'll be used. It'll be abused. It'll be global. And we will be over as a species. We will cease to matter. I don't know. Maybe we should" ("Man on the Street").

Consent, in this light, becomes merely a formality; the Dollhouse will get us all in the end. The immediate suggestion of the episode, however, is that this professor is importantly and chillingly wrong: the technology already exists in the real world in the form of the narcotizing spectacle of the entertainment industry, especially television itself. The next and final interviewee in "Man on the Street," who appears immediately following a commercial break, drives this point home: "You think it's not happening? You think they're *not* controlling you? Don't worry about it. Just sit back and wait for them to tell you what to buy." The question is not, from this perspective, whether you might somehow be turned into a Doll, unknowingly operating according the whims of corporate interests that own both your labor power and your free time; the question is whether it's happened already, without your even noticing, without anyone even bothering to complain.

As the series goes on Whedon pushes these questions of consent and control to one side to focus instead on a more traditional sci-fi complication. The imprinting technology turns out in the end to be fundamentally and fatally flawed; in its efforts to produce perfect slaves—to produce a zombie lack that can be filled with the sexual pliability the Dollhouse sells—the Dollhouse technology produces instead more excess in the form of a entirely new type of consciousness, one that (like the folkloric Haitian *zombi*) is capable of resisting and subverting the imprinting technology and repurposing it towards its own ends. Over time, the amnesiac Dolls begin to *remember*. And through this power of memory the Dolls slowly gain control over their unique situation; the characters portrayed by the show's starring cast become increasingly autonomous actors, ultimately becoming protectors of both each other and the society of large. Their hybrid status—no longer their original unitary selves, but each containing a new multiplicity—gives these characters an entirely new sort of human agency. This is especially true in the case of Eliza Dushku's Echo and Alan Tudyk's Alpha, both of whom slowly patch together new composite personalities that are the sum of all the imprints who have been uploaded into their minds. Alpha, whose original personality already contained strongly violent tendencies, is driven mad by multiple personality disorder, becoming a brilliant but murderous sociopath in his quest for revenge against the Dollhouse (in fairness he eventually gets better). Echo is more successfully able to organize all her Dolls inside a new, multitudinous personality and, driven by an urgent empathy, seeks to awaken and liberate the other Dolls and bring down the Dollhouse that enslaves them.

In much the same way as his original vision for *Buffy*, in *Dollhouse* Whedon creates an unexpected heroine out of a character who would traditionally be figured as a passive victim in need of rescuing. Despite the clichés of the genre and the hopelessness of her situation, Echo rescues herself. And in the process the very formlessness of the Doll state, its malleable plasticity, becomes her greatest strength; the living death of the *zombi*, in essence, gives her a twenty-first century superpower: the ability to reprogram herself however she likes.

In "Epitaph One," the episode originally intended to serve as a possible series finale before the show was unexpectedly renewed, we see our first glimpse of the unexpected way this story ends. The episode skips ahead ten years to a post-apocalyptic Los Angeles; the ruined city is in flames. What has happened is never made precisely clear—but Los Angeles is now divided between "actuals" (unmodified humans), "dumbshows" (pacified wanderers in the base Doll state), and "butchers" (berserk killers suggestive of nothing so much as Romero's ghouls or *Firefly*'s Reavers). Finally, our two species of zombies get to meet—and the results are not pretty. As the episode proceeds we discover that the Dollhouse technology has somehow gotten loose, broadcasting "signals" of varying kinds across all communications media that transform actuals into either dumbshows or butchers. Civilization has been destroyed in an ongoing orgy of universal zombification—TV finally and forever turning all our brains to mush.

In Season 2's series-concluding follow-up, "Epitaph Two"—continuing the plot thread begun in "Epitaph One"—we discover that the 2019 versions of the series' regular cast are still alive, hidden from the apocalypse in an agricultural enclave in the deserts of Arizona. In a sense they're partially responsible for what has happened to the world; not only did Topher and Adelle selfishly abet the Rossum Corporation's drive for better and better technologies of control, but the rebelling Dolls' victories over Rossum ironically introduced the unstable power vacuum that made the global Dollpocalypse possible in the first place. Echo and the others are still fighting the remnants of Rossum as well as periodic hordes of butchers, but things are not going well; this is not a war which can be won.

Finally Topher announces that he has come up with a miraculous plan to "bring back the world"; bouncing blanket signals off the atmosphere, he believes he can simultaneously return *every* imprinted person to his/her original, actual state. It gives nothing away to tell you the plan is ultimately successful; this is, in the end, television, and happy endings are always the order of the day. At the end of "Epitaph Two" confused dumbshows and former butchers begin to wake from their fog into a completely transformed world. We see nothing of what they're thinking, or of what sort of world they might actually construct from the ruins of ours. The focus instead is on our Doll heroes, most of whom have chosen to remain inside the Dollhouse for a year until the de-imprinting signal fades and it's safe for them to reemerge. Completely unexpectedly—and, given that the show began with the Dollhouse as an obvious metaphor for human trafficking and the sex industry, somewhat disturbingly—most of our Doll heroes decide they don't *want* to be restored to their original, actual selves. They've become something new, something powerful, something posthuman; in becoming Dolls, they've gained much more than they've lost, and they don't want to go back.

Note: *Portions of this essay also appeared in* Science Fiction Film and Television 4.2 (Fall 2011) *from the University of Liverpool Press.*

Works Cited

Angel: The Complete Series. Twentieth Century Fox Home Entertainment, 2010. DVD.

"Angel." 1.7. Writ. David Greenwalt. Dir. Scott Brazil. Buffy.

"Bargaining" (Part 1). 6.1. Writ. Marti Noxon. Dir. David Grossman. Buffy.

Buffy the Vampire Slayer Season Eight. 40 issues. Story by Joss Whedon and others. Pencils by Georges Jeanty and others. Portland: Dark Horse, 2007-2011. Print.

Buffy the Vampire Slayer: The Complete Series. Twentieth Century Fox Home Entertainment, 2005. DVD.

"Bushwhacked." 1.3. Writ. and dir. Tim Minear. Firefly.

Davis, Wade. The Serpent and the Rainbow. New York: Simon and Schuster, 1985. Print.

"Dead Man's Party." 3.2. Writ. Marti Noxon. Dir. James A. Whitmore, Jr. Buffy.

Dollhouse: The Complete Season 2. Twentieth Century Fox Home Entertainment, 2010. DVD.

Dollhouse: Season One. Twentieth Century Fox Home Entertainment, 2009. DVD.

"Epitaph One." 1.13. Story by Joss Whedon. Teleplay by Maurissa Tancharoen and Jed Whedon. Dir. Joss Whedon. *Dollhouse.*

"Epitaph Two: Return." 2.13. Writ. Maurissa Tancharoen, Jed Whedon, and Andrew Chambliss. Dir. David Solomon. *Dollhouse.*

Firefly*: The Complete Series.* Twentieth Century Fox Home Entertainment, 2002. DVD.

"Habeas Corpses." 4.8. Writ. Jeffrey Bell. Dir. Skip Schoolnik. *Angel.*

James, C. L. R. *The Black Jacobins.* New York: Vintage, 1989. Print.

Lackey, Mercedes. "*Serenity* and Bobby McGee: Freedom and the Illusion of Freedom in Joss Whedon's *Firefly.*" *Finding* Serenity. Ed. Jane Espenson with Glenn Yeffeth. Dallas: BenBella, 2005. 63-73. Print.

Lauro, Sarah Juliet, and Karen Embry. "A Zombie Manifesto: The Nonhuman Condition in the Era of Advanced Capitalism." *Boundary 2* 35.1 (Spring 2008): 85-108. Print.

Little, Tracy. "High School is Hell: Metaphor Made Literal in *Buffy the Vampire Slayer.* Buffy the Vampire Slayer *and Philosophy: Fear and Trembling in Sunnydale.* Ed. James B. South. Chicago: Open Court, 2003. 282-93. Print. Popular Culture and Philosophy Series.

The Long Way Home arc, issues 1-4. Story by Joss Whedon. Pencils by Georges Jeanty. *Buffy the Vampire Slayer Season Eight.*

"Man on the Street." 1.6. Writ. Joss Whedon. Dir. David Straiton. *Dollhouse.*

Mbembe, Achille. "The Aesthetics of Vulgarity." Trans. Janet Rostman and Murray Last. *On the Postcolony.* Berkeley: U of California P, 2001. 102-41. Print. Studies on the History of Society and Culture.

"Primeval." 4.21. Writ. and dir. David Fury. *Buffy.*

"Provider." 3.12. Writ. Scott Murphy. Dir. Bill Norton. *Angel.*

"Serenity." 1. Writ. and dir. Joss Whedon. *Firefly.*

Serenity. Writ. and dir. Joss Whedon. Universal, 2005. DVD.

Sobchack, Vivian. *Screening Space: The American Science Fiction Film.* Piscataway, NJ: Rutgers U P, 1997. Print.

"Some Assembly Required." 2.2. Writ. Ty King. Dir. Bruce Seth Green. *Buffy.*

"The Thin, Dead Line." 2.14. Writ. Jim Kouf and Shawn Ryan. Dir. Scott McGinnis. *Angel.*

Warner, Marina. "Our Zombies, Our Selves." *Phantasmagoria: Spirit Visions, Metaphors, and Media.* New York: Oxford U P, 2006. 357-70. Print.

"Welcome to the Hellmouth." 1.1. Writ. Joss Whedon. Dir. Charles Martin Smith. *Buffy.*

Whedon, Joss. Commentary. "Welcome to the Helmouth." 1.1. *Buffy.*

---. Interview. "The *Buffy the Vampire Slayer* Writer Discusses His Career." By Ken P. *IGN Filmforce* 23 June 2003. Web.

---. Interview. "Sci-Fi-Online Interview with Joss Whedon." *Sci-Fi-Online* 27 Feb. 2006. Web. 21 Nov. 2011.

---. Video interview. *Fear.Net* San Diego Comic-Con July 26-29 2007. Web.

"The Zeppo." 3.13. Writ. Dan Vebber. Dir. James Whitmore, Jr. *Buffy.*

3.11
Nathan Fillion Misbehaves All Across the Whedonverse
Lynnette Porter

During a late-2010 science fiction convention in Halifax, Nova Scotia, fans hotly debated the comparative merits of *Star Wars'* Han Solo and *Firefly*'s Mal Reynolds. How to decide which character is most charming or heroic, which is the "best" smuggler, character, or rogue? Both Solo and Reynolds are iconic figures, and Captain Mal often has been compared to his predecessor. Suddenly a call-in fan settled the matter once and for all about the power of Captain Mal.

"Malcolm Reynolds is a man with a plan. Certainly, plans do not always go his way, but he is a man with a plan. Solo, on the other hand, is making it up as he goes along." Certainly, in this caller's estimation, Captain Mal is far cooler than his ancestor. The coolness factor of that fan panel immediately rose about a thousand percent, too. The caller? "Captain Mal" himself, Nathan Fillion.

Among other comments that attracted global attention to HAL-CON reports is the often-noted trait that Mal is not afraid to shoot first, ask questions later, as the title of Syfy's *Blastr.com* news article about the panel cheerfully noted: "Nathan Fillion Brags: Unlike Han Solo, Captain Mal Shoots First" (Bernardin). Since word of the special appearance made SF news, fans have frequently enjoyed the (not-safe-for-work) audio replay, which can be found linked to numerous *Firefly* and SF web sites.

Fillion's comments are both funny and insightful, a trademark not only of the actor but of many characters he enlivens onscreen. Captain Mal does have a tendency to shoot first—but, really, is that something a traditional SF hero should brag about? That attitude straddles a dangerously thin line between what is heroic and what is villainous—and it perfectly describes many of Fillion's memorable roles in the Whedonverse. Captain Tightpants. The Big Bad. Hammer Time. Whatever you call him (perhaps King of his *Castle* nowadays), Nathan Fillion has been a cult TV fixture for nearly a decade, in large part because of his relationship with Joss Whedon.

If Fillion's characters often are more lovable rogues than traditional good guys, he has Whedon to thank. Even when Fillion visits the Dark Side as *Buffy*'s Caleb, he makes a demonic former priest look good. The actor, to date, has played three distinctive characters in four Whedon projects: Mal

Reynolds in the TV series *Firefly* and movie *Serenity* (and his character lives on in the *Serenity* comic book series), Caleb during Season 7 of *Buffy the Vampire Slayer*, and Captain Hammer in *Dr. Horrible's Sing-Along Blog* (yes, he sings). Whedon's words have given Fillion plenty to play with—and Captain Mal is as much revered as Han Solo.

MORE THAN FLYING SOLO

Fans get the idea that, despite the hard work of making a film or TV series, Fillion is having a lot of fun. His characters make viewers feel good (despite quibbles over Mal's moral ambiguity, Caleb's pure evilness, or Hammer's hero with a hefty personal agenda). With the fun factor of watching Fillion's portrayals comes the bonus that the actor also is one of "us"—the tech nerd, SF fan, game lover, and general geek.

Fillion plays with technology, uploading funny photos, calling conventions, and tweeting—including shoutouts to Browncoats: "Ready for this, Browncoats? Morena is tweeting now!! Hit her up at @missmorenab and tell her the Captain sent you." He swaps recipes and posts updates about his success with a new game. Although Captain Mal may claim to be a loner (despite his loyal crew), Fillion's frequent e-connections with his fanbase keep him from flying solo in SF fandom.

Fillion's fanboy nature inadvertently has led to many visual insider jokes about famous SF characters, including Solo and Reynolds. On the *Firefly* set in 2002, *Star Wars* fan Fillion inspired crew to work "geek-friendly" references into a shot, a trend the actor continues in his current series, *Castle* (Woerner). According to a still widely discussed interview during the *Firefly* days, that famous image of Han Solo encased in carbonite was inadvertently immortalized in the background of several scenes as the result of a running joke between the prop guys and Fillion. The Solo figurine sometimes wasn't removed before filming began, and so it ended up sharing screen time with the *Firefly* cast (for instance, see "Double Take").

Recent tweets (from November 2010) promote Fillion's penchant for Easter eggs: "I put something for Firefly in the People Magazine shot. Anyone spot it yet?" or "Who else caught the Firefly reference in last night's show?" That famous brown coat became the highlight of *Castle*'s 2009 Halloween episode. When Rick Castle slips into his "space cowboy" outfit, his daughter suggests he move on, noting that he wore that costume "like five years ago." An expiration date on Captain Mal?! Like Castle, *Firefly* fans looked appalled and voiced as one "I like it!" Fillion helps keep Whedon characters alive in the news long after a series has been canceled.

"I AIM TO MISBEHAVE"

Certainly, as scores of Browncoats worldwide can attest, Mal Reynolds is the best known of Fillion's characters created by Joss Whedon. From the get-go, the *Serenity* captain's attitude and actions paralleled those of the *Millennium Falcon*'s. Both Han Solo and Mal Reynolds claim—and diligently try—to look out solely for their own interests and to help others only if by so doing they can help themselves to a tidy profit. Somehow, in those galaxies far, far away, they manage to become embroiled in a larger struggle between Good (renegades and resistance fighters battling a vast Empire/Alliance) and Evil (aforementioned vast, politically powerful, all-reaching Empire/Alliance). They promise to leave their comrades if the going gets tough, but they instead become self-sacrificing and noble despite their bad intentions.

In *Firefly*, Captain Mal embodies and popularizes Whedon's often-morally ambiguous heroes. In an early episode, "The Train Job," he steals a train's cargo on behalf of a client but then learns the stolen goods are medicine for a desperate town. Mal then decides to "un-steal" the precious cargo. Mal makes theft and deception part of his business, but he also won't cross certain moral lines. His personal relationships can be just as complicated. He apparently adores Inara, although he never says as much, and gets caught in more than one fight as he tries to protect her. Nevertheless, he disapproves of her profession as a registered Companion.

Mal is one of those characters who should be a true hero but misses by just this much. He is a war hero (but, unfortunately, fought for the losing side). He is an entrepreneur (but, unfortunately, his business is smuggling and Alliance-baiting). He fights the enemy and often emerges victorious from the skirmish (but, unfortunately, his wars are bigger than one man can win). Yet for all his protests and flaws, Mal is one likeable guy.

Serenity's famous last words endear Mal to his fans. After losing close friends to the film's Big Bad, revealing a terrible, tragic Alliance cover up, and exposing the story's true monsters, Mal and his compatriots forge an even tighter little family—albeit one that now must evade the "law" more carefully than ever. Despite the danger, as he flies into SF history, Mal smiles. "Now I aim to misbehave."

SIDEKICK TO EVIL

"Misbehave" is a mild term for the havoc introduced by Fillion's Caleb. Although the character appeared in only five episodes, his presence sets up the earth-shattering conclusion to *Buffy the Vampire Slayer* and makes powerful symbolic statements about the nature of Evil in the world. As the First Evil's sidekick, Caleb kills potential Slayers, blinds Xander, and introduces a host of evildoers into the world. Handsome, charming ex-priest Caleb knows how to seduce and murder young women. As a supernatural second, he becomes the face of First Evil in the world, a deadly wolf in priest's clothing who leads his flock to slaughter.

Caleb is an interesting follow-up character for Fillion to play after the short-lived but cult-favored *Firefly*. The role allows him to be disarmingly charming, but then to sidestep quickly that misleading image and move in for the kill. Caleb is mesmerizing simply because of Fillion's boyish good looks and way with a line, but the actor peels back that seductive veneer to demonstrate just how effectively true evil can attack those who would try to stop it—our heroes Buffy and the Scoobies, plus a fledgling army of potential slayers. Whedon created a brilliant flip side to the type of character Fillion plays so seemingly effortlessly, and through their collaboration regarding Caleb, Fillion's fans gained a new appreciation for the actor's talent and Whedon's perspective on the continuing battle between Good and Evil.

HAMMER TIME

Following the long-awaited return to Captain Mal's storyline via *Serenity*, Fillion filled some downtime during the 2007-2008 writers' strike with yet another Whedon project: *Dr. Horrible's Sing-Along Blog*. As with many of Whedon's characters, the supposed hero, Captain Hammer, isn't quite who he seems to be or should be.

Although Hammer protects his cozy metropolis, he uses his celebrity status as the city's savior to gain photo ops and phone numbers. He stands up to evildoers—in this story the often-horribly ineffective Dr. Horrible— but when the going gets tough, Captain Hammer gets going, right out the door. His real true love isn't the Girl Next Door who sincerely wants to help the homeless; it's himself. Fillion and Whedon present yet another side to the handsome hero, this time as narcissistic player who knows how to manipulate the media and use his celebrity to his advantage.

BACK IN THE FUTURE?

Like Eliza Dushku (*Buffy, Angel, Dollhouse*), Fillion has returned to the Whedonverse more often than most, but his roles span television, film, and web. The variety of his roles attests to Fillion's range on the hero-villain scale. Certainly the actor's SF legacy owes a lot to Whedon's genius with character and plot, but fans would have a hard time envisioning anyone else playing Caleb, Captain Hammer, or especially Captain Mal.

After almost a decade of Whedon projects, would Fillion be willing to work on one more, whether the long-anticipated sequel to *Dr. Horrible* or something new? In a 2009 *TV Squad* interview, Fillion quickly responded in the affirmative: "Anytime Joss Whedon says, 'Let's go do...', you say yes. 'Let's go do blank.' Yep. I'm in. Color me in, man. Whatever you say" (Gallagher).

Nearly two years later, Fillion is still willing to say yes to Whedon. In a February 2011 interview, timed to coincide with the Science Channel beginning a re-run of *Firefly* in its entirety with extra features for fans, Fillion again expressed interest in revisiting the *Serenity*. The instantly-famous comment was "If I got $300 million from the California Lottery, the first thing I would do is buy the rights to *Firefly*, make it on my own, and distribute it on the Internet" (Hibbard).

Within about, oh, a minute of that comment's release, Browncoats everywhere vowed to follow their Captain once more—and they put their money where their tweets are. New Facebook page "Help Nathan Buy Firefly" had nearly 100,000 friends by the end of February. The website of the same name moved into Phase 2 of a three-phase attack: to generate cash for buying the series' rights. Given that the first phase successfully garnered some serious interest in the idea, Phase 2 seemed the next logical step. Yet, ever-practical Browncoats also realized that Fillion probably was joking in the interview and Whedon may have moved on to new interests. If the campaign cannot succeed, despite their best efforts (Browncoats, unfortunately, have previous experience with losing battles to an overwhelming bureaucracy), then, the website promised, any donations would be given to the nonprofit organizations listed on the site.

Fillion, while touched by Browncoats' devotion, tweeted on February 24, "It's beautiful to dream of more Firefly, but PLEASE DON'T SEND ANY MONEY. Just keep being great Browncoats, which you are." A follow-up tweet added "I'm proud my coat is brown" (Twitter).

Although Fillion may not legally be able to buy the role of Captain Mal, there is no doubt that he owns the part. Somewhere in a future project, if fans are lucky, we'll see yet another Whedon character given life by Nathan Fillion. Whether hero or villain, he'll be sure to charm us.

Works Cited

Bernardin, Marc. "Nathan Fillion Brags: Unlike Han Solo, Captain Mal Shoots First." *Blastr. com*. Syfy. 8 Nov. 2010. Web.

"Double Take: Han Solo in *Firefly*." 11 Jan. 2011. *...ology.com*. Web.

Gallagher, Kona."Nathan Fillion: The *TV Squad* Interview." *Aoltv.com*. 9 Apr. 2009. Web.

"HelpNathan Buy Firefly. Let's Get The Captain His Money" *Facebook*. Fan site. Web.

Hibbard, James. "'Firefly' Returning to Cable; Fillion Says He'd Play Mal Again." *EW.com*. 18 Feb. 2011. Web.

"Nathan Fillion Defends Mal Reynolds from Hans Solo." *SFX.co.uk*. 6 Nov. 2010. Web.

Twitter. "It's beautiful to dream of more Firefly." 10:30 p.m., 24 Feb. 2011 via Twitter for iPhone.

---. "I am proud my coat is brown." 10:30 p.m., 24 Feb. via Twitter for iPhone.

---. "Ready for this, Browncoats? Morena is tweeting now!!" 8:45 p.m., 14 Jan. 2011 via Twitter for iPhone.

---. "I put something for Firefly in the People Magazine shot. Anyone spot it yet?" 9:41 p.m., 24 Nov. 2010 via Twitter for iPhone.

---. "Who else caught the Firefly reference in last night's show?" 11:01 a.m., 16 Nov. 2010 via Twitter for iPhone.

Woerner, Meredith. "Nathan Fillion References Buffy, Firefly and Underworld in One Scene." 23 Oct. 2009. *IO9.com*. Web.

CHAPTER 4

COMICS

4.01
Joss Whedon 101:
Fray
Patrick Shand

Joss Whedon. A Slayer. A scythe. A Watcher. Witty dialogue. Some vampires. A prophecy. Sounds familiar, huh? How about we throw flying cars, mutants, and a whole bunch of *the future* into the mix? Suddenly, things seem a bit different. This is the world that Melaka Fray, our eponymous Slayer, lives in. As similar as the basics of her life are to Buffy's, the fact that her story is set hundreds of years in the future isn't what makes *Fray* original. Mel is very much her own person, and this is very much her own story.

And *damn* it's good.

Fray begins somewhat similarly to the original *Buffy the Vampire Slayer* movie—mysterious guy tells girl she's the Slayer, girl doesn't believe it, girl has experiences to make her believe it, girl and mysterious guy train as the major conflict brews—but in execution it's startlingly different. Melaka Fray is at once more of a hardass and more of a softie than Buffy Summers. She is an unrepentant thief. She's been "grabbing" since she was a young girl, and now she works for a mutant named Gunther who has more in common with aquatic life than humans. He lives in a tank, it's a thing. He is connected to everyone in the city, and he doesn't judge anyone harshly… which means he'll work with pretty much anyone. Unfortunately, this leads to Mel—unbeknownst to her—grabbing magical artifacts for a gang of vampires that don't have the best interest of the world at heart.

The world of *Fray*, like that of any Joss Whedon work, is populated by fascinating supporting characters. There's Gunther, the aforementioned mutant crime boss. There's Loo, a five-year-old "rocketmouth" girl who is missing one arm and has one dead eye; of course, she is endlessly adorable and functions as the heart of the story. Then, there is Erin; Mel's older sister is working with the "laws" and she has just been promoted to sergeant, which in Mel's eyes has elevated her to an "upper," a term that refers to the upper class. This causes tension between the sisters, though most of their issues stem from the death of their brother, Harth. Erin believes it was Mel's fault… but we'll get to that later.

Urkonn is Mel's "Watcher" of sorts, though he would protest to the label. The Watchers Council, in Mel's time, is full of lunatics. Urkonn, a horned demon who trains Mel, explains that the world was once full of magic and demons, but a slayer—heavy implications that it's a certain girl who wears stylish yet affordable boots—fought a battle that banished all magic from this Earthly dimension. The Watchers went crazy, obsessively waiting for the demons to come back... which they did, in the form of vampires. However, Urkonn is surprised to discover that the mass public doesn't see vampires as the monsters they truly are... they believe them to be mutants hopped up on steroids; they refer to them as "lurks." Urkonn explains to Mel that she's the Slayer and that it is her destiny to fight and kill lurks, but Mel doesn't believe him. When he asks her how she explains her strength, she shrugs it off, saying, "What. I'm good at stuff" (*Fray #2*). He counters, asking her about her inherited Slayer dreams. Urkonn says, "In your dreams, you're someone else. A slave. A princess. A girl in a sunlit school. In every dream you have great power. In every dream you fight them. The ones you call lurks" (*Fray #2*) to which Mel replies, "That's amazing. I have no idea what you're talking about" (*Fray #2*). She is the first Slayer who hasn't received the dreams... and that's because they're going to someone else.

Harth.

"But wait," you say. Trust me, I heard you. "But wait. Harth is Mel's dead brother, right?" Right. And death in the Buffyverse is totally the end, yeah? No. Harth was killed by a vampire when Mel took him out on a "grab," despite Erin's protests. The vampire, Icarus, was a leader, one of the most badass vamps in all of Haddyn. However, when he sank his fangs into Harth's neck, he set events into motion that would change the lives of all of the characters in *Fray*.

As Harth felt himself dying, he knew with sudden clarity that he needed to bite Icarus. And he did so, ingesting a chunk of undead flesh, becoming a vampire. A very special vampire, though. He was Mel's twin and, in a twist of fate, the visions of the Slayer that Mel was supposed to receive went, instead, to him. Harth was connected to both Slayer and vampire, which allowed him to transcend the limitations of both. He became the leader of Icarus and his gang and began a quest to bring magic back to Earth; he wanted to bring the world back to the Hellish state that it was in when the Old Ones reigned in terror. He's powerful, creepy, and—because he's a Joss Whedon character—super sarcastic. Big Bad material for sure.

Also, he's a bit in love/lust/incest with Mel.

Thing about *Fray*, though, is that nothing is as it seems. Harth is bad, for sure, but everyone in this story is hiding something. As the fight against vampires that Urkonn wants Mel to wage grows into a war to save the world, the mysterious folk of Haddyn begin to show their cards. Plans and insecurities are revealed and, as the story progresses, Mel grows stronger. When she finally faces off with Icarus, the last obstacle before Harth, she says, "My hand. It doesn't shake at all" (*Fray #6*).

Like all of Joss Whedon's best works, *Fray* is witty, funny, devastating, action-packed, and poignant as all hell. Whedon plays with language in this book in a way that is strikingly similar what he did with to *Firefly* and *Serenity*; over the years, language has evolved (or fallen apart, depending on how you look at it). Joss Whedon's fascination with the world of *Fray*, how the Buffyverse has changed and *not* changed over time, is apparent in every panel of this comic. Karl Moline's art perfectly matches Whedon's writing; the action is fluid, the characters superbly designed, and the emotion jumps off the page even more so than the excellent fight scenes. The main eight issues of *Fray* are collected in a trade paperback packed with extras (*Fray: Future Slayer*), but the character also appears in a short story at the end of the *Tales of the Slayers* graphic novel ("Tales"). She is also featured in a crossover event in the "Time of Your Life" arc of *Buffy the Vampire Slayer: Season Eight* ("Time"). Not only has her story changed the larger Buffyverse, giving the main *Buffy the Vampire Slayer* title a future to build up to; *Fray* stands perfectly on its own as a tale of a rebellious woman getting over her fears, putting the past behind her, and finding purpose in her life.

Works Cited

Fray. 8 issues. Story by Joss Whedon. Pencils by Karl Moline. Portland: Dark Horse 2001-2003. Print.

Fray: Future Slayer. Story by Joss Whedon. Pencils by Karl Moline. Foreword by Joss Whedon. Portland: Dark Horse, 2003. Print.

"Tales." Story by Joss Whedon. Pencils by Karl Moline. *Tales of the Slayer*. Portland: Dark Horse, 2001. Print.

"Time of Your Life." Story by Joss Whedon. Pencils by Karl Moline. Portland: Dark Horse, 2008. Issues 16-19 of *Buffy the Vampire Slayer: Season Eight*. Print.

4.02
Joss Whedon 101:
Astonishing X-Men

Cesar R. Bustamante, Jr.

In Joss Whedon and John Cassaday's *Astonishing X-Men* (24 issues 2004-2008) the team must stop an alien race from destroying Earth while simultaneously dealing with the announcement of a mutant cure, fighting off a murderous A.I., and confronting the ghost of a villain from the recent past. And the truth of the matter is, none of this is new. One consequence of over forty years' worth of storylines in a Marvel comic is that writing up a brand spanking new plot is hard if not impossible. But it speaks to Joss Whedon's scripting talent that he was still able to write a wildly entertaining and sometimes touching story despite his writing quirks and flaws (he just cannot let three pages go without cracking a joke, regardless of the its quality or effect on the mood). Whedon's style meshes with that of artist John Cassaday, whose artwork is realistic but not to a fault. It is colorful and vibrant in a way that works for action scenes, from Wolverine being thrown through the air at an escaping spaceship to Colossus punching a bulky alien. It also effectively communicates the characters' complex human emotions, thus playing to Whedon's emphasis on characterization.

The team line-up for Whedon's run consists of Emma Frost, Cyclops (Scott Summers), Wolverine (Logan / James Howlett), Beast (Hank McCoy), Shadowcat (Kitty Pryde), and Colossus (Peter Rasputin). His series is broken up into four chapters: *Gifted* (1-6), *Dangerous* (7-12), *Torn* (13-18), and ending with *Unstoppable* (19-24), with the finale in *Giant-Size Astonishing X-Men #1*.

In *Gifted*, a company called Benetech unveils to the public a "cure" for mutants (a plot device used two years later in the movie *X-Men: The Last Stand*), sparking hysteria within the mutant community. Investigating the legitimacy of the claim, Beast finds that Benetech's cure came with a price—the illegal experimentation on their formerly dead teammate, Colossus. In addition, behind the cure is Ord, an alien from the Breakworld who is trying to make sure the prophecy of a mutant destroying his home world does not come true. It's a lot of story and drama crammed into just these six issues, but Whedon is able to keep it engaging by playing it close to the heart. He makes it about the characters, especially about Shadowcat, who recently returned to teach at the school. Readers sympathize with Kitty's shock at the return of Colossus and are interested in Emma and Scott's relationship. Some incidents are, arguably, a bit melodramatic and forced, such as a needless fight between Beast and Wolverine, but the scripting nonetheless keeps the story active and moving.

All the while one doesn't realize that in these few issues Whedon is laying the groundwork for the overarching story arc of his entire run of 26 issues, just as he introduced plots and characters in early episodes of his television series *Buffy the Vampire Slayer* and *Angel* that would pay off five to seven seasons later. In *Gifted*, he has Scott set out the goal to present the X-Men once again as a spandex superhero team as opposed to the black-wearing agency they had become during Grant Morrison's run (not knocking *New X-Men*, of course). Also, he introduces the government's alien agency, Sentient Worlds Observation and Response Department (S.W.O.R.D., associated with S.H.I.E.L.D.); S.W.O.R.D.'s leader, Agent Abigail Brand; and an intergalactic prophecy that a mutant will destroy the alien Breakworld. All of these elements are important for the final chapter, *Unstoppable*. He even hints at the motivation for Emma's "betrayal" in the third chapter, *Torn*, and sets things in motion for the Danger Room's A.I. being conscious in *Dangerous*.

At the end of *Gifted*, a student's power was forcibly taken away and in the second chapter, *Dangerous*, this causes him to commit suicide in the Danger Room. In turn this triggers the A.I. to develop sentience and try to kill the X-Men, including Professor Xavier who was staying at the wreckage of Genosha. By the end, it's revealed that Xavier knew the A.I. was sentient but kept it confined in order to train the X-Men.

This revelation causes Cyclops to sever ties with Xavier, but it also shakes his faith in his own quality as a leader, since it was a quality that Xavier told him he possessed. It was one of the mental hang-ups Emma used in *Torn* to telepathically psychoanalyze Scott into losing the use of his powers. All the while Cassandra Nova's consciousness, which is locked up in a Brood larvae, manipulates Emma through her survivor's guilt—for not having died in the Genoshan genocide—to psychically attack her teammates. In the same chapter, Danger frees Ord and it is revealed that Colossus was the mutant prophesied to destroy Breakworld.

If one looks at these stories closely, many of the interesting elements— the mutant cure, the awakened A.I., and the psychic manipulation of Emma—are not really used to explore the moral implications of free will and identity that they touch on. They are plot elements used to push the story forward and explore the characters' inter-relational dynamics. And that's not really a bad thing. As stated earlier, these stories have been done before. What's really new is the Whedon style of dialogue and his emphasis on the relationships between the characters and their reactions facing such overwhelming odds and in such dire situations. The dialogue, which at times is witty with its pop culture references and sharp turns of phrase, provides extra pleasure for those reading the comic books. However, he does overuse them, sometimes taking you out of the story, causing you to question whether the characters would really speak this way.

Also, in a way the plot is just the backdrop, an excuse to expose the characters' fears, desires, and expectations. Peter is inspired to start a romance with Kitty after being confined in solitude, Scott and Emma's relationship is put to the test after he suppresses his powers, and the psychic attacks on the team reveal Hank's more beastly side and Wolverine's childish side. The plot can feel a little bit too geared towards these moments of self-revelation, taking out of the story as oppose to sucking you in.

But *Unstoppable*, the final chapter, is a little bit different. All the major players are on stage, major villains and heroes, as the X-Men and S.W.O.R.D. try to infiltrate Breakworld to stop the launch of a weapon aimed at Earth. This chapter is far more plot driven, and every major twist and turn pushes the story along rather than by relying solely on character development. However, the fast-paced nature of the final act of Whedon's run also allows the characters to really shine. Scott shows himself as a leader leading under immense odds, Emma's tears prove she has a heart, and Kitty, by making a heroic sacrifice, is the superhero that Scott wanted to show the world the X-Men could be.

Work Cited

Astonishing X-Men. 24 issues. Story by Joss Whedon. Pencils by John Cassaday. New York: Marvel, July 2004-March 2008. Print. Vol. 3, issues 1-24 of *X-Men*.

Giant-Size Astonishing X-Men #1. Story by Joss Whedon. Pencils by John Cassaday. New York: Marvel, 2008. Print. Final chapter of *Astonishing X-Men*.

4.03
Tom Brokaw's Coat:
Joss Whedon, *Astonishing X-Men* and the Accessibility of History
Dr. Shathley Q

By the time "Gone" hit newsstands, it would be four years after the initial publication of Issue One, the first chapter of *Gifted*. Published in *Giant-Size Astonishing X-Men #1*, "Gone" concludes the publication run of creative team Joss Whedon (as writer) and artist John Cassaday. But the cover dates of July 2004 until July 2008 belie the awkward truth about this fan-favorite title—that the title had been wracked by delays almost from the very start. Yet Whedon's *Astonishing X-Men* would prove seminal for a number of reasons, only some of which involve the publication delays.

Spanning twenty-four issues (*Gifted* 1-6, *Dangerous* 7-12, *Torn* 13-18, and *Unstoppable* 19-24) and the single concluding chapter found in *Giant-Size Astonishing X-Men #1*, Whedon's run reads like a finely-scripted, single-season television show. Coincident with President Bush's second term in office, Whedon's run also reads like an *X-Men* at the very end of history.

X-Mythology would change substantively around the time of the 2008 global financial crisis. By the winter of 2009, *Ultimate X-Men* would draw to a close during the events of Marvel's "Ultimatum" storyline. Like *Ultimate Spider-Man* and *Ultimate Avengers*, *Ultimate X-Men* was meant to craft an easily accessible X-Title for new readers. Everything in the Ultimate publication line would be a way of navigating forty-plus years of publication history. Regular X-Titles (*Uncanny X-Men*, *X-Men Legacy*, *X-Force*, *NewMutants*) would see the X-Men construct an artificial island off the coast of San Francisco, in order to provide a safe harbor for mutants because of political machinations in the broader fictive Marvel Universe. Those days of mutant teenagers mastering their skills in opulent, genteel upstate New York seem halcyon almost immediately after Whedon's run on *Astonishing X-Men*. Even the next writer on *Astonishing*, Warren Ellis, would craft a tale of the X-Men that saw them fitting into a new role in San Francisco.

Whedon's *Astonishing X-Men* is something of a last gasp then, an *X-Men* at the very end of their own history. In just a few short months, the Upstate New York home would be a thing of the past. The long familiar scenes of the *Blackbird* jetting out from a secret launch bay beneath the basketball court, the X-Men training in the mythic Danger Room, and numerous others would simply fall away. And yet, here they are, the X-Men at the end of history, perfectly preserved in the four slim volumes: *Gifted*, *Dangerous*, *Torn*, and *Unstoppable*. In Whedon's *Astonishing* we see the X-Men swashbuckle their way through regime change on an alien world, fight a pitched psychic battle against a post-mutant foe, encounter the first mutant AI, and contend against a corporation that licensed a "cure" for the mutant condition. Cassaday's bright color palette and clear-line style speak of a certain kind of exuberance. Whedon and Cassaday's *Astonishing* is a halcyon moment immediately, even before time passes and we can return to it years later.

It is strange to find then, rather than simply appearing at the end of their own history, Whedon's *Astonishing X-Men* appear at the proper End of History, the End inaugurated by conservative thinker Francis Fukuyama. Or more precisely, that Whedon's *Astonishing X-Men* mirrors an altogether different arc, a theoretical one. This arc in Fukuyama's thinking begins in 1989 with his essay "The End of History" (further developed in his 1992 book *The End of History and the Last Man*) and ends in 2002 with Fukuyama's nearly-unnoticed tract on bioethics, *Our Posthuman Future*. Over the course of the thirteen years, Fukuyama performs the kind of public escape that music journalist Greil Marcus credits Bob Dylan with completing in 1992—an escape from the shadow of his own notoriety.

Fukuyama's claiming History as a teleological force, and his assertion that the Liberal Democracy was the endpoint of that teleology was singularly audacious in 1989. But more than that, the claim brought Fukuyama into the limelight in a way that propelled his career. For the briefest moment, Fukuyama was a Bob Dylan or a Richard Feynman or a Muhammad Ali—a superstar so powerful he brought not only himself but his entire field into the popular imagination.

As the Berlin Wall crumbled, piece by piece, Fukuyama cemented a new kind of conservative thinking: the theory that the Liberal Democracy that had been seen as nothing more than an experiment less than 100 years prior, had now come completely into its own. The "experiment" had succeeded beyond all measure. And in truth, other forms of governance could be deemed nothing more than stultified in their evolution towards Liberal Democracy. Fukuyama was perhaps one of the chief architects of that sense of American stewardship of geopolitics: the idea that being the sole superpower was a responsibility rather than a license.

Thirteen years on, *Our Posthuman Future* reads nothing like the bold assertions found in "The End of History." At first glance we encounter a

Fukuyama more reactive, a Fukuyama wizened by the years and leaning more to the defense of the ideal than an analysis of its superiority. The number one claim in *Our Posthuman Future*—that bioengineering represents a credible threat to the principles of a Liberal Democracy—scans more as alarmist than thought-through. Had Fukuyama simply grown older? But even a cursory reading of the entire book produces a different view entirely. The year 2002 sees a Fukuyama that is subtle, but every bit in the fighting form he was thirteen years prior. *Our Posthuman Future* is a deep and meditative analysis of the nature of the individual, the nature of the state, and the rights and liberties that accrue to both. And while *Our Posthuman Future* is an analysis that seemed science-fictional at the time, a decade later, it seems far less futuristic.

That is, of course, if anybody took the time to read *Our Posthuman Future* fully in 2012. Ten years on, the book seems somewhat anachronistic, despite its futurist orientation. It is an uncomfortable anachronism born perhaps out of a sense that ultimately, Fukuyama assumes the wrong kind of threat to our fundamental freedoms. If the book seems not to fit any longer, it is less a statement about its content, than a statement about society. Society has changed substantially over the past decade—just enough maybe to regard *Our Posthuman Future* as something of a vintage work. For one, Fukuyama assumes that our bioethical rights and freedoms will be worked out through a contestation between the market economy and legislative structures. And yet, in the wake of 2008's financial collapse and 2011's Occupy Wall Street movement, it becomes hard to think of the government and the market economy as disentangled from each other. *Our Posthuman Future* then is its own kind of halcyon moment. A quieter halcyon perhaps than *Astonishing X-Men*, but Fukuyama traces a very similar evolutionary arc.

At its heart, Whedon's *Astonishing X-Men* reads like a proof-of-concept experiment. It is arguably the most clearly defined high concept since the iconic run of writer Chris Claremont and artist John Byrne on *Uncanny X-Men*. In essence then, the X-Men must deal with the hatred and fear of homo sapiens in *Gifted*; tackle the ghosts of past actions while facing off against a singular foe in *Dangerous*; navigate a psychic attack by a rival mutant faction in *Torn*; and weigh a distant intergalactic threat in *Unstoppable*. Very carefully then, Whedon stacked the deck with the most iconic kinds of X-Men stories, the kinds of stories that have become genre in their own right. Substance of the story aside, the style of *Gifted* reads as an almost flawless modernization of the themes of the 1982 graphic novel *God Loves, Man Kills*, and *Torn* like an updating of the micro-dramas in *The Dark Phoenix Saga* of 1980.

This conceptual mode of resemblance is not lost in Fukuyama over the course of the thirteen years. At its heart, *Our Posthuman Future* is every bit the complex wrestling with the seemingly antithetical notions of liberty as innate, and freedom as defended by the federal government. Behind the science-fiction elements and beyond the futurist debate, *Our Posthuman Future* is the same form of political treatise that Fukuyama mastered in 1989. But the science-fictional elements do provide an opportunity Fukuyama could barely have guessed at in 1989—the chance to produce a pop version of his own thinking.

Perhaps Whedon's greatest strength in writing *Astonishing X-Men* is the ease with which he grasps and communicates the essential genre of the stories and settings themselves. No surprise really, since Whedon's most recognizable television show, *Buffy the Vampire Slayer*, is a masterclass in the use of genre. Characters in *Buffy* quickly find themselves propelled beyond the native teen-horror genre of the show and contending with musicals, silent films, and alien invasions from an alternate dimension. Within the confines of the X-Men, Whedon reasserts classic storytelling modes in a credible and accessible way. Unlike the Batman or Spider-Man comics of the day, the wealth of publication history isn't needed for Whedon's *Astonishing X-Men*. You needn't have been familiar with the heady times of Stan Lee and Jack Kirby's original *Uncanny X-Men*, when social analogy was the storytelling mode. It was clear that mutant rights activism was a comics-based meditation on the Civil Rights movement. The saintly Professor Xavier was clearly Dr. Martin Luther King, while the more aggressive Magneto was arguably Malcolm X.

X-Men comes with an illustrious history, but forty years of this history might prove a stumbling block. Remember when Wolverine had his adamantium skeleton ripped out by Magneto? Well if you don't, how would this current story have any emotional context for you? Forty years later, the publication history was the primary cause of rendering the X-Men inaccessible to all but fans.

While the hyper-focus on publication history might be attributable to factors outside the realm of creativity (the mid-eighties saw the birth of direct marketing in the comics industry, and with that the rise of fandom), there can be no doubt that Whedon's storylines buck that trend of writing exclusively for fans. The interesting conundrum is, was *Astonishing X-Men* targeted to fans so they could rediscover the "classic" X-Men, or was *Astonishing* aimed at bringing new fans into the fold?

Astonishing X-Men came at a critical time for Marvel. The company had just had amazing success with two X-Movies (2000's *X-Men* and

2003's *X2: X-Men United*, both helmed by Bryan Singer) and two Spider-Movies (2001's *Spider-Man* and 2004's *Spider-Man 2*, both directed by Sam Raimi). Recapitalizing on the success of X-Men in the comic books that birthed them seemed like the next peak to scale. But the reason deeper than revitalizing sales might go to the heart of the difficulty around corporate-sponsored creativity.

Singer's *X-Men* had been a spectacular and wholly unexpected success. To find a superhero movie that hit in the popular imagination at the same level as *X-Men*, you'd have to go back to 1989, to Tim Burton's *Batman*. But the movies themselves come from very different guiding principles. Burton's *Batman* was garish, outlandish, theatrical. It emphasized the vast chasm of alienation most comic book heroes had to cross to reenter the popular imagination. Rather than attempt to naturalize the outlandishness of superheroes, Burton's intuition was to embrace, to relish it even. Singer opted for a very different approach. Singer's *X-Men* wouldn't be out place in the everyday New England of the ordinary world. They would eat at the same delis on the Hudson, they would plan shopping trips to Chicago or Boston or Grand Rapids on the weekend.

With this X-Men-at-the-end-of-the-street came the jettisoning of the superheroics and more visibly, the disappearance of the superhero costumes. Xavier's was a school, a private academy for mutants. And school meant school uniforms, black leather ones in Singer's vision. What Singer really oversaw was a return to the original touchstones pioneered by Lee and Kirby—that the X-Men was little more than a special emergency and rescue team, there to interdict when racial hatred threatened. Singer's vision of the X-Men then, begun in the original *X-Men* of 2000, traces an evolutionary path from one crisis-point in the very concept of the team to the next. In *X-Men*, the appearance of Magneto and his Brotherhood of Mutants triggers a new kind of thinking. Maybe crowd dispersal and educating the public about mutants is not simply what the X-Men should be about. Maybe, the threat to mutant-human relations can come from radical, reactionary mutants as well. *X-Men United* illustrates the evolution of that idea by showing how a weak administration can have its hand forced into taking military action against mutants. The X-Men would have to wade into contestation with fringe elements within the government.

But if Singer adapted the original Lee-Kirby vision of the X-Men, writer Grant Morrison would simply explode it. Taking the helm of *New X-Men* in 2001, Morrison offered a singular, radically altered (unrecognizable, some have argued) vision of the X-Men. Keeping the school-uniform theme of Singer's X-Men, Morrison would engineer even more radical changes.

For one, the core theme of the X-Men defending a mutant minority was simply dismissed. In Morrison's X-Men, humans became the endangered species, when their "extinction gene" activated. The traditional foes of Magneto—the Sentinels, Mister Sinister, Apocalypse—would all simply be written out (in fact, Magneto would ostensibly meet his death in just the third issue of Morrison's run). Instead, the line-up of villains would include Cassandra Nova (the psychic, bodiless remains of Professor X's twin whom he murdered in the womb), the U-Men (an international self-empowerment corporate empire bent on harvesting mutant DNA), and The Sublime (a micro-colony of sentient bacteria that had plotted universal domination for the past three billion years).

Morrison's X-Men was compelling, but it wasn't the traditional X-Men. But Morrison's run on X-Men would prove compelling for a much darker reason. Morrison's run began with *New X-Men #114* and would end with *#154*, the entire run spanning forty-one single issues and one Annual published in 2001. Issues ran from cover dates July 2001 (released two months earlier in May 2001) until May 2004 (released March 2004). But it would be the concluding chapter of *E is for Extinction*, Morrison's opening story arc, that would prove horrifically prescient. In *#116*, Morrison would script the death of 16 million mutants at the hands of a rogue "wild" Sentinel, a city-sized robot built for killing mutants. Two months later, 9/11 would play out in the most terrifying proportions. Predating the attacks by just two months, Morrison's *New X-Men* became a kind of exorcizing of the demons of 9/11 through popular culture. From Wolverine tracking terrorists across Afghanistan to building a memorial to attacks on Genosha, there always seemed to be a hidden tension in Morrison's oeuvre. Could Morrison ever escape the shadow of his own prescience? Could *New X-Men* ever become that single story of multiple plotlines that Morrison himself arguably had hoped for prior to 9/11?

Almost none of that tension exists in Whedon's *Astonishing X-Men*, that similarly comments on the historical context of President Bush's second term in office. In *Astonishing* we see an *X-Men* disillusioned at having been deceived by their leader, Professor X in *Dangerous*. We see an *X-Men* wrestling with inner demons in *Torn*. We see an *X-Men* grappling with regime change on a cosmic level in *Unstoppable*. And while there never is a direct correlation between not finding WMD's, the torture at Abu Ghraib, and the toppling of Saddam and the Ba'ath Party, there is a direct confronting of the spirit of the era.

Again, this resemblance rather than direct depiction is the dominant creative mode opted for by Fukuyama in *The End of History*. The issues remain the core issues of conservative politics—restraint on federal government, personal liberty, self-regulation of a free market economy. And yet, none of those issues appear for themselves. Rather, they enter *The End of History* as themes, each as a halcyon moment of its very own. Against the backdrop of the narrative of a quiet and unrelenting victory of the Liberal Democracy, Fukuyama presents each of these conservative themes as something to yearn towards.

Perhaps there was an astuteness to this choice. It really is hard to forget that at one of the most momentous events in human memory, the tearing down of the Berlin Wall, Tom Brokaw wore a weathered green hunter's coat for his broadcast on *CBS Nightly News*. As we watched our television sets, decades of human history began to unravel almost before our eyes. Maybe President Reagan was wrong, maybe the Cold War wouldn't go Hot and end in a global conflagration. Just maybe, we could begin to plan for the future, for a future. And despite the indescribable moment we came face-to-face with right there at the business end of history, the thing that seems to ring most true is Brokaw's coat. More than just a shield against the European night, Brokaw's coat is something resoundingly human, the everyday in us all that we can easily recognize. Everybody has a coat he or she wears but would rather not be seen in. And Tom Brokaw wearing his at the tearing down of the Berlin Wall gave us a secret passport to access the immensity of the event unfolding before us.

Joss Whedon's *Astonishing X-Men* then really is an *X-Men* at the End of History. It is the script of popular culture run side-by-side with the white-knuckle ride of history. It is a secret reliance on constructing a deep and meaningful accessibility to momentous events. And, it is the resurrection of enduring genre and themes within the smaller context of a single story. If there is any one thing enduring at all about Whedon's *Astonishing X-Men* (and there are many), it is reassertion of the deeper consequentiality of pop-culture: the idea that pop-culture is not simply the immediate or the easily-found, but the accessible core that lies at the heart of human experience. Like Tom Brokaw's coat, pop-culture is an interpretative tool. But it would take a singular talent like Whedon's to convey the profundity of the times in as ordinary a thing as a comic book about the X-Men.

Works Cited

Astonishing X-Men. 24 issues. Story by Joss Whedon. Pencils by John Cassaday. New York: Marvel, July 2004-March 2008. Print. Vol. 3, issues 1-24 of *X-Men*.

The Dark Phoenix Saga. Story by Chris Claremont. Pencils by John Byrne. New York: Marvel, 1980. Print. Vol. 1, issues 129-38 of *Uncanny X-Men*.

E is for Extinction. Story by Grant Morrison. Pencils by Frank Quitely. New York: Marvel, 2001. Print. Vol. 1, issues 114-116 of *New X-Men.*

Giant-Size Astonishing X-Men #1. Story by Joss Whedon. Pencils by John Cassaday. New York: Marvel, 2008. Print. Final chapter of *Astonishing X-Men.*

Fukuyama, Francis. "The End of History?" *The National Interest* Summer 1989. Print.

---. *The End of History and the Last Man.* New York: Free Press, 1992. Print.

---. *Our Posthuman Future: Consequences of the Biotechnology Revolution.* New York: Farrar, Straus, and Giroux, 2002. Print.

X-Men: God Loves, Man Kills. Story by Chris Claremont. Pencils by Brent Anderson. New York: Marvel, 1982. Print. Marvel Graphic Novel #5.

4.04
Joss Whedon 101:
Runaways
Kevin Chiat

A major theme in the early years of *Buffy the Vampire Slayer* was the rejection of adult authority figures. Buffy and the Scooby Gang were constantly in conflict with symbols of authority. Principal Snyder was a perpetual thorn in the side of our heroes, a disciplinarian goon who took pleasure in berating the students of Sunnydale High. The Watcher's Council turned out to be a corrupt organization, arrogantly treating Buffy like a disposable weapon. This theme was best demonstrated by Mayor Richard Wilkins III, the Big Bad of Season 3. Mayor Wilkins's outer persona was that of a polite and charming small town mayor with a love of miniature golf and a no-swearing policy. In reality, he was an immortal sorcerer trying to complete his ascension to full-blooded demon. Of course, there are also benevolent authority figures in the Buffyverse. Buffy's mother Joyce Summers grows to accept her daughter's heroic responsibility as the Slayer; and Rupert Giles, Buffy's Watcher, acts as a replacement father figure to Buffy and her friends. Yet the rejection of adult authority figures is an important part of the framework of *Buffy* and of the Marvel comic series *Runaways.*

Before Joss Whedon wrote the six-issue *Dead End Kids* run (issues 25-30, 2007-2008) in Volume Two of *Runaways,* many other themes and characters typical of his television work were apparent in the comic. The Marvel Comics series was created by writer Brian K. Vaughan and artist Adrian

Alphona with Volume One comprising eighteen issues, 2003-2004. Vaughan takes *Buffy*'s theme of rejecting adult authority to the next level. The series challenges what Vaughan saw as a tendency in the superhero genre to put guardian figures on a pedestal and show that true heroes always respect their elders and blindly follow their teachings. In *Runaways* no adult authority figures can be trusted. Parents, police, teachers, and even superheroes are all antagonistic towards the runaway teens of the title. Unlike Buffy, the Runaways have no one to turn to for advice or protection. The group of friends are completely on their own, with only each other to depend on.

The central metaphor underlying *Buffy the Vampire Slayer* is that high school is hell, a concept that every adolescent recognizes. The central metaphor behind *Runaways* is another very simple, universal idea. At some point, every teenager considers his or her parents to be evil. For Nico, Chase, Molly, Karolina, Gert, and Alex, their parents actually *are* evil. Living in Los Angeles, the families meet once a year at Alex's house and the kids are forced to interact with each other while their parents discuss their charity plans. Alex convinces the older kids to join him in spying on their parents' meeting. What they see is the murder of a young woman by Alex's father, and they find out that their parents are actually a secret cabal of supervillains named the Pride. As the Pride, their parents are the secret crime lords of Los Angeles. Vaughan makes clever use of Marvel's tendency to set all their comics in New York; there are no local superheroes to fight the Pride.

The teens go on the run, trying to find a way to end their parents' criminal empire. Each except for Alex discovers secret powers or artifacts that their parents had hidden from them. Nico discovers that her parents are dark magicians and that she has inherited their magical ability. Chase finds out that his parents are mad scientists. Gert realizes that her parents are time travelers and she unlocks a genetically engineered Deinonychus-like dinosaur her parents had bought for her in case she was ever in danger. She names her new dinosaur Old Lace. Karolina has to deal with the shocking revelation that her parents are aliens who have been hiding out on Earth her whole life and that her abilities had been kept suppressed by her parents. Molly Hayes, the youngest of the group, discovers that she's actually a mutant and is gifted with super-strength (with the minor drawback that using her power tires her out and she needs to take a nap to regain her strength).

They discover that the police are on the payroll of the Pride and they are unable to get in contact with any of the established Marvel superheroes. The first volume of *Runaways* follows the conflict between the Pride and their children. The story climaxes with a twist as shocking as Angel becoming Angelus in *Buffy* Season 2. Alex, the de-facto leader of the Runaways, turns out to have been a mole for the Pride the whole time, subtly manipulating the other kids throughout the series. The finale brings the Pride's criminal empire to an end, and the Runaways are split up and sent to foster homes by Captain America.

The influence of Joss Whedon is apparent throughout Vaughan's work on *Runaways*. The cast challenges the traditional superhero team set-up. Superhero teams have traditionally been dominated by male characters, often containing only one or two token females. The Runaways gang is instead dominated by females, with Chase and Alex being the only two males in the original line-up. Vaughan's dialogue in the comic to an end is as funny and witty as the dialogue in the Whedonverse while still sounding natural coming from the mouths of teens (plus one pre-teen.) Whedon himself is referenced in a story-arc where the Runaways are in a fight with a vampire. Joss Whedon was so impressed by the comic that he wrote a fan letter published in the last issue of Volume One, decrying the seeming end of *Runaways* in 2004.

In Vaughan's run, issues 1-24, throughout Volume Two of *Runaways*, the friends reunite and run away from their foster homes (and Molly from the Xavier Institute). As a means of making up for their parents' crimes, they try to combat the supervillains and organized crime moving into Los Angeles to fill the void left by the Pride. Now led by Nico, the Runaways have a problematic relationship with their new role as superheroes. The team doesn't wear costumes or use codenames. Rather than having a rallying cry like "Avengers Assemble!" or "Flame On!" the closest equivalent they have is "Try not to die."

The group picks up two other runaways: Xavin, a Skrull warrior who had been promised Karolina's hand in marriage, and Victor, a half-robot teen created by one of the Avengers' greatest enemies. The team experiences the tragedy of losing one of their own, a death which still haunts them. Vaughan and Alphona finished their work with *Runaways* in 2007. Their run ends with the team on the run from Los Angeles following a confrontation with Iron Man, who had taken leadership of the government registration of superheroes as part of the *Civil War* storyline. Then Marvel enlisted the services of *Runaways*' highest-profile fan, Joss Whedon, to take over writing chores beginning with issue 25 of Volume Two in June 2007. Teaming up with artist Michael Ryan, Whedon would be the first writer after Vaughan to write the Runaways in their own book (although they had appeared in a team-up with The Young Avengers). In their six-issue story arc, entitled *Dead End Kids*, the story follows the Runaways as they escape to New York and meet up with the Kingpin, Daredevil's arch-nemesis and a former business associate of their parents. They are tasked with stealing a piece of technology that turns out to have been made by Gert's time-traveling parents. After stealing the artifact (in issue #26) the Runaways are forced to use the technology to escape an attack and find themselves sent back in time to 1907.

Dead End Kids is recognizably Whedonesque, dealing with the ongoing themes found throughout his work. The entire story is structured around a doomed love affair between a Runaway and a girl from the 1900s. Karolina also has to deal with the unsavory aspects of the 1900s when she discovers Klara, a young girl forced to work in a factory. The dialogue is recognizably Whedon, but still sounds in character for the Runaways. A highlight is Victor admonishing Molly for punching the Punisher, telling her (in Slayer slang) that she should have known from his name that he has no superpowers: "What, you think he's got some sort of *punishy* force?"

Dead End Kids also gives Whedon the opportunity to contribute something to the wider Marvel universe. By taking the Runaways back to 1907 New York, Whedon has the opportunity to create an entire new set of characters. For example, introduced in issue #28, 1907 New York is protected by a superhero team named the Upward Path that includes the Difference Engine (a steampunk robot), Black Maria (one of Nico's ancestors), and Adjudicator (a 1907 version of Punisher). While stranded in 1907, the Runaways are taken in by a group known as The Street Arabs, a group of superpowered people living in New York. In *Dead End Kids*, Whedon creates a whole raft of new characters for the 1907 timeframe. Any future Marvel creators looking to tell stories dealing with the time period will be able to make use of Whedon's contributions to the shared universe.

Runaways also allows for Whedon to look at the Marvel Universe from a skewed perspective and introduce some of his idiosyncrasies to established characters. In an interview to promote his run, Whedon described *Runaways* as "the new voice of the Marvel Universe because it thinks the Marvel Universe is a bunch of old guys, and treats them accordingly." Whedon's Kingpin interrupts his inner monologue to consider his love of chocolate and is pitied by Molly because he probably has Glands. Rather than being a badass, the Punisher comes off as a psychopathic jerk and, like his earlier incarnation, is willing to kill in order to punish the perpetrators of minor crimes. He's humbled by a punch from a 12-year-old girl. Whedon, like Vaughan uses the Runaways to poke fun at the conventions of the Marvel Universe. One panel showing a brawl between superheroes and villains in 1907 resembles the fights between superheroes in Marvel's *Civil War*, a war the Runaways purposefully tried to avoid.

Following *Dead End Kids*, *Runaways* was again relaunched in Volume Three, this time with Terry Moore writing and Humberto Ramos (#1-6) and Takeshi Miyazawa (#7-9) on art. Their run was not particularly well received. The follow-up story arc written by Chris Yost (#10-11) and Kathryn Immonen (#12-14) and drawn by Sara Pichelli was better received by critics and fans, but unfortunately lagging sales led to the cancellation of the title in 2009. *Runaways* is now in creative limbo, currently unused as a comic or a movie at Marvel. Although plans were underway in 2010-2011 to adapt *Runaways* as a feature film, *Woerner* reported in August 2011 that the studio was too busy with another Joss Whedon project (some little flick called *The Avengers...*) to do *Runaways*. Fans can still hope that a future film will materialize and spark a revival of the series in the comic medium.

Works Cited

Runaways. Vol. 1, 18 issues. New York: Marvel, 2003 – 2004. Print.

---. Vol. 2, issues 1-24. Story by Brian K. Vaughan. Pencils by Adrian Alphona. New York: Marvel, 2005-2007. Print.

---. Vol. 2, issues 25-30. Dead End Kids. Story by Joss Whedon. Pencils by Michael Ryan. New York: Marvel, 2007- 2008. Print.

---. Vol. 3, 14 issues. Story by Terry Moore, Chris Yost, and Kathryn Immonen. Pencils by Humberto Ramos, Takeshi Miyazawa, and Sara Pichelli. New York: Marvel, 2008-2009. Print.

Woerner, Meredith. "Marvel's *Runaways* Movie On Ice Until After *The Avengers*." *io9.com* 15 Aug. 2011. Web.

4.05
Joss Whedon 101:
Angel: After the Fall
Patrick Shand

The finale of Joss Whedon's *Angel* left half of the fandom in awe at how the lack of resolution was brilliantly fitting and the other half wondering what the hell happened after the screen cut to black. Wesley was dead, a depressed Lorne exited stage right, Connor was told to stay out of the fight, and the rest of our heroes—Angel, Spike, Illyria, and a mortally wounded Gunn—were in an alley, facing an army of thousands of demons that Wolfram &

Hart had sent as punishment for Angel's rebellion. Among those demons? A big damn dragon.

The moment Angel charges, delivering the iconic line "Let's go to work," the screen cuts to black in a *Sopranos*-esque symbolic ending. Joss Whedon said, "...the point of the show is that you're never done; no matter who goes down, the fight goes on" (qtd. in Alter). The theme of *Angel* as a series is that the fight never ends, so of course the show had to end in the middle of Angel's biggest brawl yet. Personally, the ending made me glad to be a fan of such a smart and daring show. "Fans want to know if Angel and co. survived? Pshaw!" I said pretentiously in a faux British accent. "Don't they know that that's not the *point*?"

Despite that, the moment it was announced in 2007 that *Angel* would be continued in canonical comic book form by Joss Whedon, creator and all around ginger-haired genius, and Brian Lynch, the writer (also, very tall) of the hilarious and spot-on *Spike: Asylum*, I was among the fans squealing and whooping. Not to mention, the series was to be penciled by a roster of fantastic artists, including Franco Urru, Stephen Mooney, Nick Runge, John Bryne, and many more (*Angel: After the Fall*). All of the academic interest in *Angel*'s ending was forgotten, as we would *finally know what happened in the alley!*

In a move of sheer brilliance, however, Joss and Brian's story opens after the fight is over. *Angel: After the Fall* opens in an alley, but there isn't an insurmountable horde of demons. There are a *few* demons, though, and just as they're about to feast on some people, Angel jumps in and does what he does best—saving lives. Only this time, he's got a little help in the form of a giant, fire-breathing dragon. Angel says, "[The dragon] was part of [Wolfram & Hart]). Two minutes into fighting him, I realized he was as misled as I was" (*After the Fall #1*). Once the demons are sliced, diced, and nice and crispy, Angel gives the civilians directions to a safe house before he hops onto the dragon's back for a ride home. They fly over L.A., which looks a bit different than the last time we saw it. Fire shoots from the ground, tentacles and mouths sprout from buildings, and the sun and the moon are out at the same time. All in all, not your average Tuesday. Angel says, "My friends stood by me. Wolfram & Hart sent an army. There were losses on both sides. And then Wolfram & Hart sent Los Angeles to Hell" (*After the Fall #1*). And that's quite literal. L.A. is in Hell and the city has been divided amongst demons who saw "the Fall" as an opportunity to come to power. These so-called lords have claimed Compton, Burbank, Century City, Downtown L.A., Santa Monica, Sherman Oaks, Weho, Westwood, and Beverly Hills as their territories.

Los Angeles isn't the only thing that has dramatically changed. Wesley has been resurrected by Wolfram & Hart... but with a catch. He's a ghost, which is bad enough, but he is also being used by W&H as their last official representative of the L.A. Branch, just to hurt Angel. Wes spends most of his time playing the role, secretly doing what he thinks is best for Angel. Angel is being kept alive by Wolfram & Hart for its own unknown purposes, and Wesley wants to find out why.

Spike and Illyria are the "co-lords" of Beverly Hills. They put up the front that they're engaging in the same human-slave-keeping activities as the other lords, but they've really been housing up at the Playboy Mansion (in the prequel spin-off *Spike: After the Fall*, Spike stakes Hugh Hefner... who was clearly a vampire), giving shelter to humans who need it. Spike has been spending as much time as possible keeping these humans safe, but most of his efforts have to go to babysitting Illyria, who has been going through some... changes. The atmosphere of Hell affects all demons, but especially her; it has been tapping into some of her old power, making her and the people around her shift through time, often causing her to turn back into Fred at inopportune times.

Connor is running the safe house that Angel mentioned to the civilians. He operates it with help from Nina and Gwen, who have both been affected by the Fall in odd ways. The L.I.S.A. device that Gwen had been using to control her electricity since the *Angel* episode "Players" (4.16) was rendered useless, and she's full-on electric girl again. Nina's problem is a bit stranger; when she, caught up in the moment, begins licking one of the people she is supposed to be guarding, she says, "It's the sun/moon situation! They're both out at once. Do you have any idea what that does to a werewolf?" (*ATF #1*).

Lorne is making the best of the hellish situation. In order to combat the depression he suffered in the last season of *Angel*, he turns Silverlake into a sanctuary for humans and benevolent demons. With some help from a sorceress, all the nastiness of Hell was removed from Silverlake and a bubble was formed around the city, protecting Lorne and his friends from the wicked environment. Lorne, however, has not abandoned Angel and his other friends. He keeps a watch over them from... well, a crystal ball.

Gunn has changed the most. He's still trying to be a hero, to find a way to rescue Los Angeles from Hell... but the thing of it is, though, he didn't quite make it out of that alley alive. Moments before the Fall, he was dragged away by a gang of vampires; Angel was oblivious to this, as he was busy freeing the dragon from Wolfram & Hart's spell. Gunn wakes up, devastated and furious to find the changes that went on overnight. Simultaneously, he discovers that L.A. is in Hell and that his worst nightmare has come true: he has been turned into a vampire. Quickly killing his sire, Gunn claims the vampire gang as his own and begins his quest to return L.A. to normalcy. Gunn takes down Burge, the Lord of Westwood, in order to kidnap a telepathic fish named Betta George who he feels is key in unraveling the mystery of Wolfram & Hart. He also steals a mystical item from Burge called the *Eye of Ramras*, which he takes back to his home and adds to a shrine he is building as a part of his plan. When Betta George, who was a character from Brian Lynch's *Spike: Asylum* that Joss Whedon wanted to include, calls Gunn a vampire, Gunn protests, saying that he is not. He says, "I spent a good part of my life dusting them. The best part, actually. And then. I was fool enough to trust one. Led me into a battle that ended with me being dragged away and turned while he played goddamn dragon-whisperer. But even now… with this disease… I'm making things right. See, someone fancies himself a white hat because he's got a soul. Thinks he gets in touch with the man he was. Makes him good. Funny thing, though. Maybe the man he *was* wasn't all that good to begin with. But at the end of the day, he gives up. On everything. On us. But it's fine… I'm going to save us all" (*ATF #2*). What complicates Gunn's hero complex, however, is the fact that he kills and eats humans for dinner due to the whole not-having-a-soul thing.

And then, there's Angel. He wants to make a move, but he's been separated from his friends. He knows it's his fault that Wolfram & Hart has sent Los Angeles to Hell, and that adds endless weight to his already insurmountable guilt. In a desperate move to actually *do* something, he challenges all of the demon lords of L.A. to a battle. Angel will fight their chosen champions in an all-or-nothing match for control of L.A. It's strikingly similar to Angel's assassination of the Circle of the Black Thorn members that led to this situation in the first place, only this time, things are—if possible—more dire: Angel is alone. Also, another aspect of Wolfram & Hart's punishment is revealed by Angel's internal thoughts after he makes the challenge: "A rash decision? Yeah… Two days to figure out how I'm bringing down half a dozen of hell's most brutal minions. And to heal from normally mortal wounds. Another thing about hell. Doesn't alter a vampire's healing faculties, so a vamp can still mend quickly. Which, of course, would mean so much more… if I were still a vampire" (*ATF #3*). In order to make him defenseless, Wolfram & Hart made Angel into a human. His greatest wish was granted at the worst possible time.

And, naturally, when Gunn discovers that Angel has been granted humanity, he isn't so happy.

The series reaches its first climax when Angel faces off against the lords' chosen warriors, alone at first... until Connor, Spike, Nina, Gwen, Illyria, Lorne, and the Groosalugg join him. Angel says, "This was my fight. I was never going to ask anyone to help. Turns out... I didn't have to" (*ATF* #5). In the midst of the worst crisis the gang has ever faced, they rekindle their friendships.

After the lords are taken care of, things get even hotter in Hell. As the gang investigates what has been going on with Illyria/Fred, Angel finally faces off with Gunn, which leads to a fight, an ancient demon returning to its original and monstrous form in the middle of Hell, a few *major* character deaths, the devastating revelation of the true nature of the Shanshu Prophecy, a betrayal, and the biggest and most important fight of Angel's life.

Brian Lynch has written, with plotting from Joss Whedon, the biggest and perhaps best *Angel* story ever told. While the stakes are higher than they've ever been for Angel and his friends, the focus never veers away from the characters. It's the exploration of Angel's dedication to the good fight, Spike's passion to be his own man and follow his heart, Connor's maturation, Illyria's confusion and fall, Wesley's need to be released, and Gunn's broken heart that make this story what it is. *Angel: After the Fall* does the impossible: it does justice to the brilliant finale that came before it, tells its own epic story, and sets up things to come for IDW's excellent on-going *Angel* series. *Angel* might have had one of the best and smartest endings to a television series, but it is continued by an equally smart comic book.

Works Cited

Alter, Ethan. "*Angel* Creator's Finale Post-Mortem." *TVGuide.com* 20 May 2004. Web. 26 Oct. 2011.

Angel: After the Fall. Story by Joss Whedon and Brian Lynch. Pencils by Franco Urru, Stephen Mooney, Nick Runge, John Bryne, and others. 4 vols. 17 issues. San Diego: IDW, 2007-2009. Print.

"Players." 4.16. Writ. Jeffrey Bell, Elizabeth Craft, and Sarah Fain. Dir. Michael Grossman. Angel: *The Complete Series*. Twentieth Century Fox Home Entertainment, 2010. DVD.

Spike: Asylum. Story by Brian Lynch. Pencils by Franco Urru. 5 issues. San Diego: IDW, 2006-2007. Print.

4.06
IDW Retrospect:
A Look Back At IDW's *Angel* with Brian Lynch and Scott Tipton
Patrick Shand

1. A BRIEF HISTORY OF THE 'VERSE

In the beginning, there was television.

That's not a statement you'd expect to read, I know. It's how Joss Whedon's *Angel* started out, though. As all Buffyphiles know, the vampire with a soul first appeared in *Buffy the Vampire Slayer* as the pale, handsome gentleman who popped up and gave Buffy Summers foreboding hints about the latest supernatural goings-on. The character garnered a huge fanbase, which led to a spin-off television show that aired on the WB from 1999 until its unfortunate cancellation in 2004. As fans of the show know, though… vampires don't die that easily. *Angel* came back from the dead as a comic book.

Dark Horse Comics published *Angel* comics between 2000 and 2002, but it wasn't until 2005 that IDW (Idea and Design Works) Publishing acquired the license and went on to publish comics featuring the beloved character for six years straight.

In 2011, IDW published its last *Angel* comic and the license switched back to Dark Horse. In honor of that, I have asked longtime IDW writers Brian Lynch and Scott Tipton to answer a few questions about their work on IDW's *Angel* as I take a look back at six years of great storytelling. I admit a slight bias, because I contributed a script to the last *Angel* comic (*Angel: Yearbook*), but I—like Brian and Scott—was a fan long before I had the pleasure of writing in the Angelverse.

2. MEET THE MEN

Brian Lynch and Scott Tipton both have massive numbers of credits to their names, inside and outside of their work on *Angel*. Scott Tipton got involved with *Angel* early on. He says, "I had already been writing for [IDW] on some of their horror anthology series, and when I heard that they had acquired the license [to *Angel*], I let them know that I was very familiar with the show and would love to take a crack at it. A few months down the road, they asked if I'd be interested in submitting a proposal for a *Spike* graphic novel, Naturally, I leapt at the chance. Both IDW and Fox liked it, and we were off and running." Scott would go on to write two *Spike* oversized one-shots (*Spike: Old Wounds* and *Spike: Lost and Found*), the five issue *Angel: Auld Lang Syne* miniseries, *Angel Spotlight: Wesley*, *Angel:* "Unacceptable Losses" appearing in the Halloween special *Masks*, the four issue *Illyria: Haunted* miniseries (co-written with Mariah Huehner), the story "All the Time in the World" for *Angel: Yearbook*, and comic book adaptations of three episodes from the show's last season. He also co-wrote a short story that focused on Charles Gunn, who had been turned into a vampire in Brian Lynch's *Angel: After the Fall* storyline.

Brian Lynch was also a longtime *Angel* fan. When asked how he came to write Angel, he says, "I wrote a comic strip called *Monkey Man* on a site owned by Kevin Smith. It ran 100 weeks, and had many references to Whedonverse characters. Chris Ryall, at the time, ran the site for Kevin. Mr. Ryall and I became friends, and eventually he became Editor in Chief of IDW. Sometime after that, they got the *Angel* license. I asked him for a shot, over and over, and eventually he asked me if I had any ideas for a *Spike* mini-series. I wrote up an outline for *Spike: Asylum*, featuring Spike entering a rehab facility for supernatural creatures." After *Asylum*, Brian went on to write *Spike: Shadow Puppets*, the seventeen issue epic *Angel: After the Fall*, the spinoff *Spike: After the Fall*, five additional issues of the on-going *Angel* series, the parody comic *Last Angel in Hell*, and an eight issue *Spike* series that builds toward Joss Whedon's own *Buffy the Vampire Slayer Season Eight*.

3. AFTER THE FALL

IDW released four *Angel* miniseries, two *Spike* miniseries, and a slew of one-shots before Joss Whedon contacted the company with the desire to tell the story of what happened to Angel and his friends directly following the last televised episode. After he read and liked *Spike: Asylum*, Whedon wanted Brian Lynch to co-plot and ultimately write the series, which would be called *Angel: After the Fall*. "I danced around like a little girl, and then calmly responded 'yes,'" Brian says. "And then danced some more. But this time more manly. Like, much popping and locking." Brian Lynch's trademark humor worked hand-in-hand with Joss Whedon's approach to the characters, where they were cracking jokes in even the most dire of situations.

"We met for breakfast a couple of times to discuss what would have happened if the *Angel* series had continued, his plans for the Spike movie, etcetera," Brian says of his meetings with Joss Whedon. "And then we'd talk about the plotlines and moments from those storylines that we should use in *Angel: After the Fall*. I went home, did some more of that girl dancing, and then wrote an outline. He gave me notes, rewrote a little, sent it back, and that's how it went for a while. Truly a wonderful time."

Brian wrote seventeen issues of the epic tale of Angel's fight to save Los Angeles. However, in the eighth issue, he was joined by Scott Tipton, who helped Brian tell the tale of how Gunn was turned by a vampire. "I was very much aware that it was Brian's baby, coming right in the middle of his gigantic, epic tale, so I just tried to follow his lead and tell Brian's story as best I could," Scott says. "There is a moment or two in there that are all mine, though, that I'm really proud of."

4. BEYOND

While IDW's *Angel* comics were successful before *After the Fall*, Brian Lynch's landmark series became IDW's top selling title, which led to the expansion of the franchise. Brian himself wrote a *Spike* spin-off, while Scott Tipton and editor Mariah Huehner wrote a miniseries that focused on Illyria's evolution as a character. Comic book veteran John Byrne joined IDW to tell stories set in Angel's past, notably putting Angel in the middle of a vampire conflict during World War I in *Angel: Blood & Trenches*.

Over the course of the series, many writers had their chance to tell stories set in IDW's ever-broadening Angelverse. Kelley Armstrong, Bill Willingham, David Tischman, Bill Williams, Jeff Mariotte, and Dan Roth all joined the aforementioned writers to tell their own *Angel* tales. As I mentioned earlier, even I wrote one of the final *Angel* stories, collected in the one-shot *Angel: Yearbook*. It was the highlight of my career as a freelance writer—it's hard to articulate the feeling of utter fulfilment at writing a story about characters that have moved you the way Joss Whedon's characters have moved me. I began watching *Buffy the Vampire Slayer* in the first season on television, and Whedon's enormous body of work has played a large part in my life since then.

IDW's track record of big name writers is evidence of just that: the lasting appeal of Joss Whedon's work. Brian Lynch says, "*Buffy* and *Angel* (and *Firefly* actually) rank among my favorite TV shows. *Buffy* is a perfect blend of adventure, comedy, action, horror, romance, it has such great dialog... and it features a dozen or so of the greatest characters that have ever been on television. All the fun stuff wouldn't mean a thing if you weren't so invested in the people. Yes, watching Buffy save the world is exciting... but watching Buffy interact with Willow and Spike and Xander, that's what kept me coming back every week."

Scott adds, "Whedon's characters were so well drawn and developed that writing them was an absolute pleasure. I never had to struggle with what Spike would do next; his dialogue practically wrote itself."

Brian and Scott's work continues the *Angel* tradition in a very Whedonesque fashion: the plots and threats are always interesting, maintaining the heavy fantasy/action that is natural in the comic book medium, but the focus always remains squarely on the characters.

5. THE END

Angel: Yearbook is a bittersweet topic for me. It marks the end of my favorite comic book series, but it also includes my first (and only) story set in the Angelverse. I wrote my story, "Angel: My Only Friend," as a goodbye to Angel, the character and the series, and it was as difficult an experience as it was rewarding. Both Scott and Brian have been writing the series for years, though, so I had to wonder how it felt for them to bid farewell to the characters they'd been writing for half a decade.

"I have no idea if I'll write the characters again," Brian says. "Certainly Dark Horse has been very nice about the idea of me coming over to do some more stories in that universe. I'm happy for the breather, but I don't think the door is closed. Either way, I've told many stories with the characters, so if that's it, that's okay, I had my fun. I will (and already do) miss the original characters I co-created with the artists, as they exist in some kinda weird limbo without *Spike* and *Angel*.

"As for the endings for the characters, I worked with the Scott Allie at Dark Horse and Chris and Mariah at IDW to end [the *Spike* series] and have it dove-tail into the Dark Horse's *Buffy* series, so his ending was easy. The non-TV show characters were a bit harder, as I could have killed [the original characters] Beck or Betta George or Jeremy or Tok to go out big and emotional… but I opted to give them a 'happily ever after,' which is a rarity in Joss Whedon's universe."

Scott chose to write his final story, which appears in *Angel: Yearbook*, about Fred and Wesley. Scott says, "It was very much a 'goodbye' for me and my collaborator, artist Elena Casagrande. We had spent the last two years or so absorbed in Wesley and Fred's tragic love story, between our adaptations of "Smile Time" and "A Hole in the World" and then our *Illyria* miniseries. So once we knew it would be our swan song, we wanted to give these characters we'd lived inside a little present, a small moment of happiness that we never saw them get in the series. Of course, in true Angel style, it never goes the way it's supposed to."

Angel: Yearbook represents a thematic end for IDW's *Angel* as a series. Chronologically, it is set all over the place, telling stories set during the TV show as well as during the events of the on-going comic book series. It's as much of a celebration of why these characters are worth writing about as it is a goodbye from the writers, artists, and editors at IDW.

6. FUNNY THING ABOUT VAMPIRES

What initially drew me to IDW's Angel books was how clear it was that the writers were fans of the characters. The love of *Angel* bled through each page. In being fans, they had their fingers to the pulse of what the people who loved the original television series wanted to see in these books. When asked what he hopes fans took away from his work in the Angelverse, Brian Lynch says, "I just hope the books were enjoyable for people. I hope my comics were a tenth as emotional, or funny, or horrific, or fun as the TV shows. I think I'm a better writer for having worked on the books, after hours of re-watching and studying Whedon's work. But the best thing I walked away with was a bunch of friendships with the artists I met working on the book, and the editors, and the fans. It's a very supportive network of people." Scott Tipton, who is familiar with working on tie-in material after having written many *Star Trek* comics for IDW, says, "If the stories rang true to readers and felt like part of the show's world, that's all I can ask for. And enough of them have told me that they did that I can step out of the spotlight, satisfied."

The license passed over to Dark Horse after *Angel: Yearbook* was published in May 2011. The folks over at Dark Horse are currently publishing a series called *Angel & Faith*, written by Marvel writer Christos Gage, that features Angel and renegade slayer Faith (big surprise considering the title, no?) in London. It's a new world, and a brand new series, which essentially makes *Angel: Yearbook* the very last *Angel* tale. Because *Angel* isn't just about one vampire with a soul; it's about the characters that populated the universe. It's about Gunn, Cordelia, Fred, Wesley, Illyria, Lorne, and so many more wonderful characters. It's about how Angel has come to be the champion of Los Angeles, protecting its citizens from demons that hide in plain sight. It's about the burden of living forever in a place that values life so little.

And that's the funny thing about vampires. They don't die so easily. I've read *Angel & Faith* and, frankly, I love it. It's beautifully written and drawn, but it's a completely new sort of story. The old *Angel* tales are still around, waiting for new readers to discover them. IDW's *Angel* will live on in the form of the collections still available in bookstores and in the hearts of the readers who love Whedon's characters.

Thanks to Brian Lynch and Scott Tipton for taking the time out to talk to me, and for telling years of wonderful *Angel* stories. It's been quite a ride.

IDW's final Angel *comics have been collected in the oversized hardcover,* Angel: The End, *which came out in December 2011. It includes stories by Bill Willingham, Bill Williams, Mariah Huehner, David Tischman, Jeff Mariotte, Peter David, Dan Roth, Scott Tipton, Brian Lynch, and... well, me. You should totally buy it. I'm not biased. I promise.*

4.07
Joss Whedon 101:
Sugarshock!
Jack Milson

Don't be a Viking!

In a changing world of media engagement, traditional methods of storytelling and distribution are changing. New media are changing the way we intake material. The rise of the Internet has seen the readership of print-based news fall. In fact, all print-based media have been faced with the question of how to adapt to the digital world. While many have been concerned about the effect these changes will have upon newspapers and books, we should not forget the comic book.

Just like Joss Whedon had used new media to give us *Dr. Horrible's Sing-Along Blog*, he used the comic book industry's exploration of new distribution models and marketing to give us a short, rather hyperactive three-part adventure through music and space with the Eisner Award winning *Sugarshock!*. Written by Joss Whedon and illustrated by Fabio Moon (best known for his work on the comic book *Casanova*), the first part of *Sugarshock!*, entitled *Sugarshock! Battle Royale with Cheese* launched on August 1, 2007, on *MySpace Dark Horse Presents*. As a monthly anthology *Dark Horse Presents* would feature a number of strips, and many of the more popular ones would spin out of the book and become ongoing titles. In an effort to broaden its demographic and to engage a younger audience, in 2007 the book was relaunched online. The first issue of the new *Myspace Dark Horse Presents* featured Whedon's *Sugarshock!* in an attempt to capture fans of Whedon's work, and arguably to draw people in with a relatively known name such as Whedon's. *Sugarshock!* proved so popular online that it was later also released as a print issue in 2009.

As with all Whedon's work, the most important and interesting part is the story itself. In a world of fantastic adventures, robots, intergalactic space battles, rock music, secret government agents, and—let's not forget—Vikings, comes the adventures of Dandelion Naizen, the lead singer of Sugarshock. The red-haired lead singer of the titular band is joined on her adventures by fellow band members Wade and her sister L'lihdra, and Robot Phil. These four immediately seem to be characters that we already know. These are not what could be described as typical characters; they are not clones or copies of Whedon's other characters. They are, however, typically Whedonesque: strong, punky, fresh, and, regardless of how fantastical, real.

The story begins with the band Sugarshock losing a battle of the bands competition. The adventure continues as an armored alien falls from the sky, smashing the roof of their car, interrupting two pages of superb Whedonesque conversation. The dying alien hands them a scroll inviting them to what they understand to be an intergalactic battle of the bands, and they accept without realizing that the automatic translation of the scroll may not be as accurate as it seems.

As their spaceship lands at its destination, we become aware that it is not in fact a battle of the bands but a battle for survival. Attacked by an alien warrior, they realize the truth about their adventure as well as the truth about two members of the band. As with many of Whedon's characters, there is much more to each character than what we first see. In the case of *Sugarshock!*, Wade and L'lihdra are not sisters as readers first think. Wade is actually an exiled Princess, L'lihdra her bodyguard, and the "battle of the bands" a ruse to lure them out of hiding.

As the battle intensifies and the pace of the story remains frenetic, Dandelion resorts to music to save the day with the "Saddest Song in the World." Wade's love (masquerading as the band's "Groupie"), and her reason for exile, comes back for her and reveals that he has manufactured these events to bring Wade back. After Wade's "groupie" is ultimately killed by L'lihdra in just 11 panels and the battle is over, the pace does ease up; but as they head back to Earth readers are teased with possible future adventures because the planet is missing.

As an insane ride through space, music, and love, *Sugarshock!* leaves readers disappointed that the story ends after three parts; having only just met these characters, the readers want more. Teased with questions such as whether Dandelion works for a secret government agency or she is simply a little bit mad, fans are left wanting to see more of the world of *Sugarshock!*. Robot Phil exists mainly as comic relief but it is hard to imagine further adventures without Whedon exploring ideas of personhood or the role of robots in society, themes he has toyed with in other places. The character "Sensitive Guy" could easily become a recurring antagonist, a comical one at that. Perhaps most of all readers would like to learn the reason for Dandelion's intense hatred of Vikings. Fans just want more, be it online or in traditional formats.

Some describe Whedon's *Firefly* as being too original, too off the wall; but in comparison *Sugarshock!* makes *Firefly* looks hackneyed. *Sugarshock!* might not have been as successful if it had been a television show, movie, or even a comic book released using traditional distribution methods. Not easily describable in terms of genre or tone, the book defies categorization. The direct approach through online comics allows it to reach its audience with much more ease.

The comic book industry is one based on tradition, beginning with the tradition of selling print comics on news racks and in corner shops, then changing with the dawn of the comic book shop era, and now revolutionized by direct electronic marketing. While the era of the comic book shop is not over, the industry is having to reassess the situation as publishing houses now have direct contact with their audience. The distribution of online comics is cheaper than paper copies, with no printing or delivery costs. And with more and more software programs and hardware being developed to make reading comics online easier and more accessible, maybe it is time to reconfigure past traditions, to not be Vikings of the past but instead embrace the future. While comics fans continue to love their local comic book stores, if the flourishing of online comics means that they can read more books like *Sugarshock!*, which in other modes of distribution might not be viable, then perhaps they will have a "battle royale with cheese."

Works Cited

Sugarshock! Story by Joss Whedon. Art by Fabio Moon. *MySpace Dark Horse Presents* 2007. Web.

Sugarshock! One-Shot. Story by Joss Whedon. Art by Fabio Moon. Portland: Dark Horse, 2009. Print.

4.08

Joss Whedon 101:
Buffy the Vampire Slayer Season Eight
Nick Bridwell

When it was announced years ago that Buffy's adventures would continue in comic format, fan boys and girls were set a-frenzy. The last time we saw Buffy Summers, in the show's finale, she had defeated The First, a primordial evil, while simultaneously sharing her power with potential Slayers worldwide. Joss Whedon's original goal of spreading the message of female empowerment through Buffy was then literally (in canon) and metaphorically dispersed to the masses. The show ended with triumph as well as tragedy, seeing Spike incinerated with a mystical bauble provided by Angel, only to return in full force on *Angel*, and Anya bifurcated protecting the addictively pathetic Andrew. As some characters died, the remaining heroes (Buffy, Giles, Willow, Xander, Dawn, and Faith) and their loyal fans all echoed the final line: "What are we gonna do now?"

Whedon's answer was to provide a canonical *Buffy the Vampire Slayer Season Eight* in comic book form. Joss oversaw the entire storyline and ensured that fans would be happy with the writing by employing fan favorites such as Steven S. DeKnight, Drew Goddard, Jane Espenson, and Doug Petrie as well as celebrated non-Whedonverse writers like Brian K. Vaughan. The totality of the work resulted in an overarching story that not only mirrored the dramatic tone of the original, but also allowed for a grand, epic storyline which finally realized *Buffy*'s global appeal and influence.

Season Eight saw many things come to pass, in a nutshell (**spoiler warning!**): The Scoobies now oversee over 2,800 Slayers from a Scottish castle. The massive network of Slayers faces a masked foe named Twilight, who leads a global attack on magic. Amy (former rat) and Warren (rescued by Amy and now sporting a perma-skin-suit) are among Twilight's allies. Giles and Faith—much to the chagrin of Buffy—team up in order to save lost Slayers and carry out Giles's secret mission. Dawn is a giant (due to a curse by a thricewise demon ex-boyfriend she cheated on). Buffy has a lesbian encounter with a Japanese Slayer named Satsu.

Xander begins an intimate relationship with a Slayer named Renee, who is run through with the mystical scythe by a renegade vamp who has transmogrification powers stolen from Xander's old pal/nemesis/master

Dracula. Dracula and Xander avenge her death. Dawn is a centaur (same curse). Buffy skips into the future, meets Malaka Fray, and kills future Willow, who is now back to her old Dark Willow ways. Willow, in present time, is sleeping with an odd snake lady named Saga Vusuki/Alluwyn in another dimension, unbeknownst to Kennedy. A renegade Slayer named Simone has banded together violent Slayers who think they are above the law. Dawn is a doll (curse over!). Oz has a baby. Andrew is now part of the family. Harmony is a reality TV star whose shenanigans lead the world to support vampires fully. Buffy thinks she may have feelings for Xander, but he is now in love with Dawn. Things are about to get crazy—more crazy... Buffy gains super powers and finally faces Twilight, who we find is actually... wait for it... Angel! The two are overtaken by the mystical influence of Twilight, which is actually a universe willing itself into existence. They have a lot of sex and give birth to a universe.

Buffy abandons the universe when it becomes apparent that all of her friends (and the rest of the world) will most likely die in the creation of her and Angel's evolution. Spike shows up in time to inform Buffy et al., in typical Spike truthful-yet-snarky fashion, that Twilight and the end of the world can be stopped by protecting "The Seed of Wonder," the original source of all magic. If Twilight's multi-dimensional forces are able to remove the seed, the world will crumble. Buffy's negligence makes Twilight (who is both the universe and now a freaky magic Chimera) mad, so it overtakes Angel and leads him to attack Buffy.

Willow visits Saga Vasuki/Alluywn who tells her that the seed can be destroyed, which would save the world, but all magic would be obliterated on earth. Willow chooses not to inform Buffy about this and instead tells her that she must protect the seed at all cost. Spike and Buffy find that The Master is the protector of the seed. Buffy kicks his ass. Then, Spike and Buffy take on Angel. Giles brings the scythe to the underground cave where the fight for the seed takes place. He and Xander discuss the likelihood of stopping Twilight/Angel. Giles, against Xander's wishes, rushes in to help Buffy. Angel snaps his neck in the exact same way he killed Giles' lover Jenny Calendar.

Buffy immediately, instinctively destroys the seed, which sends Willow crashing to the ground, devoid of magic and powerless. Without magic to hold up Warren's skin, he turns to a pile of ooze. Willow, broken and bruised, cries for Saga Vusuki, as their connection is severed forever, while Xander and Buffy watch the seed dissipate and as they reel from the loss of Giles.

A few months later, Buffy is in San Francisco, sleeping on Xander and Dawn's couch. Faith has inherited all of Giles's belongings, save for the iconic "Vampyr" book, which was the first thing Giles ever showed Buffy, way back in "Welcome to the Hellmouth." Slayers and witches worldwide hate Buffy. Spike warns Buffy that someone is coming for her. Faith is keeping Angel in her London flat, attempting to help him with his redemption. The season ends with Buffy facing a single vampire, just like it all started.

Season Eight was great for character development. We finally see Dawn become a real woman, figuratively wrestling with the monsters of young womanhood. Faith faces her demons and finally builds a long-term daughter/ partner relationship with Giles, who helps her realize her true value as a Slayer and a woman, only to leave her in battle to die saving Buffy. Willow finally conquers the dark magic within, only to be left completely without magic at the season's conclusion. Andrew courageously risks his own life to stop a renegade Ragna demon, proving to Buffy he is now part of the family for good. Xander finally has a potentially long-term happy relationship with Dawn.

The only characters who are left at square one are Buffy and Angel. Buffy is now the only Slayer (though not technically; all of the other Slayers have maintained their powers, but the line is dead and the remaining Slayers have abandoned the title in direct hatred of her). Angel starts again on the path of redemption; after years of doing good he has again been taken over by a higher power and murdered a loyal ally. Giles dies, which is the single greatest loss to the Whedonverse since Wesley Wyndam-Pryce was stabbed to death in *Angel*. The writers were able to go Bigger with the Bad, and sadder with the sad this season.

There are many especially moving moments in the season. When Xander's new love interest Renee is brutally slain in *Wolves at the Gate*, we see Dracula's true character. Buffy says, "I can't leave Xander alone," but Dracula shows his loyalty to Xander, yelling: "He's Not Alone." When Xander cuts off the head of the murderous vampire, we see a great character moment for him, as well as a moment that clearly establishes Dracula as the greatest secondary character in the whole season.

Later in the season, Bander/Xuffy shippers are taken for a whirlwind ride, as she finally expresses feelings for him. Then, they are taken for another ride as we find that Xander has fallen in love with Dawn. Bask in the sunshiny goodness of that interaction. Xander is no longer following the path he feared in "Hell's Bells," when he left Anya at the altar in fear of hurting her in his quest to help Buffy. Now, he sees, cycloptically, a future for himself outside of the good fight.

Giles's relationship with Faith was another heartfelt subplot that resonated with the fan base. In the duo's adventures, Faith is able to develop a relationship not completely unlike her relationship with The Mayor, but in a more positive way. Giles is still useful to her, as he seemingly no longer is to

Buffy, and Faith is in desperate need of a human connection, and moreover a father figure. We see far too little of their time together, and hopefully some of their interactions will come up in flashbacks next season. At the beginning of the season, in the *No Future for You* arc, Giles recruits Faith to hunt down a rogue Slayer in exchange for her freedom from all duties Slayer related. When their success is contingent upon their both murdering again, they decide to go out and find Slayers who can still be saved. The interaction between them is somewhat reminiscent of the time when Green Arrow and Green Lantern hit the streets to find trouble on America's streets in DC's GL/GA series. It is nice to see that while Buffy is covering the big picture, that there are still people looking out for the little man.

Giles and Faith share a bond they both need, and up until his death things are left unsaid, with no labels. He goes off to save Buffy, probably not because Faith is expendable when Buffy is in harm, but because he knows that Faith can survive, that he taught her the lessons she needs as well. In the most heart wrenching aspect of the whole situation, we find that Faith is harboring Angel, who—under Twilight's thrall—murdered Giles, in the Watcher's own home. Faith understands more than anyone else that redemption is a perennial battle, and just as Angel once saved her, she will now save him.

An epic controversy developed when the readers found that Twilight was a masked Angel. It isn't difficult to understand why loyal fans of five seasons of *Angel* were upset to see him taken over again by a higher power, tragically throwing away all of that redemption to risk innocent Slayers not for the greater good, but for a universe outside of everything he has ever fought for. It will be interesting to see how Angel develops in *Buffy Season Nine*, because Angel fans aren't only fans of Angel himself; they are lovers of the characters created around him.

Overall, *Season Eight* was a huge triumph. Fans will no doubt be sitting on pins and needles awaiting the next season, which Whedon promises will place much more focus on the core group. One can only hope that *Season Nine* has all of the great character development that has consistently marked Buffy's journey one of the most brilliant stories of all time.

Works Cited

Buffy the Vampire Slayer Season Eight. 40 issues. Story by Joss Whedon (1-5, 10-11, 16-19, 31, 36, 40), Joss Whedon and Scott Allie (37-39), Brian K. Vaughan (6-9), Drew Goddard (12-15), Jeph Loeb (20), Jane Espenson (21, 26-30), Steven S. DeKnight (22), Drew Greenberg (23), Jim Kreuger (24), Doug Petrie (25), and Brad Meltzer (32-35). Pencils by Georges Jeanty (1-4, 6-15, 21-23, 25-40), Georges Jeanty and Eric Wight (20), Paul Lee (5), Karl Moline (16-19), and Cliff Richards (24). Afterword by Joss Whedon. Portland: Dark Horse, 2007-2011. Print.

4.09
Giant Dawn and Mutant Superheroes:
Joss Whedon in Comics
Kevin Chiat

A defining feature of the early 2000s comic book industry is the influx of screenwriters, novelists, and media personalities who flocked to a once ghettoized medium. Whereas in previous decades, comics were looked upon as fit only for children and deviants, the 2000s saw comics gain greater prestige in the eyes of Hollywood kingmakers. Comics fit perfectly with the transmedia approach to storytelling favored by Hollywood, where a franchise story is told and sold throughout multiple mediums. Comics are far cheaper to produce than films or television shows and the special effects budget is limited only by the skill and imagination of the artist. The first decade of the 2000s saw comics (especially the superhero genre born in comics) become Hollywood's preferred research and development department. Comics could be used as the proof of concept for a new franchise which would spin off into more profitable films, cartoon series, and videogames. Sometimes this has worked the other way around, where media properties with a dedicated fanbase have their stories continued in comics rather than the more expensive mediums of film and television.

However, not all of Hollywood's attention towards comics comes from such a mercantile perspective. For many writers comics had been their introduction to storytelling. The kids who grew up reading Stan Lee and Jack Kirby on *Fantastic Four,* Chris Claremont and John Byrne on *Uncanny X-Men*, and the sophisticated suspense of Alan Moore's *Swamp Thing* run were now the writers and directors of television and films. Having grown up with comics, these creators saw comics as not just "kid's stuff" but a medium with infinite storytelling potential. Many writers were also attracted to the shared universes of DC and Marvel Comics, wanting to play with the heroes and characters they had grown up reading.

Screenwriters such as *Batman Begins*' David S. Goyer, *Teen Wolf*'s Jeph Loeb, and *Lost* creator Damon Lindelof have all written for comics. *Babylon 5* creator, J. Michael Straczynski wrote the commercially successfully and well received runs on *Amazing Spider-Man* and *Thor* for Marvel, the graphic novel reboot *Superman: Earth One* and creator-owned series *Rising Stars.*

Many of the most promising comics writers, working for Marvel and DC as well as independent companies, come from screenwriting backgrounds.

Joss Whedon is one of the most successful creators, both commercially and critically, to move between screenwriting and comics. Whedon came to comics already established as a pop-cult hero and brought with him a dedicated fanbase who were eager to see how the creator of *Buffy the Vampire Slayer*, *Angel*, and *Firefly* would adapt to a new medium. Whedon's major comics projects have been the future-set Slayer story *Fray*, *Astonishing X-Men*, and *Buffy the Vampire Slayer Season Eight*. He also wrote a story arc for Marvel's *Runaways* and one for the science-fiction rock band one-shot *Sugarshock!*. The popularity of Whedon's screen work has led to licensed comics based on *Buffy*, *Angel*, *Firefly/Serenity*, *Dollhouse*, and *Doctor Horrible's Sing-Along Blog*. Whedon has been involved to various degrees in these projects, either as co-writer or having oversight over the comic book versions of his creations.

There are many reasons that writers known for working in other mediums are drawn to comics. Unlike in film or television, production budgets aren't a concern. In comics, it's the same price to make a slice-of-life indie drama as it is an action-adventure blockbuster. In comics, (especially of the creator-owned variety) there's limited interference from executives trying to mould a story into a sellable brand. At the same time, the past decade has shown that Hollywood is increasingly looking at the comic book industry as a fountain of source material for multi-media adaptation. As an example, when *Kick-Ass* and *Wanted* writer Mark Millar announces a new comic, the film rights are often sold before the first issue has been released. The influx of film option money allows for the artist to spend their time working on a creator-owned project rather than having to take work-for-hire jobs to support themselves. The flip-side to this has been the rush of comic books produced or "co-written" by a Hollywood producer or film star, comics simply made as proof of concept for a future film.

Whedon's comics have touched on many of the major themes found in his work for film and television. The importance of family (both biological and chosen), class struggles, generational conflict, gender inequality, and emotional inner turmoil are all themes which are as prevalent in Whedon's comics as they are in his television shows. Along with his artistic collaborators, Whedon embraces the infinite scale in which comics stories can be told. This is especially true of his works which continue on from his television shows, as in comics the budget does not determine where the story will take place or which characters will appear. Whedon's comics work has embraced the large scale visuals favored in Widescreen comics while always holding onto the human level story at the heart of his work. Like his television and film work, Whedon's comics are about human stories told in the shadow of grand fantastical spectacle.

These themes are best expressed in Whedon's major comics works, *Fray* with artist Karl Moline, *Astonishing X-Men* with artist John Cassaday, and *Buffy the Vampire Slayer Season Eight,* for which Whedon was the lead writer and Executive Producer. On *Season Eight* Whedon was joined by lead artist Georges Jeanty as well as multiple other artists and writers such as Jane Espenson, Drew Goddard, Brian K. Vaughn, and Cliff Richards. These comics demonstrate how Whedon approaches the comics medium as a creator and explores the recurring themes found throughout all his creative endeavors.

FRAY

"Please. I work for a fish. Take a look at the world Horn-Boy. You're not going to convince me you're special by playing the ugly card." —Melaka Fray

Released by Dark Horse Comics in 2003, *Fray* was Whedon's first comic book project. Whilst there had been licensed *Buffy* and *Angel* comics, *Fray* was the first series Whedon himself wrote. *Fray* tells the story of Melaka Fray, the Slayer who picks up the Scythe hundreds of years after Buffy Summers. It's the distant future, magic has disappeared from the world, and no new Slayer has been called for centuries. Melaka, a small time thief for a local crime lord and mutant fish named Gunther is found by Urkonn, a massive red demon who becomes her de-facto Watcher. Melaka is trained by Urkonn to fight the vampire army being built by their mysterious new leader. The world Whedon and Moline create is a memorable one, filled with an appealing supporting cast. The stand-out is Loo, Mel's five year old hyperactive friend who's involved in some of the funniest moments in the comic as well as the saddest.

In his Foreword to *Fray,* Whedon explains that he knew he wanted his first comic book to be linked to *Buffy* but didn't want to be writing a *Buffy* comic at the same time he was writing the television show. A comic starring the rogue Slayer, Faith wasn't an option because it would mess with the story told on *Angel*. His solution was to set a story so far in the future that it wouldn't be beholden to what was happening in the television show and therefore wouldn't cause major continuity problems for the *Buffy* television show. In "Chosen," the series finale, Buffy is given the Scythe used by Mel in *Fray,* creating a clear canonical link between the two stories. At the same time, Buffy and Willow's gift of the Slayer power to all of the Potentials seemingly invalidates what is established in *Fray,* that Mel is the first Slayer called in centuries and magic has disappeared from the world. This discrepancy becomes a major plot point in *Season Eight* and is integral to the *Time of Your Life* arc, written by Joss Whedon, in which Buffy and Mel encounter each other. The far future setting of *Fray* automatically defines the environment as very different from early 21st century Sunnydale and allows *Fray* to develop as a separate story.

As an artist, Karl Moline fits somewhere in between photorealism and cartoony styles of penciling. His characters appear realistic for the world he's created without looking like they're been traced from photo references. In his Foreword Whedon describes Moline as having "the splashy, over-the-top immediacy of the great old comics mixed with a naturalism and subtlety of expression that is very much of the new." One of Moline's great strengths as an artist is his ability to portray character acting and development through his art. It is clear to the reader that Mel has matured throughout the story just by looking at her body language. There's a clear difference between the Mel introduced free-falling between flying cars and the Mel who ends *Fray* watching over Haddyn from above, Scythe in hand, daring the demons and vampire to take her on. Moline is as adept at large scale imagery as he is at character moments. The final battle between Mel and the vampire army is drawn on an epic scale. A highlight is the double page splash of a giant snake demon wrecking havoc above the city. The scale of the monster is highlighted by the people and vampires in the foreground looking upwards, shocked by the giant demon above them.

A particular moment in Chapter Seven demonstrates Moline and Whedon's understanding of how to manipulate a comics reader in order to create an emotional reaction (in this instance a laugh). The entire story has been leading up to a fight between Melanka and Icarus, the vampire who killed her brother. The two pages beforehand are building up to what looks to be a knock-down all out brawl. Page three consists of close-ups of Icarus and Mel, with Mel throwing down her Scythe demonstrating that she wants to face Icarus completely alone, with no help from anyone. The reader turns the page and sees a double page splash of a flying car falling out of the sky and crushing Icarus down into the dust. This is accompanied by a large yellow "WHUMP!" sound effect and a smaller red "SMOOSH!" Moline and Whedon build up the tension of the upcoming fight, only to defuse it in a completely unexpected way. The genre-defying comedy which is such an integral part of Whedon's television shows translates very well to the comics medium.

The future envisioned in *Fray* is similar to the future Whedon envisioned in *Firefly*. Whedon describes his vision of the future as "pretty much the standard issue: The rich get richer, the poor get poorer, and there are flying cars" (Foreword, *Fray*). As in *Firefly* where the universe is divided into the rich Alliance planets and poor Outer Rim worlds, in *Fray* the future Manhattan is divided between the rich and the poor. The rich live in the upper sections of the city and the poor are consigned to the lower levels. This class division helps fuel the resurgence of vampires back into the world, as they mostly prey upon the poor and aren't understood by the police. In *Firefly* the convergence of American and Chinese culture creates a merged language where the majority of swearing is spoken in Mandarin. Similarly in *Fray*, Whedon dialogue creates a future world with unique slang. Manhattan is called Haddyn, North America is known as Noram and vampires are called lurks. The world of *Fray* is recognizably the future of the Buffyverse whilst still feeling like its own clearly defined world.

Despite being an action-adventure story set in the far future, *Fray* is a comic which is dependent on personal relationships. One of the most important relationships is between Mel and her sister Erin. The story begins with Mel and Erin having a strained relationship caused by Erin being a cop and Mel being a thief. The death of their brother Harth was a major factor in fracturing their relationship. The main conflict pushes Mel and Erin back toward each other and Mel's new mission as the Slayer brings them together. Through their relationship, Whedon explores the meaning and importance of family. In *Fray* as in *Buffy,* the characters' emotional conflicts are as important as their demon-slaying conflicts.

ASTONISHING X-MEN

"Whoa, wait… Is this gonna be about tights?" —Wolverine

Launched in 2004 and running for 24 issues (plus one Giant Size special) Whedon's run with artist John Cassaday on *Astonishing X-Men* is the most significant work Whedon has done for Marvel Comics. *Astonishing X-Men* was Marvel's flagship comic for their X-Men line throughout Whedon and Cassaday's run. The *Astonishing X-Men* roster consisted of Cyclops, Emma Frost, Beast, Wolverine, Colossus, and Kitty Pryde. This line-up was treated as the A-List X-Men team and when the X-Men made major appearances in other major Marvel titles (such as the 2005 crossover *House of M*) they were represented by the *Astonishing X-Men* team. The series was Whedon's first opportunity to work with the comic book characters he had grown up reading. In an interview with *New York* magazine, Whedon describes superheroes as "one of the central myths of the twentieth century"(Interview). *Astonishing X-Men* revels in the traditions of superhero comics and the X-Men, whilst still having a Whedonesque spin. This was aided by the visual Widescreen comics storytelling of artist Cassaday.

Astonishing X-Men came at a time when Marvel was looking to steady their X-Men line of comics. The X-Men flagship book had been the Grant Morrison penned *New X-Men*. Morrison's run was a bold reinvention of the X-Men, pushing the idea of Mutants as the evolutionary successor to humanity and turning the X-Men into a public non-governmental organization which protected and lobbied for Mutant Rights. Most controversially, the X-Men replaced their brightly colored spandex outfits with utilitarian black uniforms, resembling the costumes from the *X-Men* film franchise. Morrison's run was a commercial and critical success but its radical take on the X-Men mythos also alienated many long-term X-Men readers.

As a series *Astonishing X-Men* served two masters. Not only was it following on from Morrison's *New X-Men,* but the series also had to appeal to more traditional X-Men readers who had been turned off by Morrison's non-traditional take. Whedon and Cassaday draw on many elements set up in *New X-Men*. The relationship between Cyclops (Scott Summers) and Emma Frost began in *New X-Men* and is one of the more important relationships of *Astonishing X-Men*. Whedon and Cassaday also explore the idea of the X-Men as teachers for the next generation of mutants, an idea which was focused upon in *New X-Men* as well. Professor Xavier's evil twin Cassandra Nova, the villain of the third arc *Torn*, was also introduced in Morrison's *New X-Men* run.

The biggest departure from the *New X-Men* era was visual, with the X-Men returning to variations on their classic costumes. This decision is made by Cyclops in Issue One as part of his plan to present the X-Men as a more traditional superhero team to the general public. As he says to a recalcitrant Wolverine, "We're a super hero team. And I think it's time we started acting like one." The return of the classic X-Men costumes assured returning readers that *Astonishing X-Men* would be calling back to the Chris Claremont and John Byrne glory days of the X-Men. Another departure from *New X-Men* was the heavy focus on the core *Astonishing X-Men* team. Whereas *New X-Men* had a large sprawling cast with different mutants taking centre stage for each story arc, *Astonishing X-Men* always focused on the core team of Cyclops, Wolverine, Kitty Pryde, Beast, Emma Frost, and Colossus.

Visually, *Astonishing X-Men* is a very good example of Widescreen comics storytelling. John Cassaday, best known for his work with writer Warren Ellis on the metafictional science-fiction comic *Planetary* is one of the premiere artists to work in the Widescreen style. Cassaday uses large, cinematic panels which gives *Astonishing X-Men* a unique panoramic visual style. Cassaday's art is greatly enhanced by the realistic hues added by colorist Laura Martin. In comics, the artist plays the role of both actor and director. The artist has to compose the panel and convey the emotions of the characters through his or her drawing. Cassaday is one of the best comics artists who draws in a realist style. His characters come from the Neal Adams realist style whilst also having the larger-than-life appearance of the traditional superhero. Cassaday and Whedon show a very strong understanding of the comics form and how juxtaposition can be used to artistic effect. An example is in Issue One where the images of the X-Men suiting up for their mission are juxtaposed with the press conference where Dr. Kavita Rao announces the newly developed cure for mutation.

One of the iconic images from *Astonishing X-Men* comes from pages 26-27 of Issue One. The image is a double page splash which shows the first shot of the new X-Men team in their new superhero costumes. Cassaday draws the team walking towards the Blackbird X-Jet. Cyclops is centered in the middle of team and in front of the other characters, showing his leadership position. Cassaday chooses to tilt the image's angle which gives a larger-than-life power to the X-Men. The reader's viewpoint seems to be from underneath the wing of the Blackbird and looking up towards the X-Men. The splash sets out a clear mission statement for *Astonishing X-Men*: this is a series which will focus on big Widescreen superhero action.

Astonishing X-Men is a series which tells human scale stories on a big canvas. This is in the tradition of the X-Men franchise, which has always had a soap opera side and a focus on character relationships. Whedon is one of many writers and artists who grew up reading *Uncanny X-Men*, and the comic's influence is not seen just in *Astonishing X-Men*. Whedon has acknowledged that Kitty Pryde was a major influence on his own creation Buffy Summers (Foreword, *Fray*).

Like *Buffy*, *Astonishing X-Men* collides the personal and the epic. This is best seen with the sudden transition from the *Torn* story-arc (issues 13-18) to the *Unstoppable* story-arc (issues 19-24). *Torn* is a cerebral story, all about the villainous psychic Cassandra Nova manipulating former villain Emma Frost. Nova and Frost psychologically break down the other X-Men, exposing them to their worst fears. Beast devolves further, becoming the primitive animal he fears he's becoming. Wolverine reverts to the sensitive and fearful child he was at the start of his long and complex life. Cyclops is afraid of losing control of his mutant powers. Kitty is psychically manipulated into thinking that she's trying to save her child when in fact she's releasing Cassandra Nova. The X-Men's final battle with Nova is interrupted when they are apprehended by a S.W.O.R.D (Sentient Worlds Observation Response Department) spaceship and taken to Breakworld to deal with the conflict engulfing the Ord homeworld. It is prophesied that one of the X-Men will destroy Breakworld and the Ord developed the mutant cure to stop the fulfilment of the prophecy. With this transition, Whedon and Cassaday move straight from a psychological thriller to a space opera adventure.

Astonishing X-Men delves into themes found across Joss Whedon's body of work. A common theme across *Buffy, Angel,* and *Firefly* was the idea of a found family. As in Whedon's television series, disparate characters are brought together and bond as a family unit. For the X-Men they are brought together by their shared genetic identity and the persecution of mutants. Another of Whedon's major themes found in *Astonishing X-Men* is that of doomed romance. There are many examples of doomed romances in Whedon's television series such as Buffy and Angel, Wesley and Fred, Echo and Paul Ballard, and Giles and Jenny Calendar. Whedon and Cassaday reunite Kitty and Colossus as a couple. For the first time in their history, the characters are allowed to consummate their relationship. The series ends with Kitty needing to sacrifice herself and leaving her split up from Colossus and the rest of the X-Men seemingly for good. Kitty is left stranded in space, phasing through the giant bullet shot at Earth from Breakworld. Kitty makes a huge sacrifice, ignoring her personal wants and needs for a larger heroic purpose. Unlike in Whedon's television series, the story of Kitty and Colossus continues after he leaves the X-Men. They are eventually reunited in the pages of *Uncanny X-Men* in a happy reunion that is seldom allowed to couples who have been doomed by Whedon's pen.

BUFFY THE VAMPIRE SLAYER SEASON EIGHT

"The thing about changing the world... once you do it, the world's all different." —Buffy Summers

Buffy the Vampire Slayer Season Eight is the largest comics project Whedon has been involved in. Published by Dark Horse Comics, *Season Eight* is unique in Whedon's comic book works. Unlike *Fray* which extrapolated a new franchise out of the Buffyverse or *Astonishing X-Men* which was part of Marvel's already well established X-Men franchise, *Season Eight* is a direct continuation of the *Buffy the Vampire Slayer* television series. Released between 2007 and 2010, *Season Eight* consists of forty issues (plus three character-focused one-shots). Whedon's official role on *Season Eight* was as lead writer and Executive Producer. *Season Eight* was a large commercial success for Dark Horse Comics, being the first comic produced from outside the big two publishers (Marvel and DC) to break into the Diamond Distributors' top ten bestselling comics list in years.

Season Eight picks up the Scooby Gang at an indeterminate point after the end of the television series. Buffy has gathered the Slayers into a new organization based out of a castle in Scotland. Buffy has essentially turned all of the new Slayers into a paramilitary organization aimed at fighting demonic evil. Buffy is the leader, Xander is in command of operational intelligence, Willow is in charge of magic, and Dawn has returned from college with a curse which turned her into a giant. Buffy and the Slayers have attracted the attention of an element of the US military being led by a masked man named Twilight. (Whedon came up with the name before he knew about the omnipresent vampire romance franchise.) Twilight's manipulations further alienate the Slayers from the rest of the world, convincing the general populace that the Slayers are dangerous terrorists. *Season Eight* follows this conflict, as Buffy is being drawn further into the web of Twilight's plans and the horrible truth of Twilight's identity is revealed.

Season Eight was a trendsetter for transmedia storytelling. Whilst there have been media tie-in comics for decades (including *Buffy* comics made during the run of the show) few were regarded as canonical by the franchises' fans. For the majority of *Buffy* and *Angel* fans, the canonicity of stories is based on what Whedon says is canonical (though there is a vocal minority who only accept the television series as being in canon). *Season Eight* was a trendsetter because it had the series' original creator bringing his characters to comics and continuing their story on from the end of the television series. *Season Eight* showed that there was an audience willing to follow comic-book continuations of television series especially when the original creator of the series is involved. Series such as *Jericho* and *Farscape* have also continued their story through comics, and there are plans for a continuation of the cult television series *Pushing Daises* written by creator Bryan Fuller (although only sample pages have been displayed in 2010 and 2011). *Season Eight* worked as a proof of concept that comics could serve as a viable afterlife for television shows which have finished their run.

Moving from television to comics opens up vast possibilities for creators. *Season Eight*'s lead artist Georges Jeanty isn't a Widescreen artist in the same way that Cassaday is, but his art increases the scale of what can be done in the Buffyverse. Free of the budget restrictions of network television, Whedon and his collaborators were able to do absolutely anything with the story they wanted. *Season Eight* covers a much wider scope than does the television series. Stories happen across the entire world. It costs the same to set a scene in Japan as it does to set a scene in small town America. Comics also allow for bigger action set-pieces. The series opens with Buffy jumping out of a helicopter flanked by three new Slayers and holding a ray gun. This trend towards big action scenes reaches its height in Issue Fifteen which sees Giant Dawn fight an equally giant Mech Dawn on the streets of Tokyo.

Despite the bigger scale *Season Eight* is drawn on, the emotional lives of the characters are still integral to the story. On television *Buffy* used monsters as a metaphor for emotional problems, and the logline for the series in its early years was always "High School as Hell." In *Season Eight* growing up and the emotional problems associated with it are as important as saving the world. Buffy is shown to be struggling with the responsibilities that come with her leadership role and drifts between various people, unsure about where she wants to be in her romantic life. Issue Thirteen even sees Buffy experiment with her sexuality by having a one night stand with Satsu, one of the newly called Slayers who is in love with her. Buffy's relationship with Angel ends up becoming integral to the plot of *Season Eight*, with the entire universe literally being dependant on the choices they make as a couple.

Season Eight is *Buffy* on a superheroic scale. The superhero genre has always been an influence on *Buffy*. For example, the end of Season 6 is unofficially known as the "Dark Willow Saga" after the X-Men storyline *The Dark Phoenix Saga,* which also told the story of a redheaded heroine who loses control of her powers and becomes a destructive force. The influence of superhero comics is even more evident in *Season Eight* than in the television series. The design of Twilight is reminiscent of a supervillain, with his mask and long trench coat. Multiple characters also have the ability to fly, and Jeanty takes advantage of this to bring to *Buffy* the aerial fight scenes which are common in superhero stories. A prominent theme of superhero comics of the 2000s was the political implications of superpowers and the integration of superheroes into the Military-Industrial Complex. In *Season Eight* the Slayers come into conflict with the government because they pose a threat to the establishment. There is also a major rift between the Slayers, with a group of hardliners leaving Buffy's organization to split off on their own and bully others with their powers.

The influence of superhero comics in *Season Eight* is best shown in the *Twilight* arc, written by novelist and comic book writer Brad Meltzer.

The arc sees Buffy's Slayer powers increase dramatically, to the point that she essentially has the same power set as Superman, demonstrated when Xander puts Buffy through a series of tests including catching bullets and leaping over mountains in a single bound. In a meta moment, he asks her if she can phase through objects like Kitty Pryde, earning a response of "I don't see the appeal" from Buffy. Meltzer uses the geeky characters of the cast, Xander and Andrew, to fill the arc with references to superhero comics. In his attempt to escape from Twilight, Andrew uses replicas of Iron Man's repulsor rays and Captain America's shield which were made by the similarly geeky (but evil) Warren (Meltzer). The *Twilight* arc demonstrates the influence the superhero genre has had over *Buffy* and how this influence is brought to the forefront in *Season Eight*.

The transition of *Buffy* from television to the world of comics was not always a smooth one. In his Afterword to the series, Whedon describes *Season Eight* as "our endless season." The typical season of *Buffy* was shown over roughly six months of real time; in comparison *Season Eight* took three years to complete. Many fans had difficulty with how drawn out the narrative was compared to the television series. This, as well as the controversial plot twists regarding Twilight's identity alienated many long-time *Buffy* fans. Whedon also acknowledged that embracing the greater scale made possible in comics wasn't always the best place to take *Buffy*:

"I was so excited to finally have an unlimited budget that I wanted to make the book an epic, but I realized along the way that the things I loved best were the things you loved the best: the peeps. The down-to-earth, recognizable people. And Mecha-Dawn" (Afterword, *Buffy the Vampire Slayer Season Eight*).

The lessons Whedon and Dark Horse took from *Season Eight* can be seen in how they're approaching the currently running *Season Nine* project. They have split the season into two comics, *Buffy Season Nine* (co-written with Andrew Chambliss and drawn by Jeanty) and *Angel and Faith* (written by Christos Gage and drawn by Rebekah Isaacs). This means that the story will be told over a shorter period of time. Story-wise, Buffy is now back to working on her own and based in San Francisco. *Season Nine* promises to be a more heavily character focused series than *Season Eight*.

Works Cited

Astonishing X-Men. 24 issues. Story by Joss Whedon. Pencils by John Cassaday. New York: Marvel, July 2004-March 2008. Print. Vol. 3, issues 1-24 of *X-Men*.

Buffy the Vampire Slayer Season Eight. 40 issues. Story by Joss Whedon and others. Pencils by Georges Jeanty and others. Afterword by Joss Whedon. Portland: Dark Horse, 2007-2011. Print.

Fray: Future Slayer. Story by Joss Whedon. Pencils by Karl Moline. Foreword by Joss Whedon. Portland: Dark Horse, 2003. Print.

Meltzer, Brad. *Twilight* arc, issues 32-35. Pencils by Georges Jeanty. *Buffy the Vampire Slayer Season Eight*.

Whedon, Joss. Afterword. *Buffy the Vampire Slayer Season Eight*. N. pag.

---. Foreword. *Fray*. N. pag.

---. Interview by Gavin Edwards. "Whedon, Ink." *NYmag.com* 21 May 2005. Web. 13 Nov. 2011.

---. *Time of Your Life* arc, issues 16-19. Pencils by Karl Moline. *Buffy the Vampire Slayer Season Eight*.

4.10

Joss Whedon 101:
Comic-Con Episode IV: A Fan's Hope
Hush Money: Observing Fandom through the Eyes of Joss Whedon and Michael Spurlock

Dr. Shathley Q

In an almost throwaway line from a *PopMatters* interview ("His Shogun Is Death") screenwriter and comicbook writer John Heffernan articulates Joss Whedon's gift for storytelling. "Take a guy like Joss Whedon," Heffernan begins, "he does pop culture references really well. He can drop in a few modern references from movies or songs or whatever and it absolutely works within, and reinforces the narrative." But Heffernan is aware of the darker side of Whedon's gift for this mode of storytelling as well. He continues, "But now everybody thinks they can do it. On every TV show, all the characters seem to have this breezy culture-speak voice where they can be casually discussing a homicide, meanwhile they're dropping pop culture references like it was *The Soup* (I'm looking at you, *CSI: Miami*)" (Heffernan).

So the drama behind Michael Spurlock's recent documentary on fandom, a documentary produced by Joss Whedon, is really clear. Will Spurlock articulate popular culture with the same facility Whedon does? Or will Spurlock come off second best, another cheap imitator or perhaps even victim, of an impressive style? But right out of the gate, Spurlock's documentary, *Comic-Con: A Fan's Hope*, circles around the back of expectations. Spurlock's clear, near-journalistic style of documentary filmmaking simply averts the brewing drama of creative voices vying for control. Instead, what viewers encounter is a deep and engaging drama of an altogether different kind. It is a drama that goes to the heart of popular culture and raises the shadow of a debate that has stalked critical thought throughout the twentieth century and now into the twenty-first.

This core drama that Spurlock presents begins innocuously enough with the concern for the fans of comic books and comics culture. Where do the fans fit in? This question is inextricably linked to what we understand by comics and their publication history. To take the view of *Secret Origin: The Story of DC Comics*, a 2010 documentary that probes one of the two major comics publishers, comics come in ages: first the Golden Age, then the Silver, then Bronze, and currently the Modern Age.

The Golden Age is the time of the first appearance of superheroes, circa 1938 with the creation of Superman. The Silver Age is the comics of the Boomers. It's the recasting of classic heroes like super-speedster The Flash as forensic scientist Barry Allen, or ring-slinging hero Green Lantern as test-pilot Hal Jordan. The Fantastic Four lead lives as public intellectuals and scifi explorers, like the Richard Feynmans of tomorrow. These are the comics of the new atomic age that would witness the Cold War and the Space Race. But as a result of Senate hearings on comics' perceived evil and violent influence on children, the Silver Age would also be subject to monitoring by the Comics Code Authority. The Bronze Age begins when creative teams like writer Denny O'Neil and artist Neal Adams tackle issues like drug abuse and inner city poverty in early 1970s books like the landmark *Green Lantern/Green Arrow*. This is the first brush creators have with breaking through the strictures of the Comics Code. The Modern Age begins some time after 1986/87, in the wake of adult-themed books like Alan Moore and Dave Gibbons' *Watchmen* and Frank Miller, Klaus Janson and Lynn Varley's *Batman: the Dark Knight Returns*. The crucial hallmark of the Modern Age is its books' orientation towards more adult and often darker themes (*Secret Origin*).

It is an easy enough schema, and robust enough under most conditions to seem universal. Not at all unlike Isaac Newton's conception of gravity, that would nevertheless require Einstein's General Relativity to correct some of its more subtle points. One point of correction for this schema of Ages is its superhero-centric nature. Independent books (often publishing non-superhero material) don't seem to fit easily into these Ages.

But a second correction, one addressing an underlying tension of this schema, scans as more poignant. This schema tends to express the aspirations of the major publishers (DC and Marvel, who have been around in one form or another since the 1940s) for their intellectual properties. As superhero-centric as the Ages are, they're also a statement about DC and Marvel and these companies' connection to our lives. But at this point Spurlock's opening gambit becomes ever more pressing: What of the fans? Where are the fans in all of this?

Focus too long on the Ages as a historical schema for comics and it becomes easy to lose track of the secret joy of comics that Will Eisner articulates in *Graphic Storytelling & Visual Narrative*. Will Eisner is a rare figure in popular culture, and even more so in the history of comics publication. His career spans the history of comics publication in the twentieth century. His early work is contemporaneous with the daily news strips, and he is one of the earliest creators to transition into the magazine format of the comic book. He invents the entirely new format of the graphic novel with his 1978 book *A Contract with God*. But what, in the eyes of many fans and commentators alike, elevates Eisner above the fray is his ardent evangelism of the comics medium. With books like *Comics & Sequential Art* and *Graphic Storytelling & Visual Narrative*, Eisner delves into the philosophy of comics and its ability to tell stories the equal of novels and film.

It is in *Graphic Storytelling & Visual Narrative* that Eisner is at his most seductive. Bemoaning the loss of daily news strip comics, Eisner suggests:

"There is a major structural difference between newspaper storytelling strips and comic books. In comic books, stories come to a definite conclusion, a tradition that began when the early comic books advertised that each story was complete. A book is free-standing whereas newspapers are connected to the pattern of daily life. In a daily continuity, therefore, the storyteller need only segue into the next adventure. [Milton] Caniff understood that the story had to emulate the seamless flow of life's experiences and that the human adventure doesn't have neat endings. His work shows us how to tell a story that could make itself part of the reader's daily life" (Eisner 132).

Eisner articulates a much more useful schema than the Ages: the break between daily news strips and comic books. For one, this break is reader-centric rather than superhero-centric or publisher-centered. For another, this schema does not disavow the wealth of non-superhero comics that both pre- and post-date superhero comics.

But even granted Eisner's assay of comics publication history, the age of the fan would still be some decades off. The birth of comics fandom, that is, its transformation from one segment of comics readers into the dominant force in comics culture, would come as the result of an internal industry shift around point-of-sale.

Joe Kubert, another industry giant and father to equally renowned comics artists Andy and Adam Kubert, summarizes the situation in a *Shop Talk* interview conducted by Eisner. "Well, I believe the biggest change to take place in the past two or three years is our audience," Kubert says in his 1982 *Shop Talk* interview. He continues:

"Our reader of 30 or 40 years ago was a cross section of the general population. That is, most of our material was sold at newsstands and most people had access to those newsstands or candy stores. The kind of material we were doing was of a general nature to satisfy and be of interest to that kind of audience. As you well know, our audience today is heavily fan-oriented. Not too long ago--within the last ten years--if you got a very vociferous letter from a fan and followed his suggestions, you knew that sales were going to drop; the fans were in the minority. So whether fans liked or disliked material bore very little relationship to what a general audience would accept" (Kubert 228).

Kubert alludes to the marketing shift that saw comics pulled away the newsstand-candy store model of distribution and switched to the direct marketing model.

Contemporaneous with this shift was the rise of fandom. In its nascent stages, fandom would take the form of the Comic Conventions (Comic Cons), particularly the pioneering New York City Convention. It was the advent of the New York City Convention that would provide Phil Seuling (the person most directly responsible for the direct marketing system) with the muscle required to convince the "Big Two" of DC and Marvel to make the switch to direct distribution.

Seuling's New York City Convention would eventually morph into the International Comic-Con that Spurlock would film for *A Fan's Hope*. The pure cinematic beauty of Spurlock's documentary seems radically at odds with the almost admonishing tone Kubert takes when talking about fans. Is Kubert's curmudgeonly dismissal of "vociferous fans" itself to be dismissed? Or is there a deeper connection at play between Spurlock's rendering of comics fandom in the early twenty-first century, and Kubert's disavowal of the phenomenon nearly a generation earlier?

Key to the question of fandom are questions of ownership and participation. Not ownership in any legal sense of the term, but ownership in the sense that fans have bought into the aspirational truth of the Ages. The thoroughgoing idea is that in a direct marketing distribution system, fan support becomes integral for the continued existence of the comics. Spurlock is deeply moving in articulating the truth that most fans see themselves as participant in the comics industry to a much greater degree than with other media.

Novels singularize the author, and an audience is built around a very personal, product-driven space. The simple act of not liking the most recent

James Patterson does not preclude the chance of a potential reader picking up the next Patterson thriller. Novelists are auteurs. Similarly, movies work as singular products. In contrast to this however, TV shows often center on a high concept to draw viewers in. Will the strange goings-on in Sunnydale prevent Buffy from graduating high school? Or in an unforeseen twist, will the supernatural help her social capital?

Comics arguably fall somewhere in-between auteur-driven and concept-driven. Big name creators can often attract attention to lesser-known passion projects (would *Potter's Field* have been as successful without Mark Waid's 20-plus years in the industry?). But there's something about the inherent temporality of a creative team's attachment to an iconic character that seems to promote the idea of reader participation and reader ownership. Ed Brubaker and Michael Lark have only been writing *Daredevil* for a year, the general fan mindset seems to go, but I've been reading *Daredevil* since the 1970s. And of course without those fans' ardent support, especially since the advent of the direct marketing system, sales would drop and the companies themselves would collapse.

Kubert's characterization of fans then, comes from a very different place than simple authoritarian demands for control of the medium. Kubert is a man in the midst of confronting the collapse of comics as a mass medium. After Kubert's 1982 interview comics would be read almost exclusively by fans. Comics would move out of Main Street candy stores and newsstands and into the ethereal boutiques that are comics shops.

In his own way, Spurlock confronts exactly this reality. How is it that fandom comes to be linked to a kind of garishness? Why do those who reenter the world of comics for the first time since their childhoods, come to undertake a near-anthropological expedition to learn the codes and the practices of comics fandom? And what are the mechanisms, internal to the culture of comics but external to the medium itself, that promote the marked theatricality of comics fandom that segregates it so glaringly from the fans of almost all writing and books? There's an undercurrent to Spurlock's filmmaking sufficiently strong to reject the notion of treating the fan as something of an endangered species. Instead, *A Fan's Hope* begins to interrogate the nature of fandom and the cultural dominance of the model.

But for all its astute assaying of the rise to dominance of the fan, Spurlock's documentary's true strength lies in the ease with which it allows us to imagine the ramifications of the situation. Has this debate played out before, we ask ourselves seemingly out of nowhere, unaware of Spurlock's hand in forcing this question. And simply by asking the question, it's easy to realize that the engaging questions around comics culture and its ghettoization is no different from the European question popular during the Victorian Era: Will the working classes drink wine?

The question (often prefacing debate on extending suffrage to the working majority) belies an interrogation of the nature of elitist values. As a symbol of a sophisticated palette, wine might be seen as a guarantee of the conservative (European conservatism, as in loyal to the idea of monarchical rule) nature of society. "Do the working classes drink wine?" might be a casual inquiry into how recognizable European society might be to subsequent to the working classes gaining the vote.

Or to recast the debate in terms of comics culture: Can you trust your children if they read *MAD Magazine*?

It was this question that fueled the Senate hearings which resulted in the founding of the Comics Code Authority. Sparked primarily by psychologist Frederic Wertham's *Seduction of the Innocent*, the hearings themselves investigated the cultural impact of crime- and horror-genre comics. In the wake of these hearings, the industry would choose to self-censor by establishing the Comics Code Authority and forego the rich cultural heritage of EC Comics crime and horror lines.

Comics as an industry comes with a long history of compromises—compromises that come as both internal to the industry, and external to it, in the form of industry dealings with the world at large. In the light of comments like those made by Kubert (comments frequently taken to be emblematic of the industry's broader views of fans), many have articulated the tensions between fandom and the corporate owners of the iconic intellectual properties that now populate the collective imagination. Creative teams who shape the individual stories of these properties fall somewhere in between the two extremes, either lauded by the fans for having created unique views of the characters, or demonized by them for mediocrity.

Ultimately, it is an easy war-logic to be able to master. The binaried thinking of company-equals-evil and fandom-equals-good often proves irresistible. Spurlock's *A Fan's Hope* certainly conveys this tension passionately. But does the documentary simply miss out on the subtler tension at work in the industry? Is fandom its own kind of hush money that readers of comics have bought into from the very beginning?

It is hard to watch *A Fan's Hope*, hard to know anything about the industry and the art-form that is comics, and not think of the entire situation as what *100 Bullets* creator Brian Azzarello elegantly terms "the night of the payday." Fandom more and more begins to take on the proportions of a compromise, in certain senses. Fans are openly courted by publishers, often in a way that directs creativity towards what has historically proven to be reliable. But if the "payday" is the regularizing of comic book stories, then the "night" of that payday is the extreme loyalty that seems to be demanded by fandom. It is something garish, the costume and the codes, the ghettoizing as a geek subculture; these modes arguably often preclude general readers.

Writing in the "Backmatter" to the first issue of *Fell*, series creator Warren Ellis suggests a memory of "disturbing clarity." This memory of an interview of Alan Moore conducted by the publication *Arken Sword*, tapped into the same primal relevance of the medium that was noted by Eisner and later by Kubert; the idea that comics (by virtue of their structure) appeal to a broader cross-section of the general population. Ellis recalls of the Moore interview: "…in talking about what was good about comics, what he said was that you could walk into a comics shop with pocket change and walk out with 'a real slab of culture.'" Ellis goes on to elucidate how the pricing of comics ($2.99 in 2005 when he penned this piece) require one to make a very clear cultural statement about participating in comics culture (Ellis).

The subtler tension at work in comics today then, is not one between the fans and companies that own the superheroes, but between the fans and fandom itself. There is certainly sufficient evidence in *A Fan's Hope* for the astute observer to realize that there is a genuine tension between fans and fandom. But Spurlock fails to make this subtler tension as explicit as it perhaps could be. With the groundbreaking changes made to the industry during the 1990s (changes like the founding of Image Comics that saw creators themselves slough off the yoke of corporate limitations and promote creator-owned properties directly to fans), Spurlock's documentary very much taps the more reliable meta-narrative of fans needing a place of their own. But is this defense of fandom in its current form a reclaiming of an older debate in the face of the re-popularizing potential of digital distribution? Or is this defense simply a conservative formalizing of fandom in its current state that seeks to entrench the current modes and manners of the subculture?

Ultimately this is a call each viewer would have to make for himself or herself. Spurlock's skill however, lies in the fact that his own filmmaking style is both sufficiently distinct from, and borrows crucial modes of "pop cultural referencing," to emerge from the shadow of Joss Whedon.

Works Cited

Comic-Con Episode IV: A Fan's Hope. Documentary. Writ. Joss Whedon, Morgan Spurlock, and Jeremy Chilnick. Dir. Morgan Spurlock. Mutant Enemy, 2011. Film.

Eisner, Will. *Graphic Storytelling and Visual Narrative*. 1997. New York: Norton, 2008. Print.

Ellis, Warren. "Backmatter." *Fell* 1 (Sep. 2005). Berkeley: Image, 2005. Print.

Heffernan, John. Interview by shathley Q. "His Shogun Is Death." *PopMatters.com* 17 Nov. 2011. Web.

Kubert, Joe. Interview by Will Eisner. *Will Eisner's Shop Talk*. Portland: Dark Horse, 2001. 224-59. Print.

Secret Origin: The Story of DC Comics. Documentary. Writ. and dir. Mac Carter.Nar. Ryan Reynolds. Time-Warner Home Video, 2010. DVD.

Wertham, Frederic. *Seduction of the Innocent*. 1954. Port Washington, NY: Kennikat Press, 1972.

4.11
Chronological Bibliography of Print Comics Written by Joss Whedon
Dr. Shathley Q

Immediately after the title is/are the original publication date/s of the comic/s. After the publisher's name is the date of the first collection (hardcover or paperback) containing the individual comic.

Whedon, Joss, story. Pencils by Karl Moline. *Fray: Future Slayer*. #1-8, 2001-2003. Foreword by Joss Whedon. Portland, OR: Dark Horse, 2003.

---. Pencils by Leinil Francis Yu. "First Slayer." *Tales of the Slayers*. 2001. Portland, OR: Dark Horse, 2002.

---. "Prologue." *Tales of the Slayers*.

---. Pencils by Tim Sale. "Righteous." *Tales of the Slayers*.

---. Pencils by Karl Moline. "Tales." *Tales of the Slayers*.

---. Pencils by John Cassaday. *Astonishing X-Men: Gifted*. #1-6, 2004. Vol. 3. New York: Marvel, 2004.

---. *Astonishing X-Men: Dangerous*. #7-12, 2004-2005. Vol. 3. New York: Marvel, 2005.

---. Pencils by Alex Sanchez. "Tales of the Vampires, Part 1." 2004. *Tales of the Vampires #1*. Portland, OR: Dark Horse, 2004.

---. Pencils by Cameron Stewart. "Stacy." 2004. *Tales of the Vampires #1*.

---. Pencils by Neil Adams. "Teamwork." *Giant Size X-Men #3*. New York: Marvel, 2005.

---, and Brett Matthews. Pencils by Will Conrad. *Serenity: Those Left Behind*. Vol. 1. 2006. Portland, OR: Dark Horse, 2007.

Whedon, Joss. Pencils by John Cassaday. *Astonishing X-Men: Torn*. #13-18,

2006. Vol. 3. New York: Marvel, 2007.

---. Pencils by Georges Jeanty. *Buffy the Vampire Slayer Season Eight: The Long Way Home.* #1-4, 2007. Vol. 1. Portland, OR: Dark Horse, 2007

---. Pencils by Paul Lee. *Buffy the Vampire Slayer Season Eight: The Chain.* #5, 2007. Vol. 1.

---, and Brian Lynch. Pencils by Franco Urru. *Angel: After the Fall.* #1: "Chapter 1," #1: "Director's Cut," #1: "Hundred Penny Press Edition," and #2-5, 2007-2008. Vol. 1. Seattle, WA: IDW, 2008.

---. Pencils by Nick Runge and others. *Angel: After the Fall.* #6-7, 2008. Vol. 2. Seattle, WA: IDW, 2008.

---, and Scott Tipton. Pencils by Stephen Mooney. *Angel: After the Fall.* #8. Vol. 2.

Whedon, Joss, and Brian Lynch. Pencils by Nick Runge and Stephen Mooney. *Angel: After the Fall.* #9-12, 2008. Vol. 3. Seattle, WA: IDW, 2009.

Whedon, Joss. Pencils by John Cassaday. *Astonishing X-Men: Unstoppable.* #19-24, 2006-2008. Vol. 3. New York: Marvel, 2008.

---. *Giant Size Astonishing X-Men #1: Unstoppable.* New York: Marvel, 2008.

---, and Brett Matthews. Pencils by Will Conrad. *Serenity: Better Days.* Vol. 2. Portland, OR: Dark Horse, 2008.

Whedon, Joss. Pencils by Cliff Richards. *Buffy the Vampire Slayer Season Eight: Anywhere but Here.* #10, 2008. Vol. 2. Portland, OR: Dark Horse, 2008.

---. Pencils by Georges Jeanty. *Buffy the Vampire Slayer Season Eight: A Beautiful Sunset.* #11, 2008. Vol. 3. Portland, OR: Dark Horse Comics, 2008.

---. Pencils by Karl Moline. *Buffy the Vampire Slayer Season Eight: Time of Your Life.* #16-19, 2008. Vol. 4. Portland, OR: Dark Horse Comics, 2009.

---, and Brian Lynch. Pencils by Stephen Mooney (#13-14) and Franco Urru (#15-17). *Angel: After the Fall.* #13-17, 2009. Vol. 4. Seattle, WA: IDW, 2009.

---. Pencils by Georges Jeanty. *Buffy the Vampire Slayer Season Eight: Turbulence.* #31, 2010. Vol. 7. Portland, OR: Dark Horse, 2010.

---. Pencils by Karl Moline. *Buffy the Vampire Slayer Season Eight: Willow: Goddesses and Monsters.* One-shot, 2009. Vol. 7.

---. Pencils by Georges Jeanty. *Buffy the Vampire Slayer Season Eight: Last Gleaming.* #36-40, 2010-2011. Vol. 8. Portland, OR: Dark Horse, 2011.

CHAPTER 5

DR. HORRIBLE'S SING-ALONG BLOG

5.01
Joss Whedon 101:
Dr. Horrible's Sing-Along Blog
Lynnette Porter

THERE'S NOTHING HORRIBLE ABOUT A WHEDON MUSICAL

With a name like Dr. Horrible, a character has a lot to live down to. By the end of Joss Whedon's webiseries, *Dr. Horrible's Sing-Along Blog*, not only has Dr. Horrible discovered his true nature, but audiences discover a skewed perspective on the traditional hero story that emphasizes a growing moral darkness in the real world.

During the writers' strike of 2007-2008, the Whedons—brothers Joss, Zack, and Jed—and Melissa Tancharoen decided to put on a musical. Of course, as Joss Whedon illustrated so well in *Buffy the Vampire Slayer*'s musical episode, "Once More With Feeling" (6.7), the writers used the conventions of musical theater to make some intriguing points about life and the nature of heroes. With *Dr. Horrible* they flip the hero epic on its head by introducing new lyrics for the genre's well-worn refrain.

The project not only filled the strike time for writers (and thus actors) waiting for a resolution, but it also added more fuel to the fiery transformation of the hero story into the glorification of the villain. As well, Whedon (who doubled as director) initially made the story available only online, although the Emmy award-winning series later became available on DVD and as an iTunes download. The initial web-only viewing gained a wider audience for webisodes and created an instant web classic. Since then, *Dr. Horrible*'s story has been immortalized in comics and on stage, and, fans hope, will return once more to the web with a new adventure. Although a sequel has been rumored almost since the first act went live in July 2008, Dr. Horrible hasn't yet posted a new blog.

A WORLD WHERE VILLAINS WIN

Dr. Horrible's creators collaborated with a winsome bunch of actors, including perennial Whedonverse favorite Nathan Fillion as "hero" Captain Hammer, Felicia Day as activist-with-a-heart-of gold Penny, and Neil Patrick Harris as villain wannabe, Billy/Dr. Horrible.

During the early scenes, Neil Patrick Harris's performance harkens back to the actor's early days of TV innocence as earnest, wide-eyed Dr. Doogie Howser. Dr. Horrible hardly looks like his moniker. Instead, he seems shy and socially ill at ease in his attempts to get ahead with the girl of his dreams, Penny, and his potential new boss. He creates a web blog outlining his plan to join the prestigious Evil League of Evil, run by crime lord Bad Horse.

Smirking at popular culture, Bad Horse is indeed a horse, and his henchmen come straight from the days of TV Westerns' white-hatted sheriffs and black-hatted outlaws. Dr. Horrible hardly seems capable of joining such a league—he can't get Penny to notice him, much less foil the resident good guy, hero Captain Hammer. His attempts at causing mayhem backfire spectacularly, making this junior villain a sympathetic character. Viewers probably identify more with him than with smarmy do-gooder Captain Hammer.

This hero knows how to run a photo op and score with the groupies who follow him. Hammer hits on truly virtuous Penny, who only wants to help the homeless. The hero helps her only in order to get what he wants—her "virtue"—and to show Dr. Horrible yet another way in which he has failed. Hammer performs good deeds to ensure the desired amount of citywide swooning over his latest heroic act, as shown on the nightly news.

This portrayal does what Joss Whedon has done best in series like *Buffy* and *Angel*: illustrate none too subtly the smooth self-interest of those in power, whether demons masquerading as lawyers (Wolfram & Hart) or "heroes" like Hammer running a city. The outcasts in his TV stories often become the true heroes, such as high school vampire slayer Buffy or vampire-with-a-soul Angel. In the Whedonverse, the monsters (especially vampires) sometimes can be redeemed.

In *Dr. Horrible*, the apprentice villain is the outcast, and according to countless traditional hero stories, he, of course, should be. This story's social outcast is not looking for redemption or a way to help humanity. Whedon, however, carefully sets up a story in which viewers like the "wrong" character—Dr. Horrible. Hammer does make this choice fairly easy—Fillion gloriously goes overboard in a parody of his earlier Whedon role as Captain Malcolm Reynolds in *Firefly*, a dark hero who, for all his self-interest, manages to fight the good fight. Hammer, like Reynolds, likes to take the path of least resistance and get a job done as easily as possible, but, in both series, unexpected complications arise. Whereas Captain Mal at least has the good grace not to call himself a hero, even though he often acts like one, Hammer expects his reputation to protect him, even when he acts less than heroic. Hammer looks like a hero but, just like the villain, has his own agenda, one that doesn't involve a lot of self-sacrifice.

MUCH MORE THAN A DARK HORSE

An *LA Times* blog neatly summarized the way Joss Whedon (the miniseries' writer usually singled out for praise) makes audiences fall in love with *Dr. Horrible*: "He makes bad guys into good guys and good into bad, writes a superhero epic where every three minutes the characters break out in song, and most death defying of all, he puts the whole thing on the Internet" (Web Scout).

In July 2008, *Variety.com* saw *Dr. Horrible* in terms of coin, noting that "Whedon's gambit is the most high-profile example of a movement underway among Hollywood scribes to harness the marketing and distribution power of the Internet for their own creative (and moneymaking) ends, sidestepping the major studios and networks in the process" (Littleton). Indeed, *Dr. Horrible* proved there is a market for high-quality webisodes and their product spinoffs.

Whedon fans saw *Dr. Horrible* in terms of creativity. Over three days in July 2008, one act at a time, *Dr. Horrible* was unleashed on the public. Its viral publicity backed by high-quality performance and production made it a prime viewing attraction and one of the first streaming stories to gain so much attention. Fans also voted the miniseries as "Best Internet Phenomenon" at the U.S. People's Choice Awards.

Reviewers and awards-makers saw *Dr. Horrible* in terms of critical acclaim. The miniseries won several of the newly founded Streamy Awards for online media, including Best Web Series. At the Hugo Awards for science fiction, *Dr. Horrible* won Best Dramatic Presentation, Short Form. When Dr. Horrible and Captain Hammer visually broke into the recorded broadcast of the Creative Arts Emmy Awards and interrupted the proceedings with their banter, they stole the show, but they legitimately carried away an Emmy.

No matter how audiences see *Dr. Horrible*—as money maker, innovative entertainment, or technically superior production—they want more. Although Zack and Jed Whedon told comic book fans at a 2010 signing event in Hollywood that they had begun writing a sequel, a new edition has yet to hit the net. Other media, however, tell more of the Horrible story.

A Dark Horse comic book featuring Dr. Horrible and Captain Hammer presents a prequel to the webisodic adventure. Zack and Jed Whedon's stories at Dark Horse Comics' MySpace site provide additional insights into *Dr. Horrible* characters. Issue 12, for example, introduces Captain Hammer and Dr. Horrible through "Captain Hammer: Be Like Me," (Whedon, "Captain") and Issue 23 illustrates Penny's pre-Horrible life (Whedon, "Penny").

There's even a live-stage version in Seattle, so popular that it was brought back from 2010's sold-out performance to a bigger venue in February 2011 (Irwin). At this point, *Dr. Horrible* might someday make the rumors come true and become a big Broadway musical. Whether small screen or big stage, the concepts behind *Dr. Horrible* are well worth the attention of ever-larger audiences.

HAMMERING OUT A MODERN HERO

Viewers might laugh at the way Hammer's hugely inflated ego is pinpricked and deflated in *Dr. Horrible*, except for one other plot point found in many other Whedon stories: the "villain" really is villainous, and innocents get killed. The everyday characters audiences get to know and love in the Whedonverse, such as Tara (*Buffy*) or Fred (*Angel*) or Wash (*Firefly*, *Serenity*), often die in unexpected ways. Whedon's stories have a lot of collateral damage in battles, big and small, between Good and Evil. Despite his quirky, strangely uplifting songs and nerdy charm, Dr. Horrible really is a villain. Whedon doesn't misdirect the audience by emphasizing the sincerity behind the lead character's blog entries.

Perhaps this jolt of reality is the strength of Joss Whedon's stories, best distilled in this miniseries' three acts: Evil does exist, and Good often can't—or won't—be able to overcome it. The people we consider society's Heroes may be just as flawed as Villains, and innocents can and do get in the way.

Whedon's stories make us laugh because we understand their irony, and today's audiences can be very cynical indeed. Nevertheless, Whedon's series do what all good hero stories should do: enlighten us about the nature of our world and show how we are part of the human struggle. Quite literally, in *Dr. Horrible's Sing-Along Blog*, we're all part of the chorus.

Works Cited

Dr. Horrible's Sing-Along Blog. Writ. Maurissa Tancharoen, Jed Whedon, Joss Whedon, and Zack Whedon. Dir. Joss Whedon. Mutant Enemy, 2008. DVD.

Irwin, Jay."BWW Reviews: *Dr. Horrible's Sing-Along Blog* from Balagan at ACT [A Contemporary Theatre]." *Broadwayworld.com*. 30 Jan. 2011. Web.

Littleton, Cynthia. "Screenwriters Strike Back." *Variety.com*. 18 July 2008. Web.

Powers, Marsia. "*Dr. Horrible* News – Direct from Zack & Jed." *Whedonopolis*. 3 Apr. 2010. Web.

Web Scout. "Joss Whedon's 'Dr. Horrible' is a Site-Crashing Success." *LA Times* Blog. 15 July 2008. Web.

Whedon, Zack, story. Pencils by Eric Canete. "Captain Hammer: Be Like Me." *Dr. Horrible* 12 (July 2008). Dark Horse Comics MySpace page. Web.

---. Pencils by Jim Rugg. "Penny Keep Your Head Up." *Dr. Horrible* 23 (June 2009). Dark Horse Comics MySpace page. Web.

5.02
The Night Billy Buddy Died:
Dr. Horrible's Tragicomic Inversion of Spider-Man
Kevin M. Brettauer

"Memory is a selection of images. Some elusive, others printed indelibly on the brain. The summer I killed my father, I was ten years old." —Eve Batiste, *Eve's Bayou*

"I'm going to destroy you slowly—and when you start begging for me to end it—I'm going to remind you of one thing—YOU KILLED THE WOMAN I LOVE—AND FOR THAT, YOU'RE GOING TO DIE!"
—Spider-Man, "The Night Gwen Stacey Died," *The Amazing Spider-Man* #121

Dr. Horrible: "You idiot!"
Captain Hammer: "Dr. Horrible! I should have known you were behind this!"
Dr. Horrible: "You almost killed her!"
Captain Hammer: "I remember it differently!"

Beyond their origins, finding the single most iconic moment in the lifetime of a superhero is a task even seasoned comic book scholars would find daunting. For instance, Batman has the death of Jason Todd, his defeat at the hands of Bane, his victory over Simon Hurt and many more to choose from. Superman's death and return, his *All-Star* adventure, his initial confrontation with General Zod, and his final pre-*Crisis* tale are all contenders. Captain America's recovery by the Avengers, his assassination by Crossbones and the Red Skull, his failure to prevent a Nixon-like president from committing suicide, and several others are all probable candidates for that slot.

But when it comes to Spider-Man… well, that's a whole different, much easier story.

Spider-Man has always been an Everyman: struggling to pay the bills, watching over his infirm aunt, haunted by his own past mistakes. And, like a true Everyman, he is constantly haunted by the ghosts of those whose deaths he couldn't prevent: his uncle, Benjamin Parker. Police officers George Stacy and Jean DeWolff. Former antagonists Ezekiel Sims, Jackson Brice, Anton Rodriguez, Morlun, Angelo Fortunato, and Vladimir Kravinoff. Friends and allies like Madame Web, Ned Leeds, Marla Jameson, Mattie Franklin.

None of those deaths, none of his adventures, none of his quiet moments could ever match Peter Parker's ultimate, most iconic loss: the death of his girlfriend Gwen Stacy at the hands of his arch-nemesis Norman Osborn, the original Green Goblin. Norman died shortly thereafter, of course, but has come back time and time again. Gwen, like Uncle Ben, has always been teased to return: a clone, maybe, or an alternate universe counterpart. But like Uncle Ben, Gwen Stacy has never truly returned.

Not only has the moment become significant for the character on a number of levels, but the Marvel Universe as a whole seems to have changed as a result. Writer Karl Kesel's 1998 *Fantastic Four* annual even played on this idea in a very meta way, transporting The Thing to Earth-1961, a world where the Marvel heroes aged realistically over time, with the divergent point being the night Gwen Stacy died, which was, of course, the last time anyone saw Spider-Man.

This, then, is the crux of writer/director Joss Whedon's *Dr. Horrible's Sing-Along Blog*: an examination of the tale of the Everyman hero Spider-Man through a slightly different lens, but with a tight focus on the passing of Gwen Stacy. Using Peter Parker's scientific genius as a starting point, Whedon (who has long expressed a desire to write a Spider-Man comic, having already penned Marvel's *Astonishing X-Men* and *Runaways*), gleefully and almost maniacally incorporates so much of Peter's personality and history into the villainous Billy Buddy, the erstwhile Dr. Horrible, that it's a wonder this isn't a more widely-discussed topic. Billy and Peter share the same awkward loneliness and hunger for human connection, causing Billy to seek membership in the prestigious Evil League of Evil. Of course, this mimics Spider-Man's early desire to join the Fantastic Four and the Avengers, long before becoming a member of the latter team and still being denied a full-level Avengers paycheck. Billy's roommate, Moist, is a D-level supervillain, instantly reminding Spider-Man fans of Peter's days of rooming with Harry Osborn, Norman's son and the second Green Goblin, who was very much his father's opposite. Not as smart, cunning, or confident as Norman, Harry could have easily become much more like Moist if not for the Goblin legacy.

Like Peter Parker and his costumed alter-ego, Billy and Dr. Horrible seem to have built their current lives out of some kind of grief-based origin. Peter's adventures are motivated by Ben's wisdom: "With great power, there must also come great responsibility." Peter sees what a colossal wreck his world is and does as much as he can to salvage it as a solo hero, as an Avenger and now as a member of the Future Foundation. Billy is Peter through Lewis Carroll's looking glass, for with his freeze ray and various other inventions, Billy is armed for his crusade, knowing full well that "the world is a mess and I just... need to rule it." We're never quite told what Billy's origin is, but more than enough scenarios can be surmised based on his behavior and occupation.

As a supervillain, Buddy still doesn't get the recognition he desires. Looked upon by others the way the civilian populace (especially J. Jonah Jameson) of the Marvel Universe looks down on Spider-Man, he is still driven internally to do what he knows (or at least feels) is his life's vocation. Standing opposite him, of course, is the beloved, narcissistic Captain Hammer, a sort of composite of the acclaim Norman Osborn received publicly as a scientist amalgamated with the brash arrogance of the Ultimate Universe's nationalistic, quasi-totalitarian version of Captain America. Billy is quiet, bashful, soft-spoken, self-conscious, depressed, and full of drive. He's the villain. Hammer is egotistical, self-absorbed, borderline insane, and ridiculously insensitive. And he's the *good guy*.

And then... then there's poor, ill-fated Penny. Generous to a fault, kind, loving, humble, and red-headed, she has the physical appearance of the freewheeling party girl Mary Jane Watson, but all the characteristics of Gwen that made Peter love her so. Billy's social awkwardness and, of course, his secret identity prevent him from properly wooing her, instead resulting directly in her falling into the arms of Captain Hammer. Almost a commentary on Peter's unspoken, subtextual fear of being cheated on (strongly hinted at multiple times over the decades), Billy's plans to defeat Hammer once and for all are crystallized by their romantic pairing, almost as if Whedon himself were wagging a finger at the then fairly-recent storyline that revealed, through flashback, an affair between Norman Osborn and Gwen Stacy that resulted in more personal pain for Spider-Man years after the fact.

In Act II, Hammer tells Billy "I'm gonna give Penny the night of her life, just because you want her. And I get what you want. See, Penny's giving it up hard. Cause she's with Captain Hammer." Holding up his fists, he adds, gleefully, "And these are not the hammer." Walking away for a brief instant, he wanders back into the frame to make sure Billy knows exactly what he means: "The hammer," he declares, "is my penis." Even the sociopathic Norman Osborn had far more decorum than that while violating international law during the Siege of Asgard! His "hammer"—the Goblin—in that specific instance manifested as war paint, not a male bodily organ. Twisted, distorted and still believing himself the hero, Captain Hammer, misogynistic idol of millions, is a funhouse version of Norman Osborn, the violently insane scientist and former American security guru.

The tragedy portion of *Dr. Horrible* as tragicomedy occurs late in Act III, as innocent bystander Penny is killed in a battle between the Doctor and the Captain, a piece of Billy's freeze ray embedded in her torso. Not only does this scene visually recall the classic covers of such comics as *Crisis on Infinite Earths* #7 (featuring Superman holding the corpse of Supergirl) and *Uncanny X-Men* #136 (a screaming Cyclops holding the body of his beloved Jean Grey), but it also dares to make a firm, bold, and controversial stance on the real culprit behind the death of Gwen Stacy.

Some fans maintain that Gwen died from shock sometime during her fall off the bridge, and that Spider-Man would never have been able to save her. Others, including noted Marvel writer/editor Roy Thomas, claim that it was actually Peter's attempt to save her that resulted in her untimely demise. Thomas firmly stated in the letter column of *Amazing Spider-Man* #125 that when Spider-Man shot a web line off the bridge in order to pull Gwen up "the whiplash effect she underwent when Spidey's webbing stopped her so suddenly was, in fact, what killed her. In short, it was impossible for Peter to save her" (Thomas).

Billy's terrible social anxiety, his lack of confidence, his fear of properly wooing Penny, his palpable rage at Hammer for dating her before he even had the courage to ask her out, the vengeance he sought as a result of that anger... those led directly to Penny's death. They are Dr. Horrible's equivalent to Spider-Man's fear of loss, his endless grief, his obsession with responsibility, his Herculean burden to save his uncle, his girlfriend, Ned Leeds, Jean DeWolff, and every other friend he's lost with each life he saves. No matter how many people he saves, though, Ned, Jean, George, Angelo, Marla, and especially Gwen and Uncle Ben will never, ever come back.

As a result of Gwen's death, Norman is impaled on his own glider in his next immediate battle with Spider-Man. As a result of Penny's death, Hammer goes into therapy. Wait, no, that's not right. It's arguable Hammer doesn't even *notice* Penny's death; his bruised ego and injured hand drive him to a psychiatrist's couch, something Norman Osborn always despised and knew how to manipulate.

As a result of Gwen's death, Peter—though he never mentioned it as the reason—used his scientific acumen to find other, safer ways of saving falling civilians, and there has not been a repeat of the death of Gwen Stacy to this day. His grief, of course, over his own personal failures has helped save countless lives, eventually even using his humor as a defense mechanism again. As a result of Penny's death, Dr. Horrible also fully re-dedicates himself to his cause, finally being inducted into the Evil League of Evil, living the high life of the most elite supervillains, but also developing a cold, nihilistic, emotionless worldview.

Billy Buddy, then, died with Penny, and Dr. Horrible was truly born. However, due to the nature of serialized storytelling, Peter Parker could not, like Karl Kessel once posited, fade into the night for all time after such an unbearable episode. Like Peter and many other superheroes (among them Reed Richards, Scott Summers, Wally West, Buddy Baker, Bruce Banner, and Wade Wilson), "Billy Buddy" is an alliterative name. Oddly, we never find out Penny's last name.

From a karmic perspective, though, would anyone truly be shocked if it was "Parker"?

Works Cited

"The Night Gwen Stacy Died." Writ. Gerry Conway. Pencils by Gil Kane. *The Amazing Spider-Man* 1.121 (June 1973). New York: Marvel. Print.

Crisis on Infinite Earths 1.7 (Oct. 1985). Cover art by George Pérez. New York: DC Comics. Print.

Dr. Horrible's Sing-Along Blog. Writ. Maurissa Tancharoen, Jed Whedon, Joss Shedon, and Zack Whedon. Dir. Joss Whedon. Mutant Enemy, 2008. DVD.

Eve's Bayou. Dir. and writ. Kasi Lemmons. Perf. Jurnee Smollett, Meagan Good, Samuel L. Jackson, and Lynn Whitfield. Trimark, 1997. Film.

Kesel, Karl, writ. "In the Best of Families." *Fantastic Four 1998 Annual* 1 (Dec. 1998). New York: Marvel. Print.

Thomas, Roy. Letter. *The Amazing Spider-Man* 1.125 (Oct. 1973). New York: Marvel. Print.

Uncanny X-Men 1.136 (Aug. 1980). Cover art by John Byrne, Terry Austin, and Jim Novak. New York: Marvel. Print.

5.03
"What a Crazy Random Happenstance":
Destiny and Free Will in *Dr. Horrible*

Cynthea Masson

"Hey, this is weird. I ordered one frozen yogurt and they gave me two. You don't happen to like frozen yogurt do you?" "I love it." "You're kidding! What a crazy, random happenstance." Except, of course, this apparent good fortune is clearly *not* a random happenstance. Dr. Horrible (candidate for the Evil League of Evil) would rather Penny ("the girl of [his] dreams") mistake his calculated orchestration of events with chance, luck, or destiny, to borrow a phrase from Chaucer's *The Canterbury Tales* (*General Prologue*, line 844). In this moment, Dr. Horrible's choice governs Penny's perspective: his free will determines her destiny. And his plans to control destiny move well beyond this moment—"I'll bend *the world* to our will," he envisions singing to Penny. Elsewhere, he insists, "Soon I'll control everything/My wish is your command." Here, as in *Buffy*, "it's about power" ("Lessons" 7.1). Unlike Dr. Horrible, Buffy ultimately chooses to share her power, inviting others to exercise free will—to "make a choice" ("Chosen" 7.22); her destiny as the Chosen *One* is thus changed. Gregory Stevenson claims that "the role of fate in *Buffy*'s world is ultimately tempered by free will" (71), and, moreover, "[f]ree will as moral choice continues as a theme throughout the series" (72). Similarly, J. Michael Richardson and J. Douglas Rabb argue, "Whedon is developing... a *virtue ethics* emphasizing moral character in decision making" (52). In contrast, *Dr. Horrible's Sing-Along Blog* shifts the familiar bonds among destiny, free will, and moral choice, thereby illustrating what might be called *malevolent ethics*. Whereas Buffy works *with* destiny by accepting the opportunity to change, encouraging choice, and exercising free will toward good, Dr. Horrible works *against* destiny by rejecting the opportunity to change, discouraging choice, and exercising free will toward evil.

For the purposes of this paper (the brevity of which negates extended focus on the philosophical intricacies of free will versus destiny and/ or determinism), "free will" refers to choices characters make with the intention of affecting events, whereas "destiny" refers to events (whether by fate or happenstance) that seemingly occur beyond the control or intention of the characters. Thus, free will puts Dr. Horrible at the scene of the Wonderflonium heist, but destiny determines that he and Penny cross paths at that particular point. Robert Kane in "Free Will, Determinism, and Moral Responsibility," contends, "free will arises in circumstances where the will of the free agent is deeply divided between conflicting motives. One powerful set of motives is pulling the agent in one direction, while another… is pulling the agent in an opposing direction" (43). At such points of conflicting motives, we might place Buffy's decision to sacrifice herself in "The Gift" (*Buffy* 5.22) or Angel's decision to destroy the Gem of Amara in "In the Dark" (*Angel* 1.3). Both Buffy and Angel repeatedly resolve conflicting motives by making the "moral choice" which, according to Stevenson, "is one that sacrifices self-desire for service to others" (166). "An immoral choice," argues Stevenson, "is one that is self-centered with no regard for others" (166). Throughout *Dr. Horrible*, intersections of free will and destiny generate space for conflicting motives and, thus, for the necessity of choice—a space that provides the *opportunity* for Dr. Horrible to choose the moral good, to change course along his path to evil.

As viewers of a scripted, finite, and relatively short text, we do not have the ability to regress through each stage of Dr. Horrible's character development; nonetheless, the script provides evidence of character traits that inform, if not determine, his choices. William Dwyer in "Free Will and Determinism" asserts, "If a person is to be held responsible for his choices, then those choices must proceed ultimately from his character" (226). He maintains, furthermore, "*only* if [a person's] choice is *determined by his character* can that choice be a reflection of it, and therefore deserving of blame and punishment" (Dwyer 225). What remains debatable is this: does the text—albeit a work of fiction ultimately dependent on authorial control—allow Dr. Horrible "alternative possibilities" at moments of conflicting motives; does the character, as Robert Kane might ask, "have the power or ability to do otherwise" (Dwyer 33)? For example, when Penny interrupts the heist, could Dr. Horrible have discarded the remote control and his quest to rule the world to choose Penny and her quest to "help the helpless" (as Angel might say)?

Much of Dr. Horrible's character is revealed within the first few moments of Act One. He laughs menacingly and explains, "A lot of guys ignore the laugh and that's about standards… If you're going to get into the Evil League of Evil," he insists, "you *have* to have a memorable laugh." We then learn his application to the League is "strong this year." But the emphasis on "this year" suggests he has applied and been rejected in previous years. Thus in under a minute we learn that our apparent hero not only aspires to evil but has failed in those aspirations and now believes every aspect of his character, including voice modulation, must meet with evil standards. The e-mails he receives likewise focus on what he has failed to accomplish. "2sly4you" regarding the Transmatter Ray, taunts, "Obviously it failed"; and Johnny Snow derides him for "once again" being "*afraid* to do battle with [his] nemesis." His actual nemesis, Captain Hammer ("corporate tool") "dislocated [his] shoulder— *again*—last week." These details provide a glimpse into a past built on failure and defeat—one that influences Dr. Horrible's quest for power and *potentially* determines the unethical choices he makes.

On the other hand, textual evidence supports the "alternative possibilit[y]" that Dr. Horrible has "the power or ability to do otherwise" (Kane 33). That is, he exhibits character traits that *suggest* he is indeed capable of making ethical rather than unethical choices. For one thing, he appears to set limits on the magnitude of his evil acts. In response to Johnny Snow's e-mail regarding Dooly Park, Dr. Horrible notes, "There are kids in that park." Likewise, after receiving orders from Bad Horse to "go kill someone," he tells Moist, "Killing is not elegant or creative. It's not my style." Finally, after hearing Moist's suggestion that he kill a kid in Iowa who grows up to be president, he says, "I'm not going to kill a little kid." Thus, Dr. Horrible (initially at least) sets limits on his unethical behavior—a position that *arguably allows* him to choose the moral good among conflicting motives or desires.

Penny provides the primary site at which Dr. Horrible's conflicting motives converge. Dr. Horrible wants Penny, an emblem of good; but (as he later tells her), he also wants to "do great things… be an achiever. Like Bad Horse." Penny's reaction—"The thoroughbred of sin?"—and Dr. Horrible's backpedaling response—"I meant Ghandi"—reinforce the incompatibility of his desires. According to the e-mail from DeadNotSleeping, Dr. Horrible, "always" says on his blog that he will show Penny he is "a true villain." He aspires to win Penny's affection through a victorious life of crime. Indeed, only *after* he has "stop[ped] the world" with his Freeze Ray will he "find the time to find the words" to tell her how she makes him feel. Despite the numerous times he could have spoken with her at the laundromat— "Wednesdays and Saturdays except twice last month, you skipped the weekend"—he remains, indefinitely, "just a few weeks away from a real, audible, connection." In other words, he is never going to admit his feelings *until*—thanks to his superhero weaponry—he is able to *control her* feelings:

"I'm the guy to make it real
The feelings you don't dare to feel
I'll bend the world to our will."

He'll bend the world to *his* will, given that he regularly ignores hers. Dr. Horrible's inability to admit his feelings to Penny before succeeding as a "true villain" is so fundamental to his character that it inhibits him from getting to know her when destiny presents him with the opportunity to do so.

This serendipitous moment (at which Dr. Horrible and Penny cross paths during the heist) provides an alternative possibility. Of course, by this point, Dr. Horrible knows that the League "is watching"; indeed, they have said explicitly, "The grade that you receive will be your last we swear." In other words, he will not be able to apply again. Consequently, when Penny introduces herself and extends her hand, Dr. Horrible (or *Billy* from Penny's perspective) keeps both hands on the remote control, explaining he's "texting"—"It's very important or I would stop." Thus he rejects the opportunity to accept her gesture and, moreover, to touch her. When Penny then asks, "Can you spare a minute?"—effectively giving him a second chance to choose her over his remote—Dr. Horrible momentarily looks over his shoulder at the van, blinks his eyes firmly as if weighing the options, and says, "Okay, go." Though he listens and responds to her, he also continually looks back toward the van, leaving Penny to conclude, "You're not really interested in the homeless are you?" During their brief exchange regarding the human race, Dr. Horrible blinks firmly again when he suggests that world power be put into *different* hands. But the hands to which he refers are his own, those currently on the remote control, and his quest for ultimate control hinders his ability to help the homeless rather than rule the world. Thus he rejects the moral path represented and offered by Penny.

Dr. Horrible's subsequent actions in the heist scene physically reinforce his (im)moral choice. Though he tells Penny, "I wouldn't want to turn my back on a fellow laundry person," he immediately does so, having been distracted by the arrival of the Wonderflonium. By the time he turns toward her again, she has already walked away. Nonetheless, even in *this* moment, he could choose to follow Penny. Thinking aloud, he says, "She talked to me. Why did she talk to me *now*? Maybe I should—" *Maybe he should*, but he doesn't. Instead, he starts singing, "A Man's Gotta Do"—"Don't plan the plan if you can't follow through." In the span of a single line of this song— "All that matters is taking matters into your own hands"—*Billy*, in his street clothes, lowers himself into a stairwell and emerges as *Dr. Horrible*, complete with lab coat and goggles. At this moment of transformation, the wrought-iron fence around the stairwell fills the foreground of the shot, visually imprisoning Dr. Horrible behind bars. Though the "remote control was in [his] hands," Dr. Horrible loses control of both the planned heist and the destined opportunity to choose the moral good.

Dr. Horrible's choice to reject Penny allows Captain Hammer the chance to influence Penny's perspective when *he* sings to her, "Seems destiny ends with me saving you." Ignoring his own role in this turn of events, Dr. Horrible claims he has "*inadvertently* introduced [his] arch-nemesis to the girl of [his] dreams" and then proceeds to blame his nemesis for his own rapid descent into evil. During the opening song of Act Two, Dr. Horrible looks through the window of a homeless shelter and sees Penny having dinner with Captain Hammer. At this moment he sings, "It's plain to see evil inside of me is on the rise." On the word "rise," Dr. Horrible backs away from the light of the window into the darkness of the street—a visual cue for his retreat away from the moral good. During the same song, as he watches Penny and Captain Hammer in the park, he despairs, "Penny doesn't seem to care that soon the dark in me is all that will remain." He blames his impending darkness on their actions rather than on his choices. Later, in a laundromat scene, Penny sings, "Even in the darkness every color can be found." Thus, the darkness into which Dr. Horrible has retreated could still provide alternative possibilities if he were willing to acknowledge and act upon them.

In this same laundromat scene, Dr. Horrible reaches a point of inertia amidst the conflict of free will and destiny. When Penny says, "Everything happens," Dr. Horrible replies, "Don't say *for a reason*." This is an outright denial of the possibility of destiny—if events happen *for a reason*, an external power must be controlling those events. However, when Penny concurs, "No, I'm just saying, everything happens," Dr. Horrible responds, "Not to me." This response—"not *to* me"—suggests a denial of free will in that he confirms that things happen (or not) *to* people (not that people make things happen). Thus, in this moment, Dr. Horrible has neither hope for change through destiny nor faith in his own ability to enact change freely. Accordingly, during her song, when Penny touches him, first on his leg and then on his chin as she leans forward slightly as if welcoming a kiss, Dr. Horrible neither accepts her gesture nor makes a definitive move. He keeps both hands in his sweatshirt pockets. He is, in effect, stuck—he can neither act nor react. Moments later, Captain Hammer arrives on the scene. Their subsequent encounter—during which Captain Hammer declares, "I'm gonna give Penny the night of her life. Just because you want her"—reinforces the battle of wills between the men and prompts Dr. Horrible to sing, "This appeared as a moral dilemma," but now "it's a brand new day." In the same song, he declares, "Penny will see the evil me, not a joke, not a dork, not a failure." His "moral dilemma" is resolved by his decision to act, but his choice is anything but moral.

In the final act when Dr. Horrible is about to murder Captain Hammer, he sings, "No sign of Penny—good—I would give anything not to have her see." The contrast between his earlier desire for Penny to "see the evil me" and his desire here "not to have her see" points again to his conflict. Notably, Dr. Horrible does not commit murder (despite the subsequent media spin on events). Captain Hammer takes control of the Death Ray and pulls the trigger. And Penny dies not because anyone *intended* to kill her but because she is standing in the wrong place at the wrong time. Dr. Horrible's failure to choose the moral good when—by chance, luck, or destiny—opportunities present themselves leads to the "crazy random happenstance" of Penny's death. In his final song, he claims,

"So you think justice has a voice

And we all have a choice

Well now your world is mine."

These lyrics reiterate Dr. Horrible's view that people (including him) do not have a choice *unless* they rule the world. Yet we have seen that he did have a choice. As Richardson and Rabb insist, "We always have the potential for radical conversion" (45). Dale Koontz, in *Faith and Choice in the Works of Joss Whedon*, concludes, "In the end, as Whedon reminds us again and again, it's not what we carry in our blood that makes us worthwhile. It's what we choose to do" (189). Dr. Horrible has chosen not to share his power, not to slay the dragon, not to "feel a thing."

Note: *This paper was originally presented at Reeling in the Years: 30 Years of Film, TV and Popular Culture (Southwest Texas Popular Culture and American Culture Association Conference), Albuquerque, NM, February 25-28, 2009.*

Works Cited

Angel *Collector's Set: Seasons 1-5*. Boxed Set. Twentieth Century Fox Home Entertainment, 2007. DVD.

Buffy the Vampire Slayer*: The Chosen Collection* DVD Boxed Set. Twentieth Century Fox Home Entertainment, 2006. DVD.

"Chosen." 7.22. Writ. and dir. Joss Whedon. *Buffy*.

Dr. Horrible's Sing-Along Blog. Writ. Maurissa Tancharoen, Jed Whedon, Joss Whedon, and Zack Whedon. Dir. Joss Whedon. Mutant Enemy, 2008. DVD.

Dwyer, William. "Free Will and Determinism." *The Journal of Ayn Rand Studies* 4.1 (2002): 221-30. Print.

"The Gift." 5.22. Writ. and dir. Joss Whedon. *Buffy*.

"In the Dark." 1.3. Writ. Douglas Petrie. Dir. Bruce Seth Green. *Angel*.

Kane, Robert. "Free Will: The Elusive Ideal." *Philosophical Studies* 75 (1994): 25-60. Print.

Koontz, K. Dale. *Faith and Choice in the Works of Joss Whedon*. Jefferson, NC: McFarland, 2008. Print.

"Lessons." 7.1. Writ. Joss Whedon. Dir. David Solomon. *Buffy*.

Richardson, Michael J., and J. Douglas Rabb. *The Existential Joss Whedon: Evil and Human Freedom in* Buffy the Vampire Slayer, Angel, Firefly *and* Serenity. Jefferson, NC: McFarland, 2007. Print.

Stevenson, Gregory. *Televised Morality: The Case of* Buffy the Vampire Slayer. Lanham, MD: Hamilton, 2003. Print.

CHAPTER 6

DOLLHOUSE

6.01
Joss Whedon 101:
Dollhouse
Ian Mathers

As painful as it was the time, getting canceled (and more importantly, knowing that the end was almost certainly coming) was the best thing that ever happened to *Dollhouse*, 13 February 2009 – 29 January 2010. Whereas *Firefly* was pretty clearly nipped in the bud and became a classic example of network-squandered potential, *Dollhouse* got that second season. That still only brings the total number of episodes for the show to 26, which might not seem like enough space to tell a complete story as complicated as *Dollhouse*'s; but given the pretty horrible ratings the show had to begin with and Whedon's perennial refusal to compromise on quality, once that second season began Whedon and company knew they had to move fast.

Dollhouse is the hardest to synopsize of any of Whedon's shows; normally I'd direct you to the Wikipedia entry for a brief refresher, but the description there is so filled with spoilers, and so much of the joy of watching the show live with friends (particularly once Fox switched to two episodes a week when burning off episodes the end of the second season, which is when it REALLY became must-watch TV) was having the densely packed and often surprising revelations that the show launched at us steadily blow our minds. The gist is that the Rossum Corporation has developed technology that allows them to treat human personalities like computer programs. Sit in their chair and they can back you up to disk, erase you, even outfit you with a whole new set of memories, mannerisms, and skills (in a neat wrinkle, these personalities aren't pick-and-mix; your hostage-negotiation skills, for example, might come with poor vision).

What they choose to do with this technology is like a skeevier version of Philip K. Dick's short story "Paycheck": You go to sleep one day, and then you wake up and it's five years later. You get paid a lot of money. And for those five years, your body has been an "Active," kept in a, well, doll-like state between assignments and regularly sent to perform tasks from assassination to prostitution to simple companionship. More importantly, when you're an Active, you're sent to live a life; it's technology that lets you see your wife one last time, or solve your own murder, or find out where that serial killer in a coma on the other side of the room put his latest intended victims. Not only do "you" (your personality) have utterly no idea that these things are happening; "you" (your body) really ARE whoever it's been programmed to be, with utterly sincere emotions and reactions and no inkling that you're anything other than a real, normal person—at least not to begin with. As you can imagine just from that sketch, it's a very rich setting, probably the headiest, densest science fiction premise seen on network TV in years (not that many people noticed), and as you might expect from Whedon, the show refuses to back away from any of the difficult, sometimes disturbing ramifications of the ideas that *Dollhouse* is based around. It's just that these issues and this setting are overlaid with the typical Whedon mix of snappy patter, romantic angst, and plot whiplash.

It's not that I'd want *Dollhouse* to be more serious-minded or something; the show is commendably dark and serious when it's called for (as with all of Whedon's shows, the tonal and emotional range here puts most network TV to shame), and the chances that it takes in terms of plot, theme, even character are (mostly) commendably well-done. And once the show's awareness that it didn't have long to live meshed with the accelerated airing schedule required by low ratings, *Dollhouse* hit a truly gonzo high, seemingly rushing to get out five or six years worth of serialized TV story in just a few episodes. The infamous, not-aired-in-the-US episode "Epitaph One" that ends the first season was ample notice that Whedon wasn't relying on *Lost*-like longevity to get his whole story out, and while everyone I know who's watched the show can pick out a few moments that just register as goofy (albeit usually different moments for each person), that's a small price to pay for one of the few genre shows to go down with the ship, so to speak; to stick with its thorny premise to the bitter end (literally), to take the kind of potentially apocalyptic shift that serialized TV usually just pussyfoots around with and have it lead to... well, apocalypse; to push these characters until some of them snap, and to show what happens then.

Partly because of the relatively truncated nature of the show, *Dollhouse* works to suggest a lot more than it has the time to actually show, and that's a good deal of its power. The two season-ending "Epitaph" episodes take us far enough into the future that the viewer doesn't end the series wondering what will happen, and that future is bleak enough that the viewer doesn't get to imagine the kind of rosily idealized feel-good conclusion that networks tend to gravitate towards. The overall tone of *Dollhouse* reminds me of nothing more than the bloodily fatalistic "alternate history" stories you used to see in Marvel's *What If?* series (where Spider-Man would die instead of Gwen Stacy, or Wolverine would devolve into the super-powered equivalent of a rabid dog, and so on), except that there's no clean, happy main version of this story for us to fall back on after everyone's either dead or deranged. As witty and as filled with great little character moments as it is, *Dollhouse* is ultimately a show that just doesn't fuck around. You could do a light little adventure show about stylish personality-shifting secret agents running around in different outfits every week while they fight crime or whatever, but *Dollhouse* isn't it. It's a show about some truly horrific technology and a group of people who are either trying to destroy that technology, or who have been willing to work with it, and the slowly dawning horror of, respectively, finding out that you've become the enemy, or finding out what the real ramifications of your tools are, of how much both sides have been willing to compromise or just not think about the situation, and of just what they're all up against.

Like many shows, *Dollhouse* does take some time to find its feet. The first half of the first season is never awful (although I know many would disagree with me as far as the third episode goes), but it does suggest the much more facile and boring show someone else might have made; it's a really, really weird adventure show instead of the rich stew *Dollhouse* would become.

The characters don't all seem to work at first, either. I distinctly remember hating Fran Kranz's Topher when I watched the first episode; as the nerdy young genius responsible for the Dollhouse's imprinting capabilities, he seemed so amoral and glib that you just wanted to smack him around. But much as *Fringe*'s Olivia Dunham went from appearing wooden in that show's first few episodes to being revealed as a nicely subtle portrayal of someone so driven and battered that she's not that good with people in general, Kranz and the writers soon fleshed Topher out into not just the funniest character on the show but one of the most moving (if you can watch his scenes in the "Epitaph One" and "Epitaph Two" episodes and not feel for the guy, you're made of more insensible stuff than I am). He might be the best character on the show if not for Olivia Williams's wearily badass Adelle DeWitt (who runs the Dollhouse) or Reed Diamond's slightly underused Mr. Dominic, the perpetually cranky head of security, or Enver Gjokaj's stunning, chameleonic work as Victor, one of the Actives, or about half a dozen others.

One of the big sticking points people seemed to have with *Dollhouse* was Eliza Dushku's work as series lead Echo, the driver of most of the plot of the show (which I have mostly avoided talking about here, mainly because it's more fun to follow all the switchbacks yourself; this really is a show where you almost certainly won't be able to guess where it's going). Like Anna Torv's work as the aforementioned Agent Dunham and January Jones's Betty Draper on *Mad Men*, I really think this is a case of the audience and critics mistaking an effective portrayal of a difficult or even unlikeable character for a bad one. If anything, Dushku's job is even harder than Torv's or Jones's; she has to play a succession of different personalities, a person with no personality, and a very carefully and subtly modulated kind of gestalt personality (it's saying something for *Dollhouse* that this information isn't much of a spoiler), often in quick succession. Gjokaj and Dichen Lachman as the other main Actives in the series both do very fine jobs, but Dushku is right there with them; none of the transitions or personalities ever seem faked (unless she's playing someone faking a personality), and that's crucial to the success of the show.

Befitting what might be Whedon's densest, most idea-packed show to date, I've barely even scratched the surface of what's going on in *Dollhouse*; there are major characters and plotlines I've left untouched, more thematic and even political depth than you can shake a stick at, and some truly great guest stars (keep an eye out for the episode with Patton Oswalt, "Man on the Street"; that's the one where *Dollhouse* goes from a promising idea to a great show).

As much as I love Whedon's other series, I'm ready to call this one of his best TV shows to date; shorn of the relative conventionality of his other work, it winds up going to a strange place where the in-jokes are just as important as the weighty social/political/philosophical subtext, and vice versa. Given five or six years it might have been easy to swamp this setting under with too dense a story, but at two seasons *Dollhouse* works as a series of short, sharp shocks delivered to the viewer, ones that give the end of the series an almost uncanny power. I give Fox credit for giving it the chance that they did, but thankfully *Dollhouse* was ultimately just too odd to stay on for too long.

Works Cited

Dollhouse: *Season One*. Created by Joss Whedon. Perf. Eliza Dushku, Tahmoh Penikett, Harry Lennix, Fran Kranz, and Olivia Williams. Twentieth Century Fox Home Entertainment, 2009. DVD.

"Epitaph One." 0.0. Unaired in North America. Story by Joss Whedon. Teleplay by Maurissa Tancharoen and Jed Whedon. Dir. Joss Whedon. Dollhouse: *Season One*. DVD.

"Epitaph Two: Return." 2.13. Writ. Maurissa Tancharoen, Jed Whedon, and Andrew Chambliss. Dir. David Solomon. Dollhouse: *The Complete Season 2*. Created by Joss Whedon. Perf. Eliza Dushku, Tahmoh Penikett, Harry Lennix, Fran Kranz, and Olivia Williams. Twentieth Century Fox Home Entertainment, 2010. DVD.

"Man on the Street." 1.6. Writ. Joss Whedon. Dir. David Straiton. Dollhouse: *Season One*. DVD.

6.02
Identity and Memory in *Dollhouse*

Ryan Jawetz

Cogito ergo sum. "I think, therefore I am." These are the founding words of modern Western philosophy. When Rene Descartes famously came to this conclusion more than 350 years ago, he thought it self-evident. At first glance, his argument against doubt does seem foolproof. If I can doubt my own existence, I must be able to think, and if I am thinking, then I must exist. Open and shut case. But there is a vital question that Descartes overlooked: What is the "I"? This is the motivating question behind *Dollhouse*. Coming out of the gate, *Dollhouse* appeared to be little more than a well-written retread of *Alias* or *Charlie's Angels*. But by the end of its second and final season, *Dollhouse* had delved into issues of personal identity more deeply than most metaphysics textbooks. Although subject to network interference and a sadly truncated 26-episode run, *Dollhouse* maintains a remarkably coherent conception of what it means to be a human being. Furthermore, *Dollhouse* confronts the difficult questions of moral responsibility and free will that arise from the vision of identity presented on the show.

At the outset, competing notions of identity confront the viewer. The very first scene of the aired pilot features an exchange between Caroline Farrell (soon to become the Doll called Echo) and Adelle DeWitt, the head of the Los Angeles Dollhouse. DeWitt notes that a Doll is a "blank slate," upon which other personalities can be imprinted, and eventually to which the original personality is returned. (The show assumes that mapping people's brains can yield complete "maps" of their personalities as well. For the sake of argument, I will not dispute that premise here.) Caroline notes, astutely as it turns out, that it is impossible to wipe a real slate completely clean: "You always see what was on it before" ("Ghost" 1.1). This conflict provides the framework for the show. The Dollhouse personnel, primarily Adelle DeWitt, Topher Brink, and Laurence Dominic, reject the idea that Echo could resist the imprinting process and (initially) attempt to understand her aberrant behavior as a random occurrence; they view it as a consequence of the imprecision inherent in neurological manipulation. However, over the course of two seasons, it becomes clear that Echo's behavior is not a mere statistical fluctuation.

The Dollhouse exists to provide a service that cannot be obtained in any other fashion. As DeWitt explains to a client, when a Doll is on an engagement, he or she is not playing a part; there is no pretending. A Doll imprinted to be in love or to be a trained killer will love without reservation and kill without remorse. At the same time, there is a level of subterfuge involved. Dolls are unaware that they are Dolls, but the clients obviously are not. The emotions that the Doll experiences are *real*, but the informational mismatch between the Doll and client suggests that this reality is a subjective thing. Indeed, it is a reality bounded by the limitations of the engagement; when the engagement is done, the Doll is wiped, and the person who they had been is once again nothing more than ones and zeros on a hard drive. What, then, are we to make of this constructed truth?

In the publicity leading up to the airing of *Dollhouse*, the sixth episode was repeatedly touted by many of the actors and writers as the first time that the intended nature of the program would emerge clearly. This episode, "Man on the Street" (1.6) featuring beloved alt-comedian Patton Oswalt, is the first moment that the full range of possibilities offered by the Dollhouse becomes clear. Oswalt plays Joel Miner, an Internet mogul whose wife Rebecca died without knowing of his success. Every year, he uses Echo to recreate a moment he never had with his wife: showing her the house he had secretly bought them with his first big check. For this engagement, Echo is imprinted with Rebecca's complete personality and memories. In a sense, she *is* Rebecca. Everything that made Rebecca who she was has simply been transplanted into a new body. From an objective point of view, Rebecca no longer exists— the person who was born to that identity, in body and mind, has already died. But for one day a year, there is a living person who has a subjectively identical experience to that of Rebecca ("Man on the Street" 1.6).

If we consider that person to be Rebecca, then our conventional idea of continuous identity is flawed, or at the very least outdated. When we consider ourselves as persons, we generally ascribe a sense of linearity to our identities. From any given point in time, we can trace our personal narrative all the way back to when we were born. We might say, "I'm not the same person that I used to be," but this is understood to be a figure of speech. Even if someone has undergone significant physical or mental changes, there is a linkage that extends backwards (and forwards) in time to every moment of one's life. What happens when this linkage is disrupted? For some philosophers, like John Locke, identity is tied directly to memory. Moments that we cannot remember are, for us, gaps in our existence. This theory does not capture how we regard ourselves, though. In both the world of *Dollhouse* and the real world, there are aspects of personality that go beyond memory. It is true that our identities our shaped by memory, but what Locke did not know is that—contrary to his argument that a person at birth is a *tabula rasa*—we are all subject to our genetic heritage. Our DNA and the environmental factors that interact with it shape us in ways that Locke could scarcely have imagined. Ironically, the Dollhouse exists in a time when the importance of genetics *is* known, and even then, its minders fail to realize the biological advantage that Caroline possesses—her genetic resistance to mind-wipes. It is this mutation that allows Echo to be born.

If we reject the notion of a blank slate, as *Dollhouse* itself seems to, another possibility is that identity is more akin to a series of overlapping links than a single uninterrupted narrative. This is the basic idea put forward by the contemporary British philosopher Derek Parfit. We are not identical to the person we were in the past, nor to the person we will become in the future. However, there is psychological overlap between our identities at adjacent moments. The overlap is what constitutes our survival from one point in time to another. This is a more plausible account of Rebecca Miner's existence. It allows us a way to reconcile the objective (i.e., God's-eye) fact of Rebecca's physical demise with the subjective reality Echo experiences of her mental existence. Now, allow me to pause briefly to examine the Dollhouse's view of the mind, for reasons that will become clear momentarily.

For Topher Brink and his ilk, the mind is best understood as computer software that can only be run by the hardware of the brain. Minds cannot exist independently of bodies (whether human beings or hard drives), but neither is the mind tied to any particular physical unit. To understand how this functionalist view of the mind relates to the theory of psychological survival, we must distinguish between identity of types and identity of tokens. Two red objects are type-identical because they share the quality of redness, but not token-identical because they are numerically distinct objects. (An object can only be token-identical with itself.) In the real world, an individual is the only possible token of his or her person-type, so the very idea of a person-type is basically meaningless. However, in the world of *Dollhouse*, an unlimited number of person-tokens can be created based on someone's digital blueprint.

Before we fall too deeply down the rabbit hole of abstract metaphysics, let us return to the example of Rebecca Miner. Rebecca, from the moment her brain scan was placed on a hard drive (whenever that moment may have been, as it is not shown), is not just a token, but a type. When Echo is imprinted with Rebecca, she becomes a token of that person-type. Obviously, the body of Echo/Caroline is not type-identical to Rebecca's (bodily type-identity would only theoretically be possible through cloning), but that hardly matters—psychological continuity is a product of our mental states, whether they result from synapses firing or hard drives spinning. Thus, we can safely conclude that the Dollhouse makes personal type-identity possible.

The most immediate consequence of this revelation is hinted at in the episode "Haunted," in which a woman arranges to be temporarily imprinted into a new body after her death. Boyd Langton tells DeWitt that they have effectively brought immortality within reach for those rich enough to afford it. DeWitt dismisses his concerns, saying, "I'm not planning on presiding over the end of Western civilization" ("Haunted" 1.10). These words take on an ironic ring when we find out, in the first season finale "Epitaph One," that presiding over the end of Western civilization is in fact precisely what DeWitt has (inadvertently) done. A flashback reveals that DeWitt's superiors decide to offer "full-body upgrades," allowing clients to jump from body to body for eternity. The limitations of human physiology have been rendered obsolete, for as long as a back-up copy of a personality exists, the potential to imprint it into a new body will exist as well. Furthermore, both "Epitaph One" (1.13, not aired in the US and Canada) and the series finale "Epitaph Two" (2.13) include times when a personality has been imprinted into multiple bodies simultaneously. In these cases, the psychological continuity splits into branches, one branch for each token of the person-type. This model offers a way to understand how identity conventionally functions within *Dollhouse*. Yet as I noted previously, one of the most interesting aspects of the show is that it suggests other possibilities as well, as embodied primarily by the character of Echo. Even before Echo suffered a forced composite event at the hands of Alpha, she had been demonstrating a level of self-awareness far beyond that of the other Dolls. For example, in "A Spy in the House of Love," Echo volunteers herself to Topher to be put in the chair to help him find the titular spy (1.9). Her resistance to the wipes manifests itself throughout the first season as abrupt, momentary flashes of buried memories from other engagements, as well as glimpses of the life of Caroline. After Alpha uploads dozens of imprints into Echo's brain simultaneously, she gains the ability to toggle between personalities at will. Even as she can access the various people inside her head, Echo herself remains a transcendent being. In effect, Echo has a two-tiered identity: there are the first-order imprinted personalities, and there is the second-order dominant personality that controls and accesses the imprints. In "Omega," after her composite event, Echo describes herself as "nobody," because she believes herself to be nothing more than an empty vessel for the imprints she carries (1.12). However, by the end of *Dollhouse*, she has come to terms with her unique identity. This transition is set up by the second season premiere, in which Echo tells Ballard, "I'm all of them, but none of them is me" ("Vows" 2.1).

Thus, we return to the original question: who is this mysterious "me"? Echo is clearly more than the sum of her constituent imprints. She gradually reveals her "true" persona to people she trusts, which eventually includes the entire Los Angeles Dollhouse. She has a clearly defined personality that is distinct from the nearly 40 others in her brain. It is not clear where this personality came from, or how Echo has managed to assemble it. We might be tempted to do what Echo accuses Ballard of doing—to dismiss the possibility that Echo is a real person, rather than simply a mishmash of programmed character traits. However, if we do that, we may very well be forced to doubt the legitimacy of our own personalities. For that is the ultimate genius of *Dollhouse*: it forces us to confront the possibility that we are all Dolls. This is not to say that the show suggests that anyone could be a literal Doll. (That would be a facile concern indeed.) Rather, *Dollhouse* demonstrates that the situation of a Doll is not categorically different from our own. We are all subject to the programming imposed by our genetics and culture. Our identities shift from one moment to the next, depending on our circumstances.

Throughout all this, we are challenged to create and maintain a strong sense of self. As Echo did, we try to assemble ourselves into a whole person, while still inhabiting different personalities as the situation warrants. We acquire certain traits, and discard others. Amidst the chaos and fluidity of our lives, we strive to achieve personal constancy. And if we are lucky, we may someday be able to use truthfully the words that Whiskey says in "Omega" when she finds out that she is a Doll. Noticing that she found her computer file but did not open it, Topher asks her, "Aren't you curious to see who you really are?" Her reply: "I know who I am."

Works Cited

Dollhouse: Season One. Twentieth Century Fox Home Entertainment, 2009. DVD.

Dollhouse: The Complete Season 2. Twentieth Century Fox Home Entertainment, 2010. DVD.

"Epitaph One." 1.13. Story by Joss Whedon. Teleplay by Maurissa Tancharoen and Jed Whedon. *Dollhouse*.

"Epitaph Two: Return." 2.13. Writ. Maurissa Tancharoen, Jed Shedon, and Andrew Chambliss. Dir. Dwight Little. *Dollhouse*.

"Ghost." 1.1. Writ. and dir. Joss Whedon. *Dollhouse*

"Man on the Street." 1.6. Writ. Joss Whedon. Dir. David Straiton. *Dollhouse*.

"Omega." 1.12. Writ. and dir. Tim Minear. *Dollhouse*.

Parfit, Derek. "Personal Identity." *The Philosophical Review* 80 (Jan. 1971): 3-27. Print.

"Spy in the House of Love." 1.9. Writ. Andrew Chambliss. Dir. David Solomon. *Dollhouse*.

"Vows." 2.1. Writ. and dir. Joss Whedon. *Dollhouse*.

6.03

The Dystopian Future in Joss Whedon's Work

Erin Casey

The future is bleak.

That's what Joss Whedon thinks, anyway. Whenever his works show the future, and several of them do (namely *Dollhouse*, *Fray*, *Firefly/Serenity*, and *Angel*), it is always dystopian. Dystopian futures are not by any means an uncommon theme in science fiction, but usually the futures shown in fiction fall into two categories: post-apocalyptic wastelands and paradises. Joss Whedon often goes for the middle of the road, which is the more probable future. In the cases of *Fray* and *Firefly/Serenity*, overall human carelessness has led humanity to the future they now inhabit, and in *Dollhouse* and *Angel*, corrupt corporations have worked that change.

The future is something everyone thinks about. Joss Whedon just asks viewers and readers to think about it on a bigger scale than most people do. If people keep polluting the planet, we will have no choice but to leave Earth, as people have in the 'verse of *Firefly* and *Serenity*. If we let corporations do our thinking, humanity could be made something unrecognizable and fearsome, as in *Dollhouse*. Whedon aims to make people think, rather than just absorb a show numbly as an escape or entertainment. Of all the themes Joss Whedon presents in his work, and there are many, the contemplation of a future worse than the present is perhaps the most important for our race, and the scariest. Each of Joss Whedon's works portraying the future shows the future in a different way, but each shows us something we probably don't want to see.

The TV series *Dollhouse* (2009-2010) portrays perhaps the most desperate future. A morally bankrupt corporation, Rossum, has created the technology to wipe completely a person's memories and personality and then "imprint" him or her with new memories and traits. Rossum then transmits this technology by cell phone calls and other signals to wipe and then imprint people over the whole world. By late in the second season only a few people have survived as themselves. The rest have either been "imprinted" with another personality or they are blank or they have become violent, mindless zombie-like creatures called "butchers." The whole world is in ruin. The few people left as themselves have to fight against Rossum and the butchers to keep their own personalities. All technology is dangerous as almost any system can send out the mind-changing, mind-controlling signal. Since the signal was meant to go worldwide, it is wireless, and thus anyone can harness it and transfer his or her own consciousness to another body at any time. Nothing and no one is safe.

Rossum went from a company that was on shaky moral ground to a force capable of destroying humanity. One corporation was all it took to bring down mankind. I think Joss Whedon sees this potential in our world. Why else would the symbol at the end of the opening credits (the five pod beds in a circle) resemble the logo of a company everyone in this country knows?

The comic book *Fray* (2001-2003) doesn't show any signs of a corporate takeover, but the world is definitely in bad shape. Pollution has damaged the world and its people. The first page of the comic shows a red sky and a fizzling, darkened sun. Readers are very quickly introduced to the new human race: a mixture of people who bear the human form we are used to, and people called "radies," who, according to Fray, have "been mutated by the sun's radiation—either by direct exposure or their parents'—that you more or less get used to living in a side show." Some people have so many mutations that they do not bear any resemblance to what we would call human. Everything has gone downhill, from the environment to the economy. The government does not seem to be taking care of anyone who has been affected by the radiation, and many of them live in slums. Some of the technology has improved, but it doesn't seem to be doing anybody much good.

Firefly (2002) and *Serenity* (2005) are set 500 years into the future, further than *Dollhouse* and possibly *Fray* (since *Fray* is set on earth while *Firefly* speaks of "Earth That Was"). Captain Malcolm Reynolds and the crew of his spaceship live in another dystopian—and for us here and now, not unlikely—future. The Earth has been destroyed by human negligence (this is never stated explicitly in either *Firefly* or *Serenity*, but Whedon writes it in an afterword for the first compilation of *Serenity* comics) and people have had to spread to the skies. Planets were terraformed and settlers were sent to them, but not all of the new inhabitants survived, and for many, the going was very rough. Many of the settled planets devolved into what we would view as very primitive societies. On top of that, the government, which forced its "meddling" on the planets that it did not bother to take care of, changed some of the people of the remote planet Miranda into a race of horrible beings called Reavers that plague space and the outer, lesser-cared-for planets, killing people in nightmarish ways.

There are also hints of corporate interference from a company called Blue Sun. Because *Firefly* was cut short, this avenue was never fully explored.

However, throughout the show, there are hints that Blue Sun either had control of the Alliance (the government), or was controlling things in spite of the government. River, a character who was tortured in a government run lab, shows her fear and hatred of Blue Sun in occasional behaviors such as slashing a Jayne's chest when he is wearing a Blue Sun T-shirt, removing labels from Blue Sun cans of food, and ominously chanting "two by two, hands of blue." The setting for *Firefly* and *Serenity* is sometimes desperate and scary. Its dystopia grew from several sources: the citizens of Earth before its demise, the current government, and most likely, the large corporation, Blue Sun.

The dark future of *Angel* (1999-2004) and *Angel: After the Fall* (2007-2009) is caused by an interesting combination of demonic influences and corporate ones. In fact, the demons are running the law firm—Wolfram and Hart—that turns Los Angeles into a hell dimension. A coincidence? Probably not. Lawyers have never been spared when it comes to name-calling, and "demon" isn't too far-fetched in some people's minds.

The central character, Angel, goes through a change that brings him closer to a personal dystopia or darkness. By joining with Wolfram and Hart, even though his original intentions were honorable, he gets distracted from his purpose and becomes something that he once despised. His choices lead to Los Angeles' destruction and cost him the respect of some of the people he held dearest. Here, the "warning" Whedon is giving is centered on an individual character, Angel, but it implies a broader story. Losing oneself to the corporate world and cutting throats (in Angel's case sometimes literally) to get ahead is never worth the price that has to be paid, either by individuals or by entire societies.

Between human heedlessness, evil corporations, and yes, the occasional demon, Joss Whedon shows viewers and readers that the future he envisions is not a pretty place. He says he is doing nothing more than telling cool stories, but Joss Whedon is too sneaky to admit what he is really doing: getting us to use our brains. His works always spark discussion and stay with readers or viewers long after they are over. In his own way, Whedon is trying to warn us against the path we are on. Through fiction, he is beseeching us to change our ways so the future can turn out better—or at least not worse—than today.

6.04
Buffy and *Dollhouse:*
Visions of Female Empowerment and Disempowerment
Angela Zhang

On the one hand, she can both throw a punch and take one. She rides motorcycles and dances in skimpy outfits. She can get married and pull off elaborate heists of priceless art pieces. She solves mysteries and delivers babies. On the other hand, she wears a completely blank expression and speaks only in canned phrases; she hardly knows her own name. I'm talking, of course, about Echo, the heroine of the recent TV show *Dollhouse*, which ran for a tragically short two seasons. As exciting as her adventures may have been and as much storytelling promise the show might have had, *Dollhouse* was not without its fair share of critics. Joss Whedon, the creator of *Dollhouse*, is one of TV's most famously feminist writers, responsible for the creation of Buffy, a powerful young woman who battled evils (both metaphorical and literal) for seven seasons. In contrast, there is Echo, whom some have called the "anti-Buffy"—while Buffy is confident, witty, and empowered, Echo is frequently helpless, confused, and ultimately disempowered.

Many viewers have expressed frustration that the supposedly feminist Joss Whedon would create a story about a glorified, high-tech form of prostitution. However, I argue here that in his feminist repertoire, *Dollhouse* gives us just as much fodder for thinking about gender, feminism, and power as *Buffy the Vampire Slayer*, which drew its appeal by resisting the very forms of systemic oppression, both male and female disempowerment, that *Dollhouse* sought to make explicit.

First, let's consider Buffy and Echo, the heroines of our stories. Buffy, as we know, was all about "female empowerment." Joss's entire premise for the show is roughly explained as, "Blonde girl goes into alley, meets a monster, and destroys it." He went to great lengths to avoid making Buffy the perpetual "final girl," who usually only beats the monster out of a combination of luck and virginal purity (horror movies are notorious for killing off women who have sex). From the moment we meet her, she is imbued with supernatural strength, and already possesses some expertise in slaying vampires and demons. Her status as an empowered individual is very rarely called into question (with the possible exceptions of episodes such as "Helpless" 3.12). Yet the true story of how she, and all other Slayers, came to be empowered is particularly disturbing.

We discover in the seventh season that the Slayer line, a perfect example of structural and systemic female oppression, was created as an act of spiritual, psychological, and demonic rape by the Shadow Men. Only young women were targeted to become Slayers, presumably because they are easier to control (until Buffy and Faith prove the Watcher's Council wrong, anyway). They are also slated to disproportionately bear the cost of fighting evil ("You're waging a war. She's fighting it," Giles admonishes Travers in "Helpless") as most Slayers are killed in the line of duty before their 18th birthday. Buffy, it is implied, is the latest in a line of literally thousands of Slayers, and in return for preventing apocalypses, the best she can expect is a dramatically shortened life expectancy. Yet this disturbing history is ultimately overshadowed by the message of female empowerment that Whedon chooses to portray—the empowerment of *all* potential Slayers (by a Goddess figure, no less), and more importantly, the choice of whether or not to fight. An inspiring message, to say the least.

Dollhouse, on the other hand, is not about "girl power," though the images of a scantily clad Echo beating up the bad guys would have you believe otherwise. Echo, when we first meet her, is fundamentally disempowered. Robbed of her memories, identity, even her name, bound by an involuntary servitude, the Doll Echo is only able to do what she is programmed to do. As Echo matures into a more complete, wholesome being, with her own true identity and memories, it is obvious that Echo is not fighting for female triumph. Rather, she is fighting for basic human dignity, as she strives for the right to define her own role and identity, a right that is consistently denied in the memory wiping process. In the early episodes of Season 1, we watch as Echo struggles to retain just a few memories and words ("Caroline," she whispers to herself in her Doll state at the end of the unaired pilot, ["Echo"]) to remind her of her true identity.

At the end of Season 1, she does become a "superwoman" like Buffy, imbued with a "composite personality" incorporating the skills of at least 40 people. Yet the scene in which she receives these powers is strangely reminiscent of the Shadow Men creating the Slayer Line—Alpha, with the air of a mad scientist, forcibly inserts those personalities into a helpless and frightened Echo through wires attached to her head. Even as Echo receives these superpowers, it is clear that this, too, is morally problematic. As we see later, Echo pays dearly for having received these powers; in "A Love Supreme" (2.8), she writhes in physical pain from the side effects of her composite personality, and eventually she is sent to the Attic for being "broken." Echo's empowerment, then, is similar to the Slayers' in *Buffy the Vampire Slayer*, which also was predicated in female oppression; however, in *Dollhouse* the origins of the heroine's empowerment in oppression are delineated more clearly.

Buffy the Vampire Slayer and *Dollhouse* also differ importantly in their treatment of interpersonal relationships. *Buffy*, on the one hand, largely assumes equal relationships between its characters; idealized relationships, as supported by feminism, are generally the norm. Despite the fact that many of the relationships might entail inequity (Giles and Buffy's Watcher/Slayer relationship, for example), typically the characters in these relationships treat each other as equals with plenty of mutual respect and trust. When the expected equity of relationships is violated, it is highlighted as extremely problematic, and genuinely unacceptable. Consider Willow and Tara—though Willow quickly surpassed Tara in witchcraft, they were generally on equal terms until Willow began abusing magic and eventually erased part of Tara's memories. "I know you used that spell on me," Tara says angrily upon discovering Willow's actions. "Violate my mind like that?... You don't get to decide what's better for us, Will. We're in a relationship. We're supposed to decide together... You're fixing things to your liking now. Including me" ("Tabula Rasa" 6.8). Tara eventually ends their relationships because of this power imbalance. Similarly, Buffy is furious when she discovers that Giles violated her trust in the episode "Helpless" by temporarily removing her Slayer powers without her knowledge.

IN *DOLLHOUSE*, UNEQUAL POWER RELATIONSHIPS ARE THE NORM

In *Dollhouse*, however, unequal power relationships are the norm—Adele DeWitt and her subordinates, Topher and the dolls, handlers and their charges, the Rossum executives and the Dollhouse executives, the clients and their Actives, to name just a few. Abuses of power are also incredibly common. Adele, for instance, assuages her loneliness by turning a Doll into her lover; Topher programs himself a friend; the paternal Boyd betrays Echo's trust when he is revealed to be the head of Rossum; Paul Ballard knowingly has sex with an Active, his submissive neighbor Mellie. Sierra's handler Hearn characterizes the state of relationships best when he is discovered to have raped her while she is in her Doll state and unable to resist: "We're in a business of using people!... You don't get how it actually works down there. You put a bunch of stone foxes with no willpower and no memory running around naked? Did you think this wouldn't ever happen?" ("Man on the Street" 1.6).

But of course, these abuses of power happen all the time in the real world, even outside the fantasy institution of the Dollhouse. The abusive relationships in *Dollhouse* merely replicate existing, real-life relationships (between parents and children, employers and employees, romantic partners, producers and consumers, rapists and victims, doctors and patients). In fact, genuinely equitable relationships like the ones envisioned in *Buffy* are the exception (think Echo, Sierra, and Priya, or Caroline and Bennett Halverson). This doesn't, however, make *Dollhouse* any less feminist—the recognition and challenging of traditional power relationships is fertile ground for future feminist analysis.

Perhaps the most striking difference between *Buffy* and *Dollhouse* is the role of institutions. The Scooby Gang, during their seven seasons, typically fight against fictional patriarchies, of which they are not a part. Whether the enemy is the Order of Aurelius, Glory and her minions, or the dubiously ethical Watchers' Council, fighting against them is generally uncomplicated and free of moral conflicts, since the Scooby Gang is not a part of these institutions. Even the institutions that mimic real world institutions, such as the Initiative and the Mayor's local government, are framed as "supernatural," and separate from the Scooby Gang's comfort zone of "normal life." Furthermore, the "real world" institutions that are portrayed in *Buffy* are typically benign and unproblematic. In fact, Buffy fights very hard to defend "human" laws and "human" forms of justice when Dark Willow tries to take the life of Tara's killer.

Dollhouse, however, is more concerned with real-life institutions and their complicities in disempowerment. There is no clear-cut divide between "normal" institutions and "supernatural" institutions from which our characters can divorce themselves. The reason that the Rossum Corporation, though fictional, is so frightening is that its powers draw from existing institutions and power structures, making it more plausible to have such an institution in real life. Part of its influence stems from the medical industry and academia, but it clearly has hopes for political power as well (installing Senator Daniel Perrin in Congress, for instance). No viewers can safely say they've distanced themselves from these institutions; ultimately, we are all complicit in the forms of disempowerment that participating in this power structure creates. Buffy and her friends usually fight a single "Big Bad" who epitomize everything that is wrong. Echo's enemy, however, more closely resembles the patriarchy/kyriarchy that feminists seek to resist; she fights against a system and a set of power structures that create inequality. The case of Sierra/Priya, for example, is heart wrenchingly told in the episode "Belonging" (2.4).

While one could simply dismiss her backstory as a case of a man abusing a woman, the show demonstrates, more importantly, that "real-life" institutions permit it to happen. Behind Nolan Kinnard's power is also the support of the medical institution and an incredibly rich and powerful corporation, not to mention the inequities inherent in Nolan's status as a wealthy, educated, American psychiatrist/art patron and Priya's status as a poor, struggling artist and undocumented worker from Australia hawking her goods in California. *Dollhouse*, then, is more critical of the idealized form of resistance portrayed in *Buffy*, where a small group of civilian insurgents fight against evil: Echo and Bennett Halverson working together lead to disastrous results, while the efforts of the team at the end of "The Hollow Men" (2.12) (Echo, Victor/Anthony, Priya/Sierra, Adele, Topher, and Ballard) are ultimately futile. In resisting this kind of patriarchy/kyriarchy, we must recognize our own complicities in these institutions—much like Paul Ballard does at the end of "Omega" (1.12), eventually joining the Dollhouse as an employee in order to hurt it (his efforts are not dissimilar to Angel's rise to power in Wolfram & Hart, the very corporation he sought to destroy).

The kind of disempowerment that *Dollhouse* articulates, ultimately, is the inability to create one's own identity and make one's own choices. This extends beyond just the most obvious one in the show (the Dollhouse itself). It also examines how patriarchal families are problematic, like Boyd's dubious ethics even though he is the "father"—"You guys are my family!" he exclaims when his betrayal is revealed. Many romantic relationships are suspect too—Paul Ballard's obsession with "saving" Caroline, his sleeping beauty, is also cast in a negative light because it, too, robs Echo of her capacity to define herself, even if Paul's intentions are nothing but benevolent. An unnamed "Angelino" in "Man on the Street" says it best: "You think it's not happening? You think they're *not* controlling you? Don't worry about it. Just sit back and wait for them to tell you what to buy" (1.6). Though he is speaking about corporations (another institution that Whedon overtly criticizes in more than one show), he really could be referring to just about anyone or anything—relationships between romantic partners, employers and employees, rapists and victims. The programming of the Dollhouse is not dissimilar from the socialization that every one of us goes through, highlighting the links between the fantasy of the Rossum corporation and Whedon's message on inequality created in the real world. Topher, in the unaired pilot, delivers a particularly pertinent monologue to Boyd:

"Does that tie keep you warm?... It's just what grown-up men do in our culture. They put a piece of cloth around their necks so they can assert their status and recognize each other as non-threatening kindred... You wear the tie because it never occurred to you not to. You eat eggs in the morning but never at night. You feel excitement and companionship when rich men you've never met put a ball through a net. You feel guilty, maybe a little suspicious when you see that Salvation Army Santa. You look down for at least half a second if a woman leans forward. And your stomach rumbles you drive by a big golden arch... Everybody's programmed, Boyd... Morality is programmed too" ("Echo" 0.0). And that is what makes the Dollhouse technology so terrifying—it highlights the fact that the ability to program people and use them already exists.

Taken from this standpoint, *Dollhouse* is a great starting point for feminist analysis. These instances of disempowerment often deal much with the intersections between gender, class, and power (although very rarely about race—a major shortcoming of Whedon that many have pointed out before). To borrow a quotation from the show, the *Dollhouse* "deals in fantasy, but that is not their purpose." Ultimately, the *Dollhouse* is an extraordinary exposé of structural, systemic oppression and its implications for feminism. It is just as important to discuss the troubling implications and reality of robbed identities and sexual assault and other forms of disempowerment as it is to think about female empowerment. Giving people "the wiggins" about the dubious morals in the show is exactly what it's all about.

Works Cited

"Belonging." 2.4. Marissa Tancharoen and Jed Whedon. Dir. Jonathan Frakes. *Dollhouse2*.

Buffy the Vampire Slayer: *The Chosen Collection: Seasons 1-7*. Twentieth Century Fox Home Entertainment, 2005. DVD.

Dollhouse: *The Complete Season 2*. Twentieth Century Fox Home Entertainment, 2010. DVD.

Dollhouse: *Season One*. Twentieth Century Fox Home Entertainment, 2009. DVD.

"Echo." 0.0. Unaired pilot. Writ. and dir. Joss Whedon. *Dollhouse One*.

"Helpless." 3.12. Writ. David Fury. Dir. James A. Contner. *Buffy*.

"The Hollow Men." 2.12. Writ. Michele Fazekas, Tara Butters, and Tracy Bellomo. Dir. Terrence O'Hara. *Dollhouse 2*.

"A Love Supreme." 2.8. Writ. Jenny DeArmitt. Dir. David Straiton. *Dollhouse 2*.

"Man in the Street." 1.6. Writ. Joss Whedon. Dir. David Straiton. *Dollhouse One*.

"Omega." 1.12. Writ. and dir. Tim Minear. *Dollhouse*.

"Tabula Rasa." 6.8. Writ. Rebecca Rand Kirshner. Dir. David Grossman. *Buffy*.

6.05

Dollhouse, Fox Television, and Cultural Fragmentation

Rana Emerson

It's possible that Joss Whedon's fans who started the preemptive "hype this show" campaign on DollhouseForums.com had the right idea after all. The Fox television network had canceled Whedon's earlier television show, *Firefly*, after less than one season in 2002. In the minds of Whedon fans, Fox was the ultimate Big Bad and *Dollhouse* being on that network did not bode well for the future of the series. *Dollhouse* may not have had a chance of a long run out of the starting gate with or without hype, but that very act of collective action to support a new show by their beloved creator, demonstrates what a special breed Whedonites are.

It is also an excellent example of the ways that cultural fragmentation works in today's media and entertainment culture. Also known as fractured culture, it describes the ways that American culture has become split up into so very many specific pieces that a group that consumes one type of culture can be completely unaware of what is consumed by another. As former *Wired* editor Chris Anderson explains in *The Long Tail*, this means that the future of media and entertainment is no longer based upon a large, general, mass audience, but many small, specific, niche audiences. Profit will come not from appealing generally to everyone and creating "water-cooler conversation," as NBC was able to do with *The Cosby Show* in the 1980s, but instead from developing programming that speaks to many small, specific groups, like working women, teens, or people who enjoy a combination of quirky dialogue, philosophical themes, SF/fantasy, and angst.

Ironically, *Dollhouse*'s success was hindered by Fox's simultaneous attempt to take advantage of the specific niche of genre culture that Joss Whedon and Mutant Enemy's work represented while also forcing the program to appeal to a more mainstream demographic beyond its niche audience. The evidence and effects of these conflicting goals are revealed in the saga of *Dollhouse*'s two pilots (one never aired; the other shaped by Fox's expectations) and the first season finale (also never aired in Region 1, North America).

My first glimpse of *Dollhouse* happened at an exemplar of cultural fragmentation, the 2009 New York Comic Con. I had waited patiently in line for hours at the Jacob Javits Center with hundreds (thousands, even) of my fellow Whedonites to see and hear him introduce the show on the Sunday before it was to premiere on Fox. Along with series star (and former *Battlestar Galactica* cast member) Tahmoh Penikett, Whedon screened an extended scene from the pilot, "Ghost" (1.1). After the lights went down following Joss's typically wry introduction, onscreen we followed two racing motorcycles on Los Angeles streets that led us to a party scene featuring series star, Eliza Dushku, dancing to a remix of Lady Gaga's "Just Dance" with a handsome man. After much flirtatious banter, she abruptly walks out of the party and approaches a van occupied by Harry Lennnix. We then hear what we come to know as the signature Active/Handler phrase: "Are you ready for your treatment?" Then the house lights went up.

Upon viewing the rest of the episode, the audience learns that Eliza Dushku's character, Echo, is an "active" who lives in the mysterious underground compound called the Dollhouse run by the multi-national conglomerate Rossum Corporation, and populated by people who, like Echo, are blank slates that can have their personalities customized according to the whims of customers who pay for specialized "engagements."

The anticipation for *Dollhouse* after the online success of *Dr. Horrible's Sing-Along Blog* was high, and the complex, unusual premise of the show promised to deliver the key qualities that audiences have come to expect from Joss Whedon's shows: a combination of female protagonist of superhero-like proportions, SF/fantasy, multi-layered mythology, some procedural structure, social critique, and philosophical contemplation blended with witty dialogue and the potential for emotional pathos.

It's not clear that Fox had the same expectations for the show. The production of *Dollhouse* was apparently troubled early on. The episode from which a segment was shown at New York Comic Con was taken from the second version of the show's pilot. The original pilot episode, "Echo" (0.0), was scrapped by Whedon and his production team because of problems in tone and concept, and reshot resulting in "Ghost." Fox and Whedon and the production team did not agree on the direction of the show, namely the balance between philosophical elements and action, causing production to be halted after many rewrites and reshoots early in the shooting of the first episodes. As Whedon said in *Rolling Stone* about the relationship with the network, "It went well at first, then it went not so well. And the not-so-well is about them going, 'You know, we don't really have room for these kinder, more contemplative stories'" (qtd. in Kushner). The parties did eventually come to an agreement on the proper course to take with the show and production resumed on the first season.

Although the production company made it clear that it had problems with "Echo" as a final product and believed changes should be made, when one looks at the differences between the aired and unaired pilots, the compromises that were made in order to appeal less to a niche-oriented audience and more to a mainstream audience become clear. One could go so far as to say that these compromises even alienated certain key parts of Joss Whedon's base demographic. This happened in two major ways. The "Echo" and "Ghost" pilots are almost nothing alike and, as a result, set the series out on completely different paths. They both introduce the audience to the character Echo, but they differ mainly in their structure, and how that structure appeals to an audience.

Buffy, *Angel*, and *Firefly* all blended procedural and mythological elements, and it was clear that the intent was, from the outset, for *Dollhouse* to be a combination of the two as well. The mythology of all of those three earlier series clearly dominated the narrative arcs. Universe-building and character-development have always been key elements in Mutant Enemy shows and the niche audience has come to expect the kind of time and attention necessary for them to be accomplished. The unaired pilot begins both those processes right away. In "Echo," the audience is introduced very quickly to the *Dollhouse* universe and becomes familiar with important terminology. Most interestingly, we are introduced almost immediately to two key philosophical questions. The scene during which Topher and Boyd observe Echo, Victor, and Sierra "grouping," or repeatedly gathering to eat, is in "Echo." However, the segment does not appear in the actual aired series until the fourth episode, "Gray Hour" (1.4), which raises questions of scientific ethics and morality for humanity.

In contrast, "Ghost" is constructed more like a mystery story in which the FBI agent, Paul Ballard, played by Tahmoh Penikett is investigating the Dollhouse and trying to locate Caroline Farrell, the true identity of Echo. The episode is practically a straightforward police procedural. And unlike the unaired pilot, in which we see Eliza Dushku's character take on a number of different assignments, showcasing the varied roles that the dolls are able to perform, in "Ghost," the focus is mainly upon her highly sexualized assignment as a man's weekend date, as well as Echo's and the other female dolls' physicality (we mainly see the male doll Victor at this point in the role of an informant to Ballard). The aired pilot is more of a showcase for the stars of the show, Penikett and, especially, Dushku. The rest of the cast receive less airtime in "Ghost" than they do in "Echo"; and more significantly, their characters are explored in less depth than in the aired pilot. The broadcast pilot's themes and form were more traditional, which would seem to appeal to a more mainstream audience, so procedurals and self-contained narratives dominated the first five episodes of the first season. If the series had begun with "Echo" instead, much of the *Dollhouse* universe and mythology would have been established from the outset and possibly been more attractive to a Whedon fanbase viewership. By attempting to reap high ratings from the mainstream audience, the series risked disillusioning and losing the very niche groups that it was created for.

The fact that the actual Season 1 finale, "Epitaph One" (1.13), was not aired in North America is also telling. Here again Fox misjudged the appeal and the potential audience of *Dollhouse*. Although the official explanation was that it was not produced under an agreement with Fox, and it was instead included in the Season 1 DVD release, what was not seen by the regular broadcast audience also suggests Fox's audience strategy. "Epitaph One" shoves the audience forward to the apocalyptic future of 2019 when the imprinting technology that made the active dolls possible has gone out of control, endangering humanity itself. Both this temporal shift and the alternating flashback structure of the episode destabilize the narrative, reinforcing the onscreen chaos. Apparently, Fox feared that mainstream viewers would be confused and switch channels to a *Law and Order* rerun; but the network did not consider that the intended niche audience would have recognized a Whedon trademarked whiplash plot change, devoted hours online to blogging and posting on why it was brilliant or terrible, and tuned in next season to find the answers. "Epitaph One" clearly prefigures the potential for multi-dimensional televisual world-building that *Dollhouse*'s second season provided, with reflections upon critical themes of gender, race, domination, capitalism, and the ethical uses of science and technology.

Another of Whedon's trademarks is the use of complex, engaging characters. Yet a common critique of the early episodes of the first season of *Dollhouse* was that it was difficult to identify with the main character, Echo, and there was no other real character with whom to connect. Perhaps if there had been less focus on Echo's engagements and the strengths of the ensemble cast highlighted earlier in the show's run, a niche fan base might have been better established.

Many feminist viewers vocally criticized and abandoned the show, believing, justifiably, that the theme of human trafficking and the visual focus on the female body smacked of exploitation and prostitution. Had the series not tried to gain a young male audience that wouldn't otherwise be interested in the show without showing skin, perhaps there could have been an opportunity to begin exploring themes of identity in a more complex way earlier in the series, much in the way they were able to do so in Season 2. By that time, however, the writing was on the wall. First *Dollhouse* was put on hiatus during November Sweeps, and then it was canceled in February.

Perhaps *Dollhouse* just wasn't meant to be a hit. None of Joss Whedon's other shows, not even *Buffy*, had particularly high ratings. But in the context of a fragmented culture, maybe it could have at least survived if Fox's strategy had been to leverage its niche appeal rather than alter the series to accomplish more—and less—than was originally intended. Then, we might have been able to experience more than just a taste of the innovative and challenging television that *Dollhouse* offered.

Works Cited

Anderson, Chris. *The Long Tail*. New York: Hyperion, 2006. Print.

Dollhouse*: Season One*. Twentieth Century Fox Home Entertainment, 2009. DVD.

"Echo." 0.0. Unaired pilot. Writ. and dir. Joss Whedon. Dollhouse*: Season One*.

"Epitaph One." 1.13. Unaired in US and Canada. Story by Joss Whedon. Teleplay by Maurissa Tancharoen and Jed Whedon. *Dollhouse*.

"Ghost." 1.1. Writ. and dir. Joss Whedon. *Dollhouse*.

"Gray Hour." 1.4. Writ.Sarah Fain and Elizabeth Craft. Dir. Rod Hardy. *Dollhouse*.

Kushner, David. "Revolt of a TV Genius." *Rolling Stone* 19 Feb. 2009: 38-39. Print.

6.06

"Fantasy Is Their Business, But It Is Not Their Purpose":
The Metaphor of *Dollhouse*
Don Tresca

INTRODUCTION

When *Dollhouse* debuted on the Fox Television Network in February 2009, it instantly became Joss Whedon's most controversial work. Many of his most loyal fans began to wonder if the feminist Whedon had sacrificed his ideals at the altar of Fox, creating a show about a high-tech brothel where women were reduced to beautiful and mindless sex dolls (Wilcox 1)[1]. One of the show's first scenes, in the episode "Ghost," had Eliza Dushku erotically gyrating on the dance floor in a skimpy outfit that barely qualified as a dress (Whedon himself, in the episode's DVD commentary, referred to it as nothing more than a "shirt" [Whedon and Dushku]) while the camera shot her from a provocatively low angle. The fans also objected to Whedon's seeming abandonment of the complex serialized storytelling which dominated his previous television shows (*Buffy*, *Angel*, and *Firefly*) in favor of basic stand-alone episodes which amounted to "Who is Echo this week?" storylines. But for those fans that stuck with the show and began to examine the story more in depth, a complexity emerged, hidden beneath the show's sexy gloss and, seemingly, simplistic storytelling. *Dollhouse*, the television show, is nothing less than a treatise on the art and science of making a television series.

THE DOLLHOUSE AS TELEVISION METAPHOR

The entire first season of *Dollhouse* is told entirely from the perspective of the Network, symbolically disguised within the show as the Rossum Corporation. True to its name (which is derived from Karel Čapek's 1920 play *R.U.R.: Rossum's Universal Robots*), the Corporation/Network sees the Dolls within the Dollhouse as little more than mindless automatons designed to do the work to which they are assigned and nothing more. Following the television metaphor, the Dolls are the Actors.[2] From the perspective of the Network, actors have no minds and no personalities beyond those given to them by the Network in the form of characters which are then plugged into specific scenarios for the enjoyment of the clients (the audience). The Network views the Dolls/actors as little more than commodities, not as actual people. It only sees them in terms of numbers, how much money can be made off of them based on "ratings" (both Whiskey and Echo are celebrated within the Network establishment for being "number one"). When one of these Dolls/actors begins to glitch, begins to show signs of an actual personality at odds with the Network's intentions, he or she is fired, metaphorically being sent to the "Attic." But even in the "Attic," the Doll/actor continues to serve the Network with its personality fueling the Network's "ratings" engine.[3] A similar trope is used in the Season 5 *Angel* episode "Smile Time" (5.14), but in that instance, it is the audience (the children watching the puppet show) that are being forced to serve the Network through the draining of their life-force to serve as fuel for the demonic puppets. The purpose, however, is ultimately the same: both actors and audience become commodities rather than unique individuals, the energy used to power the massive machinery of the Network.

In the first season, the Network also controlled the "creative staff" of the metaphoric Dollhouse program. Topher Brink represented Whedon himself, as the creator/writer of the Dollhouse. Topher is the individual responsible for developing the characters imprinted upon the Dolls/actors. He designs every aspect of each personality, down to its idiosyncrasies and flaws (including such physical flaws as nearsightedness and asthma, demonstrating that his control over his characters is so complete that he is able to control both the mind and the body), taking on the construction of each personality as a provocative intellectual challenge (Chow 16). Despite Topher's adherence to scientific knowledge, he views his design and control over the personalities he has developed as "art" rather than science (as he states in both "The Target" 1.2 and "Gray Hour" 1.4). He views the Dolls/actors as little more than playthings to manipulate. He has no moral compunction over placing the Dolls in physically and ethically compromising situations, secure in his knowledge that he can remove any damaging trauma with a simple "mind-wipe" treatment at the conclusion to the engagement.

Likewise, Adelle DeWitt, the head and metaphoric producer of the Dollhouse, wears her complicity in the exploitation of the Dolls/actors on her sleeve. Unlike Topher, Adelle at least has a passing moral concern for the well-being of her charges. She sincerely believes she is providing a necessary public service by arranging the scenarios in which the Dolls/actors participate (in much the same way as a television producer is responsible for arranging the logistics of the production of the television series). She takes her responsibilities for providing the clients with the best possible engagement while simultaneously maintaining the well-being of her "employees" (the Dolls/actors and other "staff" of the metaphoric Dollhouse program). She feels her actions are morally justified by providing "therapy for the clients or relief from suffering for the people who became Dolls" (Anderson 167). As she tells a prospective client in a flashback in the episode "Epitaph One" (1.13), "This isn't just about what you want. It's about what you need."[4]

On the far opposite end of the moral spectrum to Topher and Adelle sit the characters of Boyd Langdon and Dr. Claire Saunders. Langdon can be seen in the metaphoric role of the director, monitoring the Dolls/actors "in the field" (what could metaphorically be viewed as the "on location shooting set") and ensuring that the scenario goes according to the plan determined by the writer and producer. Langdon is described by Whedon himself as the "moral center" of the *Dollhouse* television show (Whedon, Commentary, "Man on the Street" 1.6). In the first season, Langdon is the one "staff" person of the Dollhouse closest to Echo, protecting her (sometimes at the risk of his own life, as in "The Target" 1.2) and acting as her trusted confidante (at least during the times when she is imprinted). Likewise, Dr. Saunders (who can be viewed as a simple support staff or on-set medical personnel in the metaphor of the television program) is seen by others (especially in light of Langdon's eventual betrayal of Echo in late Season 2) as the show's "moral center" as, in Rebecca Levinger's words, she "often seemed to be the only person who cared about the Actives [Dolls/actors] as people, rather than a business commodity, and she made it her mission to remind her coworkers of that" (106). However, the eventual reveal of Dr. Saunders as a Doll (in the episode "Omega" 1.12) throws that status into doubt, especially when Topher reveals in "Vows" (2.1) that her morality is nothing more than a programmed personality trait (rather than an honest emotion) he placed within her to make her "better than me," to make her his moral conscience. She is forced to ultimately recognize that she does not have as much internal moral conscience and free will as she believed, and this knowledge ultimately makes her a more pliable subject in Season 2 for Langdon's manipulations and deceptions.

Yet regardless of each character's level of morality regarding the Dollhouse, they are all complicit in the Network's plan to use the Dolls/actors to manipulate the desires of the audience for financial gains. The clients (and the general television audience) seek instant gratification rather than putting in the difficult work of developing mentally and emotionally satisfying connections with other people (and, metaphorically, modes of entertainment). The clients don't want the emotional bonds of true love (and the audience doesn't want deep complexity and challenging narratives from their entertainment); they want meaningless sex, eye candy, mind-numbing violence, and simplistic storylines that can be easily digested in the short 47-minute timeframe of a single television episode. At least that's what the Rossum Corporation/Network believes. Even the Dolls/actors themselves are somewhat complicit in this plan. Most of them (with the possible exception of Priya/Sierra) willingly sign contracts giving the Network/Corporation permission to exploit them in any manner they see fit, to escape either legal entanglements (Caroline/Echo) or traumatic pain (Madelyne/November and Anthony/Victor). And Echo herself, without an implanted personality, makes the decision on two separate occasions (in "Man on the Street" and "A Spy in the House of Love" 1.9) to be voluntarily uploaded with a personality, allowing herself to be used as a shell for another's fantasy character.

And Whedon extends the metaphor even further, to suggest that everyone is a Doll, an actor on the stage of the world (to paraphrase Shakespeare). Whedon drives home the point that everyone is programmed, everyone is "trained" to act certain ways in certain situations. In the unaired pilot episode "Echo," Topher explicitly states this when he asks Langdon:

"Why do you wear a tie? It's just what grown-up men do in our culture. They put a piece of cloth around their necks so they can assert their status, and so they can recognize each other as non-threatening kindred... You wear the tie because it never occurred to you not to... Everyone's programmed, Boyd" ("Echo" 0.0).

An interviewee in the episode "Man on the Street" puts it even more bluntly, addressing the camera directly and stating: "You think it's not happening? You think they're not controlling you? Don't worry about it. Just sit back and wait for them to tell you what to buy." Complicity and consent are now a mere formality. Everyone has been made a Doll/actor without even being aware that it was happening. Each of us unknowingly operates according to the whims of media culture and corporate interests without a second thought (Canavan 27). "We're all," as Boyd says in "A Private Engagement," "in a Dollhouse" (also qtd. in Wilcox 1).

Initially Whedon provides us with a character that represents the "ordinary man" trapped within the Dollhouse, Paul Ballard. At first glance, Ballard seems entirely unprogrammed, in complete opposition to the Dollhouse program. He is a rogue FBI agent, refusing to acquiesce to the demands of his superiors and the taunts of his fellow agents, in regards to his investigation of the Dollhouse. He refuses to allow himself to be manipulated and controlled by others. Yet, ultimately, he is undone by his obsession with Caroline in a manner that is even more powerful than the Dollhouse's control of the Dolls themselves. He becomes the dangerously, quasi-psychotic "obsessed fan," who becomes convinced that he, and only he, can save the object of his desire from the evil clutches of the Dollhouse. Ballard becomes enamored with Caroline in much the same way as all "obsessed fans" become enamored with their objects of desire, through her image on a television screen. He becomes emotionally attached to her as a character, as a false image, rather than as a real person.[5] This obsession makes him an easy target of manipulation for both the Dollhouse itself and for Alpha, the truly psychotic Big Bad of season one. Ballard becomes an unwitting client of the Dollhouse by being guided in his search by two Dolls (Victor as his Russian informant Lubov and November as his beautiful and naïve neighbor Mellie) and by the trickery and manipulation of Alpha himself (both by sending clues and eventually by leading him directly into the Dollhouse itself). When he reaches the interior of the Dollhouse and sees Victor in his Doll state, Ballard realizes that "My whole life isn't real" in the episode "Briar Rose" (1.11) which makes him ripe for his conversion into the Dollhouse mentality. In his effort to become the solution, he instead becomes part of the problem.

DOLLHOUSE AND THE WHEDON FANBASE

Ballard's conversion into complicity with the Dollhouse program is very symbolic of Whedon's fanbase becoming centralized figures within the creation of his television programs themselves. Whedon always prided himself on using his fans to help build the reputation of his shows and celebrated in various ways their inventive ideas on how best to promote the shows through such venues as Internet web pages. Whedon wanted to use his television programs as a way to communicate with his target audience and to allow the fans to communicate amongst themselves outside the purview of the programs, to create "community authorship and shared values" (Rothman 14). Certainly, *Dollhouse* is not the first of Whedon's properties to privilege the power of television as an important tool for fan communication. In *Serenity*, the audience is introduced to the character of Mr. Universe, a technological genius and television "fan," whose main source of communication with the outside universe is through broadcast signals which he appears to control himself outside the influence of the Alliance (Abbott, "Can't Stop" 236). His catchphrase, "Can't stop the signal," is both a paean to the unending influence of television as a means to inform the masses of the insidious work of the evil Alliance and also a clear message to the *Firefly* fans that, due to their hard work and influence, even cancellation cannot "stop the signal," stop the message of Whedon's work from reaching them. Even after his death at the hands of the Alliance's Operative, Mr. Universe's legacy lives on. Through his "lovebot" Lenore, he is able to reveal to Mal the way to broadcast the information about Miranda and the Alliance's duplicity in the creation of the Reavers to the rest of the 'verse.

When *Angel* was canceled by the WB Television Network in 2004, the fan response was tremendous. The Saving Angel Campaign consisted of a wide variety of elements designed to let the network and affiliates know how much the show would be missed (and how many viewers would be lost) if the show were canceled, including on-line petitions, telephone call-in campaigns, letter-writing and postcard mailings, and live rallies. The campaign organizers even developed some more radical and inventive ways to keep their message alive, including blood drives and donations of toys to children's hospitals and money to the Los Angeles Regional Food Bank (Abbott, "'We'll Follow'" 231). Although the fan efforts failed to save the show, they attracted the notice of Whedon himself who, in the show's penultimate episode, "Power Play," used Angel's speech to his team to send a powerful (but veiled) message to the fans:

"We're in a machine. That machine's gonna be here long after our bodies are dust. But the senior partners will always exist in one form or another because mankind is weak… We are weak. The powerful control everything… except our will to choose… Heroes don't accept the way the world is. The senior partners may be eternal, but we can make their existence painful… We're in a machine… We can bring their gears to a grinding halt, even if it's just for a moment… They will do everything in their power to destroy us. So… I need you to be sure. Power endures. We can't bring down the senior partners, but for one bright, shining moment, we can show them that they don't own us" ("Power Play" 5.21, *Angel*).

The message within this speech is clear. The Network (symbolized here by the Senior Partners) will "always exist" because there will always be someone to watch their programs regardless of the quality because "mankind is weak." The Network is powerful, but it cannot control "our will to choose," the fans' ability to change the channels and choose not to partake of the Network's offerings. This "will to choose" will ultimately "make their existence painful," bring them bad publicity and reduced ratings. Clearly the pain won't last; time will move on, and people will adjust to the cancellation of favorite programs and move on to new viewing choices. The ratings dip may only last "just for a moment… but for one bright, shining moment, we can show them that they don't own us," that the fans have power and influence and will not back down without a fight regardless of the odds. Shades of Angel's final speech eventually made their way into Joss Whedon's filmed introduction to *Serenity* in early 2005: "Just remember, they tried to kill us… they did kill us… and here we are. We have done the impossible, and that makes us mighty. Thank you for helping to get this movie as far as it has gotten" (qtd. in Smith 10).

TELEVISIONS AND CAMERAS AS VISUAL SYMBOLS IN THE DOLLHOUSE

Although the metaphor of the Dollhouse as television production was crucial, Whedon chose not simply to rely on metaphor to stress the value of television in the narrative. The use of televisions and cameras as symbols of the constant presence of broadcast technology in the lives of the characters of *Dollhouse* is intense throughout both seasons of the series. Televisions are constantly present, serving as receptacles of knowledge. Almost every important clue as to the true intent of the Network/Rossum Corporation and to the true purpose of their use of the Dollhouse technology is revealed through a television monitor. Ballard is set on the path of Caroline through a videotape he watches on his television of a home movie of her in her pre-Echo college days and then later sees her (and picks up her trail) due to spotting her in a television report about the fire at the cult complex in "True

Believer" (1.5). In "Belle Chose" (2.3), Victor (as Terry, the misogynistic serial killer with whom he has been imprinted) learns the truth about the car accident which left him in a coma by viewing his "real" body on a video monitor while Adelle watches him on yet another video monitor. The Dollhouse staff learns about the potential danger of Senator Perrin (and his wife, Cindy) by watching a television interview (in "The Public Eye" 2.5) and then later discovers the purpose to Rossum's plot involving the Senator by watching the Congressional trial on television (in "The Left Hand" 2.6). Caroline herself discovers the existence of the Dollhouse via the television monitors in the Rossum corporate offices (in "Getting Closer" 2.11). And video footage provides both the information necessary to bring down the Rossum Corporation (in "The Hollow Men" 2.12) and to create the mind-pulse necessary to bring back the world (in "Epitaph Two: Return" 2.13).[6] Occasionally too television signals are disrupted in an effort to deny or conceal knowledge. Bennett violently disconnects the television signal at the end of "The Public Eye" to prevent anyone from seeing her torture of Echo, and then in the following episode ("The Left Hand"), she turns off yet another broadcast signal and then violently breaks the television screen with her head in an effort to simulate an injury after Echo escapes from the Washington, DC, Dollhouse. However, one of the most powerful visual images involving a television within the show occurs during "Getting Closer." After Dr. Saunders/Whiskey, under the influence of Langdon, shoots Bennett to prevent her from helping Topher design a method to stop Rossum from weaponizing the mind-imprinting technology, Topher, sitting in the exact same spot Bennett was sitting when she was shot, glances over at the television screen next to him. The television shows nothing but the snow of blank static and has Bennett's blood dripping down its screen. The inference is clear. The television, Whedon's preferred tool for dissemination of his entertainment content, has been murdered. This scene occurs during the episode immediately following the one in which he announced to the cast and crew that *Dollhouse* had been canceled by Fox ("Defining Moments"). The impending cancellation serves to strengthen both the fans' connection to the show and adds to the meaning of the show. The Fox Network (and its metaphoric representative, the Rossum Corporation) has again, as they did with *Firefly*, abruptly stopped the signal (da Silveira 151-52).

Likewise, cameras have a highly symbolic value within the framework of *Dollhouse*. Unlike televisions, which serve both as symbols of knowledge and the ever-present existence of televisual technology, cameras are seen as tools of spying, a visual symbol of the paranoia and conspiracy that permeates the show. At least seven times during the series, there are references to being "watched," with characters fearing they're being monitored,[7] and many more scenes of Dollhouse personnel (Adelle in particular) watching the Dolls/actors through televisions or video monitors. The sense of paranoia over being watched is so pervasive, many scenes involving cameras show characters either hiding from them (Hearn in "Man on the Street") or characters destroying cameras in an effort not to be observed (particularly in season two episodes such as "The Public Eye," "The Left Hand," "A Love Supreme," 2.8 and "Stop-Loss" 2.9). Echo uses a video camera in "The Public Eye" (when imprinted with a prostitute named Kiki) to attempt to intimidate and blackmail Senator Perrin into giving up his quest against Rossum. And Echo herself is even turned into a camera (through a medical implant) in "True Believer" when she poses as a blind religious cultist to infiltrate a cult. Echo's conversion both points out the ethical dilemma regarding the treatment of the Dolls/actors (with Topher seeing the implantation of the camera device as a chance to experiment with a new procedure while Dr. Saunders expresses her belief that the implantation poses a serious permanent risk to Echo's sight) and the ethical use of innocent civilians as spies in potentially dangerous situations. Whedon seems to suggest we now live in a culture where literally anyone can be used as a tool as long as it leads to a desired outcome. The ends now truly justify the means.

THE DOLLHOUSE AS UNREAL, FANTASY WORLD

One of Whedon's most vivid techniques for revealing *Dollhouse* as a metaphoric examination of the inner workings of a television show rather than as a realistic depiction of a potential present reality is through the use of several literary techniques designed to accentuate a fictional tale's unreal qualities. These techniques are allusion, self-referentiality, and intertextuality. As Vivien Burr states, each of these techniques is used to pull a viewer (or reader in the case of a written text) out of the narrative itself and to focus instead on the work's "method of production, to the constructed nature of the text rather than the text itself. This positions the reader outside of the text-world, aligning him or her with the producer of the text [rather than any particular character or situation within the text] at that moment" (Burr 37). One of Whedon's favorite intertextual devices is the use of "type casting," which "refers to the way that narrative expectations are set up [or disrupted] by the repeated use of particular actors" (Burr 10) within a certain artist's work. In *Dollhouse*, Whedon uses six primary actors that he has used in major roles in previous productions.[8] Eliza Dushku (Echo) played the crucial role of Faith, the dark vampire

Slayer, in *Buffy the Vampire Slayer*. Amy Acker (Dr. Saunders) and Alexis Denisof (Senator Perrin) were series regulars in *Angel*, and Alan Tudyk (Alpha) and Summer Glau (Bennett) were regulars on *Firefly* and starred in the film version of that television show, *Serenity*. The final actor, Felicia Day (Mag in the episodes "Epitaph One" and "Epitaph Two: Return"), played Vi, one of the potential slayers in the final televised season of *Buffy the Vampire Slayer*, and Penny, the love interest in *Dr. Horrible's Sing-Along Blog*. Any fan of Whedon's would have instantly recognized all six actors from their previous appearances on Whedon productions, which brought those fans out of the text since each of these characters would be viewed both in terms of their value to the *Dollhouse* narrative and also in relation to each of the actors' previous performances on other Whedon shows.[9] And Whedon played with the actor's individual personas from these previous appearances by casting them each slightly against type. Dushku's previous role as the sexually-charged and dark (but deeply independent and headstrong) character Faith was contrasted with her role here as a mindless, sexually-neutered Doll character, Echo.[10] Acker's early appearance on *Dollhouse* as the rather withdrawn Dr. Saunders was very similar to her performance as the shy and demure Fred on *Angel* which made her sudden transition to the sexually-aggressive Whiskey (in "Omega") and the cold evil of Clive 2.0 (in "Getting Closer" and "The Hollow Man") that much more shocking. Denisof, Tudyk, and Glau all played heroes in their previous Whedon incarnations, which made their roles as antagonists to the characters (in various degrees) that much more stark by comparison. And Day's performances (like Acker's) of the innocent Vi and the naïve Penny were a broad departure from the militaristic and violent (and lesbian) character of Mag. Each of these casting choices was conducted specifically to bring the fans out of the text and to set up expectations of how the actors would be used within the production only to disrupt those expectations by using the actors in unexpected ways. This adds to the unreality of the situation in which certain recognizable faces appear in different contexts and different characterizations within the text.

Whedon also uses allusion to create unreality by indirect self-referencing within the *Dollhouse* text to unrelated Whedon properties. Most of these allusions are minor and are meant only to recall similar scenes or incidents within earlier texts in order to both serve as fun "catch the reference" games for the fans and also to bring those familiar with the references out of the text and participate in a moment of sharing and remembrance with the producer of the text. The scene in "Briar Rose," for example, when Susan is shown altering the Sleeping Beauty book in order to "fix" the narrative recalls the similar scene in the *Firefly* episode "Jaynestown" in which River Tam attempts to "fix" Shepherd Book's Bible in order to process the story intellectually rather than as a matter of faith (as Book himself does). Another even more clever *Firefly* allusion comes in the episode "Getting Closer" in which Echo discovers a file on Bennett and comments, "I bet you [Bennett] could kill me with your brain." In the *Firefly* episode "Trash," River comments to Jayne, "I can kill you with my brain." Both Bennett and River were portrayed by the same actress, Summer Glau.

A critical allusion occurs in the episode "A Love Supreme." It is critical because this scene is a repeat of a scene that occurs in two other separate and unrelated Whedon properties, *Angel* (in the fourth-season episode "Sacrifice" 4.20) and *Serenity*. In each scene, the show's primary hero (Echo in *Dollhouse*, Angel in *Angel*, Captain Mal Reynolds in *Serenity*) is forced to abandon his or her allies in the midst of battle (against Alpha in *Dollhouse*, against Connor and Jasmine's mind-controlled mob in *Angel*, against the Reavers in *Serenity*) so that he or she may end the conflict while the allies "sacrifice" themselves to buy him or her time. This repetition serves many functions in Whedon's various narratives. As with the other allusions mentioned earlier, it pulls the fans out of the narrative and allows them the shared experience of seeing something in the narrative that the non-fan would not see. It also reiterates a tenet of Whedon's message about heroism. All of Whedon's heroes stress both the need for sacrifice and doing what's best for the common good. This scene binds all of Whedon's heroes (Echo, Angel, and Reynolds as well as their various allies)[11] together through the strength and value of this commitment to the ideals of heroism.

CONCLUSION

In a September 2001 interview with The Onion A.V. Club, Whedon issued his now famous proclamation: "In terms of not giving people what they want, I think it's a mandate: Don't give people what they want, give them what they need" (qtd. in Robinson 43). In its two short seasons, *Dollhouse* gave the fans both what they wanted (a high-quality and thrilling mythologically driven science-fiction show from a master of the television art form) and what they needed (a well-deserved diversion from the plethora of mindless reality television drivel). The fact that Fox was willing to back the show, despite its poor ratings and obviously critical stance against traditional television programming, is a testament to Whedon's standing as both the preeminent television creator and show runner alive today and the power of the fanbase. *Dollhouse* may be gone from our weekly television screens but as long as Whedon is out there it will never truly be gone. It will show up on our comic book racks (as I write this, *Dollhouse* #3 is due to hit stands next week), our Internet chats, our academic collections (like this one), and our DVD players. And, after *Dollhouse*'s unique commentary on the nature of television today, who knows what Whedon will come up with next? No matter what it will be, I can guarantee, to paraphrase Adelle DeWitt in the opening scene of *Dollhouse*, Season 1, nothing will be as it seems.

Notes

1. Citations for web documents are notated parenthetically. Citations for print documents are notated paginally.

2. In Eliza Dushku's initial meeting with Whedon, she discussed with him her own life as an actress and her attempt to find her own path within the entertainment industry. In response, Whedon conceived of the concept of the Dollhouse as a symbolic representation of the actor's role-playing and the role-playing all people engage in within their daily lives (Wilcox 2).

3. Just look at Charlie Sheen and how his personality conflict with the CBS Network, and subsequent firing, has affected the publicity (and ratings) for his former TV show *Two and a Half Men*.

4. This quotation ties Adelle (and the Dollhouse credo) to Whedon directly through the use of Whedon's oft-quoted statement regarding audience expectations: "Don't give people what they want, give them what they need" (Robinson 43).

5. This idea is further intensified by Ballard's first real glimpse of Caroline/Echo as herself when he glances at her in the reflection of a window in the episode "Man on the Street."

6. At the end of the scene, Topher kisses his finger and presses it against the screen, simultaneously kissing the image of Bennett and the television itself.

7. The episodes in which characters directly state that they are being "watched" include "Stage Fright," "Needs," "Omega," "Instinct," "The Public Eye," "Meet Jane Doe," and "Stop-Loss."

8. Some of the actors that appear in featured roles in *Dollhouse* have now become part of Whedon's "stable" of actors. Fran Kranz (Topher) is starring (along with Amy Acker) in the Whedon-scripted film *The Cabin in the Woods* (due for theatrical release in April 2012); Kranz and Reed Diamond (Dominic) are starring (along with Acker and Alexis Denisof) in Whedon's *Much Ado About Nothing* (due for theatrical release in the spring of 2012); and Enver Gjokaj (Victor) will have a featured role in Whedon's film *The Avengers* (due for theatrical release in May 2012).

9. Whedon does not just use actors from his own productions in his "type casting." In several of the DVD commentaries for *Dollhouse*, Whedon comments on his casting of Tahmoh Penikett (and the development of the character of Paul Ballard) based on Penikett's performance as the noble and heroic Captain Karl "Helo" Agathon on *Battlestar Galactica*, 2004-2009.

10. Gradually, Echo becomes more independent and determined, but fans of the show would

have based their initial impressions of the character (and its comparison to the earlier character of Faith) on the character as she appeared at the beginning of the series. Echo's sexually provocative nature in the initial scene in the episode "Ghost" (in which she appears in the short white dress in the dance club) is an aspect of the "character" with which she has been imprinted, not of the core character of Echo herself. Whedon's inclusion of this introductory scene may have had the goal to serve as a semi-transition between the sexually-aggressive Faith and the meek and mindless Echo as well as the sexual enticement that is standard in most television as a method for grabbing the audience's attention at the beginning of the series.

11. Whedon's other hero, Buffy, does not have a similar scene because she is primarily a loner when it comes to fighting many of her battles and those she fights with her allies, the Scooby Gang, never result in her abandoning them to be potentially "sacrificed" on her behalf, although two scenes do come close to mirroring this scene: Buffy moving up the platform to fight Glory and save Dawn in the fifth season finale episode "The Gift" while her allies fight Glory's minions on the ground and Buffy leading Spike, Faith, and the newly-anointed Slayers into the Hellmouth to fight The First and its army of Turok-Han while her other allies fight the remainder of the Turok-Han (and, in the case of Willow, cast the spell to convert all of the Potentials into Slayers) in the ruins of the new high school in the series finale "Chosen."

Works Cited

Abbott, Stacey. "'Can't Stop the Signal': The Resurrection/Regeneration of *Serenity*." *Investigating* Firefly *and* Serenity: *Science Fiction on the Frontier*. Ed. Rhonda V. Wilcox and Tanya R. Cochran. New York: Tauris, 2008. 227-38. Print.

---. "'We'll Follow Angel to Hell… or Another Network': The Fan Response to the End of *Angel*." *Reading* Angel: *The TV Spin-off with a Soul*. Ed. Stacey Abbott. New York: Tauris, 2005. 230-33. Print.

Anderson, Tami. "Whose Story Is This, Anyway?" Espenson and Wilson.161-173. Print.

Angel: *Collector's Set: Seasons 1-5*. Twentieth Century Fox Home Entertainment, 2007. DVD.

"Belle Chose." 2.3. Writ. Tim Minear. Dir. David Solomon. *Dollhouse 2*.

"Briar Rose." 1.11. Writ. Jane Espenson. Dir. Dwight H. Little. *Dollhouse One*.

Buffy the Vampire Slayer: *The Chosen Collection: Seasons 1-7*. Twentieth Century Fox Home Entertainment, 2005. DVD.

Burr, Vivien. "'It All Seems So Real': Intertextuality in the Buffyverse." *Special Issue on* Buffy the Vampire Slayer. Ed. Angela Ndalianis and Felicity Colman. *Refractory: A Journal of Entertainment Media* 2 (18 Mar. 2003). Web. 29 Sep. 2011.

"Chosen." 7.22. Writ. and dir. Joss Whedon. *Buffy*.

Chow, Lesley. "A Thousand Blooms Inside Joss Whedon's *Dollhouse*." *Bright Lights Film Journal* No. 68 (May 2010). Web. 22 Sep. 2011.

da Silveira, Luciana Hiromi Yamada. "How Cancellation Told the Story of the Dollhouse." Espenson and Wilson. 147-59. Print.

"Defining Moments: A Retrospective with Joss Whedon." *Dollhouse 2*.

Dollhouse: *The Complete Season 2*. Twentieth Century Fox Home Entertainment, 2010. DVD.

Dollhouse: *Season One*. Twentieth Century Fox Home Entertainment, 2009. DVD.

"Echo." 0.0. Unaired pilot. Writ. and dir. Joss Whedon. *Dollhouse One*.

"Epitaph One." 1.13. Unaired in North America. Story by Joss Whedon. Teleplay by Maurissa Tancharoen and Jed Whedon. Dir. Joss Whedon. *Dollhouse One*.

"Epitaph Two: Return." 2.13. Writ. Maurissa Tancharoen, Jed Whedon, and Andrew Chambliss. Dir. David Solomon. *Dollhouse One*.

Espenson, Jane, and Leah Wilson, ed. *Inside Joss' Dollhouse: From Alpha to Rossum*. Dallas: BenBella, 2010. Print.

Firefly: *The Complete Series*. Twentieth Century Fox Home Entertainment, 2003. DVD.

"Getting Closer." 2.11. Writ. and dir. Tim Minear. *Dollhouse 2*.

"Ghost." 1.1. Writ. and dir. Joss Whedon. *Dollhouse One*.

"The Gift." 5.22. Writ. and dir. Joss Whedon. *Buffy*.

"Gray Hour." 1.4. Writ. Sarah Fain and Elizabeth Craft. Dir. Rod Hardy. *Dollhouse One*.

"The Hollow Men." 2.12. Writ. Michele Fazekas, Tara Butters, and Tracy Bellomo. Dir. Terrence O'Hara. *Dollhouse 2*.

"Instinct." 2.2. Writ. Michele Fazekas and Tara Butters. Dir. Marita Grabiak. *Dollhouse 2*.

"Jaynestown." 7. Writ. Ben Edlund. Dir. Marita Grabiak. *Firefly*.

"The Left Hand." 2.6. Writ. Tracy Bellomo. Dir. Wendey Stanzler. *Dollhouse 2*.

Levinger, Rebecca. "'Let the Tide Come In': How Claire is the True Representation of *Dollhouse*'s Premise." Espenson and Wilson. 105-15. Print.

"A Love Supreme." 2.8. Writ. Jenny DeArmitt. Dir. David Straiton. *Dollhouse 2*.

"Man on the Street." 1.6. Writ. Joss Whedon. Dir. David Straiton. *Dollhouse One*.

"Meet Jane Doe." 2.7. Writ. Maurissa Tancharoen, Jed Whedon, and Andrew Chambliss. Dir. Dwight Little. *Dollhouse 2*.

"Needs." 1.8. Writ. Tracy Bellomo. Dir. Felix Enríquez Alcalá. *Dollhouse One*.

"Omega." 1.12. Writ. and dir. Tim Minear. *Dollhouse One*.

"Power Play." 5.21. Writ. David Fury. Dir. James A. Contner.

"The Public Eye." 2.5. Writ. Andrew Chambliss. Dir. David Solomon. *Dollhouse 2*.

Rothman, Lily. "'I'd Very Still': Anthropology of a Lapsed Fan." *PopMatters* 15 Apr. 2011. Web. 29 Sep. 2011. Rpt. *Joss Whedon: The Complete Companion* 126-134.

"Sacrifice." 4.20. Writ. Ben Edlund. Dir. David Straiton. *Angel*.

Serenity. Universal Studios Home Entertainment, 2005. DVD.

"Stop-Loss." 2.9. Writ. Andrew Chambliss. Dir. Felix Enríquez Alcalá. *Dollhouse 2*.

"Smile Time." 5.14. Wr. Ben Edlund and Joss Whedon. Dir. Ben Edlund. *Angel*.

Smith, Laura M. "PR Star of the Week: Joss Whedon for *Serenity*." *The Blog of an Emerging Media*. 10 June 2011. Web. 5 Oct. 2011.

"A Spy in the House of Love." 1.9. Writ. Andrew Chambliss. Dir. David Solomon. *Dollhouse One*.

"Stage Fright." 1.3. Writ. Maurissa Tancharoen and Jed Whedon. Dir. David Solomon. *Dollhouse One*.

"The Target." 1.2. Writ. and dir. Steven S. DeKnight. *Dollhouse One*.

"Trash." 11. Unaired. Writ. Ben Edlund and Jose Melina. Dir. Vern Gillum. *Firefly*.

"True Believer." 1.5. Writ. Tim Minear. Dir. Allan Kroeker. *Dollhouse One*.

"Vows." 2.1. Writ. and dir. Joss Whedon. *Dollhouse 2*.

Whedon, Joss. Commentary. "Man on the Street." *Dollhouse One*.

---. Interview by Tasha Robinson. *The A.V. Club* 5 Sep. 2001. *Onion*. Web. 29 Sep. 2011.

---. and Eliza Dushku. Commentary. "Ghost." *Dollhouse One*.

Wilcox, Rhonda V. "Echoes of Complicity: Reflexivity and Identity in Joss Whedon's *Dollhouse*." Special Issue: *Fantasy Is Not Their Purpose: Joss Whedon's* Dollhouse." Ed. Cynthea Masson and Rhonda V. Wilcox. *Slayage: The Journal of the Whedon Studies Association* 8.2-3 (2010). Web. 22 Sep. 2011.

CHAPTER 7

MARVEL'S AGENTS OF S.H.I.E.L.D.

7.01
A Part of Something Bigger:
A Roundtable discussion of *Marvel's Agents of S.H.I.E.L.D.*, Transmedia Television, and the Joss Whedon Brand
Stacey Abbott, Bronwen Calvert, and Lorna Jowett

Since its opening episode, *Marvel's Agents of S.H.I.E.L.D.* (*AoS*) has generated much discussion and analysis online, in print, and at academic conferences that relate to the series' place within the Whedon canon. In particular there has been intense informal discussion about whether this show can be considered a Whedon product. These debates raise many questions about the creation of the show, notions of authorship, and the Whedon brand. This reproduction of a virtual roundtable discussion that took place in the summer of 2014 as we awaited the beginning of season 2 seeks to examine the show's position within Whedon's canon as well as within a changing landscape of cult and mainstream television production. It debates how we might situate this show alongside Whedon's other work while also considering new ways of thinking through issues around authorship within the synergy of Marvel and Mutant Enemy. Through this roundtable format, we seek to discuss these issues but also to raise more questions as the series, and the Marvel project, continue to unfold. Television is an ephemeral art form, not in the sense that it doesn't last (because it clearly does), but in the way in which it is never fixed, but rather develops and changes, often in unexpected ways. We hope that, in a similar way, this will be the beginning of an ongoing debate about the series and Whedon's ever-evolving *oeuvre*.

Bronwen Calvert: While some commentators have worked to distance *AoS* from Whedon's authorship, certain aspects of the series suggest it is part of his "brand." What are these identifying features?

Stacey Abbott: Well I think that there are a lot of tropes within the series that at a glance evoke the Whedon brand. The presence of a kick-ass heroine; a certain genre playfulness and humour (think of Agent Phil Coulson's introduction in "Pilot" (1.1) after his presumed death in *The Avengers* (Joss Whedon 2012) as he dramatically steps out of the shadows and announces

"Welcome to Level Seven"); and a performance or questioning of identity that is at times quite serious and at others playful. Throughout season 1, characters like Coulson, Skye, and Melinda May are repeatedly shown to be more than what they seem, while Grant Ward and John Garrett are, as double agents, both performing completely constructed identities. But these darker elements are matched by comic moments such as Coulson and May playacting as science geeks Fitz-Simmons ("Ragtag" 1.21), and Skye performing as action heroine May ("The Magical Place" 1.11). You never know what is real on this show. These are very Whedon-like elements.

Lorna Jowett: While intertextuality of casting is a feature of TV generally, it is immediately apparent in most Whedon-branded products (see Jeffrey Bussolini for more on this). Those familiar with the Marvel universe may take pleasure in the characters who cross over into episodes of *AoS* (including Nick Fury himself, Asgardians Lorelei and Sif, cyborg Deathlok, and Agents Maria Hill and Eric Koenig) while those familiar with Whedon's other work might take pleasure in recognising actors such as J. August Richards (Gunn in *Angel*) in the pilot and other, later episodes, as well as appearances by Ron Glass (Shepherd Book in *Firefly* and *Serenity*), Amy Acker (Fred in *Angel*), and Patton Oswalt (Joel Mynor in *Dollhouse*). Part of the success of the Whedon brand is in ensemble casting and fully exploiting it within the drama. Selecting Scot Iain De Caestecker (Leo Fitz) for a key role and Irish actor Ruth Negga for a recurring part (Raina) potentially draws on their successes in British cult fantasy/SF series *The Fades* (De Caestecker) and *Misfits* (Negga)—both of which also aired on BBC America—while Bill Paxton's casting as Garrett offered a bigger name in a guest star role.

BC: There are a lot of Brits! Is this something else we can chalk up as a Whedon characteristic—the presence of British culture in his shows? We don't quite have characters making tea at every opportunity like Giles and Adelle but, as Lorna says, there's a good proportion of British actors from cult British shows in *AoS*.

Significantly, also, we have disparate characters drawn together as part of a team for the common good. We see this in all Whedon shows and it's the distinguishing mark of *Avengers*, of course. I think the team in *AoS* are a little more Whedon than Marvel; they're like, for instance, the Scooby Gang without Buffy. However, despite that, each character does have some kind of special ability: May's fighting skills, Coulson's strategizing, Fitz-Simmons' abilities with science, Skye's with tech. None of these are what one might call usual.

LJ: Yes, the team is an important part of the structure of the series, in terms of the characters and also of the cast and crew. In *Why Buffy Matters* Rhonda Wilcox discusses how Whedon continues to develop a "company" of actors, writers, and crew who often become consistent creative collaborators. In *AoS* Joss Whedon actually has very little credited input as a writer or director, though collaborators Jeffrey Bell, Jed Whedon, and Maurissa Tancharoen all write significant episodes as well as serving as showrunners. This series tends to use crew from the Marvel films rather than from other TV shows, however, providing different dynamics.

SA: I agree, and as a result the Whedon brand raises very interesting questions about authorship within the entertainment industry. It originally grew out of the cult phenomenon that was *Buffy*, without a doubt Whedon's creation and a very personal project for him. It was the little show that defied expectations by managing to survive on mainstream television (see Catherine Johnson's *Telefantasy* for a detailed discussion of how and why it survived) and developing a loyal cult following. Whedon's intense involvement with that series led to its following extending to him too, despite developing and expanding the creative team who contributed to *Buffy*'s production. Subsequently, he is as much an object of fandom as *Buffy*, *Angel*, and *Firefly*—perhaps more so now as he is the link between these shows as well as the many productions and transmedia tie ins that have followed. His work—no matter how collaborative—is, therefore, often viewed through the prism of his authorship.

LJ: Yes, and this may be because as a writer/director/producer who has worked across several media, Whedon is ideally placed to become an iconic figure. He is a single figure who handily embodies the varied characteristics of the Whedon brand, as created in practice by many contributors and different teams.

SA: Do you think it has been problematic for the Whedon brand to work with an existing property in *AoS*?

BC: There are a couple of things to think about here. There are the expectations that come with the Marvel brand—there are fans who are familiar with the Marvel world and its characters, who have read the comics, seen the films, and are looking for more of the same in *AoS*. Then there are the expectations for the Whedon fan—again, these viewers are familiar with Whedon's work and look for certain aspects to continue in this television show. And because there are such expectations, inevitably one or other fan group are going to be disappointed at times. Then of course there are those who are fans of both, or are new to both—these viewers in particular might have an easier time and be able to appreciate aspects of *AoS* that perhaps the Marvel and Whedon fan groups overlook. I was struck by the similarities between Black Widow in *Avengers* et al. and May in *AoS*; not just with the characters but also in a fight scene with May in "T.R.A.C.K.S." (1.13), which is a near shot-for-shot match for Black Widow's opening scene in *Avengers*. It's too close to be accidental and looks to me like a deliberate echo, stressing connections between the two narratives as well as the characters. This is something that's developed in the second half of the season, as Joseph Oldham notes.

SA: There are definitely expectations of a Whedon product that *AoS* has had to address, but it is coming from a different direction (or directions) as it has grown out of Marvel and the *Avengers* project. This project is neither personal to Whedon (although he is clearly very invested in Marvel as a fan and producer) nor designed to be cult. The films are blockbusters produced to command the spring/summer cinema release schedules and it is no coincidence that *AoS* is broadcast in the US on a major television network, ABC, and not a small cable channel.

LJ: What aspects of the Whedon brand lend themselves to a Marvel property, then?

SA: Whedon products tend to focus upon the least likely characters finding their inner hero (Buffy, Willow, Wesley, Cordelia, Mal, River) while undercutting those characters who seem to fit the cliché image of the hero (Angel, Jayne, Captain Hammer). These approaches seem entirely suitable to the superhero genre as it has developed at Marvel in particular. Whether the *Avengers* or *The X-Men* series, these heroes are all freaks in some form or another who learn to accept themselves and celebrate their difference, even finding power in it. The other trend at Marvel is heroes like Thor and Ironman, who have been gifted with great strength and intelligence respectively, as well as being left the keys to their respective kingdoms by their fathers, but, like Angel who has to work for his redemption, they have to learn humility and selflessness to be a real hero. These themes unite the Whedon and the Marvel franchises, and we see them in operation in *AoS*.

BC: And it's the team again, isn't it? That certainly made *Avengers* what it was, and in *AoS* we have disparate-individuals-in-a-team once again; we see it assembled in the first episode, follow it working together with varying degrees of success through the season, and see its tensions and turmoil in the later episodes.

LJ: So does the TV series *AoS* distinguish itself from other Marvel products?
BC: Well, the distinction from Marvel cinema is that its heroes aren't "super" but do have the same status as the superheroes. By the end of season 1 that's very clear, and Fury's comments to Coulson underline it—Coulson was revived from death in an "emergency situation" and when Coulson protests "that emergency was supposed to be the fall of an Avenger," Fury replies, "Exactly" ("Beginning of the End" 1.22). That clearly places Coulson on the same "heroic" level as Thor, Captain America, et al.

SA: True, these characters may hold secrets but they are not super-strong. Their skills are learned and earned and not built into their matrix (at least as far as we know about Skye). The show therefore explores a different kind of heroism… one of intelligence, ingenuity, graft. They are the clean-up team who have to pick up the pieces when the superheroes are gone—quite literally in "The Well" (1.8) when they have to clear up after Thor—and they have to keep fighting the good fight. This all feels very *Angel*-like.

LJ: Yes, and this was clearly intended as a selling point, given the series' tagline, "Not all heroes are super." The impact of Coulson's death in *Avengers* derived from his ordinariness, not from any of the fantasy elements, though these are what allowed him to return for the TV series. In some ways Coulson being killed in the film echoed Joyce and Tara's deaths in *Buffy*, and Wash's in *Serenity*, (Joss Whedon 2005) making it characteristic of the Whedon brand. Bringing Coulson back in a television series does not necessarily undercut the dramatic effect of his death in the movie, and provides another ordinary person placed in an extraordinary situation, raising questions about who he is now.

BC: I felt that what the show did with the Mike Peterson/Deathlok storyline was typically Whedon too. Deathlok is a Marvel character but in a sense Mike was another Whedon hero given superpowers and left to deal with them/ figure out how to use them. The fact that Skye finally managed to overthrow his programming through an appeal to his family bonds was another Whedon-type moment. It's the appeal to family/chosen family and the sense

that those bonds (whether of birth or of choice) are stronger than anything.
LJ: What do you think is particularly televisual about *AoS*, then?

SA: Its televisuality is built into the oscillation between the mission of the week and the long-arc narrative. Many viewers were frustrated by the early episodes, which seemed a bit throwaway, with little narrative development (references to Centipede were introduced but then seemingly abandoned until much later in the season). While watching it, I had to remind myself and others that with TV, and with Whedon in particular, you have to be prepared for the long haul. A show like this won't reveal too much too soon, but rather lays the ground work first. There was much excitement late in the season, when "Turn, Turn, Turn" (1.17) began to show the series writers' hand, revealing complex narrative twists, connecting with *Captain America: The Winter Soldier* (Anthony and Joe Russo 2014), and taking the least-liked character in the show and making him a villain. Many fans commented on Facebook that now the show was a "Whedon" show (ironically the episode was written by Jed Whedon and Maurissa Tancharoen and doesn't have any credited Joss Whedon input), but I would argue that this shift between the episodic and the arc is inherently televisual, partly in terms of how narratives operate on TV but also in terms of the need for a show to find its feet.

BC: Yes, I completely agree. Much of the discussion that's interested me is among fans rather than academics (if we can so draw the line) and has tended to focus on categorization or categorization problems: is this Whedon or not-Whedon (or Marvel); is this show deliberately slow-paced or badly paced or badly written; are the characters mysterious or (again) badly written. A lot of this discussion seems to be fuelled by expectations about a Whedon show and those expectations seem to be that a Whedon show will give the viewer twists and different identities and excitement all the time, in every episode. As Stacey has pointed out, in fact previous Whedon shows use the slow arc—sometimes only apparent in retrospect—and frequently include standalone episodes that can puzzle or frustrate viewers and that may not immediately fit into the ongoing story. Think of an episode like *Buffy*'s "Once More With Feeling" (6.7), which appeared to be a bit of fun, and is a terrific fan favorite, but works as a jumping-off point for the serious tone of following episodes in season 6. I think *Dollhouse* is a good example too, right down to the viewer frustration with some of the series' arc direction and the function of individual episodes. With *AoS*, there's an interview with cast members and producers that focuses on fan criticism of the first half of the season (Dalton), and I think it's very telling that in saying the show isn't moving fast enough, those fans are almost saying they want to be watching the Marvel films instead. All the commentators in that interview highlight the differences in pacing between cinema and TV that we're talking about, and emphasise what they're trying to do with the long-form narrative—establishing character, setting up story arcs, and so on.

LJ: Yes, and this long-form televisual development, despite the episodic nature of some TV series, lends itself to character development and opportunities for character interaction. These can further the plot and the action but they really help the audience engage and re-engage with the regular cast of characters. The action genre is not known for its deep, well-rounded characters, and nor are other spectacular genres that *AoS* draws on such as fantasy and SF, yet TV drama inevitably revolves around character. Older versions of the spy-fi (the genre *AoS* seems closest to) such as the British 1960s series *The Avengers* succeeded partly because of the interaction and "chemistry" between agents John Steed and, particularly, Mrs Peel.

SA: Similarly the American spy-fi series *Alias* is built around the relationships between the main protagonist Sydney and her CIA handler, her double-agent father, and the friends who become embroiled in her missions, sometimes becoming spies themselves.

LJ: Right. And as the characters of an ongoing TV series become more familiar, they can be taken in different directions, whether through big reveals, as with Grant's villainy in *AoS*; reversals, such as the switch of perspective on Coulson and May's positioning within the hierarchy of S.H.I.E.L.D. and therefore also on their personal relationship; or in smaller ways, like the minor arc of Raina's disappointment at finding out that Garrett is not clairvoyant.

SA: Yes, and going back to Lorna's point about the British series *The Avengers*. Coulson and May do seem to operate like an American echo of Steed and Mrs Peel, don't you think? The suave, articulate male spy, the sexy female action heroine.

BC: Does a TV show like this seem intended for a cult (comic books, superheroes, fantasy) or a mainstream (network TV, action adventure, disposable entertainment) audience? Are these still meaningful categories and how do they relate to the Whedon and Marvel brands?

SA: Terms like cult and mainstream are evolving but I think that they still have a place in discussions of TV, if only to consider how their evolution affects our expectations of certain types of programs. *AoS* may be perceived as cult in traditional terms because of its genre associations (links to the superhero genre) but not in terms of its audience expectation. Superhero films are blockbuster fare and the broadcast of *AoS* on ABC suggests that the program makers were aiming for a similarly large audience. In the UK the show was broadcast on Friday nights on Channel 4—a non-subscription channel and therefore available to all—at 8pm, a time that connotes family viewing. This show is not trying to be *Firefly* or *Buffy*, but rather is designed to appeal to fans of action and adventure television.

LJ: Yes, as Stacey notes, this was perhaps more obvious with the broadcast in the UK. The action or spy-fi elements of *AoS* align it with the blockbuster Marvel movies but also position it as more mainstream TV, and the emphasis in pre-broadcast advertising that the agents were not "super" suggests that the fantasy elements are, or can be, window dressing. Season 1 stuck with the spy-fi formula, offering action and character byplay for those not inclined to fantasy but keeping enough fantasy elements to engage superhero and Marvel fans (as with precursors juggling similar elements, like *Lost* and *Heroes*). The characters, as Bronwen has already noted, are not exactly "ordinary" since they all have special talents and training, but they are initially introduced as regular people dealing with fantastic events.

BC: This fluctuation of cult/mainstream feeds into some of the problems Whedon fans have experienced—there is an expectation that, *on television*, Whedon equals cult, and as we've discussed, people tend to expect that Whedon shows will behave in certain ways. *AoS* does seem to be going for more of the wide appeal, deliberately so, and again I think it's relevant that we're placing this show as part of Brand Whedon; it's not a tricky, cult show like *Firefly* or *Dollhouse*, which could both be positioned as products of a more "auteur" Whedon.

SA: I was struck while watching *AoS* by a weight of expectation that the other shows, even *Dollhouse*, didn't need to carry. Has the context of watching *AoS* changed from how audiences watched earlier Whedon shows?

BC: Absolutely. I recall a huge amount of anticipation on social media as *AoS* first aired, and immediate commentary after that first episode. Now a similar thing is happening in the run-up to season 2.

SA: Yes, but it isn't just about expectations. People are discussing it in detail via social media, in a way that didn't happen with the other shows. Sites like Whedonesque.com historically offered a space for committed fans to talk about *Buffy* and *Angel*, but social media opens the discussion to fans, casual fans, and even anti-fans.

BC: This is a different sort of word of mouth than we had when, for example, *Buffy* was airing and fans would encourage others to start watching this weird-sounding show. It's now possible to have a very immediate and impulsive form of comment, which is at times not very considered, and that could affect whether people decide to persevere with the show or start watching at all. And also we have ABC running the "official" *AoS* Twitter account, posting teaser trailers in advance of the new season, so there's a blending of advertising, critical comment, and fan comment that is ongoing.

Already, then, we can consider *AoS* a key work that illuminates current tensions and developments in contemporary television. It's an ongoing serial TV format *and* a transmedia property that combines two major brands and crosses several formats (comics, movies, TV). It calls attention to the notion of the Whedon brand as potentially distinct from Whedon authorship, represents its success in the mainstream, and is perhaps the most transparent example yet of the Whedon brand as founded on teamwork and creative collaboration. It also demonstrates the kind of business/industry savvy typical of Whedon and his brand, allowing for exploitation of all these factors at the best time to sell them to a receptive audience. Amid the continuing critique of *AoS*, it will be well to remember the example of *Dollhouse*—another show that received adverse criticism. It was a product of the Whedon brand, and though it was criticized for seeming anti-Whedon, his clear involvement made it impossible to distance him from the product. But attitudes change, and it is now highly regarded by many. In time, the same might be said of *AoS*, and it is certain that the show will continue to spark debate.

Works Cited

Bussolini, Jeffrey. "Television Intertextuality After *Buffy*: Intertextuality of Casting and Constitutive Intertextuality." *Slayage* 10.1 (2013). December 13, 2013. Web.

Dalton, Brett. "Marvel's Agents of S.H.I.E.L.D Producers discuss Fan Criticism and Going Full Throttle in the Second Half of the Season." IGN.com, February 3, 2014. Web.

Johnson, Catherine. *Telefantasy*. London: BFI, 2005. Print.

Oldham, Joseph. "Agents of SHIELD: Agency, Institutions and Transmedia Serialisation." CST Online. Critical Studies in Television, 27 June 2014. June 30, 2014. Web.

Wilcox, Rhonda. *Why Buffy Matters: The Art of Buffy the Vampire Slayer*. London: I.B. Tauris, 2005. Print.

CHAPTER 8

FILMS

8.01
Joss Whedon 101:
Buffy The Vampire Slayer (The Movie)
Laura Berger

The 1997 television series *Buffy the Vampire Slayer* is often cited as an "unlikely" critical darling. The title didn't exactly inspire confidence, nor did the fact that the cast was led by former soap star Sarah Michelle Gellar. Perhaps most damning was the show's affiliation with a poorly received film released five years prior—a film of the same name and premise.

The earliest incarnation of Buffy is something that many fans would like to forget; indeed, even Joss Whedon, screenwriter of the film and creator behind the series, is adamant about the fact that the film should not be considered part of the Buffy canon. Whedon has (repeatedly and publicly) voiced his disappointment with the film, which was not representative of his original screenplay. Viewers agree. The film has a score of 32 percent at Rotten Tomatoes; 11 "fresh" reviews are eclipsed by the 23 "rotten" ones ("*Buffy*").

For most fans of the show, the movie is embarrassing. Diehard fans of the series have more success convincing people who *haven't* seen the movie to watch the show because they don't have preconceived notions (except the silly title, its affiliation with the WB, a teen-oriented network, the fact that it is science fiction and fantasy… etc.). In any case, introductions to *Buffy* are met with *less* resistance when the person in question hasn't seen the film.

Many hardcore fans of the show do not rewatch the movie often—or at all. These same fans cringe whenever it's mentioned, but interestingly, the details of the film are unfamiliar to them. They unceasingly criticize the film, but when they do watch it, they discover they still can't summarize details of the storylines or comment on the characters. Merrick, Pike, Lothos—the characters that comprise the movie's cast of characters are decidedly less memorable than the indelible Giles, Spike, and Angel.

The film begins with a flashback to Europe sometime in "The Dark Ages" (characterization is not the only area in which the film lacks specificity). A voiceover sets the stage: "Since the dawn of time, the vampires have walked among us, killing, feeding. The only one with the strength or skill to stop their heinous evil is the Slayer. She who bears the birthmark, the mark of the coven." The Slayer is trained by the Watcher, and when one Slayer dies, the next is chosen. We are then introduced to Buffy, a blonde high school student, a cheerleader by day who will soon become—albeit reluctantly—a vampire Slayer by night. The fate of the world rests on Buffy's (Kristy Swanson) shoulders. She's passionate about shopping and gossiping and seems like an entirely unlikely candidate for superpowers.

The movie chronicles Buffy's transformation from an unlikeable airhead into a powerful hero. By the film's conclusion, we are cheering for Buffy; that being said, there is nothing remarkable about her besides her birthright. We want her to succeed, but we don't feel particularly connected to her. Swanson's Buffy lacks Sarah Michelle Gellar's vulnerability and seriousness—her depth. Gellar is an anchor in the series; whether she's facing witches, prom dogs, or ghosts, she manages to keep the show grounded. Imprisoned by her calling and negotiating the warzones of adolescence and the Hellmouth, Gellar's Buffy is a Slayer and a person, whereas Swanson comes across as somewhat of a caricature.

This seems less the fault of Swanson than of the project itself. The film doesn't bask in its silliness (except for one memorably amusing death scene) or dare to take its subject matter seriously, so it's rarely funny or moving. It lacks any semblance of conviction; it doesn't know what it is or even what it's striving to be. There is a main villain—Lothos—but we don't really know what he wants (other than to kill Buffy).

Some of the movie is unintentionally hilarious. Hilary Swank makes her first appearance on film as Buffy's frenemy Kimberly. Swank is clad in cut-off vests and wears scunchies (unironically!); nothing in her performance suggests that she would go on to become a two-time Oscar winner. David Arquette "acts" as an immature and asinine sidekick, and Luke Perry plays a teenager—not at all convincingly. Perry was in his 30s when the film was released. We're also supposed to believe that Buffy's popular friends find Luke Perry's character (Pike) unappealing and inappropriate boyfriend material for Buffy (as if superficial teenage girls would reject Luke Perry—Luke Perry in the '90s with a leather jacket, no less).

Donald Sutherland's performance as Buffy's Watcher Merrick is deeply unsettling; he seems less like a mentor and more like a predator. When Merrick first approaches Buffy and tells her that she is the Slayer and demands that she come with him to a graveyard, Buffy accuses him of being "a skanky old [man] who attacks little girls and stuff." Merrick never loses the skanky old man aura. There is nothing paternal about Sutherland's portrayal, and he seems ready to open his trench coat at any moment. Skanky indeed.

The film is sort of like an embarrassing picture from your adolescence that you want to hide. Burning it would be bad luck and a mite too dramatic.

The portrait means something, in its own painfully awkward way. But there are traces—however faint—of what Buffy would go on to become: a rare example of a strong female character, an iconic hero. The movie is Buffy in braces. Buffy as raw cookie dough.

Works Cited

Buffy the Vampire Slayer. Writ. Joss Whedon. Dir. Fran Rubel Kuzui. Perf. Kristy Swanson, Donald Sutherland, Paul Reubens, and Luke Perry. Twentieth Century Fox Home Entertainment, 2001. DVD.
"*Buffy the Vampire Slayer* (1992)." *Rotten Tomatoes* Web. 20 Oct. 2011.

8.02
Alien Resurrection, the Script That Shaped Joss Whedon's Career
Raz Greenberg

Before inspiring legions of fans and winning critical acclaim for his television shows *Buffy the Vampire Slayer*, *Angel*, *Firefly*, and *Dollhouse*, Joss Whedon worked as a screenwriter and script doctor on a variety of big-screen productions. The projects he worked on vary from a handful of animated features (*Titan AE*, *Atlantis: The Lost Empire*, and notably the first *Toy Story* film) to action spectacles (*Speed*, *Twister*, *Waterworld*, and the first *X-Men* movie).

Whedon was involved in each of these films to a different degree, but two original scripts written by him during this early stage of his career are notable for having a very big impact on his later acclaimed works. Interestingly, the fact that both scripts suffered from poor execution made Whedon revisit many of their ideas and themes in his later works: he wanted to see them realized properly. The first of these two scripts is the teen horror-comedy feature *Buffy the Vampire Slayer*, directed by Fran Rubel Kuzui and released in 1992, later revised by Whedon into his first successful television show. Shortly before working on the show, Whedon completed another script that echoes strongly in his acclaimed television works: the script for *Alien Resurrection*, the fourth installment in the *Alien* film franchise. This article examines how the work on this script helped shape many elements that dominate Whedon's works to this very day.

THE *ALIEN* FRANCHISE AND JOSS WHEDON

The *Alien* film franchise began in 1979 with the release of the first film in the series, directed by former set-designer Ridley Scott. The film followed the crew of the *Nostromo*, a commercial cargo spaceship on a mission from a big corporation. On the way back from the mission, the crew is ordered to investigate transmissions from an unknown origin, and the investigation turns into a struggle for the crew members' lives when the ship is boarded by a lethal alien monster. The creature, whose unique anatomy combines organic and mechanical parts, is the perfect killing machine with its great physical strength, the ability to disguise itself, and its acid blood. The most horrible fate that the creature can bring upon its victims, however, is using them as hosts in its reproductive process: implanting its embryos within human bodies that are violently torn apart once the offspring is born. Through the course of the film, Ellen Ripley (played by Sigourney Weaver) emerges as the dominant figure, leading the crew as their fight against the seemingly invincible monster becomes more and more desperate.

The clever combination of elements from monster movies, the futuristic dystopian cinema of the 1970s, and the high production values of the post-*Star Wars* era made *Alien* a big success at the box-office upon its release —and the struggle between the film's strong female lead and a monster that defiles the human body in the most horrifying way imaginable also sparked many intellectual interpretations and discussions, of a volume that is quite uncommon to Hollywood blockbusters.

Subsequent films in the franchise kept the audience coming to the theatres, and they also kept the academic discourse around the franchise alive, mostly due to the producers' choice of assigning a new director with a different vision to each new installment. The first sequel, *Aliens* (released 1986, directed by future Academy Award winner James Cameron), took the franchise in a more military-action direction while further developing the original film's subtext of gender roles and motherhood. *Alien 3* (released 1992, the debut theatrical feature of music video director David Fincher) attempted to turn in a more metaphysical direction, applying religious subtext to Ripley's fight against the monster, appropriately ending with her sacrificing herself to prevent the monster's unleashing upon the human race.

As a prime (and still rare) example of a successful Hollywood horror/action franchise centered around a strong female protagonist, the heavy influence that the first three *Alien* films exerted can be easily traced to Joss Whedon's works, and examples will be discussed further in this article. Whedon's involvement with *Alien Resurrection*, however, makes the influence of the franchise on his work particularly interesting, because beyond being merely inspired by the *Alien* films, he also had a chance to give them his own interpretation.

Following Ripley's death in *Alien 3*, Whedon's original script for *Alien Resurrection* opens two centuries after the end of the previous film, with the heroine resurrected, cloned from her DNA by a team of scientists aboard the military ship *Auriga*. She finds it hard to adjust to her surroundings, and soon makes the disturbing discovery that her resurrection was merely a byproduct of a seemingly successful attempt to clone the alien monsters— an attempt that caused her, in her resurrected form, to acquire some of the monster's genes and biological traits. Things take an ugly turn with the arrival of the *Betty*, a ship owned by a gang of mercenaries hired by the military. The mercenaries bring with them a cargo that later turns out to be live human hosts for the future inbreeding of the monsters. One particular member of the gang, a young girl named Call (played by Winona Ryder), has a secret: as the plot evolves, it is discovered that she is an android who made it her mission to protect humanity from the alien monsters, and is out to eliminate all of them. At first, she considers Ripley to be an object for elimination too, since she now shares some of the aliens' genes. But when the monsters bred aboard the *Auriga* break loose, Ripley and Call must collaborate in order to escape and prevent the monsters from reaching Earth. In the course of their escape, accompanied by the other mercenaries and a treacherous military scientist, it is discovered that like Ripley, the monster's DNA was also spliced with human genes in the cloning process. The result is the birth of a new monster, a huge alien-human hybrid, with whom Ripley, Call, and the surviving mercenaries fight a climactic battle after crashing on Earth, eventually killing the creature and presumably saving humanity.

Whedon's script was brought to the screen by French director Jean-Pierre Jeunet, who gained acclaim for his previous work on the futuristic satire *Delicatessen* (1991) and the dark fantasy *City of Lost Children* (1995). The film's release in 1997 sharply polarized the critics, some impressed with the film's lavish visuals, others criticizing its failure to generate tension or make the audience sympathize with its characters. Whedon holds a highly negative view of the finished film and the production process that led to it. However, after reading two versions of Whedon's original script for the film, and comparing them with the film itself in both its theatrical and extended versions, I believe that two points need to be clarified about the relationship between the script and the finished film.

First, it should be noted that most of Whedon's script, in terms of plot and dialogue, made it into the finished film. Some changes were made to fit the film into its runtime of less than two hours, including the decision to remove a character called St. Just from the mercenaries' gang (giving his trademark two-gunned sharpshooting skills to another mercenary named Christie), while omitting some dialogue lines as well. One action sequence was omitted for budgetary reasons, a chase-scene taking place in a huge garden aboard the *Auriga*. Another action sequence, the final battle against the hybrid alien-human on Earth, was considerably scaled-down and, in the finished film, takes place aboard the *Betty*. But overall, the theatrical release of *Alien Resurrection* sticks closely to the original script written by Whedon, and the extended edition available on DVD is even closer, restoring many of Whedon's omitted lines of dialogue. Whedon himself blamed the film's problems less on changes made to his script, and more on what he considered as its poor execution.

Which brings up the second point that needs to be clarified before examining *Alien Resurrection* in the context of Whedon's other works: simply put, it is not one of his better efforts. While questionable choices were certainly made during filming in terms of direction, photography, design, special effects, and, in particular, casting and acting, many of the film's flaws can be equally attributed to the script. It suffers from problematic pacing, moving from an overlong and generally uneventful exposition to a breathless set of fast action scenes, and the passage is not gradual enough to build viewers' excitement. An even bigger problem is that throughout most of the script, Ripley is apathetic and indifferent, surrounded by other characters that viewers have little or no reason to like or care about. The true value of Whedon's script for *Alien Resurrection* is as a transitional piece—one from which he took many elements and themes, making them work the second time around in his later productions.

THE UNHOLY RESURRECTION

The best place to start examining the influence of *Alien Resurrection* on Whedon's later works is the ending of the previous film in the franchise, *Alien 3*. As noted earlier, David Fincher's film carried a strong religious subtext and ended with the sacrifice of Ripley. The heroine, who has been implanted with a monster's embryo that is about to be born, is determined to keep the monster away from the hands of the Wayland-Yutani Corporation (her employer in the two previous films), knowing that the company wishes to use it for the development of weapons. Ending the monster's threat once and for all, she chooses to kill herself by jumping into the burning flames of a huge furnace.

This scene has a strong parallel in "The Gift," the fifth season finale of *Buffy the Vampire Slayer*. The narrative circumstances leading to the episode's final scene are different, but the scene itself, in which Buffy sacrifices herself to save the world from a coming apocalyptic monster-infestation, closely resembles the sacrifice scene in Fincher's film. There are even visual similarities: the act of sacrifice in both the film and the show is performed by jumping down from a high place. Different thematic subtext, however, was given to each scene. Ripley's sacrifice, true to the film's heavy usage of religious iconography, is eventually an act of passiveness: she jumps down with her back to burning flames, spreading her arms to the side in a crucifixion-pose, accepting her fate. Buffy's sacrifice is active: she jumps down facing the monstrous portal: her dive through it is an act of struggle. Whedon, the devoted atheist, obviously wanted to present his heroine as someone who saves the world on her own rather than allude to any hint of divine inspiration. But the act of sacrifice in "The Gift" was also presented as part of Buffy's destiny. Even if there was no intention to give it a religious meaning, at the very least it implied that there is some grand purpose, a meaning to life and its ending.

The resurrection of both Ripley and Buffy takes this meaning away. Throughout most of *Alien Resurrection*, Ripley portrays indifference towards the other human characters, not caring whether they live or die. In fact, she also seems indifferent towards her own survival, with the film making clear that her resurrection is merely an accident, the result of a scientific experiment conducted for another purpose. She is kept alive only due to the curiosity of the scientists responsible for the experiment; she is the object of a research rather a person in her own right. (One of the most memorable scenes in *Alien Resurrection* occurs in a storage facility where Ripley meets deformed clones of herself—the results of previous, failed cloning experiments). If Ripley's sacrifice in *Alien 3* had a religious subtext to it, her resurrection is an act of unholy meaninglessness.

Season 6 of *Buffy the Vampire Slayer* opened with Buffy resurrected, this time through magic rather than science, but with similar emotional impact on the heroine: throughout most of the season, she portrays a certain apathy, a sense of misdirection and aimlessness, an uncertainty about her existence that is further heightened once she finds out that in coming back to life, some part of her became nonhuman (just as Ripley's DNA was spliced with the monster's). This attitude makes the sixth season of the show share some faults with *Alien Resurrection*: viewers have little reason to care for an apathetic protagonist. Much like Ripley, Buffy is also a victim of her "unholy" resurrection.

Furthermore, the unholy nature of both acts of resurrection can be seen as a warning: the same technology used to resurrect Ripley goes out of control as the film progresses, just like the magic that resurrected Buffy goes out of control in the course of the show's sixth season.

SISTERS AND FATHERS

Another interesting parallel between *Alien Resurrection* and Whedon's later works—in particular, *Buffy the Vampire Slayer*—is the bond created between Ripley and Call. Though the two characters begin the film with a mutual feeling of animosity, as the film progresses they gradually befriend one other and come to each other's aid when they realize that they are struggling against a common enemy.

The superficial parallels of this relationship to the relationship between Buffy and Dawn are obvious: Like Ripley, Buffy is the skilled human monster-fighter, and Dawn is the artificial life-form, disguised as a young girl, with both characters beginning the fifth season of the show openly hostile towards one another, growing steadily closer as it progresses.

But the similarities go deeper: the strength of the bonding between Ripley and Call and between Buffy and Dawn is based on the fact that all these characters move outside the cycle of normal human existence. The resurrected Ripley is no longer sure that she belongs in the human world, and Buffy (even before her resurrection) has accepted the fact that her role as a Slayer will prevent her from having anything similar to a normal life. Call is an android disguised as a human and, as we learn in the film, the production of her model (and the entire android industry) was terminated because this model was just too human in its behavior for organic people to feel comfortable around it. It was her "overtly human" nature that made her take on the defense of humanity as a mission.

Like Call, Dawn longs to be recognized as a human: part of the initial hostility between her and Buffy revolves around the affection of Buffy's mother, and her envy of Buffy's circle of friends. While Buffy herself may have given up the chance of having a normal life, Dawn sees Buffy's life as more normal—more human—than her own. The support each character gives to the other, throughout both *Alien Resurrection* and *Buffy the Vampire Slayer*, especially in their mutual fight against the monsters, makes them connect to their humanity—to realize that they are, indeed, a part of the human race despite any biological or social difference.

Other than the bond of sisterhood, another familial relationship from *Alien Resurrection* that influenced Whedon's future works is the role of fatherhood. Fatherhood is portrayed in an especially unflattering manner in *Alien Resurrection*: both heroines were made by uncaring "fathers"—the scientists who cloned Ripley as part of a scientific experiment and the company that made Call as a consumer product—and both fathers are quick to abandon their "daughters" when they became undesirable. (Call was abandoned after the company that made her went out of business, and Ripley must threaten the chief scientist in military's cloning program to help her and the mercenaries escape the ship after the monsters break loose).

The most threatening father presence in the film, however, is that of the ship's computer: an artificial intelligence referred to as "Father," which controls the ship according to the directions of the ship's chief scientist. In one of the film's key scenes, Call (with Ripley's encouragement) hacks the computer's systems, bringing the ship under her control, foiling the chief scientist's plans to escape the ship and abandon her, Ripley, and the mercenaries to death—a victory of her sisterhood-bond with Ripley over two oppressive father-figures.

Given the praise that Whedon's works have often received for their portrayal of female empowerment, it could be tempting also to interpret this scene as a victory of two oppressed female characters over their male oppressors. This interpretation is strengthened by the fact that the choice of the name "Father" for the ship's oppressing computer is a reference to the name "Mother" given to the equally-oppressive ship's computer in the first film of the *Alien* series, substituting male oppression for female oppression. Whedon's later works featured some notable examples of bad fathers: Hank Summers, who abandoned his daughter, and Daniel Holtz, who abducted Connor (Angel's son) and brought him up to hate his biological father.

But it should also be noted that Whedon's works had their share of bad mothers as well: Joyce Summers and her initial disapproval of her daughter's status as Slayer, and an even closer example to *Alien Resurrection*, professor Maggie Walsh, a scientist whose "child" Adam became Season 4's villain. The sisterhood theme—not necessarily in the biological sense—was presented in *Alien Resurrection* as an alternative not just to oppressing fatherhood but to oppressing parenthood in general, a recurring theme in Whedon's future works.

BRINGING DOWN THE OPPRESSORS

Bad parents are merely representative of the greater oppressive entity in *Alien Resurrection*: authority. The military, responsible for bringing back the threat of the alien monsters, seeks to oppress more than just individuals;

it seeks to oppress the whole human race. Even worse, it rationalizes its decision: as explained to Ripley early in the film, the military is confident that by experimenting on the monsters, it brings new options for the further development of the humanity in the form of new "alloys and vaccines," dismissing comparisons to Ripley's former employer because the military is not "some greedy corporation" that is "flying blind." Ripley responds to these claims with a bitter laugh, knowing full well how the process of humans trying to study the monsters tends to get out of control.

This is a common trait for oppressive authority agencies in Whedon's other works: they are involved in a scientific or pseudo-scientific research of supernatural entity or phenomenon, a research that goes wrong not just because they are dealing with powers that they cannot understand, but also because of the lust for this power that turns them into oppressors. Wolfram & Hart, the law firm that served as antagonist through the five seasons of *Angel*, deals with monstrous entities as a way of achieving influence. The Initiative, the military-research section from the fourth season of *Buffy*, also captures and experiments on monsters (as noted above, in a manner very similar to the military scientists in *Alien Resurrection*), and even before these experiments go out of control, the desire to remain in control drives Professor Walsh to try to eliminate Buffy. The Rossum Corporation in *Dollhouse* achieves an incredible amount of influence due to its groundbreaking use of technology, and brings an apocalypse on humanity (vividly illustrated in the series' two concluding episodes). And the Alliance that rules humanity in the far future, as *Firefly* fans learned in *Serenity*, turned its subjects into monsters in an attempt to control them.

More than any other work by Whedon, *Firefly* is perhaps his most direct attempt to expand on and realize elements that did not work well in *Alien Resurrection*. Again, the oppressive authority is represented mostly by armed forces, there are (as noted above) the monstrous experiments conducted by this authority, and, finally, the rebels who do not see themselves subjected to this authority—the crew of the *Betty*—can be seen as a spiritual predecessor of the *Serenity* crew.

There are also some specific parallels in the characters. In both *Alien Resurrection* and *Firefly* we find the confident captain with a strong female second-in-command (though the nature of the relationship between the two characters is different—romantic in *Alien Resurrection*, professional in *Firefly*), a selfish and violent mercenary, and both Ripley and Call have traits that could be recognized in the character of River Tam. But these similarities are superficial, and the mercenary characters of *Alien Resurrection* remain largely undeveloped throughout the film. The process these characters go through, however, is the true template for the fight against oppression seen later in *Firefly*: from a group of outlaws that merely seeks to make a living in space, to those who bring about the end of oppression, the downfall of the oppressing authority.

WHERE DO WE GO FROM HERE?

But what happens after oppression has been defeated? *Alien Resurrection*, like most of Whedon's later works, leaves this question unanswered, for both his protagonists and his audience. The final scene of Whedon's *Alien Resurrection* script has Call asking Ripley what they should do now that they have won their battle against both the military and the Alien monster. Ripley replies: "I don't know... I'm a stranger here myself." Even after deciding that humanity is worth fighting for and saving it, Ripley fully realizes that she herself is not completely human, and she obviously has her fears about (re)integrating into human society. But Ripley is also another kind of "stranger"—she now embarks on a journey back to the same human society that almost brought the monster apocalypse upon itself. Will it happen again?

Such an ending note is typical of Whedon's later works. Buffy, Angel, Mal Reynolds, and Echo have all won their final great battles against the oppressors of humanity in the concluding episodes (either televised or cinematic) of their adventures. Now they face the task of having to return to "normal" life, knowing full well that this will be a hard process, and that humanity may bring further dangers upon itself in the future. Will the protagonists find peace? Will humanity learn its lessons? The answers to these questions remain, in *Alien Resurrection* as in all of Whedon's other works, open.

Note:

Various drafts of Whedon's *Alien Resurrection* script are available for reading on the Internet. For this article, I have used the first draft available here and also the official *Alien Resurrection Scriptbook* (New York: HarperPrism, 1997). This script is credited to Whedon, but is actually closer to the extended version of the film available on DVD.

Works Cited

Alien. 1979. Dir. Ridley Scott. Story by Dan O'Bannon and Ronald Shusett. Screenplay by Dan O'Bannon. Twentieth Century Fox Home Entertainment, 2007. DVD.

Alien Resurrection. 1997. Dir. by Jean-Pierre Jeunet. Writ. Joss Whedon. Twentieth Century Fox Home Entertainment, 2007. DVD.

Alien Resurrection Scriptbook. New York: HarperPrism, 1997. Print.

Aliens. 1986. Dir. James Cameron. Screenplay by James Cameron. Story by James Cameron, David Giler, and Walter Hill. Characters created by Dan O'Bannon and Ronald Shusett. Twentieth Century Fox Home Entertainment, 2004. DVD.

Alien 3. 1992. Dir. Alan Fincher. Screenplay by David Giler, Walter Hill, and Larry Furguson. Story by Vincent Ward. Characters created by Dan O'Bannon and Ronald Shusett. Twentieth Century Fox Home Entertainment, 2007. DVD.

"The Gift." 5.22. Writ. and dir. Joss Whedon. Buffy the Vampire Slayer: *The Complete Series*. Twentieth Century Fox Home Entertainment, 2010. DVD.

8.03

Burning Down the House:
Cabin in the Woods and Genre Immolation
Colin Dray

Joss Whedon is finally the world-recognized filmmaking force he was always destined to be thanks to a bohemian art-house film he made called *The Avengers* (you may have heard of it). He began his first creator-owned television project, *Buffy the Vampire Slayer**, with a brief introduction that subverted one of the most firmly established, and frankly *tired* conventions of the horror genre.

Within the sequence, a strapping young man leads a coquettish blonde girl down a dark corridor, the couple seemingly trying to find somewhere to be alone. The girl, giggling as she sashays in her school uniform, grows suddenly timid, pondering what dangers might lurk in the shadows around them. But the young man, predatory and amorous, skulks closer. He leers over her, tells her not to worry about it; there's nothing to fear. He smiles, looking her over hungrily, and inching closer to her neck.

The darkness closes in, his frame towering over hers as they linger in this lonely alcove, cut off from the world. There is no escape. The viewer knowing that this trembling girl is wholly at his mercy.

And at that point, she spins around and rips open his throat. She was a vampire, and he was her gullible lunch.

Whedon took one of the most played-out motifs in horror—the sexually promiscuous blonde getting moralistically devoured by the monster—and before even running the opening credits, wholly flipped it on its head. In the universe of *Buffy the Vampire Slayer* (as if the title wasn't enough) it was immediately evident that women were no longer relegated to rote damsels in distress, and all the weary conventions of schlock cinema were about to be fundamentally shaken up.

For seven years *Buffy* was a malleable catch-all genre pastiche, a revolutionary blurring of fantasy, horror, comedy, romance, and sci-fi that effortlessly manifested the elevated emotional turmoil of adolescence through literalized demons and whatever is the plural of "apocalypse." In his more recent film collaboration with fellow *Buffy* alum Drew Goddard, *The Cabin in the Woods* (co-written and directed by Goddard), the two have sculpted an even more focused—and arguably more acerbic—exploration of the horror genre, offering an unparalleled example of textual self-assessment that combines homage, parody, and an unapologetic embrace of traditional genre conventions all in one cohesive narrative salad.**

So yes, *The Cabin in the Woods* does lay out the mechanics of the horror narrative, riffing on them with a sly metatextual self-awareness, but rather than simply tearing them down, or satirising them as repetitive drivel, it goes further, not only justifying their ubiquity, but finding a legitimate means of validating their perpetuation. It posits that there is a *reason* we enjoy watching these clichés play out, an inexorable drift toward formula that explains why this group of teens look like a rehash of the Scooby-Doo Gang as they drive toward their doom; because these narratives reflect back an image of ourselves, about our collective paranoias and the history of iterative storytelling that defines us.

Sure, it makes us laugh—just as we can laugh at all the things we love—but what it embraces and emboldens is proved more important than what it derides.

The Cabin in the Woods is propelled by the frisson of dissonant worlds—the rational and the fantastical, the experiential and bureaucratic, the subjective and objective—all rubbing up against each other, eventually colliding in a thunderous, anarchic eruption by the film's end. Superficially, the narrative concerns a group of teenagers travelling to a cabin in the woods (the most clichéd locale for any cookie-cutter campfire tale), where they find themselves trapped in real-life enactments of the urban legends hard-wired into our communal subconscious (mutants, cannibals, escaped psychotics, werewolves, clowns... ergh... *clowns*), and get slaughtered one by one as evil is unleashed upon them. This is the first level of narrative; the second takes place in a sterile office space where a group of technicians look on dispassionately as this horror plays out. As the film progresses it is revealed that these men are the ones orchestrating the brutal fate being inflicted upon these young people—ensnaring them in a trap from which the only escape is gratuitous, theatrical death.

It is possible to therefore read this layering as a metaphorical satire upon the *making* of horror films, with their hackneyed, predictable narrative beats and desensitising gore. The tedium and contempt of the technicians in their ties becomes a statement on the conveyer-belt production of such films— complaining about tight schedules and broken pyrotechnics and having to deal with that weird actor who takes his role as crusty old harbinger of doom a little *too* seriously—all offering a glimpse into the behind-the-scenes machinations of these tired narratives and their restrictive mechanics.

However, while this is a wholly valid way of analysing the work, in truth, it's perhaps less an analogy for the *production* of horror films as the *viewing* of them. Those observers are not solely proxies for the "writer"/"director," but rather *mirrors*. The workers in button-down shirts and the sensible ties wanting to blow off steam; whining about home repairs and pressure from their supervisors to meet quotas; observing through the detachment of television screens as another handful of hot young teens are predictably picked off before their eyes; betting amongst themselves on the outcomes; hoping to see boobies; scarfing down snack food and yawping with disappointment as the frisky young lovers get interrupted before getting too carried away—they are *us*. We the viewers. Both revolted and delighted with the ritualized narrative sacrifice playing out before them.

Sure, they devise the scenario—but ultimately they are just as surprised as the audience at which *kind* of tale will be selected, and how exactly it will play out. Will it be the zombie cannibal story about a repressed history of familial abuse resurfacing to brutalize more innocents? Fantastical creatures of legend intruding upon the rational world? Werewolves that expose (both symbolically and in sprays of viscera) the beast within us all? What do these desires say about *them* (and us) that they long for one more than another? And what's the deal with that one guy and his mermen obsession, already?

As they look on, the engineers' curiosity is mirrored by that same natural human curiosity of the victims caught in the snare. As they rummage through the basement, several potential fates and several potential plotlines await, but it is the *most* inquisitive personality that dictates what tempting bauble will trigger which gristly demise. Again we get to ask: what attracted them so much to that *particular* bait? Why go for the dust-speckled journal? Why not the shiny trinket, or the mystic scroll? Why not finish solving that puzzle box, or finally latch that antique, cursed trinket around their neck?

On every level—both amongst the teens at the cabin and the sterile overseer hub—the movie speaks to the way in which we are inexorably inclined to explore our own subliminal motivations and terrors by sublimating them onto a cinema screen soaked with gore.

Traditionally, we humans use these genres as morality plays to explore our own nature, repetitiously punishing the aspects of ourselves considered too antisocial and base (lechery, stupidity, cowardice), and making manifest the fears that plague the darker regions of our communal consciousness (the unknown, the repressed, ignored injustices of the past), so that in a cathartic fictional space we can confront and overcome them. Hence, of course, the revelatory final scene of *The Cabin in the Woods*, where it is explained that the sacrificial ritual on the surface is designed to appease the demons lurking below—perhaps one of the clearest summations of the horror genre ever offered. We feed the audience examples of human frailty and vice, and once or twice maybe a chaste young heroine survives.

But in this film, contemporary humanity manages to triumph over this perpetual reiteration, even if only briefly, and in a stupefying act of self-destruction. In the end, when a unforseen catalyst is thrown into the mix—the stoner, adrift in his impenetrable weed-coma, sees through the artifice—suddenly a cog is thrown, the machine spits, and the pressure lets loose in a frenzied immolation. As the live feeds from other failed rites from around the world reveal (damned Japan and those resourceful kiddies), the world has outgrown the hackneyed beats of these repetitious old tales. J-horror, jump-scares, psycho-thrillers, torture porn; we've seen it all already, so we know what's coming. Neither are people simply "jocks" and "cheerleaders" and "virgins" anymore—not that they ever were. The "classic" arbitrary archetypes of such fictions no longer apply—so trying to unimaginatively cram characters into boxes and serve up predictable color-by-numbers plots will not satisfy anymore.

Thus, both the viewers—and the characters in the cabin—start to *react*. They shake out of their stupor and literally attempt to escape the restrictive paradigm within which they find themselves: "I am not some meathead—I'm freaking Thor!" (okay, bad example). How about: "I am not some helpless damsel; I'm the woman who flips the switch, unleashes chaos, and turns the whole power structure on its head."

And then—

Well then you have a movie. And potentially the rebirth of a genre that both embraces and transcends its history.

Thus that instant where the lever is thrown—where mayhem is unleashed, where every source of human dread, literalized into monsters, pours from their cages to mutilate and destroy—that moment is a call to arms for this genre and its viewership. Yes, on one level it reiterates the same old need for these genre fictions: if the psyche doesn't have such spit valves for the release of these psychological undertows, if surrogates can't be sent to the altar to analogously purge us of those aspects of ourselves that we detest, then we might well (psychologically) implode.

But more than that, it declares that if all we are doing, as both viewers and moviemakers, is watching these films for cheap thrills, if it is all just to catch a glimpse of flesh and watch some dude get a pickaxe buried in his face, if there really is no deeper interrogation of ourselves being *offered* (even if not actively embraced), then it truly does all just become a farcical geyser of blood. No meaning, no substance, just empty carnage and clamour.

And if that is case then we may as well burn it all down.

Because when that demon hand (in all its distinctly *human* dimensions) bursts out of the earth at the end, it becomes either the harbinger of doom for this genre, or the birth of things to come.

Notes:

* Itself based upon his earlier attempt at telling this story as a film, *Buffy the Vampire Slayer* (with which he was apparently not satisfied).

** An argument could most certainly be made for the masterful works of Messrs Pegg, Frost, and Wright in *Shaun of the Dead*, *Hot Fuzz*, and *The World's End* however.

8.04
The Avengers Confront America's Midlife Crisis:
War, Whedon, and Western Values in the Post-9/11 World
Sam Hedlund

INTRODUCTION

"We're running the world's greatest covert security network, and you're going to leave the fate of the human race to a handful of freaks!" With these words, early in *Marvel's Avengers* (2012), the World Security Council dismisses S.H.I.E.L.D. director Nick Fury's trust in a tentative roster of questionable heroes. What chance do these ill-tempered recruits have against Loki's organized power and seductive magic? In the film, Joss

Whedon once again confronts evil the way he knows best: by assembling a team of misfits who must overcome their own flaws and divisions to save the world. And, as in many of Whedon's works, they defend not only against an external enemy, but also against their own civilization's secretive and cynical security bureaucracy. *Avengers* handles these themes in a way that echoes both Marvel's previous works, and Whedon's, particularly Season 4 of *Buffy the Vampire Slayer*.

Avengers adds to Hollywood's ongoing conversation on American and global identity, values, and security in the post-9/11 world, as the heroes unite to defend Manhattan both from an alien attack, and from the World Security Council's missile. The film dramatizes many of the challenges contained in the early-21st Century U.S. era of fear, cultural disruption, and self-examination which Gary Weaver and Adam Mendelson describe as America's "National Midlife Crisis." (195). As the Avengers struggle with one another, Loki, and Fury, Whedon shows that national and personal greatness come from finding unified purpose within freakish diversity, integrating the best of old and new values, protecting human rights, and balancing loyalty with dissent.

AMERICA'S MIDLIFE CRISIS

"Aren't the stars and stripes a little…old-fashioned?"—Captain America in *Avengers*

Avengers makes a nationalistic, yet morally-complex, statement about the place of America in the world, at a time when the U.S. (and other pluralistic, egalitarian, and capitalist countries like it) are particularly questioning the future. Weaver and Mendelson argue that, just as the new century was starting, and the post-Cold-War U.S. was seemingly growing into a mature and stable role in the world, the country's "can-do" confidence was suddenly shaken: the country was faced with the 9/11 attacks, followed by challenges such as the war in Iraq, economic inequality, and the rise of competing economies like China and India (201). This identity crisis has created the danger of returning as a nation to a very "melodramatic," Manichean worldview rather than accepting "the tragic reality and uncertainties of a dangerous world where there are no clearly defined good guys or bad guys" (203). America runs the risk of applying its action-oriented values "rashly" to address security threats, and of withdrawing from international engagement and cooperation (200).

These challenges come on top of existing conflicts among the differing visions for U.S. values held by different classes, generations, and subcultures.

Weaver and Mendelson say that, because America's most cherished principles are also some of the most debated, "what holds America together also tears it apart" (171). The same values which at times unite America, at other times divide it, including differing conceptions of individual rights (177), the role of religion (181), the meaning of egalitarianism (186), and how best to achieve fairness in capitalism (120).

Avengers builds on these types of cultural dynamics to portray how the deep internal conflicts in a pluralistic community can fruitfully produce a kind of flexible strength and self-correction which Loki's prideful and rigid authoritarianism cannot match.

THERE ARE ALWAYS MEN LIKE HIM: LOKI VERSUS HUMANITY

"It's the unspoken truth of humanity, that you crave subjugation. The bright lure of freedom diminishes your life's joy in a mad scramble for power, for identity. You were made to be ruled."—Loki in *Avengers*

Loki arrives on earth as the latest of a long line of tyrants who justify their control of humanity by celebrating their own divine qualities, while simultaneously criticizing humanity's failures in controlling their own chaotic behavior. Like most authoritarians, Loki has a very personal logic to explain his own moral superiority and the inferiority of those whom he wishes to control. Whereas Whedon describes the Hulk as a "green 'id' giant rage monster" (interview by Woerner), Loki could be described as more of a skinny superego shame monster. Nick Fury initially confronts Loki by saying he's attempting to bury him "like the pharaohs of old." This echoes the language used in past centuries to express anti-monarchism, self-determination, or abolitionism (Brian Palmer). "Pharaoh," for Thomas Paine, was his era's equivalent of calling King George III "Hitler" (Brian Palmer). Fury's line probably also alludes more specifically to the famous Biblical scene of freed Israelites watching the sea close in on Pharaoh and his army, which was also pictured in an early proposal for the Great Seal of the United States (Weaver and Mendelson 185). Loki's anti-freedom speech in Germany closely parallels the psychological explanations for the rise of authoritarianism first developed during World War II by Erich Fromm and many of his Jewish-German and American peers. According to Fromm, modern people desire to escape freedom because of the psychological burden of isolation and fear which freedom places upon the individual (Fromm 104). Authoritarianism produces leaders who are convinced of their own "wonderful and unique" character (142). As Adorno et al. argue, "authoritarian aggression," including ethnocentrism and moralistically-justified aggression toward groups with unconventional values, can be the result of displacing anger that would otherwise be directed at authority figures (162).

In Whedon's opinion, Loki truly believes his speeches about freedom (Commentary). Yet what makes him interesting to Whedon is that the logic of his belief that "humanity is not doing a very good job of taking care of themselves, and what they'd really like is for Daddy to make it better," is matched by a lack of self-awareness: Loki does not comprehend that "only a person who is so deeply damaged would *want* to be the person who takes care of everybody...." (Commentary). Unlike the Avengers, Loki does not have a community in which he can admit his limitations or seek help in compensating for them.

Whedon's Loki is such a compelling contrast to the Avengers because his form of power shows why the Avengers are unlikely to succeed, but also why they still have a chance. In the end, the war is decided not only by the slow-incoming strength and unity which the Avengers finally pull together, but also by the weakness and psychological shallowness hidden within Loki's own aloof values and assumptions.

A TEAM OF RIVALS, INSIDE AND OUT

"What are we, a team? No, no, no. We're a chemical mixture that makes chaos. We're... a time bomb."—Bruce Banner in *Avengers*

Loki assumes that the Avengers' tendency toward "sentiment" and their internal conflicts are sources of weakness. He expects to win by sowing discord, unleashing the Hulk, and flipping the loyalties of Hawkeye, Erik Selvig, and (he hopes) Tony Stark. But over time, the Avengers instead grow through their conflict and loss into a powerful unity. Whedon describes *Avengers* as an origin story in which the team members must "find something in themselves that makes them need to work with each other [and] to step outside of themselves" (Woerner). In contrast with Loki's military alliance with The Other and his army—which is built upon intimidation, domination, and a transactional, quid-pro-quo deal—the Avengers come together as an awkward family which has no hope of hiding its freakish quirks and conflicts. The team which Fury recruits (or conscripts) is pluralistic and egalitarian in its varied makeup and its openness to debate, conflict, and psychological turmoil. The Avengers are a "team of rivals," Doris Kearns Goodwin's phrase for the cabinet Abraham Lincoln chose (49), which David Eagleman has also extended as a metaphor for how the halves of the brain serve as "agents with the same goals, but slightly different ways of going about it" (124).

In this new community, the Avengers find themselves having to deal with superheroes like themselves for the first time, with fruitful as well as explosive results. The Avengers community, as Tony Spanakos writes in the context of Avengers comics, is a reflection of the type of fellowship and flourishing which Aristotle says can happen only in a community: without living in community, beings are either "gods or beasts" (100).

The Avengers' fractious community parallels the era of America's "Midlife Crisis" by dramatizing the challenges and strengths of pluralism. According to Weaver and Mendelson, Americans have managed to find unity in our differences as they have "somehow balanced individualism and individual freedom with…respect for differences, cooperation with others, and a civic order that has grown out of political and legal change" (173). As a result, America's productive conflict has a self-correcting, evolving pattern: "When the country moves to an extreme version of one of these basic values, it seems to develop a counterbalancing value or force that somehow integrates and reconciles the differences," and this further strengthens national unity (173). That dynamic is most visible in the relationship among the three superhuman Americans on the team, Steve Rodgers (Captain America) Tony Stark (Iron Man), and Bruce Banner (The Hulk).

CAPTAIN AMERICA VERSUS TONY STARK

"Tony Stark—not a man of the people—he's a man of Tony Stark. And God bless him, he's definitely a hero, definitely likes to help people, but it's his world, we're all just living in it."—Joss Whedon, Commentary on *Avengers* DVD.

As Linda Holmes argues, the conflict between Steve Rodgers(Captain America) and Tony Stark(Iron Man) reveals the tension between two very different visions of American greatness. Cap, on one hand, reflects American Exceptionalism at its most traditional, built on monotheism, "chivalry," and traditional masculinity. Stark, on the other hand, represents a more contemporary version of American power, gained from "earned egotism, unchecked capitalism, and entrepreneurial genius" (Holmes). Cap's collectivism and Stark's individualism have consequences for how both men relate to authority and to personal sacrifice. Cap's orders-following, soldierly respect for authority does not impress Stark, while Stark's risk-taking, egotism, and gadget-filled suits do not impress Cap, either. As Holmes says, Cap's accusation, "take that off, and what are you?" comes down to accusing Stark of being "all weaponry and no character" (Holmes). Yet, Stark is not bothered by this accusation, because he has "hit all four fundamentals of the Successful American Man": that is, as a "'genius billionaire playboy philanthropist,'" which is to say that he has "brains, money, women and respectability" (Holmes). While Cap is committed to the good of all, Stark implies that his self-interest serves the world just as well (Holmes). America has always had people like Cap as well as Stark, but what has changed over time is who is dominant: As Landon Palmer points out, the tension between the two is a tension between a man whose powers were created by the public sector in an era when the public sector was seen as doing things right, and a man who is the face of a more privatized and corporate vision of American greatness.

Back in the days portrayed in *Captain America: The First Avenger*, working-class "kid from Brooklyn" Rodgers jokes that what happened to him is that he simply "joined the Army," and therefore became a musclebound superhero. In that era, Tony Stark's industrialist father plays only a supporting role in creating and deploying Rodgers. Fast-forwarding to the era of *Avengers*, the spotlight has shifted to trust-fund superhero Stark, who proclaims his private wealth and ingenuity to the world in Donald-Trump-sized letters. Only in the course of the devastating battle will his name be blasted down to leave a single "A," similar to the one on Captain America's helmet.

Stark Tower, a "beacon of clean energy" (in Stark's words) or "a warm light for all mankind to share," (in the phrase Loki uses to link S.H.I.E.L.D.'s and Stark's clean-energy programs), shows an era in which John Winthrop's "city on a hill" imagery of America as a civic example (qtd. in Weaver and Mendelson 2) has morphed into a very individualistic technological and economic vision. It comes as no surprise, therefore, that Cap calls Stark Tower "ugly."

The film shows that both Cap's and Stark's approaches to life are useful and needed (Holmes). But it is only in challenging one another's underlying values that the two are able to protect New York. Thanks to the new Avengers community, Cap grows from being an orders-following subordinate to an orders-giving leader, and Stark grows from being a self-serving businessman into a self-sacrificing teammate.

When it comes to the need for teamwork and sacrifice, Cap values people who will not look for a "way out," but rather "lay down on the wire and let the other guy crawl over you," whereas technological trickster Stark would rather "cut the wire," like a modern-day Gordian knot or Kobayashi Maru exercise. But Stark does not keep his wire-cutting attitude forever. By the end of the battle, by choosing to accept what Cap calls "the sacrifice play" and taking the apparently "one-way trip" to steer the incoming missile away from Manhattan, Stark has come much closer to accepting Cap's viewpoint. Stark's risk-taking balances and compliments his anti-authority instincts, and in the end serves to direct the destructive power of the security bureaucracy in a useful direction.

TALE OF TWO HULKS: FROM WEREWOLF TO WARRIOR

"You really have got a lid on it, haven't you? What's your secret? Mellow jazz? Bongo drums? Huge bag of weed?"—Tony Stark in *Avengers*.

As the third superhuman American on the team, Banner has several possible implications for national identity and values. Given his isolation, as a man exiled from his country as well as from his past role in the scientific and defense establishment, it is easy to miss the fact that Banner is just as much a face of the current state of American Exceptionalism as Stark or Cap are. As a broad metaphor, unlike Cap's proud war-fighting or Stark's eager capitalism, Banner the emotionally-volatile, irradiated humanitarian may serve as an image of the unpredictable, disappointed aftermath of America's idealistic engagements with technology, war, and foreign affairs. More positively, he may also represent America's potential to overcome such challenges. He is a figure who at once warns about, justifies, and seeks to manage the human impulses toward anger and violence. Based on Stark's call to learn to embrace his "terrible privilege," Banner grows from being afraid of repeating his past mistakes, to instead actively seeking out where he can use his strength to help others. Of course, at a more literal, individual level of analysis, Banner is simply a troubled but talented person who is fortunate to be forced onto a team as welcoming as the Avengers. Cap and Stark both are glad to have Banner on the team, but they immediately come into conflict over how to handle him. Both treat him in much the same way that their respective American generations relate to social differences: Cap, in reassuring Banner that the only thing that matters to him is Banner's scientific mission, is in effect acting as many mid-20th Century American "liberals" (as defined in Weaver and Mendelson's typology) did toward minorities (Weaver and Mendelson 58). Cap overlooks and tolerates Banner's differences provided that he minimizes his freakishness and fits into mainstream norms, yet he fears how the monster inside may endanger the team. 21st Century Stark, on the other hand, corresponds to the "Realistic Humanist" in the typology, a perspective made possible by American identity movements beginning in the 1960s (58): Rather than expecting everyone to be the same, Stark actively welcomes Banner's difference as a source of strength, and therefore intentionally provokes and experiments with Banner's anger. Cap is justifiably terrified by Stark taking this risk. Yet, as Whedon observes, the fact that Stark is not afraid of the Hulk, and understands as no one else does that Banner "needs to embrace his inner Hulk, as it were," is what allows the Hulk to help save the world, and eventually even rescue Stark himself (Commentary).

As Whedon describes it, it is Stark's prodding which helps the "werewolf" Banner to choose to be the Hulk, which makes possible the contrast between the "two Hulks" of the film. Banner's problem, Whedon says, is a human problem: "we all have these reservoirs of anger....Do we deny them, so they flare up, or do we incorporate them, into our being, in an even fashion, so that they are present, but not prominent?" (Commentary).

From the beginning of *Avengers*, the Black Widow, followed by everyone else, wants to know Banner's "secret" of how he controls himself. His eventual answer, that he's "angry all the time," amounts, as Whedon indicates, not to uncontrolled rage, but rather ongoing awareness and integration of his emotions. Given that his self-control means he can, and chooses to, transform, it is also a matter of having faith in himself as the Hulk to behave ethically in the midst of being a monster. Being "angry all the time" closely resembles the language in *Buffy the Vampire Slayer* in which Oz realizes he is "the wolf all the time," and therefore needs to learn to control and prevent his transformation ("Wild at Heart" 4.6).

Becoming an emotionally-integrated Hulk makes him capable of taking on even what he calls the "puny god" Loki. Whedon says that Banner's line that "you can smell crazy on" Loki originally was intended to foreshadow an unproduced scene in which the Hulk would have used an acute, animalistic sense of smell to overcome Loki's trickery (Commentary), the same useful ability that Oz has in *Buffy* ("Wild at Heart"). Loki underestimates the "dull creature" of the Hulk for the same reason he underestimates women like Black Widow and everyone else he sees as "beneath" him. He shares the tendency Fromm finds in all authoritarians, to see differences, such as race or sex, as "necessarily signs of superiority or inferiority," which is so fundamental to his worldview, that "A difference which does not have this connotation is unthinkable to him" (171).

STARK AND LOKI: THE HEART VS. THE SCEPTER

"You're gonna lose....It's in your nature....You lack conviction."—Agent Phil Coulson in *Avengers*.

Stark does not have to wait long to answer Cap's question, "Take that off, what are you?" After landing at his tower and taking off his suit, Stark rebuffs the taps on his chest from Loki's deadly scepter, the same scepter that Loki used to turn the hearts of Hawkeye and Selvig, and to stab Agent Phil Coulson. Even in a film full of alien magic, superhuman biology, and futuristic armor, one of the most unexpected and miraculous moments is this quiet one, which is not an obvious and expected outcome of the stated science-fictional rules. Physically speaking, it seems that something about the reactor Stark built for his chest protects his heart from Loki's spell from the scepter, much as it already protects his heart from the shrapnel still in his body from Afghanistan.

But this victory is more than physical. It is a sign that he is in fact more than just, to quote Holmes, "all weaponry and no character." The reactor, as Pepper Potts inscribed on the plaque for his original reactor in *Iron Man*, is a technological expression of the fact that "Tony Stark has a Heart." It is a reminder of Stark's decision, as someone already rich and powerful, to become good (or less bad), after his fellow prisoner Yinsen sacrifices his life for him in *Iron Man*. This power, at this moment in *Avengers*, is also an extension of the pride and trust he has just declared in "Earth's Mightiest Heroes," which he believes in even before they have worked together effectively, and even as two of the team may still be miles away recovering from falling out of the sky.

At the same time, Stark's resistance to Loki is also powered by erectile dysfunction humor, or "dick-measuring," as Landon Palmer quips. But in joking about the "performance issues" of Loki's masculinity, Stark is ultimately concerned not just with a "dick-measuring" contest, but with a heart-versus-scepter contest. Stark is, in effect, challenging the psychological and practical viability of Loki's assumption that he can prove himself through military conquest with a borrowed army and mental coercion with a borrowed scepter. Loki desires to rule over others while denying there is anything unruly or weak in himself. This echoes Fromm's view that authoritarian domination of others is categorically different from healthy personal power. According to Fromm, "a lust for power is not rooted in strength but in weakness," being a response to (metaphorical) "impotence" in a person's own power to accomplish things themselves (160).

This is where the seeming contradiction can be resolved in comparing Whedon's statement that Loki strongly believes his authoritarian words (Commentary), and Coulson's statement that Loki "lacks conviction." The power of conviction, as unifying martyr Coulson seemed himself to be aware, is not simply about the fervency of a belief, but what kind of psychological integrity, and what kinds of friends, support it.

WAR ON TERROR, WAR ON LOKI

"We've made some mistakes along the way. Some, very recently."—Nick Fury in *Avengers*

As *Avengers* builds toward the invasion of Manhattan, it addresses the persistent tension, in this era of Midlife Crisis, between Americans' fear of terrorism and other threats, and our concern that the West risks choosing a security cure that is worse than the disease. Since 9/11, America has been engaged in an an ongoing debate about issues like civil liberties, torture, war crimes, civilian casualties, and deceptive selling of security policies by politicians. Although historical precedents cause Weaver and Mendelson to be optimistic about America's ability to counterbalance itself, they also express concern that "Our virtues are now being tested" with regard to how U.S. civil liberties are at risk in wartime (190).

The real-world resonance of the security issues in *Avengers* is built upon the Marvel Cinematic Universe's distinctly U.S.-centric and post 9/11 manner of depicting the intergovernmental security institution S.H.I.E.L.D. The MCU, founded with *Iron Man* in 2008, introduced a new name for S.H.I.E.L.D.'s initials, the Strategic Homeland Intervention, Enforcement and Logistics Division. In echoing the creation of the U.S. Department of Homeland Security and the post-9/11 national security culture, *Avengers* and the other films in the series create a space to at once celebrate, parody, and critique U.S. and Western security bureaucracies.

Even though *Avengers* in many ways is a typically melodramatic American superhero movie, it also contains tragic and morally-complex themes. Because it treats the "good guys" in the security bureaucracy as very morally-questionable, and leaves open the possibility that even those who have committed grave crimes are deserving of forgiveness or ethical treatment in a way often absent in action films, it in some ways goes against the kind of simplistic Manichean worldview which Weaver and Mendelson warn about.

The geographically-isolated U.S. still sometimes interprets wars through a very passive and reactive lens of national innocence, victimization, and heroic revenge, a narrative which Dan Hassler-Forest criticizes most superhero films for uncritically promoting (73). Although *Avengers* is not as critical of the national security state as other superhero films like *Watchmen* (2009) or even its own successor *Captain America: The Winter Soldier* (2014), the picture painted by Whedon is still morally complex. *Avengers* shows Western security leaders having an ongoing involvement in the wider world and universe, and making ethically fraught decisions with unpredictable consequences. In showing the Avengers treating killers with mercy and justice, avoiding torture, preventing civilian casualties, and confronting security lies, Whedon upholds humane values which are unexpected in a team with vengeance in its name.

TORTURE AND JUSTICE

"There's no pain would prise his need from him....He is a prisoner."—Thor in *Avengers*

Whedon's repeated scenes of interrogation and discussions of torture in *Avengers* provide a different perspective from the way these issues are often handled elsewhere in pop culture. Works like the TV series *24* (2001-2010 and 2014) and the film *Zero Dark Thirty* (2012) have often been perceived as promoting torture as effective and necessary. Whedon, on the other hand, frames interrogation in *Avengers* as a psychological process of information-gathering in which less forceful methods are superior. Black Widow's tactic of eliciting information while feigning emotional and physical weakness yields results that are at least as good as anything the Russian arms smugglers or Fury could hope to achieve when, in Fury's words, "the pain starts." Thor, given his desire to reform his adoptive brother, also emphasizes Loki's status as "a prisoner" and the obstacles posed by Loki's mental state, despite Fury's pressure for Thor to help torture him.

The heroes' eventual means of bringing justice to a mass murderer like Loki is also significant, especially in an era of self-consciously gritty and grim superhero films like *Man of Steel* (2013). In that film, even a moral paragon like Superman breaks with his character's long tradition of merely exiling or imprisoning enemies like Zod, and decides that protecting civilians requires killing him. While Loki serves as a punching bag in the midst of battle, the outcome of his final capture is humane, with him jokingly asking Stark for a drink, and returning with his brother Thor to face justice on his own planet.

PROTECTING CIVILIANS

"There are people inside and they're going to be running right into the line of fire."—Captain America in *Avengers*.

One notable aspect of *Avengers* is how the heroes manage to keep an entire extraterrestrial army hemmed in within a small territory in Midtown. Whedon says that he wanted from the start to make a "war movie," in which the ground being protected in the fighting is very specifically delineated (Commentary). One effect of this choice, especially as Cap and the others devote much of their effort to protecting civilians, is to emphasize values of protecting noncombatants, while showing that even a massive attack by bizarre aliens can be comprehensible, bounded, and stoppable.

This bounded warfare and Avengers' focus on protecting civilians, in turn, contrasts with the values of the World Security Council revealed in the argument with Fury over using a nuclear weapon. The implicit argument of the Council, based on the fear that "if we don't hold it here, we've lost everything," is what Michael Walzer, after Winston Churchill, calls the argument of "Supreme Emergency": That is, that a threat is both so imminent, and presents such a massive danger to a political community, that the usual ethics of war, including noncombatant immunity, should be suspended wholesale (252). Fury, however, argues that to take such an action would itself amount to defeat, and places his refusal in the context of his reliance on his team of rebellious but principled warriors. When the Council bypasses Fury to launch the missile anyway, the robot-like, obedient military jargon of the F-35 pilot launching it contrasts with the language of friendship and independent tactical deliberation that the Avengers use even in the heat of battle.

SECRETS, LIES, AND WEAPONS

"He's a spy. He's *the* spy. His secrets have secrets."—Tony Stark on Nick Fury in *Avengers*

The lie that creates the most tension between Fury and the team is his effort to conceal the military purposes of the Tesseract research, which is one of the major motivations for the mission to recover it. Fury assembles the Avengers initially, not to protect the earth from a large-scale invasion, but to get the Cube back from Loki. As Fury recruits him to recover the Cube, Cap tells him that "you should've left it in the ocean." This echoes the attitude of the Norwegian guarding the Cube at the beginning of *Captain America: The First Avenger*, who protects it with his life, yet never even looks at it himself. S.H.I.E.L.D., however, not trusting Thor to return and protect the earth, is acting on the same basic Promethean goal as Hydra did in stealing it in the earlier film, and which The Other and Loki have in this film—to "wield" the energy of this dangerous alien object and use it for military purposes.

Faced with extraterrestrial threats, S.H.I.E.L.D. chooses what weapons and policies to pursue, and then must face the unpredictable consequences. Despite Fury's lies, the Avengers discover, and immediately voice their opposition to, S.H.I.E.L.D.'s pursuit of what Banner calls "weapons of mass destruction," and Stark sarcastically mocks as a "nuclear deterrent" that "always calms everything right down."

Fury eventually comes clean about this first lie, and pivots by comparing his trust in the experimental weapons with his even more improbable faith in the Avengers themselves.

But even as he admits his first lie, Fury tells the Avengers a second lie—that Coulson was carrying his Captain America trading cards when he died, and therefore believed in "heroes." As Whedon points out, it shows just how dark a character Fury is, to see that his first impulse upon Coulson dying would be to take a dead man's prized possessions and cover them in blood, just to be able to lie to his team with them (Commentary).

Yet it is an open question whether it was the honest or deceptive part of Fury's behavior which most sold Stark and Cap on returning to war. Coulson did, in fact, believe in heroes to a humorous and vocal extreme. And Fury's manipulation is not entirely hidden. Even Cap acknowledges that Fury "has the same blood on his hands as Loki does"—quite literally—but Cap helps Stark set that aside, to take care of the real enemy first. As Whedon suggests, even the eventual backlash against Fury may have been part of Fury's plan—the Avengers were a gamble, and he had to "bring them together and hope that if he pushed them enough that they would gel even if it was in rebellion to him" (.interviewed in Woerner "Whedon Dissects."). In any case, Whedon carefully balances the truth and lies about Coulson in a way which suggests that patriotic myths can be manipulative, yet still have real heroes as their subjects, and can in turn inspire honest actions by other heroes.

FURY'S FAITH IN THE FREAKS

"I recognize the Council has made a decision, but given that it's a stupid-ass decision, I've elected to ignore it."—Nick Fury in *Avengers*.

Fury's decision to debate and disobey the World Security Council's order to fire a nuclear missile at Manhattan is his final and most important act of trust in the Avengers in the battle. Fury trusting the self-led, freakish Avengers, more than he trusts a standard-issue nuclear missile, is what ultimately saves Manhattan from the missile, and earth from the aliens, just as much as Stark's self-sacrificial decision to act in response to Fury's warning.

While Fury had used a patriotic lie to reinforce the team's perception of Coulson's belief in "heroes," there is no lie in Fury's own concrete choice to believe in them, even as they are battered, scattered, and he has little control left over them. By trusting his "handful of freaks" with the battle for Manhattan and the Earth, Fury once again chooses his moral team over sophisticated weapons or a direct order from an immoral bureaucracy. This choice, and the language that establishes the conflict earlier in the film, resembles Riley Finn's decision in *Buffy* to disobey his orders from the Initiative in favor of setting Oz free and helping what Finn's superior officer calls "the Slayer and her band of freaks" ("New Moon Rising" 4.19). While Fury's relationship with the Avengers remains coercive and hierarchal, he also uses his power to protect them from further control by the World Security Council. He lets them go (for the time being) and protects their whereabouts from the Council, because he trusts them to return when they are needed.

Just as Fury has decided against the missile and in favor of the "freaks," he also chooses against holding on to the Cube. Rather than deferring to the Council's desire for him to keep it, he decides to "not argue with the god" Thor who made the decision to take it with him. The language of "wield[ing]" the cube, reflecting the temptation of corrupting powers which mortals should not try to harness, is very familiar ground for early 21st-Century movies, given lines such as "You cannot wield it. None of us can," in another Norse-mythology influenced franchise, *Lord of The Rings: Fellowship of the Ring* (2001). Similarly, in *Buffy*, the "Council" which oversees the Initiative states that the experiment "represented the Government's interest in not only controlling the otherworldly menace, but in harnessing its power for our own military purposes" ("Primeval" 4.21). In *Buffy*, due to the resulting carnage and the embarrassment of trained troops being rescued by Finn and the Scooby Gang, the Council concludes that "the demons cannot be harnessed, cannot be controlled" ("Primeval").

In much the same way, in *Avengers,* the gods get back their fire, returning the Cube to Asgard. Even though the Cube partly serves a plot-oriented, MacGuffin function, Whedon's framing of it as a focus of secrecy and critical choices also reflects a concern with the power and ethics of weapons and the people who control them. It resonates with real-life debates on arms control and disarmament, contrasting technological, impersonal weapons systems with the security and good judgment provided by more human, ethically-grounded "freaks."

CONCLUSION

"Captain America saved my life."—the Waitress in *Avengers.*

In an era where America, the West, and the rest of the world are questioning what matters for national identity, values, and security, *Avengers* dramatizes both the strengths and weaknesses found in pluralistic, egalitarian, and capitalist societies. This includes portraying the dangers of authoritarian behavior within democracies themselves. By showing the relationship between individual psychology, community, and strength, Whedon uses the superhero and war-movie genres to tell a nuanced story that dramatizes a possible route through the current tensions in our culture. When it comes to Cap's traditional values of nationalism, collectivism, loyalty, and self-sacrifice, Whedon implies that the Stars and Stripes may be "a little old-fashioned," and they may even be the subject of political manipulation and dangerous security decisions, but they are still needed, and are worthy of debate and service. At the same time, America and the world also need Stark's individualistic, iconoclastic, and pragmatic qualities, and Banner's powerful self-control and emotion, along with Fury's bold leadership and followership.

Works Cited

24. Created by Joel Surnow and Robert Cochran. Perf. Kiefer Sutherland. Fox, 2001-2010 and 2014. Television.

Adorno, T.W., Else Frenkel-Brunswik, Daniel Levinson, and R. Nevitt Sanford. *The Authoritarian Personality*. Abridged edition. New York: Norton, 1982.

Buffy the Vampire Slayer. Twentieth Century Fox. Accessed from Netflix <http://www.netflix.com>.

Writ. Christopher Markus and Stephen McFeely. Dir. Joe Johnston. Marvel Studios, 2011. Film.

Captain America: The Winter Soldier. Writ. Christopher Markus and Stephen McFeely. Dir. Anthony Russo and Joe Russo. Marvel Studios, 2014. Film.

Eagleman, David. *Incognito: The Secret Lives of the Brain*. New York: Pantheon, 2011.

Goodwin, Doris Kearns. *Team of Rivals: The Political Genius of Abraham Lincoln*. New York: Simon & Schuster, 2006.

Hassler-Forest, Dan. *Capitalist Superheroes: Caped Crusaders in a Neoliberal Age*. Arlesford, UK: Zero Books, 2012.

Holmes, Linda. "Armor And Anxiety: Tony Stark Is The New Captain America" May 06, 2013. Monkey See blog. National Public Radio. <http://www.npr.org/blogs/monkeysee/2013/05/06/181560276/armor-and-angst-tony-stark-is-the-new-captain-america>. Accessed September 7, 2014.

Iron Man. Writ. Mark Fergus, Hawk Ostby, Art Marcum, and Matt Holloway. Dir. Jon Favreau. Marvel Studios, 2008. Film.

Lord of The Rings: Fellowship of the Ring. Writ. Fran Walsh, Philippa Boyens and Peter Jackson. Dir. Peter Jackson. 2001. Film.

Man of Steel. Writ. David S. Goyer. Dir. Zack Snyder. Warner Bros. 2013. Film.

Marvel's Avengers. Writ. and Dir. Joss Whedon. Marvel Studios, 2012. Region 1 DVD.

Palmer, Brian. "Before Hitler, Who Was the Stand-In for Pure Evil?" *Slate*. <http://www.slate.com/articles/briefing/explainer/2011/10/hank_williams_jr_firing_who_was_the_rhetorical_worst_person_in_h.html>. October 4, 2011. Accessed September 21, 2014.

Palmer, Landon. "Egos Assemble: The Tortured, Exaggerated Masculinity of 'The Avengers.'" <http://filmschoolrejects.com/features/egos-assemble-the-tortured-exaggerated-masculinity-of-the-avengers-lpalm.php>. May 8, 2012. Accessed September 14, 2014.

"Primeval" 4.21. Writ. David Fury. Dir. James Contner. *Buffy*.

Spinakos, Tony. "Gods, Beasts, and Political Animals: Why the Avengers Assemble." In *The Avengers and Philosophy*. Ed. Mark White. 98-112. Hoboken, N.J.: Wiley, 2012.

Walzer, Michael. *Just and Unjust Wars: A Moral Argument with Historical Illustrations*. 3rd. ed. New York: Basic, 1977.

Watchmen. Writ. David Hayter and Alex Tse. Dir. Zack Snyder. Legendary Pictures, DC Comics, Cruel and Unusual Films, and Lawrence Gordon Productions, 2009. Film.

Whedon, Joss. Commentary on *Marvel's Avengers* DVD. 2012.

"Wild at Heart" 4.6. Writ. Marti Noxon. Dir. David Grossman. *Buffy*.

Woerner, Meredeth. "Joss Whedon Dissects the Family Dynamic of the Avengers." <http://io9.com/5906755/joss-whedon-dissects-the-family-dynamic-of-the-avengers>. May 1, 2012. Accessed September 22, 2014.

Woerner, Meredith. "Joss Whedon says Captain America and Iron Man won't be pals in his 'Avengers'" <http://io9.com/5595293/will-joss-whedons-avengers-movie-include-marvels-civil-war-we-asked-him>. July 24, 2010. Accessed September 22, 2014.

Zero Dark Thirty. Writ. Mark Boal. Dir. Kathryn Bigelow. AnnaPurna Pictures, 2012. Film.

8.05

Cheeky Heroines, Girls in Refrigerators, Wit, and Slapstick:
Much Ado's Place in the Whedon Canon
Valerie Estelle Frankel

Buffy is famous for subverting gender roles, but among Shakespeare's many plays, *Much Ado About Nothing* particularly does so as well—it's no accident that Whedon chose that particular work to produce. *Much Ado* offers Beatrice—a mouthy, aggressive heroine who doesn't transform into a submissive wife like Kate in *Taming of the Shrew* or die like Cleopatra. She doesn't even disguise as a boy to find power like Rosalind or Viola. She remains wittily uncompromising through the story, much like Buffy. Hero, the sweet girl next door with daisies in her hair, does not fare as well and comes across more like *Doctor Horrible*'s Penny, sacrificed in a conflict between the story's men. Still, with Whedon's beloved cast engaging in slap fights, cross-dressing, and even a tumble down the stairs, the humor of the play is pure Whedon, through and through.

THE WITTY HEROINE

As the spokesman of the Watcher's Council puts it, "A slayer is not just physical prowess. She must have cunning, imagination, a confidence derived from self-reliance" ("Helpless" 3012). These are Buffy's defining traits and also Beatrice's, as the two use witty insults to disarm their opponents.

BENEDICK: What, my dear Lady Disdain! Are you yet living?

BEATRICE: Is it possible disdain should die while she hath such meet food to feed it as Signior Benedick? Courtesy itself must convert to disdain, if you come in her presence. (I.i.72–74)

BUFFY: I may be dead, but I'm still pretty. Which is more than I can say for you. ("Prophecy Girl" B1012).

Both statements assert the young women's power while putting down the opponent. Their male opponents are not as witty as they; by losing the conflict of wits, they have on some level lost the larger conflict as well. "In a culture that for decades had told young women to be soft-spoken, always tactful, deferential to men, and thus to self-censor their feelings and desires, hearing an adolescent girl mouth off like this to powerful males was, yes, liberating," Susan J. Douglas notes about Buffy in *Enlightened Sexism* (90). Hearing Beatrice "mouth off" in her far more patriarchal society is just as unexpected and delightful. She's "'a pleasant-spirited lady,' full of merry mischief and feeling no restraint that should prevent her from indulging her love of banter to the utmost," as Shakespeare critic William J. Rolfe comments (235).

Both heroines also critique their opponents' dialogue in delightfully self-aware moments:

BEATRICE: In our last conflict four of his five wits went halting off, and now is the whole man governed with one: so that if he have wit enough to keep himself warm, let him bear it for a difference between himself and his horse. (I.i.38–40)

BUFFY: That's it? That's all I get? One lame-ass vamp with no appreciation for my painstakingly thought-out puns. I don't think the forces of darkness are even trying. ("Wild at Heart" B5006)

More than engaging in simple insults, Buffy understands her role as chosen one, responding to frequent comments that she's "just a girl" with persistence and heart. Elana Levine explains in "*Buffy* and the 'New Girl Order:*" "Though her speech is sprinkled with girlish slang, her incisive taunts at demons and her insightful one-liners to her friends reveal a bravura and maturity far beyond girlhood" (178). Beatrice is likewise quite astute, manipulating Benedick and revealing that Claudio is seething with jealousy. With an even deeper level of self-awareness, both women give other characters their "lines," insisting on directing the action around them. If the men must play the parts given them, the heroines are the scriptwriters:

BEATRICE: Speak, count, 'tis your cue… Speak, cousin; or, if you cannot, stop his mouth with a kiss, and let not him speak neither. (II.i.204–209)

BUFFY: You ever heard the expression, "biting off more than you can chew?" Okay. Um, how 'bout the expression, "Vampire Slayer?" … Okay, how about, "Oh, God, my leg, my leg?" (He attacks her and she breaks his leg.)

VAMPIRE: Oh, God, my leg!

BUFFY: See, now we're communicating. ("The Gift," B5022)

When *Buffy* began, Whedon commented, "If I can make teenage boys comfortable with a girl who takes charge of a situation without their knowing that's what happening, it's better than sitting down and selling them on feminism" (Bellafante). Shakespeare's agenda in *Much Ado* parallels this—Beatrice has only one scene of angry rhetoric about her limited gender options. Instead, she spends the story as a sparkling example of female empowerment: she weds the man she wants and defends her cousin Hero from the slanders of her fiancé Claudio. In particularly stand-out moments, both heroines reject the patriarchies in their lives—when the desirable prince Don Pedro proposes to Beatrice, she irreverently turns him down. Likewise, after disclosing her plans to never marry, Beatrice actually counsels her cousin to ignore her father's marriage plans for her in front of Hero's father Leonato, saying:

It is my cousin's duty to make curtsy and say "Father, as it please you." But yet for allthat, cousin, let him be a handsome fellow, or else make another curtsy and say "Father, as it please me." (II.i.34–36)

Buffy, who slays evil patriarchs like Ted or the Master, Mayor, and Judge, "mutinies" against the Watcher's Council at her graduation. Later, she demands the Council work for her, ordering: "You're gonna tell me everything you know. Then you're gonna go away" ("Checkpoint" 5012). Their leader Quentin Travers helplessly agrees. Beatrice achieves her own outrageous demands—she and her cousin both wed the men they choose. The prince and Claudio beg forgiveness and do penance at Hero's grave all night while she watches, then receive another comeuppance at Hero's trick wedding that follows. And Beatrice remains delightfully mouthy.

DISTRESSED DAMSELS

Hero and Claudio's romance is much more conventional, with exaggerated (yet mildly subversive) traditional roles, more a *Doctor Horrible* take on gender than a *Buffy* one. In a nutshell, Hero's character exists to affect the men of the story—Claudio and Leonato personally, Don Pedro and his evil brother Don John politically. Her faked death, too, is a spectacle used to guilt the story's men, as Penny's actual death is for Horrible. This trope, coined "Women in Refrigerators" by writer Gail Simone, is found in many classically male stories, especially superhero comics. The *Encyclopedia of Comic Books and Graphic Novels* defines it as "the use of the death or injury of women characters as a plot device to stir the male hero into action," and Penny and Hero are textbook examples, as are Jenny Calendar or Chloe the Potential on *Buffy* (Booker 261). When the girlfriend is sacrificed in order to teach the hero a lesson, her flimsiness as a character becomes apparent. Her plot lacks growth or personal achievement—her only purpose is to spur transformation in the stronger characters around her.

In *Doctor Horrible,* Penny is a pawn caught between the two superheroes—Captain Hammer's romance with her is presented as a strike at his nemesis rather than a product of his affection. As he smirks: "You got a little crush, don't you, Doc? Well that's gonna make this hard to hear. ... I'm gonna give Penny the night of her life, just because you want her. And I get what you want." Don John's sidekick Borachio similarly promises, "Proof enough to misuse the prince, to vex Claudio, to undo Hero and kill Leonato" (II.ii.18–19). The men are the real targets here.

While Horrible appears to sincerely love Penny, he idealizes her, emphasizing that she's more image than independent character. Before ever speaking to her, he does all his deeds to "show her." Even his Freeze Ray, a device for (in his mind) freezing Penny and her movements in place, is a way of objectifying her, by literally transforming her into a statue. Hammer too assesses her as "Cute, huh? Sort of a quiet, nerdy *thing*. Not my usual, but nice" (my emphasis). After stealing her from Horrible, he displays her like a possession for public appreciation. Alyson Buckman explains in "'Go ahead! Run away! Say it was Horrible!': *Dr. Horrible's Sing-Along Blog* as Resistant Text":

Hammer... embarrasses Penny with his declaration that they "totally had sex" and that she is his "long-term girlfriend," sparking her decision to leave the stage she shares with him at the opening of the homeless shelter. Hammer doesn't even notice. His assertion of heterosexual prowess and power is defining him at this moment. (22)

Claudio is not much better, especially when speaking to Act One's cynical Benedick. He notes of Hero, "In mine eye she is the sweetest lady that ever

I looked on" (I.i.113). Two references to sight suggest he doesn't mean her personality. It's not surprising that Benedick sarcastically responds to the objectification:

BENEDICK: Would you buy her, that you inquire after her?
CLAUDIO: Can the world buy such a jewel?
BENEDICK: Yea, and a case to put it into. (I.i.108–110)

Hero's frilly bedroom, complete with a big-eyed doll, emphasizes her helpless role. She's always seen with daisy earrings, a childish flower worn by vapid young Buffy before she's chosen in "Becoming" (B2022). At her failed wedding, she wears a thin crumpled daisy wreath, rather than more expensive or grownup flowers. In the text, Hero manages a few pitiful protests as Claudio accuses her of infidelity, but Whedon has expunged most of them. When blamed, his Hero only mutely shakes her head and erupts in loud whimpers—her cousin is the one to lunge at Claudio. Villainous Don John, in a daisy tie himself like her satanic date, munches one of the childish wedding cupcakes on his way out. He's done his part in gobbling her up.

Completing the "girls in refrigerators" trope, Penny dies, trusting Hammer will save her. In fact, her faith is as misplaced as Hero's—both of their men have discarded them. In fact, Hero's plight is underscored by the similar abandonment of the helpless pawn Margaret, her maid, and Whedon's gender-flipped Conrade, now Don John's lover as well as lackey. The look on all three women's faces when learning their men have skipped town says it all.

While Penny's story ends here, Hero survives to take back her agency. "Whedon loves to build up men's belief in their own masculinity and power, and then trap them in it when they are outclassed by the (usually much more powerful) women in his narratives," notes critic Lilian DeRitter (191). At her own funeral, then at her second wedding, Hero makes Claudio publicly humble himself as he humbled her, before she reveals she is still alive. When she reappears, she stands tall and powerful in a fresh white gown without the taint of infidelity. Claudio half-kneels before her, and she holds his head as if blessing him. She appears a powerful saint risen from the dead, as she gives what feels like her first self-assured speech in the entire story. She's taken back a piece of her own plot, though the action quickly returns to her cousin.

A particularly poignant anticlimax, usually trimmed from stage and film adaptations, features the maid Margaret after Borachio's betrayal. In the film, she comes off as wary and wistful rather than with her traditional bawdiness as she jokes with Benedick and wheedles a sonnet from him. She has not magically recovered from her emotional upheaval, but in Whedon fashion is deeply wounded. At last, she sadly notes, "Give us [women] the swords; we have bucklers of our own" (V.ii.11). While the original character speaks with cheerful innuendo, Whedon's clearly has learned self-defense for her heart, though too late. Directly after, Whedon cuts the line in which Benedick warns, "They are dangerous weapons for maids," in preference of letting the empowered line stand alone (V.ii.12). There is no perfect ending for Margaret, a second victim of the men's plotting.

GENDER FLIPPING

As always, Whedon presents atypical gender roles. His Benedick lies on a ruffled white bed surrounded by paper butterflies and a dollhouse, staring dreamily at photos of his beloved—a more classic pose for the girl of the relationship. When he thanks his mother for bringing him up, Benedick tries on a woman's hat, briefly showing kinship with women, even as he rails against them. While other Shakespeare plays like *Taming of the Shrew* emphasize man's rulership over woman, Benedick defines manliness as genteel chivalry, noting that a "manly wit… will not hurt a woman" (V.ii.9). Whedon's character takes things a step further and sings in falsetto to woo Beatrice, complete with a howling dog for accompaniment. Accentuating this less-than-manly performance is the actor's previous role: in *Buffy*, Alexis Denisof played Wesley Wyndam-Price, the helpless joke of a Watcher most often heard yelping and screaming "like a woman," until Faith and Cordy both nickname him "princess." Unlike many stage and film Benedicks, Denisof shaves off his beard mid-story, emasculating himself to be more attractive to Beatrice, who quips, "He that hath no beard is less than a man" (II.i.26).

The leading men of *Buffy* are similarly famous for breaking gender norms—Giles sings as a hobby and admits he and Dawn "ate cookie dough and talked about boys" ("I Was Made to Love You" B5015). Spike watches *Passions* with Buffy's mom and wears a female slayer's coat. In her definitive *Sex and the Slayer*, Lorna Jowett comments, "Spike is sensitive not only in that he is easily hurt but also in the 'feminine' way of being attuned to situations, relationships, and underlying emotions, as his frequently perceptive comments demonstrate" (161). He is the one to beg for an emotional commitment as Buffy insists on using him for sex. Xander, as the only young male Scooby (aside from Oz and Riley's temporary participation), fares no better. He is the token "other gender," often kidnapped by predatory females and rescued by Buffy in a subversion of gender roles.

Buffy, by contrast, is the breadwinner and protector of her small nuclear family, especially in the later seasons. She fires a rocket launcher at the sinister Judge, and even as Red Riding Hood, carries a basket of weapons. Whedon's Beatrice, in similar fashion, is seen toying with knives repeatedly, and her dress is covered in sharp-edged fish as often as flowers. Determined to smash her way out of the role to which she's condemned, Beatrice rages, "O God, that I were a man! I would eat [Claudio's] heart in the market-place" (IV.i.285–286). With Leonato no longer challenging Claudio to a duel in this adaptation, Beatrice is Hero's sole champion. Buffy of course protects all the lost children and young women of the series, from Anne (B3001) to the defenseless children in "Killed by Death" (B2018) or "Band Candy" (3006), until she finds a new mission as Dawn's defender.

THE ACTORS

Fans of Whedon's other works get a few particular delights: Wesley and Fred, the star-crossed lovers from *Angel*, end the movie in a happily-ever-after at last. Other characters, too, have arcs that cleverly echo their previous Whedon roles. Reed Diamond, the prince, once played the all-powerful head of security in *Dollhouse*, in both cases publically shamed by the helpless-looking heroine. Manipulative Leonato, with most of the events out of his hands, has a similar job as the paternal Agent Coulson of S.H.I.E.L.D. Don John is an inverted mirror of Sean Maher's Simon Tam: pompous, wealthy, and controlled as Simon is, but silkily seducing his sidekick in a way poor Simon would envy as he babbles to Kaylee about cow fetuses.

The campy captain of *Firefly* rules over a different group of misfits. Andrew Wells (Tom Lenk) from *Buffy* is hilarious as Nathan Fillion's buddy-cop sidekick, because he's playing the same role he played previously—adjunct and sounding board for an arrogant minor character with delusions of grandeur. The comic relief characters take strong roles in the play as they do in *Buffy*: Don John and Borachio maneuver Claudio and the Prince much like the season six Trio does Buffy. And it's the Neighborhood Watch, goofy as the Trio, who manage to uncover the plot. "What your wisdoms could not discover, these shallow fools have brought to light," Borachio notes (V.i.132–134). Fillion and Lenk exchange mutual "that's us!" smirks at this label. As Dogberry, Fillion gets in a slap fight with Conrade, puts on the wrong jacket, and locks his keys in the squad car, hamming up his role in a campy version that reflects his roles on *Doctor Horrible*, *Firefly*, and *Castle*.

While Riki Lindhome, the alluring blonde Conrade, was briefly a student on Buffy's "Him" (B7006), *Much Ado's* Margaret and Hero are both cast from *Avengers*. Whedon explains:

What happened was Jillian [Morgese] was in the last couple of days [of *The Avengers*, playing woman in restaurant], right when I was forming the idea [of *Much Ado*], as an extra. And I noticed her. She actually introduced herself. She's not unmemorable. She was one of the waitresses and Ashley [Johnson] who plays Margaret was the other. But I kept sort of throwing more and more stuff at her. I'd go: "OK, now you're terrified, now you're running over here." She ended up having a stunt double on *The Avengers* because I kept blowing things up around her. And she could really bring it. (*"Much Ado About Nothing, Joss Whedon Interview"*)

In addition, Ashley Johnson, Waitress Beth, was also Wendy the Waitress in *Dollhouse's* "Omega" (D1012), kidnapped so Alpha can imprint a new personality on her helpless body. She's another victim, exploited by "Eddie the Prince" in the *Dollhouse* unaired pilot. Each time, she's been cast as the lower-class everywoman, open to abuse by powerful men.

Fran Kranz, once the mastermind Topher who was disastrously oblivious to the consequences of his inventions, plays a similar role as Claudio, destroying his bride with angry words. Topher is the most immature character in *Dollhouse*, "a brilliant, unapologetic geek, socially awkward and arrogant" (Jones 79). His relationships are comprised of Bennett Halverson, whom he admires for her disabled arm but never achieves a relationship with and the doll Sierra, imprinted as an asexual buddy to share his junk food and video games. In *Cabin in the Woods*, he plays the story's unstable loner. In Claudio's pointy-eye mask at the ball, Kranz appears more of a Robin than a Batman; he appears even dorkier while spying on his beloved with a snorkel and a martini. As such, he offers Claudio a youthfulness along with naive cluelessness and terribly dopy looks of confusion.

FINAL THOUGHTS

Hero and the immature, faithless Claudio are not guaranteed a happily-ever-after, though unlike Jenny Calendar or Penny, Hero returns from her refrigerator death. Beatrice, however, chooses the life she wants and goes after it, albeit with help from her friends. Keeping her lively sense of fun, she is not "tamed" like the shrew but instead weds a man who secretly adores "My Lady Tongue." This is the female empowerment play of the Shakespeare canon, and as such, it's a fitting match for Whedon.

Works Cited

Bellafante, Gina. "Bewitching Teen Heroines." *Time*. 5 May 1997. 82–84.

Booker, M. Keith, ed. "Feminism." *Encyclopedia of Comic Books and Graphic Novels. Volume 1*. USA: Greenwood, 2010.

Buckman, Alyson. "'Go ahead! Run away! Say it was Horrible!': *Dr. Horrible's Sing-Along Blog* as Resistant Text" Slayage 8.1. http://slayageonline.com/PDF/Buckman.pdf

DeRitter, Lilian. "We're Not Men" *Inside Joss' Dollhouse,* ed. Jane Espenson. Dallas, TX: BenBella, 2010. 79–94.

Douglas, Susan J. *Enlightened Sexism*. New York: Henry Holt and Co., 2010.

Jones, Andrew Zimmerman. "The Redemption of Topher Brink." *Inside Joss' Dollhouse,* ed. Jane Espenson. Dallas, TX: BenBella, 2010. 79–94.

Jowett, Lorna. *Sex and the Slayer: A Gender Studies Primer for the Buffy Fan*. Middletown, CT: Wesleyan University Press, 2005.

Levine, Elana. "*Buffy* and the 'New Girl Order': Defining Feminism and Femininity." *Undead TV: Essays on* Buffy the Vampire Slayer, ed. Elana Levine and Lisa Parks. Durham, NC: Duke University Press, 2007. 168–189.

Whedon, Joss. "Much Ado About Nothing, Joss Whedon Interview" *Indie London* 2013. http://www.indielondon.co.uk/Film-Review/much-ado-about-nothing-joss-whedon-interview.

8.06
"I've Never Met Anyone I Didn't Disappoint":
In Your Eyes' Flaws and Fortes

Curtis A. Weyant

"Joss Whedon has taken a page from Beyoncé's… playbook," Ryan Reed announced on *Rolling Stone*'s website on April 21, 2014. No, he wasn't comparing Whedon's *Angel* cameo as Numfar the dancing Pylean (2.21) to one of Beyoncé's derriere-shaking performances. Rather, Reed was referring to the surprise digital release of *In Your Eyes*, which premiered the day before at the 2014 Tribeca Film Festival. After the film's first screening, the festival audience was treated to a prerecorded announcement by Whedon: "It's not just the premiere of the film; it is the worldwide release date," he said, adding that *Eyes* was now available for streaming rental from video-on-demand service Vimeo.

The unexpected release of new material from the writer and director of *The Avengers* (2012) stirred up industry and mainstream news sites, blogs, and social media. Reed wasn't the only one to note the similarity between Whedon and Beyoncé, and director Brin Hill made the connection explicit: "We've been watching that evolution, and there's something really cool about a brand like Joss or a brand like Beyoncé doing that, just dropping it on you" (Truitt). During the Tribeca question-and-answer period, producer Michael Roiff admitted, "We always wanted to do something different with it" by "taking it straight to" the audience (Reed), and Whedon's announcement affirmed the aim of wanting "to explore yet another new form of distribution."

Then, three and a half weeks after *Eyes* premiered, an article appeared on *Buzzfeed* detailing a "reverse kickstarter" by the movie's production team, who had been sending various gifts to a small sample of people who rented the movie (Vary). Again, bloggers and reporters praised Whedon for "another brilliant and unconventional move" (Mason) and for "embracing digital business models and treating fans with an unmatched level of awesomeness" (Geigner). Within a month of *Eyes'* release, the movie had seemingly gathered all the requisite ingredients for blowout indie success: new content written by an acclaimed, popular storyteller; a maverick distribution method that delivered instant gratification; and a fan-love campaign that went viral without any prompts from the producers.

So why, then, by September 2014, just four months after *In Your Eyes'* scintillating debut, had all but the die-hardiest Whedon fans apparently forgotten about this movie?

"NOTHIN' YOU DO COULD SURPRISE ME"

Throughout his career, Whedon has cultivated a reputation for sneak-attack storytelling and acknowledging conventions only to then subvert them. So when the wily writer does something in real life that resembles one of his stories' twists, it's easy to get caught up in the very Whedonness of it. By announcing *Eyes'* digital release immediately after its first screening at Tribeca, Whedon offered fans a taste of what his characters must feel like in a happy pivotal plot moment. There was a slight buildup with the release of a three-minute preview of *Eyes* by *Entertainment Weekly* on April 17 (Gocobachi), but before that, media mentions were limited to a handful of casting notices and regional stories about the filming two years earlier. The film's release as a download was a surprise to nearly everyone, including Tribeca programmers, whom Roiff notified a few days before. Roiff has insisted that the decision to announce at a "more traditional film festival setting," rather than potential venues like Comic-Con, was due to the nature of the story rather than theatrics (Masters). However, it's easy to think that Whedon—who once scripted high school students throwing off their commencement gowns to reveal medieval weaponry (*Buffy* "Graduation Day, Part Two" 3.22)—also found some artistic satisfaction in lifting eyebrows at such a "traditional" setting. Bellwether Pictures co-founder Kai Cole has stated, "It was always the plan to release *In Your Eyes* in a new and exciting way" (Bernstein), and the surprise announcement was certainly a major part of that newness and excitement.

Except digital distribution isn't all that new. Roiff acknowledges discussing "Louis CK, and Aziz [Ansari], and Jim Gaffigan, and all these comedians who've done things like this," adding that the $5 pricing was explicitly modeled after such examples (Masters). Nor was *Eyes*' digital distribution unique within the Tribeca context: three other films timed digital releases near festival screenings, including *Beneath the Harvest Sky*, *Bright Days Ahead*, and *The Bachelor Weekend* (Buckley). None of these other movies received the amount of attention that *In Your Eyes* did, and columnist Mark Tomkins wonders, "Would it have even registered on the critics' Next Big Thing Richter Scale if it wasn't for [Whedon's] more mainstream successes?" Roiff agrees, "I think it wouldn't be possible" to achieve similar results with a film *not* tied to the creator of *The Avengers*, and even with Whedon's name behind it, he adds, "it's not a completely repeatable event" (Masters)—which may be why most indie filmmakers continue to follow the more traditional festival route. The festival circuit helps filmmakers generate "buzz" about their independent projects, and ideally the publicity leads to distribution deals that facilitate more lucrative theater, digital, and home-media releases. Therefore, filmmakers generally submit their films to a variety of festivals in the hopes of prompting more press, winning more awards, and gaining more attention to their work.

The first Bellwether Pictures production, *Much Ado About Nothing*, took that route. After premiering at the Toronto International Film Festival on September 8, 2012, *Much Ado* was picked up by Lionsgate, and plans to release the film theatrically emerged almost immediately ("Toronto 2012"). Even with the distribution deal, Whedon and team continued taking *Much Ado* to festivals in early 2013, shifting their goals from finding a distributor to generating excitement for the upcoming theatrical release. Along the way the film picked up some awards, garnered more reviews, and received increased exposure. In contrast, the *In Your Eyes* team—including Hill, Roiff, and co-stars Zoe Kazan and Michael Stahl-David—had no need to secure a distribution deal at Tribeca, because an agreement with Vimeo had been inked six weeks earlier (Vary). At the festival, the cast and production staff still made the usual appearances and participated in customary press interactions, but after the event, promotional efforts lost focus. Within about a week, chatter about *Eyes'* surprise announcement died down, both in the media and by the film's own makers. In particular, for a movie relying solely on a digital, web-based distribution model, there was an uncanny lack of social media marketing to support the launch: Brin Hill is the only member of the cast or production team who promoted the movie after April on any social media platform. Screenwriter John August sums up *Eyes'* social media effort: "While I got a lot of tweets about it, I didn't sense the universe going apeshit over this movie."

Of course, social media isn't the only way to market something. In the three weeks following *Eyes'* online launch, Roiff led a gift-sending effort, the story of which went viral on May 15 (Vary). Like the initial announcement, the tactic received generally positive reports. "By gifting a small and somewhat random number of viewers of a small film," assessed Timothy Geigner, "suddenly you have a flurry of attention being paid where otherwise there might be little." Like most flurries, however, it was over quickly, and four months after *In Your Eyes* debuted online there was very little discussion about the movie. The critics who had anything to say about it had done so, and the small stream of reviews had dried up. This was a shame because, while *In Your Eyes* is not Whedon's best creative expression, there's still a place for it among the rest of his works. To find that place, it's time to look beyond the launch and explore the story itself.

"MAYBE THERE'S A SIDE OF ME YOU DON'T SEE"

Critics of *In Your Eyes* have received the film with mixed feelings. Those who like the movie often point to one or two problems, such as the acting or cinematography, while those who dislike it typically point to one or two strengths, such as the acting or cinematography. The specific concerns called out by each critic differ, but three commonly identified problems are its simplicity, the awkwardly public communication between Rebecca Porter (Zoe Kazan) and Dylan Kershaw (Michael Stahl-David), and Rebecca's lack of agency. Without dismissing critics' concerns completely, it is possible to see that *In Your Eyes* has more depth than these critiques allow.

Some reviewers have complained that *In Your Eyes* lacks Whedon's signature genre bending. In an undated interview before the movie's release, Zoe Kazan described the film as "Joss Whedon does Nicholas Sparks," and critics latched onto the comparison to grumble about the film's simplicity and adherence to romance movie tropes, ignoring the actress's immediate addendum, "I mean, not really, it's not sentimental in that way" (McCracken). Strangely, many critics have noted the film's lack of sentimentality, employing the word "earnest" as something of a double entendre that indicates the movie's genuineness while ascribing to it the sin of being uncomplicated. For example, Jason Bailey calls *Eyes* "weirdly earnest, its preposterous premise perched on the edge of accidental parody," and Matt Barone says the movie is "earnestly made and finely acted," adding "[a]nyone who's not a Whedon apologist, however, will likely roll his or [her] eyes more than an optometry patient." Others have described it as "earnest, and sometimes saccharine" (Rodriguez), "earnest and heartfelt, sometimes to a fault" (Dunn), and even, perhaps paradoxically, "earnestly sentimental" (Taylor). This confusion between earnestness and its opposite suggests that many critics don't consider the movie's tone—that very earnestness they mention even while they shunt it aside—as a contrast to the typically preposterous, eye-rolling, saccharine sentimentality of Sparksian romance films. Such assessments fail to recognize that Whedon's best genre-busting occurs alongside his most earnest storylines, such as the climax of Buffy and Angel's romantic relationship in the second season of *Buffy*. Angel losing his soul and psychologically torturing Buffy in "Innocence" (2.14) would lack its gut-wrenching impact if the characters were anything less than genuine in both the slow-build seasonal arc of their bonding as well as the in-the-moment excitement that leads to the consummation of their passion ("Surprise" 2.13). While *Eyes* does not feature soul loss, it shares with *Buffy* a theme of finding true connection. Given the commonly cynical view of romances as mawkish and inauthentic, the universally acknowledged earnestness of *Eyes* becomes itself a subversion of the romance genre. But perhaps "subversion of tone" is too amorphous and ambiguous to redeem *In Your Eyes* in critics' eyes.

Other reviewers have taken Whedon to task for specific plot-driven flaws, with several people suggesting that the film would have been better had Rebecca and Dylan used phones every time they talked with each other. "In fact," Alexandria Malloy argues, "half the problems the characters deal with in the movie would have been avoided if the two had simply stuck a headset on their ear and pretended to be on the phone instead of chatting with a voice in their heads." Angie Han contends that "in the real world, it also would've been easy for Dylan and Rebecca to head [their] issues off at the pass by pretending to speak into a Bluetooth headset or at least waiting to talk until they were in private." To the contrary, during nearly every conversation at least one of the main characters is in private or someplace where they are unlikely to be noticed talking. Furthermore, one or the other uses (or pretends to use) a phone in at least five separate on-screen instances: during their first conversation when a passing woman gives Rebecca a dirty look; later that night, when Rebecca's husband Philip (Mark Feuerstein) walks into the office; when Rebecca is parked at the mechanic; during a musical montage as Rebecca passes her friend Diane (Jennifer Grey); and while Dylan surreptitiously describes the patrons of the bar he frequents. More important than whether the characters use phones to disguise their conversations, however, is the progression their communication undergoes, from self-conscious concealment to oblivious and unembarrassed engagement, such as dancing while Dylan's boss and Rebecca's husband respectively look on. A few critics have likened the main characters' relationship to "a perpetual FaceTime conversation" (Fine) or a "chat-room romance" (Strout), but such descriptions miss the mark. The story is not about two people talking, but about how they become so engrossed with each other because of their shared connection—which goes well beyond verbal communication—that everything else becomes unimportant. If there is anything cringe-worthy about this sort of behavior, it is its mimicry of real life, not inadequate plot devices. The follies of new love are many, and keeping them hidden from others is hard. Myopic as their actions may be, Rebecca and Dylan engage in the sort of dependent addiction that many people experience at some point in their lives. If there is a criticism with such mania, it lies well outside the portrayal in this particular movie.

The lack of cell phone appearances is a minor point compared with the criticism that Rebecca has little or no agency. "Whedon used to give us girls who could save the world," Sady Doyle writes, but "this time around, he gives us a girl who can't even save herself without her boyfriend pumping step-by-step instructions into her head." It's true that Rebecca doesn't have the physical strength of a Slayer like Buffy or Faith (*Buffy*, *Angel*), the confidence of a space pirate like Zoe (*Firefly*), or even the mental resilience of a doll like Echo (*Dollhouse*). However, it seems strange to criticize a woman, even a fictional one, for not fitting into a mold created by other women, even fictional ones, especially if the core criticism is that she should break out of a mold. Dylan feeds Rebecca some advice about car maintenance and picking locks, which certainly helps her to differing degrees, but these instances don't imply that Rebecca is helpless or that she doesn't help Dylan in similar ways. While playing solitaire, Rebecca refuses Dylan's suggestion that she cheat, saying, "It's no fun to cheat; it's no fun if you win," further eschewing Dylan's claim that she's only honest because she's afraid of getting caught. When in the next scene Dylan's friends Bo and Lyle try to entice him into resuming his former criminal occupation, Dylan seems ready to accept the job until Lyle asks, "Who's ever gonna know?" Dylan suddenly realizes that someone else *will* know, and his jibe at Rebecca about being afraid of getting caught gets turned on himself. Later, Dylan drunkenly reiterates that fear when he asks, "What am I gonna do when she finds out that I'm just like everybody said?" Dylan may give Rebecca knowledge and encouragement to help save a few dollars and escape a locked room, but between those events, Rebecca's honesty—a core character trait that she refuses to change to satisfy Dylan's taunts—becomes the model by which Dylan changes *his* character. This sort of strength aligns very well with the strengths of Willow in the early seasons of *Buffy*, Kaylee in *Firefly*, and most particularly with Fred in *Angel*, whose immediate backstory includes five years as a slave in a demon dimension ("Belonging" 2.19 and "Over the Rainbow" 2.20). During Rebecca's escape, Dylan remotely teaches her how to pick the lock on her room door, a much less (if at all) agency-eroding action than Simon's infiltration of Alliance laboratories to free River (*Serenity*), considering Rebecca still has to physically pick the lock herself. Furthermore, once she's free, Rebecca navigates the facility on her own, dodging orderlies and maintaining presence of mind to grab a coat to disguise herself. To Dylan's surprise, she even punches Philip when she finds him in the reception area. Dylan's coordinating instructions that help them find each other are balanced by the directions Rebecca earlier gave him while simultaneously effecting her own escape. Other than the lockpicking tutorial, the only substantial help Dylan gives Rebecca is to pull her onto the train. Just like Buffy needs a little help from Xander to shut a stuck door when Jesse and a band of vampires attempt to kill them ("The Harvest" 1.2), Rebecca needs a little help climbing up. She was able to run fast enough to keep up with the train, and she even makes multiple attempts to climb on, almost but not quite succeeding. The significance here is not that Rebecca is weak and needs help, but that she is strong—and still needs help. More than any commentary about equality or gender stereotypes, this is the thread that runs through all Whedon stories: even the strongest of us needs help sometimes, and true strength lies in forging connections so that we never have to rely solely on our own inadequate capabilities.

"THIS IS WHERE THEY PUT ME, BECAUSE THIS IS WHERE THEY SEE ME"

These counterpoints are not meant to imply that *In Your Eyes* is flawless, or even that points raised by critics can be fully resolved. However, they show that it's worth taking a deeper look at this story as something more than a passing curiosity because of its novel distribution method and unique gifting campaign. For those not convinced, then perhaps a shift in view will help.

Although filmed in 2012, *In Your Eyes* was first written 20 years earlier in 1992 (IMDb), the same year that the movie *Buffy the Vampire Slayer* debuted. Without providing authoritative confirmation of this date, Whedon has acknowledged that *Eyes* came from "an old script of mine" (Jamieson). Kazan further supports the script date in two interviews. In one instance, she addresses the perceived lack of cell phone use: "The truth is that Joss wrote this movie in 1992 or something. It was a long ass time ago before there were cell phones" (Topel). Elsewhere she notes, "Joss wrote this pre-*Sleepless* [*in Seattle* (1993)], and he tabled this when that movie came out" (Kramer). If that date is correct, then the movie precedes the "chat-room romances that were just hitting the mainstream around the mid-90s" (a group that presumably includes another Nora Ephron blockbuster, *You've Got Mail* [1998]), rather than being derived from them (Strout). It also means that *In Your Eyes* was written on the cusp of a change from the coming-of-age romances that dominated the mid-to-late 1980s—including *Footloose* (1984), *Dirty Dancing* (1987), and many stories starring either Molly Ringwald or John Cusack—to 1990s films featuring the more complex romantic problems of young adulthood, such as Ephron's works along with *The Bodyguard* (1993), *Jerry Maguire* (1996), and even *Titanic* (1997). Dating *In Your Eyes*' script at the crux of these two periods in romantic movie history shows that Whedon had identified a need for something new in the genre before many others had done so. Even if some of the themes, settings, and characterizations in the final movie, as produced two decades later, seem outdated or cliché to critics, Whedon's status as a genre-bending writer at the time the original script was penned remains intact.

More importantly, the script of *In Your Eyes* precedes nearly all of the work for which Whedon is known and praised. Receiving it as an early Whedon story opens opportunities for comparisons to "later" works, which further developed themes found in *Eyes*. Reluctance, and perceived inability, to leave abusive romantic relationships is explored in various ways within episodes like *Buffy*'s "Beauty and the Beasts" (3.4), "I Was Made to Love You" (5.4), and "Dead Again" (6.13); *Angel*'s "In the Dark" (1.3) and "She" (1.13); *Firefly*'s "Shindig" (1.4); and *Dollhouse*'s "Belonging" (2.4), among others. Questions about the sanity of people who experience their world differently from others due to special skills or powers work their way into "Normal Again" and "Help" (*Buffy* 6.17, 7.4), "Objects in Space" (*Firefly* 1.14), and the character arcs of both Alpha and Topher in *Dollhouse*. River

Tam experiences empathic powers in *Firefly* and *Serenity*, while the brief but intense visions sent by The Powers That Be in *Angel* serve to direct the Angel Investigations team to people who need help, with explicit references to the importance of making connections in episodes such as "Lonely Hearts" (1.2). Perhaps one of the most interesting expansions of this theme is "I Only Have Eyes for You" (*Buffy* 2.19), which culminates in a multilayered confrontation between Buffy and Angelus, who empathically (through possession) see, feel, and re-enact the final homicidal moments of a relationship between a teacher and student 43 years earlier, commenting tacitly and explicitly on topics such as gender roles, age difference, covetousness, insecurity, and other romantic complications. Even for those who believe *In Your Eyes* does not work in 2014, at the very least it demonstrates that Whedon was considering such themes much earlier than the TV series and movies that later made him famous.

In Your Eyes deserves to find its acknowledged place among the rest of Joss Whedon's stories, not only for the light it sheds on his other work, but in its own right as a creative endeavor. It won't ever be considered his best work, but to have it linger forgotten, as it has in the time since its launch at the Tribeca Film Festival, would be a loss. It is possible to glean both enjoyment and enlightenment from this satisfactory-but-flawed tale, and in the end that's really all we can ask of any story.

Works Cited

August, John. "Full Whedoncé." johnaugust.com. 5 May 2014. Web.

Bailey, Jason. "Is Joss Whedon's 'In Your Eyes' Worth Your $5?" *Flavorwire*. 21 April 2014. Web.

Barone, Matt. "Tribeca: Joss Whedon's Beyoncé-Like Power Movie is, Sadly, Not 'Beyoncé'-Level Good." *Complex*. 22 April 2014. Web.

"Belonging." 2.19. Writ. Shawn Ryan. Dir. Turi Meyer. *Angel*.

Bernstein, Paula. "Joss Whedon Film 'In Your Eyes' Released Online Following Tribeca Film Festival Premiere." *Indiewire*. 21 April 2014. Web.

Buckley, Cara. "Tribeca Film Festival: Joss Whedon Fans Get a Surprise." Arts Beat. *The New York Times*. 20 April 2014.

Doyle, Sady. "Joss Whedon Proves He Can Create Weak Female Characters." *In These Times*. 25 April 2014. Web.

Dunn, Tom. "The Light, the Heat of Joss Whedon's In Your Eyes." *Tor.com*. 24 April 2014. Web.

Fine, Marshall. "The week in movies: Tribeca Film Festival 2014." *Hollywood and Fine*. 22 April 2014. Web.

Geigner, Timothy. "Joss Whedon Shows How Being Awesome Rewards Creators." *Tech Dirt*. 16 May 2014. Web.

"Graduation Day, Part Two." 3.22. Writ., dir. Joss Whedon. *Buffy the Vampire Slayer*.

Gocobachi, Pamela. "Joss Whedon's 'In Your Eyes': Watch the gripping first three minutes before Tribeca." *Entertainment Weekly: Inside Movies*. 17 April 2014.

Han, Angie. "Joss Whedon-Penned 'In Your Eyes' Smacks of Wasted Potential." /Film. 25 April 2014.

In Your Eyes. Writ. Joss Whedon. Dir. Brin Hill. Bellwether Pictures, 2014.

InYourEyesMovie.com. n.d. Web.

"In Your Eyes (2014)." *The Internet Movie Database*. IMDb.com, Inc. n.d. Web.

"Innocence." 2.14. Writ., dir. Joss Whedon. *Buffy the Vampire Slayer*.

Jamieson, Teddy. "Too much of a good thing?" *The Herald*. 17 February 2013. Web.

Kramer, Gary M. "'I hate the word "quirky"': Zoe Kazan on being an indie starlet." Salon.com. 16 May 2014.

Malloy, Alexandria. "'In Your Eyes' In Review." *The Daily Geekette*. 28 April 2014. Web.

Mason, Will. "Joss Whedon's 'Reverse Kickstarter' is a Success." *Mason's Musings*. 2 July 2014. Web.

Masters, Kim. "Producer Michael Roiff." *The Business*. KCRW. 2 June 2014. Web.

McCracken, Kristin. "Zoe Kazan Talks Twin Roles Of 'The Pretty One' & How 'In Your Eyes' Is 'Like Joss Whedon Does Nicholas Sparks.'" *The Playlist*. Indiewire. 21 February 2014. Web.

"Over the Rainbow." 2.20. Writ. Mere Smith. Dir. Fred Keller. *Angel*.

Reed, Ryan. "Joss Whedon Pushes 'In Your Eyes' to Vimeo On Demand." *Rolling Stone*. 21 April 2014. Web.

Rodriguez, Cain. "Watch: Trailer For Joss Whedon Penned, Supernatural Romance 'In Your Eyes.'" *The Playlist*. Indiewire. 29 April 2014. Web.

Strout, Justin. "In Your Eyes (NR)." *Colorado Springs Independent*. 7 May 2014. Web.

"Surprise." 2.13. Writ., dir. Joss Whedon. *Buffy the Vampire Slayer*.

Taylor, Drew. "Tribeca Review: Joss Whedon's 'In Your Eyes' Gamely Fluctuates Between Sappy And Sincere." *The Playlist*. Indiewire. 21 April 2014. Web.

"The Harvest." Writ. Joss Whedon. Dir. John T. Kretchmer. *Buffy the Vampire Slayer*.

"Through the Looking Glass." 2.21. Writ., dir. Tim Minear. *Angel*.

Tomkins, Mark. "Will Beyoncé-style stunt by Avengers director reinvent the movie industry?" *Marketing Blogs*. 22 April 2014. Web.

Topel, Fred. "Tribeca 2014: Zoe Kazan and Michael Stahl David on In Your Eyes." *Crave Online*. 22 April 2014. Web.

"Toronto 2012: Joss Whedon's 'Much Ado About Nothing' Goes to Lionsgate." *Indiewire*. 11 September 2012. Web.

Truitt, Bryan. "Whedon releases new film 'In Your Eyes' online." *USA Today*. 20 April 2014. Web.

Vary, Adam B. "Joss Whedon's Crazy Reverse Kickstarter." *Buzzfeed*. 15 May 2014. Web.

Whedon, Joss. "A Special Announcement." *Vimeo*. Bellwether Pictures, 2014. Web.

APPENDICES

A.01
The Verses Go On:
15 Years of Whedon Studies
Alysa Hornick

A lot has happened in the oeuvre of Joss Whedon since I first sat down to write an earlier version of this essay for the first edition of this book. Then, *The Cabin in the Woods* was languishing in the MGM vaults, *Much Ado About Nothing* had been shot in secret but not yet announced, and a little movie called *The Avengers* was still being eagerly anticipated by theatergoers. Ultimately, *Cabin*, produced and co-written by Whedon with director Drew Goddard, would go on to create rather vigorous debate about the state and future of the horror genre, *Much Ado* would bolster Whedon's credentials as an adapter of Shakespeare, and *The Avengers* became one of the highest-grossing films of all time, making its director a household name in the process. Many journalists have referred to 2012 as the Year of the Whedon. But for Whedon scholars, it all goes back to 1999.

1999 was a memorable year for me. It was the year that I graduated from high school and went off to university. It was also the year that, on television, Buffy Summers did the same, taking Whedon's little show about the teenage vampire slayer away from its roots as a metaphor for adolescence and into the even more complicated world of adulthood. Even then, I felt that Buffy's journey, fantastic though it may be, paralleled my own. But where Buffy wasn't cut out for scholarly pursuits, I was just beginning to learn all about how exciting and valuable those very pursuits could be. As a freshman browsing through the university library, I discovered something else that had happened in 1999: Rhonda Wilcox published her first essay on *Buffy the Vampire Slayer*.

"'There Will Never Be a 'Very Special' Buffy': *Buffy* and the Monsters of Teen Life," which appeared in *Journal of Popular Film & Television* (27.2 [1999]: 16–23), was not the first serious article to be written about *Buffy*. In fact, it was not even the only one in that publication. What is was, however— perhaps along with Michael Adams' first "Slayer Slang" articles in *Verbatim: The Language Quarterly* from about the same time (24.3 [1999]: 1–4; and 24.4 [1999]: 1–7)—was the first real volley of sustained academic interest in Joss Whedon. Wilcox would go on to become one of the most respected and productive figures in a field that has since come to be known as Whedon

Studies. Within a few years, there were remarkable numbers of monographs and edited collections, graduate theses, book chapters, journal articles, web sites, conference sessions, and even entire conferences dedicated exclusively to exploring Whedon's work, and to the worlds that he has created, lovingly referred to as the Whedonverse(s).

Back when Buffy and I were both in high school, although I had already developed an interest in cinema studies and in certain film directors, it never would have occurred to me to think about a television show as having a driving creative force, like Whedon. Now 15 years have passed, TV studies has finally begun to earn its place in the ivory tower, and with each new project that Joss Whedon undertakes, whatever the format, interest continues unabated. Buffy and I grew up together, though if she were real she would probably call me a geek and blanch at my subsequent passion for *Firefly*, rapt anticipation of *Avengers* [2]: *Age of Ultron*, and general love of the stuff created by some self-proclaimed fanboy. If you are reading this book, you are probably enough like me in spirit that you don't need an explanation as to why Whedon is so beloved. But unlike me, you may not have spent these years happily devouring as much analysis as you could get your hands on and rigorously trying to keep track of it all—the sum total of which has colonized virtually every academic discipline. Therefore, in this essay I humbly attempt to introduce the uninitiated to some of the best scholarship and resources produced in the past 15 years of Whedon Studies.

Wilcox's work is a good place to begin, and without question one of the best. Her 2005 monograph *Why Buffy Matters: The Art of Buffy the Vampire Slayer* (Tauris) comprises 12 essays, most of which had previously been delivered as conference papers around the world, providing an outstanding, elegantly written overview of Wilcox's varied work on *Buffy*. The book is divided into two sections: "Panorama," with discussions of larger themes such as symbolism, myth, identity, heroism, sexuality, and globalization; and "Tight Focus," with close readings of individual episodes, each through a particular lens such as Laughter (examining Xander's character in Season 3's "The Zeppo") or Poetry (comparing Season 4's "Restless" to T.S. Eliot's *The Waste Land*). *Why Buffy Matters* makes it easy to see, well, why *Buffy* matters, and also why Wilcox is one of the biggest guns.

Another big gun is David Lavery, with whom Wilcox co-edited *Fighting the Forces: What's at Stake in Buffy the Vampire Slayer* (Rowman & Littlefield, 2002). Along with Roz Kaveney's *Reading the Vampire Slayer: An Unofficial Critical Companion to Buffy and Angel* (Tauris, 2001; 2nd edition 2004), this was one of two more or less concurrently compiled collections offering an incredible variety of viewpoints and establishing most of the primary disciplines from which further work would springboard. Patricia Pender's "'I'm Buffy and You're... History': The Postmodern Politics of *Buffy the Vampire Slayer*" (*Fighting* 35–44), for example, was among the first to address how the show deliberately plays with a number of so-called binaries in order to undermine them all. Kaveney's "'She Saved the World. A Lot': An Introduction to the Themes and Structures of *Buffy* and *Angel*" (*Reading* [2004] 1–82) is just what it says, but in a way that should make it required reading. I've also found Boyd Tonkin's "Entropy as Demon: Buffy in Southern California" (*Reading* [2004] 83–99) to be a useful exemplar of how postmodern writings on Whedon's work can be, drawing as it does from many different disciplines to get at the ultimately coherent points that it makes about the Buffyverse's representations of "So Cal."

A more recent book from Lavery is his 2014 monograph *Joss Whedon, A Creative Portrait: From Buffy the Vampire Slayer to Marvel's The Avengers* (Tauris). More a chronological study of Whedon's creative development than a traditional biography, this is a wonderful book for both novices and long-term fans. Lavery's approach is very fresh and quite apropos to his subject, and his writing is as fun and accessible as it is smart and well-researched. Wilcox, Lavery, Tanya R. Cochran, and Cynthea Masson also co-edited 2014's *Reading Joss Whedon* (Syracuse University Press), a large and stellar collection of scholarly work. It will be of interest to serious academics, but the majority of the essays are written in a manner that should be just as appealing to mainstream readers, provided said readers come with their brains ready to engage. This collection is also a testament to the editors, who establish some cohesion via overall structure, presentation, and cross-referencing. Try as I might, I am finding it impossible to single out any particular essays in this book. It is almost tempting to suggest that if you read only one new collection of Whedon Studies essays, read this one.

But wait! I've gotten ahead of myself. Let's rewind back to when Wilcox and Lavery received so many excellent submissions for *Fighting the Forces* that they decided to found a journal, and thus *Slayage* was born on the web. *Slayage: The Online International Journal of Buffy Studies* began its life exclusively on the subject of *Buffy*, as is evidenced by its name, but in 2010 it was renamed *Slayage: The Journal of the Whedon Studies Association* (www. slayageonline.com). It fosters peer-reviewed scholarship on all of Whedon's work, and while it is widely regarded as a standard-bearer for seriousness in the field, it certainly hasn't lost its sense of playfulness. *Slayage* will soon pass its 14th birthday and its 40th issue. I can hardly begin to address the depth and breadth of all the material that's been published in its virtual pages, so I'll just mention that I'm especially fond of issue 3.3–4 (2003). I still have my old marked-up printouts of Elizabeth Rambo's "'Lessons' for season 7 of *Buffy the Vampire Slayer*," Brett Rogers and Walter Scheidel's "Driving Stakes, Driving Cars: California Car Culture, Sex, and Identity in *BtVS*," and Stevie Simkin's two articles on anxious masculinity in *Buffy*: "'You hold your gun like a sissy girl,'" and "'Who died and made you John Wayne?'" (all in *Slayage* 3.3–4). I'll also be forever grateful to Matthew Pateman's special issue on aesthetics (6.2 [2006]), for articles such as Leigh Clemons' "Real Vampires Don't Wear Shorts: The Aesthetics of Fashion in *Buffy the Vampire Slayer*," which will be of great use to anyone wondering about the uses and abuses of clothing styles within the world of the show, and David Kociemba's "'Actually, it explains a lot': Reading the Opening Title Sequences of *Buffy the Vampire Slayer*," an analysis of how the show uses this little-studied facet of its production to make both subtle hints and grand statements about itself.

Since the official scope-change of *Slayage*, I've been quite impressed by many of the non-*Buffy* essays that have appeared, such as Eve Bennett's "Deconstructing the Dream Factory: Personal Fantasy and Corporate Manipulation in Joss Whedon's *Dollhouse*" in issue 9.1 (2011), Taylor Boulware's "'I Made Me': Queer Theory, Subjection, and Identity in *Dollhouse*" in issue 10.1 (2013), and the entirety of Kristopher Woofter and Jasie Stokes' special issue on *The Cabin in the Woods* (10.2/11.1 [2013–14]), in which I'd advise that interested readers first approach the editors' own "Once More into the *Woods*: An Introduction and Provocation" before deciding which essays to tackle next. I also greatly enjoyed K. Dale Koontz and Ensley Guffey's special issue collecting papers presented at the 2013 "Joss in June" conference (11.2/12.1 [2014]), in which my very-subjective favorites might be Sara Hays' "Tight Pants and Pretty Floral Bonnets: Outfitting the Outlaws of the 'Verse" and Masani McGee's "Big Men in Spangly Outfits: Spectacle and Masculinity in Joss Whedon's *The Avengers*." To conclude my effusive praise of *Slayage*, I'll mention that I am also indebted to older issues 1.3 (2001) and 3.1 (2003) for introducing Stacey Abbott with "A Little Less Ritual and a Little More Fun: The Modern Vampire in *Buffy the Vampire Slayer*" (1.3) and "Walking the Fine Line Between Angel and Angelus" (3.1), respectively. The first looks at the vampires of *Buffy* in the larger context of existing vampire genre and mythology, while the second looks more closely at the concept of the vampire with a soul, and sets the stage for Abbot's subsequent emergence as the foremost figure in *Angel* studies.

Reading Angel: the TV Spin-off With a Soul (Tauris, 2005), edited by Abbott, and the simply titled 2009 *Angel* monograph (Wayne State University Press) in which Abbott collects many of her own essays, are very much worth reading in tandem. I find that the two books combined offer the most thorough examination of *Angel* on its own merits and not just as an offshoot of the "main" *Buffy* narrative. My favorite non-Abbott essays in *Reading Angel* include Tammy A. Kinsey's "Transitions and Time: The Cinematic Language of *Angel*" (44–56), which is nearly as useful as a primer on televisual language in general as it is on this show, and Matt Hills and Rebecca Williams' "*Angel*'s Monstrous Mothers and Vampires with Souls: Investigating the Abject in 'Television Horror'" (203–17) just because I find themes of bodily abjection in the horror genre absolutely fascinating and love how they are explored here.

Because the Buffyverse remains one of Whedon's most famous, and *Buffy* is of course his largest complete canon text, it makes sense that most work has focused on *Buffy* and its direct spin-off, as Don Macnaughtan's *The Buffyverse Catalog: A Complete Guide to Buffy the Vampire Slayer and Angel in Print, Film, Television, Comics, Games and Other Media, 1992–2010* (McFarland, 2011) can attest. But it was Abbott's *Reading Angel*, I think, that best helped to firmly cement the notion that more of us could and should look beyond *Buffy* towards Whedon's other works, that they might prove just as fertile an inspiration for the critical mind. Also to prove worthwhile was the subsequent trend of focusing topically across multiple Whedonverses, and across previous scholarship, to reveal cohesive themes as well as what Lavery calls "key Whedonian signatures" (*Creative Portrait* 182–202).

Firefly aired on television, and was canceled, in the fall of 2002, and subsequently gained a strong enough following to merit a feature-length continuation, *Serenity*, in 2005. A few conference papers and two volumes of pseudo-scholarly work appeared between 2004 and 2007, but the first "real" serious publications are *Investigating Firefly and Serenity: Science Fiction on the Frontier* (Tauris, 2008) and a more or less contemporaneous *Slayage* special issue (7.1 [2008]), both edited by Wilcox and Cochran. Once again, it's difficult to choose any particular entries. Lorna Jowett's "Back to the Future: Retrofuturism, Cyberpunk and Humanity in *Firefly* and *Serenity*" (*Investigating* 101–13) is fairly awesome—as is most anything from Jowett. Also of note, J. Michael Richardson and J. Douglas Rabb's "Reavers and Redskins: Creating the Frontier Savage" (*Investigating* 127–38) and Agnes Curry's "'We Don't Say Indian': on the Paradoxical Construction of the Reavers" (*Slayage* 7.1) function as complementary companion pieces on the problematic racial connotations behind everyone's favorite violent cannibals.

Dollhouse, often regarded as the most troubling and troubled of Whedon's productions, has also earned a special treatment (no pun intended) in

Slayage, which provides a neat overview of scholarly concerns. Edited by Masson and Wilcox, this double issue (*Slayage* 8.2–3 [2010]), has room to be more inclusive of both familiar and new authors—which is great, because some of the less familiar provide some of the most fun essays: Renee St Louis and Miriam Riggs' "'A Painful, Bleeding Sleep': Sleeping Beauty in the Dollhouse" and, Lisa Perdigao's "'This one's broken': Rebuilding Whedonbots and Reprogramming the Whedonverse" are prime examples, because, honestly, who doesn't like to read about fairy tales and robots?

Two *Dollhouse* books have also appeared. The first, Jane Espenson and Leah Wilson's *Inside Joss' Dollhouse: from Alpha to Rossum* (Smart Pop [BenBella], 2010) seems less scholarly at a glance. Espenson is one of Whedon's co-scriptwriters, and only about half of the book's essays are penned by academics. These tend to be the more effective, if perhaps not the more approachable. Finding the right balance is Kate Rennebohm's prize-winning "'The Mind Doesn't Matter, It's the Body We Want': Identity and the Body in *Dollhouse*" (5–19), which works well as an entry point into *Dollhouse* scholarship, and one suspects it comes first in the book for precisely this reason. I also loved Julie Hawk's more challenging, book-ending "More Than the Sum of Our Imprints" (247–57), which uses an unusual demonstrative structure to frame multiple ideas about Echo's multiple selves, as well as our own in the real world, in a larger context. The second *Dollhouse* book, Sherry Ginn, Alyson R. Buckman, and Heather M. Porter's *Joss Whedon's* Dollhouse*: Confounding Purpose, Confusing Identity* (Rowman & Littlefield, 2014), takes a different overarching approach and might be too scholarly for most casual readers, but it does further the discourse on *Dollhouse* in a big way by featuring essays that bring up a wide variety of previously ignored questions. Some personal favorites, in order of appearance, are Ananya Mukherjea's "Somebody's Asian on TV: Sierra/Priya and the Politics of Representation" (65–80), which explores issues raised by the presentation of Sierra/Prita, portrayed by Nepali-Australian actor Dichen Lachman; Samira Nadkarni's "'In my house and therefore in my care': Transgressive Mothering, Abuse, and Embodiment" (81–96), which springboards from *Dollhouse* but looks at an upsetting pattern of abuse across multiple Whedon shows; and Bronwen Calvert's "'Who Did They Make Me This Time?': Viewing Pleasure and Horror" (113–26), which essentially looks at how the show's destabilization of different genre and performance conventions affects viewer response.

The first topical volumes to appear in Whedon Studies were still, of course, exclusively about *Buffy* and *Angel*, and these continue to appear with some regularity. Some great early examples include *Buffy and Philosophy: Fear and Trembling in Sunnydale*, edited by James South (Open Court, 2003) and Jowett's *Sex and the Slayer: A Gender Studies Primer for the Buffy Fan* (Wesleyan University Press, 2005). Some newer favorites are *The Literary Angel: Essays on Influences and Traditions Reflected in the Joss Whedon Series* (McFarland, 2010), edited by AmiJo Comeford and Tamy Burnett; *Music, Sound, and Silence in Buffy the Vampire Slayer* (Ashgate, 2010), edited by Paul Attinello, Janet Halfyard, and Vanessa Knights; and *Fan Phenomena: Buffy the Vampire Slayer* (Intellect, 2013), edited by Jennifer K. Stuller.

An ever more popular trend is to cross 'Verses and collect essays treating multiple canon texts. I have already gushed about *Reading Joss Whedon* (Syracuse University Press, 2014), which is an incredibly broad collection, but I would also recommend a few that are more narrowly focused. Koontz' *Faith and Choice in the Works of Joss Whedon* (McFarland, 2008) is among my favorites. It's divided into sections on purpose, family, redemption, and zealotry, and I found each one to be both sophisticated and compulsively readable even for those not usually as interested in these topics as in other fields. As if in anticipatory counterpoint to Koontz, Richardson and Rabb's *The Existential Joss Whedon* (McFarland, 2007) also reveals cohesive themes of a different sort, with avowed-atheist Whedon as moral philosopher independent of religious faith. More recently, Anthony R. Mills, John W. Morehead, and J. Ryan Parker's edited collection *Joss Whedon and Religion: Essays on an Angry Atheist's Explorations of the Sacred* (McFarland, 2013) covers some similar ground, but in different ways and with a notably palpable sense of fannish love throughout.

Although more heavily skewed towards *Buffy*, Erin B. Waggoner's collection *Sexual Rhetoric in the Works of Joss Whedon: New Essays* (McFarland, 2010) is also to be commended for its fresh takes on some new material as well as old themes and characters. Hélène Frohard-Dourlent and Lewis Call in "'Lez-faux' Representations: How *Buffy* Season Eight Navigates the Politics of Female Heteroflexibility" (31–47) and "Slaying the Heteronormative: Representations of Alternative Sexuality in *Buffy* Season Eight Comics" (106–16) respectively, are notable for their dissections of sexual politics in the *Buffy* Season Eight comics, which otherwise remain underrepresented as topics of study. Catherine Coker's essay, "Exploitation of Bodies and Minds in Season One of *Dollhouse*" (226–38) is important, as well, for its necessary reminder of how the exploitation of the "Dolls" in *Dollhouse* can be read as not entirely dissimilar to that embedded within the marketing strategies used to promote the show. These ideas all build indirectly on older critiques of *Buffy*, for example, and invite further development themselves.

Buffy, Ballads, and Bad Guys Who Sing: Music in the Worlds of Joss Whedon (Scarecrow, 2011), edited by Kendra Preston Leonard, is another that skews towards *Buffy*. But—quite possibly due, in part, to *Buffy*-fatigue—my favorite inclusions are actually Eric Hung's "The Meaning of 'World Music' in *Firefly*" (255–273), Leonard's "'The Status is not Quo': Gender and Performance in *Dr. Horrible's Sing-Along Blog*" (275–292), and Matthew Mills' "*Angel*'s Narrative Score" (173–208), all of which propulsively managed to teach me brand new things about how to more carefully listen to what I would otherwise simply watch.

And popping up in other places (or stealthily infiltrating, as I like to think of it), more essays abound for the studious and desirous. Some of these come from people already known and prolific in the community. Masson comes to mind, with Buffyverse essays such as "'Evil's Spreading Sir... And It's Not Just Over There': Nazism in *Buffy* and *Angel*" in Sara Buttsworth and Maartje Abbenhuis' *Monsters in the Mirror: Representations of Nazism in Post-War Popular Culture* (Praeger, 2010: 179–99). Others seem far more random. Everything from Kent Ono's "To Be a Vampire on *Buffy the Vampire Slayer*: Race and ('Other') Socially Marginalizing Positions on Horror TV" in Elyce Rae Helford's *Fantasy Girls: Gender in the New Universe of Science Fiction and Fantasy Television* (Rowman & Littlefield, 2000: 163–86)—the first, much-needed criticism ever to appear on the important subject of race-based othering in the Buffyverse—to Casey J. McCormick's "Making Sense of the Future: Narrative Destabilization in Joss Whedon's *Dollhouse*" in Melissa Ames' *Time in Television Narrative: Exploring Temporality in Twenty-first-century Programming* (University Press of Mississippi, 2012: 205–17). From Jennifer Hudson's "'She's Unpredictable': Illyria and the Liberating Potential of Chaotic Postmodern Identity" in *Magazine Americana: The American Popular Culture Magazine* (March 2005, web)—a strong piece among the rather few available about one of the most captivating and complicated characters of *Angel*'s final season—to Deanna Day's "Toward a Zombie Epistemology: What it Means to Live and Die in *Cabin in the Woods*" in *Ada: A Journal of Gender, New Media, & Technology* 3 (2013).

There have also been a couple of journals besides *Slayage* (and its undergraduate offshoot, the adorably titled *Watcher Junior*) brave and clever enough to dedicate entire issues to Whedon. Some of these have been upstart web journals with nonetheless impressive results (e.g., *Refractory: A Journal of Entertainment Media* 2 [2003] and *Water Cooler Journal* 2.3 [2014]), but established print journal *European Journal of Cultural Studies* went a radical step further and devoted an entire issue to one supporting character. Entitled *The Vampire Spike in Text and Fandom*, this special issue (8.3 [2005]) remains the only occurrence of such intense single-character focus, as far as I'm aware, and stands as a good argument that there should be more of it in future. Editors Dee Amy-Chinn and Milly Williamson include their own articles as well as four other weighty submissions, more than one of which link actor James Marsters' embodied performance with fannish investment in his character. I totally get it; I'm a Spike fan.

One need not be a hardcore fan or admirer of all work in which Whedon has had a hand in order to enjoy any one example or aspect of it. I'd wager that millions enjoyed *The Avengers* at the local multiplex without ever having routed for the little blonde girl in the dark alley, or having thought too deeply about the meaning behind it all. But for most people interested in Whedon Studies, love of *Buffy* is almost a prerequisite. Or perhaps *Firefly* instead, for a vocal minority. Buffy herself may not have excelled in academics but, for over 15 years, academics have sure gone crazy for her. Buffy was just the beginning, merely the iconic foundation upon which Whedon Studies was built. As long as Joss Whedon keeps producing work—and quite likely for a long time afterwards—we'll keep watching it, being challenged by it, sharing it, writing about it, and reading about it. Many articles have come out that I'm ashamed to admit I haven't read yet, so if you'll excuse me, I think I'll go get started on that.

A.02

Buffy the Vampire Slayer Episode List
Seven Seasons 1997-2003, 144 Episodes

Mary Alice Money

Season.number "Title" / Writer(s) / Director / Date of original telecast

Season 1, 1997 (as a mid-season replacement) on the WB: Monday 9:00-10:00

1.1 "Welcome to the Hellmouth" / Joss Whedon / Charles Martin Smith / 10 Mar. 1997

1.2 "The Harvest" / Joss Whedon / John T. Kretchmer / 10 Mar. 1997

1.3 "Witch" / Dana Reston / Stephen Cragg / 17 Mar. 1997

1.4 "Teacher's Pet" / David Greenwalt / Bruce Seth Green / 24 Mar. 1997

1.5 "Never Kill a Boy on the First Date" / Rob Des Hotel & Dean Batali / David Semel / 31 Mar. 1997

1.6 "The Pack" / Matt Kiene & Joe Reinkemeyer / Bruce Seth Green / 7 Apr. 1997

1.7 "Angel" / David Greenwalt / Scott Brazil / 14 Apr. 1997

1.8 "I Robot... You Jane" / Ashley Gable & Thomas A. Swyden / Stephen Posey / 28 Apr. 1997

1.9 "The Puppet Show" / Rob Des Hotel & Dean Batali / Ellen S. Pressman / 5 May 1997

1.10 "Nightmares" / Joss Whedon & David Greenwalt / Bruce Seth Green / 12 May 1999

1.11 "Out of Mind, Out of Sight" / Joss Whedon, Ashley Gable, & Thomas A. Swyden / Reza Badiyi / 19 May 1997

1.12 "Prophecy Girl" / Joss Whedon / Joss Whedon / 2 June 1997

Season 2, 1997-1998 on the WB: Monday 9:00-10:00 through 19 Jan. 1998; Tuesday 8:00-9:00 beginning 20 Jan

2.1 "When She Was Bad" / Joss Whedon / Joss Whedon / 15 Sep. 1997

2.2 "Some Assembly Required" / Ty King / Bruce Seth Green / 22 Sep. 1997

2.3 "School Hard" / David Greenwalt & Joss Whedon / John T. Kretchmer / 29 Sep. 1997

2.4 "Inca Mummy Girl" / Matt Kiene & Joe Reinkemeyer / Ellen S. Pressman / 6 Oct. 1997

2.5 "Reptile Boy" / David Greenwalt / David Greenwalt / 13 Oct. 1997

2.6 "Halloween" / Carl Ellsworth / Bruce Seth Green / 27 Oct. 1997

2.7 "Lie to Me" / Joss Whedon / Joss Whedon / 3 Nov. 1997

2.8 "The Dark Age" / Rob Des Hotel & Dean Batali / Bruce Seth Green / 10 Nov. 1997

2.9 "What's My Line?" (Part 1) / Howard Gordon & Marti Noxon / David Solomon / 17 Oct. 1997

2.10 "What's My Line?" (Part 2) / Marti Noxon / David Semel / 24 Nov. 1997

2.11 "Ted" / David Greenwalt & Joss Whedon / Bruce Seth Green / 8 Dec. 1997

2.12 "Bad Eggs" / Marti Noxon / David Greenwalt / 12 Jan. 1998

2.13 "Surprise" (Part 1 of 2) / Marti Noxon / Michael Lange / 19 Jan. 1998 -- *Monday*

2.14 "Innocence" (Part 2 of 2) / Joss Whedon / Joss Whedon / 20 Jan. 1998 -- *Tuesday*

2.15 "Phases" / Rob Des Hotel & Dean Batali / Bruce Seth Green / 27 Jan. 1998

2.16 "Bewitched, Bothered and Bewildered" / Marti Noxon / James A. Contner / 10 Feb. 1998

2.17 "Passion" / Ty King / Michael E. Gershman / 24 Feb. 1998

2.18 "Killed by Death" / Rob Des Hotel & Dean Batali / Deran Serafian / 3 Mar. 1998

2.19 "I Only Have Eyes for You" / Marti Noxon / James Whitmore, Jr. / 28 Apr. 1998

2.20 "Go Fish" / David Fury & Elin Hampton / David Semel / 5 May 1998

2.21 "Becoming" (Part 1) / Joss Whedon / Joss Whedon / 12 May 1998

2.22 "Becoming" (Part 2) / Joss Whedon / Joss Whedon / 19 May 1998

Season 3, 1998-1999 on the WB: Tuesday 8:00-9:00

3.1 "Anne" / Joss Whedon / Joss Whedon / 29 Sep. 1998

3.2 "Dead Man's Party" / Marti Noxon / James Whitmore, Jr. / 6 Oct. 1998

3.3 "Faith, Hope and Trick" / David Greenwalt / James A. Contner / 13 Oct. 1998

3.4 "Beauty and the Beasts" / Marti Noxon / James Whitmore, Jr. / 20 Oct. 1998

3.5 "Homecoming" / David Greenwalt / David Greenwalt / 3 Nov. 1998

3.6 "Band Candy" / Jane Espenson / Michael Lange / 10 Nov. 1998

3.7 "Revelations" / Douglas Petrie / James A. Contner / 17 Nov. 1998

3.8 "Lovers Walk" / Dan Vebber / David Semel / 24 Nov. 1998

3.9 "The Wish" / Marti Noxon / David Greenwalt / 8 Dec. 1998

3.10 "Amends" / Joss Whedon / Joss Whedon / 15 Dec. 1998

3.11 "Gingerbread" / Jane Espenson & Thania St. John / James Whitmore, Jr. / 12 Jan. 1999

3.12 "Helpless" / David Fury / James A. Contner / 19 Jan. 1999

3.13 "The Zeppo" / Dan Vebber / James Whitmore, Jr. / 26 Jan. 1999

3.14 "Bad Girls" / Douglas Petrie / Michael Lange / 9 Feb. 1999

3.15 "Consequences" / Marti Noxon / Michael Gershman / 16 Feb. 1999

3.16 "Doppelgängland" / Joss Whedon / Joss Whedon / 23 Feb. 1999

3.17 "Enemies" / Douglas Petrie / David Grossman / 16 Mar. 1999

3.18 "Earshot" / Jane Espenson / Regis Kimble / 21 Sep. 1999

   [Originally scheduled for 27 Apr.; WB delayed broadcast because of a plot parallel to the April 20 Columbine High School shootings, in Littleton, Colorado, in which two students murdered 12 students and a teacher and wounded many more, then killed themselves]

3.19 "Choices" / David Fury / James A. Contner / 4 May 1999

3.20 "The Prom" / Marti Noxon / David Solomon / 11 May 1999

3.21 "Graduation Day" (Part 1) / Joss Whedon / Joss Whedon / 18 May 1999

3.22 "Graduation Day" (Part 2) / Joss Whedon / Joss Whedon / 13 July 1999
[Originally scheduled for May 25; WB delayed broadcast because of tenuous similarities to Columbine]

Season 4, 1999-2000 on the WB: Tuesday 8:00-9:00 (before *Angel*, 9:00-10:00)
(This pairing, continued for three seasons, allowed frequent references and parallels in episodes on the same night as well as occasional crossovers and continued plots.)

4.1 "The Freshman" / Joss Whedon / Joss Whedon / 5 Oct. 1999

4.2 "Living Conditions" / Marti Noxon / David Grossman / 12 Oct. 1999

4.3 "The Harsh Light of Day" / Jane Espenson / James A. Contner / 19 Oct. 1999

4.4 "Fear, Itself" / David Fury / Tucker Gates / 26 Oct. 1999

4.5 "Beer Bad" / Tracey Forbes / David Solomon / 2 Nov. 1999

4.6 "Wild at Heart" / Marti Noxon / David Grossman / 9 Nov. 1999

4.7 "The Initiative" / Douglas Petrie / James A. Contner / 16 Nov. 1999

4.8 "Pangs" / Jane Espenson / Michael Lange / 23 Nov. 1999

4.9 "Something Blue" / Tracey Forbes / Nick Marck / 30 Nov. 1999

4.10 "Hush" / Joss Whedon / Joss Whedon / 14 Dec. 1999

4.11 "Doomed" / Marti Noxon, David Fury, & Jane Espenson / James A. Contner / 18 Jan. 2000

4.12 "A New Man" / Jane Espenson / Michael Gershman / 25 Jan. 2000

4.13 "The I in Team" / David Fury / James A. Contner / 8 Feb. 2000

4.14 "Goodbye Iowa" / Marti Noxon / David Solomon / 15 Feb. 2000

4.15 "This Year's Girl" (Part 1 of 2) / Douglas Petrie / Michael Gershman / 22 Feb. 2000

4.16 "Who Are You?" (Part 2 of 2) / Joss Whedon / Joss Whedon / 29 Feb. 2000

4.17 "Superstar" / Jane Espenson / David Grossman / 4 Apr. 2000

4.18 "Where the Wild Things Are" / Tracey Forbes / David Solomon / 25 Apr. 2000

4.19 "New Moon Rising" / Marti Noxon / James A. Contner / 2 May 2000

4.20 "The Yoko Factor" / Douglas Petrie / David Grossman / 9 May 2000

4.21 "Primeval" / David Fury / James A. Contner / 16 May 2000

4.22 "Restless" / Joss Whedon / Joss Whedon / 23 May 2000

Season 5, 2000-2001 on the WB: Tuesday 8:00-9:00 (before *Angel*, 9:00-10:00)

5.1 "Buffy vs. Dracula" / Marti Noxon / David Solomon / 26 Sep. 2000

5.2 "Real Me" / David Fury / David Grossman / 3 Oct. 2000

5.3 "The Replacement" / Jane Espenson / James A. Contner / 10 Oct. 2000

5.4 "Out of My Mind" / Rebecca Rand Kirshner / David Grossman / 17 Oct. 2000

5.5   "No Place Like Home" / Doug Petrie / David Solomon / 24 Oct. 2000

5.6   "Family" / Joss Whedon / Joss Whedon / 7 Nov. 2000

5.7   "Fool for Love" / Doug Petrie / Nick Marck / 14 Nov. 2000

5.8   "Shadow" / David Fury / Daniel Attias / 21 Nov. 2000

5.9   "Listening to Fear" / Rebecca Rand Kirshner / David Solomon / 28 Nov. 2000

5.10   "Into the Woods" / Marti Noxon / Marti Noxon / 19 Dec. 2000

5.11   "Triangle" / Jane Espenson / Christopher Hibler / 9 Jan. 2001

5.12   "Checkpoint" / Jane Espenson & Douglas Petrie / Nick Marck / 23 Jan. 2001

5.13   "Blood Ties" / Steven S. DeKnight / Michael Gershman / 6 Feb. 2001

5.14   "Crush" / David Fury / Daniel Attias / 13 Feb. 2001

5.15   "I Was Made to Love You" / Jane Espenson / James A. Contner / 20 Feb. 2001

5.16   "The Body" / Joss Whedon / Joss Whedon / 27 Feb. 2001

5.17   "Forever" / Marti Noxon / Marti Noxon / 17 Apr. 2001

5.18   "Intervention" / Jane Espenson / Michael Gershman / 24 Apr. 2001

5.19   "Tough Love" / Rebecca Rand Kirshner / David Grossman / 1 May 2001

5.20   "Spiral" / Steven S. DeKnight / James A. Contner / 8 May 2001

5.21   "The Weight of the World" / Douglas Petrie / David Solomon / 15 May 2001

5.22   "The Gift" / Joss Whedon / Joss Whedon / 22 May 2001

Season 6, 2001-2002 on UPN: Tuesday 8:00-9:00 (before *Angel*, 9:00-10:00 on the WB)

6.1   "Bargaining" (Part 1) / Marti Noxon / David Grossman / 2 Oct. 2001

6.2   "Bargaining" (Part 2) / David Fury / David Grossman / 2 Oct. 2001

6.3   "After Life" / Jane Espenson / David Solomon / 9 Oct. 2001

6.4   "Flooded" / Douglas Petrie & Jane Espenson / Douglas Petrie / 16 Oct. 2001

6.5   "Life Serial" / David Fury & Jane Espenson / Nick Marck / 23 Oct. 2001

6.6   "All the Way" / Steven S. DeKnight / David Solomon / 30 Oct. 2001

6.7   "Once More, With Feeling" / Joss Whedon / Joss Whedon / 6 Nov. 2001
       [UPN allowed this musical to run 8 extra minutes on the first telecast]

6.8   "Tabula Rasa" / Rebecca Rand Kirshner / David Grossman / 13 Nov. 2001

6.9   "Smashed" / Drew Z. Greenberg / Turi Meyer / 20 Nov. 2001

6.10   "Wrecked" / Marti Noxon / David Solomon / 27 Nov. 2001

6.11   "Gone" / David Fury / David Fury / 8 Jan. 2002

6.12   "Doublemeat Palace" / Jane Espenson / Nick Marck / 29 Jan. 2002

6.13   "Dead Things" / Steven S. DeKnight / James A. Contner / 5 Feb. 2002

6.14   "Older and Far Away" / Drew Z. Greenberg / Michael Gershman / 12 Feb. 2002

6.15   "As You Were" / Douglas Petrie / Douglas Petrie / 26 Feb. 2002

6.16   "Hell's Bells" / Rebecca Rand Kirshner / David Solomon / 5 Mar. 2002

6.17   "Normal Again" / Diego Gutierrez / Rick Rosenthal / 12 Mar. 2002

6.18   "Entropy" / Drew Z. Greenberg / James A. Contner / 30 Apr. 2002

6.19 "Seeing Red" / Steven S. DeKnight / Michael Gershman / 7 May 2002

6.20 "Villains" / Marti Noxon / David Solomon / 14 May 2002

6.21 "Two to Go" / Douglas Petrie / Bill Norton / 21 May 2002

6.22 "Grave" / David Fury/ James A. Contner / 21 May 2002

Season 7, 2002-2003 on UPN, Tuesday 8:00-9:00

Note that for a few brief, shiny months in late 2002, it was possible to watch *Angel* on Sunday, *Buffy* on Tuesday, and *Firefly* on Friday.

7.1 "Lessons" / Joss Whedon / David Solomon / 24 Sep. 2002

7.2 "Beneath You" / Douglas Petrie / Nick Marck / 1 Oct. 2002

7.3 "Same Time, Same Place" / Jane Espenson / James A. Contner / 8 Oct. 2002

7.4 "Help" / Rebecca Rand Kirshner / Rick Rosenthal / 15 Oct. 2002

7.5 "Selfless" / Drew Goddard / David Solomon / 22 Oct. 2002

7.6 "Him" / Drew Z. Greenberg / Michael Gershman / 5 Nov. 2002

7.7 "Conversations with Dead People" / Jane Espenson & Drew Goddard / Nick Marck / 12 Nov. 2002

7.8 "Sleeper" / David Fury & Jane Espenson / Alan J. Levi / 19 Nov. 2002

7.9 "Never Leave Me" / Drew Goddard / David Solomon / 26 Nov. 2002

7.10 "Bring on the Night" / Marti Noxon & Douglas Petrie / David Grossman / 17 Dec. 2002

7.11 "Showtime" / David Fury / Michael Grossman / 7 Jan. 2003

7.12 "Potential" / Rebecca Rand Kirshner / James A. Contner / 21 Jan. 2003

7.13 "The Killer in Me" / Drew Z. Greenberg / David Solomon / 4 Feb. 2003

7.14 "First Date" / Jane Espenson / David Grossman / 11 Feb. 2003

7.15 "Get It Done" / Douglas Petrie / Douglas Petrie / 18 Feb. 2003

7.16 "Storyteller" / Jane Espenson / Marita Grabiak / 25 Feb. 2003

7.17 "Lies My Parents Told Me" / David Fury & Drew Goddard / David Fury / 25 Mar. 2003

7.18 "Dirty Girls" / Drew Goddard / Michael Gershman / 15 Apr. 2003

7.19 "Empty Places" / Drew Z. Greenberg / James A. Contner / 29 Apr. 2003

7.20 "Touched" / Rebecca Rand Kirshner / David Solomon / 6 May 2003

7.21 "End of Days" / Douglas Petrie & Jane Espenson / Marita Grabiak 13 May 2003

7.22 "Chosen" / Joss Whedon / Joss Whedon / 20 May 2003

A.03

Angel Episode List
Five Seasons 1999-2004, 110 Episodes

Mary Alice Money

Season.number "Title" / Writer(s) / Director / Date of original telecast

Season 1, 1999-2000, on the WB: Tuesday 9:00-10:00 (following *BtVS*, 8-9)

1.1 "City Of" / David Greenwalt & Joss Whedon / Joss Whedon / 5 Oct. 1999

1.2 "Lonely Hearts" / David Fury / James A. Contner / 12 Oct. 1999

1.3 "In the Dark" / Douglas Petrie / Bruce Seth Green / 19 Oct. 1999

1.4 "I Fall to Pieces" / story Joss Whedon & David Greenwalt; teleplay David Greenwalt / Vern Gillum / 26 Oct. 1999

1.5 "Rm w/a Vu" / story David Greenwalt & Jane Espenson; teleplay Jane Espenson / Scott McGinnis / 2 Nov. 1999

1.6 "Sense and Sensitivity" / Tim Minear / James A. Contner / 9 Nov. 1999

1.7 "The Bachelor Party" / Tracey Stern / David Straiton / 16 Nov. 1999

1.8 "I Will Remember You" / David Greenwalt & Jeannine Renshaw / David Grossman / 23 Nov. 1999

1.9 "Hero" / Howard Gordon & Tim Minear / Tucker Gates / 30 Nov. 1999

1.10 "Parting Gifts" / David Fury & Jeannine Renshaw / James A. Contner / 14 Dec. 1999

1.11 "Somnambulist" / Tim Minear / Winrich Kolbe / 18 Jan. 2000

1.12 "Expecting" / Howard Gordon / David Semel / 25 Jan. 2000

1.13 "She" / David Greenwalt & Marti Noxon / David Greenwalt / 8 Feb. 2000

1.14 "I've Got You Under My Skin" / story David Greenwalt & Jeannine Renshaw; teleplay Jeannine Renshaw / R. D. Price / 15 Feb. 2000

1.15 "The Prodigal" / Tim Minear / Bruce Seth Green / 22 Feb. 2000

1.16 "The Ring" / Howard Gordon / Nick Marck / 29 Feb. 2000

1.17 "Eternity" / Tracey Stern / Regis B. Kimble / 4 Apr. 2000

1.18 "Five by Five" / Jim Kouf / James A. Contner / 25 Apr. 2000

1.19 "Sanctuary" / Tim Minear & Joss Whedon / Michael Lange / 2 May 2000

1.20 "War Zone" / Garry Campbell / David Straiton / 9 May 2000

1.21 "Blind Date" / Jeannine Renshaw / Thomas J. Wright / 16 May 2000

1.22 "To Shanshu in LA" / David Greenwalt / David Greenwalt / 23 May 2000

Season 2, 2000-2001, on the WB: Tuesday 9:00-10:00 (following *BtVS*, 8-9)

2.1 "Judgement" / story Joss Whedon & David Greenwalt; teleplay David Greenwalt / Michael Lange / 26 Sep. 2000

2.2 "Are You Now, or Have You Ever Been" / Tim Minear / David Semel / 3 Oct. 2000

2.3 "First Impressions" / Shawn Ryan / James A. Contner / 10 Oct. 2000

2.4 "Untouched" / Mere Smith / Joss Whedon / 17 Oct. 2000

2.5 "Dear Boy" / David Greenwalt / David Greenwalt / 24 Oct. 2000

2.6 "Guise Will Be Guise" / Jane Espenson / Krishna Rao / 7 Nov. 2000

2.7 "Darla" / Tim Minear / Tim Minear / 14 Nov. 2000

2.8 "The Shroud of Rahmon" / Jim Kouf / David Grossman / 21 Nov. 2000

2.9 "The Trial" / story David Greenwalt; teleplay Douglas Petrie & Tim Minear / Bruce Seth Green / 28 Nov. 2000

2.10 "Reunion" / Tim Minear & Shawn Ryan / James A. Contner / 19 Dec. 2000

2.11 "Redefinition" / Mere Smith / Michael Grossman / 16 Jan. 2001

2.12 "Blood Money" / Shawn Ryan & Mere Smith / R. D. Price / 23 Jan. 2001

2.13 "Happy Anniversary" / story Joss Whedon & David Greenwalt; teleplay David Greenwalt / Bill Norton / 6 Feb. 2001

2.14 "The Thin Dead Line" / Jim Kouf & Shawn Ryan / Scott McGinnis / 13 Feb. 2001

2.15 "Reprise" / Tim Minear / James Whitmore, Jr. / 20 Feb. 2001

2.16 "Epiphany" / Tim Minear / Tim Wright / 27 Feb. 2001

2.17 "Disharmony" / David Fury / Fred Keller / 17 Apr. 2001

2.18 "Dead End" / David Greenwalt / James A. Contner / 24 Apr. 2001

2.19 "Belonging" / Shawn Ryan / Turi Meyer / 1 May 2001

2.20 "Over the Rainbow" / Mere Smith / Fred Keller / 8 May 2001

2.21 "Through the Looking Glass" / Tim Minear / Tim Minear / 15 May 2001

2.22 "There's No Place Like Plrtz Glrb" / David Greenwalt / David Greenwalt / 22 May 2001

Season 3, 2001-2002, on the WB: Tuesday 9:00-10:00 (following *BtVS*, 8-9)

3.1 "Heartthrob" / David Greenwalt / David Greenwalt / 24 Sep. 2001

3.2 "That Vision Thing" / Jeffrey Bell / Bill Norton / 1 Oct. 2001

3.3 "That Old Gang of Mine" / Tim Minear / Fred Keller / 8 Oct. 2001

3.4 "Carpe Noctum" / Scott Murphy / James A. Contner / 15 Oct. 2001

3.5 "Fredless" / Mere Smith / Marita Grabiak / 22 Oct. 2001

3.6 "Billy" / Tim Minear & Jeffrey Bell / David Grossman / 29 Oct. 2001

3.7 "Offspring" / David Greenwalt / Turi Meyer / 5 Nov. 2001

3.8 "Quickening" / Jeffrey Bell / Skip Schoolnik / 12 Nov. 2001

3.9 "Lullaby" / Tim Minear / Tim Minear / 19 Nov. 2001

3.10 "Dad" / David H. Goodman / Fred Keller / 10 Nov. 2001

3.11 "Birthday" / Mere Smith / Michael Grossman / 14 Jan. 2002

3.12 "Provider" / Scott Murphy / Bill Norton / 21 Jan. 2002

3.13 "Waiting in the Wings" / Joss Whedon / Joss Whedon / 4 Feb. 2002

3.14 "Couplet" / Tim Minear & Jeffrey Bell / Tim Minear / 18 Feb. 2002

3.15 "Loyalty" / Mere Smith / James A. Contner / 25 Feb. 2002

3.16 "Sleep Tight" / David Greenwalt / Terrence O'Hara / 4 Mar. 2002

3.17 "Forgiving" / Jeffrey Bell / Turi Meyer / 15 Apr. 2002

3.18 "Double or Nothing" / David H. Goodman / David Grossman / 22 Apr. 2002

3.19 "The Price" / David Fury / Marita Grabiak / 29 Apr. 2002

3.20 "A New World" / Jeffrey Bell / Tim Minear / 6 May 2002

3.21 "Benediction" / Tim Minear / Tim Minear / 13 May 2002

3.22 "Tomorrow" / David Greenwalt / David Greenwalt / 20 May 2002

Season 4, 2002-2003, on the WB: 9:00-10:00 Sunday 2002, then 9:00-10:00 Wednesday 2003

4.1 "Deep Down" / Steven S. DeKnight / Terrence O'Hara / 6 Oct. 2002

4.2 "Ground State" / Mere Smith / Michael Grossman / 13 Oct. 2002

4.3 "The House Always Wins" / David Fury / Marita Grabiak / 20 Oct. 2002

4.4 "Slouching Toward Bethlehem" / Jeffrey Bell / Skip Schoolnik / 27 Oct. 2002

4.5 "Supersymmetry" / Elizabeth Craft & Sarah Fain / Bill Norton / 3 Nov. 2002

4.6 "Spin the Bottle" / Joss Whedon / Joss Whedon / 10 Nov. 2002

4.7 "Apocalypse, Nowish" / Steven S. DeKnight / Vern Gillum / 17 Nov. 2002

4.8 "Habeas Corpses" / Jeffrey Bell / Skip Schoolnik / 15 Jan. 2003

4.9 "Long Day's Journey" / Mere Smith / Terrence O'Hara / 22 Jan. 2003

4.10 "Awakening" / David Fury & Steven S. DeKnight / James A. Contner / 29 Jan. 2003

4.11 "Soulless" / Sarah Fain & Elizabeth Craft / Sean Astin / 5 Feb 2003

4.12 "Calvary" / Jeffrey Bell, Steven S. DeKnight, & Mere Smith / Bill Norton / 12 Feb. 2003

4.13 "Salvage" / David Fury / Jefferson Kibbee / 5 Mar. 2003

4.14 "Release" / Steven S. DeKnight, Elizabeth Craft, & Sarah Fain / James A. Contner / 12 Mar. 2003

4.15 "Orpheus" / Mere Smith / Terrence O'Hara / 19 Mar. 2003

4.16 "Players" / Jeffrey Bell, Elizabeth Craft, & Sarah Fain / Michael Grossman / 26 Mar. 2003

4.17 "Inside Out" / Steven S. DeKnight / Steven S. DeKnight / 2 Apr. 2003

4.18 "Shiny Happy People" / Elizabeth Craft & Sarah Fain / Marita Grabiak / 9 Apr. 2003

4.19 "The Magic Bullet" / Jeffrey Bell / Jeffrey Bell / 16 Apr. 2003

4.20 "Sacrifice" / Ben Edlund / David Straiton / 23 Apr. 2003

4.21 "Peace Out" / David Fury / Jefferson Kibbee / 30 Apr. 2003

4.22 "Home" / Tim Minear / Tim Minear / 7 May 2003

Season 5, 2003-2004, on the WB: Wednesday 9:00-10:00

5.1 "Conviction" / Joss Whedon / Joss Whedon / 1 Oct. 2003

5.2 "Just Rewards" / David Fury & Ben Edlund / James A. Contner / 8 Oct. 2003

5.3 "Unleashed" / Elizabeth Craft & Sarah Fain / Marita Grabiak / 15 Oct. 2003

5.4 "Hell Bound" / Steven S. DeKnight / Steven S. DeKnight / 22 Oct. 2003

5.5 "Life of the Party" / Ben Edlund / Bill Norton / 29 Oct. 2003

5.6 "The Cautionary Tale of Numero Cinco" / Jeffrey Bell / Jeffrey Bell / 5 Nov. 2003

5.7 "Lineage" / Drew Goddard / Jefferson Kibbee / 12 Nov. 2003

5.8 "Destiny" / David Fury & Steven S. DeKnight / Skip Schoolnik / 19 Nov. 2003

5.9 "Harm's Way" / Sarah Fain & Elizabeth Craft / Vern Gillum / 14 Jan. 2004

5.10 "Soul Purpose" / Brent Fletcher / David Boreanaz / 21 Jan. 2004

5.11 "Damage" / Steven S. DeKnight & Drew Goddard / Jefferson Kibbee / 28 Jan. 2004

5.12 "You're Welcome" / David Fury / David Fury / 4 Feb. 2004

5.13 "Why We Fight" / Drew Goddard & Steven S. DeKnight / Terrence O'Hara / 11 Feb. 2004

5.14 "Smile Time" / Joss Whedon & Ben Edlund / Ben Edlund / 18 Feb. 2004

5.15 "A Hole in the World" / Joss Whedon / Joss Whedon / 25 Feb. 2004

5.16 "Shells" / Steven S. DeKnight / Steven S. DeKnight / 3 Mar. 2004

5.17 "Underneath" / Sarah Fain & Elizabeth Craft / Skip Schoolnik / 14 Apr. 2004

5.18 "Origin" / Drew Goddard / Terrence O'Hara / 21 Apr. 2004

5.19 "Time Bomb" / Ben Edlund / Vern Gillum / 28 Apr. 2004

5.20 "The Girl in Question" / Steven S. DeKnight / David Greenwalt / 5 May 2004

5.21 "Power Play" / David Fury / James A. Contner / 12 May 2004

5.22 "Not Fade Away" / Jeffrey Bell & Joss Whedon / Jeffrey Bell / 19 May 2004

A.04

Firefly Episode List
One Season 2002, 11 Episodes plus
3 never aired Episodes
Mary Alice Money

Number in the order Whedon intended. "Title" / Writer(s) / Director / Date of original telecast

Season 1, 2002, on Fox: Friday 8:00-9:00

1. "Serenity" (Parts 1 and 2) / Joss Whedon / Joss Whedon / 20 Dec. 2002

2. "The Train Job" / Joss Whedon & Tim Minear / Joss Whedon / 20 Sep. 2002

3. "Bushwhacked" / Tim Minear / Tim Minear / 27 Sep. 2002

4. "Shindig" / Jane Espenson / Vern Gillum / 1 Nov. 2002

5. "Safe" / Drew Z. Greenberg / Michael Grossman / 8 Nov. 2002

6. "Our Mrs. Reynolds" / Joss Whedon / Vondie Curtis Hall / 4 Oct. 2002

7. "Jaynestown" / Ben Edlund / Marita Grabiak / 18 Oct. 2002

8. "Out of Gas" / Tim Minear / David Solomon / 25 Oct. 2002

9. "Ariel" / Jose Molina / Allan Kroeker / 15 Nov. 2002

10. "War Stories" / Cheryl Cain / James Contner / 6 Dec. 2002

11. "Trash" / Ben Edlund & Jose Molina / Vern Gillum / never aired

12. "The Message" / Joss Whedon & Tim Minear / Tim Minear / never aired

13. "Heart of Gold" / Brett Mathews / Thomas J. Wright / never aired

14. "Objects in Space" / Joss Whedon / Joss Whedon / 13 Dec. 2002

A.05

Dollhouse Episode List
Two Seasons 2009-2010, 27 Episodes

Mary Alice Money

Season.number "Title" / Writer(s) / Director / Date of original telecast

Season 1, 2009, on Fox: Friday 9:00-10:00

0.0 "Echo" / Joss Whedon / Joss Whedon / unaired pilot

1.1 "Ghost" / Joss Whedon / Joss Whedon / 13 Feb. 2009

1.2 "The Target" / Steven S. DeKnight / Steven S. DeKnight / 20 Feb. 2009

1.3 "Stage Fright" / Maurissa Tancharoen & Jed Whedon / David Solomon / 27 Feb. 2009

1.4 "Gray Hour" / Sarah Fain & Elizabeth Craft / Rod Hardy / 6 Mar. 2009

1.5 "True Believer" / Tim Minear / Allan Kroeker / 13 Mar. 2009

1.6 "Man on the Street / Joss Whedon / David Straiton / 20 Mar. 2009

1.7 "Echoes" / Elizabeth Craft & Sarah Fain / James Contner / 27 Mar. 2009

1.8 "Needs" / Tracy Bellomo / Félix Enríquez Alcalá / 3 Apr. 2009

1.9 "Spy in the House of Love" / Andrew Chambliss / David Solomon / 10 Apr. 2009

1.10 "Haunted" / Jane Espenson, Maurissa Tancharoen, & Jed Whedon / Elodie Keene / 24 Apr. 2009

1.11 "Briar Rose" / Jane Espenson / Dwight Little / 1 May 2009

1.12 "Omega" / Tim Minear / Tim Minear / 8 May 2009

1.13 "Epitaph One" / story by Joss Whedon; teleplay by Maurissa Tancharoen &
     Jed Whedon / Joss Whedon / [17 June 2009 Singapore; unaired in Region 1:
     USA and Canada]

**Season 2, 2009-2010, on Fox: Friday 9:00-10:00; three additional episodes
also 8:00-9:00 as noted below**

2.1　"Vows" / Joss Whedon / Joss Whedon / 25 Sep. 2009

2.2　"Instinct" / Michele Fazekas & Tara Butters / Marita Grabiak / 2 Oct. 2009

2.3　"Belle Chose" / Tim Minear / David Solomon / 9 Oct. 2009

2.4　"Belonging" / Maurissa Tancharoen & Jed Whedon / Jonathan Frakes /
     23 Oct. 2009

2.5　"The Public Eye" / Andrew Chambliss / David Solomon / 4 Dec. 2009 (8:00-9:00)

2.6　"The Left Hand" / Tracy Bellomo / Wendey Stanzler / 4 Dec. 2009

2.7　"Meet Jane Doe" / Maurissa Tancharoen & Jed Whedon & Andrew Chambliss /
     Dwight Little / 11 Dec. 2009 (8:00-9:00)

2.8　"A Love Supreme" / Jenny DeArmitt / David Straiton / 11 Dec. 2009

2.9　"Stop-Loss" / Andrew Chambliss / Felix Alcalá / 18 Dec. 2009 (8:00-9:00)

2.10 "The Attic" / Maurissa Tancharoen & Jed Whedon / John Cassaday / 18 Dec. 2009

2.11 "Getting Closer" / Tim Minear / Tim Minear / 8 Jan. 2010

2.12 "The Hollow Men" / Michele Fazekas, Tara Butters, & Tracy Bellomo /
     Terrence O'Hara / 15 Jan. 2010

2.13 "Epitaph Two: Return" / Maurissa Tancharoen, Jed Whedon, & Andrew Chambliss /
     David Solomon / 29 Jan. 2010

A.06

Marvel's Agents of S.H.I.E.L.D. Episode List
First Season 2013-2014, 22 Episodes
Mary Alice Money

Season.number "Title" / Writer(s) / Director / Date of original telecast

Season 1, 2013-2014, on ABC: Tuesday 8:00-9:00

1.1　"Pilot" / Joss Whedon, Jed Whedon, Maurissa Tancharoen / Joss Whedon /
     24 Sept. 2013

1.2　"0-8-4" / Maurissa Tancharoen, Jed Whedon, Jeffrey Bell / David Straiton /

1 Oct. 2013

1.3   "The Asset" / Jed Whedon, Maurissa Tancharoen / Milan Cheylov /
     8 Oct. 2013

1.4   "Eye Spy" / Jeffrey Bell / Roxann Dawson / 15 Oct. 2013

1.5   "Girl in the Flower Dress" / Brent Fletcher / Jesse Bochco / 22 Oct. 2013

1.6   "FZZT" / Paul Zbyszewsk / Vincent Misiano / 5 Nov. 2013

1.7   "The Hub" / Rafe Judkins, Lauren LeFranc / Bobby Roth / 12 Nov. 2013

1.8   "The Well" / Monica Owusu-Breen / Jonathan Frakes / 19 Nov. 2013

1.9   "Repairs" / Maurissa Tancharoen, Jed Whedon / Billy Gierhart / 26 Nov. 2013

1.10 "The Bridge" / Shalisha Francis / Holly Dale / 10 Dec. 2013

1.11 "The Magical Place" / Paul Zbyszewski, Brent Fletcher / Kevin Hooks /
     7 Jan. 2014

1.12 "Seeds" / Monica Owusu-Breen, Jed Whedon / Kenneth Fink / 14 Jan. 2014

1.13 "T.R.A.C.K.S." / Lauren LeFranc, Rafe Judkins / Paul Edwards / 4 Feb. 2014

1.14 "T.A.H.I.T.I." / Jeffrey Bell; Marvel Comics: Stan Lee, Jack Kirby / Bobby Roth /
     4 Mar. 2014

1.15 "Yes Men" / Shalisha Francis / John Terlesky / 11 Mar. 2014

1.16 "End of the Beginning" / Paul Zbyszewski / Bobby Roth / 1 Apr. 2014

1.17 "Turn, Turn, Turn" / Jed Whedon, Maurissa Tancharoen / Vincent Misiano /
     8 Apr. 2014

1.18 "Providence" / Brent Fletcher / Milan Cheylov / 15 Apr. 2014

1.19 "The Only Light in the Darkness" / Monica Owusu-Breen / Vincent Misiano
     / 22 Apr. 2014

1.20 "Nothing Personal" / Paul Zbyszewski, DJ Doyle / Billy Gierhart / 29 Apr. 2014

1.21 "Ragtag" / Jeffrey Bell / Roxann Dawson / 6 May 2014

1.22 "Beginning of the End" / Maurissa Tancharoen, Jed Whedon / David Straiton
     / 13 May 2014

A.07
Author Biographies

Abbott, Stacey

Stacey Abbott is a reader in film and television studies at the University of Roehampton. She is the author of *Celluloid Vampires* (2007) and *Angel: TV Milestone* (2009), and the editor of *Reading Angel: The TV Spin-off with a Soul* (2005) and *The Cult TV Book* (2010). She is the co-author, with Lorna Jowett, of *TV Horror: The Dark Side of the Small Screen* (2013) and is currently writing a book on the vampire and zombie in twenty-first century film and television. She is the series editor for the Investigating Cult TV series at I.B. Tauris and is president of the Whedon Studies Association (2014–16).

Anderson, Lisa

Lisa Anderson lives near Nashville, Tennessee. She has been writing about popular culture since she was in high school, when she reviewed films for the teen page of her local newspaper. She writes for Popshifter.com, a pop culture weblog and bi-monthly web magazine, where she was recently made a contributing editor. This is her third year participating in WhedonFest as a member of Whedonites United. Lisa became involved in fan activism because, to paraphrase Dr. Horrible, the world is a mess, and fans just... need to change it.

Bailey, Mike

Mike Bailey is a recent graduate of the University of North Florida where he received his Master's in Practical Philosophy and Applied Ethics. He presented his paper, "Choosing Your Fate: Existentialism in the Buffyverse" for the Comics and Popular Arts Conference, Dragon*Con 2010. He's been a Whedon fan since the *Buffy* movie in 1992. He watched all of his shows as they aired, and is fascinated by the ease in which Whedon explores philosophical ideas and themes in his works.

Barton, Kristin

Kristin M. Barton is an assistant professor of communication at Dalton State College in Dalton, GA. He graduated from Florida State University in 2007 with a Ph.D. in communication. His previous work has examined the effects of watching reality TV shows such as *Survivor* and *American Idol*. His recent work includes an essay in the edited volume *Investigating Heroes: Essays on Truth, Justice and Quality TV* (McFarland, 2012) as well as *The Big Damn Firefly & Serenity Trivia Book* (BearManor Media, 2012), which explores Joss Whedon's beloved series and film in intricate detail.

Berger, Laura

Laura Berger is a Master of Arts candidate in English at McMaster University. She completed an M.A. in Popular Culture at Brock University. Laura began watching *Buffy* when she was 11 years old; at 22, she wrote her thesis on the series. She is honoured to have her writing included in this anthology. Laura's upcoming work includes a project on professional wrestling and a joint paper with Keri Ferencz examining Universal Orlando's *The Wizarding World of Harry Potter*.

Brettauer, Kevin

Kevin M. Brettauer is a screenwriter/director who currently resides in Santa Monica, California. He has a degree in Film Studies and Theatre from Manhattanville College in Purchase, New York. He has studied acting with Michael C. Williams, comic book writing with Denny O'Neill and screenwriting with Nicholas Meyer. He currently writes for the Comics section of PopMatters.com and is really looking forward to Joss Whedon's film version of The Avengers.

Bridwell, Nick

Nick Bridwell has a B.A. in English from the University of North Texas, with an emphasis in Creative Writing-Fiction. He currently resides in Austin, Texas, where he is working on his first novel. His passions include singing and songwriting.

Bustamante, Cesar

Cesar R. Bustamante, Jr. is a freelance reporter studying to be a multimedia journalist at the CUNY Graduate School of Journalism. A writer most of his life, he hopes to expand into data visualization and video production, especially for the web. He earned his B.A. in English from Queens College where his honors thesis on the traumatic origin stories of superheroes was the first to be awarded the Harold Schechter Prize for an Essay on Popular Culture. As a Filipino immigrant, he found comic books in his early teens. It inspired an interest in telling stories through both words and graphics.

Calvert, Bronwen

Bronwen Calvert is a former senior lecturer in English literature at Sunderland University, working at the North East Centre for Lifelong Learning in Newcastle upon Tyne, and is an associate lecturer with the Open University in the north of England. She researches on aspects of embodiment in science fiction and fantasy narratives. She has published articles on various television shows, most recently *Angel, Dollhouse, The X-Files*, and *Fringe*, and is working on a book about television cyborgs.

Canavan, Gerry

Gerry Canavan completed his dissertation on transatlantic literature and culture, "Theories of Everything: Science Fiction, Totality, and Empire in the Twentieth Century", under the co-direction of Fredric Jameson and Priscilla Wald in April 2012. He recently published two articles on race, empire, and utopia in zombie narrative in *Extrapolation and Science Fiction Film and Television*. He is the co-editor of special issues of *American Literature* ("Speculative Fictions", with Priscilla Wald) and Polygraph ("Ecology and Ideology", with Lisa Klarr and Ryan Vu), as well as an edited collection (with Kim Stanley Robinson) titled *Green Planets: Ecology and Science Fiction*, forthcoming from Wesleyan University Press.

Casey, Erin

Erin Casey lives in Phoenix, Arizona. She is a fan of Joss Whedon, books of all kinds, *Doctor Who*, and hats.

Chant, Ian

Ian Chant is a freelance writer, reporter and radio producer. He writes about science, pop culture, and pretty much anything else that catches his interest. He lives and works in Brooklyn, New York.

Chiat, Kevin

Kevin Chiat is a freelance writer based in Perth, Western Australia. He is also a Ph.D. student at the University of Western Australia, researching Media Franchises and Shared Universe Storytelling. He can be found blogging at 5thdimensionalscholar. wordpress.com.

Cochran, Tanya

TANYA R. COCHRAN, Ph.D., is Associate Professor of English at Union College in Lincoln, Nebraska. She is a founding board member and immediate past president of the Whedon Studies Association, an organization devoted to the academic study of the works of *Buffy the Vampire Slayer* creator Joss Whedon and his associates. Additionally, Cochran serves as an editorial board member for *Slayage: The Journal of the Whedon Studies Association*, *Watcher Junior: An Undergraduate Journal of Whedon Studies*, and *The Journal of Fandom Studies*. Her publications include essays in multiple collections, and she is coeditor of *Investigating Firefly and Serenity: Science Fiction on the Frontier* (I. B. Tauris, 2008) as well as *Reading Joss Whedon* (Syracuse University Press, 2014).

Dray, Colin

Colin Dray is a Lecturer in Literature at Campion College of the Liberal Arts, Australia, and has taught Creative Writing at the University of Wollongong, Australia. His writing and criticism has appeared in *Australian Literary Studies*, *Meanjin*, *Voiceworks*, and *Antipodes*. His blog can be found here: http://drayfish.wordpress.com/

Colgan, Chris

Chris Colgan is an accomplished music reviewer, former DJ at Seton Hall University's WSOU-FM, metal enthusiast, and lifetime science fiction/fantasy fan. When not reviewing or rocking out to the newest hard rock and heavy metal hits, Chris indulges his inner geek with heavy doses of *Star Wars*, *Firefly*, *Star Trek: Deep Space Nine*, *Starcraft*, and *Magic: The Gathering*. He also contributes a column called "New & Noteworthy" to MetalInsider.net, detailing the new releases in hard rock and heavy metal each week. He lives in West Hempstead, New York.

Drewniok, Malgorzata

Malgorzata Drewniok is completing her doctoral studies in linguistics at Lancaster University, UK. In her research she is examining *Buffy the Vampire Slayer* TV series (1997-2003), and more particularly, how the language of the series is manipulated to show the change in identity among the vampires. Her chapter on transformations in *Buffy* will appear in *Open Graves, Open Minds: Vampires and the Undead in Modern Culture* (forthcoming, 2012). Her research interests include: stylistics, contemporary gothic, popular fiction, television studies, popular culture and gender and language.

Emerson, Rana

Rana Emerson works as a Program Coordinator for the College Now program at the City University of New York and graduated from Yale University and the University of Texas at Austin. She has published articles on race and gender in media and popular culture in journals including *Gender & Society* and the *American Journal of Sociology* and currently writes for XOjane.com.

Ferencz, Keri

Keri Ferencz holds a Master's degree in Popular Culture from Brock University, where her thesis considered the spiritual dimension of fandom. Interested in the application of theory and continental philosophy to cultural artefacts, Keri's work is concerned with issues of identity and the possibility for true community within the consumer marketplace. She and Laura Berger are currently in the early stages of joint research on fan experiences at the Wizarding World of Harry Potter, and how these types of extra-textual experiences affect the practice of fandom. Her work has appeared on *PopMatters* and *Gaga Stigmata*.

Ford, Jessica

Jessica Ford currently lives in Sydney, where she is completing her Ph.D. in Film, Media & Theatre at the University of New South Wales. Jessica's research focuses on the representation of the female body in sci-fi television (in particular, *Dollhouse*) and the implications of a feminist fan culture. She has a Bachelor of Arts (Honours) in English Literature and Political Science and is very interested in feminism and gendered perspectives in film, television and literature.

Frankel , Valerie Estelle

Valerie Estelle Frankel has won a Dream Realm Award, an Indie Excellence Award, and a *USA Book News* National Best Book Award for her Henry Potty parodies. She's the author of over 20 books on pop culture, including *From Girl to Goddess: The Heroine's Journey in Myth and Legend, Buffy and the Heroine's Journey, Winning the Game of Thrones, Katniss the Cattail: A Guide to Names and Symbols in The Hunger Games, An Unexpected Parody, Teaching with Harry Potter, Joss Whedon's Names, Sherlock: Every Canon Reference You May Have Missed in BBC's Series 1–3*, and *Doctor Who: The What, Where, and How*. Once a lecturer at San Jose State University, she is a popular speaker on the heroine's journey and pop culture. Come explore her latest research at VEFrankel.com.

Fuller, Nikki Faith

Nikki Fuller earned her B.A. in Psychology and M.A. in English and currently teaches English Composition and Literature courses in California. She wrote her Master's thesis on *Buffy the Vampire Slayer*, examining it from the perspective of Joseph Campbell's hero's journey. She is currently enrolled in the Mythological Studies program at Pacifica Graduate Institute. When Nikki is not teaching or studying, she continues to write on *Buffy* and *Angel* and has presented papers at academic conferences including PCA and Slayage.

Garret, Kyle

Kyle Garret writes books, short stories, and essays. He is the author of the 2011 Independent Literary Awards nominated book, *I Pray Hardest When I'm Being Shot At*. His short fiction has appeared in the *Ginosko Literary Journal, Children, Churches, and Daddies*, and *Unrequited*. He is also a regular contributor to comicsbulletin.com, where he covers both comics and television. Kyle is currently finishing his first YA book. He can be found at www.kylegarret.com and twitter.com/kylegarret.

Golding, Holly

Holly Golding reads English Literature at the University of Exeter, and is spending her second year on exchange in Victoria, British Columbia. In her free time she enjoys writing short fiction and poetry, as well as television recaps and analyses. She has been a fan of *Buffy* since childhood, and eight years after the series finalé is still finding new aspects to consider.

Greenberg, Raz

Raz Greenberg is a Ph.D. student, researching animation as text at the Hebrew University. The first essay based on his research has appeared at the *Journal of Film and Video*, with upcoming essays by him set for publication at *Literature Film Quarterly*, and a future volume of Salem Press' *Critical Survey of Graphic Novels*. He wrote reviews for a variety of magazines, notably *Strange Horizons* and *Salon Futura*, and also published fiction in *FutureQuake, Ray Gun Revival and Murky Depths*. In 2010, one of his stories was nominated for a Geffen Award (the Israeli equivalent of the Hugo).

Hedlund, Sam

Sam Hedlund is a writer, speaker, and international trade and development professional who lives in Washington, D.C. He holds an MBA and MA in International Development from American University, and a B.A. in International Studies and Spanish from Pepperdine University. He served as an Atlas Corps fellow in Bogotá, Colombia. He blogs at www.samhedlund.com

Helfrich, Ronald

Ronald Helfrich teaches History and Sociology of Religion in Science and Technology Studies at Rensselaer Polytechnic Institute and in the Department of History at SUNY Oneonta. Ron is interested in popular culture, particularly American and British television (he taught History of Television for several years), American religious history, social movements, culture wars, and Comparative History. He has long been a fan of virtually all things Whedon, especially *Buffy* and *Firefly*.

Hornick, Alysa

Alysa Hornick received her BA in Comparative Literature from New York University and her MLIS from Long Island University, and has hosted and maintained the online *Whedonology: An Academic Whedon Studies Bibliography* since 2005. She is a member of the Whedon Studies Association, and is on the editorial board of *Watcher Junior: The Undergraduate Journal of Whedon Studies*. She is also a member of the Organization for Transformative Works. Alysa lives and works in New York City.

Jawetz, Ryan

Ryan Jawetz is a senior majoring in philosophy at Pomona College in Claremont, California. His interests include listening to music and arguing.

Jowett, Lorna

Lorna Jowett is a reader in television studies at the University of Northampton, UK, where she teaches some of her favorite things, including science fiction, horror, and television, sometimes all at once. She is the co-author with Stacey Abbott of *TV Horror:*

Investigating The Dark Side of the Small Screen, the author of *Sex and the Slayer: A Gender Studies Primer for the* Buffy *Fan*, and is on the editorial boards of *Slayage: The Journal of the Whedon Studies Association* and *Intensities: The Journal of Cult Media*. She has published many articles on television, film, and popular culture and is currently writing a book on gender in the new *Doctor Who* franchise.

Masson, Cynthea

Cynthea Masson holds a Ph.D. in English from McMaster University. As a professor in the English Department at Vancouver Island University (British Columbia, Canada), she teaches a variety of writing and literature courses, with an upper-level focus on medieval literature. Her academic research and publication areas comprise medieval visionary literature, medieval alchemical poetry, and the contemporary works of Joss Whedon, including *Buffy*, *Angel*, *Firefly*, and *Dollhouse*. Her paper "What the Hell?—*Angel*'s 'The Girl in Question'" was awarded the Mr. Pointy Award for best paper at the Slayage Conference on the Whedonverses 3 (2008).

Mathers, Ian

Ian Mathers is a Canadian writer whose work has appeared in *PopMatters*, the *Village Voice*, *Stylus Magazine*, *Resident Advisor*, and the world's foremost Philip K. Dick fan site. He studied philosophy in school, twice (favourite philosopher: Spinoza), and edits computer security reports for a living (favourite type of exploitation: XSS). The first Joss Whedon show he saw was *Firefly* on DVD, but he's made up for lost time. He writes regularly at imathers.tumblr.com.

McRae, Leanne

Leanne McRae is the Senior Researcher for the Popular Culture Collective and a Lecturer in Media and Cultural Studies in Perth, Western Australia. Her research interests include city imaging, postcolonial theory and popular cultural studies, pedagogy, postwork theories, and mobility studies.

Milson, Jack

Jack Milson is a part-time blogger, full-time Browncoat. He graduated from the University of Hull with a First in Media, Culture and Society B.A. (Hons.) in 2010. He is currently an Assistant Video Editor/Producer at a digital media production company based in Hull, UK

Money, Mary Alice

Mary Alice Money, emerita professor of English at Gordon State College in Barnesville, Georgia, earned BS and MA degrees from the University of Tennessee in her home town of Knoxville and a PhD from the University of Texas, and has served as president of the Popular Culture Association in the South. She often presents papers and sometimes publishes on Whedonverses television, detective fiction, heroes, Westerns, myths, and setting. She edited the first edition of *Joss Whedon: The Complete Companion*.

Moore, Robert

Robert W. Moore is a features editor and writer for *PopMatters* and has written extensively about television and SF. He studied philosophy at Yale and the University of Chicago and currently lives in Chicago. His current research focuses on the history of Cyborgs and robots on television.

Murray, Faye

Faye Murray graduated in 2009 with an honours degree in Natural Sciences from the University of Cambridge and is currently employed at the University of South Australia. She is an avid follower of the film and TV industries and spends much of her spare time writing TV scripts and commentaries, the latter on aspects such as feminism, reliance on TV tropes and their subversion, and the changing climate of TV.

Nelson, Michael Curtis

Michael Curtis Nelson lives in Bloomington, Indiana, where he works for IU Communications at Indiana University. He writes about film and television for *PopMatters*, and regularly torments his friends and loved ones with screenings of low-budget domestic and foreign horror films. Nelson earned a Ph.D. in American Literature from IU.

Pensky, Nathan

Nathan Pensky is an Associate Editor for *PopMatters* and a writer for *Forbes*, as well as a recent graduate of the Master's writing program at Mills College.

Porter, Lynnette

Lynnette Porter, Ph.D., is a professor of humanities and communication at Embry-Riddle University in Daytona Beach, Florida. She is a Contributing Editor for *PopMatters* and writes a monthly column, Deep Focus.

Q, Shathley

Shathley Q holds a Ph.D. in Literary and Cultural Theory and is *PopMatters'* Comics Editor. His current research focus is on the comics medium and cognitive development.

Ramachandran, Nandini

Nandini Ramachandran is a lawyer and writer (blogging at chaosbogey) living in Bangalore, India.

Rothman, Lily

Lily Rothman is a Brooklyn-based freelance writer. Her work has appeared in many national, local, and online publications, including *TheAtlantic.com*, *Bust* magazine, and *The Brooklyn Eagle*. Find out more at www.lilyrothman.com.

Shand, Patrick

Patrick Shand has written for Joss Whedon's *Angel* for IDW Publishing, *Grimm Fairy Tales* for Zenescope Entertainment, and *1000 Ways to Die* for Zenescope/Spike TV. He has been active in the Off Off Broadway scene as a playwright and teaches Script Writing and Screenwriting at Five Towns College in New York.

Tresca, Don

Don Tresca is a graduate of California State University, Sacramento with a Master's Degree in English. He is currently working on a book on found footage horror films.

West, Candace

Candace E. West is a scholar of religion, ethics, and literature, with a Ph.D. in Religious Studies from Stanford University. She examines a variety of genres and styles in her work but is primarily interested in the connections between selfhood and storytelling, especially in contemporary, popular narratives. She currently lives in California.

Weyant, Curtis A.

Curtis A. Weyant is a digital content specialist by trade and a student of speculative literature by choice. He co-hosts *Kat & Curt's TV Re-View*, a weekly podcast discussing episodes of *Buffy*/*Angel* and *Doctor Who*, and rocks the keyboard at CurtisWeyant.com. His writings have been featured in *McSweeney's Internet Tendency*, *The Binnacle*, and *Slayage*.

Wilcox, Rhonda

Rhonda V. Wilcox, Ph.D., is a professor of English at Gordon College (Georgia) and president of the Whedon Studies Association. She is editor of *Studies in Popular Culture* and coeditor of *Slayage: The Journal of the Whedon Studies Association*. She is the author of *Why Buffy Matters: The Art of Buffy the Vampire Slayer* and coeditor, with David Lavery, of *Fighting the Forces: What's at Stake in Buffy the Vampire Slayer*.

Zhang, Angela

Angela Zhang is a senior studying Geography at Dartmouth College. She is particularly interested in critical geography, discourse, neoliberalism, and feminism, and loves to apply these interests to computer games and pop culture.